Supreme Decisions

Great Constitutional Cases and Their Impact
Volume 1: To 1896
Volume 2: Since 1896

Melvin I. Urofsky

Virginia Commonwealth University

WESTVIEW PRESS

A Member of the Perseus Books Group

Volume 1:
For my children
Philip and Melissa, Robert and Leslie
And for their children

Volume 2:
For my grandchildren
Emma, Chloe, and Aaron
And for their parents

Combined Volume:
For my children, my grandchildren,
and as they requested,
for all the pooches as well

———————

Westview Press was founded in 1975 in Boulder, Colorado, by notable publisher and intellectual Fred Praeger. Westview Press continues to publish scholarly titles and high-quality undergraduate- and graduate-level textbooks in core social science disciplines. With books developed, written, and edited with the needs of serious nonfiction readers, professors, and students in mind, Westview Press honors its long history of publishing books that matter.

Copyright © 2012 by Westview Press
Published by Westview Press,
A Member of the Perseus Books Group

Find us on the World Wide Web at www.westviewpress.com.

Every effort has been made to secure required permissions for all text, images, maps, and other art reprinted in this volume.

Westview Press books are available at special discounts for bulk purchases in the United States by corporations, institutions, and other organizations. For more information, please contact the Special Markets Department at the Perseus Books Group, 2300 Chestnut Street, Suite 200, Philadelphia, PA 19103, or call (800) 810-4145, ext. 5000, or e-mail special.markets@perseusbooks.com.

A CIP catalog record of this book is available from the Library of Congress.
Supreme decisions: great constitutional cases and their impact (volume 1, volume 2, combined volume), Melvin I. Urofsky
Paperback ISBNs: Volume 1: To 1896: 978-0-8133-4731-8; Volume 2: Since 1896: 978-0-8133-4733-2; Combined Volume: 978-0-8133-4735-6 (alk. paper)
E-book ISBNs: Volume 1: To 1896: 978-0-8133-4732–5; Volume 2: Since 1896: 978-0-8133-4734-9; Combined Volume: 978-0-8133-4736-3

10 9 8 7 6 5 4 3 2 1

Contents

Reviewer Acknowledgments   xiii

Introduction   xiv

Volume 1: To 1896

C h a p t e r   o n e

**The Case of the Disappointed Office-Seeker:
Marbury v. Madison (1803)**   **1**

The Judiciary Act of 1801 and the Midnight Judges   2
William Marbury   2
The First Step—Repeal of the 1801 Judiciary Act   3
Marbury v. Madison   6
The Politics and Logic of Marshall's Opinion   8
The Republicans Continue Their Attack   10
The Impeachment of Justice Chase   11
Defining Treason   13
Aftermath   15
Cases Cited   16
For Further Reading   16

C h a p t e r   t w o

**The Case of the Larcenous Cashier: *M'Culloch v.
Maryland* (1819)**   **17**

Interpreting the Constitution: Jefferson versus Hamilton   17
James McCulloh—Cashier Extraordinaire   20
Arguments before the Court   22
Decision   25

The States' Rights Attack   28
John Marshall's Defense   29
Citizen McCulloh   30
Cases Cited   31
For Further Reading   31

C h a p t e r   t h r e e

The Case of the Rival Steamboat Operators: *Gibbons v. Ogden* (1824)   **33**

Mr. Fulton's Steamboat   33
The Steamboat Monopoly   35
Enter Gibbons and Ogden   38
Creating a Question for the Federal Courts   40
Arguing before the Supreme Court   41
The Decision   42
The Legacy of the Case   43
Cases Cited   45
For Further Reading   45

C h a p t e r   f o u r

The Case of the Missionary to the Cherokee: *Worcester v. Georgia* (1832)   **47**

Setting the Stage   47
Taking Indian Land   48
Challenging Georgia Law in the Supreme Court   51
Samuel Worcester Goes to Georgia   52
The Georgia Law before the Supreme Court   54
The Failure of Law and a Political Compromise   57
Cherokee Removal   58
Aftermath   59
Cases Cited   60
For Further Reading   60

C h a p t e r   f i v e

The Case of the Zealous Slave Catcher: *Prigg v. Pennsylvania* (1842)   **61**

The Fugitive Slave Act of 1793   61

Personal Liberty Laws 62
Edward Prigg and Margaret Morgan 65
The Supreme Court Rules 66
After *Prigg:* George Latimer 70
The Fugitive Slave Act of 1850 71
Cases Cited 73
For Further Reading 73

C h a p t e r   s i x

The Case of the Slave Who Would Be Free: *Dred Scott v. Sandford* (1857) **75**

Dred Scott and His Travels 75
The Case in the Missouri State Courts 77
The Growing Storm over Slavery 79
The Compromise of 1850 80
Dred Scott in the Missouri Supreme Court 81
A Diversity Case—or Not 82
Before the Supreme Court 83
"The Self-Inflicted Wound" 85
Aftermath 87
Cases Cited 90
For Further Reading 90

C h a p t e r   s e v e n

The Case of the Antiwar Agitator: *Ex parte Milligan* (1866) **91**

The Making of a Copperhead 91
Opposing the War 93
Military Trial 95
Ex parte Merryman 96
Ex parte Vallandigham 98
Arguing the Case 100
The Court's Decision 102
Milligan in History 103
Milligan after the Case 105
Cases Cited 105
For Further Reading 106

C h a p t e r e i g h t

The Case of the New Orleans Butchers: The *Slaughterhouse Cases* (1873) — 107

A Simple Health Regulation in an Unhealthy City — 108
The Butchers Fight Back — 110
Defining Rights — 113
In the Louisiana Courts — 116
Justice Joseph Bradley, on Circuit — 119
Before the U.S. Supreme Court — 120
A Closely Divided Court Decides — 123
Aftermath — 125
Cases Cited — 126
For Further Reading — 126

C h a p t e r n i n e

The Case of the Woman Who Wanted to Be a Lawyer: *Bradwell v. Illinois* (1873) — 127

Myra Bradwell — 127
The *Chicago Legal News* — 128
The Nascent Women's Movement — 130
A History of Legal Discrimination — 131
Small Doors in the Wall — 133
A Person of Good Character—but Not Eligible — 133
On Appeal to the Supreme Court — 136
The Decision — 138
Moving On, and Triumphing — 141
Cases Cited — 142
For Further Reading — 142

C h a p t e r t e n

The Case of the Devout Bigamist: *Reynolds v. United States* (1879) — 143

Mormon Beliefs — 143
The Growing Opposition to the Faith — 145
George Reynolds — 146
The Test Case — 147
The Supreme Court Decides: Belief versus Practice — 148
Reaction to the Decision — 150

The Persecution and Prosecution of the
   Mormons   151
The End of Plural Marriage   154
Continuing Questions   156
George Reynolds's Last Years   156
Cases Cited   157
For Further Reading   158

C h a p t e r   e l e v e n

The Case of the Reluctant Strike Leader: *In re Debs* (1895)   **159**

George M. Pullman and the Palace Car   159
Pullman, Illinois   161
Eugene Victor Debs   162
The American Railway Union   164
The Pullman Workers Strike   165
The Boycott   166
Violence   167
Judge Grosscup Issues an Injunction   168
The Trial of Eugene V. Debs   170
The High Court Rules   171
Aftermath   173
Cases Cited   174
For Further Reading   174

C h a p t e r   t w e l v e

The Case of the Almost-White Traveler: *Plessy v. Ferguson* (1896)   **175**

The Freedmen after the Civil War   175
The Beginnings of Jim Crow   178
Challenging the Separate Car Act   179
Enter Homer Adolphe Plessy   182
The Separate Car Act in the Courts   183
The Supreme Court Decides   184
Justice Harlan's Dissent   187
Plessy's Bitter Fruits   188
Coda   189
Cases Cited   190
For Further Reading   190

Volume 2: Since 1896

C h a p t e r   t w e l v e

The Case of the Almost-White Traveler: *Plessy v. Ferguson* (1896)   **175**

The Freedmen after the Civil War	175
The Beginnings of Jim Crow	178
Challenging the Separate Car Act	179
Enter Homer Adolphe Plessy	182
The Separate Car Act in the Courts	183
The Supreme Court Decides	184
Justice Harlan's Dissent	187
Plessy's Bitter Fruits	188
Coda	189
Cases Cited	190
For Further Reading	190

C h a p t e r   t h i r t e e n

The Case of the Stubborn Baker: *Lochner v. New York* (1905)   **191**

Industrialization and Protective Legislation	191
Substantive Due Process versus the Police Power	192
Bakeshops at the Turn of the Century	194
Trying to Clean Up the Bakeshops	197
Joseph Lochner Challenges the Law	199
The Supreme Court Hands Down a Surprise Decision	202
Lochner's Aftermath	206
Cases Cited	207
For Further Reading	208

C h a p t e r   f o u r t e e n

The Case of the Gentle Anarchist: *Abrams v. United States* (1919)   **209**

World War I and Speech	209
Jacob Abrams Opposes the War	211
Theories of Speech and the Bad Tendency	213

Schenck and "Clear and Present Danger" 214
Holmes Learns from His Critics 215
Abrams: Fighting Faiths 218
Reaction to Holmes's Dissent: Pro and Con 221
The Sad End of Jacob Abrams 222
Cases Cited 223
For Further Reading 224

C h a p t e r   f i f t e e n

The Case of the High-Tech Bootlegger: *Olmstead v. United States* (1928) **225**

The Road to the Noble Experiment 225
Prohibition in Practice 227
The Olmstead Ring in Seattle 229
The Meaning of the Fourth Amendment 231
Chief Justice Taft's Opinion 233
Justices Butler and Holmes Dissent 235
The Brandeis Dissent and the Right of Privacy 236
Roy Olmstead Reforms 239
Cases Cited 240
For Further Reading 240

C h a p t e r   s i x t e e n

The Four Horsemen's Last Ride: *The New Deal Cases* (1930s) **241**

The Great Depression 242
The Court and State Measures to Combat the Depression 243
The New Deal Begins 244
Going Off the Gold Standard 247
The National Industrial Recovery Act 248
The *Schechter* Case 249
The New Deal Farm Program and the Court 252
The Attack on the New Deal Continues 254
The Court-Packing Plan 255
Elsie Parrish Wants Her Money 256
Cases Cited 258
For Further Reading 258

C h a p t e r   s e v e n t e e n

The Case of the Conscientious Schoolchildren:
The Flag-Salute Cases **(1940 and 1943)**   **259**

Lillian Gobitas Acts on Her Faith   259
The Witnesses in Federal Courts   260
The Witnesses in the High Court: Round I   262
The Violent Response to the Decision   267
Expanding the Boundaries of the First Amendment   268
The High Court: Round II   270
Aftermath   273
Cases Cited   274
For Further Reading   274

C h a p t e r   e i g h t e e n

The Case of Too-Long-Delayed Equality: *Brown v.*
Board of Education **(1954 and 1955)**   **275**

Linda Brown and the Other Plaintiffs   275
From *Plessy* to *Brown*   277
The Arguments   280
The Decision   281
The Response   283
Remedies and *Brown II*   284
Moving—but Slowly   286
Ike and Little Rock   287
The Beginnings of Desegregation   288
Cases Cited   289
For Further Reading   290

C h a p t e r   n i n e t e e n

The Case of the Robust Press: *New York Times v.*
Sullivan **(1964)**   **291**

Merton Nachman Reads the Newspaper   291
The Struggle for Civil Rights in Alabama   292
L. B. Sullivan and Law Enforcement in Montgomery   295
The Sit-in Movement Comes to Alabama   296
"Heed Their Rising Voices"   297
A Brief History of Libel Law   299

The *Sullivan* Case 301
The Supreme Court and the Press Clause 303
"Debate on Public Issues Should Be Uninhibited, Robust, and
  Wide-Open" 303
Aftermath 306
Cases Cited 307
For Further Reading 307

C h a p t e r   t w e n t y

The Case of the Uninformed Rapist: *Miranda v. Arizona* (1966)   309

The Victim 310
Ernesto Miranda and His Confession 310
The Due Process Revolution Begins: *Gideon v. Wainwright* 312
The Fifth Amendment's "Great Right" 313
Connecting the Fifth and Sixth Amendments: *Massiah* 314
Strengthening the Connection: *Escobedo* 316
"You Have the Right to Remain Silent" 318
The Success of *Miranda* 320
Refining *Miranda* 321
Miranda's End 322
Cases Cited 323
For Further Reading 323

C h a p t e r   t w e n t y   o n e

The Case That Aroused Great Passions: *Roe v. Wade* (1973)   325

Abortion Legislation: A Brief History 325
Growing Support for Abortion Rights 329
Establishing the Right to Privacy 333
Sarah Weddington Meets Norma McCorvey 334
Jane Roe Wins Round One 336
Abortion in the Supreme Court before *Roe* 338
Roe v. Wade and *Doe v. Bolton* 339
The Response to the Decisions 341
Aftermath 343
Cases Cited 344
For Further Reading 344

C h a p t e r   t w e n t y   t w o

Coming Out of the Closet and into the Courts: *The Gay Rights Cases* (1986–2003)   **347**

Michael Hardwick Is Arrested	347
Hardwick Goes to Court—Charting Unfamiliar Territory	349
The Gay Rights Movement	350
Hardwick in the Supreme Court	352
The Court Tries to Find Its Way	355
A Ray of Hope—*Romer v. Evans*	357
John Geddes Lawrence Is Arrested	360
The Supreme Court Decides	361
The Aftermath of *Lawrence*	364
Cases Cited	365
For Further Reading	366

C h a p t e r   t w e n t y   t h r e e

The Constitution Besieged: *The War on Terror Cases* (2000s)   **367**

Rounding Up Suspected Aliens	367
Zacarias Moussaoui	370
Enemy Combatants	371
The Prisoners of Guantánamo	373
The Supreme Court Issues a Warning	376
Hamdan v. Rumsfeld	377
Another Rebuke from the Court	379
Aftermath	381
Cases Cited	382
For Further Reading	382

Constitution of the United States	C-1
Glossary	G-1
Index	I-1

Reviewer Acknowledgments

I would like to thank the reviewers whose feedback on the manuscript was so helpful, including:

Robert Allison, *Suffolk University*
Gordon Bakken, *California State University, Fullerton*
Elizabeth Dale, *University of Florida*
Thomas J. Davis, *Arizona State University, Tempe*
Sally Hadden, *Western Michigan University*
Eric R. Jackson, *Northern Kentucky University*
Patricia Minter, *Western Kentucky University*
Yvonne Pitts, *Purdue University*
Richard Polenberg, *Cornell University*
John C. Putman, *San Diego State University*
John E. Semonche, *University of North Carolina* [retired]
Christopher Waldrep, *San Francisco State University*
Laura Wittern-Keller, *University of Albany*

Introduction

TODAY ALL OF US RECOGNIZE that the Supreme Court plays an important part in our daily lives, as it defines what rights belong to the citizens of this country, what Congress and state legislatures can and cannot do, how far presidential authority extends, and what is the proper balance between the powers of the national government and those of the states. But when George Washington took the oath of office in 1789 as the first president under the Constitution, he had difficulty finding men to serve as justices of the Supreme Court that Congress had created. During its first decade, although the Court handed down some important decisions, few people in the country thought of the judicial arm as a coequal partner in the national government, comparable to the executive or legislative branch. The first chief justice of the United States, John Jay, resigned to become governor of New York, and Associate Justice John Rutledge left to become chief justice of South Carolina. The constitutional declaration in Article III that "the judicial power of the United States shall be vested in one Supreme Court, and in such inferior courts as the Congress may from time to time ordain and establish," seemed to many an afterthought.

That, of course, changed when John Marshall became chief justice in 1801. Just as Washington had clothed the bare-bones description of the presidency with the flesh and blood of practice, so Marshall gave life to some of the key phrases of the Constitution, and in doing so made the Supreme Court not only a significant player in the affairs of the national government but also the final arbiter of what the Constitution means. For more than 210 years it has been what the Court says that has influenced major trends in our historical development, and has defined the important phrases in the Constitution. We understand what interstate commerce, freedom of speech, and equal protection of the law mean because of what the Court has said.

Each generation of Americans brings new questions before the courts, and the flexibility that the Framers built into the Constitution has allowed it to respond to issues that the founding generation never even imagined. Sometimes the decisions have been controversial, and there have been some false starts. But for the most part, the justices have done a good job of reading the words of an eighteenth-century document to cover the contingencies raised in the ensuing decades.

Although the U.S. Supreme Court is one of the most powerful constitutional courts in the world, it can only decide those issues that come within its jurisdiction. In the early nineteenth century the French traveler Alexis de Tocqueville declared that in the United States all important political questions ultimately wind up as judicial questions. But the justices cannot just reach out and decide an issue; they must wait until a "case or controversy" is properly brought before them, and then they carefully weigh just which questions they wish to answer.

These cases and controversies are not abstract, and they involve real people—the men and women who brought the issues into the courts to begin with—people like William Marbury challenging the authority of a president, Dred Scott claiming to be free, and Myra Bradwell believing that women ought to be allowed to practice law. In more modern times we find Jacob Abrams arguing that the First Amendment gave him a right to voice unpopular opinions, Lillian Gobitas refusing to salute the flag because of her religious beliefs, and Oliver Brown wanting his daughter Linda to go to a desegregated school.

When I studied constitutional history in graduate school, and later on in law school, the emphasis was on the case holding. In this case the Court decided that a particular clause of the Constitution meant a certain thing, and therefore the statute in question was either constitutional or not. We never met the litigants, other than in one or two sentences at the beginning of the opinion setting out how the case began. One could read through such famous decisions as *Marbury v. Madison* (1803), *Plessy v. Ferguson* (1896), *Olmstead v. United States* (1928), and *Roe v. Wade* (1973) and know absolutely nothing about William Marbury, Homer Plessy, Roy Olmstead, and Norma McCorvey (Jane Roe). Who were these people? What were the circumstances that brought their cases into court? What were the larger social, economic, and political developments that lay behind their cases?

The so-called new constitutional history that began in the late 1970s and early 1980s demanded that teachers and students pay more attention to such questions. Great scholars such as E. S. Corwin and Willard Hurst had always done so, but they had been a minority. Now men and women who had been trained in law and history or law and political science entered the field who articulated the need to understand not just the jurisprudence of a case, but the social conditions that surrounded it. One could not discuss the *Plessy* case, for example, and ignore the growth of segregation after the Civil War, or why someone like Homer Plessy challenged it. Nor could one deal with *Abrams* without understanding the fear of radical ideas during wartime and the fact that ideas regarding free speech—ideas we now all take for granted—were not yet part of the constitutional dialogue.

One of my teachers, John A. Garraty, edited the first effort to provide these stories to students, and his *Quarrels That Have Shaped the Constitution* had a long and successful run as a supplemental text in college courses. That book has long been out of print, and I am grateful to Westview Press, and especially to my editor, Priscilla McGeehon, for agreeing with me that a new text was needed—one that would tell the stories behind some of the most important cases in our history. I would also like to thank Marcelle Maginnis and Laura Stewart for their editorial assistance.

One of the problems for anyone trying to tell constitutional stories is choosing which ones to include. Every teacher of constitutional history in the country has his or her "favorite" cases, and all would be legitimate contenders for inclusion. In this collection I have tried to provide cases that handle issues that not only were important in the past but still resonate today—issues of privacy, free speech, and race; treatment of women, Native Americans, and gays; and rights of people accused of crimes. There are other cases that also address these questions—and indeed many more as well—but a choice had to be made both among the topics to consider and which stories to tell. These are my choices, and in the selection I relied heavily on my own experience in teaching constitutional history and law. My hope is that others will find the tales as compelling as I do.

Melvin Urofsky
Virginia Commonwealth University

Supreme Decisions

The Case of the Disappointed Office-Seeker

Marbury v. Madison (1803)

LOOKING BACK, we can see that the election of 1800 was an important step forward in the growth of an American democratic state. For the first time in Anglo-American history, a government had been turned out by the people at the polls, and its leaders peacefully handed over power to the opposition. This, however, did not seem so clear at the time. Although the Jeffersonian Republicans had won control of the executive and legislative branches, the judiciary remained firmly in the hands of the defeated Federalists. The idea of a divided government was foreign to Americans at the time; in the English tradition the king chose the prime minister and appointed the judges.

Thomas Jefferson believed that he would not able to implement the democratic policies he favored so long as the Federalists controlled the judiciary, and especially with his cousin and rival, John Marshall, as the new chief justice of the Supreme Court. The battle between Jefferson and the judiciary played out in several venues during the eight years of Jefferson's presidency, and included the abolition of some courts, the impeachment and near-conviction of Justice Samuel Chase, and the treason trial of Aaron Burr. None of them, however, would have a greater influence on American constitutional development than William Marbury's case. It was not the opening gun of the war between Jefferson and the Court, but it was the most decisive. Aside from political differences, much of the situation resulted from efforts by John Adams and the Federalists to retain control of the judiciary, and Jefferson's determination not to let that happen.

The Judiciary Act of 1801 and the Midnight Judges

In the months after the Federalists lost the election of 1800, but before Jefferson took over the White House, the Federalist-controlled Congress passed the Judiciary Act of 1801 along with the Organic Act for the District of Columbia. Along with other provisions, both laws created a number of new judicial offices, which the outgoing president, John Adams, proceeded to fill mostly with members of his own party.

At the time, the newly created District of Columbia consisted of two counties, Washington (the present-day area of Washington, D.C.) and Alexandria (which is now Alexandria, Virginia). On March 2, 1801, Adams nominated twenty-three men to be justices of the peace in Washington County and nineteen in Alexandria County. After the Senate confirmed these appointments on March 3, Adams signed the official commissions, not finishing until late into the night of his last day in office (hence the group came to be known as the "Midnight Judges"). Secretary of State John Marshall, who had just been named chief justice of the Supreme Court, affixed the great seal of the United States, and that same evening his brother, James Marshall, delivered some of the commissions to men in Alexandria, who ultimately served their term in office. But none of the twenty-three justices of the peace in Washington County received their commissions before Adams left office at noon on March 4.

When Jefferson took office he discovered the signed, sealed, but as yet undelivered commissions. He reappointed the six Republicans who had been on Adams's list, as well as six of the Federalists, but refused to name the remaining eleven men. Most of the Federalists who did not receive their commission accepted their fate passively, but not William Marbury. Without the commission—without the actual parchment and seal—he could not serve in the office. So Marbury went to court to force the Jefferson administration to deliver the commission. The resulting case led to one of the most important decisions in American constitutional history.

William Marbury

William Marbury had been born in 1762 on a small tobacco plantation in Piscataway, Maryland. His career progressed slowly in the 1780s, since Maryland government and politics were in a constant turmoil. Not until the adoption of the U.S. Constitution and the establishment of a new national government did Maryland's economic fortunes revive; when that occurred, Marbury, aligned with the leading Federalists in Maryland, stood ready to prosper. In 1796 Marbury was named agent of the state of Maryland, the most powerful unelected office in the state. Although he and his colleagues in the office apparently did not shirk from using their positions to advance their own fortunes—a practice not uncommon then or now—unlike many other Maryland officials at the time, Marbury was never tainted with even the slightest tinge of corruption. He prospered not only because of the new federal government's successful fiscal policies, but also because of his financial acumen. In addition, he helped other important members of the Maryland elite to realize profit from the federal plan, earning their trust and gratitude.

In the bitterly contested presidential election of 1800, Marbury declared his support for John Adams, and when Congress finally chose Thomas Jefferson as the winner on February 17, 1801, a mob ran through the capital demanding that everyone put candles in their windows to indicate support for the new president. When they came to Marbury's house, he would have none of it, and stood up to the mob's leaders until they finally moved on, leaving him in peace. To reward Marbury for his loyalty, Adams named him one of the forty-two justices of the peace Congress had authorized for the capital. Many, like Marbury, had been staunch supporters of John Adams and his party. Although Jefferson did not revoke the commissions of all of Adams's appointees, he believed the new city did not need so many justices of the peace. The new president believed—correctly—that Marbury had been one of the Federalist Party's most partisan supporters, and withheld his commission. And, because John Marshall had not delivered the commission, technically Marbury had never held the office.

But Marbury wanted it, both for its prestige and political influence, which could translate into wealth. But although the commission had been signed and sealed, it had not been delivered, and without the document itself, Marbury could neither exercise the powers of the office nor collect the fees for his services. He needed the actual commission, and decided to go to court to get it. Under the provisions of the Judiciary Act of 1789, Congress had given the Supreme Court the power to issue writs of mandamus, which in effect direct a public official to carry out an act or duty. Marbury sought such a writ against Secretary of State James Madison to force him to hand over the commission that Adams had signed. The whole situation resulted from efforts by Adams and the Federalists to retain control of the judiciary, and Jefferson's determination not to let that happen. The politics involved in the effort to control the judiciary explains much of what followed.

The First Step—Repeal of the 1801 Judiciary Act

The Judiciary Act of 1801 created sixteen new circuit court judges, an expansion of the court system that the growing nation needed. But those benefits have been obscured by charges that the Federalists, ousted from authority by the people, sought to cling to power by packing the courts with their allies. In Jefferson's words, the Federalists "retired into the judiciary as a stronghold." Had these appointments been available to the Republicans, their complaints might not have been so loud, for many in that party also recognized the need to correct the deficiencies in the system. On the other hand, had the goal of Adams and his party been only judicial reform, the retiring president might have been wise enough to leave a few of the new judicial seats vacant, allowing Jefferson the opportunity to make some selections. But Adams appointed men to all the vacancies—and with great haste—filling the judiciary with dozens of Federalists, many of whom would have tenure for life.

In 1801 not a single Republican sat on a federal court, and nothing but death or resignation—both unpredictable factors—would allow Jefferson to rectify that situation. Adams's appointment of John Marshall as chief justice did not please the new president at all, for there had long been ill will between them, and Marshall's federalism—centered on a strong national government with extensive constitutional powers— stood solidly opposed to Jefferson's belief in a limited national government with the majority of power lodged in the states. Something had to be done, Jefferson believed, to prevent the Federalist bench from hindering democracy. As Republican representative William Giles asserted, "[T]he revolution is incomplete, so long as that strong fortress is in possession of the enemy." Giles advocated that Jefferson remove "all of [the judges] . . . indiscriminately."

Any proposed solution raised constitutional questions. Since judges served for life, no one knew if Congress could simply abolish judgeships in order to get rid of particular judges. Certainly if this were possible, then the whole idea of life tenure for judges would be in doubt. Nothing would prevent Jefferson and his allies from abolishing all existing courts, including the Supreme Court, and then re-creating them a short time later, so that the new president could appoint his allies to the bench. The process might well be repeated whenever a new administration took office. Such political tinkering with the courts strikes modern ears as unfathomable, but since the Republicans proceeded to do just that, it is clear that they worried very little about the constitutionality of an act that fired judges.

Jefferson, who often claimed to be a strict constructionist when it came to reading the Constitution, nevertheless saw no constitutional problems with the idea. His plan was to abolish the new courts and, in the process, eliminate the judges. Shortly after his inauguration, Jefferson told a friend that "the judge of course stands till the law is repealed, which we trust will be at the next Congress." On January 6, 1802, John Breckinridge of Kentucky, a strong supporter of Jefferson, introduced a bill in the Senate to repeal the Judiciary Act of 1801. After intense debate, the Repeal Act narrowly passed the upper chamber, 16–15, on February 3; the House, where the Republicans enjoyed a large majority, enacted the Senate bill without amendment on March 8, 1802.

Congress then passed the Judiciary Act of 1802, increasing the number of circuits from three to six, with each Supreme Court justice assigned to only one, where he would hold court with the local district judges on circuit twice a year. In addition, the new law provided for only one term of the Supreme Court each year instead of the two terms that had been in effect since 1789, thus further reducing the physical strain on the justices by eliminating an arduous trip to the capital. The new term would begin on the first Monday of every February. This provision, which certainly made sense in light of the Court's caseload, nonetheless provoked much criticism. Because this act was passed in April 1802, the Supreme Court would not meet again until February 1803. Since the last meeting had been in December 1801, this meant that the Supreme Court would not meet for fourteen months, and tensions simmered in the interim.

Critics of the 1802 act claimed that the Republicans feared that the Supreme Court at the anticipated June term would have found the Repeal Act unconstitutional. Jefferson's friend James Monroe, now governor of Virginia, warned that if the public viewed the postponement as "an unconstitutional oppression of the judiciary by the legislature," then it might also see the Repeal Act as unconstitutional. He urged the president to veto the bill, but Jefferson believed that the delay would work in the party's favor; by the time the Court met in 1803, the president predicted, the furor would have died down.

Chief Justice John Marshall privately "doubted the constitutionality of the repeal." But Marshall was shrewd enough as a politician to know when he could not win. He told Justice William Paterson that he would "be bound by the opinion of the majority of the Judges," knowing that in fact within the Court only Justice Samuel Chase publicly argued against the constitutionality of the repeal. When a specific challenge did reach the Court in *Stuart v. Laird* (1803), the Court, in an opinion by Paterson, affirmed the constitutionality of the repeal. What had seemed so grave a question at the time passed quickly into obscurity. One reason for Marshall's acquiescence may have been his desire to avoid a direct confrontation with President Jefferson in a manner that would allow Jefferson to obstruct the Court's opinion. Instead, Marshall found a better way to challenge Jefferson, in an opinion delivered six days before the decision in *Stuart v. Laird.* In *Marbury v. Madison,* Marshall confronted Jefferson—and beat him on a major constitutional point—in such a manner that Jefferson could not respond.

Marbury v. Madison

Jefferson claimed that delivery was essential for a commission to be valid, just as for a deed or bond, and that by withholding the document, the entire nomination had been voided. Marbury and his lawyer, former attorney general Charles Lee, argued that signing and sealing the commission completed the transaction, and that delivery constituted a mere formality. But formality or not, without the actual piece of parchment, Marbury could not enter into the duties of office. The Court, aware of Jefferson's hostility, might well have dismissed the suit immediately for lack of jurisdiction, but instead it aroused Republican resentment by agreeing to hear the case at its next term. When Marshall convened the Court in February 1803, *Marbury v. Madison* stood on the docket.

Some scholars have questioned whether Marshall should have removed himself from this case because of his prior involvement as Adams's secretary of state. Certainly, later judicial standards would have called for recusement, but at the time only financial connections to a case led judges to step aside, as Marshall did in suits regarding Virginia lands in which he had an interest. The Jeffersonians, always quick to criticize Marshall, did not even raise the issue of his sitting in the *Marbury* case.

The merits of the case, by any reasonable interpretation, can only be described as minor. By the time the Court heard it, the wisdom of Jefferson's reducing the number of justices of the peace had been confirmed; Marbury's original term was almost half over; and most people, Federalists and Republicans alike, considered the issue moot. But Marshall, despite the political difficulties involved, recognized that he had a perfect case with which to expound a basic principle, and by his persistence, he utilized it to lay the foundation for the Court to assume the primary role in constitutional interpretation.

It is questionable if Marshall had planned any grand strategy when he and the Court agreed to hear the case. By the time the justices heard arguments, however, the chief justice recognized the hostility of the Jeffersonian Republicans and the dilemma it posed to the Court. If it issued the mandamus, the Court had no power to enforce it, and Jefferson would certainly ignore it. If, on the other hand, the Court refused to issue the writ, it would appear that the judiciary had backed down before the executive, and this Marshall would not allow. The solution he chose has properly been termed a tour de force. In one stroke, Marshall managed to establish the power of the Court as the ultimate arbiter of the Constitution, to chastise the Jefferson administration for its failure to obey the law, and yet to avoid having the Court's authority challenged by the administration.

Marshall, adopting a style that would mark all his major opinions, reduced the case to a few basic issues. He asked three questions: Did Marbury have the right to the commission? If he did, and his right had been violated, did the law provide him with a remedy? If so, did mandamus from the Supreme Court constitute the proper remedy? The last question, the crucial one, dealt with the jurisdiction of the Court in a particular case, and should normally have been answered first, since a negative response would have obviated the need to decide the other issues. But that would have denied Marshall the opportunity to criticize Jefferson for what the chief justice saw as flouting the laws.

For the most part, following the arguments of Marbury's counsel on the first two questions, Marshall held that the validity of a commission existed once a president signed it and transmitted it to the secretary of state to affix the seal. Presidential discretion ended there, for the political decision had been made, and the secretary of state had only a ministerial task to perform—delivering the commission. In this, the law bound him, like anyone else, to obey. Marshall drew a careful and lengthy distinction between the political acts of the president and the secretary, in which the courts had no business interfering, and the simple administrative execution that, governed by law, the judiciary could review. "The province of the court," he wrote, "is, solely, to decide on the rights of individuals, not to inquire how the executive, or executive officers, perform duties in which they have a discretion. Questions in their nature political, or which are, by the constitution and laws, submitted to the executive, can never be made in this Court."

Having decided that Marbury had the right to the commission, Marshall next turned to the question of remedy, and once again, it appeared that the Court would find for the plaintiff. Mandamus would require Secretary Madison either to provide the original commission or secure a copy from the record. So far, those sitting in the courtroom listening to the chief justice read the opinion in his hard, dry voice must have assumed that Marbury had won his case. But then, having lectured Jefferson and Madison for their sins in "sport[ing] away the vested rights of others," Marshall turned to the crucial third question. Now at last, he declared that Congress, in granting the Supreme Court the power of mandamus in original jurisdiction in Section 13 of the Judiciary Act of 1789, had violated the Constitution. That document defined the original jurisdiction of the Court—that is, cases the Court could hear directly rather than on appeal from a lower court. The Constitution did not grant the Court the power of mandamus, and therefore Congress could not do so either. In effect, he told Marbury: "Plaintiff, your rights have been violated by Jefferson and mandamus is your proper remedy, but we are sorry; this Court cannot help you." Marshall thus had his cake and ate it too; he castigated the administration, but avoided a confrontation with Jefferson that the Court could not win.

The Politics and Logic of Marshall's Opinion

The politics of *Marbury v. Madison* have been widely hailed. In view of the attacks the Jeffersonians launched against the judiciary, Marshall had to make a strong statement to maintain the status of the Court as a coequal branch of government. By asserting the power to declare acts of Congress unconstitutional, a power that the Court would not exercise again for more than a half-century, Marshall claimed for the Court the paramount position within the government in constitutional interpretation. Marbury set the abiding precedent for the Court's power in this area, and even today the case is cited as authority whenever a law comes before the Court for constitutional review.

The judicial logic of Marshall's argument, however, has been questioned over the years, especially at times when Court decisions have been unpopular. The proper initial question for any court to ask is whether it has jurisdiction over a particular case; if the answer is no, it need not—and should not—decide the merits. In *Marbury*, the Court decided it had no jurisdiction to decide the two questions it had already decided. Marshall stood the normal procedure on its head in order to make his political points.

There is also some support for the idea that Marshall wrongly interpreted the Constitution. Article III, Section 2, of the Constitution gives the Supreme Court original jurisdiction in a limited number of cases, and then gives the Court "appellate Jurisdiction" in "other cases" but "with such Exceptions, and under such Regulations as the Congress shall make." Many modern scholars argue that "such Exceptions" can be interpreted to allow Congress to *expand,* but not contract, the original jurisdiction of the Court. If this were so, then Congress did have the constitutional authority to give the Court the right to issue a writ of mandamus. Had Marshall been arguing from a position of strength, perhaps with a supportive president in office, he might have made such an interpretation. But, given the political realities of the case, he could not do so.

Beyond the immediate issue, Marshall also claimed for the Court two far-ranging powers. The first of these, judicial review of legislation, was not that revolutionary, despite the absence of a specific delegation of this authority in the Constitution. Marshall carefully justified the Court's power through a commonsense reading of Articles III and VI. Article III provided that "the judicial Power of the United States, shall be vested in one supreme Court, and in such inferior Courts as Congress may from time to time establish." This grant of judicial power provided a broad mandate, intended to include all functions normally performed by courts, and therefore had to be read in light of customary usage and other provisions of the Constitution. Article VI, the supremacy clause, established a hierarchy of law, with the Constitution at the apex, superior to acts of Congress. Whenever the two conflicted, the lesser (legislation) had to give way to the greater (the Constitution). The power of courts to nullify legislative acts, while admittedly not exercised frequently, existed in English and American legal traditions, and sufficient examples, many fresh in memory, supported the power. Finally, the Constitution, although the fundamental law of the land, remained a law; as such, it had to be interpreted, and courts had always been the accepted interpreters of the law.

While these arguments supported Marshall's claim for the Court to decide the merits of a particular case, he assumed a second and even larger power. Not only did judges take an oath to support the Constitution, but the legislative and executive officers did so as well. Why did they not have an equal authority to decide on the constitutionality of a measure? Would not a major consideration of Congress in drafting a bill, and the president in signing it into law, be the validity of the statute in light of constitutional provisions? Marshall conceded that in certain areas the Court would defer to the other branches, but some agency had to decide which of the arms of government should pass on a specific measure. The question of "Who decides who decides?" is thus the most important of all, and Marshall assumed for the Court the power to determine when it would determine the merits and when it would make the judgment that Congress or the president had the responsibility.

Although *Marbury v. Madison* has remained the key precedent for judicial review, the debate, even if diminished in volume, has continued for nearly two centuries. The Republicans condemned the decision, and Jefferson, until the end of his life, derided the opinion. In 1823 he told Justice William Johnson that the decision was "merely an obiter dissertation of the Chief Justice." In 1825 Justice John Bannister Gibson of the Pennsylvania Supreme Court, dissenting in *Eakin v. Raub*, argued against Marshall's logic, claiming that courts lacked the power of judicial review unless it was specifically granted in a constitution.

It is likely that the debate will never be fully resolved, and the literature about judicial review will continue to grow. But the fact remains that the Court has claimed and exercised the power through most of our country's history—and, as Judge Learned Hand noted over a century later, the country is used to it by now. Moreover, it does fit into a government of checks and balances, as Hamilton had explained in *Federalist* No. 78. Finally, one can hardly argue with Marshall's statement of principle near the end of his opinion, "that a law repugnant to the constitution is void, and that courts, as well as other departments, are bound by that instrument."

The Republicans Continue Their Attack

The Republican attacks on the judiciary did not result from *Marbury,* or even begin with the case, although Marshall's tongue-lashing of the administration exacerbated the tensions. While the Repeal Act and a few new appointments whittled down Federalist strength in the judiciary, Federalists still controlled a major branch of government. Jefferson would ultimately make three appointments to the Supreme Court, but no vacancy occurred until 1804, the last year of his first term. Republicans resented this situation, and beyond their hunger for office, feared that Federalist judges would undermine Republican programs. In fact, the only excuse for this otherwise indefensible assault on judicial independence is that in fact some Federalist judges did abuse their positions.

At about the same time the Republican Congress was passing the Repeal Act, Republicans began an assault on Alexander Addison, a Federalist judge in Pennsylvania's western district. Addison infuriated the Republican majority in the state legislature with his frequent political harangues from the bench attacking Jefferson and the Republicans, while denying a Republican colleague the right to address a grand jury. Although judges in Pennsylvania could be removed by a simple majority vote of both houses, that was not enough for the Republicans, who decided that Addison's behavior deserved impeachment, a process that resembled a criminal trial. The state Republicans hired Alexander J. Dallas, whom Jefferson had appointed as federal district attorney, to manage the prosecution, and in January 1803, Dallas secured Addison's removal from office.

Shortly afterward, Jefferson sent a letter to the House of Representatives about complaints he had received concerning District Judge John Pickering of New Hampshire. Since the matter did not lie "within Executive cognizance"—that is, there was nothing he could do about it—the president forwarded the materials to Congress for whatever action it deemed appropriate. There is no question that Pickering played politics from the bench. The case that triggered the complaint involved a Republican-appointed customs collector's seizure of the ship *Eliza,* owned by a Federalist merchant, for allegedly carrying illegal goods. At the trial, an obviously drunken Pickering ruled for the ship owner and then verbally abused the Republican district attorney when he sought to appeal the decision. The elderly judge, who had served the state for many years and had been an active patriot during the Revolution, appeared to be mentally deranged as well as chronically inebriated. Pickering should have been removed from the bench, but instead this sad case became enmeshed in partisan strife.

Unfortunately, the Constitution made no provision for the removal of judges, or any official, in such a situation, and not until the Twenty-fifth

Amendment (1967) did the nation address this problem for the presidency. The Constitution noted that judges "shall hold their Offices during good Behaviour" but did not define this phrase. Elsewhere, the document provided for the impeachment of the president and "all civil Officers of the United States" for "Treason, Bribery, or other high Crimes and Misdemeanors." But no one seriously suggested that Pickering's conduct fell into this category. The president considered impeachment "a bungling way" to remove judges, and suggested a constitutional amendment to permit the chief executive, upon petition of Congress, to remove federal judges. Pickering's case might have offered the opportunity to amend the Constitution to provide for such cases, but the intense partisan bitterness over the judiciary at this time made any change impossible. At Jefferson's request, the judge's friends tried to persuade him to resign, but Pickering refused, in part because he was no longer mentally competent to make such a decision.

In the end, Pickering was removed from office without much partisanship. Of the thirty-six Federalists in the House, only eight voted against his impeachment. Of the nine Federalists in the Senate, only one voted to acquit him. However, instead of voting him guilty of "high crimes and misdemeanors," the senators voted that he was only "guilty as charged." Even the most partisan Republicans could not declare the obviously insane Pickering guilty of a "high crime."

The Impeachment of Justice Chase

The Pickering case proved but a rehearsal for the next act of the drama, the impeachment of Supreme Court Justice Samuel Chase. A patriot and signer of the Declaration of Independence, Chase had enjoyed a long and distinguished career that was blemished, however, by more than one untoward incident. He had not been averse to rioting during the anti-British agitation, and during the war he had engaged in some questionable financial operations, leading Alexander Hamilton to condemn him as "universally despised." Chase had originally opposed the Constitution, and later became a staunch Federalist. His combative nature was well-known. As a state judge he narrowly escaped removal from the Maryland bench when the legislature failed to muster the two-thirds vote necessary for his impeachment. Despite these liabilities, George Washington had appointed him to the Supreme Court in 1796.

Of all Federalist officials, none had earned greater dislike from the Republicans than Chase, who had presided over the highly political trials of Republican journalists Thomas Cooper and James Callender, who were found guilty of sedition and later pardoned by Jefferson. Lawyers feared

Chase's frequent browbeating, and he often used jury charges to vent his spleen on political opponents. In fact, the impeachment stemmed directly from his charge to a grand jury in Baltimore in May 1803, in which he intemperately condemned the Repeal Act, as well as recent proposals to broaden the suffrage in Maryland, which he claimed would only lead to "mobocracy" and the destruction of peace, order, freedom, and property.

Jefferson originally tried to ignore Chase, and some of the party leaders, aware that some Republican judges also used state benches for political purposes as well, hesitated to take action. But the groundswell of opposition, fueled by an aggressive Republican press, finally led Virginia representative John Randolph of Roanoke in January 1804 to call for an investigation of Chase's conduct. At the request of Pennsylvania Republicans, the committee also looked into the activities of Richard Peters, a district judge in that state. No one expected Peters to be impeached, and the House committee rapidly cleared him, but Republicans hoped that the threat of impeachment would teach him and other Federalist judges some caution. The committee did, however, recommend impeachment proceedings against Chase, and on March 11, by a vote of 73–32, the House approved the committee's recommendations.

On March 12, 1804, the same day that the Senate voted to remove Judge Pickering, the House impeached Justice Chase. It appeared the Republicans were going to dismantle the federal judiciary, one judge at a time. Chase's trial began in the Senate on February 4, 1805, presided over by Vice President Aaron Burr. Although the Republicans had been almost unanimous in their pursuit of Chase in the House, their ranks broke in the upper chamber. Sen. William Giles of Virginia made his feelings clear: "A removal by impeachment [is] nothing more than a declaration by Congress to this effect: You hold dangerous opinions, and if you are suffered to carry them into effect you will work the destruction of the nation. *We want your offices,* for the purposes of giving them to men who will fill them better." Some Republicans, however, no matter how they despised Chase, feared such a bald attack on the independence of the judiciary, and Giles evidently hinted that once they removed Chase, they would go after Marshall and the rest. Events in Pennsylvania at this time, where Republicans were attempting to impeach all but one of the judges on the state's highest court, underscored the seriousness of the threat. The effort there failed, but only by a narrow margin.

These fears led enough moderate Republicans to defect, so that after a bitter and sensational trial, the Senate failed to muster the two-thirds majority necessary to convict Chase. Unlike Pickering, who was too incompetent to mount a defense, Chase defended himself before the Senate with great vigor, arguing that "no judge can be impeached and removed from office for any act or offense for which he could not be indicted." Despite their overwhelming control of the Senate, the

Republicans got only a tiny majority—nothing close to the required two-thirds vote—to vote for two of the eight charges of impeachment. On one count, only four Republicans voted to convict, and on another the Senate was unanimous in voting for acquittal. Chase had no doubt abused his office—he even admitted that his conduct on the bench had, on occasion, been "improper and dangerous," but he had not acted criminally, and that, in essence, became the standard for removal of federal judges. But Chase was superb in his own defense, and in the process shaped the law of impeachment for the next two centuries.

Following Chase's acquittal and the failure to impeach the Pennsylvania judges, the Republicans' assault on the judiciary ebbed to some extent. The question of how to remove judges who were no longer capable of fulfilling their duties, or who abused the position but fell short of criminal behavior, remained unanswered. Shortly after Chase's trial, John Randolph proposed a constitutional amendment allowing the president to remove a federal judge on joint address of both houses of Congress. Although a majority of the Senate indicated its willingness to consider the motion, the idea never caught on. Jefferson, who did not take an active role in the proceedings, continued to worry about an irresponsible judiciary. Having found impeachment an empty threat, he wrote in 1820 that judges "consider themselves secure for life; they skulk from responsibility to public opinion. . . . A judiciary independent of a king or executive alone, is a good thing; but independence of the will of the nation is a solecism, at least in a republican government."

While losing the battle over Chase, Jefferson nevertheless made an important contribution to the development of American courts and constitutional law. Following the trial, federal judges began to avoid flagrantly partisan acts. If nothing else, the attack on the judiciary helped create a federal bench that concentrated on the law and left overt politics to the elected representatives of the people.

But it would be impossible for the bench to avoid the political fall-out from all controversies. When such a situation arose, the judges had to exercise their political skills, as well as display their legal knowledge. Chief Justice Marshall would soon face such a challenge during the treason trial of Vice President Aaron Burr.

Defining Treason

Burr had once been a close ally of Jefferson and served as his first vice president, but in 1804 he ended what little chance he had for any future political career by killing Alexander Hamilton in a duel. His fortunes in ruin, Burr embarked upon an ill-conceived scheme to capture and settle territory in Spanish-held western lands. His exact plans are shrouded in confusion, since he kept a number of options open. But whatever his plans may have been, the whole scheme fell apart when his chief confederate, General James Wilkinson, the governor of Louisiana (and secretly in the pay of Spain), denounced Burr to Jefferson, suggesting that Burr's actions could provoke a war with Spain. The army seized Burr as he floated downstream on a flatboat to New Orleans, and then brought him to Richmond to stand trial for treason in the U.S. Circuit Court.

Convicting Burr became an obsession for Jefferson, and by extension, for the entire Republican Party. The president publicly denounced Burr in a letter to Congress, kept in close touch with the proceedings throughout the case, and personally directed the government prosecutor. His disdain for the guarantees of a fair trial, his suggestion that habeas corpus be suspended, and his veiled threats that if Burr went free the entire Supreme Court should be impeached all reveal what one historian has termed "the darker side" of a man venerated in history as the great apostle of individual liberty.

Since Burr was captured in a territory where there was no federal court, he was brought to the nearest site of a federal court that could hear the trial, namely Richmond, and Jefferson's fury at Burr quickly encompassed John Marshall, who presided over the trial as circuit judge for Virginia. (At that time, circuit courts had original jurisdiction to try treason cases; the Supreme Court has never had that power. Marshall presided because of his dual role—as a member both of the Supreme Court and of one of the circuits.)

Painfully aware of the political ramifications of the trial, Marshall also recognized the serious legal issues involved. Historians have in general given him high marks for his handling of the case, as well as for the law he propounded during its proceedings. The chief justice, however, does not completely escape criticism. Several times during the trial he took the occasion to chastise the government for its apparent vendetta against Burr and its disregard for the essential safeguards of a fair trial. Rather indiscreetly, he even attended a dinner given by Burr's counsel in honor of the defendant! Little wonder, then, that Jefferson saw Marshall as attempting to coddle traitors and embarrass his administration.

Above all, the chief justice wanted to depoliticize the case, an effort doomed to failure from the beginning. On April 1, Marshall dismissed the charge of treason against Burr. The Constitution (Article III, Section 3) defines treason as "only in levying War against [the United States], or in adhering to their enemies, giving them Aid and Comfort." To support the charge of treason, therefore, war actually had to take place. Conspiracy to make war, while certainly a crime, did not meet the definition of treason. This definition of treason as only related to war remains valid to this day.

Despite a reference to the "hand of malignity," which must not be permitted to "grasp any individual against whom its hate may be directed, or whom it may capriciously seize, charge him with some secret crime, and put him on the proof of his innocence," Marshall's opinion displayed prudence and legal exactitude. A careful review of the evidence failed to prove treason, for actual war had not been levied against the United States. The government would, however, be allowed to try Burr for assembling a military expedition against a country with whom the United States was then at peace, and if it could gather any evidence that Burr had intended to wage war against the United States, it could then seek a grand jury indictment for treason.

A furious Jefferson wrote to Senator Giles that the day could not be distant when the Constitution would be amended so as to remove "the error . . . which makes any branch independent of the nation." With more passion for vengeance than sensitivity to legal rights, the president personally took direction of the prosecution. Witnesses would be produced, he assured Giles, as well as evidence to "satisfy the world, if not the judges," of Burr's treason. He immediately sent out a call for anyone who could testify to the former vice president's guilt, promising pardons to anyone connected with the affair if they would cooperate. Jefferson even instructed George Hay, the government attorney, to introduce Marshall's opinion in *Marbury* and then denounce it "as not law." Hay wisely declined to do so, and ultimately, after much maneuvering on both sides, the jury found Burr not guilty.

Although the Burr trial took place in circuit court, the ruling is properly viewed as part of John Marshall's tenure on the Supreme Court, for, as much as any case he participated in, it helped to develop the power of the judiciary and strengthen the rule of law. Despite Marshall's occasional slaps at Jefferson, he remained for the most part highly sensitive to the overcharged political atmosphere in which the trial took place. He worded his rulings carefully and displayed meticulous attention to legal principles; despite the confusion that still exists regarding Burr's intentions, there is little doubt that treason, as defined by the Constitution, had not occurred. The Jeffersonians, as expected, reacted strongly to the acquittal. The president sent several hundred pages of supporting materials to Congress, urging it to consider the appropriate steps that should be taken—hoping that one would be the removal of John Marshall from the bench. But increased tensions with Great Britain and France soon diverted the administration's attention to other matters, and the Burr issue was dropped.

Aftermath

Marbury received much less attention in 1803 than it did in succeeding years, in part because the result of the case—that Marbury never got his commission—was uncontroversial. Jefferson, who had no intention of granting the commission, was off the hook, and the Federalists were pleased enough with Marshall's deft handling of the case not to be too sorry about the result.

Following the case, William Marbury faded from public view, his political fortunes declining alongside those of the Federalist Party. He remained a well-to-do banker, and although he did not recognize it at the time, his name would live on, as his case is studied by succeeding generations of students and cited by federal courts. He is the only disappointed office-seeker whose portrait hangs in the Supreme Court building. Chief Justice Warren Burger designated the justices' private dining room as the "John Marshall Room," and in it, side by side, are portraits of William Marbury and James Madison. Marbury's portrait was painted by Rembrandt Peale, a cousin of his wife's, and it depicts a prosperous banker, well satisfied with his world. The disappointment of not getting his commission does not appear on his face.

Cases Cited

Eakin v. Raub, 12 S. & R. (Pa. 1825)
Marbury v. Madison, 5 U.S. (1 Cr.) 137 (1803)
Stuart v. Laird, 5 U.S. (1 Cr.) 299 (1803)

For Further Reading

Certainly the best book on the subject is William E. Nelson, *Marbury v. Madison: The Origins and Legacy of Judicial Review* (2000), although the older Robert L. Clinton, *Marbury v. Madison and Judicial Review* (1989), is still useful. Information about the plaintiff is drawn primarily from David F. Forte, "Marbury's Travail: Federalist Politics and William Marbury's Appointment as Justice of the Peace," 45 *Catholic Law Review* 349 (1996). For John Marshall, see R. Kent Newmyer, *John Marshall and the Heroic Age of the Supreme Court* (2001), and Charles F. Hobson, *The Great Chief Justice: John Marshall and the Rule of Law* (1996). For Jefferson's conflict with the judiciary, see Richard E. Ellis, *The Jeffersonian Crisis: Courts and Politics in the Young Republic* (1971). The story, with more of an emphasis on the political and philosophical differences, is also told in James F. Simon, *What Kind of Nation: Thomas Jefferson, John Marshall, and the Epic Struggle to Create a United States* (2002). For the Burr trial as well as the Chase impeachment, see also Joseph Wheelan, *Jefferson's Vendetta* (2005).

The Case of the Larcenous Cashier

M'Culloch v. Maryland (1819)

ONE OF THE MOST CONTENTIOUS political and constitutional battles in the early decades of the United States concerned a bank, and whether under the Constitution Congress had the power to charter banks and other institutions. The case that ultimately resolved these issues bore the name of James William McCulloh, a man of modest means, boundless energy and ambition, and few scruples. The decision by Chief Justice John Marshall is considered one of the foundation stones of American constitutional development.

Interpreting the Constitution: Jefferson versus Hamilton

The question of whether Congress had the power to charter banks had first arisen when Alexander Hamilton, secretary of the Treasury under George Washington, proposed a three-part plan to solve the nation's economic woes. The Constitution had, in large part, come about because of the financial problems besieging the federal government under the Articles of Confederation. The Confederation Congress had had no independent taxing power, and so it had been unable to pay the mounting debt owed to European nations as well as to its own citizens.

Hamilton presented his "Report on the Public Credit" to Congress when it convened in January 1790. He proposed to convert more than $13 million in unpaid interest into principal, and then fund the entire debt at par—that is, one hundred cents on the dollar. A certain part of the government's revenue from its new taxing power under the Constitution would be pledged to paying this debt, which would also include bonds issued by the states to help finance the Revolution. As Hamilton well understood, the plan would bring influential and wealthy citizens who held the debt into closer ties and greater support for the new national government.

Hamilton proposed using a tariff on imported goods to provide the revenue to pay the $80 million national debt, and the funding and assumption of prior state and federal debts would indeed bring order out of the government's financial chaos. But the nation also lacked an adequate circulating currency and a central bank, and for the third part of his plan Hamilton looked to the model of the Bank of England, which served as the main depository of government funds, the issuer of currency, and a regulator of smaller banks. Hamilton's proposed Bank of the United States would do all this and more; it would be the fiscal agent of the government, facilitate tax collection, and stimulate the flow of capital into and around the country. As he noted, the Bank, which would be privately owned but responsible to the government, would be "a political machine of the greatest importance to the State."

Despite spirited opposition from southern representatives and senators who questioned whether the national government had this power, the bank bill easily passed both houses of Congress. Although President Washington felt disposed to sign the bill, some of the objections raised in the congressional debate about the constitutional power of Congress to charter a bank bothered him. So, as was his custom, he sought advice. He asked James Madison to prepare a veto measure should he decide against the measure, and also sought the views of Attorney General Edmund Randolph and Secretary of State Thomas Jefferson.

The views of Jefferson and Hamilton provided the first great debate on the meaning of the Constitution after it had been adopted and the new government established. Jefferson conceded that the proper construction of the Constitution "where a phrase will bear either of two meanings, [is] to give it that which will allow some meaning to the other parts of the instrument, and not that which would render all the others useless." But, he argued, neither the taxing power nor the necessary and proper clause supported justification for a bank charter. Jefferson claimed that the Constitutional Convention had not intended to give Congress a free hand, but to "lace them up straightly within the enumerated powers." The necessary and proper clause meant no more than that Congress could enact measures *indispensable* to carrying out the enumerated powers in a narrowly defined manner. In other words, Congress could do only what the Constitution expressly permitted it to do, and nothing else. He claimed that the convention had not given

Congress the authority to grant charters because it feared that Congress would do just what Hamilton proposed—charter a bank.

(On this Jefferson was wrong. In the debates at the Philadelphia Convention delegates had rejected a proposal to put in a clause expressly giving Congress the charter power—not because it wanted to deny that power, but because it was assumed that any sovereign had the authority to issue a charter. It was not necessary to spell out a power already there.)

Washington then showed Hamilton the objections and invited a reply. The Treasury secretary quickly prepared a 15,000-word "Opinion on the Constitutionality of the Bank," a document considered by scholars to be the most forceful argument ever written that the frugal words of the Constitution "ought to be construed liberally in advancement of the public good." The necessary and proper clause meant that Congress had to have the fullest authority possible to carry out the general goals of the Constitution, such as the common defense and the general welfare, "by all the means fairly applicable to the attainment of those ends."

Where Jefferson had argued that Congress could only do what the Constitution expressly permitted it to do, Hamilton claimed that Congress could do everything except what the Constitution specifically forbade. Rather than a statute, which is to be interpreted literally and applies to a specific matter, the men at Philadelphia had wanted to provide a broad framework for a government, and so had provided not only express powers but implied ones as well. Congress had the express power to lay and collect taxes, to coin money, and to regulate trade, so therefore it had to have the implied power to create an appropriate mechanism to exercise those functions—in this instance, a bank.

The debate between Hamilton and Jefferson represented far more than differing modes of textual interpretation. Jefferson and his fellow Virginian and ally, James Madison, feared a strong national government, and although they recognized the need for some central authority, they wanted that government to do no more than what was absolutely necessary lest it endanger the liberties of the individual. Hamilton did not want to restrict individual rights, but he had seen the chaos of the confederation, and believed that only a powerful central agency would ensure the economic stability on which the nation's future prosperity and happiness depended. A government by its nature had to be able to govern, and while he recognized constitutional limits—he had, after all, helped to draft the document—he claimed for the government all other powers inherent in sovereignty.

Hamilton's view prevailed; Washington signed the measure, and the Bank of the United States began business with a twenty-year charter. It proved very successful, and functioned exactly as Hamilton had hoped. But when its charter expired in 1811, James Madison occupied the White House, the Jeffersonian Republicans controlled Congress, and they refused to renew the charter. The nation's finance grew muddled, and local state banks—free from the regulations enforced by a central bank—flooded the nation with cheap and sometimes worthless currency that fueled land speculation in the West.

Then came the War of 1812, and the Madison administration was embarrassed by the lack of a national bank, both as a source for borrowing and as a means of transferring funds from one part of the country to another. Whatever their earlier beliefs about the constitutionality of the bank, Madison and the younger Republicans faced up to its necessity. The issue, he told Congress, had been settled "by repeated recognitions . . . of the validity of such an institution in acts of the legislative, executive and judicial branches of the Government . . . accompanied by . . . a concurrence of the general will of the nation." Congress agreed, and in 1816 issued a twenty-year charter for a new second Bank of the United States modeled after Hamilton's original, but capitalized at $35 million instead of $10 million.*

Many of the older states' rights Republicans still opposed a charter, as did New England Federalists, who did not want to see the nation's banking center shift from Boston to Philadelphia. While no one had ever challenged the first Bank in the courts, no one doubted that there would be a suit this time, due in part to a growing fear in southern states about the increased power of the national government. Despite Madison's assertion, the Supreme Court had never passed on the legitimacy of the bank or of congressional power to charter such an institution.

James McCulloh—Cashier Extraordinaire

In 1818 the Bank, anticipating an economic downturn, began calling in loans, and in doing so caused a number of overextended local banks in the South and West to fail. The Panic arrived, but many people blamed the Bank for causing it, and under pressure from jealous local banks, seven states passed laws restricting the Bank's operations within their borders; in some instances they taxed banknotes issued by non-state-chartered institutions. (Prior to the passage of the Federal Reserve Act in 1913, paper currency consisted primarily of denominational certificates, i.e., banknotes, issued by private banks.)

In February 1818 the Maryland legislature passed a measure that had but a single purpose—to banish from the state the "monstrous"

---

* Jefferson had also been forced to adopt a Hamiltonian interpretation of the Constitution in 1803 when he purchased the Louisiana Territory from France, an action that could not be grounded in a specific clause of the Constitution but could be rationalized through use of the necessary and proper clause.

second Bank of the United States—through the device of levying high taxes on the Bank's notes. Such a tax would cost consumers far more to use Bank of the United States notes than those from local Maryland banks, which were untaxed. The law especially targeted the large Baltimore branch of the Bank, run by its president, James A. Buchanan, and its cashier, James William McCulloh. (As in a number of cases, the clerk of the Supreme Court misspelled the name, and the case has come down as *M'Culloch v. Maryland.*)

A native of Philadelphia, McCulloh had until this time lived primarily in obscurity. He may—or may not—have served with a group of Baltimore volunteers during the War of 1812, and appears to have been wounded when the British invaded Maryland. Returning to Baltimore, he entered the banking firm of Smith and Buchanan, and had progressed to the position of cashier, which paid him a salary of $4,000 a year. Although at the time a man of modest means, McCulloh had ambition and talents just waiting to be tapped. Rapid growth in postwar Baltimore provided opportunity not only for the hardworking, honest businessman, but also for those of another stripe. In Baltimore, John Quincy Adams noted, prosperity and profligacy had become intertwined, and when the Bank of the United States opened a Baltimore branch, Buchanan and McCulloh seized the opportunities to pursue personal enrichment at the expense of sound financial management.

Buchanan, McCulloh, and a third person, George Williams, formed a separate company in late 1816 or early 1817 for the sole purpose of acquiring and trading the Bank's stock. They soon understood that the central office in Philadelphia had neither the interest nor the ability to curb their activity, and they used their positions as officers of the Baltimore branch to manipulate the price of the stock in the open market. They made substantial loans to themselves, sometimes secured by the stock but more often with no collateral at all.

McCulloh, as the Baltimore branch cashier, played the key role. In his official capacity as an officer of the Bank he spoke critically of the central management in Philadelphia, calling it too conservative. In a letter to the secretary of the Treasury in 1817, he spoke approvingly of a "system of permanent loans adopted toward individuals and likewise to banks." He failed to mention, however, that most of these loans had been made without any collateral security, and to individuals like him and his partners whose sole purpose was secret profit. McCulloh had, in fact, approved unsecured loans to himself totaling $500,000, part of the $3 million he and his confederates eventually stole from the Bank.

Shortly after the Maryland tax law went into effect in early 1818, McCulloh approved the issuance of banknotes to George Williams on unstamped paper—that is, paper on which the state tax had not been paid. On May 18, 1818, John James, the Maryland state treasurer for the Western Shore, brought an action against the Bank to recover $2,500 in penalties owed on these notes. There is some evidence that McCulloh and James acted collusively in the matter, planning to set up a confrontation to test the legality of the second Bank. There had always been questions about constitutionality, but the second Bank, unlike the first, had become widely unpopular because of poor management almost from the time it had opened for business. McCulloh had no real interest in protecting the Bank; he had already stolen about as much as he could, and if the Bank were declared unconstitutional, he could walk away with his ill-gotten gains and no one would be the wiser.

The case proceeded quickly through the Maryland courts. In June the Baltimore County Court found that the Bank owed the tax, a judgment confirmed by the Maryland Court of Appeals. The Supreme Court placed the case on its docket on September 18, 1818, and set argument for the following February. During this time the schemers' plans began to unravel, as the central bank began trying to get control over the loans issued by the branches. The head office demanded a list of all the stock loans made by the Baltimore branch. McCulloh, at his partners' urging, stalled, only to have the officers in Philadelphia insist more forcefully. He began falsifying records and managed to hide his chicanery until January 1819, when one of his partners, William Jones, the president of the Baltimore branch, resigned. Soon news about the frauds became common knowledge, but that played no role when Daniel Webster rose before the Court to argue the constitutionality of the second Bank of the United States.

Arguments before the Court

Oral argument lasted nine days before an attentive Court and an appreciative audience. Justice Joseph Story noted to a friend that the case involved a "great question" and was argued before "a crowded audience of ladies and gentlemen; the hall was full almost to suffocation, and many went away for want of room." The Court itself, Story said, recognized that this was a "case involving a constitutional question of great public importance, and the sovereign rights of the United States and the State of Maryland." Because of its significance, the Court did away with its usual rule of allowing only two lawyers to argue for each side, and so it heard a total of six people make their cases.

Certainly the best known of the advocates, and one who regularly drew a large crowd whenever he appeared before the Court, was Daniel Webster. Called by some the "Godlike Daniel" and by others "Black

Dan," the Boston attorney (he would later be a senator and also serve as secretary of state) was a physically commanding figure with black hair and a large head in which were set a pair of piercing eyes. Well conscious of his appearance, he always came before the Court impeccably attired in the latest fashion. But his greatest asset was his voice, which according to one Englishman who heard him speak, "when animated, it rings on the ear like a clarion."

Webster framed the issues simply: Did Congress have the power to create the Bank? If so, could Maryland levy a tax on it? In those days the justices did not pepper attorneys appearing before them with questions, but sat silently listening to the arguments. So they listened attentively as Webster led them through the case for the Bank, claiming that by this time it ought to be beyond question that Congress had the power, and that the Bank itself was constitutional. Since neither the executive nor the legislative branch had ever expressed an opinion against the Bank's constitutionality, then neither should the Court, "unless [the Bank's] repugnancy with the constitution were plain and manifest."

But even though he claimed that the constitutionality of the Bank and congressional power to create it were clear to all, he rehearsed those arguments again so as to make them even clearer to the justices. The Bank was a means, not an end—a mere adjunct to Congress carrying out powers given to it directly by the Constitution. That being the case, then the states could not tax the Bank: "An unlimited power to tax involves, necessarily, a power to destroy." If the Court upheld the Maryland tax, then the taxing power could be applied by the states to all branches of the national government, including the courts. Such a power could not be countenanced.

Following Webster came the first attorney for Maryland, Joseph Hopkinson, a distinguished Philadelphia lawyer who in other cases had been Webster's ally. A thoughtful and refined man, he was described by contemporaries as a skilled advocate, with a "beautiful and highly trained mind." Hopkinson did not accept the argument that the constitutionality of the Bank had long been established. Indeed, there had been a running debate on that question almost from the time Alexander Hamilton had proposed it. But even if one accepted the argument that the government needed some agency to hold and disburse tax monies, that agency did not have to have branches. Those branches existed for one purpose only—to make money for the stockholders.

This brought him to the question of taxation, which Hopkinson declared implicated "the highest attributes of sovereignty, the right to raise revenue; in fact, the right to exist; without which no other right can be held or enjoyed." Banks were not immune from taxation, and there was no reason the Bank of the United States should be. Even though it carried out certain tasks for the government, it was essentially a private corporation, a status that the great Hamilton himself had characterized as necessary. Take away the official-sounding name and it is "a mere association of individuals, putting their money into a common stock, to be loaned for profit, and to divide the gains." Such a corporation deserved no special immunity from taxation.

Hopkinson did not shirk from the key constitutional issue, whether the "necessary and proper clause" expanded the reach of specific delegated powers or whether it was a mere truism. He condemned the very idea of a government of ill-defined but apparently all-encompassing authority, and declared that the only proper way to interpret the Constitution and the powers it gave Congress was as narrowly as possible.

Webster and Hopkinson laid out the major arguments for the Bank and for Maryland, and for the most part the other attorneys rang changes on these themes. William Wirt, the attorney general of the United States, also argued on behalf of the Bank. He explained that "necessary and proper" is equivalent to "needful and adapted." This, he claimed, was consistent with both the common understandings of the terms and the manner in which the Constitution had intended them to be interpreted. Wirt also went into the history of the Bank, and noted the great distress faced by the government during the years between the expiration of the first Bank and the chartering of the second.

Wirt was followed by Walter Jones, a Washington attorney and the least known of the six advocates, who nonetheless enjoyed a reputation as a "legal genius." He brought nothing new to the arguments, but expounded at length on the compact theory of government, by which he claimed that ultimate authority rested not in Congress but in the states who had joined together through the Constitution (a compact) and in which sovereignty rested with the states and not with the national government. (This theory would be a key feature in the Southern states' rights argument leading up to the Civil War.)

The last two speakers between them took up five days—Luther Martin, the attorney general of Maryland, and William Pinkney, an acerbic but highly effective litigator. A later chief justice, Roger Brooks Taney, said, "I have heard all of the greatest advocates of the United States, but I have seen none equal to Pinkney." Martin mounted an extensive attack on the very idea of implied powers, and that one could not, by a fair reading of the Constitution, find in it one power more than those expressly described. Pinkney declared that it was beneath his dignity, and that of the Court, to even waste time on such a claim, since both the text and experience had shown that the government not only had but needed the implied powers to carry out its duties. He attacked the claim that states could tax at their will, and closed the ninth day declaring that "no other alternative remains, but for this Court to interpose its authority, and save the nation from the consequences of this dangerous attempt."

Decision

After the attorneys had finished, it seemed clear that the Court had to resolve two questions: Did Congress have the power to charter the Bank? And if so, did Maryland have the right to tax its operations within the state? Although the questions appeared simple enough, the answers—and the form they took—would have far larger implications. Few people expected the Court to rule against congressional authority to charter the Bank. In the arguments before the bench, counsel for both sides apologized about repeating contentions that had now grown "threadbare" since the debate between Hamilton and Jefferson more than a quarter-century earlier. Why should the Court adopt Jefferson's views when even his own party had abandoned them? Madison had certainly been right when he noted the "concurrence of the general will of the nation" in the Bank's legitimacy. For most observers, only the constitutionality of the state tax on a valid organ of the national government seemed in doubt.

The opinion came down quickly—so quickly that some people speculated that a draft had been prepared even before the Court heard oral argument. Chief Justice John Marshall's opinion in *M'Culloch v. Maryland* went far beyond the two basic questions. His "state paper," as it has been properly called, put forth theories of national sovereignty and federal power that over the next century and a half would be used to justify the growth of the central government and its involvement in nearly every aspect of national life. *M'Culloch* would help make the Constitution support the "great national interests," in Justice Joseph Story's words, "which shall bind us in an indissoluble chain." Speaking for a unanimous Court, Marshall quickly demolished Maryland's assertions of state sovereignty. While conceding that the federal government had limited powers in a federal union of divided sovereignty with the states, within its assigned spheres of power, the national government reigned supreme. Whenever legitimate federal power conflicted with state authority, the latter had to give way. The federal government took precedence over the state, because it derived its mandate from the people: "It is the government of all; its powers are delegated by all; it represents all, and acts for all."

But if the state could not restrict a legitimate act of Congress, did Congress have the power to charter a bank in the first place? Such authority had admittedly not been included among the enumerated powers of Article I, Section 8, but Marshall still held that it came within the parameters of the Constitution. Relying on William Pinkney's argument for the Bank, as well as Alexander Hamilton's justification for the first Bank of the United States, Marshall set out a broad interpretation of constitutional power.

To begin with, he declared that "[w]e must never forget that it is a constitution we are expounding." If every power necessary to the federal government had to be listed, the Constitution would be nothing more than a legal code, whose prolixity "could scarce be embraced by the human mind." The enumerated powers merely pointed out obvious traits of government, but they had to be interpreted liberally, so that the government could act without undue restraint in any area of its responsibilities. The Framers had been too wise to anticipate all contingencies, and so they had provided, along with enumerated powers, the power to pass "all laws which shall be necessary and proper for carrying into execution the foregoing powers."

The word *necessary* should not be construed, as Maryland urged, as a restriction, but rather as an addition to the enumerated powers. Congress thus had discretion over which means it would choose to implement "those great powers on which the welfare of the nation essentially depends." Then, in one of his most oft-quoted passages, Marshall declared: "Let the end be legitimate, let it be within the scope of the constitution, and all means which are appropriate, which are plainly adapted to that end, which are not prohibited, but consist with the letter and spirit of the constitution, are constitutional." Any other reading would reduce the Constitution to a "splendid bauble," and not a great charter of government "intended to endure for ages to come, and, consequently, to be adapted to the various crises of human affairs."

But could the Bank (which had barely been mentioned so far) be taxed? Marshall had made clear the supremacy of the national government when operating within its broadly defined parameters; now he set about preventing the state's conceded sovereignty from clashing with that of the federal government. The Constitution, the chief justice noted, did not expressly limit the state's power to tax, but by a series of inferences, he solved that problem. If the government had the power to create an agency, then it obviously had the means to preserve it. But "the power to tax involves the power to destroy . . . and render useless the power to create." How could the federal government be supreme within its area of competency if another sovereign could exercise a power capable of reaching into and destroying creations authorized by the Constitution? Marshall did not discuss whether the Maryland tax actually threatened the Bank with destruction; the *potentially* injurious power of the tax alone invalidated it on constitutional grounds. Declaring it as a broad principle, Marshall concluded that "[s]tates have no power, by taxation or otherwise, to retard, impede, burden, or in any manner control the operation of the constitutional laws enacted by Congress to carry into execution the powers vested in the general government."

The impact of *M'Culloch* lay less in its specific holding than in the bold and expansive manner in which the chief justice interpreted federal power. The decision heartened the Bank but did not prove decisive. Within a few years, the exact same issue came back before the Court in *Osborn v. Bank of the United States* (1824), when Ohio, in defiance of a circuit court injunction, levied and collected a tax on the Bank. Once again John Marshall, this time with Justice William Johnson dissenting, upheld the constitutionality of the Bank and gave another strong lecture on national supremacy. Moreover, despite the Eleventh Amendment, which had been passed to prevent private entities, such as people and companies, from suing states in federal courts, he ensured the Bank's access to the federal courts to defend itself against similar attacks by a state. Even more important, he ruled that agents of the state were personally liable for damages inflicted while executing an unconstitutional statute.

There could not have been much surprise at the ruling. After all, the first Bank had lasted twenty years, and the second Bank, despite intense hostility from local interests, had already gained recognition as an important and useful feature of the nation's economic life. Charges that the Bank had caused the Panic of 1819 had led to an attempt in the House of Representatives to revoke the charter, but a majority in Congress considered the Bank too valuable for such a severe action. So "the Bank Case" would never have become "the Great Case" just for its validation of the Bank's legitimacy.

It became a great case—one of the most important in American constitutional development—because John Marshall justified the Bank's legitimacy on the basis of a broad and flexible interpretation of the Constitution, arguing that a constitution could not be expected to list every power of government, and that Congress therefore enjoyed large discretion in determining the means it would use to achieve its ends. His analysis provided the foundation for broadly conceived national action that has been drawn upon ever since as the government expanded its activities. Moreover, Marshall's decision came at a time of government retrenchment after a period of nationalistic expansion during and after the War of 1812; it did not serve to justify current activity so much as provide the jurisprudential basis for future growth.

The States' Rights Attack

To many Republicans, however, *M'Culloch* sounded an alarm, and their response triggered an event unique in American constitutional history—a justice defending a decision publicly albeit pseudonymously. William Brockenbrough attacked the decision in a series of essays in the *Richmond Enquirer* beginning at the end of March 1819, under the pseudonym "Amphictyon." (As was common from colonial times through the early Republic, famous people writing essays on matters of public policy often took the names of ancient Greeks or Romans. Amphictyon had been king of Athens, and had created an alliance with neighboring city-states for common defense.)

Brockenbrough, a member of the Virginia elite, served on the circuit court in Richmond, an important tribunal just one step below the court of appeals. He belonged to the Richmond Junto, a powerful secretive group that controlled Virginia politics for many years, and he spoke for other states' rights advocates who feared the Court under Marshall would build up the power of the national government to the point where it could conceivably attack the institution of slavery.

He began by criticizing the manner in which the Court had decided the case, through a "unanimous and decided opinion." This echoed the longtime lament of Thomas Jefferson that under John Marshall the Court had abandoned the English practice of *seriatim* opinions, in which each justice spoke for himself. Brockenbrough believed the public should have the benefit of each member's views, rather than just hearing from the arch-nationalist Marshall. Creating a more powerful national government, he charged, is "a subject which has employed [Marshall's] thoughts, his tongue, and his pen, as a politician, and an historian, for more than thirty years." No doubt the opinion was very able, "as everyone must admit," for after all, it had come from a man of "gigantic powers." But *M'Culloch* should be seen for what it really was—a political rather than a legal resolution of the important issues raised by the Bank.

The crux of the Amphictyon essays involved what Brockenbrough saw as the threat to states' rights posed by the Court's decisions under Marshall, and the great powers they confirmed in Congress that had not been given to that body in the Constitution. He saw two great dangers:

> The first is the denial that the powers of the federal government were delegated by the states; and the second is, that the grant of powers to the government, and particularly the grant of powers "necessary and proper" ought to be construed in a

liberal, rather than a restricted sense. Both of these principles tend directly to the consolidation of the states, and to strip them of some of the most important attributes of their sovereignty.

These arguments continued the constitutional debate that had occupied the country since 1787, and Brockenbrough charged that the Court had gotten it wrong when it declared that the powers of the national government came from the people rather than from the states.

The case, therefore, had not really been about the Bank; Brockenbrough conceded that the debates surrounding the establishment of the first Bank in 1791 and the Second Bank in 1815 had resolved the constitutionality of that institution. The core issue involved the powers of the states, and the notion that in a federal system all sovereignty flowed from the states. It would be a claim maintained by the Southern states until the Civil War bloodily resolved the matter, and even beyond.

John Marshall's Defense

Although Marshall had not responded to earlier criticisms of his decisions, he felt compelled to answer Amphictyon, and in many ways the nine essays he published as "A Friend of the Constitution" in the *Philadelphia Union* in late April were a continuation and expansion of his opinion in *M'Culloch*.

Unlike the states' rights Republicans, Marshall believed that the power of the national government came from the people, not from the states, and the people bestowed on that government certain powers as well as certain limits—the powers to make sure that the government could function successfully in their best interests, and the limits so as to preserve their liberties. He addressed specifically the claim that the Constitution made the national government one of limited authority, delineated by those powers specifically listed, and nothing else. "The power to do a thing," he claimed, "and the power to carry that thing into execution, are, I humbly conceive, the same power, and the one cannot be termed with propriety 'additional' or 'incidental' to the other." This, of course, was the heart of both Hamilton's defense of the Bank and the opinion in *M'Culloch*—a power, even if expressly declared, was of no value if it could not be implemented, and the implementation could take whatever form Congress chose.

The heart of his arguments, which drew from his opinion, dealt with the nature of the Constitution. It was not "a contract for a single

object, every thing relating to which, might be recollected and inserted."
It is a constitution, a document that is

> the act of a people. The powers of this government are
> conferred for their own benefit, are essential to their own
> prosperity, and are to be exercised for their good, by persons
> chosen for that purpose by themselves. The object of that
> government is not a single one which can be minutely
> described, with all its circumstances. The attempt to do so,
> would actually change its nature, and defeat its purpose. It is
> intended to be a general system for future times, to be adapted
> by those who administer it, to all future occasions that may
> come within its view. From its nature, such an instrument can
> describe only the great objects it is intended to accomplish,
> and state in general terms, the specific powers which are
> deemed necessary for those objects.

It would ultimately take a civil war to swing the argument in favor
of Marshall's nationalistic interpretation of the Constitution, but in the
end his views—and those of Alexander Hamilton—prevailed.

Citizen McCulloh

Two months after the decision, news about the full extent of
McCulloh's fraud became widely known, and the Bank's directors forced
him to resign. The losses at the Baltimore branch eventually exceeded
$1.5 million (equivalent to more than $26 million in current dollars),
and while McCulloh and his cronies were not the only ones to abuse the
Bank and manipulate the stock, their activities far outpaced those of
other schemers. McCulloh, Buchanan, Williams, and Jones became
emblematic of all the wrongs that people associated with the second
Bank of the United States, including the belief that its policies had triggered the Panic of 1819.

The decision in the Supreme Court, of course, did not speak to the
criminal culpability of Bank officers, and Nicholas Biddle, soon to
become president of the Bank, worried about the possibility that
McCulloh and others like him could "defraud the institution of millions
and escape the criminal law of the United States." His concerns proved
justified. McCulloh, Buchanan, and Williams were indicted for conspiracy to defraud the Bank and its investors. At the initial trial in Hartford
County Court in 1820, the judges dismissed the indictment after accepting defense arguments that conspiracy to defraud was neither a crime

recognized by statute in Maryland nor an offense at common law. In December 1821 the Maryland Court of Appeals reversed and ordered that the case go to trial on the merits—that is, to determine the guilt or innocence of the defendants.

After a bench trial (one tried by a judge without a jury) in March 1823, McCulloh and Buchanan were acquitted and the indictment against Williams dismissed. As the historian Mark Killenbeck noted, "[T]he results almost certainly reflected a verdict against the Bank itself, rather than a judgment that the three had not engaged in massive fraud." The three men had portrayed themselves as "victims," caught up in the "hopes and calcula-tions in which the whole community indulged." Had the value of the Bank's stock increased, they maintained, they would have been looked upon as "nobles, as the architects of their fortunes, by the very men who persecuted them, and lauded to the skies as possessing spirits fraught with enterprise." This defense conveniently ignored the fact that much of the collapse in bank share values came about because of their failed speculation.

In the 1820s the second Bank of the United States prospered might-ily, only to fall victim to Andrew Jackson's ill-founded hatred of all banks. In 1832 he vetoed the recharter of the Bank, calling it a "mon-ster" and a "hydra of corruption" that must be eliminated. The country found itself without an adequate central bank until 1913, when the modern Federal Reserve System began.

James William McCulloh also prospered. Condemned as a "destroyer of Widows and Orphans" in 1819, he won election to the Maryland House of Delegates from Baltimore County soon after his acquittal, and served as speaker of that house in 1826. In the 1830s, his past all but forgotten by contemporaries, he became an influential lobbyist, and worked assiduously for the Chesapeake and Ohio Canal Company in pursuit of government support for the canal and other such enterprises. He lived out his life as a successful businessman and lawyer and a respected citizen until his death in 1861.

Cases Cited

M'Culloch v. Maryland, 17 U.S. (4 Wheat.) 316 (1819)
Osborn v. Bank of the United States, 22 U.S. (9 Wheat.) 738 (1824)

For Further Reading

The best books on the subject are Mark R. Killenbeck, *M'Culloch v. Maryland: Securing a Nation* (2006), and Gerald Gunther, *John Marshall's Defense of M'Culloch v. Maryland* (1969). The first covers all aspects of the matter, including the activities of the Bank and the chicaneries of McCulloh and his fellow culprits; the second focuses more on the decision in the case, the series of articles attacking it, and the essays that John Marshall wrote anonymously in its defense. The classic work on banking in the early United States that explores both the first and second Banks is Bray Hammond, *Banks and Politics in America from the Revolution to the Civil War* (1957), but it should be supplemented by Edward S. Kaplan, *The Bank of the United States and the American Economy* (1999), and by Robert V. Remini, *Andrew Jackson and the Bank War* (1967).

The Case of the Rival Steamboat Operators

Gibbons v. Ogden (1824)

THE CONSTITUTION of the United States grants to Congress the power "to regulate Commerce with foreign Nations, and among the several States, and with the Indian Tribes" (Article I, Section 8). Until 1824, however, neither Congress nor the Supreme Court defined what is meant by the regulation of commerce. In that year, thanks to a dispute between two rival steamboat operators, the Supreme Court had the opportunity to define the power, and John Marshall's broad interpretation turned what might have been a neglected clause into one of the most important constitutional provisions for justifying a broad exercise of congressional power. His was not the last word on the subject, however, for the debate continues to this day.

Mr. Fulton's Steamboat

On August 17, 1807, the *North River Steamboat** made an upriver voyage from New York to Albany in thirty-two hours. Designed by Robert Fulton, a gifted engineer and shameless self-promoter, and financed by his partner, Robert Livingston, the steam-powered boat, able to sail

---

* There is a debate over exactly what Fulton and Livingston named the boat, with various sources giving the *North River Steamboat,* the *North River,* the *North Rover Steamboat of Clermont,* or simply the *Steamboat.* Apparently only after the successful voyage did the public start referring to it as the *Clermont.*

inland waterways without the need for wind or currents, would revolutionize transportation in the United States in the early nineteenth century. It would become the dominant means of transportation of agricultural goods to market, as well as of travelers, until the explosion of railroads at the time of the Civil War. Every schoolchild is taught that Fulton invented the steamboat; it would be more accurate to say that he built upon the work of others, perfected the idea, and made it into a workable reality.

Twenty years earlier, at the time of the Constitutional Convention in 1787, while the Committee on Detail put together the various provisions that had been agreed upon, a number of delegates went down to the Delaware River to view the launch of an experimental steamboat, *Perseverance,* built by the inventor John Fitch. Absent from that group was the one delegate who might well have been expected to be most interested in such an invention, Benjamin Franklin. But Franklin had given his support to another man working on a steamboat, James Rumsey. Although both Fitch and Rumsey had promising designs, and both received patents on their designs, neither could secure the financial or political patronage necessary to raise the large capital investment needed to turn their primitive prototypes into commercially viable steamboats. It remained for the team of Fulton and Livingston to make the steamboat financially viable.

Robert Livingston had been born into one of the great New York families, and enjoyed social status, political influence, and, of course, wealth. He had a successful law career, rising to become the first chancellor of the state, its highest judicial office. He was also an enthusiastic amateur scientist, and pursued a number of experiments, such as building gristmills so as to eliminate the friction between stones, and crossing cows with elk at his estate at Clermont on the Hudson. He followed the efforts of Fitch and Rumsey, but refused to invest in them, believing they had not developed a design that would prove commercially feasible. But he did perceive that if a steamboat could be perfected, it would have an enormous impact on the country, and make its inventor and sponsors a lot of money.

He conducted some experiments with his neighbors and fellow amateurs, John Stevens (who would later do pioneer work in railroads) and Nicholas Roosevelt. In 1801 Thomas Jefferson appointed Livingston as one of the ministers to France to negotiate what would ultimately become the Louisiana Purchase. When he departed, he despaired that he would ever see the steam engine developed. In Paris, however, he met the man who would do what others before him had failed to accomplish.

Robert Fulton had grown up in Lancaster, Pennsylvania, and for many people he embodied the energy and self-confidence of the young nation. He had been a locksmith, a gunsmith, a draftsman, and a portrait painter; in fact, he had gone to England to study painting with Benjamin

West. While there he also developed an abiding interest in submarines and torpedoes. As one scholar noted, it might be doubted whether Fulton's lifelong purpose was to put boats upon the water or to blow them out of it. Fulton, however, had a gift of taking different strands of thoughts and the ideas and inventions of other people and putting them together in a way that would work. The work of other inventors existed only to be borrowed. "All these things," he declared, "being governed by the laws of nature, the real invention is to find [such laws]."

In Paris, Fulton and Livingston built an experimental steamboat and successfully sailed it on the Seine. With Livingston's financial backing, Fulton then went to England and managed to talk the British government into allowing the Boulton & Watt Company to build a steam engine to his specifications and for export. On April 23, 1807, Fulton claimed the engine at the New York Custom House, and took it over to his carpenter, who built a boat under Fulton's guidance to house the engine.

The boat's inaugural voyage took her through the highlands of the Hudson, and without a moon to illuminate the river, it seemed as if a volcano were sailing up the river spewing smoke and sparks. It apparently excited great terror among some of the farmers along the banks. One reportedly raced home, barred the doors, and declared that the Devil himself was going up to Albany in a sawmill.

In February 1809 the U.S. government gave Fulton a patent on his design. The issuance of a patent is designed, among other things, to confer a monopoly on the inventor for a period of time. The value of a patent and the exclusivity it provides, however, are directly proportional to the patent-holder's ability to raise the necessary capital to develop the invention into a commercially feasible operation. He must also be prepared to prosecute infringers of his rights, successfully market the invention to the general public, and then license its use to those who would compete with him for the business.

The Steamboat Monopoly

In 1798 the New York legislature granted monopoly rights to John Fitch for steamboat navigation on the Hudson River, which flows for nearly three hundred miles within New York before forming the border between New York and New Jersey at its mouth. Fitch's monopoly also included other New York waters, such as the upstate lakes. When Fitch could not raise the money to perfect his invention, however, the politically well-connected Livingston secured the monopoly rights for the partnership he had with Fulton. After Fulton demonstrated the success of his boat, the legislature extended the franchise for another twenty years, until 1838. The law gave Fulton and Livingston exclusive rights of steamboat navigation on all state waters, including the adjacent coastal waters, and on the lower Hudson River, where it runs between New York and New Jersey. The Fulton-Livingston group assigned licenses to a number of individuals to run steamboats in New York waters, collecting goodly sums of money in the process. This gave it the resources it needed to fight off efforts to break its monopoly, especially in the courts.

The profitability of a steamboat between New York City and the state capital in Albany led to the first serious challenge to the Fulton-Livingston group. The steamboat cut the time it took to get between the two cities from several days to a little more than one day, and in May 1811 a group of Albany businessmen, led by James Van Ingen, decided to start their own steamship line without getting a license. The Fulton-Livingston interests immediately sued in the federal circuit court of New York, only to have the case thrown out for lack of jurisdiction. Justice Henry Brockholst Livingston, whom Thomas Jefferson had appointed to the Supreme Court in 1806, was sitting on circuit, and pointed out that all of the parties involved were citizens of New York, and therefore the case could not be tried in a federal court because there was no diversity of citizenship. Because of the very complexity of the various patents involved, including some filed by earlier inventors and from which Fulton had borrowed, the Fulton-Livingston interests did not want to use what would have been their other—and legitimate—grounds for going into federal court: namely, the defense of a patent.

Instead, they went into a New York court seeking an injunction against Van Ingen to stop his company from plying the Hudson River in a steamboat. In October 1811 John Lansing Jr., a former mayor of Albany and a successor to Livingston as chancellor, denied the injunction, for what appeared to be political as much as legal reasons. The Fulton-Livingston group then went to the Court of Impeachment and Errors, at that time the state's highest court. Composed of justices from the New York Supreme Court as well as a few members of the state senate, the Court of Errors heard the appeal, and in 1812 handed a significant victory to Fulton in *Livingston v. Van Ingen*. The case is important not only because it came from the pen of one of the most highly respected jurists of the time, Chief Justice James Kent, but also because it laid out with great clarity the status of the commerce clause at the time, as well as relations between the federal government and the states over who could exercise authority in specific areas.

The Court of Errors might have confined itself to a very narrow reading of the case—namely, did Van Ingen, by establishing a nonlicensed steamboat service, violate the rights granted to the Fulton-Livingston group? This was clearly the case, and the court could have ignored all other matters, such as whether New York even had the power to establish a monopoly, or if the lower Hudson River, where it ran between New York and New Jersey, came under control of the federal government. Kent and his colleagues, however, did not ignore these issues, nor did they ignore the question of whether a monopoly served the public interest.

In their opinions, Joseph Yates and Smith Thompson (whom James Monroe would appoint to the Supreme Court in 1823) strongly endorsed the legitimacy of New York granting exclusive privileges to the Fulton-Livingston group. The award of a monopoly for a period of years to reward inventors was a common policy. The franchise covered only the territorial waters over which New York normally exercised jurisdiction, a power traditionally associated with state sovereignty that pre-existed the adoption of the Constitution. Moreover, the federal Constitution only allowed patent rights to inventors and authors (copyright), and said nothing about what New York had awarded—the right to navigation. The state had originally made that award to John Fitch, and then had, through an official act of the legislature, transferred it to Fulton and Livingston. Neither Yates nor Thompson saw any conflict between state grants of monopolies and either the patent provisions or the commerce clause of the Constitution. The federal government controlled one area, and the states held sovereignty over another.

Chief Justice Kent, on the other hand, did not draw a bright line between state and federal authority, but pointed out that up until that time Congress had enacted no legislation regulating commerce. This meant that the Fulton-Livingston monopoly did not come within the ambit of congressional authority so far, but he speculated that it might do so in the future, depending on how Congress chose to exercise the powers of the commerce clause. "It may be difficult," he noted, "to draw an exact line between those regulations which relate to external and those which relate to internal commerce, for every regulation of one will, directly or indirectly, affect the other." Until Congress acted, therefore, it would be a "monstrous heresy" to interfere with an existing state grant in the absence of either federal legislation or a specific constitutional prohibition.

All three judges agreed that should there be a conflict between a state law and federal action, the latter would prevail under the supremacy clause. None of the three judges, however, knew whether federal power over commerce was exclusive (that is, it could only be exercised by Congress) or concurrent (where both the states and the national government shared authority). In words that Chief Justice John

Marshall, a champion of a strong national government, might have employed, Kent noted that "the legislative power, in a single, independent government, extends to every proper object of power, and is limited only by its constitutional provisions, or by the fundamental principles of all governments, and the unalienable rights of mankind." The monopoly New York had granted to Fulton and Livingston pertained only to steamboat travel within the state, and so the question, according to Kent, was not what powers Congress had, but rather what powers remained with the state. If, he concluded, a power that originally belonged to a state had not been ceded to Congress, and the Constitution did not specifically prohibit it to the states, then the states could continue to exercise that power until and if it came into conflict with federal laws.

Kent believed the commerce powers were concurrent—that is, both the states and the national government had authority in this area. In looking at the Constitution, he found only one clause that related directly to the states and commerce, the provision prohibiting states from imposing tariffs or taxes on exported goods (Article I, Section 9). The narrowness of this provision, he suggested, indicated that many other commerce-related powers remained within state control. In fact, the limits of the federal patent power indicated that the Framers of the Constitution expected that states would take steps to enhance the value of inventions, much as New York had done.

Although Kent's extensive dictum on the relation between state and federal power might have been unnecessary to resolve the case, it did send a powerful message to others who might want to challenge the Fulton-Livingston monopoly: New York had acted within its authority, and the monopoly would resist all legal challenges.

Enter Gibbons and Ogden

While the Court of Errors was resolving the dispute with Van Ingen, Livingston and Fulton had to defend their monopoly from other interlopers. In 1800 Aaron Ogden, the former governor of New Jersey, had begun a wind-powered ferry between Elizabethtown, New Jersey, and New York City, an enterprise that did not trespass on the Fulton-Livingston monopoly. In 1812, however, he converted to steam, and that triggered litigation between Ogden and the Livingston-Fulton group. The parties settled that suit in 1814, Ogden became a licensee of Fulton's franchise, and under the terms of their agreement he had the sole right to run a steam ferry between Elizabethtown and New York.

This license made Ogden an ally of Fulton and Livingston. The latter, however, had died in 1813, leaving the large Livingston family to squabble over who owned his estate, and after Fulton's death in 1815, Ogden—now allied with the Fulton interests—became the primary defender of the patent and monopoly rights. Thus he, and not Fulton, sued Thomas Gibbons when the latter established a competing steam ferry on the New York–Elizabethtown route in 1816, a suit that eventually wound up in the U.S. Supreme Court.

Gibbons had been a Tory Loyalist during the Revolution, and then a land speculator in Georgia, where some of his activities were considered unethical if not completely illegal. In 1801 he relocated to New Jersey, where his somewhat shady past would be less known. When he learned about the profitability of the wind-powered ferry lines established by Ogden and others, he secretly purchased the shares owned by Jonathan Dayton, one of Ogden's investors; became a partner in the firm; and, utilizing Ogden's social and political contacts, soon became a successful businessman. At this time Ogden had not yet secured the franchise from the Fulton group, and he and Gibbon decided to challenge the Fulton-Livingston chokehold on ferry lines in the New York City area, and persuaded the New Jersey legislature to enact legislation that levied fines and forfeiture on Fulton-Livingston vessels operating in New Jersey waters.

They then planned to attack the New York monopoly on three fronts. First, they would try to have the New York legislature rescind its grant. Second, they would challenge the monopoly in both the New York and the New Jersey courts. Finally, if the first two efforts failed, they would go into federal court and claim that the state-granted monopoly violated the commerce clause of the Constitution. Thanks to Livingston's influence with the New York legislature, Ogden and Gibbons got nowhere trying to get the New York assembly to repeal the grants; similarly, Ogden's position in New Jersey (as a former governor) ensured that that state's legislature would not repeal its law.

Before the two could start judicial proceedings, however, a personal feud erupted between them, as Ogden took umbrage over how Gibbons treated his married daughter, and this led to the breakup of their business arrangements. Ogden then started his own steamboat ferry and, as noted above, became a licensee of the Fulton group. In 1816 Gibbons established his own steamboat company, with the specific intent of challenging Ogden's monopoly over the lucrative Elizabethtown–New York City route. The death of the original franchise holders and internal feuding in the Livingston family left Ogden, who still held a license from the Fulton-Livingston group, in the position of having to defend it in order to maintain the profitability of his own ferries.

If this had been a normal patent case, the Fulton group could have gone into federal court to defend it against infringement by Gibbons and others. But the Fulton patent did not cover all of the technology involved in the steamboat. He had contributed a great deal to the successful design, but as noted earlier, he had built upon the work of others, and there were a number of devices covered by both American and European patents that he had utilized. None of the parties, therefore, wanted to go into federal court to argue about which patents prevailed and who owned them.

Creating a Question for the Federal Courts

In fact, the Fulton-Livingston strategy had always relied less on the technical accomplishments of the inventor and more on the political influence of his partner, Chancellor Robert Livingston. It had been Livingston's connections, as well as his family's wealth, that had financed Fulton's successful development of a workable design and secured the New York monopoly. With Kent's opinion in *Van Ingen,* the franchise had seemed impregnable.

Gibbons, however, had a strategy in mind to get around this impasse. Ogden secured an injunction from Kent (now chancellor) in 1816 to prevent Gibbons from operating his steamboats, and Kent also denied Gibbons's request to move the suit to federal court. Gibbons then secured a coasting license under the Coasting Act of 1793—a license allowing him to operate boats in coastal waters under the jurisdiction of the federal government—and went back to the state court, arguing that the federal license took precedence over New York's power to regulate the lower Hudson River.

Once again, in *Gibbons v. Ogden* (New York, 1820) Kent upheld the monopoly, refusing to believe that a simple coasting license, obtained "as a matter of course, and with as much facility as the flag of the *United States* could be procured and hoisted," could enable its holder to flout an act of New York's sovereign legislature. But Gibbons now had his federal question, and he retained the renowned lawyers Daniel Webster and William Wirt to appeal the case to the U.S. Supreme Court. The Supreme Court, however, initially refused to hear the case on the technical grounds that Chancellor Kent's opinion was not a final decree, and therefore not appealable. The Court of Errors affirmed Kent's ruling in January 1822, and Gibbons again appealed to the Supreme Court. This time the justices accepted the case, and heard six days of oral argument beginning on February 4, 1824.

Arguing before the Supreme Court

Webster began by noting that New York's law, which had invited retaliatory legislation by Connecticut and New Jersey, imposed just those barriers to interstate commerce that had existed during the confederation and which the Constitution had intended to remove. Unlike taxation, in which the federal and state governments enjoyed concurrent power, the Constitution had granted full power to the national government in this area. If Congress failed to exercise its authority, then the states remained free to act. But Congress had not been silent on this issue; through the 1793 Coasting Act, it had stated its intention to bring coastal trade under federal control. The New York assembly had exceeded its acknowledged power to police trade within its borders, and in effect regulated commerce between states, a power reserved exclusively to Congress. Webster claimed that Gibbons's coasting license gave him a right to "navigate freely the waters of the United States," a right that New York now attempted to take away from him.

On behalf of Ogden, former representative Thomas J. Oakley urged the Court to view the regulation of commerce as a concurrent power. While not going as far as some states' rights advocates did, Oakley also maintained that in 1787 the states had reserved certain powers and had not ceded their sovereignty in all matters to the federal government. Moreover, interstate commerce had always been viewed as the transportation of goods and not, as in this case, the movement of passengers, and thus did not apply. Oakley's associate, Thomas A. Emmet, the longtime counsel for the Livingston family (who clearly had an interest in the case), then proceeded to list numerous areas that affected interstate commerce and that had always been considered within the purview of the states, such as quarantines, pilotage, lighthouses, turnpikes, and even Indian trade. These had all been pursued for the general welfare of the people, and not only as police measures to protect their health and safety.

Emmet's arguments led Webster's colleague, Attorney General William Wirt, to suggest that Webster had never intended that the state have no powers in regulating trade. Although Wirt appeared in court in a private capacity, as counsel to Gibbons, he also spoke for the federal power, and he urged the Court to draw a line between those activities deriving from the commerce power, which were exclusive to the federal government, and those regulations over primarily intrastate commerce growing out of the police powers, which might indirectly affect interstate trade. This compromise position might have pleased the Fulton-Livingston interests, which drew the bulk of their income from activities north of New York City, where the Hudson flowed entirely within state borders. From their point of view, Ogden's license between New York and New Jersey could easily be sacrificed, providing the monopoly remained intact elsewhere.

The Decision

The decision came down less than a month later. Chief Justice John Marshall initially approached this case with caution. He had great respect for Chancellor Kent, who had been a leader of the Federalists in New York, and was probably the most prominent and able state judge in the nation. Kent's lower court opinion could not be cavalierly brushed aside. The commerce clause itself had received practically no judicial explication, and no one knew how far it reached. Marshall, as he did in other cases (see the next chapter), intended to expand and consolidate the powers of the national government. He casually stated it as a "well-settled rule" that enumerated powers, such as federal control over interstate commerce, had to be construed both by the language of the Constitution and in light of the purpose for which they had been conferred. The Article I powers, including control over commerce, had been granted to further the "general advantage" of the whole American people. Although not infinite in its reach, in delegated areas "the sovereignty of Congress, though limited to specified objects, is plenary as to those objects."

Commerce, a vital aspect of national life, included not just the exchange of goods, but "every species of commercial intercourse" among the states. The key word *among* meant not only "between" but "intermingled with," so that the power of Congress did not stop at state lines, but extended into the interiors of the states as well. Reaching all aspects of trade, the congressional power to regulate commerce "[is] complete in itself, may be exercised to its utmost extent, and acknowledges no limitations other than are prescribed in the Constitution." The wisdom of Congress and of the electorate in choosing appropriate policies shaped its exercise.

Marshall no doubt sympathized with Webster's view of the commerce power as exclusive—that is, solely a function of the federal government—but he recognized that some nod had to be made to at least a limited claim of state sovereignty. His opinion thus held that both state and national governments had concurrent powers over commerce but that the former always had to give way to the latter in case of conflict. Through a broad reading of the Coasting Act of 1793, the chief justice ruled that the statute constituted a guaranty against state interference with interstate commerce. The New York law contradicted this intent, and was therefore void. In an aside, Marshall hinted that the mere grant of the commerce power might have been sufficient to reach this result, even in the absence of a specific congressional statute such as the Coasting Act.

Scholars consider Marshall's acknowledgment that the states could control commerce that was wholly internal to have been an assurance to the slave states that they could regulate free blacks, slaves, and the slave trade within their borders. The chief justice was reacting to a recent controversy in South Carolina, which had incarcerated a free black sailor when his ship docked in Charleston. Justice William Johnson had written a bitter circuit court opinion in *Elkison v. Deliesseline* (1823) denouncing South Carolina's position, and in *Gibbons* he entered a concurrence that took a stronger position than Marshall on the supremacy of federal power. In fact, one could surmise that Marshall could soft-pedal his usually strong nationalistic view since Johnson, a Jefferson appointee, said it for him.

The Legacy of the Case

The *Gibbons* decision had both immediate and long-range consequences. It proved to be extremely popular, since it broke up what had become an unpopular monopoly and prevented a looming transportation war between the states. Although it diminished state power, it did so in the area of transportation, in which most Americans, even states' rights localists, wanted a free market. The case treated the nation as a single commercial entity, and prevented states from fragmenting the national economy. The broad interpretation of what constituted interstate commerce permitted the government to adapt its policies to new technologies in transportation and communications, and except for a relatively brief period in the early twentieth century, allowed the continuous expansion of federal regulation over the nation's commerce, banking, industry, and labor. Beyond that, the analysis applied to the commerce power could be used to expand the scope of the other constitutionally enumerated congressional powers as well.

Three years later, in *Brown v. Maryland* (1827), the Court again emphasized the national character of commerce when it voided a Maryland statute that imposed a tax on importers of out-of-state goods.

Congress had not addressed itself to the issue of taxes (as it supposedly had in the steamboat case with the Coasting Act), and Marshall enlarged on his earlier *obiter dicta* (comments in an opinion as opposed to a finding of law) that the commerce power by itself might preclude a state from any interference in interstate trade. Although the states still enjoyed authority over primarily intrastate activities, the new demarcation line would be what Marshall dubbed the "original package" doctrine. So long as goods crossing state lines remained in their original packages, they could not be taxed or otherwise regulated by the states, a doctrine that remained in effect for over a century.

For reasons that are not entirely clear, Justice Smith Thompson of New York did not participate in *Gibbons*. If he had, he might well have dissented, since in *Van Ingen* he had shown a strong propensity to allow states great control over commerce within their borders. In the *Brown* case, he did dissent, arguing that once an imported good passed into Maryland's jurisdiction, it became fully subject to the licensing and taxing laws of that state. In many ways his *Brown* dissent tracked the same views he had explicated while on the New York court, that a state had full discretion over how it chose to regulate commerce within its borders.

But if Congress had the broad power, the Supreme Court retained the ultimate authority to determine when and if that power had been applied appropriately. In *Willson v. Black Bird Creek Marsh Co.* (1829), Marshall sustained a Delaware law authorizing damming a creek to keep out marsh waters, even though the creek was navigable and had at times been used in coastal trade. Willson had registered his boat under the same 1793 law as Gibbons, and following the reasoning of the earlier cases, Marshall might have held that the mere existence of either the commerce power or the statute invalidated the Delaware law. But, according to the Court, Congress had not acted specifically in this matter, and thus the Court reserved the right to determine whether congressional silence permitted state action or if the commerce power precluded it.

After the conclusion of the case, Aaron Ogden and Thomas Gibbons continued their personal vendetta, and some sources say that the fight left Ogden near bankruptcy for a while. Ogden ran his steamboat ferry for another few years, and then moved to Jersey City and resumed the practice of law. In 1830 President Andrew Jackson named him to the post of collector of customs for the city, and he served in that post until his death in 1839. The political gene seemed to have been very strong in the Ogden family. His son, Elias, served as a justice of the New Jersey Supreme Court from 1842 to 1865. His grandson, Frederick, was mayor of Hoboken for one term, and his nephew, Daniel Haines, was twice elected as governor of New Jersey.

Thomas Gibbons also abandoned the ferry route and went on to become a very successful businessman, and at the end of his life owned extensive property in South Carolina, Georgia, and New Jersey. Cornelius Vanderbilt, who did business with Gibbons, said, "I think he was one of the strongest minded men I ever was acquainted with; I never knew any man that had control over him." At the time of Gibbons's death in 1826, Vanderbilt said that his mind was as capable as ever.

The debate over the meaning of interstate commerce and the extent of federal power in that area has continued to be an issue for which there seems to be no final answer. Seventy years after John Marshall's very broad interpretation of the commerce clause in the steamboat case, conservative jurists at the end of the nineteenth and in the early twentieth century took a far narrower view, one that gave the federal government a relatively cramped space for economic regulation. That changed in the 1940s, when the Court once again began to view commerce as Marshall had done, and Congress utilized the commerce clause over the next several decades—with the Court's approval—to justify everything from airline regulation to civil rights legislation. In the 1980s conservative justices tried to impose some limits, and denied that the clause could be used to ban guns on school playgrounds (*United States v. Lopez* [1995]) or make abuse of women a matter for federal courts (*United States v. Morrison* [2000]). No doubt the debate will continue into the foreseeable future, as Congress and the courts deal with changing modes of commerce, such as the Internet.

Cases Cited

Brown v. Maryland, 25 U.S. (12 Wheat.) 419 (1827)
Elkisob v. Deliesseline, 8 F. Cas. 493 (1823)
Gibbons v. Ogden, 17 Johnson's Reports 488 (New York, 1820)
Gibbons v. Ogden, 19 U.S. (6 Wheat.) 449 (1821)
Gibbons v. Ogden, 22 U.S. (9 Wheat.) 1 (1824)
Livingston v. Van Ingen, 9 Johnson's Reports 507 (New York, 1812)
United States v. Lopez, 514 U.S. 549 (1995)
United States v. Morrison, 529 U.S. 598 (2000)
Willson v. Black Bird Creek Marsh Co., 27 U.S. (2 Peters) 245 (1829)

For Further Reading

The most complete treatments of the case are Herbert A. Johnson, *Gibbons v. Ogden: John Marshall, Steamboats, and the Commerce Clause* (2010), and the older but still very useful Maurice G. Baxter, *The Steamboat Monopoly:* Gibbons v. Ogden,

1824 (1972). An extensive examination of the case covering the complex set of commercial, economic, and personal relations involved is Thomas H. Cox, *Gibbons v. Ogden, Law, and Society in the Early Republic* (2009). To understand the case in the broader context of Marshall Court decisions, see G. Edward White, *The Marshall Court and Cultural Change, 1815–1835* (1988), and David P. Currie, *The Constitution in the Supreme Court: The First Hundred Years, 1789–1888* (1985). The history of the steamboat is well told in Andrea Sutcliffe, *Steam: The Untold Story of America's First Great Invention* (2004).

The Case of the Missionary to the Cherokee

Worcester v. Georgia (1832)

F ROM THE TIME EUROPEAN settlers came to the Americas, there had been tension between them and the Native Americans who lived here, a tension that often exploded into violence and warfare. By the early nineteenth century the superior arms of the white settlers, as well as the diseases they carried for which the Indians had no immunity, had decimated the tribes on the East Coast of the United States. Many had been pushed west into lands supposedly protected by treaty with the federal government against further incursions by whites.

But the West to which the Indians in the Southeast had retreated was merely the western portion of the original southern colonies, such as Georgia, and as the states grew, white farmers and plantation owners cast covetous eyes on the rich land held by the Indians. The issue came to a head in the late 1820s and early 1830s, and led to the ejection of Indians from lands they had been promised would belong to them forever. The events of the 1820s set the stage for the Cherokee cases in the 1830s, and then the tragic Cherokee removal under President Martin Van Buren.

Setting the Stage

The early 1820s saw the Court's first significant attempt to define the relationship between the United States and the native Indians in *Johnson and Graham's Lessee v. M'Intosh* (1823), which provided the constitutional basis for taking all lands from the Indians. In 1775 the Piankeshaw Indians sold land in present-day Illinois to a group of speculators, including one Thomas Johnson. Prior to the adoption of the Articles of Confederation, Virginia claimed the land in this part of the Northwest Territory. In 1783, as part of the conditions set by smaller states for ratifying the Articles, Virginia ceded ownership to the national government. In 1818, William M'Intosh bought more than 11,000 acres of that land from the federal government. The same lands, however, were also claimed by Johnson's heirs, Joshua Johnson and Thomas Graham, who lost their cases in the lower courts, and then appealed to the Supreme Court.

The Court heard the case in early 1823, and despite its record of supporting property rights, ruled against Johnson's descendants, even though their claims predated those of M'Intosh by nearly fifty years. Chief Justice John Marshall rejected the idea that Indians could have any claims to land and therefore the right to sell land. He argued that when Europeans arrived in the New World they gained title to all lands they occupied through a right of "discovery." This discovery gave the British and then the Americans "an exclusive right to extinguish the Indian title of occupancy, either by purchase or by conquest; and gave also a right to such a degree of sovereignty as the circumstances of the people would allow them to exercise." The British, therefore, had an "absolute title of the crown" in the lands, which then transferred to the newly independent United States.

The contemptuous attitude that many Americans had toward the Indians came through clearly in Marshall's opinion, when he wrote that "the tribes of Indians inhabiting this country were fierce savages, whose occupation was war, and whose subsistence was drawn chiefly from the forest." The Indians were to be protected if they lived peaceably on the land, but they were "incapable of transferring the absolute title to others." The Piankeshaw Indians had held no property rights in the land they occupied, and therefore could not sell or otherwise transfer them. By this reasoning, no Native American could lay any claim to lands they occupied. The decision helped set the stage for the dispute among Georgia, the Cherokee, and the U.S. government in the 1830s.

Taking Indian Land

The policy of removing Indians from their lands had begun with Thomas Jefferson and had been part of the administration of every president who preceded Andrew Jackson. During and immediately after the War of 1812, then-general Andrew Jackson secured treaties with most of the southeastern Indian tribes, in which they agreed to move to territory in present-day Oklahoma. Under these treaties the Creek, Choctaw,

Chickasaw, and some members of the Seminole and Cherokee moved west, although not to Oklahoma at this time. Some of the Cherokee settled in the western part of what is now Georgia, while the remaining Seminole retreated into the interior of Florida, where they successfully resisted numerous military assaults on them.

In 1825 a federal Indian commissioner negotiated the fraudulent Treaty of Indian Springs, tricking the Creek chiefs into ceding 4.7 million acres in Georgia to the federal government. President John Quincy Adams signed the treaty, but upon learning of the deception, he withdrew it and secured the less stringent Treaty of Washington the following year. The Georgia legislature declared that Adams's annulment of the earlier treaty was invalid, and characterized his action as a violation of states' rights. In the 1783 agreement giving up claims to western lands beyond its current boundary to the national government, Georgia had been promised that the federal government would, as soon as possible, secure for the state all the Indian lands within its borders. The Cherokee and Creek tribes had resisted efforts to be moved, and Georgia used the false treaty as the lever to get Indian lands that white settlers had long coveted. Gov. George M. Troup threatened to call out the militia if Adams did anything to prevent enforcement of the Indian Springs Treaty. Adams caved in and left the Creek to their fate.

Andrew Jackson's position on Indian affairs reflected the attitude of the West in general—Indians should get out of the white man's way. In the earlier Creek and Seminole wars, he had shown both his valor as a fighter and his inclination to move the natives off their ancestral lands. Indeed, as a general he had negotiated scores of treaties with Indians leading to the successful and relatively peaceful movement of thousands of Indians to what later became Oklahoma. By 1828 Jackson had fully endorsed the notion that a "just, humane, liberal policy" required that Indians be moved west of the Mississippi. He believed that through this policy the Indians could live within their own culture, without worrying about white incursions on their land, while whites could have access to the rich farmlands of Georgia, Mississippi, Alabama, and Tennessee previously occupied by the Indians.

This policy had been crystallizing since Jefferson's purchase of Louisiana in 1803, and had been fully articulated by Secretary of War John C. Calhoun as early as 1823. But as president, Jackson made it the official policy of the government, and in the Indian Removal Act of 1830, Congress appropriated a half-million dollars to facilitate massive tribal transfers. The administration negotiated over ninety treaties in the next few years, and in 1836 the president announced that all but a few tribes had accepted the program.

In all these negotiations, however, the national government had failed to bargain with the tribes in good faith and never carried out its obligations or fulfilled its promises to them. Furthermore, the federal government made little or no effort to control the states, whose citizens could not wait for the Indians to move before rushing in to grab their lands. In the North, weak tribes either gave way before the white settlers or were tricked or bribed by federal Indian commissioners to give up what little they had. The struggle they occasionally put up often ended in disaster, as in the Black Hawk War of 1832, with its gruesome massacre of Sauk and Fox women and children trying to flee across the Mississippi.

Stronger tribes in the southern states put up a stiffer resistance. The Florida Seminoles fought a guerrilla war in the Everglades swamps from 1835 to 1842, and were never actually defeated, although military engagements dissipated after American soldiers treacherously seized their chief, Osceola, under a flag of truce. The Cherokee, more than any other tribe, had adopted aspects of white culture. They had a written constitution; had divided tribal land into individually owned farms; and had even followed the southern practice of slaveholding, as had the other "civilized Tribes" of the old Southwest, the Creek, Choctaw, Chickasaw, and Seminole. They grew cotton and corn, and tried to blend into the South while occupying large tracts of land in northern Georgia and western North Carolina that had been guaranteed to them by a 1791 treaty. In 1827, when the Cherokee adopted a constitution, it was based on their treaty rights, which not only affirmed their claims to the land, but also insisted that, as an independent nation, they were not subject to the laws of any other state or nation. Georgia responded the following year with a statute declaring that after June 1, 1830, state law would extend over all the Cherokee living within the state's borders. With the discovery of gold deposits in 1829, white settlers and prospectors began crowding into Indian country.

Georgia had forced John Quincy Adams to back down from his efforts to revise the Indian Springs Treaty, which had pushed the Cherokee into a narrow strip of land on the western and northern borders of the state. Georgia had no constitutional right either to claim jurisdiction over the Indians or to negotiate with them on land or other matters. Under the Articles of Confederation, the states had negotiated directly with Indian tribes, but the Constitution ended this, and Article I, Section 8, reserved the power to regulate trade with the Indian tribes to the Congress. Treaties negotiated by the United States took priority, under the supremacy clause, over state laws.

Since the time of the adoption of the Articles of Confederation, however, American governments had dealt with various tribes as autonomous nations, and even while trying to remove the Indians from the path of settlement, they had at least heeded these formalities. But the status of the tribes remained vague at best, and the manner in which the federal government tried to manage Indian policy depended on whether the vigor of a president in exercising federal prerogatives outweighed the determination of the states to gain control of tribal lands.

In President Jackson, the southern states recognized a man who sympathized with their desire to remove the Indians, and who, they correctly anticipated, would not oppose them if they did not directly challenge his authority. Jackson made no comment on the 1830 Georgia law claiming jurisdiction over lands ceded to the Cherokee under the Treaty of Hopewell (1785) and the Treaty of Holston (1791), nor did he oppose the state's subsequent seizure of much of that land. The state found the Supreme Court somewhat less sympathetic, but it did not really matter; Georgia, in the end, successfully defied the judicial power of the United States, with the tacit support of Jackson.

Challenging Georgia Law in the Supreme Court

The first case to test the Georgia law involved the state murder prosecution of a Cherokee named George Corn Tassels, under Georgia's newly proclaimed authority over the Indians. Corn Tassels, in turn, argued that Georgia had no jurisdiction over him. The Supreme Court agreed to review the case, but Georgia refused to acknowledge the Court's jurisdiction. Governor Troup, backed by the legislature, declared that he would fight off any attempt to interfere with the state's court system. Corn Tassels, who may or may not have been guilty, was soon tried, found guilty, and executed.

Although Jackson refused to interfere, Georgia's actions and the breach of treaty obligations led the Cherokee to seek an injunction to prevent the state from seizing Indian lands or enforcing its law over the tribes. An aging John Marshall tried once again to walk the political tightrope he had so successfully traversed for three decades. In *Cherokee Nation v. Georgia* (1831), the Court held on the one hand that the Indian tribes constituted neither a state of the Union nor a foreign nation, and they therefore could not pursue an action in the federal courts. On the other hand, the chief justice defined the Indians as "domestic dependent nations" under the jurisdiction of the United States, and were in fact "in a state of pupilage"—that is, still in need of supervision by the federal government. He found that the relation between the federal government and the tribes "resembles that of a ward to his guardian." Although he conceded that the tribes could not be forced to give up their lands except through voluntary cession, "this is not the tribunal in which those rights are to be asserted." Since Marshall essentially concluded that the Court had no jurisdiction to decide the issues, Georgia could easily ignore its implications. The Court's decision helped seal the fate of the Cherokee, and abdicated any judicial responsibility for the enforcement of treaty rights or for the protection of Indian lands or peoples.

Justice Smith Thompson, joined by Joseph Story, dissented. He argued that the Court indeed had jurisdiction since the Georgia law overturned treaties made by the United States. Furthermore, as a suit between a foreign nation (the Cherokee nation) and a state, it was not barred by the Eleventh Amendment, which prohibited suits by citizens against a state in federal courts. Thompson offered a detailed and convincing analysis showing that in light of congressional actions, treaties, and common usage of language, the Indian tribes were "nations" within the meaning of Article III of the Constitution. This brought the case within the original jurisdiction of the Court. He then argued that on the merits of the case, the Cherokee were entitled to relief. This issue seemed obvious: under various treaties the tribe had claims to certain lands, and Georgia had violated these rights.

Thompson's analysis was more logical and persuasive than that of the chief justice; it was also more reasonable and humane. However, because it backed Indian claims, it was politically unacceptable to a majority of Americans, to the land-hungry citizens of Georgia, and to President Jackson. Although Marshall may have been sympathetic to Thompson's argument, the elderly jurist was not prepared, at least this time, to take on a political fight he had no hope of winning.

The issue of Indian sovereignty, however, came back to the Supreme Court just a year later in *Worcester v. Georgia* (1832), thanks to the efforts of a missionary named Samuel Austin Worcester.

Samuel Worcester Goes to Georgia

Worcester was a New England Yankee who seemed destined to champion Cherokee rights as a matter of principle. Born in 1798 into a Vermont family that included a number of leading congregational ministers, he was educated by his father, the Rev. Leonard Worcester, then at the University of Vermont (of which his uncle was president), and then graduated in 1823 from the Andover Theological Seminary. A year later he married Ann Orr of New Hampshire. The couple learned missionary principles and methods at Boston's American Board of Commissioners for Foreign Missions, an early Christian mission agency active both domestically and overseas. When Samuel was ordained in 1825, his father preached the sermon at the ceremony. The married couple then left to begin their ministry with the Cherokee in the South.

Worcester and his wife accepted several assumptions held by the American Board of Commissioners. First, the Cherokee should be educated, which of course meant European-American education. Second, newspapers, schoolbooks, and sermons should initially be in the native language of the tribes, with the Indians eventually learning to speak, read, and write in English. Third, Indian autonomy from hostile power— safety from domination—was the key to conversions, education, and development. Worcester's uncle, Dr. Samuel Worcester, had argued for these principles since 1817.

These formal principles, however, covered up the fact that most missionaries imposed their own views and prejudices on their work. Leonard Worcester's ordination sermon praised his son's mission "to the heathen." The American Board's agenda for Native Americans assumed that they would change how they lived in ways the missionaries approved. The Worcesters had no qualms in accepting their charge from the board: "To make the whole tribe English in their language, civilized in their habits, and Christian in their religion." Beyond that, however, missionaries faced the usual challenge of outsiders. How far would they go to help those different from themselves, and how far would their superiors or the Indians allow them to go? No matter how noble their intentions, the practicalities and especially the politics could be very dangerous.

The Worcesters first went to Brainerd, Tennessee, in 1825, and then to New Echota, Georgia, in 1827. By then missionaries from other denominations had established themselves in Cherokee country, and had already converted some of the Indians to Christianity. Worcester was soon accepted by the tribe as A-tse-nu-sti ("the messenger"), and he quickly developed education and conversion tools. He had learned woodworking and typesetting from his father, so he soon mastered Cherokee letters and printed the *Cherokee Phoenix* (1828–1834), to which he contributed articles and editorials in English. He started translating the Bible into Cherokee, and also worked on translating hymns and sermons. And, because education stood foremost in his priorities, he began to build schools.

Samuel Worcester's duties as a minister seemed unlikely to lead him to be imprisoned or to take an appeal to the U.S. Supreme Court. There is no question that Worcester's actions reflected his religious principles, but his beliefs about Indian sovereignty and independence differed significantly not only from white Georgians but also from most white Americans. The treaties the Cherokee relied upon led Andrew Jackson and the Georgia leaders to charge that the Indians wanted to erect a state within a state—an *imperium in imperio*. The Cherokee believed that they had prior domain over the land, and did not see themselves as trying to create a state within a state. But the arguments by Jackson and Georgia politicians, and their proposed remedy—Indian removal—were very popular with the general public, especially those who wanted to get their hands on the fertile lands held by the tribe.

This popular appeal is why Jackson's opponents in the 1828 presidential campaign failed to hurt him by attacking his Indian policy. Jackson advocated Indian removal in his first annual message to Congress in December 1829, and in May 1830 Congress passed the U.S. Indian Removal Act. That fall the American Board of Commissioners for Foreign Missions issued resolutions opposing the removal, and Worcester not only drafted resolutions but spoke publicly against the Georgia policies.

The sequence of events that led Samuel Worcester to jail and to the high court began in late 1830, when he wrote a document signed by about a dozen Christian ministers protesting Georgia's encroachments on Cherokee territory. All of the ministers detested President Jackson's efforts to force Indian removal, and all were familiar with Georgia's attempts to hasten it. Only one of them, however, Elizur Butler, joined Worcester in the penitentiary after Georgia incarcerated them because they deliberately remained with the Cherokee nation after the March 1, 1831, deadline for all white men to leave or secure a license and swear an oath to abide by Georgia law. Worcester intended to provoke a Supreme Court case and, by winning, ensure the Cherokees' protection by federal law.

Worcester stood prepared for a moral and legal battle, but some of his earlier allies had begun to desert him. Three Georgia-based missionaries who had previously opposed removal decided against joining Worcester and Butler as their fight became more public. Worcester attacked Georgia governor George R. Gilmore when the latter accused the missionary of "opposition to the humane policy which the General Government has adopted for the civilization of the Indians" and criticized his "effort to prevent their submission to the laws of Georgia." Worcester responded, declaring, "If I am correct in the apprehension that the state of Georgia has no rightful jurisdiction over the territory where I reside, then it follows that I am under no moral compunction to remove, in compliance with her enactments."

For his failure to obey the law, Georgia authorities arrested Worcester, and after a jury found him guilty, he entered prison in September 1831, and stayed there for sixteen months. In prison he improved his woodworking and cabinetmaking skills, talents he would put to good use later on in the Oklahoma Indian Territory. He also appealed to the U.S. Supreme Court.

The Georgia Law before the Supreme Court

The Court accepted the case in early January 1832, and set February 20 as the first day of oral argument. William Wirt, John Sergeant, and

Elisha W. Chester appeared that day, the first two representing the Cherokee and the latter on behalf of Samuel Worcester. Wirt was one of the best-known lawyers in the country, a veteran of many Supreme Court cases, and he had represented the Cherokee in the earlier case. But in 1824, as attorney general, he had issued an opinion denying the Cherokee government the power to impose a licensing tax on white traders doing business with the tribe. Wirt wrote that it was "fallacious" to view the Cherokee as having sovereignty equal to that of the United States. "By the treaties they have entered with us," he declared, "they have placed themselves under the protection of the United States." Now, of course, he would have to argue just the opposite.

Wirt had had a difficult time finding cocounsel, in part because many lawyers had no desire to represent Indians, and in part because loyal Democrats feared crossing Andrew Jackson. Finally, he secured the services of the wealthy Philadelphia lawyer and representative John Sergeant, an ardent anti-Jacksonian. Worcester hired Elisha W. Chester, a New England acquaintance who was practicing law in Georgia, but in general, Chester, who had little experience in appellate work, took his guidance from Wirt.

Georgia, as it had done the year before in *Cherokee Nation v. Georgia*, refused to send any representative, in effect declaring that it did not recognize the authority of federal courts in what it considered internal matters. Georgia was not alone at this time in challenging federal power on the basis of states' rights, and its decision reflected a long-standing objection to the idea of federal judicial supremacy over the states. It had, in fact, been Georgia that first challenged the Supreme Court's authority to hear a suit by a citizen against a state, in *Chisholm v. Georgia* (1793), a decision that led to the adoption of the Eleventh Amendment barring such suits. The failure to even attend the proceedings, however, boded ill for Worcester and the Cherokee, since even if they won in the high court, Georgia would undoubtedly ignore the decision.

Sergeant laid out the case for Worcester and for the Cherokee on February 20, and Wirt took over the next day, expanding on Sergeant's outline, and finishing on February 23 (the Court adjourned on February 22 to attend a service in the Capitol in honor of the centennial of George Washington's birth). Justice Joseph Story reported to his wife that "both of the speeches were very able, and Wirt's, in particular, was uncommonly eloquent, forcible, and finished."

Sergeant took a straightforward approach, without the rhetorical flourishes favored by Wirt, and set out a simple legal argument—the Court had the power to hear the case. That is, it had jurisdiction; the Eleventh Amendment did not bar appeals to the high court in which a federal question had been raised. He then turned to the merits of the case, which he asserted derived directly from treaties made with the

Indian tribes and that had been ratified by Congress. While Congress could repeal laws it had passed, it could not unilaterally abrogate a treaty, and neither could any individual or state.

Sergeant described the rights of the Cherokee as having been violated, but he always spoke of tribal claims as secondary to the issue of federal authority. As for the Indians' political status, he cautiously cited Chief Justice Marshall's language in *Cherokee Nation v. Georgia*: "As to the Cherokees themselves, they are a State—a community. Within their territory, they possess the powers of self-government. . . . They are domestic, dependant nations."

On March 3, 1832, the Court, as Wirt and Sergeant had expected, ruled against the state of Georgia. Writing for the Court, Chief Justice John Marshall first asserted the Court's jurisdiction to hear the case. Worcester and other missionaries could, as citizens of the United States, properly challenge their convictions under earlier Court decisions affirming the high court's national judicial power. "It is too clear for controversy," he asserted, "that the act of Congress, by which this court is constituted, has given it the power and the duty of exercising jurisdiction in this case." (While Marshall may have been reminding Congress that it had conferred upon the judiciary the authority for hearing such cases, and that the Court had not seized it, it did sound a false note, since just the previous year the Court had denied that it had any "duty" to hear the *Cherokee Nation* case.)

He then turned to the merits of the case, and declared that Georgia's laws and actions were "repugnant to the constitution, laws, and treaties of the United States." Worcester and Elizur Butler had been arrested and imprisoned under an unconstitutional law, and should therefore be freed immediately. The opinion, however, did not stop there, as it well might have, since the missionaries were contesting only their convictions and imprisonment. Marshall went on to declare all of Georgia's harassing legislation unconstitutional, and he did so in sweeping terms. The state's laws violated the authority of the United States and the rights of the Cherokee, who constituted a distinct political entity with full control over their territory, over which "the laws of Georgia can have no force, and which the citizens of Georgia have no right to enter but with the assent of the Cherokees themselves."

As he had in so many controversial cases, Marshall deftly avoided a direct confrontation with either Georgia or the U.S. government. His opinion was clearly an affront to the state of Georgia—much the same way his opinion in *Marbury* had been an affront to Jefferson. Here he was implicitly ordering the state to release Worcester, but he could not have expected any cooperation from Georgia. Indeed, Marshall's closest confidant on the Court, Justice Joseph Story, predicted that Georgia probably would "resist the execution" of the Court's judgment. For Story, and perhaps Marshall, the symbolism of the opinion was enough. "Thanks be to God," Story wrote to his wife, "the Court can wash their hands, clean of the iniquity of oppressing the Indians and disregarding their rights." Story was proud that the "Court has done its duty."

The Failure of Law and a Political Compromise

While his opinion required Georgia to set Worcester free, Marshall never issued a final order in the case directing the state to do so. Instead, the day after the decision, the Court adjourned. The opinion of the Court was sent to Georgia, to be implemented by that state's government. If Georgia failed to act, which is what everyone assumed, then Worcester could return to the Court the following term, in January 1833, to ask for some process to secure his release. This left Worcester in the odd position of having won a favorable decision but without any specific order or writ that he could ask someone to serve on Georgia authorities. Marshall strongly implied in his opinion that the president had a duty to enforce federal law and treaty obligations, but he did not order Jackson, or anyone else, to do anything.

According to the journalist Horace Greeley at the time, Jackson declared that "John Marshall has made his decision, now let him enforce it," but despite the constant repetition of this alleged response, there is no evidence that Jackson said anything of the sort. Marshall had issued no mandate requiring that the president or anyone else take any action. Jackson did, however, write to a longtime friend that "the decision of the supreme court has fell still born, and they find that they cannot coerce Georgia to yield to its mandate." Moreover, Jackson did not believe he could force Georgia to act, nor was there sufficient military or political power to "preserve [the Cherokee] from destruction," if it came to that. Thus Jackson took no direction action in response to the decision, and as one historian has noted, "Jackson's silence on the Court's decision appears to have been astutely planned."

In the months following the decision in *Worcester,* President Jackson was deeply immersed in three other issues:

1. The upcoming election of 1832, where he would run for reelection.
2. The developing conflict between the national government and South Carolina over tariffs, which would lead to the state's effort to nullify a federal law later that year.
3. The debate over the recharter of the Bank of the United States, which would lead to Jackson's famous Bank Veto in July (see Chapter 2 for more about the Bank).

Shortly after Jackson signed the compromise tariff bill in July 1832, Vice President John C. Calhoun resigned his office in July to publicly oppose Jackson's policies and to advocate for the right of states to nullify federal laws. By the fall of 1832 all three issues complicated any resolution of the *Cherokee* case, while South Carolina's movement toward nullification—with an ordinance passed on November 24, 1832—threatened the entire nation.

Under these circumstances, Jackson could hardly risk a confrontation with Georgia over the Cherokee. Rather, he needed the support of Georgia and the rest of the South in his emerging confrontation with South Carolina. At the same time, he could hardly chastise South Carolina for its nullification of a federal law while Georgia defied the U.S. Supreme Court's assertion that Worcester's imprisonment violated the U.S. Constitution and the federal treaties with the Cherokee.

In the late fall of 1832 a series of compromises emerged. Jackson and his new vice president, Martin Van Buren, worked with Gov. Wilson Lumpkin of Georgia to arrange to have the legislature repeal the statute under which Worcester had been convicted. The board of ministers that Worcester worked with agreed to end the litigation. Governor Wilson met with the wives of Reverend Worcester and his codefendant, Reverend Butler. Then, in response to petitions to release Worcester and Butler, Lumpkin was able to act in a "humanitarian" way to set the men free. By January 1833 Worcester and his colleague were out of jail. Lumpkin offered to pardon Worcester and Butler; they would not accept the pardon (since that would have implied that they had been in the wrong), but they did accept the humanitarian release and promised to leave the state, which they did. With this issue moving toward settlement in late 1832, Andrew Jackson was now free to turn his attention to crushing the nullification movement in South Carolina, with the full support of Georgia.

Cherokee Removal

In these negotiations, Jackson promised Georgia that the federal government would finally remove the Cherokee. He thus pressured the tribe into signing a new treaty. In 1835 a group of Cherokee signed a treaty in which the tribe agreed to vacate the land they occupied in Georgia in exchange for land in a newly designated "Indian Territory" in present-day Oklahoma, along with $5 million and expenses for transportation. The negotiators who signed the treaty did not represent the majority of the Cherokee nation, and actually had no authority to act on behalf of the nation. The overwhelming majority of the Cherokee opposed the treaty, and many refused to comply with the requirements, even when faced with the overwhelming force of the U.S. Army. Thus most of the Cherokee made no preparation to leave until 1838, when the army forcibly moved most of the Georgia Cherokee west in what is known as the "Trail of Tears." Nearly 4,000 Cherokee died in internment camps before they were relocated, along the way, or shortly after their arrival in the Indian Territory. Inadequate food and shelter, as well as the strenuous journey, caused most of these deaths. Only 17,000 Cherokee reached Oklahoma. On the trail, they were subjected to humiliating treatment by the soldiers supposedly guarding their way, to pilferage from civilian contractors on whom they relied for supplies, and to the open scorn of whites along the route. A few Cherokee, known as the eastern band, remained in Georgia, and eventually settled on a reservation in North Carolina.

The Cherokee removal illustrates how whites as individuals, and collectively through the federal and state governments, maltreated the Indians in the nineteenth century. It remains a blot on the national heritage. It also points up one of the gray areas of the Constitution, which at this time provided little protection for Indians or other minority groups. The inherent racism of whites toward Indians influenced policy and actions from the time of the early settlements until well into the twentieth century, despite the efforts of some whites (and, later on, activist Indians as well) to secure justice and fair treatment for the tribes. Most of the states supported Georgia's flouting of the Supreme Court, as well as Jackson's policy to force the tribes, against their will, to give up fertile lands that they had long inhabited and had been granted in treaties, to move to the barren reaches of the Great Plains. Just as ominously, Georgia's assertion of state sovereignty against the federal judicial power anticipated a major constitutional crisis involving federal tariff policy.

Aftermath

Samuel Worcester moved to the Indian Territory in 1835, ahead of the Cherokee who came on the Trail of Tears. There he continued his work as a newspaper publisher, minister, and supporter of Indian education, and finished his translation of the Bible into Cherokee. His granddaughter, Alice M. Robertson, would be elected to Congress from Oklahoma in 1920.

In November 1992, Gov. Zell Miller of Georgia issued a full and unconditional pardon to Samuel Worcester and Elizur Butler, the two missionaries whom the state had imprisoned more than a century and a half before. He relied upon an earlier recommendation issued just two months earlier by the State Board of Pardons and Paroles, which read in part:

Today, the State Board of Pardons and Paroles acts to remove a stain on the history of criminal justice in Georgia. The U.S. Supreme Court did what it could 160 years ago to reverse the wrong committed against Reverend Worcester and Reverend Butler. Believing justice ought to be denied no longer, by this Order the State Board of Pardons and Paroles unconditionally and fully pardons Samuel Austin Worcester and Elizur Butler.

In a ceremony at the state capital, Governor Miller presented the posthumous pardons to state representative Bill Dover, chief executive officer of the Georgia Tribe of Eastern Cherokee, the descendants of that small remnant who had not traveled the Trail of Tears.

Cases Cited

Cherokee Nation v. Georgia, 30 U.S. (5 Pet.) 1 (1831)
Chisholm v. Georgia, 2 U.S. (2 Dall.) 419 (1793)
Cohens v. Virginia, 19 U.S. (6 Wheat.) 264 (1821)
Johnson and Graham's Lessee v. M'Intosh, 21 U.S. (8 Wheat.) 543 (1823)
Marbury v. Madison, 5 U.S. (1 Cr.) 137 (1803)
State v. George Tassels, 1 Dud. 229 (Georgia 1830)
Worcester v. Georgia, 31 U.S. (6 Pet.) 515 (1832)

For Further Reading

On the cases, see Jill Norgren, *The Cherokee Cases: The Confrontation of Law and Politics* (1995), and Theda Perdue, *The Cherokee Removal: A Brief History with Documents* (1995). Tim Alan Garrison, *The Legal Ideology of Removal: The Southern Judiciary and the Sovereignty of Native American Nations* (2002), offers an important study of the state litigation leading to the Cherokee cases, including Corn Tassels' case. Ronald N. Satz, *American Indian Policy in the Jacksonian Era* (2002), provides detailed scholarship on the questions. Robert Remini, *Andrew Jackson and His Indian War* (2001), is a complex analysis of Jackson's career in relation to Indians. Also useful, but controversial, is Michael P. Rogin, *Fathers and Children: Andrew Jackson and the Subjugation of the American Indian* (1975). On Worcester, see Althea Bass, *Cherokee Messenger* (1936), and William G. McLoughlin, *Cherokees and Missionaries, 1789–1839* (1984).

The Case of the Zealous Slave Catcher

Prigg v. Pennsylvania (1842)

N O ISSUE ROILED the American Republic in the first part of the nineteenth century as did slavery, and this was true in the courts as well. So long as the political system was able to tamp down the tensions—as it did in the 1820 Missouri Compromise—then the judiciary could ignore what its defenders euphemistically called "the peculiar institution."

By the 1830s, however, antislavery sentiment had grown, and would continue to intensify until the Thirteenth Amendment finally abolished involuntary servitude. As the compromises over slavery that had been made at the 1787 Constitutional Convention began to unravel, issues that had been overlooked for decades could no longer be put aside. In *Prigg v. Pennsylvania* the justices wrestled with the problem of runaway slaves, the demands made by slave owners for the return of their "property," and efforts by the North to allow those who had escaped from bondage to remain in freedom.

But the efforts by the judiciary, both in *Prigg* and in *Dred Scott* (see next chapter), to resolve the thorniest problem in American history both came to naught. If anything, they only fanned the flames of sectional tension.

The Fugitive Slave Act of 1793

At the 1787 Constitutional Convention in Philadelphia, the delegates had to overcome a number of serious differences in order to finally agree on a document that could be sent out to the states for ratification. Some of these are familiar, such as the agreement to base membership in the House of Representatives upon population, while each state received two senators. One of the most divisive issues involved slavery, with Southern states demanding protection for their "peculiar institution." Although the words *slave* and *slavery* do not actually appear in the Constitution, there are several clauses that embodied the compromises made between the slaveholding states of the South and the free states of the North.

At the heart of the debate was the question of whether slaves should be considered "persons" and "property." The North argued that if slaves were property, as Southerners claimed, then they should not be included as part of the population count used to determine representation in the lower house of Congress, but should be counted solely for purposes of taxation. Southerners argued that slaves not only produced great wealth but were a form of wealth themselves, and therefore required representation in Congress. The compromise in this area counted slaves on a three-fifths basis—that is, for terms of representation as well as taxation, five enslaved persons would count as three free persons. The agreement was a compromise over political power. The South had won extra representation for its slaves, even though the people filling the seats in Congress would always vote against the personal interests of the slaves.

The South also demanded, and won, a provision regarding runaway slaves in Article IV, Section 2: "No Person held to Service or Labour in one State, under the Laws thereof, escaping into another, shall, in Consequence of any Law or Regulation therein, be discharged from such Service or Labour, but shall be delivered up on Claim of the Party to whom such Service or Labour may be due."

Since runaway slaves crossed state lines, and only the federal government had the power to enforce this provision, Congress passed the Fugitive Slave Act in 1793. Under the terms of this law, owners or the slave hunters they hired could capture an escaped slave in any territory or state of the Union, and all they had to do was swear orally before a state or federal judge that the person was a runaway. The captive was not entitled to a trial by jury, and the judge's decision was final; the slave could not appeal to any other court. In addition, a person hiding an escaped slave could be fined $500—a very expensive penalty in those days.

Personal Liberty Laws

At the time of the adoption of the 1793 act, slavery was widespread not only in the Southern states but in the Northern ones as well. Within a few decades, however, slavery had died out in the North; by the 1840s all Northern states had enacted laws freeing remaining slaves and forbidding slavery within their borders. The Missouri Compromise of 1820 also prohibited slaves in the vast Louisiana Territory above the southern border of Missouri. The eradication of slavery throughout the nation became one of the chief reforms of the Jacksonian era, and the growing abolition movement not only exacerbated tensions between North and South, but undoubtedly contributed to the coming of the Civil War.

As long as the constitutional provisions on slavery remained intact, though, there was little opponents of slavery could do on the federal level. In the Northern states, however, they achieved success in four general areas. First, they succeeded in eliminating whatever remnants of slavery existed within the North. Second, through political activism and litigation, opponents of slavery convinced most of the free states to emancipate any enslaved persons brought within their borders. In this area they relied on English law that slavery could only exist where positive—that is, legislatively enacted—law supported it. In the absence of positive law, they argued, there could be no slavery, and any slave entering the jurisdiction would be free. Chief Justice Lemuel Shaw ruled in *Commonwealth v. Aves* (1836) that slaves brought into Massachusetts by the voluntary action of their masters became immediately free. Soon nearly every Northern state had adopted this law, and it became the basis for the suit by Dred Scott seeking his freedom (see next chapter). As late as 1860, New York's highest court ruled that a slave brought into the state for only one day became free (*Lemmon v. The People*). The Virginia owner no doubt intended to take this case to the U.S. Supreme Court, but the Civil War prevented any appeal.

Third, opponents of slavery worked to improve the condition of free blacks in the North. Many states still had "black codes" on their books from the time when slavery had been legal, and these codes restricted the rights of free blacks just as did the counterpart codes in the South. Although the Massachusetts Supreme Judicial Court upheld the segregation of black children in public schools in *Roberts v. Boston* (1850), within five years the state legislature banned the practice. In 1857 a new constitution in Iowa removed the word *white* from provisions dealing with public education, and on the eve of Abraham Lincoln's election in 1860, blacks could find some form of public education open to them in almost all of the Northern states.

Finally, starting in the 1820s and continuing until the Civil War, Northern legislatures passed "personal liberty laws" to prevent the kidnapping of free blacks by Southerners hunting for fugitive slaves. From the beginning, opponents of slavery, and especially Northern free blacks, had been concerned that the lax standards of proof in the federal Fugitive Slave Act would lead to the kidnapping of free blacks. All a slave catcher had to do was swear before a magistrate that the captive was an escaped slave, and there was nothing—under federal law—that the black man or woman could do to prove otherwise. The federal law, however, contained no guidelines on procedures states should follow, and so opponents of slavery stepped in to secure laws aimed at preventing free blacks from being taken, and also to ensure that fugitive slaves would not be removed without a fair hearing and clear evidence that they were, indeed, runaway slaves.

In the 1820s, New Jersey, New York, and Pennsylvania passed "personal liberty laws" providing fugitive slaves with basic legal protections. They could not be removed from the state without a fair hearing and clear evidence that someone identified as a runaway slave was indeed that person. Antislavery lawyers used the personal liberty laws to protect both free blacks and fugitives in their states. They also mounted a broad attack on the federal Fugitive Slave Act and showed that, on this issue at least, they could be as ardent defenders of states' rights and strict constitutional construction as their Southern counterparts.

They questioned the power of the federal government to pass such a law, since the Constitution did not specifically grant to Congress authorization to implement the fugitive slave clause. The wording of the clause is quite vague as to who—if anyone—has responsibility to "deliver up on Claim of the Party to whom such Service or Labour may be due." The Constitution, they claimed, made it clear when Congress could and could not act. The necessary and proper clause (Article I, Section 8) gave Congress the power only to implement powers specifically delegated to the national government. The full faith and credit clause (Article IV, Section 1) required states to honor the legal actions taken in other states, but congressional action was needed to establish a procedure for just how that should be done. Opponents of slavery challenged the constitutionality of the Fugitive Slave Act, and took a page directly from Southern defenders of states' rights, who argued vociferously that Congress could enact only such laws as the Constitution specifically provided. Even John Marshall's broad interpretation of the necessary and proper clause in *McCulloch v. Maryland* (1819) (see Chapter 2) only extended to the delegated powers of Congress; it did not create new powers, but only gave Congress great latitude in how it would implement its authority.

The response in state courts to this reasoning was mixed. Before 1820, the high courts in Pennsylvania and Massachusetts upheld the constitutionality of the Fugitive Slave Act. Then, starting in the 1830s, the supreme courts of New York, New Jersey, and Pennsylvania all adopted the position that Congress lacked power to pass such a law. Chief Justice Joseph C. Hornblower of New Jersey declared that the lack of a jury trial under the federal law undermined its constitutionality. In 1837 a young Cincinnati lawyer named Salmon P. Chase—who would later be a U.S. senator, governor of Ohio, secretary of the Treasury in the Lincoln administration, and then chief justice of the United States— took on the case of the slave Matilda Lawrence. Lawrence had escaped from Kentucky into Ohio, and her owner claimed her under the Fugitive Slave Act. Chase developed an elaborate attack on the law, claiming that it violated the Fourth Amendment protection against unreasonable search and seizure, the procedural guarantees of the Fifth Amendment's due process clause, and the protections of jury trial and habeas corpus embodied in the Northwest Ordinance (of which Ohio was originally a part). Although the local court ordered Lawrence handed back to her owner, Chase's arguments accurately reflected the sentiments of the antislavery community and its opposition to the federal law. They were printed up and received wide circulation throughout the North. At this point it was only a matter of time before the constitutionality of the Fugitive Slave Act and of the personal liberty laws would reach the Supreme Court.

Edward Prigg and Margaret Morgan

A Maryland farmer named John Ashmore had owned Margaret Morgan's parents, but sometime before 1812, Ashmore had allowed the two to live in virtual freedom. Although Ashmore never formally manumitted the two slaves, he had on numerous occasions declared he "had set them free." The two blacks raised their daughter Margaret as a free person. When Ashmore died in 1824 the inventory of his estate listed only two slaves, both young males, and at the time no claim was made by Ashmore's heirs on either Margaret or her parents. Margaret believed herself to be free, married a free black named Jerry Morgan, and was assumed to be free by most people in the community. In the early 1830s the Morgans, who by then had two children, moved to Pennsylvania, where they had two more children. (No matter what the courts might later determine about Margaret's status, there should never have been a legal question that her children born in Pennsylvania were free.)

In 1837 Ashmore's niece and heir hired Edward Prigg, a Maryland farmer, to go into Pennsylvania along with his neighbor, Nathan Beemis (who was Ashmore's son-in-law), and two other men to capture Margaret Morgan, her husband Jerry, and her children, and to bring them back to the niece, who claimed to be the rightful owner. When the two men arrived in Pennsylvania, they applied to a justice of the peace for a warrant to arrest Margaret Morgan as a fugitive slave. After obtaining the warrant, Prigg arrested Morgan and her children and brought her back to the court in order to obtain a certificate of removal under the 1826 Pennsylvania personal liberty law. Given the circumstances of the family, it is not surprising that the magistrate refused to issue the certificate. At this point Prigg, Beemis, and the two other men forcibly removed Margaret and her children from Pennsylvania. The niece, who apparently wanted their monetary value more than slaves, turned Margaret and her children, including those born in Pennsylvania, over to slave traders, and they were never heard from again.

Prigg and his cohorts were indicted for kidnapping in Pennsylvania by a York County grand jury, but Maryland initially refused to extradite the men, even though the Maryland governor privately conceded they had broken the law. After extensive negotiations between Maryland and Pennsylvania officials, the Pennsylvania legislature passed an act that provided that any of the four defendants could post a thousand-dollar bond until a final decision would be reached. Maryland then handed Prigg over to Pennsylvania authorities for trial, with the assurance that if convicted at a jury trial, he would not be punished until after the Supreme Court had ruled on the matter. As expected, a York County jury found Prigg guilty of kidnapping, and Prigg appealed to the Pennsylvania Supreme Court. Under the terms of the agreement, if this court found in Prigg's favor, he would be turned loose and the case would be dismissed. By this time, however, officials in Pennsylvania and Maryland, as well as in other states, wanted a ruling on the constitutionality of the Fugitive Slave Act and the personal liberty laws. The Pennsylvania high court issued a short summary judgment affirming the conviction so that the issue could be taken to the U.S. Supreme Court.

The Supreme Court Rules

Seven justices wrote opinions in *Prigg*—a majority opinion, five concurrences, and a dissent, which tied it for the most opinions up to that time in any Supreme Court case. By the standards of the nineteenth century this was truly extraordinary. While multiple opinions today are commonplace, they were rare in the antebellum period. After Chief Justice John Marshall abolished the practice of *seriatim* opinions (in which each justice writes a separate opinion), justices rarely wrote individual opinions except to dissent from the result of the case. The vast majority of decisions were unanimous. In 1832, for example, the Court decided fifty-five cases. Forty-six were unanimous, and eight cases contained a single dissent. In 1842 the Court decided forty-three cases, including *Prigg*. Thirty-eight contained only a single "opinion of the court." In four other cases, there were two opinions. This contrasts sharply with the seven opinions in *Prigg*. In the entire period from 1801 until 1842 no case had more than seven opinions, and only one besides *Prigg* had that many. That case, *Groves v. Slaughter*, decided a year before *Prigg*, also involved slavery.

The many opinions in *Prigg*, as well as the wide range of those opinions, suggest its importance. Speaking for the Court, in what was understood at the time to be an overwhelmingly proslavery decision, was Joseph Story of Massachusetts, whom many believed to be at least nominally opposed to slavery. Story, in his younger days, had attacked the institution, and even after his appointment to the high court had criticized the African slave trade. But he was also hostile to abolitionists, and while he was against slavery, had never showed any sympathy to the plight of the slaves themselves.

In his opinion for the Court, Story reached four major conclusions, all of which combined to give Southern slaveholders a significant victory. Everyone on the Court except Justice John McLean agreed with the outcome—that Prigg's conviction was invalid—and with Story's major points that (1) the Fugitive Slave Act of 1793 was constitutional; (2) state personal liberty laws that interfered with the rights of slave owners under the Constitution were unconstitutional; (3) the Constitution gave masters a common-law right to recapture a fugitive slave without resorting to any legal process, if it could be done without a "breach of the peace"; and (4) no fugitive slave was entitled to any due process hearing or trial beyond a summary proceeding to determine if the person seized was the person described in the affidavit or other papers provided by the claimant.

Although the least surprising of the holdings, it was by no means inevitable that the 1793 law would be found constitutional. Pennsylvania had argued that Congress had no authority to legislate on the subject because it was not one of its powers as enumerated by the Constitution. Although the fugitive slave clause appeared as part of the comity provisions in Article IV (which provided for legal reciprocity among the states), the clause did not directly give Congress specific powers to enforce it. In addition, the 1793 law might also have been invalidated because it violated other parts of the Constitution. It denied free blacks and alleged slaves the rights to a jury trial, habeas corpus, double jeopardy, and other Bill of Rights protections. Although the runaway slaves had not been charged with "crimes," it would not have been unreasonable for the Court to demand that persons who potentially faced a life of involuntary servitude ought to have at least minimal due process safeguards.

Story's assertion that exclusive jurisdiction over fugitive slaves lay with the federal government should not have been surprising, given his strong nationalist ideology. In some ways this ran counter to the Southern states' rights doctrines, but the South welcomed the opinion because it gave strong support for slavery. Pennsylvania's personal liberty law, like those of other Northern states, encroached upon what Story saw as the exclusive domain of congressional power. Contemporaries as well as historians since have seen Story's opinion as supporting the system of slavery with the power of the federal government, and putting those who opposed the return of fugitive slaves in the awkward position of following their conscience, and thus seemingly violating not only federal law but the Constitution as well. In fact, *Prigg* is the first Supreme Court decision to explicitly recognize slavery as a constitutionally protected institution within the Union.

Story's conclusion that a master had a personal right to recapture his slave without following any more than the most summary judicial procedure was in some ways the most unexpected part of his opinion, since it went much further than the Court had ever gone in dealing with the rights of slave owners, and even further than the case required. Under the fugitive slave clause, Story found "a positive and unqualified recognition of the owner in the slave, unaffected by any state law or regulation whatsoever." This being the case, "the owner must, therefore, have the right to seize and repossess the slave, which the local laws of his own state confer upon him as property; and we all know that this right of seizure and recaption is universally acknowledged in all the slaveholding states." Story then declared that under the comity provisions of Article IV, all other states had to recognize that an owner is clothed with the full legal authority to seize and recapture his property. So long as this recapture did not breach the peace or instigate illegal violence, it required no aid in the form of state or national legislation. By the same token, neither state nor national legislation could impinge on that right. As critics immediately noted, this was an open invitation for the kidnapping of free blacks, since they had no recourse to the courts to prove their status; a slave owner's declaration that a person was a slave trumped everything else.

Most significantly, Story's opinion effectively made the law of the South the law of the nation. In the South, race was a presumption of enslaved status, and by giving masters and slave hunters a common-law right of recapture, Story nationalized this presumption. As a result, slave catchers could operate in the North without having to prove the seized person's enslaved status. The consequences for the nearly 175,000 free blacks in the North were dire. Even if they were not personally threatened with recapture, the anxiety must have been great.

The only controversy among the majority justices centered on the role of the states in the return of fugitive slaves. Justice Story believed that state officials *ought* to enforce the fugitive slave law by passing implementing legislation authorizing state officials to act in support of slave catchers. But the federal government could not require states to do so. Story, in what was probably the earliest use of the "preemption doctrine," asserted that because Congress had passed legislation on this subject, the states were preempted from acting in any way contrary to federal policy. This ruling dovetailed with Story's lifelong goal of nationalizing law and allowing for the development of a federal common law.

Chief Justice Roger B. Taney, while concurring with Story's general conclusions, nonetheless objected to this portion. Story had in effect said that while states could choose to help enforce the federal law, they did not have to do so. Taney immediately saw the danger in this— namely, that Northern states would refuse any aid to the slave owners or their agents, and could, by refusing to cooperate, effectively nullify the law. The chief justice argued that states were obligated to help enforce the law, and they could and should enact more elaborate legislation to assist in the recapture of runaways.

In dissent, Justice McLean warned that the decision would lead to the enslavement of free blacks. Indeed, Justice Story's refusal to consider the status of the Pennsylvania-born children of Margaret Morgan illustrates that the dangers set out in McLean's opinion were far from hypothetical.

The importance of *Prigg* had been apparent as soon as the Court had announced that it would hear the case. In January 1841, over a year before oral argument, John Quincy Adams—who had become one of the most vocal opponents of slavery—had made two trips to the Court to secure a printed copy of the record so he could study it. The abolitionist leader Theodore Dwight Weld had predicted that "the decision will involve the Constitutionality of the laws of Mass., N.Y., and other northern states. . . . Of course the trial is of immense importance."

Following the decision on March 1, 1842, newspapers hailed or damned it as a victory for slavery. The conservative New York *Herald* thought it would "have the most salutary effect in repressing the incendiary movements of the abolitionists, and in quieting the just apprehensions entertained at the South." William Lloyd Garrison's *Liberator,* the most fiery of all the antislavery organs, responded by predicting that the decision would "treble the present number of abolitionists and serve to raise their zeal to a pitch, and that will not exactly quiet the apprehensions of the South."

After *Prigg:* George Latimer

Story doubtless hoped that his opinion would reduce sectional tensions and give the South a greater sense of security in the nation. This goal, however, backfired. *Prigg* failed to settle the issue because of strong public sentiment against it in the North. This opposition manifested itself in Boston later in 1842, in the case of a runaway slave named George Latimer. Initially, Latimer was confined in the local jail while his owner, James B. Gray, waited for proper documentation of Latimer's status to arrive from Virginia. Abolitionists appealed to Chief Justice Shaw for a writ of habeas corpus, but Shaw refused, claiming that Latimer was legitimately held under the Fugitive Slave Act of 1793. Local abolitionists, however, convinced the county sheriff that he could not hold a slave in a Massachusetts jail. Faced with the prospect of trying to keep Latimer in a Boston hotel, Gray agreed to sell Latimer—for far less than the slave was worth—to agents of his defense committee, who immediately freed him.

The most common reaction in the North was, as Taney had feared, seizure upon Story's dictum that states did not have to take positive steps to implement the law. Massachusetts, Vermont, Connecticut, New Hampshire, Pennsylvania, and Rhode Island all enacted legislation prohibiting state officials from enforcing the federal statute. Ohio repealed a statute that had required state officials to enforce the law. Although a Democratic governor of New York urged the assembly to repeal the state personal liberty law since it was unconstitutional after *Prigg*, the legislature refused to do so, and the New York law remained in force until the Civil War.

Northern legislatures, in fact, took Story's comments literally— namely, that while they could enforce the federal law, they did not have to, and in fact could direct state officers *not* to participate in abetting the slave catchers. In 1843, Massachusetts passed the "Latimer Law," which prohibited the use of any state facility for holding a fugitive slave and prohibited all state employees from participating in the return of a slave. Even more important, the Latimer incident highlighted the growing dilemma for abolitionists and lawyers between obedience to law and adherence to what many perceived as a higher moral duty. The moral repugnance of slavery led the abolitionists, especially the more radical followers of William Lloyd Garrison, to mount an outright attack on the Constitution and on those federal and state laws that enforced its slavery provisions. A majority of lawyers and judges, however, opted for obedience to the law, taking refuge in strict adherence to the letter of the state statute. This formalistic view permitted some of them to find, in the absence of positive state law upholding slavery, the means to free some individual fugitives. Most, however, even when pronouncing their personal opposition to slavery, argued that they could not prevent the return of blacks to their owners until the laws had been changed.

Even without legislation, antislavery judges and lawyers found *Prigg* a useful tool for opposing the rendition of fugitive slaves. State judges could declare that they had no authority to hear cases involving fugitives, and to suggest that claimants seek a remedy in federal court, even though the nearest federal court might be hundreds of miles away or not even in session. The slave, of course, could be returned to the South under the self-help rule—that is, capture by the owner or a slave catcher—but without access to jails and aid from local officials, it could be difficult or impossible for an owner to bring his property back home.

The Fugitive Slave Act of 1850

The growing creativity of Northern opponents of slavery made it increasingly hard for Southerners to capture runaway slaves, as the Latimer incident showed. Abolitionists across the North created the "underground railroad," which helped escaped bondsmen get to Canada, where they were beyond the reach of American law. The growing tensions between North and South over issues such as the slave trade and the existence of slavery in the western territories nearly led to the rupture of the Union in early 1850. An aging Henry Clay, who had forged the Missouri Compromise of 1820, helped broker another agreement to keep the Union together, one that included a new Fugitive Slave Act.

The 1850 law was a supplement to the original 1793 act rather than a replacement for it, and it immediately inflamed the North—with good reason. The new statute completely favored the slave catcher or owner and denied the alleged runaway even minimal recourse to due process. Under this law owners or professional slave catchers could seize a black person without a warrant; once in custody, the slave catcher could secure a rendition certificate, either from a federal judge or a new class of commissioners named by the federal courts; the alleged slave could not testify on his own behalf; no legal process, including habeas corpus, could interfere with returning a captured slave; an alleged slave was not allowed to test his freedom, or even his identity, before a jury; federal marshals and commissioners could form a posse, asking all "good citizens" to help catch a runaway slave; and obstruction of the law, or rescue of a runaway, could be punished by a fine of $1,000 and six months in jail.

A Georgia convention declared that "upon the faithful execution of the Fugitive Slave Bill by the proper authorities, depends the preservation of our Union," and in 1860–1861 a number of Southern states would cite the failure of the North to obey this law as a reason for secession. On the other hand, Rep. George W. Julian of Indiana spoke for many Northerners when he declared that "a more heartless and cold-blooded" law had "never disgraced the legislation of a civilized people."

The terrible one-sidedness of the law gave abolitionists one of their greatest propaganda weapons. Denouncing "this filthy enactment," the essayist and poet Ralph Waldo Emerson urged his neighbors to break it "on the earliest occasion." Clergymen across the North echoed these sentiments, and many Northerners needed little encouragement. Yet, despite this public opposition, there was little interference with the law, and few successful rescues of fugitives who were seized under the law. Between 1850 and 1860 at least 366 fugitive slaves were returned to the South while only 23 were either rescued or escaped from federal custody. These rescues, however, and subsequent escapes gained the headlines and gave the impression of massive Northern resistance to the law. Moreover, vigilance committees formed by free blacks, fugitive slaves, and their white allies made enforcement dangerous or impossible in many places in the North. Southerners estimated that there were at least 10,000 fugitive slaves in the North, and thus a return of fewer than 400 suggests that the law worked poorly. Many Northerners would have agreed. The great black abolitionist Frederick Douglass noted in his memoirs that after the successful "Jerry rescue" in Syracuse, New York, in 1851, the law was a "dead letter" throughout upstate New York. In that incident, a mob, which included the mayor and the city's leading minister, removed the fugitive slave Jerry McHenry from the custody of a U.S. marshal. Abolitionists later successfully took McHenry to Canada.

The Fugitive Slave Act had its greatest impact, one evidently unforeseen by the South, in spreading revulsion against slavery throughout the North, and in politicizing Northerners who had previously ignored the issue of slavery. Both moral and legal considerations governed the views of many Northerners. When Sen. William H. Seward of New York attacked the 1850 compromise, he declared, "There is a higher law than the Constitution!" That phrase became the allying cry for opposition to the Fugitive Slave Act.

The act led to a variety of legal responses. The Chicago City Council passed a resolution declaring the law null and void. The Ohio legislature passed a resolution holding the act unconstitutional because Congress lacked the power to pass such a law and because it violated the

Bill of Rights. Initially, the states took a wait-and-see attitude toward the law. Between 1854 and 1858, however, in response to both increasingly vigorous federal enforcement and the Kansas-Nebraska Act of 1854, all six of the New England states, as well as Ohio, Michigan, and Wisconsin, passed new personal liberty laws. Most of these states also closed their jails to slave catchers. In 1855, Massachusetts passed the most radical and comprehensive of these new personal liberty laws, which gave runaway slaves the right to appointed counsel, jury trials, habeas corpus, and even the writ of personal replevin, an old procedural device to free a person from prison or from the custody of another. The law also prohibited any lawyer in the state from representing a slave owner and any state official from acting under the law. Since most of the federal commissioners in Massachusetts were also state officeholders and lawyers, enforcing the federal law could cost them their regular jobs, as well as their right to practice law.

Prigg, like *Dred Scott*, can be seen as an effort by the courts to resolve the growing tension between North and South over the issue of slavery. Justice Story in *Prigg*, and Chief Justice Taney in *Dred Scott*, both underestimated the growing revulsion against slavery in the North and the almost hysterical demand in the South that the full power of the federal government be brought to bear to protect the "peculiar institution." In the end, it took a war to finally resolve the question of slavery.

Cases Cited

Commonwealth v. Aves, 35 Mass. 193 (1836)
Dred Scott v. Sandford, 60 U.S. (19 How.) 393 (1857)
Groves v. Slaughter, 40 U.S. (15 Pet.) 449 (1841)
Lemmon v. The People, 20 N.Y. 562 (1860)
McCulloch v. Maryland, 17 U.S. (4 Wheat.) 316 (1819)
Prigg v. Pennsylvania, 41 U.S. (16 Peters) 539 (1842)
Roberts v. City of Boston, 59 Mass. 198 (1850)

For Further Reading

The literature on American slavery is immense and growing. For good overviews, see Kenneth M. Stampp, *The Peculiar Institution* (1956), and Ira Berlin, *Generations of Captivity: A History of African-American Slaves* (2003). Similarly, the scholarship on slavery and the law is also burgeoning. Paul Finkelman, *Slavery in the Courtroom* (1985), and Mark V. Tushnet, *The American Law of Slavery, 1810–1860* (1981), are very useful. For the *Prigg* case, see Finkelman, "Story Telling on the Supreme Court: *Prigg v.*

Pennsylvania and Justice Joseph Story's Nationalism," 1994 *Supreme Court Review* 247 (1995), and for a broader context, his *An Imperfect Union: Slavery, Freedom, and Comity* (1981). For fugitive slaves, see John Hope Franklin and Loren Scheninger, *Runaway Slaves: Rebels on the Plantation* (1999), and for Northern law, see Thomas D. Morris, *Free Men All: The Personal Liberty Laws of the North* (1974). The complexities of the 1850 compromise are examined in Holman Hamilton, *Prologue to Conflict: The Crisis and Compromise of 1850* (1964).

The Case of the Slave Who Would Be Free

Dred Scott v. Sandford (1857)

THE *DRED SCOTT* DECISION holds a unique place in American constitutional history as the worst example of the Supreme Court trying to impose a judicial solution on a political problem. No other case called down such opprobrium upon the Court in its own time, nor has this criticism abated since. A later chief justice, Charles Evans Hughes, famously characterized the decision as the Court's great "self-inflicted wound."

The case involved not just the efforts of one enslaved man to be free, but the larger political debate then roiling the country—what would be the future of slavery—a question that ultimately would be resolved in a civil war. The decision might have been ignored had not Chief Justice Roger Brook Taney tried, in a single opinion, to resolve the nation's most intractable problem.

Dred Scott and His Travels

Dred Scott was born a slave in Southampton County, Virginia, around 1800. His original owner, Peter Blow, moved to Alabama in 1818, and then relocated again to St. Louis, Missouri, in 1830, taking with him his property—including his slaves—as he moved west. Blow died in 1832, and Dr. John Emerson, an army surgeon, purchased Scott. From December 1, 1833, until May 4, 1836, Emerson served as the post physician at Fort Armstrong, Illinois, near the present city of Rock Island. Scott lived with Emerson on the army post.

Because Illinois was a free state, he could have claimed his freedom during these years. The illiterate Scott did not do so, however, perhaps because he did not know that a slave in a free state had a right to be free, and that therefore he could have sued for his freedom. It is also possible that Scott found Emerson a tolerable master, and that being a free black on the Illinois frontier did not seem attractive to him.

In 1836 Scott accompanied Emerson to the doctor's new posting at Fort Snelling in the Minnesota Territory, now St. Paul. Minnesota was part of the Louisiana Territory, and the Missouri Compromise of 1820 "forever prohibited" slavery in the area. Two weeks before Emerson and Scott left Illinois, Congress passed the Wisconsin Enabling Act to govern the region that includes the present-day states of Wisconsin, Minnesota, and Iowa. The new law repeated the Missouri Compromise ban on slavery, and also applied the provisions of the Northwest Ordinance of 1787. Article VI of that law, passed by the Confederation Congress and reaffirmed by the new Congress after the ratification of the Constitution, declared, "there shall be neither slavery nor involuntary servitude in the said Territory, otherwise than in the punishment of crimes, whereof the party shall have been duly convicted."

Despite slavery's illegality in the territory, Scott remained a slave at Fort Snelling from his arrival in May 1836 until his departure in April 1838. During those two years he met and married Harriet Robinson, a slave owned by Major Lawrence Taliaferro, the Indian agent stationed there. Taliaferro, who also served as a justice of the peace, performed a formal wedding ceremony for the two slaves. Some scholars speculate that since formal weddings between slaves were rare and because Emerson and Taliaferro both agreed to the ceremony, they might have believed that Harriet and Dred were in fact free. Even if the masters did not agree, the wedding ceremony itself might have been interpreted as a de facto emancipation, especially since Taliaferro had acted in his official capacity to perform the rite. Nonetheless, neither Scott nor his wife claimed freedom at the time, and at some point Harriet's ownership passed into Emerson's hands.

In November 1837 the army transferred Emerson to Fort Jesup in Louisiana, where he met and married Eliza Irene Sanford, who preferred to be called "Irene." Emerson then sent for his slaves, and the Scotts traveled down the Mississippi to Louisiana, meeting up with Emerson in April. The two passed through free territories and states on the voyage, and at almost any of those stops could have gone ashore and claimed freedom. They did not.

Even after they arrived in Louisiana, they could have sued to be free. For more than twenty years, Louisiana courts had upheld the freedom of slaves who had previously lived in free jurisdictions. Had the Scotts pursued their freedom in 1838, it would have been an easy case with a foregone conclusion. They did not do this, and one again has to speculate why. Did they not know about the law? It is hard to believe that the Scotts had not met free blacks on their travels who would certainly have told them that free states make free men and women. Perhaps they did not know about Louisiana law, or even if they had, perhaps they were not bold enough to go this route.

Not until Emerson died did the Scotts begin their efforts to gain their freedom, and this may indicate that the two had not found servitude under Emerson onerous. He had, after all, agreed to their marriage, kept them together, and apparently treated them well—or well enough—that they did not try to escape or sue in court. There is also speculation that he may have promised them eventual freedom, and this convinced them to wait until they had secured a legal manumission. Unfortunately, we just do not know what the Scotts thought during this time.

In October 1838 Emerson was transferred again, and the Scotts moved with him back to Fort Snelling. On the trip up the Mississippi Harriet gave birth to their first daughter, whom they named Eliza after Dr. Emerson's wife. The child was born between the free state of Illinois and the free territory of Wisconsin, and by all rights should therefore have been free.

A year and a half later, when the army sent Emerson to Florida to serve during the Seminole War, he settled his wife and slaves in St. Louis, Missouri. After the fighting ended, Emerson went to the Iowa Territory, but the Scotts remained in St. Louis, where they apparently hired out their services to various people. In December 1843 Emerson suddenly died, leaving his estate—including the Scotts—to his widow. For the next three years the Scotts worked as hired slaves, with the money they earned going to Irene Emerson. Not until February 1846, however, did Scott first seek freedom for himself and his family. The evidence indicates that Scott may have been advised to do so by a white abolitionist lawyer or by a former slave, the Rev. John Anderson, the pastor of the black Baptist church where Harriet Scott worshipped. Scott offered to purchase his freedom, but Irene Emerson refused to sell him to himself, and in April 1846 he began the legal proceedings that would eventually bring his case to the Supreme Court.

The Case in the Missouri State Courts

An attorney pleading the case at the time would have considered Scott's argument an easy one to win, since the precedents were unambiguous. In 1824, in *Winny v. Whitesides,* the Missouri Supreme Court had declared that an enslaved person who had been taken to the free territory of Illinois had become a free person. Over the next dozen years, there were other such cases, and in every one the Missouri courts ruled that a slave working or living in a free jurisdiction for a reasonable period of time became free. As late as 1836, in *Rachel v. Walker,* the court held that a slave named Rachel became free when her owner took her to military bases in the North and in the western territories where slavery was prohibited. During this time the Missouri courts were among the most liberal in the nation on this question, but they were not alone even among the slave states. Similar cases had arisen in Kentucky, Louisiana, and Mississippi, and courts in those states had upheld claims of slaves that residence in a free state or territory made them free.

The courts in these cases nearly always referred to the leading English decision of *Somerset v. Stewart* (1772). There the British court had declared that the status of a slave was so contrary to both common law and natural law that it could not be maintained except through the passage of legislation specifically allowing it. Under *Somerset,* when a master took a slave into a jurisdiction that did not have laws authorizing slavery, the slave automatically reverted to his status as a free person. Well into the 1840s, courts in Missouri, Louisiana, and Kentucky freed slaves who had worked or lived in free jurisdictions. Under *Somerset, Winny,* and a dozen other precedents, Scott should have won his case and his freedom.

He lost the first round in June 1847 only because of a technicality. He sued Irene Emerson, but had no witness who could testify that she in fact owned him. In December the judge ordered a new trial in St. Louis Circuit Court, but a failed appeal from Mrs. Emerson to the Missouri Supreme Court, two continuances, a major fire, and a cholera epidemic all combined to delay the case until January 1850. After hearing the evidence, the judge charged the jury that residence in free jurisdictions destroyed Scott's status as a slave, and that if they determined that he had lived in a free state or territory, they should find him free. The twelve jurors—all white men—found for Scott, and the judge ordered him, his wife, and their two daughters freed.

Reluctant to lose her four slaves, Mrs. Emerson instructed her lawyers to appeal to the state's high court. Not just the ownership of Scott, his wife, and their children was at stake. In addition, since the litigation had begun in 1846, Scott had been hired out and all his wages were being held in escrow. This was a tidy sum, and Mrs. Emerson wanted it. In early 1850 she left Missouri for Springfield, Massachusetts, and that fall married Dr. Calvin Chaffee, a physician with antislavery leanings who later became a Republican representative. Although no longer in Missouri, she was the titular owner of the Scotts, and so her name remained as defendant. Her brother, John F. A. Sanford, a prosperous New York merchant with extensive personal and professional contacts in St. Louis, agreed to act on her behalf.

Absent any errors of law on the part of the trial judge, an appellate court should have routinely confirmed the decision since it was fully based on Missouri precedent. But there had been a seismic shift in the debate over slavery in the previous three decades, and the judges on the state's high court responded to the political pressures the whole country—and especially the slave states—were feeling.

The Growing Storm over Slavery

Slavery had been part and parcel of American history since the first boatload of African prisoners had been sold in Virginia in 1619. By the time of the Revolution the debate over slavery had begun, and at Philadelphia, representatives of the Southern colonies refused to sign the Declaration of Independence unless any references to slavery were deleted. The announcement that "all men are born free" rang hollow with those held in bondage because of the color of their skin.

At the Constitutional Convention of 1787, one of the great compromises involved slavery. The word itself is never used, but one provision called for the enactment of laws to recover "persons held to service or labor in one state" escaping to another state (Article IV, Section 2), while another declared that for purposes of taxation and representation, such persons shall be counted as "three fifths of all other persons" (Article I, Section 2).

In the early years of the Republic, as Northern states did away with slavery, a rough balance existed between the slaveholding South and the mercantile North in Congress. Then in 1819, as the House of Representatives considered the enabling legislation to admit Missouri to the Union, New York representative James Tallmadge Jr. offered an amendment prohibiting the further introduction of slaves into Missouri and emancipating all children born to slaves there once they reached their twenty-fifth birthday. The Tallmadge amendment passed the House by a narrow vote, and when news of it reached former president Thomas Jefferson at Monticello, he likened it to "a firebell in the night," and "considered it at once as the knell of the Union." The threat the Tallmadge amendment posed led the Senate to develop the Missouri Compromise as an alternative.

Although the Tallmadge amendment addressed only Missouri, Southerners immediately assumed that it would be the first in a series of laws not only limiting slavery in the growing western territories but potentially striking at the very existence of the "peculiar institution" (as it was euphemistically called) where it already existed. Moreover, with the North growing in population far faster than the South, the balance of power in the House of Representatives had already shifted away from the slave states. If slavery could be prohibited in the territories, then at some day in the not too distant future, the parity that existed between the two sides in the Senate would be gone, and there would be no barrier to stop the attack on slavery.

The Missouri Compromise of 1820 addressed all these issues. Missouri would be admitted to the Union without restrictions—that is, as a slave state—while Maine, until then part of Massachusetts, would enter as a free state. Slavery would be excluded in the rest of the Louisiana Purchase territory north of 36°30', the southern border of Missouri. Since previous army explorations had termed the Midwest the "great American desert," unsuitable for settlement, this left only the Arkansas Territory open to slavery. The South saw the compromise as a victory, while many in the North denounced it. Thanks to the efforts of Henry Clay of Kentucky, both houses adopted the measure.

For the next two decades the Missouri Compromise governed the politics of slavery. States came into the Union in pairs, one free and the other slave, thus preserving the balance in the Senate. In the 1840s the structure collapsed. The war with Mexico brought in very large tracts of land in Texas, California, and the Southwest. The "great American desert" proved to be fertile beyond belief, attracting new settlers by the thousands. Perhaps most ominous to the South, the growing sentiment against slavery and the abolitionist movement threatened the slaveholding states and their reliance on the "peculiar institution." Whigs and many Northern Democrats began to call for "free labor" and "free soil," and opposed the expansion of slavery into the western territories.

The Compromise of 1850

In the middle of the *Dred Scott* case, the issue of whether the territories would be slave or free came to a boil following the election of Zachary Taylor as president in 1848. In his first annual message to Congress, Taylor endorsed statehood for California and urged that "those exciting topics" that had caused such apprehension be left to the courts. He opposed any legislative plan that would address the problems that so agitated Northerners and Southerners, thus preventing Henry Clay from pushing ahead with another compromise plan that, he hoped, would settle the issue for at least a generation, as had the Missouri Compromise thirty years earlier. Then Taylor died just sixteen months into his term, and his successor, Millard Fillmore, saw the wisdom of Clay's proposal and encouraged him to continue.

The plan that Congress adopted had several parts: California came in as a free state, upsetting the equilibrium that had long prevailed in the Senate; the boundary of Texas was fixed along its current lines; Texas, in return for giving up land it claimed, received $10 million, enough to pay off the state debt; the area ceded, New Mexico, became a recognized territory, as did Utah, and in neither case was slavery mentioned; the slave trade, but not slavery itself, was abolished in the District of Columbia; and finally, Congress passed a new and stronger Fugitive Slave Act, taking the matter of returning runaway slaves out of the control of states and making it a federal responsibility.

The political system, already weakened by a decade of stress over the slavery issue, had seemed to work, and many Americans greeted the Compromise of 1850 with relief. President Fillmore called it "a final settlement," and the South certainly had nothing to complain about. It had secured the type of fugitive slave law it had long demanded, and although California came in as a free state, it elected proslavery representatives. New Mexico and Utah enacted slave codes, technically opening the territories to slavery. Nothing, however, was said about the Missouri Compromise, and it was assumed that the proscription against slavery in the larger territories to the north and west remained in place.

Dred Scott in the Missouri Supreme Court

Dred Scott's case reached the Missouri Supreme Court in 1852, and was tied to the political issues surrounding the Compromise of 1850. The court was dominated by recently elected judges who were aggressively proslavery. They were prepared to reject the rulings in *Winny v. Whitesides* and *Rachel v. Walker,* and did so in *Scott v. Emerson* (1852). Speaking for the court, Chief Justice William Scott emphatically rejected the doctrine of "once free always free," and held that regardless of the law of Illinois or the Missouri Compromise, the policy of Missouri would govern. The judges not only defended slavery but also vigorously attacked those who opposed it:

> Times are not now as they were when the former decisions on this subject were made. Since then, not only individuals but States have been possessed with a dark and fell spirit in relation to slavery, whose gratification is sought in the pursuit of measures, whose inevitable consequence must be the overthrow and destruction of our Government. Under such circumstances, it does not behoove the State of Missouri to show the least countenance to any measure which might gratify this spirit. She is willing to assume her full responsibility for the existence of slavery within her limits, nor does she seek to share or divide it with others. . . . We will not go to [the Northern state courts] to learn law, morality or religion on this subject.

What had started out as a simple freedom suit had led to a sea change in Missouri law. It was about to evolve into a major political and legal issue.

A Diversity Case—or Not

Scott's story might have ended in the Missouri courts. The case had been decided by a state court under state law, and no issue involving the U.S. Constitution had been raised. Section 25 of the Judiciary Act of 1789 permitted appeal from a state court only if the appellant could show that a federally guaranteed right had been impinged. In determining that Scott was still a slave, the Missouri court had blatantly ignored a federal statute: the Missouri Compromise of 1820. It seemed unlikely that the U.S. Supreme Court would have considered an appeal based on Missouri's interpretation, or misinterpretation, of the Missouri Compromise without a more specific constitutionally based claim. Clearly, Scott did not have such a claim, and thus the case seemed over.

However, after Mrs. Emerson remarried and moved to Massachusetts, she transferred ownership of Scott to her brother, John F. A. Sanford, who had been taking care of the case for her.* Then the children of Peter Blow, Dred Scott's original owner, entered the scene. Taylor, Peter, and Henry Blow had been childhood playmates of Dred Scott, a not uncommon situation; young black and white children often played together until the enslaved children were old enough to start helping in the field and the whites learned their place in the social and economic hierarchy of plantation life. The Blows had fond memories of Scott, and when they learned that their brother-in-law, Charles Edmund LeBeaume, was renting the Scotts and that Scott was trying to secure his freedom, they came to his aid. LeBeaume also joined in the effort, and helped obtain the services of Roswell Field, a Vermont-born lawyer with strong antislavery convictions. Field brought the case into federal court in May 1854, where Scott sued Sanford for battery and false imprisonment, and demanded $9,000 in damages. The complaint was based on Scott's presumed status as a free man being held against his will by a slave owner, but this tactic allowed him to get the case into federal court. Since all of his avenues of legal redress in Missouri had been blocked, he used a claim of diversity of citizenship of the parties. Diversity jurisdiction allows a federal court to hear a case in which the parties are residents of different states and thus transcend a state court's jurisdiction. Scott claimed to be a free citizen of Missouri, while Sanford was clearly a citizen of New York.

Sanford's lawyer filed a "plea in abatement," arguing that the case should be stopped. "Dred Scott is not a citizen of the State of Missouri, as alleged in his declaration, because he is a negro of African descent; his ancestors were of pure African blood, and were brought into this country and sold as negro slaves." Because Scott was "a negro of African

---

* Sanford spelled his name with one "d," but the Supreme Court reporter mistakenly spelled it "Sandford," and the case has since been known as *Dred Scott v. Sandford.*

descent," Garland declared, he could never be a citizen of the United States, and therefore could never sue in diversity. Judge Robert W. Wells, a slave owner originally from Virginia, ruled that if Scott were free, then he was enough of a citizen of Missouri to sue in diversity in federal court. After hearing the case, however, Wells instructed the jury that Scott's status under Missouri law had been determined by the Missouri Supreme Court, and federal courts were bound to accept that result. Wells did not consider whether the Missouri courts had improperly interpreted the Missouri Compromise. The jury found for Sanford, and Scott now had only one last chance to secure his freedom in court: an appeal to the U.S. Supreme Court.

Before the Supreme Court

The appeal to the high court would be expensive and cost more than Scott's friends the Blows could afford. Fortunately for Scott, Montgomery Blair, a Washington lawyer connected to Missouri politics, agreed to take the case without fee. Blair did not oppose slavery where it existed, nor did he care how slavery affected blacks. He belonged, however, to the Free Soil wing of the Democratic Party, and opposed the spread of slavery into the territories. If the courts abandoned the "once free, always free" rule, then Southerners could take their slaves into the western territories with impunity, confident that their slaves could not sue them for freedom. Blair unsuccessfully sought some other lawyers to help him, but no one stepped forward. Most attorneys believed that the Supreme Court, dominated by Southern members, would reject Scott's appeal and do so on narrow grounds that would set no new precedent.

Sanford also secured a new legal team. Missouri senator Henry S. Geyer, a strong advocate of slavery, and Reverdy Johnson of Maryland, one of the nation's leading constitutional lawyers and a close friend of Chief Justice Taney, joined Garland. According to one historian, Johnson "added luster to any legal cause that he undertook," and "made opposing attorneys apprehensive."

Blair filed the appeal in December 1854, claiming that Judge Wells had erred in charging the jury that Scott was not free. The papers reached Washington too late for the 1854 term, so the Court held it over for the December 1855 term and finally heard oral arguments in *Dred Scott v. Sandford* in February 1856.

At oral argument, which lasted four days, both sides addressed the central questions of whether blacks could be citizens of the United States, and whether Congress had the power to prohibit slavery in the territories, as it had done in the 1820 Missouri Compromise. Geyer and Johnson claimed that blacks could not be citizens and that Congress had no power to enact legislation affecting the status of slaves as private property in the federal territories. The Missouri Compromise had, therefore, never been constitutional, and Scott's sojourn in free territory did not affect his status as a slave. Blair, to the contrary, upheld the constitutionality of the Missouri Compromise and argued that free blacks could indeed be citizens.

The Court could not reach agreement after the first hearing, and ordered reargument for December 1856. In addition to divisions within the Court, the justices wanted to avoid a ruling before the presidential election of 1856. The Court asked the attorneys on both sides to focus on (1) whether the plea in abatement (upheld in the district court) was legitimately before the Supreme Court, and (2) whether a free Negro could be a citizen of a state or of the United States, and as such bring a suit in diversity in federal court. Both of these issues involved questions of the jurisdiction of the Supreme Court, and if the Court answered no to either one, it could and should simply dismiss the suit. But the justices also wanted to hear further argument on the constitutionality of the Missouri Compromise. This argument went beyond the 1820 act, however, and by extension dealt with the power of Congress to legislate on slavery in all the territories. If the 1820 act was unconstitutional, so were the acts banning slavery in the recently created Minnesota and Oregon Territories.

Also at stake was the whole idea of popular sovereignty. "Territorial" or "popular sovereignty" generated a lot of enthusiasm, and Sen. Stephen Douglas of Illinois, a rising star in the Democratic Party, had adopted it as the vehicle on which he hoped to ride into the White House. Rather than Congress legislating whether a particular territory would be free or slave, it should be left to the settlers in those areas acting through their territorial legislatures. This plan was questionably constitutional, however, since it gave the people of a territory the type of sovereign powers normally reserved to the states. Popular sovereignty had some supporters both in the North and the South, and it seemed to some the ideal way to resolve the issue—leave it to the people who actually settled in a territory. If the Court held, however, that Congress could not ban slavery in the territories, then territorial legislatures, created by Congress, would also be precluded from doing so.

From the outset, many commentators have argued that if ever a case called for judicial restraint and a narrow ruling, this one cried out for it. Although framed in constitutional terms, the questions confronting the Court had already torn gaping holes in the political and social fabric of the Union. The tense national atmosphere precluded any definitive judgment of the Court from being accepted by a large part of the nation, yet many people prayed for a final ruling by the Court. The political system seemed incapable of handling the issue of slavery in the territories, but a Court ruling might end debate and allow the nation to get back to the business of building railroads, settling new lands, and bringing prosperity to its white inhabitants. Taney and his brethren had an opportunity, so they thought, to render a great service to the nation by finally ending the debate over slavery in the territories.

At first, the Court leaned toward evading the territorial issue. Justice Samuel Nelson of New York drafted an opinion that affirmed the Missouri court's interpretation of state law and reaffirmed that states had the power to determine the status of all people within their jurisdiction. Nelson deliberately avoided the questions of black citizenship, the constitutionality of the Missouri Compromise, and the power of Congress to legislate on slavery in the territories. The four Southern justices—James Wayne of Georgia, John Catron of Tennessee, Peter V. Daniel of Virginia, and John A. Campbell of Alabama—insisted, however, that the Court decide these issues. Taney agreed with them, and the chief justice drafted an opinion that dealt with every one of the major slavery issues.

The importance of the case led President-elect James Buchanan to write to Justice Catron of Tennessee, asking if the Court would reach its decision in time for him to refer to it in his inaugural address. In mid-February, Catron told Buchanan that the Court would address the constitutionality of the Missouri Compromise, and he suggested that in his inaugural the president tell the nation that the issue of slavery in the territories should be settled by the "appropriate tribunal"—the Supreme Court. In his inaugural address, Buchanan did just that, asserting that the issue of slavery in the territories was a "judicial question, which legitimately belongs to the Supreme Court of the United States."

Catron also asked Buchanan to bring pressure on his fellow Pennsylvanian, Robert Grier, to join the majority so that the final decision would have less of a sectional character. Buchanan promptly did so, hoping fervently that a definitive ruling from the Court would spare his administration the problems that had plagued his predecessor.

"The Self-Inflicted Wound"

On March 6, Taney handed down the decision of the Court, although each of his eight colleagues also wrote an opinion. While the opinions differ in many respects, the following is clear: seven of the justices agreed that Scott was still a slave, six agreed that blacks could not be citizens of the United States, and five or six agreed that the Missouri Compromise was unconstitutional. Two justices, John McLean of Ohio and Benjamin R. Curtis of Massachusetts, dissented from all these positions.

Taney's opinion is the worst he ever wrote; he ignored precedent, distorted history, imposed a rigid rather than flexible construction on the Constitution, ignored specific grants of power in the document, and tortured meanings out of other, more obscure clauses.

Taney's logic on the citizenship issue was perhaps the most convoluted. He admitted that blacks could be citizens of a particular state, and that they might even be able to vote, as they did in some states. But he argued that state citizenship had nothing to do with national citizenship, and that blacks could not sue in diversity because they could not be citizens of the United States. He dismissed Scott's suit, therefore, for lack of jurisdiction. On this point, Taney stood on shaky constitutional ground; if one state considered a black person a citizen, then the Constitution required that all states, and by inference, the federal government, had to accord that person "all Privileges and Immunities of Citizens in the several States" (Article IV, Section 2), which included the right to sue in federal court. Furthermore, Article III gave the courts jurisdiction over suits "between Citizens of different States," and did not discuss federal citizenship at all. But even with this weak argument, Taney could have been accused of no worse than faulty reasoning, if he had stopped there; if Scott was not a citizen, he could not sue in federal court, and therefore the Court could dismiss the case.

But Taney had determined to impose a judicial solution on the slavery controversy. Although later courts would adopt the policy of deciding constitutional questions on the narrowest possible basis, the pre–Civil War courts often decided all issues that could support their rulings. So Taney continued, holding that Scott had never been free. Congress had exceeded its authority in the Missouri Compromise, Taney stated, because it had no power to forbid or abolish slavery in the territories. The Missouri Compromise, which had served as the accepted constitutional settlement for nearly four decades, thus fell. Even the substitute of territorial sovereignty that Stephen Douglas had written into the 1854 Kansas-Nebraska Act lacked constitutional legitimacy: "The only power conferred [on Congress] is the power coupled with the duty of guarding and protecting the owner in his rights." Taney thus voided the principles of free soil, territorial sovereignty, and indeed every aspect of antislavery constitutional thought. Nor could Scott claim freedom based on his residence in Illinois. Whatever status Scott might have had while in a free state or territory, once he had returned to Missouri, his status depended entirely on local law. The Missouri court had declared him to be a slave and therefore property, and no federal court could challenge that ruling. The doctrine of "once free, always free" had no validity.

Taney would have been on strong ground if he had simply upheld the lower court decision based on the idea that status was to be determined by states. He similarly would have been correct to hold that Dred Scott could not sue Sanford in federal court through diversity of citizenship. Even if free, he could not be a citizen of Missouri because Missouri did not allow free blacks to be citizens. Had Taney limited himself to this analysis and this result, the case would barely be remembered. But Taney outraged much of the North by asserting that blacks could *never* be citizens of the United States, and that Congress had no power to ban slavery in the territories.

Two justices, McLean of Ohio and Curtis of Massachusetts, wrote devastating critiques of the Taney opinion. Curtis in particular undercut most of Taney's historical arguments, showing that blacks had voted in a number of states at the founding. "At the time of the ratification of the Articles of Confederation," he wrote:

> All free native-born inhabitants of the States of New Hampshire, Massachusetts, New York, New Jersey, and North Carolina, though descended from African slaves, were not only citizens of those States, but such of them as had the other necessary qualifications possessed the franchise of electors, on equal terms with other citizens.

Thus, Curtis argued, they were members of the nation, and could not now be denied the right to claim citizenship. The majority decision violated both history and precedent.

Aftermath

The South could not have asked for more. "The Southern opinion upon the subject of Southern slavery," trumpeted one Georgia newspaper, "is now the supreme law of the land," and opposition to it is "morally treason against the Government." The view that Southern ideologues such as John C. Calhoun had argued for more than a decade—that the federal government had a positive, indeed a constitutional, obligation to defend slavery—had apparently triumphed.

The North, of course, exploded in denunciations of Taney's opinion. Several sober appraisals in the Northern press decimated the chief justice's tortured legal reasoning. The Republican editor Horace Greeley published Justice Benjamin R. Curtis's dissent as a pamphlet to be used in the elections of 1858 and 1860. The press and pulpit echoed with attacks on the decision as heated as Southern defenses of it. Taney's hopes of settling the issue lay smashed; if anything, *Dred Scott* inflamed passions and brought the Union even closer to the breaking point. As for Scott himself, Taylor Blow, one of his champions throughout the long legal battle, purchased him from Sanford and emancipated him; he died a free man two and a half years after the Supreme Court had pronounced him a slave.

For all practical purposes, Northern courts and politicians rejected *Dred Scott* as binding. In an advisory opinion, Maine's high court declared that blacks could vote in both state and federal elections. The Ohio Supreme Court ruled that any slave coming into the state with his master's consent, even as a sojourner, became free and could not be re-enslaved upon returning to a slave state; the New York Court of Appeals handed down a similar ruling in *Lemmon v. The People* (1860). In several states, legislatures resolved to prohibit slavery, in any form, from coming onto their soil, and enacted legislation freeing slaves coming within their borders.

The case also raised fears in the North that the decision would impose slavery on the free states. Indeed, some extreme Southern spokesmen argued that the Constitution would protect them in taking their slaves anywhere, even for sale in the North. Sen. Robert Toombs of Georgia supposedly declared that one day he would call the roll of his slaves at Boston's Bunker Hill. In the Lincoln-Douglas debates in the Illinois senate race of 1858, Lincoln put Douglas on the defensive by several times referring to the possibility that the Supreme Court could nationalize slavery by forbidding states to exclude bondage within their borders. In his famous "House Divided" speech in June 1858, Lincoln predicted that there would be "another Supreme Court decision declaring that the Constitution of the United States does not permit a State to exclude slavery from its limits." He argued, "Such a decision is all that slavery now lacks of being alike lawful in all the States. Welcome, or unwelcome, such decision is probably coming, and will soon be upon us, unless the power of the present political dynasty shall be met and overthrown. We shall lie down pleasantly dreaming that the people of Missouri are on the verge of making their State free, and we shall awake to the reality instead, that the Supreme Court has made Illinois a slave State."

In his debate with Douglas at Galesburg, Illinois, he spelled out the reasoning that many Northerners now deemed well within the realm of the possible: nothing in the Constitution or laws of any state can destroy a right distinctly and expressly affirmed in the Constitution of the United States. Since the right of property in a slave is distinctly and expressly affirmed in the Constitution of the United States, nothing in the Constitution or laws of any state can destroy the right of property in a slave.

Stephen Douglas appeared to be the major political loser as a result of *Dred Scott*. He had gambled his career on popular sovereignty, hoping that the flexibility of the formula would win him enough support in both the North and the South to propel him into the White House. The Supreme Court's ruling had destroyed the entire basis of his proposed constitutional settlement. Yet he continued to insist that popular sovereignty would still work. In their debate at Freeport, Lincoln asked him how he could reconcile popular sovereignty with *Dred Scott;* Douglas responded that it did not matter what the Supreme Court said on the abstract question of slavery in the territories. The people would still decide, for "slavery cannot exist a day or an hour anywhere, unless it is supported by local police regulations." The territorial assemblies could, therefore, adopt unfriendly legislation to discourage slave owners from bringing in their slaves. The so-called Freeport Doctrine, with its open invitation to disregard *Dred Scott,* infuriated the South, which now insisted that the Court's decision meant Congress and the territorial legislatures had to protect slavery. Douglas won the senatorial election, but lost any chance he might have had for the presidency.

The decision in *Dred Scott* did not cause the Civil War; slavery and the opposition to slavery led to secession and conflict. The effort of the Court to resolve the debate, and the passions and fears it ignited in the North, must, however, be treated as a contributing factor. Roger Taney, who many historians believe was a good chief justice through most of his nearly thirty-year tenure, is remembered now almost solely for the blatantly proslavery decision he wrote, and his demeaning comments about African Americans. When he died in 1864 he was roundly denounced and vilified in the North. The fact that he had written *Dred Scott* was enough for many senators to oppose having Taney's bust placed alongside those of other departed justices. Sen. Charles Sumner of Massachusetts predicted that "the name of Taney is to be hooted down the page of history," and that prediction seemingly has come true. Whatever else he may have done, his name will always be linked with that of a black slave who wanted nothing more than his freedom.

Dred Scott did, in fact, get his freedom, but not through the courts. Irene Emerson's second husband, the abolitionist doctor Calvin Chaffee, now a Massachusetts representative, learned that his wife owned the most famous slave in America in February 1857, just before the Court decision. Defenders of slavery ridiculed the hypocrisy of a man who owned slaves and yet spoke out against slavery. Since at that time a husband controlled his wife's property, Chaffee immediately transferred ownership of Scott and his family to Taylor Blow in St. Louis; Missouri law only allowed a citizen of a state to emancipate a slave there. Irene Emerson Chaffee insisted, however, that she receive the wages the Scotts had earned over the past seven years, a sum of $750 that had been tied up because of the court proceedings. Since according to one estimate Scott and his wife were worth about $350 apiece on the slave market, Mrs. Chaffee came out a little bit ahead.

On May 26, 1857, Dred and Harriet Scott appeared in the St. Louis Circuit Court and were formally freed. Scott then took a job as a porter at Barnum's Hotel in the city, and became a sort of celebrity there. Harriet took in laundry, which her husband delivered when he was not working at the hotel. Unfortunately, Dred Scott did not live to enjoy his free status very long; on September 17, 1858, he died of tuberculosis.

His wife, Harriet, lived until June 1876, and saw the Civil War and the Thirteenth Amendment finally abolish slavery in the United States.

Cases Cited

Lemmon v. The People, 20 N.Y. 560 (1860)
Rachel v. Walker, 2 Mo. 350 (1836)
Scott v. Emerson, 15 Mo. 576 (1852)
Somerset v. Stewart, 98 Eng. Rep. 499 (K.B. 1772)
Winny v. Whiteside, 1 Mo. 472 (1824)

For Further Reading

Don E. Fehrenbacher, *The Dred Scott Case: Its Significance in American Law and Politics* (1978), is a classic and puts the case in its wider social, political, and economic context. For a somewhat different context, see Austin Allen, *Origins of the Dred Scott Case: Jacksonian Jurisprudence and the Supreme Court, 1837–1857* (2006). Walter Ehrlich, *They Have No Rights: Dred Scott's Struggle for Freedom* (1979), provides a careful and detailed narrative of the case, with a useful reminder that whatever other people made of it, Scott only wanted to be free. Paul Finkelman, Dred Scott v. Sandford: *A Brief History with Documents* (1997), provides a short analysis and explanation of this case, together with relevant documents. William M. Wiecek, "Slavery and Abolition before the United States Supreme Court, 1820–1860," 65 *Journal of American History* 34 (1978), argues that the *Scott* decision was not an anomaly, but emerged from doctrines the Court had been expounding for twenty years. David T. Konig, Paul Finkelman, and Christopher A. Bracey, eds., *The Dred Scott Case: Historical and Contemporary Perspectives on Race and Law* (2010), provides an interdisciplinary approach to the case through a collection of essays by numerous scholars and judges. A somewhat revisionist view is Mark A. Graber, *Dred Scott and the Problem of Constitutional Evil* (2006). There is no modern biography of Taney, but Carl Brent Swisher, *Roger B. Taney* (1935), remains useful.

The Case of the Antiwar Agitator

Ex parte Milligan (1866)

THE OUTBREAK OF THE CIVIL WAR in April 1861 found a country strongly divided over what course of action to follow. While a majority in the North supported Abraham Lincoln's decision to use force to put down the insurrection of the Southern states, a significant majority opposed the president's policy. Mainly Democrats and in most instances proslavery, they believed the secessionist states had been right to oppose federal policy aimed at restricting the growth of slavery in the western territories, and would not only have allowed the states to secede, but in some instances wanted to forge alliances between parts of the Northern states with the new Confederacy.

One of the men agitating for such a course was Lambdin P. Milligan, an Indiana lawyer and politician whose outspoken opposition to the war and alleged ties to a secret association called the Sons of Liberty led to a conviction for treason by a military tribunal. The Supreme Court overturned his conviction in a decision that continues to influence our jurisprudence, especially in the war on terror.

The Making of a Copperhead

Born in Ohio in 1812, Milligan never received a formal education. His father, however, had a good library and encouraged his son to read widely. When he turned eighteen, Milligan left home to study medicine, but almost immediately changed his mind to pursue a legal career. As was usual at the time, he read law (i.e., apprenticed) in a practicing attorney's office, and in 1835 he was admitted to the Ohio bar and married Sarah Ridgeway. He was not terribly successful, and after several years he moved to Indiana to try his hand at farming. He had to abandon the farm because he suffered from epilepsy, and decided to make one more effort at the law. This time he proved successful, and soon achieved prominence at the Indiana bar and became active in the state Democratic Party.

During most of the 1850s Milligan led a relatively quiet life, enjoying his family and his success as a lawyer. But as the Union threatened to break apart in 1860, Milligan became involved with an antiwar group in the Indiana Democratic Party. The strong pro-Union forces in the state soon condemned the Peace Democrats as "Copperheads," implying their disloyalty to the true principles of the Union and comparing them to poisonous snakes. (The Peace Democrats accepted the label, but for them the copper "head" was the likeness of Liberty, which they cut from copper pennies and wore proudly as badges.) But at least before the firing on Fort Sumter in April 1861, groups in both the North and the South sought peaceful means to resolve the growing tensions and avoid a war. America was at the time an overwhelmingly agrarian nation with limited industrial capacity, and farm crops in the North and the South accounted for much of the states' wealth. The core of antislavery sentiment could be found in the Northeast, especially New England. Most western farmers had nothing against slavery; with the exceptions of some areas of Ohio, the states of the Northwest Territory did not lean toward abolition. Strong political as well as economic ties to the South led many to sympathize with the South's alleged grievances, and abolitionist efforts to make headway in this area proved futile.

Democrats in the West and Midwest shared another characteristic with Southern planters—a healthy distrust of easterners. Although many of the states in the old Northwest Territory had been settled by New Englanders, there was a strong belief that the growing industrial interests in the Northeast wanted to dominate national politics at the expense of agricultural interests. Lambdin Milligan was a true Jeffersonian Democrat who believed that the ideals of the American republic could best be maintained by an agrarian society, with the states holding more power within the federal system than the national government. If the South seceded, he and other Peace Democrats believed that an ensuing war would isolate westerners as the only remaining agrarian interest in the remnant of the Union, easy prey to domination by New England industrial and mercantile interests.

Their fears seemed justified when, in 1861 and 1862, Congress passed new tariffs on household items such as coffee, tea, sugar, and spices, increasing the cost of living for western farmers and laborers during an economic downturn caused by the onset of the war. Milligan publicly denounced as protectionists the factory owners and bankers of New England who, he charged, were trying to maintain their manufacturing monopolies without regard for the economic interests of the western and agrarian part of the nation. The Peace Democrats also charged New Englanders with promoting the war, provided the West supplied the soldiers to fight and the tax monies to fund it.

Not all Peace Democrats shared this sense of economic exploitation. For many, other considerations also mattered greatly. Some feared that a war would end the American democratic experiment and lead to the establishment of a dictatorship. In the early years of the war, economic depression affected the upper Mississippi Valley far more than it did other parts of the North, further dampening enthusiasm for fighting. Some people simply hated the whole idea of war, of the death, destruction, and bloodshed. Not the least consideration among the Peace Democrats was their intense dislike, one might even say hatred, of the abolitionists. Even those who personally did not care for slavery thought it a lesser evil than war, and they charged that peace and compromise between the North and South could easily have been achieved had the abolitionists not interfered. Peace Democrats were more than willing to tolerate slavery in the South if it meant reconciliation and economic recovery for the region.

Opposing the War

In 1862 the war was not going well for the Union, and in that year's elections the Indiana Democrats seemed poised to take over the state government from the Constitutional Union Party, a branch of the national Republican Party. The strong antiwar sentiment led Milligan to make a bold proposal. The best way to get New England to consider peace would be for the Midwest to threaten to secede and establish a western confederation. Other Peace Democrats took up the cry, and called for a national convention to discuss whether the Union could be saved, and by what means.

Then, on September 22, 1862, President Abraham Lincoln announced that he would issue a formal proclamation freeing all the slaves in any state of the Confederacy that had not returned to the Union by January 1, 1863. This proved to Milligan that Lincoln had fallen under the control of the New England abolitionists, men determined to profit from the war and extend their industrial economy over the West. The war, he believed, would eventually destroy the importance of agriculture in the nation's economy and the influence of the agrarian sectors in its government.

If the Democrats could negotiate a peace with the South, Milligan believed that the agricultural West (by which he meant what we would now term the Midwest as well) could join with the plantation South, and together they could defeat the destructive influence of New England. The Emancipation Proclamation went into effect on January 1, 1863, and soon afterward Milligan began openly advocating for an armistice. Democrats, he claimed, needed to protect their constitutional rights "at all costs," including the use of arms.

Even as Milligan grew more outspoken, the Peace Democrats were losing political ground. The Emancipation Proclamation had converted the war from a fight to preserve the Union to one that also had the great moral weight of freeing the slaves. Milligan failed to win the Democratic nomination in Indiana's 1864 gubernatorial race. The Peace Democrats were ostracized by the mainstream of the Democratic Party, which, whatever their views in 1860 and 1861, now strongly supported the war, the Union, and the abolition of slavery. In addition, their clumsy efforts to form secret societies that would work behind the scenes to win over public sentiment backfired, and Republicans had a field day mocking them.

Milligan, Indianapolis printer Harrison H. Dodd, John C. Walker, a lawyer, and others had helped organize these societies. From all evidence the groups formed by the Peace Democrats did not plan armed revolt, but instead intended to generate publicity to win over the people to the cause of peace and reconciliation. Some argued that the Republicans had formed similar societies, which they needed to counteract. The societies enjoyed a short spurt of popularity; at one time the Peace Democrats claimed membership of some 18,000 men. Interest, however, usually proved short-lived, they had little money, and the various local societies could not seem to agree on any statewide organization.

In 1863 Milligan became involved in a new secret society, the Order of the American Knights, which later evolved into the Sons of Liberty, named after the Revolutionary era patriots. Harrison Dodd served as the grand commander, and the organization claimed to be a Democratic club to aid the party's future political campaigns. The regular Democrats would have nothing to do with it, and some historians believe the Sons of Liberty was more of a construct of Dodd's imagination than a viable organization. Dodd also tried to give it a military character, which discouraged men who might have sympathized with its alleged civilian purpose. Dodd also appointed Milligan as a "major general" of the society, although Milligan later swore he knew nothing about the organization.

A military investigation determined that Dodd had received at least $10,000 from Confederate agents in Canada to organize a northwest confederacy that would actively aid the rebellion.

The supposedly "secret" Sons of Liberty did not remain a secret very long. News of the rituals and proceedings soon leaked out to the public, and the society became a target for the Republican Party. The Republican governor of Indiana, Oliver P. Morton, a staunch supporter of the war and of Lincoln, and General Henry Carrington, the military commander of the district of Indiana, quietly employed detectives to infiltrate the group. (Military districts existed in all states that bordered on the Confederacy, and while they were not in control of the civil government, they could act in matters the commanders believed affected military security.) The most effective of these operatives, a Kentuckian named Felix Stidger, gathered evidence against Milligan, Dodd, and other members of the Peace Democrats. Although Stidger relied on hearsay and exaggerated much of what he heard, his reports led to Dodd's arrest and, subsequently, the arrest and treason trials of others, including Milligan.

Military Trial

In October 1864 the military arrested Milligan for a speech he had given the preceding August in which he had openly criticized Lincoln's conduct of the war. Milligan and five others were charged with conspiring to seize munitions at federal arsenals and to liberate Confederate prisoners being held in Northern prison camps. In December, after a trial that lacked many safeguards of due process, such as a grand jury indictment and restrictions on the type of evidence that could be used, the military court found all of the defendants guilty of treason, and sentenced Milligan, along with Dr. William Bowles, Andrew Humphreys, and Stephen Horsey, to be hanged.

Almost immediately doubts about the guilt of the defendants surfaced, and Governor Morton, who had originally pushed strongly for the trials, urged President Lincoln to pardon the men. Lincoln promised to issue the pardons when the war ended, and in the meantime Secretary of War Edwin Stanton granted the condemned men stays of execution. Before he could carry out his promise, Lincoln was assassinated, and President Andrew Johnson commuted Milligan's sentence to life imprisonment. Milligan, however, wanted his freedom, and applied to a federal circuit court for a writ of habeas corpus, on the grounds that although civil courts had remained open in Indiana throughout the war, Milligan and his codefendants had been tried before a military commission. The two judges on the circuit court disagreed on the issue, and the case went to the U.S. Supreme Court, which heard oral argument in early 1866.

Ex parte Merryman

There was little in the jurisprudence of the Court, or indeed of the young country, to govern the situation. The last time that any part of the United States had been under military control was during the War of 1812, when British troops had occupied some areas. No charges of treason against American citizens had arisen during that war, and the Madison administration had seen no need to establish military commissions.

Two earlier cases, however, had arisen during the Civil War. Shortly after the attack on Fort Sumter in April 1861, Lincoln had ordered the suspension of habeas corpus in Maryland, fearing that the border state might well try to secede and join the Confederacy. This allowed the military to round up and hold people suspected of disloyal activities and prevented their release by court order until a determination could be made on their potential to cause future trouble. All told, the military arrested about 18,000 civilians in the Northern states during the war. Many were arrested for evading military service. Most of the others regained their freedom within a few days of taking an oath to abstain from further secessionist activities. Although the action shocked many, the government did not abuse its extraordinary power; not a single person suffered torture or execution.

Lincoln resorted to this drastic tactic because substantial sympathy for the secessionists existed at first, especially in the border states, and because he could not rely on local law enforcement officials, many of whom shared secessionist sentiments, to keep order. When the war began, there were very few federal criminal laws, nor was there any federal police force, like the modern FBI. Thus, when Confederate sympathizers attempted to disrupt rail service, prevent troops from marching to defend the national capital, or even organize treasonous conspiracies to make war on the United States, Lincoln could not turn to any existing law or law enforcement agencies. His only tool for suppressing the rebellion was the army, and to use the army against civilians in the United States he had to declare martial law, which he did early in the war. Congress would later approve these actions.

In Baltimore, local mobs, abetted by officials, attacked troops passing through the city on the way to Washington, D.C. Acting on Lincoln's orders, the army began arresting some of the troublemakers, including one John Merryman, a well-known Baltimore social figure, a member of the state legislature, a colonel in the militia, and an ardent secessionist. Merryman was trying to organize troops to fight for the Confederacy and to destroy railroad lines and bridges to cut off Washington, D.C., from the rest of the nation. Thus he was arrested by the army and held in Fort McHenry.

Despite Lincoln's suspension of habeas corpus, which authorized the military to arrest him, army officers allowed Merryman access to counsel, who quickly filed for a writ of habeas corpus. Since the local military commander had ignored a similar writ issued by District Judge William F. Giles (in the case of a minor who had enrolled in Union forces without the consent of his parents), Merryman's attorney decided to present the petition directly to Chief Justice Taney, in his capacity as the circuit justice for Maryland. On May 26, 1861, when Taney arrived in Baltimore to sit as circuit judge, he learned that Merryman had been charged with various acts of treason, and that, in light of the current crisis, the president of the United States had suspended habeas corpus in the area. The commander of the Fort McHenry military district, General George Cadwalader, ignored the writ and refused to present the prisoner.

Two days later, Taney, now in his chambers in Washington, delivered an impassioned opinion asserting that the suspension of habeas corpus, while permitted by the Constitution (Article I, Section 9), belonged within the powers of Congress, and that the president could not suspend the writ on his own authority or authorize any military officer to do so. Taney declared that he would write out his opinion fully, have it delivered to the president, and call on him "to perform his constitutional duty to enforce the laws. In other words, to enforce the process of this Court," and obey writs of habeas corpus.

Anti-administration newspapers in the North hailed the chief justice as the defender of the Constitution; the South greeted the decision as equivalent to a military victory. Lincoln's supporters, on the other hand, criticized Taney severely and pointed out the inconsistencies in his career: for example, he had supported strong executive action, except when such actions might harm slavery. They also quoted his earlier opinion in *Luther v. Borden* (1849), that "power in the President [is said to be] dangerous to liberty, and may be abused. All power may be abused if placed in unworthy hands. But it would be difficult, we think, to point out any other hands in which this power would be more safe and at the same time equally effectual."

A majority of the Court realized that Lincoln would not obey this order, and the associate justices refused to go along with Taney in his demand that the Court confront the president. Hostilities had begun, and Lincoln had wide support in the North for his measures taken to prevent the rebellion from spreading. Lincoln would suspend habeas corpus again, from time to time, in some parts of the North, especially those areas harboring pro-Confederate sentiment or exposed to invasion, and in March 1863, Congress finally enacted a habeas corpus statute, retroactively authorizing the president's actions from the start of the war.

As for Merryman himself, it appears that he might have been released earlier had the chief justice not intervened. Criticism of his arrest had harmed the Union cause, and the administration, unsure about what course to follow, had even considered backing off from habeas corpus suspension. Taney's attempt to turn Merryman's case into a conflict between the executive and the judiciary stiffened the administration's resolve, and in fact led to widespread support of the policy. In the end, the administration got rid of the problem by having Merryman indicted for treason in civil court. He was released on bail in July 1861, and his case, like that of many others similarly indicted, hung in the fire for the rest of the war. But although Taney's draft opinion had never been adopted by the Court, the justices in 1866 recognized the validity of what he had written, especially as it applied to the *Milligan* case.

Ex parte Vallandigham

A second case, which was even more relevant to Lambdin Milligan's petition, involved a racist, proslavery Ohio politician and Confederate sympathizer named Clement Vallandigham. A shrewd and clever man, Vallandigham always prefaced his tirades against Lincoln, the draft, emancipation, and the use of black troops with the caveat that of course people should not directly break the law. Even as he ratcheted up the fervor of his tirades against the administration and its policies, Vallandigham made sure to distance himself from possible charges of treason by reiterating that he never, ever urged illegal activities.

The administration considered this all a ruse, and in 1863 military authorities in Ohio arrested and tried Vallandigham for publicly declaring that the Civil War "was a wicked, cruel, and unnecessary war, one not waged for the preservation of the Union, but for the purpose of crushing out liberty and to erect a despotism; a war for the freedom of blacks, and the enslavement of the whites, and that if the administration had not wished otherwise, that the war could have been honorably terminated long ago." He also accused Lincoln of trying to set up a monarchy and destroying the liberties of the American people. Vallandigham's goals were clear, despite his claims that he did not encourage illegal actions. He wanted to stop conscription, end the war effort, and prevent emancipation of the slaves. While he was technically innocent of inciting resistance, everyone understood that, in fact, that was what he wanted people to do.

At his trial Vallandigham refused to enter a plea. He asked for counsel, but the three lawyers he chose refused to enter the courtroom to represent him. So he conducted his own defense, called only one witness to testify for him, and ended by reading a long statement challenging the military's authority to try him. The court found him guilty and sentenced him to be confined to a military prison.

In a brilliant move, Lincoln commuted his sentence to exile, and he was handed over to the Confederacy. "Must I shoot the simpleminded soldier who deserts," declared Lincoln, "while I must not touch the hair of a wily agitator who induces him to desert?"

Before his exile, Vallandigham petitioned the Supreme Court for a writ of *certiorari,* demanding that it review his case. The Court granted the writ, but concluded that it had no jurisdiction to review the proceedings of a military tribunal, noting that the actions of a military court were not "judicial," and therefore a writ of *certiorari* could not be directed at it. This, of course, made no sense since the Court had already allowed the writ, but in this way sent the message that in wartime the justices would not second-guess the military, a posture the Court would resume during later conflicts. The justices had no desire to challenge presidential authority in the midst of a conflict, but parts of Justice James Moore Wayne's opinion were noteworthy for the limits the Court placed on itself.

It could not issue a writ of *certiorari* because a military tribunal did not constitute a proper court—that is, an Article III court within the constitutionally authorized structure of the federal judiciary. This implied, of course, that if the appeal had come from a lower, non-military federal court, the Supreme Court could issue the writ. In *Ex parte Vallandigham* the justices found a technicality to avoid confronting the administration in wartime. But the argument they used, once the fighting had ended, worked in Milligan's favor—he had gone through a civilian court, and thus his appeal was not directly from the military tribunal that had tried him, but from a regularly constituted Article III court.

Arguing the Case

Now that the war had ended, Milligan's allegedly treasonous behavior, as well as his clearly outspoken antiwar and pro-Confederacy positions, could be put aside, and the justices could address the issue they had so studiously avoided in the *Merryman* and *Vallandigham* cases, namely the extent of military authority. Four of the most distinguished lawyers in the country appeared for Milligan—James A. Garfield (then a member of the House of Representatives and a future president), Jeremiah S. Black (a former attorney general), Joseph Ewing McDonald (a former Indiana attorney general and a future U.S. senator), and David Dudley Field (a leading legal reformer). Representing the government were James Speed (a former attorney general under Lincoln), Henry Stanbery (the attorney general under Andrew Johnson), and Benjamin F. Butler (a Massachusetts lawyer and future governor whose harsh attitudes toward southerners during the war had earned him the nickname "Beast Butler").

Although both sides focused on the question of the extent of military authority, there was a secondary question below the surface. The Republican-controlled Congress and Andrew Johnson had been at odds almost since he took office upon Lincoln's assassination. Congress wanted to ensure that the former Confederate states would respect the rights of the newly freed slaves, and intended to do so through a series of stringent laws. Johnson opposed this policy, wanted the former rebellious states readmitted to the Union with no strings attached, and would have left the fate of the freedmen to their former owners. The fight between the executive and legislative branches of government would lead to the impeachment and near-conviction of the president, the imposition of harsh measures in congressional reconstruction, and the passage of the Fourteenth and Fifteenth Amendments.

Many Republicans in Congress viewed the *Milligan* case as a test of whether the Supreme Court would attack their Reconstruction policies. If the Court ruled against Milligan, then Congress could assume that there would be no judicial objections to a strong Reconstruction policy that might well involve (as it eventually did) military governments in the former Confederate states. If the Court decided for Milligan, however, this might mean that the Court would take a very narrow view of what restrictions Congress might impose on the rebellious states before admitting them back into the Union. While clearly the justices could have ruled for Milligan (whose facts arose from wartime policies) and not viewed this decision as having anything to do with postwar Reconstruction (which in fact is what happened), few people believed that when the Court heard the case.

During the oral presentations, the weight of the arguments clearly went against the government. Field showed that when Milligan's military trial began, no known armed enemy could be found in the state of Indiana; in fact, none could be found within hundreds of miles. On the day originally set for Milligan's execution, a date allegedly set out of military necessity, Confederate resistance had collapsed, and all Confederate armed forces had surrendered throughout the area of the former rebel states. Jeremiah Black noted that in an earlier uprising, the Whiskey Rebellion of 1794, President George Washington had called out the militia to quell the insurgents, but had never thought of suspending constitutional guarantees in Pennsylvania. During the Civil War, members of the House of Representatives had attached a rider to an appropriation bill declaring that, except for military personnel or alleged spies, "no person shall be tried by court-martial or military commission in any State or Territory where the courts of the United States are open," and that measure passed.

Milligan's lawyers also argued that precedents from Anglo-American history supported their case. In 1745 a Lieutenant Frye, serving on a British warship in the West Indies, had been ordered to arrest another officer, but doubting the legality of the action, demanded that his superior provide him with a written directive. For this Frye was himself arrested and tried by a naval court, which sentenced him to fifteen years in prison and disbarred him from any future service in His Majesty's forces. He immediately went to civil court in England and brought suit against the president of the navy tribunal, who was arrested. The judges of the civil court awarded him damages of 1,000 pounds for illegal detention and sentencing, and told Frye that he could arrest and sue any member of the naval court. An irate Frye immediately had two more members arrested.

Upon receiving this news, fifteen officers, including a rear admiral, met and publicly denounced, as a gross insult to His Majesty's Navy, that any civil officer should cause the arrest of a navy officer for any official act. Thereupon the lord chief justice had all fifteen officers—including the admiral—arrested and brought before him. Their efforts to have the king intervene on their behalf failed, and after two months of examination in the civil court, the fifteen signed a humble letter of apology acknowledging the supremacy of civilian courts over military tribunals.

In the face of these and other arguments to show that the history of Anglo-American law did not recognize military authority when civilian courts remained open, the government's lawyers could do little other than argue that courts should not be second-guessing decisions made by the military during a conflict, and that the nature of Milligan's crimes warranted the imposition of military justice. The justices did not concur.

The Court's Decision

All the justices agreed that the military court had failed to live up to the terms of Congress's 1863 act suspending habeas corpus. Specifically, while Congress and the president certainly had a right and a duty to suspend habeas corpus where the civil courts were closed, they could not do so where the civil courts remained open. The Constitution, declared Justice David Davis, "is a law for rulers and people, equally in war and peace, and covers with the shield of its protection all classes of men, at all times, and under all circumstances." He asserted that "civil liberty" and "martial law cannot endure together." Davis acknowledged that in an emergency it was permissible to suspend habeas corpus, and thus Merryman's arrest had been permissible. But, Davis argued, there was a clear difference between arrest in an emergency and the trial of civilians by military courts when the civilian courts could operate. Envisioning future emergencies and the possibility that at other times executives might want to avoid civilian courts, Davis noted:

> This nation, as experience has proved, cannot always remain at peace, and has no right to expect that it will always have wise and humane rulers, sincerely attached to the principles of the Constitution. Wicked men, ambitious of power, with hatred of liberty and contempt of law, may fill the place once occupied by Washington and Lincoln; and if this right is conceded, and the calamities of war again befall us, the dangers to human liberty are frightful to contemplate.

While the Court was unanimous in believing that Milligan should have been tried in a civilian court, the justices divided over who had the power to decide when a crisis justified the expediency of imposing martial law. Davis unnecessarily noted that a military commission did not meet the Article III constitutional description of a court created by Congress, and he doubted that Congress had the power to create such tribunals. This led four justices to enter a partial dissent, in which they claimed Congress did have the power to determine when military justice should be established, even in areas remote from the actual theater of war. This debate within the Court was not, in fact, about Milligan at all, but about the power of Congress to regulate trials in the postwar South, where Ku Klux Klan terrorism was rampant. Although a Lincoln appointee and in fact a close friend of the slain president and the executor of his estate, Davis was unsympathetic to issues of black freedom and more inclined to support an early return of white rule to the South.

Chief Justice Salmon Chase wrote a concurring opinion that rested on a different reasoning. Chase believed that congressional war powers could authorize military trial of civilians even if the civil courts still functioned. The 1863 Habeas Corpus Act, however, stated that civilians detained by the military had to be released if grand juries failed to indict them—and since grand juries were not part of the military justice system, the act not only protected civilians' rights to trial in civil courts, but actually mandated the civil courts as the required venue for those trials.

When the decision came on April 3, 1866, some commentators believed that the opinion called into question Congress's power over the South. Justice Davis later voiced his dismay at this reaction, since the Court diligently avoided saying a word about Reconstruction. Yet Secretary of War Stanton told the president that in view of *Milligan,* his department could not "determine what cases, if any . . . can be acted upon by the military authority." Even normally acute constitutional scholars like Francis Lieber accused the Court of undermining congressional policy, when in fact it had not done so.

Milligan in History

Milligan then and afterward has been hailed as a landmark in constitutional protection of civil rights, and its language certainly allows the courts to interpose themselves between the citizenry on the one hand and Congress, the president, and the army on the other. There is little doubt that the Lincoln administration occasionally overreacted to threats of potential disorder and pro-Confederate activity in the Northern states. The arbitrary use of executive authority—often without congressional approval—can only be justified by the unique conditions surrounding the war. Davis, with the benefit of hindsight after the war, could claim it had been unnecessary for the government to react so strongly to disloyalty in the North. Lincoln, having to act in the midst of crisis, knew that Southern sympathizers had already provoked violence in several areas and had no assurances that it would not happen again. If the imposition of military law later seemed too strong a step, Lincoln's policy did work and forestalled civil disorder. Moreover, as in other areas, Lincoln scrupulously avoided going too far; he utilized martial law sparingly and never attempted to impose a permanent military regime.

In many instances *Milligan* provided a useful limit on the use of the military in civilian areas. During the internment of Japanese Americans during World War II, however, *Milligan* proved to be unhelpful. In *Hirabayashi v. United States* (1943) and *Korematsu v. United States* (1944) the Court easily distinguished between the trial of civilians by the military in *Milligan* and civilian authorities using the military to detain and guard civilians. Although the facts were quite different, the Court might have used *Milligan* for the theory that incarceration by the military, even under congressional authority, is unnecessary as long as the civil courts are open to try people who are accused of committing crimes or making plans to do so. However, in the Japanese internment cases, the Court refused to second-guess military decisions in the midst of conflict.

More recently, the actions of the George W. Bush administration in the early years of the Afghanistan and Iraq Wars, in detaining civilians and so-called enemy combatants and refusing to allow them to be tried in civilian courts, brought the issue of the extent of military authority back to the high court. In *Rasul v. Bush* (2004)—decided along with *Al Odah v. United States*—a 6–3 majority made it clear that the Bush administration had gone too far in seeking unchecked power to detain and interrogate individuals in its war on terror. The detainees were entitled to review by neutral adjudicators, either in civilian or in special military tribunals, and in a direct rebuff to the administration, reminded it that the Supreme Court, and no one else, is the final arbiter of the boundaries among the branches, in wartime as well as in peace.

The Court was even more explicit in *Hamdi v. Rumsfeld* (2004), a case involving an American citizen captured with the Taliban in Afghanistan. "We have long since made clear that a state of war is not a blank check when it comes to the rights of the nation's citizens," wrote Justice Sandra Day O'Connor. "The threats to military operations posed by a basic system of independent review is not so weighty as to trump a citizen's core rights to challenge meaningfully the government's case and to be heard by an independent adjudicator." Even the dissenters in that case opposed the administration's argument of military necessity. Justice Antonin Scalia said the Constitution offered only one way to achieve the administration's goal—suspension of habeas corpus by a vote of Congress, a step that has not been taken in the contiguous states since the end of Reconstruction. "If civil rights are to be curtailed during wartime," Scalia wrote, "it must be done openly and democratically as the Constitution requires."

When Congress and the Bush administration tried to sidestep the Court by stripping it of the jurisdiction to hear appeals from newly created military commissions, they received a stinging rebuke in *Hamdan v. Rumsfeld* (2006). The Court declared that the military tribunals convened by the Defense Department did not measure up to any standards provided for either under civilian courts or military courts convened under the Military Justice Act, and in fact lacked any constitutional base whatsoever. Speaking for the majority, Justice John Paul Stevens used a separation-of-powers argument to note that Congress and the executive could not strip federal courts and the Supreme Court of jurisdiction to hear cases involving basic rights.

Milligan after the Case

Lambdin Milligan was released from prison only a few days after the high court ruled in his favor. He immediately denounced Governor Morton and his use of a military commission to achieve political ends, and he made it clear that he wanted redress for his time behind bars. Republicans still controlled the Indiana legislature, and in March 1867 moved to protect Morton and other Indiana officials from damage claims for actions taken in their official capacity during the war. Under the act, the state provided free counsel to the defendants.

In 1868 Milligan filed suit in Huntington County Court against Morton, the twelve members of the military commission that had found him guilty, and nine other men whom he considered responsible for his arrest, and asked for damages totaling $500,000. During the trial, Milligan testified that he had never been an officer in the Sons of Liberty or even a member of that organization. He won the case, and the jury awarded him the statutory limit of five dollars in damages plus costs.

Despite his failure to win the large sum he had sought for damages, Milligan considered the trial result a victory and a vindication of his antiwar beliefs and actions. He returned to Huntington, where his fellow townsmen hailed him as a hero. He rebuilt his law practice there and remained politically outspoken for the rest of his life. He died on December 21, 1899, at the age of eighty-seven.

Cases Cited

Al Odah v. United States, 542 U.S. 466 (2004)
Ex parte Merryman, 17 F. Cas. 144 (1861)
Ex parte Milligan, 71 U.S. (4 Wall.) 2 (1866)
Ex parte Vallandigham, 68 U.S. 243 (1 Wall.) 243 (1864)
Hamdan v. Rumsfeld, 548 U.S. 557 (2006)
Hamdi v. Rumsfeld, 542 U.S. 507 (2004)
Hirabayashi v. United States, 320 U.S. 81 (1943)
Korematsu v. United States, 323 U.S. 214 (1944)
Rasul v. Bush, 542 U.S. 466 (2004)

For Further Reading

The fullest examination of the episode is Samuel Klaus, *The Milligan Case* (1970). Two sources that put *Milligan* into larger, and differing, contexts are Jennifer L. Weber, *Copperheads: The Rise and Fall of Lincoln's Opponents in the North* (2006), and Frank L. Klement, "The Indianapolis Treason Trials and *Ex parte Milligan*," in Michal R. Belknap, ed., *American Political Trials* (rev. ed. 1994), 97–118. For the issues as they reappeared in modern times, see Jonathan Mahler, *The Challenge:* Hamdan v. Rumsfeld *and the Fight over Presidential Power* (2008). A contrarian view from one of Bush's legal advisers is John Yoo, "*Merryman* and *Milligan* (and *McCardle*)," 34 *Journal of Supreme Court History* 243 (2009).

The Case of the New Orleans Butchers

The *Slaughterhouse Cases* (1873)

As A RESULT OF THE CIVIL WAR, Congress proposed and the states ratified three amendments to the Constitution, sometimes known as the Reconstruction or Civil War Amendments. The Thirteenth Amendment, ratified in 1865, did away with slavery and involuntary servitude, the Fourteenth (1868) defined citizenship and its privileges, while the Fifteenth (1870) gave the former slaves the right to vote. The Thirteenth Amendment, enforced as it were by the results of the Civil War, proved immediately effective, and the institution of legalized slavery on the basis of race disappeared from the Union. Eventually the Fourteenth and Fifteenth Amendments would be the constitutional basis for the great civil rights revolution in the mid-twentieth century.

In the decade following the South's surrender at Appomattox, however, no one could be sure exactly what the amendments actually meant. Later, scholars and activists searched the records of the congressional debates for clues to the Framers' intent, and found a bewildering array of comments. Did the guarantees of freedom apply only to the former slaves, or did they have a larger meaning? Did the definition of national citizenship do away with or even affect the earlier rights associated with state citizenship? What did terms such as *due process, privileges and immunities,* and *equal protection* mean, and did they apply the Bill of Rights to the states as well as to the federal government?

The Supreme Court, as the interpreter and arbiter of the Constitution, did not immediately answer these questions. It had to wait until cases raising these issues appeared on its docket, and the most important of the early decisions involved not the rights of former slaves, but a complaint by white butchers against a Louisiana law they claimed established a monopoly over slaughtering livestock in New Orleans. The decision would affect the course of American constitutional history for the next six decades, and in many ways, the *Slaughterhouse Cases* marked the beginning of a seismic shift in the high court's jurisprudence.

A Simple Health Regulation in an Unhealthy City

The law that eventually led to the Supreme Court struck many people as little more than a commonsense health regulation. New Orleans city officials had been trying to remove slaughtering operations from inside city limits since 1804, but their efforts had had little effect. As the city grew, so did the number of butchers and stock dealers, as well as their political influence. By the 1860s, butchers slaughtered more than 300,000 animals a year in New Orleans and adjacent Jefferson City. New Orleans had no public sewer system, so commercial as well as household wastes were either dumped in uninhabited locales such as the Mississippi River levees or into open gutters. The offal from the slaughterhouses went into the river or, in many cases, onto the streets.

The area's natural environment—high humidity and temperature and marshy swamplands—made conditions worse. Physicians tagged New Orleans—also known as the Crescent City because of the Mississippi River's path around it—as the dirtiest and most unhealthy city in America. The city had an extremely high death rate, as epidemics of yellow fever and cholera repeatedly decimated its residents. In 1867 Dr. E. S. Lewis testified before a state legislative committee that "barrels filled with entrails, liver, blood, urine, dung, and other refuse portions in an advanced stage of decomposition, are constantly being thrown into the river . . . poisoning the air with offensive smells and necessarily contaminating the water near the bank for miles."

Given this situation, it is little wonder that in April 1862 the city council of Jefferson City, which contained both the stock landing (the dock area where livestock were brought into the city) and the largest slaughterhouses in the Crescent City area, took the first step that eventually led to the Supreme Court litigation. It awarded an exclusive franchise to three businessmen—William Hepp, Albin Rochereau, and Raymond Pochelu—plus others who might join with them, to build at their own expense a "general slaughterhouse" and "to have and enjoy, during twenty-five years from the completion thereof the exclusive privileges of slaughtering animals within the limits of Jefferson City." The city council, upon completion of the building, would give public notice for thirty days and then all other slaughterhouses within the city limits would be closed. All slaughtering would have to take place in the general facility, and there would be a $100 fine for each violation of slaughtering an animal elsewhere.

The vote in the city council appears to have been unanimous, and there was little opposition noted in the city's three newspapers. The ordinance would have given the franchise holders the exclusive right to run a slaughterhouse in Jefferson City, the building would have been subject to health inspections, and other butchers in the city would be able to slaughter livestock only at this one site. In all ways, it anticipated the legislation seven years later that would be challenged. The chief reason no opposition arose is that the facility was never built. Three weeks after the passage of the measure General Benjamin Butler and Union forces occupied New Orleans, and as one of the attorneys in the later litigation noted, the city "was cut off from trade and commerce [and] walled in by military rule. Is it a wonder, then, that Hepp and Rochereau could not use the powers and privileges conferred upon them?"

During the military rule the army enforced stringent sanitary controls similar to those in Northern cities, and New Orleans escaped yellow fever and cholera epidemics while under occupation. When civilian rule was restored in March 1866, however, despite the pleas of the mayor that the citizens continue to follow these sanitary policies, New Orleans soon reverted to its old, dirty self. By August a local medical journal complained, "This city is now filthy in the extreme." That summer, cholera struck the area, and yellow fever returned with a vengeance a year later.

For the next three years various interests in the city fought over what should be the proper sanitation policy, with the butchers, of course, acting as if it were still 1860 and throwing their offal wherever they wanted. A state committee proposed regulations, but the New Orleans city council refused to cooperate. Citizens signed petitions demanding that the large number of abattoirs, or slaughterhouses, near the municipal waterworks be closed. Two entrepreneurs approached the city council with offers to build a centralized slaughterhouse at their own expense in the sparsely populated Third District, below the city, so that refuse could not contaminate the water supply. In return, all of the facilities above the city would have to close, and the butchers would have to use the new building. Opposition to the proposals was immediately forthcoming from the Butchers' Benevolent Association, and Councilman John Kaiser, who represented the Fourth District where many of the livestock operations were located, successfully blocked all proposals to either centralize slaughtering or close particular operations. He had lived in the Fourth District for more than thirty years, and did not believe there was anything unhealthy about an abattoir. Despite public sentiment in favor of regulation, efforts in the state legislature to push through a centralized facility came to naught because of political pressure from the butchers and their allies. Thus, when the first state legislature to meet under the 1867 Reconstruction Act convened, Republicans immediately began pushing for what many people considered a necessary and long-overdue reform.

In March 1869 the legislature passed "An Act to Protect the Health of the City of New Orleans, and to Locate the Stock Landings and Slaughterhouses." The measure incorporated seventeen men into the Crescent City Live Stock Landing and Slaughter-House Company, and gave the firm "the sole and exclusive privilege" for twenty-five years of landing, keeping, and slaughtering animals for food in the adjacent parishes of Orleans, Jefferson, and St. Bernard. The company had to erect, no later than June 1, 1869, "a grand slaughterhouse of sufficient capacity to accommodate all butchers," as well as stockyards to receive all animals brought or shipped into the port. Once the new facility opened, no stock could be slaughtered anywhere else in the city.

The law, however, did not give the incorporators exclusive control over the butchering, only over where it would take place. The management could not refuse to allow healthy animals to be slaughtered in the new facility, and had to permit access to all who wished to use it. If the company refused access to a butcher, or denied him the right to slaughter a healthy animal, it could be fined $250 in each case. The company would make its money from a detailed schedule of fees that the legislature authorized it to charge and also allowed it to keep a portion of each animal for its value as raw material for agricultural fertilizer. To ensure sanitary conditions as well as the health of the livestock, the governor would appoint an inspector, who would have to issue a certificate of good health before an animal could be slaughtered. There would be a fee for such inspections, to be divided equally between the company and the state.

The Butchers Fight Back

The butchers had not protested against the earlier Jefferson City ordinance, primarily because it had never gone into effect. But they organized against the 1869 statute, and for several reasons.

First, they sought to protect their own economic self-interest. Because of the fees, all of the butchers would have to pay more to use the central slaughterhouse than for their own facilities, and in many instances it would cost them more to transport the livestock further and then have to carry the dressed beef back to their local shops. Moreover, many businessmen anticipated that with new interest in Texas beef, New Orleans might become the major southern meatpacking center now that the Civil War had ended. The East Coast seemed starved for meat, and because normal markets had been closed during the fighting, Texas herds had grown so that some estimated that as many as six or eight million head roamed the plains in 1865, nearly twice the prewar number. New Orleans had been the chief market for Texas cattle before the war, but that trade had been a relatively small-scale effort, and without a railroad connecting eastern and central Texas to Louisiana, it would be impossible to move more than a small number of animals on a cattle drive. So far only a single line with limited capacity ran west from New Orleans.

As a result, in 1866, Texas ranchers began the first of the cattle drives that would take livestock north, first to Sedalia, Missouri, and then in a few years to Abilene, Kansas, where they would be put on the Union Pacific Railroad to Chicago. The first efforts were a disaster, with the ranchers losing many head to bad weather, rough terrain, and thieves. New Orleans saw this failure as a good omen, and assumed that Texas ranchers would have no choice but to look east to the Crescent City. When that happened, there would be so many cattle to slaughter that the central abattoir would be unable to handle the business. So the plan had to be stopped, the butchers reasoned, until the wisdom of multiple slaughterhouses handling tens of thousands of Texas beeves could be shown. There was also an assumption that the Texas–to–New Orleans railroad would expand and be able to transport thousands of head of cattle.

Second, the Jefferson City measure had been a local ordinance, and to some extent there had been recognition that localities could enact sanitary measures to protect the health and safety of their citizens. The new law had been passed by the state, however, and in the 1860s the extent of the state's police powers was still undetermined. As early as 1851, Chief Justice Lemuel Shaw of the Massachusetts Supreme Judicial Court wrote in *Commonwealth v. Alger* that "every holder of property, however absolute and unqualified may be his title, holds it under the implied liability that his use of it may be so regulated, that it shall not be injurious to the equal enjoyment of others . . . nor injurious to the rights of the community." As the century continued, other state courts confirmed the powers of the legislature to protect the community. In a case involving slaughterhouses, the California Supreme Court upheld a law regulating the placement, operation, and even the prohibition of such facilities if "expedient for the preservation of the public health" (*Ex parte Shrader* [1867]). Louisiana courts had yet to rule on the extent of the state's police powers, though, and there was no certainty that they would follow the examples of other states.

Third, the whole episode stank of bribery and corruption. The Louisiana government during this time was neither better nor worse than any of the other Reconstruction regimes in the South—or, for that matter, many governments in the North. (This was, one should recall, the heyday of Boss Tweed and Tammany Hall in New York.) Gov. Henry C. Warmoth, a twenty-six-year-old carpetbagger from Illinois, became the youngest governor in the nation's history. Upon taking office he reported that "New Orleans was a dirty, impoverished, and hopeless city with a mixed, ignorant, corrupt and bloodthirsty gang in control. . . . Many of the city officials, as well as the police force, were thugs and murderers." Warmoth proposed that the legislature adopt an antibribery law, but it refused to do so. In fact, Warmoth's administration is considered one of the most corrupt in Louisiana history, and he was later impeached.

The butchers attacked the method of incorporating the new abattoir and within a few months of its passage local courts heard a number of stockholder suits claiming that some of the slaughterhouse company's organizers were being denied their rightful number of shares. Both Judge William H. Cooley of the Sixth District Court and the Louisiana Supreme Court (which did not review the cases until 1875) came to the same conclusion: that a stock fund had been "created for the purposes of corrupting and improperly influencing members of the Legislature in their action on a matter of legislation before them." The courts dismissed the suits, declaring, "We will have nothing to do with it."

Fourth, the butchers and others opposed the law because half of the organizers were carpetbaggers—men who had come in from the North to exploit the economic opportunity they believed existed in the war-ravaged and defeated South—and the other half were scalawags—Southerners who cooperated with Reconstruction governments for their own benefit. It was not entirely true, as one conservative newspaper claimed, that all of the organizers were "newcomers here. Not a name among the seventeen is familiar to any old citizen." But while few of the men had deep roots in the city, their real sin lay in their willingness to work with the new government, an attitude reviled by many of the city's white citizens.

Finally, we come to what may be the most important reason for the animosity against the Slaughterhouse Act—that it had been passed by the Reconstruction legislature and signed by a carpetbag governor. Butchers probably would have opposed a centralized abattoir at any time, but if it had been passed by a prewar legislature, or one that would have been elected after Reconstruction, they would have at the least recognized the legitimacy of the measure. This legitimacy they refused to extend to the Reconstruction government, and their animosity fed their anger toward the law establishing a centralized abattoir.

The resentment also had roots in racism and bitterness toward the national government. In 1868 a convention met under federal protection to draft a new constitution for Louisiana, one that embodied many of the Reconstruction goals of the Republican-dominated U.S. Congress. The new state constitution abolished black codes; provided for universal integrated education; prohibited racial discrimination in public places; and, for the first time, contained a bill of rights. With the former slaves casting ballots in their first election, the voters returned an integrated legislature. Thirty-five of the 101 members of the house were black, as were seven of the thirty-six state senators—and all of the black members were Republican. No matter what the quality or justification for the laws this assembly passed—and many of them were both necessary and beneficial—white Louisianans opposed them. All laws emanating from this body, declared the *New Orleans Bee,* "are of no more binding force than if they bore the stamp and seal of a Haytian [*sic*] Congress of human apes." Other papers chimed in, urging citizens across the state to fight any and all acts passed by the new assembly, which, they claimed, were merely a parody of legislation. The slaughterhouse measure itself, declared one newspaper, was just the sort of law that one came to expect from a legislature organized "under the oppressive usurpations of the federal Congress." The measure had been "conceived in iniquity and carried through by the boldest and most unscrupulous of means," all to the benefit of carpetbaggers who would keep their money in "capacious iron safes, located in colder climes." The exposure of the stock fund scandal merely confirmed these views.

When the slaughterhouse bill cleared the state senate on February 17, 1869, the *Picayune* charged that "300,000 people are to be heavily taxed upon their necessities for the benefit of a dozen, and this should bring from the Governor his refusal to sign and approve the bill." There was little chance of that happening, though, and Governor Warmoth signed the bill into law on March 8. The fight, however, was far from over. The combination of economic self-interest, demand for a long-overdue sanitation measure, uncertainty about the extent of the state's police power, widespread corruption, resentment against carpetbaggers and scalawags, and the whole notion of allowing former slaves to participate in government combined to drive litigation against the Slaughterhouse Act, a litigation that would eventually end at the Supreme Court.

Defining Rights

The challenge to the law came from the butchers and their well-financed and well-organized trade group, the Butchers' Benevolent Association of New Orleans. Within days of the measure's passage the association organized a protest meeting and nailed up placards all over the city inviting citizens to attend. The group also raised $40,000 to hire lawyers to fight the statute in court. From the beginning the butchers and their allies portrayed the fight as one of individual rights. At a mass meeting on June 18, the 1,000 or so attendees resolved that they "held these truths to be self-evident," that "every man in this community has a property in his person and his faculties. That no less sacred than this is his right to the product of those faculties which implies a right to the possession of property, to accumulate property by his labor, and to employ those faculties in any lawful avocation without the control, domination, or direction of any other person or persons in the community for their own emolument." In a separate resolution, the butchers declared that they would not "submit patiently to a measure which invades their natural and constitutional rights."

Although these arguments would sound familiar by the end of the nineteenth century, they were still inchoate in the years immediately following the Civil War. The notion of "vested rights" could be traced back to the Revolutionary generation, many of whom believed that many rights—especially those of property and its concomitant, the right to ply one's business freely—were "natural," inherent in the social contract that bound society together. Take away these vested rights and anarchy would reign. The people of the United States, asserted Justice Samuel Chase in *Calder v. Bull* (1798), created a government to establish justice, promote the general welfare, secure the blessings of liberty, and "protect their *persons* and *property* from violence." Any legislative act that failed to further these goals and that detracted from one's rights in property, Chase declared, had no force, for it violated the basis of the social compact. A formal vested rights doctrine went into decline during the Jacksonian era, but the ideas of protecting property—broadly defined—never completely vanished. In the first half of the nineteenth century, Chancellor James Kent of New York and Supreme Court justice Joseph Story, both noted legal scholars, extolled the common law as a source of property rights and protections, and warned against ill-conceived reforms to abrogate the "wisdom of the centuries."

A related idea, the due process of law, also had ancient roots, reaching back to the Magna Carta's "law of the land." From its beginnings, due process has meant a bundle of procedural rights, some of which are spelled out in constitutions, statutes, and regulations, and some of which are of common-law derivation. (To understand the difference, how a trial is conducted, the rules of evidence, and jury selection are matters of procedure; the right to a trial itself is a substantive right.) The idea that due process of law might also include *substantive* as well as *procedural* rights had appeared in only a few cases before the Civil War. In the best-known state decision, *Wynehamer v. People* (1856), the New York high court read due process to prohibit certain types of legislative interference with business, regardless of the method used. The following year, in *Dred Scott*, Chief Justice Roger Taney commented without elaboration that an "Act of Congress which deprives a citizen of the United States of his liberty or property . . . and who had committed no offense against the law, could hardly be dignified with the name of due process of law."

But if due process of law might include substantive rights, in 1869 lawyers and judges would have been hard-pressed to explain how and when it could be applied, where its justifications originated, or how, exactly, it could be used to protect property and the right of individuals to engage in a legitimate business of their own choosing. If the jurisprudence of the state's police powers lacked clarity in these years, so too did rights theories such as those the butchers hoped to invoke.

The association would ultimately hire three different law firms to make its case, but the lead attorney turned out to be the legendary John Archibald Campbell. The son of a Georgia lawyer-planter, Campbell had begun practicing law at the age of eighteen in 1829. The following year he relocated to Alabama and quickly established himself as a leader of the legal and commercial community in Mobile. Campbell's reputation rested on his courtroom abilities as an advocate and his extensive knowledge of the law. He owned what may have been the largest personal law library in the United States, and his knowledge of Anglo-American law was reputed to rival that of Joseph Story. A Democrat, he allied himself with the branch of the party that favored both a strong Southern rights position as well as commercial development—one loosely tied to John C. Calhoun of South Carolina and the cause of Southern nationalism, a position that later led to the secession of Southern states from the Union. In 1853 President Franklin Pierce named Campbell to the U.S. Supreme Court, reportedly on the advice of sitting members of the Court who had been impressed after hearing him argue six separate cases during the December 1851 term. Campbell freed his own slaves upon his nomination, but although considered pro-slavery on the bench, he occasionally worried about the impact of the "peculiar institution" on Southern society.

Opposed to secession but loyal to the South, he resigned from the Court in 1861 with "a heavy heart," and was quickly recruited to serve as assistant secretary of war in the Confederacy. After the war he resumed the practice of law in New Orleans, and Campbell, Spofford, and Campbell (his son) quickly became one of the leading firms in the city. He also resumed his advocacy before the Supreme Court, and when he died in 1889, Justice Joseph B. Bradley wrote to a local newspaper that "[t]he esteem in which he was held by members of the Supreme Court amounted to reverence. For myself, from the time I first heard him . . . until his death, he was the *beau* idea of forensic perfectness." Bradley, as we shall see, agreed with Campbell's arguments in the *Slaughterhouse Cases,* and this may account for some of his admiration. Justice Samuel Miller, who did not accept those arguments, had little good to say of Campbell, and charged that he had "made himself an active leader of the worst branch of the New Orleans democracy."

While the butchers held rallies and secured counsel, the Crescent City Company bought land and prepared to build the "grand slaughterhouse" opposite the city on the west bank of the Mississippi at Slaughter House Point in Algiers, the same site where abattoirs had been confined in the colonial era. The location met both sanitary and commercial criteria. It was away from the city's waterworks, and near to the railhead of the New Orleans, Opelousas, and Great Western Railroad, which ran westward to Texas. In addition, two river ferries operated nearby. The location of the facility inflamed the butchers even more, for once operations began they would have to commute to the stock pens across the river and pay additional fees to have the meat brought to local markets. The company also took out an ad in the local newspapers announcing that it would be prepared to open for business as required on June 1, 1869.

In the Louisiana Courts

As the building rose, so too did the opposition, and butchers both individually and as a group filed suit in local courts to halt construction and invalidate the law. Ultimately six of these suits were consolidated into what came to be known as the *Slaughterhouse Cases*.

The first case to be filed, and the one that brought all of the constitutional arguments to bear, began on the morning of May 26, 1869, when the association brought a suit in the Sixth District Court seeking an injunction to prevent the Crescent City Company from asserting any of the rights granted to it under the March law. The Butchers' Benevolent Association claimed that its members engaged in a "lawful and necessary" trade that had been conducted for more than three decades in the parishes covered by the new law. A thousand people, supposedly, including four hundred members of the association, had invested both money and labor in building these businesses, now valued at more than a half-million dollars. The court should declare the Slaughterhouse Act null, because it destroyed important property rights for the benefit of a few adventurers.

The most innovative part of the butchers' brief, however, came when it charged that the act violated the privileges and immunities clause of the newly ratified Fourteenth Amendment, which "secures to all protection from state legislation that involves the right of property the most valuable of which is to labor freely in an honest avocation." In addition, because cattle came in from Texas, association lawyers charged that the statute also encroached upon the power of Congress to regulate interstate commerce.

In a second case, initiated only a few hours later, the Crescent City Company sought and secured an injunction against the Butchers'

Benevolent Association to stop it from attacking the company in the exercise of its legal rights and to leave the company free to assert those rights. Another injunction would have prevented association butchers from selling meat after the new abattoir opened. The president of the association denied the validity of the writ and was temporarily jailed for violating the injunction, but when he came out he urged butchers to continue selling meat through their own facilities. Since the injunction won by the company was against the association, and did not bind butchers not affiliated with it, he urged individual butchers to resign from the association and continue to ply their trade.

In the next several weeks, the general district courts in New Orleans were besieged by lawyers for the butchers and the company filing one motion after another. An injunction given in one court would be nullified by a counter order in another. By the end of June, counsel for the butchers had filed at least 170 suits and secured about 500 injunctions, while the company secured over 200 injunctions of different kinds against the association as well as individual butchers. One of the company's actions was filed against the steamboat *B. L. Hodge No. 2* and its owner for landing 226 head of cattle at a place other than the company's pier, and thus avoiding wharfage fees. It would become one of the five cases included in the appeals to the high court. By the end of June, only a month after the Crescent City Company had opened the state-authorized abattoir, it was clear that the merits of the arguments would have to be decided by the state supreme court.

What is extraordinary about all of these actions is that while both sides sought to cripple the other through the use of various injunctions—orders to stop doing something—neither the butchers nor the Crescent City Company seemed willing to debate the merits of the cases. And while the litigation dragged on, the butchers launched an end run around the state-authorized slaughterhouse.

In nearly all the butcher suits one theme appeared over and over—the state had created a monopoly, and in so doing had transgressed both common law and constitutional restraints. The *Picayune* reminded the butchers that it was this issue, and this issue only, that had popular support. The public, according to the paper, did not want slaughterhouses near the water supply, and there was nothing in the law to prevent the butchers from selling beef slaughtered outside the three parishes covered by the law inside New Orleans. The butchers got the hint, and in mid-July a group of stock dealers and butchers bought land in St. Bernard Parish for the purpose of erecting a slaughterhouse. By relocating outside the city, there could no longer be any health questions, although the distance to this location was for nearly all of the butchers as great or greater than that to the Crescent City facility. This new group then secured an injunction to prevent the Crescent City Company from interfering with its plans, and challenged the constitutionality of the law on both state and federal grounds. In January 1870, just days before the Louisiana Supreme Court heard arguments, the newly formed Live Stock Dealers and Butchers Association staged a grand opening of its almost finished facility. The festivities included a parade through the city with a brass band, droves of cattle, and dozens of butchers dressed in the colorful European costumes of their trade. Everyone, including the judges, knew that a new and up-to-date slaughterhouse existed below the city.

The state court refused to hear all of the various pleas and counterpleas, and ordered both sides to consolidate their arguments into manageable cases—three actions initiated by the Butchers' Association against the Crescent City Company, and three by the company against the butchers, including the suit against the steamboat. Both sides filed dozens of formal exceptions, with an eye to keeping these minor issues alive in case of an appeal. On January 27 and 28, 1870, the Louisiana Supreme Court heard the arguments.

John Campbell spoke as the lead attorney for the butchers, and he stressed three major points—both procedural and constitutional. First, the statute in question had been enacted through bribery of members of the legislature, and could therefore be put aside for fraud. Second, the statute violated the Louisiana constitution because the governor had signed it after the legislature had adjourned and not within the five-day period the constitution mandated. Third, the statute was unconstitutional because it created a monopoly, a power that exceeded the legislature's authority. In all, Campbell took a very Jeffersonian approach, arguing for a very limited view of governmental powers.

Where Campbell raised constitutional questions, Louisiana attorney general Simon Belden tried to dismiss them as irrelevant. The statute was a pure and simple police measure promoting the health and cleanliness of the city. Since this was clearly within the province of the state's authority, so then was the means it chose to carry it out. That it could do so by insisting on a central abattoir was so reasonable that no one could deny the justness of the solution. No one had taken away the right of a person to be a butcher; the state had simply insisted that all butchering be done in a central, sanitary place in order to protect the health of the city.

Randell Hunt, one of the attorneys for the company, took on the task of answering Campbell's constitutional arguments, and responded in the same manner that Alexander Hamilton and then John Marshall had done decades earlier. In words reminiscent of Marshall's argument in *M'Culloch v. Maryland* (1819), he argued that the state had all powers necessary to carry through a legitimate purpose, and what could be more legitimate than protecting the health and safety of the people? He then attacked Campbell for his argument that the incorporators deserved to be in a penitentiary for corrupting the legislators, calling it a libel, an accusation for which Campbell had not the slightest shred of evidence.

In a 3–1 opinion the state high court upheld the validity of the statute, ruling in favor of the Crescent City Corporation. For the most part, Chief Justice John Ludeling brushed aside the butchers' arguments as inconsequential. The heart of their arguments—that the act deprived them of their livelihood in violation of the new state bill of rights as well as the Fourteenth Amendment, and that it created a monopoly—failed to convince the judges. They accepted the state's argument that this was a needed sanitary measure, fully compatible with the state's police powers, and that it had not created a monopoly. Butchers were still free to ply their trade, but they had to do so in a centralized location. Ludeling quoted from Thomas M. Cooley's *Constitutional Limitations* (1868), a new volume already recognized as authoritative, that "[t]here are, unquestionably, cases in which the State may grant to specified individuals, privileges, without violating any constitutional principle, because, from the very nature of the case, it is impossible that they be possessed and enjoyed by all."

This should have ended the matter. Both sides had agreed to abide by the decision of the Louisiana Supreme Court, and while not specifically precluding an appeal to the U.S. Supreme Court, no one believed they would be able to get that tribunal to accept such a seemingly inconsequential matter. But as soon as the state court handed down its decision upholding the statute as a legitimate exercise of the police power, the attorneys for the butchers ignored the agreement and initiated an appeal to the federal courts. Much to everyone's surprise, Justice Joseph Bradley, sitting on circuit, agreed to hear the case.

Justice Joseph Bradley, on Circuit

On June 8, 1870, spectators crowded into the courtroom to hear John Campbell denounce the bill, claiming that both the Civil Rights Act of 1866 and the Fourteenth Amendment had been designed to secure all citizens equality of civil rights. (The irony of the former Confederate official invoking laws passed by the hated Republican Congress was not lost on the city's newspapers, who, if they opposed the law, wanted some other justification for scuttling it than one that seemingly acknowledged the legitimacy of the federal government's power.) Opposing counsel William Hunt denounced the butchers for reneging on their agreement, and argued that the Civil Rights Act and the Fourteenth Amendment had never been intended for the purposes Campbell claimed. Moreover, he asked, where had anyone lost his rights? There was no monopoly, since all butchers could ply their trade. The state had done no more than legitimately enact a health measure requiring a centralized slaughterhouse.

Campbell had not tried to hide what he thought of the Reconstruction legislature and the foisting of an interracial legislature on Louisiana, and he knew that Bradley, a New Jersey lawyer who had only been on the Court six months, believed that the South should be left alone to deal with internal matters. Campbell's ploy worked. Bradley ruled that the 1866 Civil Rights Act had no bearing on the case, since it had been enacted to secure to citizens of every race and color the same civil rights, and not to enlarge or modify the rights of white citizens. The Fourteenth Amendment, however, did bear on the matter, and the privileges and immunities clause served as an absolute barrier to the states' infringing on those rights. "There is no more sacred right of citizenship," Bradley held, "than the right to pursue unmolested a lawful employment in a lawful manner. It is nothing more nor less than the sacred right of labor." As such, he found the 1869 statute unconstitutional.

Although Bradley accepted practically all of Campbell's arguments and held the law unconstitutional, a technical matter prevented him from giving the butchers the relief they sought. A 1793 act of Congress forbade federal courts from granting an injunction to stay proceedings in state court. As such, he could not overturn the Louisiana court's judgment, and the parties would have to appeal to the U.S. Supreme Court for relief. With this decision, Bradley made it not only possible but inevitable that the issue would go to the high court.

Before the U.S. Supreme Court

The justices heard arguments in the case in January 1872, with the ailing Samuel Nelson absent. Apparently the remaining justices split 4–4, and rescheduled arguments the following term. On February 3, 1873, lawyers for both sides began three days of argument before a full Court, with Ward Hunt replacing Nelson, who had retired.

The Court that John Campbell faced in 1873 was far different from that on which he had sat in the 1850s. Only one man, Nathan Clifford, remained from the bench from which Campbell had resigned. That Court had consisted entirely of appointees named by Democratic presidents, and their jurisprudence had been proslavery, pro–states' rights, and in opposition to a strong national government. In 1873 all but Clifford had been named by Republican presidents, and they looked at the world and at the Constitution differently. A bloody war had been fought to eliminate slavery, and states' rights—at least as far as the Southern states were concerned—did not rank high in their consideration. The expansion of power by the federal government to meet the emergency of rebellion did not mean that the role of the states had been abolished, but a new balance was being created in the federal system, one that was more sympathetic to national power. And, of course, the Civil War amendments meant something, but exactly what they meant remained to be determined. The *Slaughterhouse Cases* would be the first opportunity for the Court to weigh in on this question.

Campbell had a dual agenda. On the one hand, like any lawyer, he wanted to win the case for his clients. But he had a subtler goal—namely, to use the Reconstruction amendment to put an end to Reconstruction. Campbell hated the occupation of the South by Union troops, and the role of the former slaves that, as he saw it, had been forced onto the new state government. He wrote to his daughter, "We have the African in place all about us. . . . Corruption is the rule." As far as he was concerned, the 1869 statute had no merit at all because it had been enacted by the hated mixed-race assembly and signed into law by the carpetbag governor. If he could convince the Court that the Fourteenth Amendment protected white people against what he saw as arbitrary and corrupt government, then much of Reconstruction would be voided as unconstitutional.

He first argued that the Slaughterhouse Act had been enacted by "legislative caprice, partiality, ignorance or corruption," and here as in the lower courts Campbell appealed to what he saw as the righteousness of the old ways. It may have been an emotionally powerful plea, but it had little jurisprudential force. In 1810 the Court had heard a case involving thirty-five million acres of the Yazoo land grants in what is now Alabama and Mississippi that had been procured through bribery and corruption of the Georgia legislature. In *Fletcher v. Peck* Chief Justice John Marshall said that the Court would not look into charges of chicanery in a state legislature; such problems had to be corrected by the people themselves through the political process. Chief Justice Roger Taney also refused to look into problems with state assemblies. When rebellion broke out in Rhode Island because of the virtual disenfranchisement of more than half the citizenry, Taney declared that such matters were "political questions" that the judiciary could not resolve, but had to be left to the people (*Luther v. Borden* [1849]). Campbell hoped, however, that by painting as unpalatable a picture of the Louisiana assembly as possible, he might gain sympathy for his second, and critical, argument.

The "first great principles of the social contract," he claimed, were that legislatures could not act outside their legitimate spheres of power. This had always been implicit in American law, and the new constitutional amendments now made that explicit. It did not matter that the amendments may have been originally proposed as a protection for the former slaves: "We have never supposed that these Constitutional Amendments had any particular or limited reference to Negro slavery," he said. The wording of the documents—involuntary servitude, equal protection, due process of law, privileges and immunities—applied to all men, white as well as black. This assertion, of course, flew in the face of history and the fact that nearly all Americans, North and South, understood that they had in fact been drafted to deal with slavery and the freedmen.

Campbell then proceeded to argue that the 1869 law subjected his clients to a form of involuntary servitude, in that the butchers were forced to ply their trade at the central abattoir. This also violated their privileges and immunities, since "no kind of occupation, employment or trade can be imposed upon him, or prohibited to him, as to avoid all choice or election on his part." He totally ignored the fact that the people had been seeking this type of health regulation for decades, or that the state had police powers to protect its citizens. Campbell took a law that did not prohibit his clients from practicing their vocation and made it sound as if they had to butcher animals while chained to a post and under the lash. Finally, the law had what he believed to be a fatal constitutional flaw in that it created a monopoly, a device hated in both English and American law since Elizabethan times, and he contended that every holding in the great English *Case of Monopolies* (*Darcy v. Allein*) of 1588 applied here as well.

Campbell did more than merely distort the Slaughterhouse Act and try to portray it as an affront to traditional tenets of Anglo-American law; he out-and-out lied. He falsely asserted that no question of health had ever been raised before the Louisiana Supreme Court, or that the pollution of the Mississippi had ever been mentioned in connection with the city's water. This travesty of a law, he claimed, and the great harm it inflicted on his clients all resulted from the further travesty of Reconstruction, which had not only upended the traditional "social order and conditions," but had deprived its citizens of their rights.

In rebuttal, Thomas Durant, counsel for the company, argued that the law was nothing more or less than a valid exercise of the state's police powers to protect the health and welfare of its citizens. From a precedential point of view, Durant easily had the stronger position. The Supreme Court had on several occasions upheld state acts as legitimate expressions of this power, including the right to incorporate a private entity for the attainment of such goals. Time and again Durant emphasized that the law was a health measure, and that no sane person could interpret it any other way. The butchers had not been made slaves, they had not been deprived of their livelihood; they merely had to practice their craft with due regard to the health of their fellow citizens. As for the Fourteenth Amendment, Durant thought it clear to everyone that

Congress in proposing it, and the states in ratifying it, had the protection of the former slaves in mind.

A Closely Divided Court Decides

On April 14, 1873, the Supreme Court handed down its decision in the *Slaughterhouse Cases.* Justice Samuel F. Miller spoke for the 5–4 majority, and his background made him very familiar with public health issues. Prior to his appointment to the Court he had lived in Keokuk, Iowa, a town on the Mississippi that had once been the sixth-busiest pork-packing center in the country. Miller, who had been a doctor before taking up the law, well knew the nature of the slaughtering business, and had seen how Keokuk had successfully regulated the abattoirs there.

Miller summarized Campbell's extensive charges about the creation of a monopoly and the deprivation of the rights of the butchers, and then dismissed them. "A critical examination of the act hardly justifies these assertions," he said. The law, as Durant had emphasized, determined the place where livestock could be landed and butchered, but did not prevent anyone from plying their trade. With this point made, of course, the rest of Campbell's argument fell by the wayside. The state had acted not only reasonably, but within its authority—that, of course, being the police power. That power had been exercised in the past, and no doubt would be in the future, through the creation of private corporations to carry out a legitimate goal of government.

Miller could have, and perhaps should have, stopped here without going into a full-scale repudiation of Campbell's constitutional arguments. If there had been no deprivation of vocation, then there had been no "involuntary servitude," no violation of privileges and immunities, no creation of a monopoly. But he knew that four members of the Court had accepted those arguments, so he felt constrained to answer them, and he did so by going into the history of the Civil War amendments and declaring that they had been enacted for the sole purpose of freeing the slaves and then protecting their legal rights. Clearly the wording was expansive, and Miller did not deny that the rights could be invoked by others who had not been slaves, but the Framers of the amendments had not been concerned with butchers having to work in a central slaughterhouse but with the rights of millions of ex-slaves.

In his exegesis of the privileges and immunities clause, the first time the Court had addressed the issue, Miller declared that if one adopted Campbell's arguments, the Court would become a perpetual censor of all state legislation, and that was clearly neither desirable nor the intent of the amendment. The limit imposed upon the states did not mean that all protections for civil rights and liberties were now transferred to the national government; rather, it imposed just one more limitation upon the states, similar to others. States would remain the primary defenders of the rights of their citizens; the Fourteenth Amendment was intended to clarify those duties, and not diminish the role of the states in the federal system.

Scholars parsing Miller's opinion find a tentativeness in it, a reluctance to follow through on some of his assertions, perhaps because if he had done so, he might not have reached the conclusions he did. While he had no problem with asserting the power of the states to enact measures under the police powers, and to see the Louisiana law as a health measure, his sections on who would protect the rights of citizens, whether the Fourteenth Amendment expanded upon the rights of national citizenship as opposed to those of state citizenship, and whether there had been an alteration in the dynamics of the federal system are far less assertive.

The same could not be said of Justice Stephen J. Field's dissent, joined by Chief Justice Chase and Justices Swayne and Bradley. The latter two also entered separate and bitter dissents, but the key opinion is that of Field, because it would, in the end, be triumphant and dramatically affect the future course of American jurisprudence. They did not fear that the federal courts would become the censors of state action; in fact, they welcomed such a development. Field argued that the Fourteenth Amendment protected the basic rights of all Americans, not just the ex-slaves, and this meant that the New Orleans butchers could not be denied their economic rights without due process of law. As Field noted, the issue was "nothing less than the question whether the recent amendments to the Federal Constitution protect the citizens of the United States against the deprivation of their common rights by State legislation." The Fourteenth Amendment, in this view, provided that protection.

The privileges and immunities designated in the amendment "are those which of right belong to the citizens of all free governments," and among these was the right "first to pursue a lawful employment in a lawful manner, without other restraint than such as equally affects all persons." The amendment required that all state legislation protect liberty and equal rights for all citizens, and that all laws had to be "just, equal, and impartial." Under the supremacy clause of the Constitution, the Court had the power through the new amendments to strike down offending state legislation that did not comply with this standard.

In essence, Field argued that the Fourteenth Amendment had now created a new standard of rights, those enjoyed by citizens of the United States, and that these rights not only had to be respected by the states, but they could be enforced by federal courts. Most commentators now agree that the Fourteenth Amendment was, in fact, designed to apply the Bill of Rights to the states, and this created a common standard of rights throughout the nation.

This idea took a while to catch on, but eventually, through the process of incorporation of the Fourteenth Amendment's due process clause, the Court did apply most of the provisions in the Bill of Rights to the states. More important, Field's exegesis of what due process of law meant, and that it included substantive economic rights, also won over the Court. By 1897 the notion of substantive due process, incorporating economic liberty and standing as a bar against regulation of property or the labor force, had become enshrined in the law, and would remain there until the great constitutional crisis of the 1930s. It should be noted, however, that Field as much as Miller recognized the need for state police powers, but Field seemed willing to allow the states wider latitude in striking a balance between individual freedom and the need to preserve social order and promote the general welfare. That part of Field's opinion got lost as later conservative justices emphasized property rights and denied government its traditional powers to protect the citizens.

Aftermath

By the time the Court decided the *Slaughterhouse Cases*, Reconstruction was beginning to run down, as Southern opposition and growing Northern indifference to the fate of the freedmen fused into a political bargain in 1876 that gave the presidency to the Republicans and removed all Northern troops from the South. The freedmen soon found themselves tied up in a system of apartheid that, if not outright slavery, nevertheless kept them in legally enforced inferiority until the 1950s.

Once freed from federal control, Louisiana adopted a new constitution in 1879 that attempted, as much as it could, to reestablish the old order. Blacks did not fare well, there were no protections for civil rights, the power of the government was limited, and the only legitimate role of government was "to protect the citizen in the enjoyment of life, liberty, and property." The state government was prohibited from creating corporations, or granting to any corporation already in existence any special or exclusive rights. The regulation of slaughtering was given to parish and city governments, but they could not do so by means of monopoly or exclusive privileges, and any designation of specific places for abattoirs had to be approved by the board of health.

Over the next decade the Crescent City Company fought to keep its privileges, and even took a case up to the Supreme Court on the basis of the contract clause, which forbids states from retroactively changing the terms of a contract, claiming that what the legislature had once created it could not now take away. Other abattoirs were created, and came and went with monotonous regularity. Periodically, New Orleans newspapers would complain about the stench and ill effects of local slaughterhouses.

The Crescent City Company, in one corporate form or another, stayed in business until the 1920s. The last slaughterhouse in New Orleans closed in 1963.

Cases Cited

Calder v. Bull, 3 Dall. 386 (1798)
Commonwealth v. Alger, 61 Mass. 53 (1851)
Darcy v. Allein (Case of Monopolies), 9 Coke's Reports 84 (1588)
Dred Scott v. Sandford, 19 How. 393 (1857)
Ex Parte Shrader, 33 Cal. 279 (1867)
Fletcher v. Peck, 6 Cranch 87 (1810)
Luther v. Borden, 7 How. 1 (1849)
McCulloch v. Maryland, 4 Wheat. 316 (1819)
Slaughterhouse Cases (The Butchers' Benevolent Association of New Orleans v. Crescent City Live-Stock Landing and Slaughter-House Company), 16 Wall. 36 (1873)
Wynehamer v. People, 13 N.Y. 378 (1856)

For Further Reading

The most comprehensive look at these cases and the issues they raised is Ronald M. Labbé and Jonathan Lurie, The Slaughterhouse Cases: *Regulation, Reconstruction, and the Fourteenth Amendment* (2003). The best survey of constitutional development in this period remains Harold M. Hyman and William Wiecek, *Equal Justice under Law: Constitutional Development, 1835–1875* (1982). The spread of due process jurisprudence and its influence for the next sixty years is explored in William Wiecek, *The Lost World of Classical Legal Thought: Law and Ideology in America, 1886–1937* (1998). The expansion of police powers is detailed in William Novak, *The People's Welfare: Law and Regulation in Nineteenth Century America* (1996). For the butchers' leading lawyer, see R. J. Saunders, *John Archibald Campbell: Southern Moderate, 1811–1899* (1997). For Stephen J. Field, see Paul Kens, *Justice Stephen J. Field: Shaping Liberty from the Gold Rush to the Gilded Age* (1997).

The Case of the Woman Who Wanted to Be a Lawyer

Bradwell v. Illinois (1873)

STARTING IN THE 1830S, a great social revolution swept through the United States. The era of Jacksonian democracy saw the abolition of property requirements for voting, the disestablishment of official churches in the states, and the removal of religious restrictions on the suffrage. Other reforms took longer. The drive to do away with slavery picked up momentum in the 1840s and 1850s, but it would take a civil war and the Thirteenth Amendment before the "peculiar institution" could be abolished.

At the same time that reformers looked to end bondage based on skin color, many of them also sought to end the legal disabilities of women. Traditional common-law rules forbid women from voting, holding property in their own name, and making contracts. If they wanted to sue, they had to do so in their husband's name, and by law, the legal control of a husband over his wife was near-absolute.

After the Civil War the drive for women's suffrage and for the removal of other legal impediments picked up steam, but it would take many years before women would be able to cast a ballot, and even more before they achieved full equality before the law. *Bradwell v. Illinois* illustrates well the courage of women pioneering in a new field, the obstacles they faced, and the ingrained male chauvinism of the legal establishment.

Myra Bradwell

Myra Colby Bradwell had been born in 1831 in Manchester, Vermont, to upper-middle-class parents, and some people believe that she had been marked from birth to be a genteel rabble-rouser. Her strongly Baptist parents, Eban and Abigail Colby, took part in the anti-slavery agitation that roiled New England in the 1830s, and their hatred of the "peculiar institution" intensified after a proslavery mob in Illinois killed a close friend of the family in 1837. In 1843 the Colbys moved to Schaumburg Township in Cook County, Illinois, and Myra had a thorough if somewhat peripatetic education. In her teens she attended a school in Kenosha, Wisconsin, where an older sister lived, and then graduated from the Ladies' Seminary in Elgin, Illinois, and became a district schoolteacher. In May 1852, over her parents' opposition, she married the penniless but ambitious James Bradwell, who had moved to Illinois as a child with his immigrant parents.

An aspiring lawyer, James Bradwell had worked his way through part of the curriculum at Knox College. As was common in those days, before law schools came to dominate legal education, he then read law—that is, he apprenticed—in the office of a practicing attorney, but had not progressed far enough to be admitted to the bar. The young couple moved briefly to Memphis, where they established a private school that did well. But the slave culture of Tennessee offended them, and when their first daughter, who was also named Myra, was born in 1854, they moved to Chicago, where James resumed his legal studies. He was admitted to the Illinois bar a year later, and opened a law office, Bradwell & Colby, with his brother-in-law.

The partnership flourished, and Bradwell soon became a man of considerable influence in Chicago, at the time already a bustling, entrepreneurial, and growing city. He and Myra had two more children. In 1861 their first daughter, Myra, died; three years later they lost a fourth child, James.

Myra Bradwell became deeply involved in work related to the Civil War, especially with the Northwestern Sanitary Commission, organizing sanitary fairs and collection campaigns to raise money for the health care of wounded soldiers. When the Civil War ended, she volunteered at the Chicago Soldier's Home, the Soldier's Aid Society, the Illinois Industrial School for Girls, and—since her husband was a Mason—also got involved in the charitable activities of the Masonic women's auxiliaries. For the rest of her life she continued to do volunteer work, and as the family's fortunes grew, she also gained a reputation as a local philanthropist.

The *Chicago Legal News*

But Myra Bradwell had a passion to do more than volunteer work—she wanted to become a lawyer. From the earliest days of their marriage, James had tutored his wife in legal matters. In early 1868 Myra established a newspaper, the *Chicago Legal News.* Within two years the paper was carrying more advertisements than any legal newspaper in the country, and had developed a reputation for clear writing and perceptive analysis. Because of the laws regarding limitations on women owning property, the newspaper technically belonged to James, although he and everyone else knew that Myra ran it. Once she had the *News* up and running, she went to the Illinois legislature in late 1868 to obtain a special license suspending the legal disabilities associated with coverture (the legal term for the status of a married woman), such as the inability to make contracts, own property, or manage one's own money. She then openly assumed full responsibility for running the *Chicago Legal News,* its contents, finances, and daily operations.

Bradwell used the pages of the *News* not only to advance the cause of women's rights, but also for legal reform. She called for the adoption of uniform rules of legal practice throughout Illinois, and urged lawyers in the larger cities to specialize in particular areas of the law. She was fierce in her anger at disreputable lawyers, especially those who bribed jurors (a rampant practice not only in Chicago but elsewhere at the time), stole their clients' money, drank too much, or obtained quick divorces for their clients. Bradwell inveighed against jury-packing, and insisted that lawyers and judges practice good manners in the courtroom, be on time, and avoid side conversations. To raise the quality of the state's judges, she urged the legislature to raise judicial salaries and to improve courtroom conditions as well as facilities. She had nothing against judges deciding to run for elected office, but insisted that they first resign from the bench. She also supported bills that would have provided for compulsory retirement of judges at age sixty-five.

After Myra secured the private bill that allowed her to own property and manage the business, James started a spin-off publishing and bindery operation, the Chicago Legal News Company, which quickly became the city's leading provider of legal forms, stationery, and printed briefs. The company then became the state's official printer of its legal materials, guaranteeing its success. The two companies, of course, worked closely, and at the close of every legislative session Myra Bradwell could be found comparing the proofs of the printed proceedings and laws with the original handwritten texts at the state capital in Springfield. The *News* then published the latest legislation several months before the state published its own laws. As a result, no lawyer in the Chicago area, and in fact through much of Illinois, could be without the *News.*

A telling incident occurred on the evening of October 8, 1871, when Chicago's Great Fire swept through the city. Bradwell went through the house, collected a few valuables, and gave them to her husband to bury in the front lawn to save them from destruction. The couple then fled to Lake Michigan, where they and other city residents stood in shallow water that night to avoid nearby flames. The fire raged for three days, and destroyed almost the entire city. Aside from losing their house, the Bradwells did not know where their thirteen-year-old daughter, Bessie, had gone. They found her, alive and well, the following afternoon. Truly her mother's daughter, Bessie had rushed to the newspaper office to save the lengthy subscription list of the *Legal News* before the premises fell to the flames.

Nothing tangible could have been of greater value to Bradwell. With the city in ashes and most law offices and law libraries destroyed, copies of the *Legal News,* especially the back issues, became extremely useful to the survivors. Bradwell ensured that her paper became indispensable to a new group of clients—landowners—when she convinced the Illinois legislature to choose her paper as the official medium in which to publish all court records, including notices of land titles, that had been burned by the fire and then re-created through archival research. Advertisers believed her when she told them that "in no place in the world will there be such a demand for law books as in Chicago in the next few months."

Although not a practicing attorney, and certainly not a member of the bar, she wielded a great deal of influence in Chicago and Illinois legal circles. Most of the state's lawyers subscribed to the *Chicago Legal News,* and in editorials and in choosing which topics to feature as important, she helped shape opinion on matters as varied as judicial reorganization, regulation of railroads, city zoning, and women's rights.

The Nascent Women's Movement

Unlike many other feminist activists at this time, Myra Bradwell worked on the inside rather than taking part in public demonstrations. While people like Susan B. Anthony and Elizabeth Cady Stanton organized rallies and marches for women's suffrage, in early 1869 Bradwell quietly went to every judge in Cook County and secured their endorsement for giving women the vote. Stanton, who was no fan of the business-oriented Bradwell, nonetheless recognized her as a "woman of great force and executive ability," one well entrenched in the powerful circles of bench and bar.

As the drive for voting rights continued, Bradwell gradually became a more visible part of it, serving as a member of the executive committee of the Illinois Woman Suffrage Association. In late 1869 the American Woman Suffrage Association, the umbrella organization for all of the state groups, organized a conference in Cleveland, Ohio, and Bradwell not only served as the temporary chair, but then became one of the permanent corresponding secretaries.

But while she certainly favored giving women the right to vote, Bradwell was far more concerned with removing economic and occupational limits on married women, the full dimension of which she had come to know personally as she struggled to establish and manage a thriving business. The culture of the late Victorian era did not look kindly on female autonomy, and in many states the old legal rules that gave a husband complete control over his wife and her earnings were still in place.

A History of Legal Discrimination

Myra Bradwell was well aware of the disabilities the law placed on women, restrictions that had deep roots in history. Since early times, society recognized and often revered women as the unique source of human life, but at the same time considered them not only physically and intellectually inferior to men, but also the major source of temptation and evil. In Greek mythology a woman, Pandora, opens the forbidden box that brings unhappiness to mankind, while Roman law described women as children, eternally inferior to men. The early Christian fathers perpetuated these views. St. Jerome declared that "woman is the gate of the devil, the path of wickedness, the sting of the serpent, in a word, a perilous object." In the thirteenth century, Thomas Aquinas wrote that woman was "created to be man's helpmeet, but her unique role is in conception . . . since for other purposes men would be better assisted by other men."

The widely held view of women as naturally inferior to men greatly influenced their status in the law. The common law of England held that an *unmarried* woman could own property, make a contract, and sue or be sued in court. The law saw a *married woman* as one with her husband; she gave up her name, and virtually all of her property came under his control. When they married, women became subordinate to their husbands under the principle of *coverture*, a term defined by the English jurist Sir William Blackstone:

> By Marriage, the husband and wife are one person in law: that is, the very being or legal existence of the woman is suspended during the marriage, or at least is incorporated and consolidated into that of the husband; under whose wing, protection and cover, she performs everything; . . . and her condition, during her marriage is called her coverture.

Under coverture a married woman could not make contracts, write wills, sue or be sued in court, or own property. Her money and even her household goods and clothing belonged to her husband in his role as head of the household. If a woman worked outside of the house for wages, the money she brought home belonged to her spouse. If a woman came from a wealthy family, she might have some rights to property and perhaps even be given a house. Unless her father had taken the trouble and expense to draw up papers giving her management rights as well, her husband had the sole right to manage or sell such property without her permission, and to keep the profits.

This attitude crossed the Atlantic, and the common-law rules regarding women became part of the colonial legal codes. At the time of the Revolution John Adams told a friend he hoped Massachusetts would not lower its voting qualifications. "It is dangerous to open so fruitful a source of controversy," he explained. "New claims will arise; women will demand a vote." Forty years later, his friend and cosigner of the Declaration of Independence, Thomas Jefferson, still opposed opening the franchise to women:

> Were our State a pure democracy . . . there would yet be excluded from deliberations . . . women, who, to prevent depravation of morals and ambiguity of issues, should not mix promiscuously in the public meetings of men.

A married man had the legal right to sexual relations with his wife, and if she did not care for the intimacy, he could force her; the legal definition of *rape* specifically excluded husbands and wives. Just as he controlled their material wealth, the husband also had control of their children, and in the rare instances of divorce, custody automatically went to the father. English law carried over to the colonies and then to the states. During the early years of the Republic, a man virtually owned his wife and children as he did his material possessions. If an impoverished man chose to send his children to the poorhouse so he no longer had to support them, the mother legally had no standing to object.

The democratizing forces at work in the 1830s and 1840s did improve the situation somewhat. A number of states passed laws known as "married women's property acts." To some extent these laws resulted from pressure by early advocates of women's rights, but they also grew out of the need of a dynamic capitalist society to preserve property to avert the financial problems and confusion that could result if creditors seized property and broke up estates. Mississippi enacted the first property act in 1839, in order to keep plantations and their slaves intact, and to preserve the family's interests against creditors. New York followed in 1848, and Massachusetts in 1854, but despite their ability—in some states—to own property, there were still significant limitations on the ability of married women to run their own businesses, a fact that confronted the Bradwells when they established the *Chicago Legal News*.

Small Doors in the Wall

Bradwell did more than rail at these injustices. Her role as editor of the *Legal News* and the company's status as the state's printer gave her access to judges, legislators, and important attorneys that most advocates of women's rights lacked. In 1869 she drafted, and then personally lobbied the legislature to enact, a bill that allowed wives to retain a portion of their earnings. She also supported laws that set aside portions of estates for widows, permitted women to serve on elected school boards, and ensured equal custody of children after a divorce. In 1875 she successfully pushed a bill that opened the office of notary public to women, a post for which Bradwell had applied in 1868 and again in 1870, and on both occasions was denied because of her gender.

By the early 1870s, Myra and James had done well indeed. He had been named a county judge, and by any standard, she has to be counted as one of the most successful and prosperous businesswomen of the latter nineteenth century. To replace the house that burned in the 1871 fire, they built a large mansion on the shores of Lake Michigan. She wanted more, however, and inevitably Myra Bradwell thought of the law.

Again she confronted the pervasive bias against women. Although during colonial times women had been allowed to represent themselves in some courts, this had been more because of a lack of trained lawyers in America than any sensibility regarding women. Not until 1869 did the St. Louis Law School become the first law school in the United States to admit women. In 1870 an accredited institution, the Union College of Law in Chicago, awarded a woman a law degree. These were not, however, signs of a new, egalitarian age. Most states continued to exclude women from the legal profession. In Iowa, for example, the law permitted "any white male person" admission to the bar, and it took a very creative reading of that law by the Iowa Supreme Court in 1869 for the state to allow Arabella Mansfield admission to the bar, the first woman who secured that status.

A Person of Good Character—but Not Eligible

There is no question that at age thirty-eight Myra Bradwell knew as much law as any lawyer in Illinois. She had been her husband's partner on the *Legal News* as well as in the printing of state legal business and private briefs. As his business expanded he had talked to her constantly, explaining the problems before him and the legal issues involved. She wrote the editorials and, very often, the analytical articles for the paper. She saw no reason that she should not be admitted to the bar so she could actually practice law, and in 1869, knowing she would be turned down, she passed the required examination with "high honors." She applied for admission to the bar, and included the required letter from an inferior court attesting to the fact that she was a "person" of good character, only to learn, as she had expected, that she would be turned down for the sole reason that she was a woman—and a married woman—and therefore ineligible.

The Illinois Supreme Court declared that it was "compelled" to deny her application because, unlike men, she would "not be bound by the [contractual] obligations necessary to be assumed where the relation of attorney and client shall exist, by reason of the disability imposed" by her "married condition—it being assumed that you are a married woman." Because of her coverture, the committee explained, Bradwell would not have the power to uphold the implied contracts that were standard between attorneys and clients. Married women could not, under existing Illinois law, contract on their own behalf without their husband's consent, a fact Bradwell already knew.

The fact that Arabella Mansfield had gained approval to practice law in Iowa greatly heartened Bradwell. She decided to fight the decision and appealed it. In her brief, she insisted that "it is neither a crime nor a disqualification to be a married woman." Married women, she pointed out, often acted as legal agents for their husbands and under Illinois law could enter into contracts on behalf of their spouses. She saw no difference between a woman acting as a legal agent for her husband and an attorney acting as an agent for a client. Moreover, since passage of the Illinois Married Women's Property Act in 1861, a married woman could now contract with respect to any property she might hold separately from her husband.

The court's decision made little sense since Bradwell, as editor and publisher of the *Chicago Legal News,* had been doing for years what the court said she could not do—make and uphold contracts. In fact, she not only had a contract with the state legislature to publish its minutes and enactments, she had a contract with the Illinois Supreme Court to print its opinions in her paper. Bradwell argued that a woman like herself, who was legally entitled to carry out business contracts without the express consent of her husband, should be considered a *femme sole*—a single woman—under common law. Bradwell had, of course, secured the right to act on her own behalf because of a private bill enacted in the Illinois legislature—an option, she claimed, open to all married women.

If a married woman lawyer failed "to perform her duty, or to comply with all her contracts as an attorney," then the court could punish her as it would punish a man who failed in his duty, by striking his name from the roll—that is, disbarring him. She called on the court to approve her admission, claiming that in doing so it would "strike a blow [for] the rights of every married woman in the great State of Illinois who is dependent on her labor for support."

She failed, and it is worthwhile quoting from the Illinois Supreme Court's opinion to get a sense of how the male-dominated society and bar viewed the prospect of a woman lawyer:

Whether, in the existing social relations between men and women, it would promote the proper administration of justice, and the general well-being of society, to permit women to engage in the trial of cases at the bar, is a question opening a wide field of discussion, upon which it is not necessary for us to enter. It is sufficient to say that, in our opinion, the implied limitation upon our power [as a court]. . . , must operate to prevent our admitting women to the office of attorney at law. If we were to admit them, we should be exercising the authority conferred upon us in a manner which, we are fully satisfied, was never contemplated by the legislature.

It is to be remembered that at the time this statute was enacted we had, by express provision, adopted the common law of England . . . so far as they were applicable to our condition.

It is to be also remembered that female attorneys at law were unknown in England, and a proposition that a woman should enter the courts of Westminster Hall in that capacity, or as a barrister, would have created hardly less astonishment than one that she should ascend the bench of bishops, or be elected to a seat in the House of Commons.

It is to be further remembered, that when our act was passed, that school of reform which claims for women participation in the making and administering of the laws had not then arisen, or, if here and there a writer had advanced such theories, they were regarded rather as abstract speculations than as an actual basis for action.

That God designed the sexes to occupy different spheres of action, and that it belonged to men to make, apply, and execute the laws, was regarded as an almost axiomatic truth.

In view of these facts, we are certainly warranted in saying that when the legislature gave to this court the power of granting licenses to practice law, it was with not the slightest expectation that this privilege would be extended to women.

Although Bradwell had originally been turned down on the grounds that she was a married woman, the Illinois court's decision made clear that the real reason was her gender. Women—married or not—would not be allowed to practice law. There was only one resort left: appeal to the U.S. Supreme Court, relying on the wording of the Fourteenth

Amendment—"no State shall make or enforce any law which shall abridge the privileges or immunities of citizens of the United States; nor shall any State deprive any person of life, liberty, or property, without due process of law; nor deny any person within its jurisdiction the equal protection of the laws." The Supreme Court had not yet handed down any decisions interpreting the meaning of any of these clauses. The wording did not refer to "men" but to "citizens" and "persons." A plain reading of those phrases, she believed, should be enough to win her case.

On Appeal to the Supreme Court

Bradwell could not, of course, argue her own case before the Supreme Court, since women were, at the time, also excluded from admission to the Court's bar. She secured the services of Sen. Matthew Hale Carpenter of Wisconsin, an experienced advocate as well as a supporter of women's rights. It is unclear from the evidence whether Bradwell herself worked on the appellate brief, but in the preface there is a lengthy assurance that giving women the right to practice law would not imply that they should also be given the right to vote. According to Bradwell's biographer, Jane Friedman, Bradwell directed Carpenter to make that argument in order to reassure the conservative justices that they were not starting down a slippery slope to full equality. (The same Court would, in fact, soon rule unanimously in *Minor v. Happensett* [1875] that while women were citizens, the suffrage was not a privilege of citizenship.)

Other sources suggest that she may not have been consulted, but given her extensive knowledge of the law, this is improbable. Although a strong supporter of women's suffrage, Bradwell might well have chosen to compromise one goal in order to secure another. She recognized that the constitutional argument for suffrage was weak; after all, despite gaining citizenship in the Fourteenth Amendment, the former slaves had not secured suffrage until the passage of the Fifteenth Amendment in 1870. That amendment spoke to "race, color, or previous condition of servitude," and not to gender. From a legal standpoint, the argument for allowing women to make contracts seemed far stronger. We do know that Susan B. Anthony, the leader of the women's suffrage movement, believed Bradwell had a hand in the brief, and wrote her a letter scolding her for the reasoning.

Whether Bradwell advised him or not, in the end Carpenter decided to rely on the privileges and immunities clause guaranteeing citizens the same rights in every state of the Union. He claimed that admission to the bar, and the pursuit of "other ordinary avocations," belonged in those constitutionally protected privileges that a state could not abridge. He suggested that the clause should be read broadly: "If this provision does protect the colored citizen, then it protects every citizen, black or white, male or female. . . . Intelligence, integrity and honor are the only qualifications that can be prescribed as conditions precedent to entry upon any honorable pursuit or profitable avocation."

Today we look at such an assertion as commonsensical, but we are the heirs of more than six decades of equal protection jurisprudence, which has struck down invidious discrimination based on race, religion, gender, alienage, and sexual orientation. In 1873, however, Carpenter's argument was unprecedented. "Of a bar composed of men and women of equal integrity and learning, women might be more or less frequently retained as the taste or judgment of clients might dictate," the brief continued. "But the broad shield of the Constitution is over all, and protects each in the measure of success which his or her individual merits may secure."

(Carpenter, in what can only be described as a stretch, noted that Bradwell had at one time been a resident of Vermont, which had a far more liberal stance regarding the ability of women to make contracts. Since she would have been able to make contracts in Vermont, he argued, the privileges and immunities clause meant that she should also be allowed to do so in Illinois.)

Matthew Hale Carpenter rose to begin oral argument on Saturday morning, January 18, 1873. "The question does not involve the right of a female to vote," he began, echoing the opening of the brief. "It presents a narrower matter: Can a female citizen, duly qualified in respect of age, character, and learning, claim, under the Fourteenth Amendment, the privilege of earning a livelihood by practicing at the bar of a judicial court?"

Prior to the ratification of the Fourteenth Amendment, the question of privileges and immunities was strictly a matter of state law, and if a citizen left one state to live in another, he did not carry the rights he enjoyed in the first state to the second, but received only those applicable in the latter. But now the federal government ensured that the rights exercised in one state were available in all, and no state could lessen such rights.

Carpenter then went on to argue that the right of admission to the bar of a qualified person fell into this category, and could not be denied to anyone simply because of gender. Carpenter cited cases such as *Cummings v. Missouri* (1867), in which the Court had held that among the basic liberties of Americans was the right to enter an avocation, and that the right to do so could not be denied to anyone.

"The profession of the law," he argued, "like the clerical profession and that of medicine, is an avocation open to every citizen of the United States. And while the legislature may prescribe qualifications for entering upon this pursuit, they cannot, under the guise of fixing qualifications, exclude a class of citizens from admission to the bar."

As for the difficulties supposedly related to her inability to make the normal type of contract between attorney and client, Carpenter dismissed them out of hand. Once Bradwell had been admitted to the bar, she would become an officer of the court and therefore subject to its summary jurisdiction: "Any malpractice or unprofessional conduct towards her client would be punishable by fine, imprisonment, or expulsion from the bar, or by all three." In fact, the Illinois high court had, in its full opinion, abandoned the arguments that her coverture would create difficulties. It had denied her admission solely on the basis of her gender, and the Fourteenth Amendment did not permit that sort of class discrimination. "I maintain," he concluded,

> that the Fourteenth Amendment opens to every citizen of the United States, male or female, black or white, married or single, the honorable professions as well as the servile employments of life; and that no citizen can be excluded from any one of them. Intelligence, integrity, and honor are the only qualifications that can be prescribed as conditions precedent to an entry upon any honorable pursuit or profitable avocation, and all the privileges and immunities which I vindicate to a colored citizen, I vindicate to our mothers, our sisters, and our daughters. . . . The broad shield of the Constitution is over them all, and protects each in that measure of success which his or her individual merits may secure.

No one answered Carpenter's arguments because the state of Illinois did not send a lawyer to represent its high court, for reasons that are unknown. It is possible that it felt Myra Bradwell's case to be so weak that it was unnecessary to go to the expense of having counsel present. One could equally surmise that so many high officials in the state government thought so well of her that they hoped she would prevail, and thus chose not to oppose her.

The Decision

On April 14, 1873, the Supreme Court handed down its decision in the *Slaughterhouse Cases* (see preceding chapter), and there gave its first judicial interpretation of the meaning of the privileges and immunities clause. Justice Samuel F. Miller dismissed the claim of the New Orleans butchers that the Fourteenth Amendment gave them protection to carry on their professions as they saw fit without interference from the state in the form of regulations over where they could do that business. It is likely that the Court held off ruling on Myra Bradwell's petition until after it had decided the Louisiana case, which presented more complex issues than that of one woman wanting to practice law. The very next day, also speaking through Justice Miller, it ruled against her by an 8–1 vote.

Miller first dismissed what, at best, had been a somewhat frivolous claim that because Bradwell had years ago lived in Vermont, therefore Illinois had to grant her the same right to make contracts that she would have enjoyed in Vermont. Bradwell had not lived in Vermont for many years; she was clearly a citizen of Illinois, and therefore subject to the laws of that state. Miller also dismissed Carpenter's claim that among the rights and privileges belonging to all citizens in the United States was admission to the bar if they proved the requisite learning and good character required.

"There are privileges and immunities belonging to citizens of the United States," the Court agreed, and "it is these alone which a state is forbidden to abridge." Miller did not explain what these rights were, but he was quite clear that "the right to admission to practice in the courts of a state is not one of them." In fact, in many states and even in the federal courts one did not even have to be a citizen to be admitted to the bar, but that determination rested solely in the hands of the legislature, and had nothing to do with the Fourteenth Amendment.

Miller did not say more, merely noting that the opinion rendered in the *Slaughterhouse Cases* "renders elaborate argument in the present case unnecessary." The right to control and regulate the granting of licenses remained wholly within the power of the state. The Court did not need to reiterate the arguments in the earlier case. "It is sufficient to say they are conclusive of the present case."

Had the decision stopped here, *Bradwell v. Illinois* would probably be remembered today, if at all, as one more relatively minor decision that kept women in a status of legal inferiority. Instead, Justice Joseph Bradley, joined by Justices Stephen J. Field and Noah H. Swayne, entered a wholly superfluous concurrence that has earned itself a certain notoriety in American legal history. Bradley took on a far wider issue than the meaning of a clause in the Fourteenth Amendment; he addressed the whole question of equal rights for women. He conceded that in recent years there had been changes in the law that allowed women greater freedom to own property and to act for themselves in some legal transactions. Then, in extremely paternalistic tones, he declared:

> Man is, or should be, woman's protector and defender. The natural and proper timidity and delicacy which belongs to the female sex evidently unfits it for many of the occupations of civil life. The constitution of the family organization, which is founded in the divine ordinance, as well as in the nature of things, indicates the domestic sphere as that which properly belongs to the domain and functions of womanhood.

Bradley went on to explain approvingly that the common law viewed the husband as the wife's "head and representative in the social state," and the laws flowing from and depending upon this "cardinal principle still exist in full force in most States." While he noted that many women were unmarried, and therefore not affected by these "duties, complications, and incapacities," he considered these exceptions irrelevant:

> The paramount destiny and mission of woman are to fulfill the noble and benign offices of wife and mother. This is the law of the Creator. And the rules of civil society must be adapted to the general constitution of things, and can not be based upon exceptional cases.

While noting the advancement of women in certain fields, a movement, he claimed, that had his "heartiest concurrence," this did not mean that they had the right to be admitted into every office or position, especially those that required special skills or knowledge:

> This [decision] fairly belongs to the police power of the state, and, in my opinion, in view of the peculiar characteristics, destiny, and mission of women, it is within the province of the legislature to ordain what offices, positions, and callings shall be filed and discharged by men, and shall receive the benefit of those energies and responsibilities, and that decision and firmness which are presumed to predominate in the sterner sex.

Women, it seemed, were much too delicate to practice law; it took "sterner" character, the type that only men enjoyed.

The views expressed by Justices Miller and Bradley that because of the special nature of women, states could regulate their legal rights lasted well into the twentieth century. Even with the passage of the Nineteenth Amendment in 1919 granting women the right to vote, many states retained laws on the books limiting what women could do economically as well as legally. The Supreme Court in *Goesart v. Cleary* (1948) upheld a Michigan law prohibiting a woman from tending bar, unless she was the wife or daughter of the male owner. Justice Felix Frankfurter made lighthearted reference to barmaids in literature— "We meet the alewife, sprightly and ribald, in Shakespeare"—but then went on to note that, although being a barmaid had long historic roots, "Michigan could, beyond all question, forbid all women from working behind a bar [because] liquor traffic is one of the oldest and most untrammeled of legislative powers."

A little over a decade later, in *Hoyt v. Florida* (1961), the Supreme Court unanimously upheld the Florida system of jury selection that discouraged most women from service. Where all male voters were registered automatically for jury duty, women who wanted to serve had to sign up separately, leading most women not to do so. The state's justification was that it did not exclude women from jury duty, but merely spared them the obligation in recognition of their place at "the center of home and family life."

Not until *Reed v. Reed* (1971) did the Court finally begin to grapple with the question of full legal equality for women. An Idaho law dating to 1864 required that when the father and mother of a deceased person both sought appointment as administrator of the estate, the man had to be preferred over the woman. In a brief and unanimous opinion, the Idaho Supreme Court upheld the law; in an equally brief and unanimous opinion, the U.S. Supreme Court ruled the law unconstitutional under the equal protection clause. The Court had finally begun the long march away from Joseph Bradley's paternalism.

Before leaving *Bradwell,* one might note the following. There was one dissent, by Chief Justice Salmon P. Chase, who happened to be a distant cousin of Bradwell's. But because he was critically ill and would die within a few weeks, there was no accompanying opinion, just a dissenting vote. Where the Court had voted against the New Orleans butchers by a bare 5–4 majority, it was nearly unanimous in its rejection of a woman's claim to practice law. Finally, where Bradwell's attorney, Sen. Matthew Hale Carpenter, had argued energetically for her right to be admitted to the bar under terms of the Fourteenth Amendment, he had argued against the butchers in the *Slaughterhouse Cases,* believing the Louisiana law to be a simple and legitimate health regulation. Bradley, on the other hand, had been a dissenter in the Louisiana case, believing that the butchers—all male, of course—had a constitutional right to pursue any lawful employment. He joined all but one of his colleagues in their view that women had no such right.

Moving On, and Triumphing

Even while the Supreme Court pondered her appeal, Bradwell and two of her protégés, Ada Kepley and Alta Hulett, had been busy drafting and lobbying the Illinois legislature for a statute providing that "no person shall be precluded or debarred from any occupation, profession or employment (except military) on account of sex." Bradwell's reputation as well as her superb lobbying skills led the legislature to pass the measure in 1874, and then the Illinois Supreme Court had no choice but to admit—however grudgingly—women to the bar. Bradwell also drafted legislation making women eligible to hold elective office in the Illinois public school system. The bill also passed, although it would be 1892 before the assembly passed a law—also drafted by Bradwell—allowing women to vote in school board elections.

Despite having drafted and secured passage of legislation allowing all persons, regardless of sex, to pursue an occupation, Myra Bradwell never reapplied for admission to the bar. In 1890, however, the Illinois Supreme Court decided to act. It issued an order granting Bradwell's original application to practice law, and she became the first person in Illinois granted a license on the court's own motion. Two years later, on March 28, 1892, she was admitted to the bar of the Supreme Court of the United States, on the motion of Attorney General W. H. H. Miller.

Myra Bradwell died of cancer on February 14, 1894. Her daughter, Bessie Bradwell Helmer, who had heroically saved the subscription lists during the Great Fire, continued her mother's work with a career in law and as publisher of the *Chicago Legal News* until 1925. A week after Bradwell's death, Bessie published a tribute to her mother, stating: "The future historian will accord her the breaking of the chain that bound women to a life of household drudgery. She opened the doors of the professions to her sex, and compelled law makers and judges as well, to proclaim that it was not a crime to be born a woman."

Cases Cited

Bradwell v. Illinois, 83 U.S. (16 Wall.) 130 (1873)
Cummings v. Missouri, 71 U.S. (4 Wall.) 277 (1867)
Goesart v. Cleary, 335 U.S. 464 (1948)
Hoyt v. Florida, 368 U.S. 57 (1961)
In re Bradwell, 55 Ill. 535 (1869)
Minor v. Happensett, 88 U.S. (21 Wall.) 162 (1875)
Reed v. Reed, 404 U.S. 71 (1971)

For Further Reading

Bradwell's life story is told in Jane M. Friedman, *America's First Woman Lawyer: The Biography of Myra Bradwell* (1993). A good and popular overview of cases affecting women is Claire Cushman, ed., *Supreme Court Decisions and Women's Rights* (2001). The broader subject of women's rights is explored in the classic book by Eleanor Flexner, *Century of Struggle: The Women's Rights Movement in the United States* (enl. ed. 1996), and the legal impediments are well explicated in Joan Hoff, *Laws, Gender, and Injustice: A Legal History of U.S. Women* (1991). Perhaps the best book on women's changing role in the constitutional order is Linda K. Kerby, *No Constitutional Right to Be Ladies: Women and the Obligations of Citizenship* (1998).

The Case of the Devout Bigamist

Reynolds v. United States (1879)

GEORGE REYNOLDS believed firmly in his Mormon faith at a time when it was anathema to many Americans. Born in London in 1842, he converted to Mormonism at the age of fourteen, and devoted the rest of his life to his new church. He emigrated to the United States in 1865, and then trekked overland to the Utah Territory, where Mormons had migrated in the hope of establishing a new Zion. Reynolds became the first Mormon successfully prosecuted for the practice of polygamy, in a case that wound up in the U.S. Supreme Court. The doctrine enunciated in *Reynolds v. United States* (1879), separating beliefs from actions, still informs the jurisprudence of the First Amendment's free exercise clause.

Mormon Beliefs

The Mormons comprise the most populous branch of the Church of Jesus Christ of Latter-Day Saints (LDS). The movement traces back to Joseph Smith Jr., who founded the group in New York in the 1820s, and began winning its first converts as Smith translated the revelation he had received into the Book of Mormon. The sacred text of the religion is a chronicle of the early indigenous peoples of the Americas, picturing them as believing Israelites and calling for their restoration to the Christian faith. Smith claimed that he translated over five hundred pages in sixty days, and that it was an ancient record vouchsafed to him "by the gift and power of God."

Smith had his first vision in the spring of 1820 as an answer to his question of which faith he should join. He saw God the Father and Jesus

Christ as two separate entities, a major departure from orthodox Christian doctrine, which sees Father and Son as two aspects of the same deity. Although vilified by most Christian groups at the time, Smith viewed Mormonism as the rebirth of an early and unperverted Christianity, with authority residing in the Mormon prophets chosen by God. The various doctrines pursued by the Roman Catholic Church, the Eastern Orthodox Church, the Anglican Communion, and Trinitarian Protestantism were all abominations in the sight of God, and had in fact been foretold as such in the second book of Thessalonians. Mormons then and now believe in both the Old and New Testaments, although they consider the modern translations to be full of inaccuracies that were corrected by the Book of Mormon.

The disdain with which Mormonism viewed mainstream Christian faiths accounted for some of the hostility against it, as did its belief in a theocratic form of government—that is, rule of the government and society by Church leaders according to Church doctrine. Building the Kingdom of God on Earth—a truly righteous society governed by holy men—would pave the way for the second coming of Jesus and the onset of the Millennium. But the aspect of Mormonism that drew the most ire was plural marriage, or polygamy.

Joseph Smith claimed that he was told in a revelation that some Mormon men would take more than one wife. Marriages celebrated in the proper manner endured not only during the lives of the husband and wife, but throughout eternity. Only those married according to the new revelation would be exalted and reach the highest levels of salvation. According to the law of Abraham, men who were called upon by faith and church were justified in marrying more than one woman. Refusal to enter into such marriages could result in destruction and damnation. Diaries and other records from this period indicate early believers often had unhappy experiences as they tried to accommodate to the demands of the faith, since plural marriage represented such a radical departure from the monogamous family structure they had known as children. "Living the Principle," as Mormons called the demands of polygamy, often tore families apart and led to apostasy, especially in the early years of the practice. Yet as historians and Church leaders noted, despite the difficulties, plural marriage helped knit together people of diverse backgrounds into a community of faith.

Although Mormon leaders believed that the American tradition of religious pluralism would lead to toleration of their faith, this proved not to be the case. As members of the sect began to practice polygamy, they found increasingly high barriers to public tolerance, much less acceptance. Smith's followers were first driven from New York to Ohio, and then settled in Nauvoo, Illinois, in 1839. There Smith and his chief lieutenants, Brigham Young and Heber Kimball, took plural wives, leading the state of Illinois to make polygamy illegal. On June 27, 1844, a mob killed Smith and his brother. Led by Brigham Young, the Mormons trekked westward to the Utah Territory, where they established Deseret, a Mormon kingdom in the middle of the desert.

Initially it seemed that the Mormons had finally found a place where they could live in peace, and under Young's leadership they enjoyed good relations with the neighboring Indian tribes. Although the federal government did not approve of Mormon theology or practices, the distance from Utah to Washington, and the seeming isolation of the Mormon community from mainstream society, led the federal government to leave Young and his followers alone. But after the Civil War the transcontinental railroad tied East and West together; in fact, the ceremonial "golden spike" driven by Leland Stanford connecting the Central Pacific and Union Pacific Railroads took place at Promontory Summit in the Utah Territory.

The Growing Opposition to the Faith

Even before the two roads linked up, the government in Washington, under pressure from mainstream Christian groups, began a forty-year campaign to eradicate Mormon distinctiveness. Although the population of Utah soon reached the minimum required for statehood, Congress refused to admit Utah to the Union until the Mormons abandoned polygamy, which was illegal everywhere else in the United States and its territories.

Between 1862 and 1877, Congress enacted four major pieces of legislation aimed at the Mormons. Antislavery activist and representative Justin Morrill of Vermont, best known as the father of the land grant public universities, sponsored the Morrill Anti-Polygamy Act of 1862. The statute made polygamy a crime in any U.S. territory, punishable by fines of up to $500 and imprisonment for as many as five years. The act also revoked the charter given by the Utah territorial legislature incorporating the Church of Jesus Christ of Latter-Day Saints, and annulled all acts of that legislature that supported or protected polygamy in any way.

While seemingly very stringent, in fact the Morrill Act was all noise, passed to quiet some constituents who saw Mormonism as an affront to all (proper) God-fearing people. In the middle of the Civil War the Lincoln administration had more important matters at hand than the behavior of a small sect out in the desert, and the federal government turned a blind eye to Mormon practices. Members of the LDS were for the most part sober, hardworking people industriously making a desert bloom. So long as no one made a big deal out of their practices, the government saw no reason to intervene in the territorial government's running of daily affairs.

All remained quiet until the summer of 1873, when one of Brigham Young's wives renounced her faith in Mormonism and sued him for divorce. Ann Eliza Young then embarked on one of the most successful lecture tours of the nineteenth century. She told audiences that the harmony of polygamous households—so touted by Mormons in defense of the practice—was only superficial, and hid the facts of systematic torture of women, jealousy, violence, and deception.

The uproar that followed her lectures, as well as the prior lack of action by the federal government against what many non-Mormons saw as the sexual enslavement of women in the Utah Territory, prompted Congress to pass the Poland Act in 1874. The law breathed new life into antipolygamy laws already on the books, and provided for appeal of convictions to the U.S. Supreme Court. It is at this point in our story that George Reynolds walks onstage.

George Reynolds

Before he left England, Reynolds had served the Church as a missionary in London, then as an emigration clerk in Liverpool, assisting other Mormons to arrange for travel to the United States. He had a talent for writing, and also worked on various Church newspapers and publications. Reynolds arrived in Utah near the end of the Civil War, and joined a society governed almost entirely by its religious principles, which included proselytizing and polygamy. He embraced the demands of the faith, and vowed his obedience to the authority of the New Dispensation, which Mormons viewed as the communications God had made to Joseph Smith.

Church leaders quickly recognized his abilities, and Reynolds served as private secretary to a succession of Mormon Church presidents. He married Mary Ann Tuddenham and soon settled into life in Salt Lake City. In addition to his duties in the office of the Church presidency, Reynolds taught in his local Sunday school and helped edit the daily *Deseret News*. He had a facility with devotional essays, and often wrote on the duty of obedience that belonged to every saint, which is what the LDS Church called its adherents. In one of his early essays he told his fellow saints that if they asked for advice from priests, they had to obey that advice or risk divine punishment.

In 1871 the Church sent him back to England as a missionary, and while there he edited a Church newspaper in Liverpool. He also met Amelia Jane Schofield. After he returned to Salt Lake City in 1874, he wrote to her proposing that she become his second wife. She agreed, emigrated to Utah, and married him. The peaceful life in Deseret that he had described to her, however, was about to end.

The Test Case

Ann Young's lectures and the resulting Poland Act led federal prosecutors to begin harassing Mormon leaders. George Q. Cannon, Utah's territorial delegate to Congress and the LDS Church's most articulate spokesman in the Capitol, found himself under arrest in Utah on charges of polygamy shortly before he was due to depart for Washington in October 1874. The Poland Act allowed appeal to the Supreme Court, and Mormon leaders believed that since they lived in a federal territory, the First Amendment protected their religious practices. A decision was reached to have a test case, although one without a prominent Mormon leader in the suit. The Church valued Cannon's role in representing Utah in national politics, and wanted to protect him. A younger, less-known defendant might diffuse some of the political animus that a trial might generate.

A few days later, as George Reynolds and his second wife were strolling in Temple Square, they met Cannon, who informed them that Reynolds had been selected to be the model Mormon polygamist in the test case. Supposedly, an arrangement had been made with the local U.S. attorney. In his diary for October 16, 1874, Reynolds wrote, "[I]t has been decided to bring a test case of the law . . . before the court . . . and to present my name before the grand jury." Reynolds then met with the prosecutor and provided the information that resulted in his indictment. It never occurred to him that he should refuse what amounted to an order from Church officials. After his indictment, he entered a plea of not guilty and was released on $2,500 bail.

The decision to use Reynolds for the test case made a great deal of sense. Young (thirty-two years old at the time), handsome, sober, and hardworking, only had two wives, both of them near to him in age. The LDS Church was well aware of the perception held by many non-Mormons that all polygamists were old, grizzled men with a number of very young wives. Reynolds would be an effective antidote to this image, and Church leaders trusted his religious and emotional stamina to withstand the indignities and pressure of a trial. On this point they were right, but the trial itself cost Reynolds dearly—public humiliation and eventual imprisonment. The LDS Church lost as well in its bid to establish a separate and religiously governed society within the United States.

The Mormons—and Reynolds—thought that a deal had been struck with the U.S. attorney, who would prosecute the case in order to get a definitive decision from the Supreme Court on whether or not the Constitution protected plural marriage. To do this all they needed was a verdict—either guilty or not guilty—that could then be appealed; there would be no need for a jail sentence, and Mormons believed that this arrangement had been what they and the prosecutor had agreed to. However, even before the trial they became convinced that the government had reneged on the agreement. Moreover, it appeared that the U.S. attorney had also scared defense witnesses by threatening them with prosecution.

Reynolds had provided a list of witnesses to the government, but at the trial they all suffered from amnesia, and could not recall whether Reynolds had ever been married, if the LDS Church kept records of marriage, and so on. (Given the Church's belief in eternal marriage it is inconceivable that it would not keep records.) Then, at the last minute, the prosecutor called Amelia Reynolds, his second and, at the time, very pregnant wife. She had no idea of the strategy adopted by the Mormon elders, and so testified that yes, she was married to Reynolds, and the ceremony had been performed by the previous witness, a man who testified he could not recall any ceremony.

Although the defense conceded that a plural marriage had occurred, Reynolds's lawyers argued that it did not matter, since the Constitution protected practices mandated by religious beliefs. The judge dismissed this claim, ruling that matters of religious conscience had no place in a criminal trial. The jury deliberated thirty minutes and found Reynolds guilty.

The territorial court threw out the conviction on a technicality, namely that the grand jury that had indicted Reynolds had been improperly impaneled. In his diary Reynolds rejoiced at this "signal triumph" over those who "persecuted the people of God." The U.S. attorney brought him to trial a second time and again secured a conviction, the judge sentenced him to two years of hard labor and a $500 fine, and this time the territorial court upheld the verdict.

Reynolds now turned to the U.S. Supreme Court, which heard oral arguments over two days in November 1878.

The Supreme Court Decides: Belief versus Practice

The chief argument of Reynolds's lawyers was that Congress had no jurisdiction over "domestic relations" in the territories. Any other view would reduce the territories to the status of colonies, and they bolstered this view with language from Chief Justice Roger Taney's opinion in *Dred Scott v. Sandford* (1857), the infamous opinion denying Congress control of slavery in the territories. That decision, which many people believe had helped precipitate the Civil War, had been roundly denounced, and the Court was now dominated by Republicans. If the Mormon lawyers hoped to defend polygamy by relying on a notorious decision upholding slavery, they made a very poor tactical decision.

Chief Justice Morrison Waite wrote for a unanimous Court, and rather than deal with how much power Congress had over the territories, he focused on the question of whether or not a defendant in a criminal case should be able to avoid conviction because he claimed to be obeying a higher religious law when he committed the act. Although the Court had never explored the meaning of the free exercise clause of the First Amendment, Waite was undoubtedly correct in making that the key issue. In effect, the Mormons had said all along that they could freely pursue their religious beliefs, including plural marriage, because of the protection of religion provided in the Constitution. *Reynolds v. United States*, decided on January 4, 1879, is thus the Court's first explication of what free exercise of religion means.

To answer this question, Waite turned to the writings of Thomas Jefferson, the author of the Virginia Statute for Religious Freedom (1786) and a passionate advocate of the separation of church and state. According to Waite, Jefferson's Virginia provided the model to follow, since the 1786 statute was the direct forebear of the First Amendment religion clauses. Waite noted that in the three years after Virginia banned state support for the Anglican Church, it also enacted a law that imposed the death penalty for bigamy and polygamy. In 1802 then-president Jefferson, in his famous "Letter to the Danbury Baptists," declared that the religion clauses had erected a "wall of separation" between church and state, and that while religious "opinions" were absolutely protected, government could reach and punish "actions."

Developing this argument, Waite declared that the Mormons retained absolute freedom to believe in polygamy, but could be punished if they acted on this belief. This distinction between belief, protected by the Constitution, and action, which opened the believer to the law, was well founded in state law across the country, even though Waite spoke primarily about Virginia. This did not mean that the state could punish any religious-based action. But it could make illegal those practices if, and only if, they transgressed "peace and good order." Polygamy, the Court declared, was just such a transgression. Quoting from Professor Francis Lieber, a leading nineteenth-century legal scholar, Waite described a political regime that tolerated polygamy as one that would inevitably become mired in *stationary despotism,* a term that reformers and liberal politicians had long used to describe slavery. Marriage so deeply affected society that civilized nations always regulated it in the interests of social stability and progress. Reynolds's claim of religious freedom not only flew in the face of progress, it violated "the direct and serious prohibition of polygamy . . . in our law [based] on the precepts of Christianity, and the laws of our social nature, supported by the sense and practice of civilized nations."

"Congress was deprived of all legislative power over mere opinion," Waite declared, "but was left free to reach actions which were in violation of social duties or subversive to social order." He then went on to attack polygamy as "odious among the Northern and Western Nations of Europe" and, until the advent of Mormonism, "almost exclusively a feature of the life of Asiatic and African people." The late nineteenth century was an age of social Darwinism, when the rights of blacks were under constant assault and a powerful movement was building to ban Chinese immigration. By tying polygamy to Asians and Africans, Waite set the stage to denounce Mormonism as essentially "un-American" and foreign, even though the faith was entirely the product of native-born citizens of Anglo-Saxon origins. He then compared polygamy to human sacrifice and to the Hindu practice of widows throwing themselves on the funeral pyres of their dead husbands.

Having lined up Thomas Jefferson, the law, civilization, and Christianity against Mormon polygamy, the Court had no trouble finding that plural marriage satisfied the standard of an action that violated "good order" and therefore could be punished. Otherwise, Reynolds's claim of free action, if religiously directed, would undermine the power of law and eventually destroy government itself. The guilty verdict stood, although on May 5, while denying a petition for rehearing, the Court changed the punishment to imprisonment without hard labor.

Reaction to the Decision

Non-Mormons applauded the decision. The *New York Times,* for example, wrote that Mormon arguments for plural marriage as divinely sanctioned were on the same moral ground as claims that "incest, infanticide or murder was a divinely appointed ordinance." In the story about the case, entitled "A Blow against Polygamy," the *Times* expressed pleasure that the "courts have made short work of George Reynolds and his celebrated test case" and struck down this "relic of barbarism."

In Utah, of course, Mormons had a far different reaction. George Woodruff, later to be the Church president, thundered, "I will not desert my wives and my children and disobey the commandments of God for the sake of accommodating the public clamor of a nation steeped in sin and ripened for the damnation of hell." Other Mormon leaders condemned the opinion as a product of fanatical anti-Mormonism, and they swore undying resistance. George Cannon, whose arrest in 1874 had precipitated the entire affair, was especially bitter, perhaps because he felt some responsibility for what had happened to George Reynolds. He attacked the opinion and the justices as out of step with history, bigoted, and just plain wrong when it came to the meaning of religious freedom. "Liberty, then, not of mere opinion alone," he declared, "but religious liberty of practice, is my natural and indefeasible right, and with this neither the legislature nor any branch of the civil power can legitimately interfere." As for the charge that polygamy violated peace and good order, he said, "Our actions do not injure others. We do not trespass on private right or the public peace." Just because human sacrifice is wrong, he asked rhetorically, "does it necessarily follow that human propagation [through plural marriage] is wrong?"

The Persecution and Prosecution of the Mormons

Despite the decision and the federal laws, polygamy continued to thrive in Utah. Prosecutions were rare, however, because local juries refused to convict their neighbors of an action that they themselves condoned. As a result, in 1881 President Chester A. Arthur asked Congress to enact new legislation to deal with the problem of "procuring legal evidence sufficient to warrant a conviction [of polygamy] even in the case of the most notorious offenders." Congress responded with the Edmunds Act of 1882, which imposed civil liabilities on polygamists, depriving both polygamists and their wives of the vote (in Utah women had enjoyed the right to vote since 1870) as well as the ability to hold public office. The law also greatly simplified prosecution of plural marriage. To get around the problems caused by the legal distinction in the Morrill Act between *bigamy* and *polygamy*, the Edmunds Act created a new offense, *unlawful cohabitation*, for which no proof of marriage was required. All the prosecutor had to show was that a man lived in the same household with two or more women who were not his mother or daughters; a marriage license proved of little use, since the law allowed prosecutors to mix cohabitation and polygamy in the same indictment. Prosecutors could also dismiss from the jury pool for cause anyone who was or had been a polygamist, or even one who although a monogamist himself believed it acceptable to have more than one wife. Since Church policy still upheld polygamy, this in effect excluded all believing Mormons from juries hearing polygamy cases.

Still, the Mormons maintained the practice. In 1887, Congress passed its strongest measure yet, the Edmunds-Tucker Act. The law eliminated various evidentiary obligations on the part of prosecutors to prove polygamy, and repealed the common-law proscriptions barring a wife from testifying against her husband in cases involving bigamy, polygamy, or unlawful cohabitation. U.S. marshals could compel witnesses to appear in court, all marriages in the territory had to be licensed and registered, and a Utah law directing that only a spouse could bring a polygamy charge in court was annulled. In addition, and for reasons that are clearly not related to the attack on polygamy, Section 20 completely disenfranchised Utah's women. Women married to polygamists had lost the suffrage in the 1882 Edmunds Act; now, single as well as monogamous women were disenfranchised as well. Last, the Edmunds-Tucker Act stripped the Utah territorial legislature of much of its power, placed the state's school system under federal control, and dismantled the LDS Church. The act directed the attorney general to seize all Church real estate in excess of $50,000 in value. Because the Morrill Act had already revoked the charter the territorial legislature had granted to the Church, theoretically it could no longer own any property, and thus faced the potential seizure of all its assets. It can hardly be doubted that had these laws been passed today, all but the provisions outlawing polygamy would have been struck down as unconstitutional. But Congress enacted these measures in the latter nineteenth century, when many middle-class Protestants saw Mormon teachings and practices as a threat to social stability and morality.

The Mormons, of course, fought all of these laws in federal court, but to little effect. Judges in district courts shared the same prejudices as members of Congress and of the Supreme Court. The religious bias as well as the male chauvinism of the high court (which only a few years earlier had upheld an Illinois law prohibiting women from practicing law—see Chapter 9), its unquestioning acceptance of a monogamistic social order, its willful ignorance of women's interests or desires, and its underlying assumption that the United States was a Protestant Christian nation may strike the modern reader as outrageous, but they fit perfectly into the mental patterns not only of nineteenth-century judges but of the entire population of the country outside of Utah. At the time and even today, polygamy strikes most people as offensive and subversive of the social order.

After deciding *Reynolds*, the Court also heard cases arising from the Edmunds Act of 1882 prohibiting cohabitation. The statute did not provide definitions of cohabitation, and as one might expect from a Victorian-era document, it shied away from the obvious—namely that a man living with one or more women could be presumed to be having sexual intercourse with them. Angus Cannon had married three women before passage of the law; two of his three wives lived with him in separate quarters in the same house, and the third lived nearby. At his trial, Cannon claimed that after the law had been passed he had told two of his wives and their families that he intended to obey the law and not occupy their beds or have intercourse with them, but he could not afford separate houses for all of them. After having been found guilty of cohabitation, Cannon based his appeal on the grounds that the law had been aimed at sexual relationships, and that because he had declared he would not engage in sex with two of the women, he should have been found not guilty.

The Supreme Court upheld the conviction, having dismissed Cannon's testimony as unreliable. Moreover—and in this comment one can read not only the Court's moral compass but that of the country as well—"compacts for sexual non-intercourse, easily made and easily broken, when the prior marriage relations continue to exist . . . [are] not a lawful substitute for the monogamous family which alone the statute tolerates" (*United States v. Cannon* [1886]).

The Court heard several other cases deriving from the cohabitation act. Zealous prosecutors claimed that each year a man lived with more than one woman in a house constituted a separate offense, and thus Lorenzo Snow was charged with three counts of cohabitation, all with the same women, each offense relating to a different year. By the time Snow's appeal reached the high court, prosecutors had started charging cohabitation for six-month periods as separate offenses. In one of the few victories won by the Mormons, the Court in *In re Snow* (1887) found that cohabitation was a "continuous offense, having duration, and not an offense consisting of an isolated act."

Despite this one case, for the most part the Supreme Court ignored the constant dilution of evidentiary requirements needed for conviction, so that by 1890, even if a man were living with only one of his wives and had absolutely no contact with others who resided apart from him, he could still be found guilty under the cohabitation law. A man could live with only one legal wife, and the presumption seemed to be that the first woman he married occupied that position, no matter the circumstances.

In addition to violations of free exercise of religion, the courts seemed willing to tolerate restrictions of due process and criminal procedure in order to stamp out polygamy. The high court upheld the Edmunds Act exclusion of Mormons as petit as well as grand jurors (*Clawson v. United States* [1885]). In *Murphy v. Ramsey* (1884) the Court held that the Utah Commission could disenfranchise practicing polygamists as well as bar them from holding office, and a few years later, in a case from Idaho—a state known for its anti-Mormon sentiments—the Court upheld a constitutional provision barring Mormons from voting. In *Davis v. Beason* (1890), the Court not only justified the exclusion of practicing polygamists because they were little better than common criminals, but also approved the exclusion of those who believed in polygamy or supported an organization that taught about polygamy. In a little over a decade, hatred of Mormons blinded the Court to the core holding of *Reynolds*—that belief by itself could not be punished.

The End of Plural Marriage

In the end the government won its battle against polygamy through economic warfare. The Morrill and Edmunds-Tucker laws made all of the Church's real and tangible property vulnerable to confiscation. By the 1880s this property amounted to a considerable sum.

Under its original charter, issued by the Assembly of the State of Deseret in 1851, the Church had vast powers, none of which were subject to judicial review. Over the years, in part due to the theocratic nature of Mormon society, the Church became a major economic force in Utah, and as a result of Mormon communal doctrines, it held a major portion of the group's collective wealth. The seizure of those assets not only would have harmed the Church but would have dealt a devastating blow to the community. In July 1887 the U.S. attorney for Utah went into court seeking an order to dissolve the Church as a corporate entity and to recover all property held by the Church except for real property acquired before 1862 (the date of the Morrill Act) and valued at less than $50,000.

Here the Mormons should have had a sound constitutional defense, for ever since the *Dartmouth College* case in 1819, the sanctity of corporate charters had been held inviolate. Although the contract clause of the Constitution applied to states, one might have inferred from the Court's defense of property rights in this era that under the Fifth Amendment's due process clause, that same prohibition would have held against the federal government. Even if Congress had the right to nullify the charter, the property should have reverted to the Church's membership and not to the United States.

However, the Court disagreed with each of these contentions in *The Late Corporation of the Church of Jesus Christ of Latter-Day Saints v. United States* (1890). It held that the property had been donated to the Church to promote public and charitable purposes, but instead the Church had used it to spread polygamy, an evil and illegal activity. By depriving the

Church of its property, Congress was doing no more than redirecting the use of the property to its original, charitable purposes. To justify this reasoning, the Court invoked the ancient common-law doctrine of *cy pres*. Under this doctrine, if a charitable trust could not be fulfilled according to its terms, the state would apply it to those purposes most nearly like that of the original intent. The Mormon Church's continued adherence to polygamy made it impossible to return the money to its members, since that would only continue its use for illegal purposes. The majority opinion by Justice David Brewer likened polygamy to barbarism and dismissed out of hand LDS claims to religious freedom. Brewer described the plenary powers of Congress to legislate for the territories in truly sweeping terms.

Chief Justice Melville Fuller, joined by Justices Stephen Field and Lucius Q. C. Lamar, dissented. They agreed that Congress could try to erase polygamy through criminal sanctions, but they argued that it had no authority to confiscate the property either of persons or of corporations that might have been guilty of criminal practices. "I regard it of vital consequence," Fuller wrote, "that absolute power should never be conceded as belonging under our system of government to any one of its departments."

The Court remanded the case to territorial court for final disposition of property. While the lower court considered the issue, Mormon leaders officially abandoned polygamy in October 1890. Church president Wilford Woodruff issued a manifesto declaring that he was prepared to submit to the laws of the United States and that he strongly urged all members of the Church to do so as well. This action did not, however, move the Utah Supreme Court, which refused to give the assets back and named a trustee to oversee the property for the maintenance of Church structures and the relief of the poor. Eventually Congress, satisfied with its victory, and perhaps influenced by Fuller's dissent, passed a resolution returning the Church's personal property in 1894 and its real property two years later.

Congress had won its war against polygamy, and in doing so had seriously crippled the LDS. Aside from the seizure of real and personal property, there had been 1,004 convictions for unlawful cohabitation and 31 for polygamy. Moreover, under Mormon doctrine only men who were morally worthy and financially able to support large families could marry more than one woman. Thus the attack on polygamists was also an attack on Mormon leadership, and it had a devastating effect on the lives of many people. Wives who refused to testify against their husbands often wound up in jail. Many men either went into hiding or obeyed federal law and lived with only one wife, leaving numerous women abandoned and their children fatherless. Federal agents crisscrossed the

Utah Territory looking for polygamists, disrupting communities and invading the privacy of homes.

Continuing Questions

One can see how great the anti-Mormon sentiment was in the latter nineteenth century, and how far the Mormon vision of a theocratic society differed from that of mainstream Protestant America. Yet one wonders whether the Mormon plan would have been acceptable at any time in our history—even today, when pluralism is so much in vogue. There has been a resurgence of polygamy in Utah, a counterpart to the resurgence of conservative religion in other parts of the country. But whereas the Christian Right and Orthodox Judaism are seen as respectable, public opinion still runs strongly against polygamy. Even in a nation as devoted to religious freedom as the United States, the limits to this freedom are apparent.

In the middle of the twentieth century the Court and society in general began to have a greater appreciation of the relationship between religious belief and those activities that flowed directly from that belief, such as the requirement for proselytization or not working on the Sabbath day. In *Sherbert v. Verner* (1963), the Court ruled that the state had to make a reasonable accommodation to satisfy the religious practices of its citizens. But in *Employment Division v. Smith* (1990), the Court reaffirmed the belief-action dichotomy in criminal matters in a case involving the religious use of peyote. Although many constitutional scholars condemned Justice Antonin Scalia's opinion, the case firmly put the basic ruling of *Reynolds*—a distinction between religious belief and action—back at the heart of free-exercise jurisprudence.

George Reynolds's Last Years

George Reynolds himself wound up spending eighteen months in prison, first in Lincoln, Nebraska, and then in a facility outside Salt Lake City. Like most Mormons, he dismissed the Supreme Court opinion with contempt. In response to a query from a reporter, he answered that "to say the Constitution simply grants freedom of religious opinion but not the exercise of that opinion is twaddle."

Reynolds suffered in prison from loneliness and physical privation. At the time authorities did not believe that prisoners deserved anything but minimal accommodations, so during the winter they endured icy conditions, and in the summer dust and heat. But he did have many visitors, especially after being transferred to the Utah prison, and these included his family members as well as Church leaders. Authorities allowed him access to books, and he read widely and wrote on religious topics and scripture. During the period of his incarceration Mormon newspapers and periodicals carried some eighty articles that he wrote. He also began what would be his most famous work, a concordance to the Book of Mormon, which he completed just before his death.

Upon his release he returned to his former position as confidential secretary to the Mormon Church president. He continued writing religious articles, including many on Mormon history. However, the federal government found out that he was still living with both of his wives, although federal law invalidated plural marriage. It indicted him again in 1885, this time for the crime of "unlawful cohabitation." Like other Mormon leaders with more than one wife, Reynolds avoided arrest by resorting to an underground of "safe houses" in Salt Lake City. During this time, he had a "direct revelation" that led him to take a third wife.

In 1890 Reynolds, in his position as secretary to LDS president Wilford Woodruff, participated in preparing the document—known as the "Manifesto"—that officially announced the Church's accommodation to federal authority. Tensions with the larger non-Mormon society soon eased, and Reynolds devoted himself to his writing, publishing a dictionary of the Book of Mormon that identifies and describes every person and place mentioned in it, and is still widely read today. He became a "general authority" of the Church, a position of great honor that marked him as an elder statesman.

Reynolds maintained his writing schedule and other work until he suffered a stroke on New Year's Day, 1907. After that his mental and physical health deteriorated, and he died in 1909.

Cases Cited

Clawson v. United States, 114 U.S. 477 (1885)

Dartmouth College v. Woodward, 17 U.S. (4 Wheat.) 518 (1819)

Davis v. Beason, 133 U.S. 333 (1890)

Dred Scott v. Sandford, 60 U.S. (19 How.) 393 (1857)

Employment Division v. Smith, 494 U.S. 872 (1990)

In re Snow, 120 U.S. 274 (1887)

Late Corporation of the Church of Jesus Christ of Latter-Day Saints v. United States, 136 U.S. 1 (1890)

Murphy v. Ramsey, 114 U.S. 15 (1884)

Reynolds v. United States, 98 U.S. 145 (1879)

Sherbert v. Verner, 374 U.S. 398 (1963)

United States v. Cannon, 118 U.S. 355 (1886)

For Further Reading

Good introductions to the Mormon faith are Klaus J. Hansen, *Mormonism and the American Experience* (1981), and Leonard Arrington, *Brigham Young: American Moses* (1985). Bruce Van Orden has written a full and sympathetic biography in *Prisoner for Conscience' Sake: The Life of George Reynolds* (1992). The legal and constitutional issues are fully explored by Sarah Barringer Gordon in *The Mormon Question: Polygamy and Constitutional Conflict in Nineteenth-Century America* (2002), and in Edwin B. Firmage and Richard C. Mangrum, *Zion in the Courts: A Legal History of the Church of Jesus Christ of Latter-Day Saints, 1830–1900* (1988). The end of Mormon claims to polygamy is explored in Kathryn Daynes, *More Wives Than One: The Transformation of the Mormon Marriage System, 1840–1910* (2001).

The Case of the Reluctant Strike Leader

In re Debs (1895)

IN 1894 THE PULLMAN Palace Car Company, like many other firms, felt the pinch of hard times caused by the economic recession that had begun the previous year. The company had reduced wages five times within twelve months, and in May the workers went out on strike. Members of the American Railway Union, to which many of the Pullman workers belonged, soon refused to handle Pullman cars, and by the end of June, 20,000 men working on railroads emanating from Chicago went out on strike, and eventually 125,000 men and women were striking throughout the country. A boycott declared in sympathy with the Pullman workers quickly escalated into the largest labor stoppage in the country's history, even since then, and affected the nation's entire railroad system.

President Grover Cleveland declared that nothing should be allowed to halt delivery of the mails, and over the protest of Illinois governor John Peter Altgeld, Cleveland sent in troops to quell the disturbance. Federal courts issued injunctions, or orders to cease certain actions; the U.S. Supreme Court weighed in and, despite its own precedents, upheld the use of the injunction in labor disputes, giving conservative courts and industrial management a powerful tool that it would use against organized labor for the next four decades.

George M. Pullman and the Palace Car

George Mortimer Pullman (1831–1897) had come to Chicago in 1859 from upstate New York, where he had taken over and greatly expanded his father's business of physically relocating residential and business structures. He established a similar company in Chicago, and while successful, realized that as the city grew and new buildings were erected with better foundational structures, there would be less need for his services. After exploring several possibilities, he decided on the manufacture and leasing of railroad cars.

After starting modestly in the 1830s, the American railroad system had expanded enormously, as many railroad lines were constructed by private entrepreneurs to serve local and regional needs. By 1850 the nation had 9,000 miles of track, and a decade later the figure had risen to 31,000. Government aid in the form of land subsidies helped fuel the expansion, and the development of the iron business led to the replacement of the old wooden rails with stronger and more durable iron ones. In the North, railroads agreed on a standard width, so that engines and cars from one road could connect to other lines, a development that did not take place in the South until after the Civil War. Smaller lines also merged into larger ones. In 1853 seven companies joined to form the New York Central, and in that same year the Pennsylvania Railroad began running trains directly from Philadelphia to Pittsburgh. On the eve of the Civil War trains crisscrossed the Northeast and Midwest, and ran all the way to St. Joseph, Missouri. Once the Southern states seceded, Congress pushed through a subsidy bill to help build a transcontinental line, ultimately completed in 1869, connecting the West Coast to the more populous eastern part of the country.

Although the greatest impact of the expanded rail lines may have been on the transport of raw materials and finished goods, Pullman's interest lay in passenger travel. He himself frequently used railroads in pursuit of business, but did not like rail journeys. Regular cars were uncomfortable and dirty. He booked a berth in one of the new sleeping cars that were just beginning to appear, and found it unsatisfactory, with cramped beds and inadequate ventilation. He decided to build a better sleeper, one that was not only comfortable but also luxurious, and he persuaded the small Chicago, Alton and St. Louis Railroad to try out his work. The debut of the new cars came in August 1859, and they were an immediate success. Some reviews declared that the Pullman sleepers were comparable to cabins in a steamboat, and the most luxurious way to travel.

Pullman, like most well-to-do men, hired a replacement to serve in his stead in the Civil War, and devoted the years to expanding his business; he even managed to have several of his cars included in the train that bore Abraham Lincoln's body back to Illinois in 1865. He and his company survived the fire that ravaged Chicago in 1871 and the Panic of 1873. By 1879 the Pullman Palace Car Company boasted 464 cars that it leased to railroads, gross annual earnings of $2.2 million, and net annual profits of almost $1 million. In the following decade the company continued to grow. For the most part it leased rather than sold the sleeping cars, charging two cents a mile and also making money on maintenance. The company also manufactured and sold freight, passenger, refrigerator, street, and elevated cars. By the early 1890s the company had a capitalization of over $36 million, and despite the vagaries of the economy, had paid robust dividends for two decades.

Pullman, Illinois

The most unusual aspect of Pullman's business involved the construction of Pullman, Illinois. Pullman, the man, began planning the town in 1879, and in 1880 he purchased 4,000 acres adjacent to his factory and near Lake Calumet, some fourteen miles south of Chicago, for $800,000. Pullman, the town, which opened on January 1, 1881, was not a municipality in the normal sense, but an effort—as George Pullman saw it—to solve the issue of labor unrest and poverty. All 1,300 of the original structures were designed by the architect Pullman hired, and in addition to housing for the workers, included shopping areas, churches, theaters, parks, and a library. The centerpiece was a towered administration building, and the Hotel Florence, named for Pullman's daughter, was erected nearby.

Pullman believed the country air and fine facilities, with labor agitators, saloons, and red-light districts excluded, would produce a happy and loyal workforce. The model planned community became a leading attraction during the 1893 World's Columbian Exposition in Chicago, and the nation's press praised Pullman for his benevolence and vision.

What enthusiasts failed to see was that while Pullman had built a beautiful town—considered by some to be the most healthful place in the country—it was a company town that Pullman ruled like a feudal baron. Within it the housing reflected the social hierarchy of the workforce. Freestanding homes were for executives, row houses for skilled or at least senior workers, tenements for unskilled workers, and rooming houses for common laborers. Pullman prohibited independent newspapers, public speeches, town meetings, or open discussion. His inspectors regularly entered homes to check for cleanliness, and the company could terminate leases on ten days' notice. The church often stood empty because approved (Protestant) denominations would not pay the high rent, and no other congregations were allowed. Professor Richard Ely, the noted Wisconsin economist and progressive social commentator, wrote that the power exercised by Otto von Bismarck, the chancellor who had unified modern Germany, was "utterly insignificant when compared with the ruling authority of the Pullman Palace Car Company in Pullman." One worker allegedly wrote, "We are born in a Pullman house, fed from the Pullman shops, taught in a Pullman school, catechized in the Pullman church, and when we die we shall go to the Pullman Hell."

Although workers were not required to live in the town, they were strongly encouraged to do so, and while rents were higher—averaging $14 a month—many chose to reside there because living conditions were in fact better than in surrounding areas, something even Pullman's critics conceded. As pleasant as the town might be, Pullman expected it to make money. On payday he issued workers who lived in the town two checks, one for the rent and the other for the balance of the wages. A paymaster delivered the checks with a rent collector in tow, and workers had to immediately endorse and hand back the rent check. By 1892 the community was indeed profitable, and had a valuation of more than $5 million.

When business fell off in 1894, Pullman cut jobs and wages, and increased working hours in order to lower costs, but he did not reduce the rents or the prices of goods and utilities in the town. For those who lived in Pullman, wages beyond rent had been barely enough to live on in prosperous times; now there was hardly anything left afterward.

The economic depression, however, did not affect all branches of Pullman's business equally. He enjoyed a near-monopoly in the manufacture of the palace cars, and although he leased no new cars in the first part of 1894, the revenues from cars already leased and from their maintenance and repair continued unreduced. In the manufacture and sale of ordinary cars, he had to compete with other companies, and this part of his business did suffer greatly in 1893. He laid off 40 percent of his workforce and reduced wages several times, but he did not reduce dividends. The workers, driven to desperation, joined the American Railway Union. The union sent a grievance committee to confer with management, and the company fired all of the committee members. On May 11, 1894, the Pullman workers went on strike, and looked to the American Railway Union and its leader for help.

Eugene Victor Debs

Perhaps the most charismatic leader in American labor history, Eugene Victor Debs (1855–1926) would later become the head of the Socialist Party in the United States and run for president of the United States four times, the last from a federal prison cell in Atlanta.

Born in Terre Haute, Indiana, to middle-class parents who had emigrated from Alsace, he dropped out of high school at age fourteen to work as a painter in the railroad yards. He then became a railroad boilerman, and attended business school at night. In 1874 he returned to his parents' home, got a job for a while as a grocery clerk, and then became involved as a founding member and the secretary of a new lodge of the Brotherhood of Locomotive Firemen.* The personable Debs rose quickly in the union ranks, going from an assistant editor of the union magazine to editor and then to grand secretary in 1880, when he was only twenty-five years old. Debs was far from a radical at this time; he spoke out for the Protestant work ethic and civic responsibility. He seemed to be a nice young man on his way up and became well-known in the Terre Haute community, which elected him twice as city clerk and to one term as a Democrat in the Indiana General Assembly.

During these years, Debs's views on organized labor evolved. In general, labor organization in the 1880s and early 1890s was plastic and diverse, and as industrialization changed the marketplace, labor leaders seemed to be seeking some institutional form that would serve as a means of expressing and protecting labor interests. Craft unions, composed only of skilled workers from a particular trade, evolved from earlier craft guilds, but no craft union ever enrolled more than a third of the workmen in its trade, and craft union membership never exceeded 10 percent of the workforce. The Knights of Labor under the leadership of Terence V. Powderly had tried to enlist workers from every field, both skilled and unskilled, and it had reached its peak membership of approximately 730,000 in 1886, and then began a steep decline. Soon after that, Samuel Gompers succeeded in rallying the craft unions to form the American Federation of Labor (AFL), although there would continue to be cries for organizing the unskilled that would, in the 1930s, lead to the Congress of Industrial Organizations.

As general secretary of the Brotherhood of Locomotive Firemen, Debs saw the railroad brotherhoods as elite and exclusive, just the type of craft union that Gompers wanted in the AFL. The brotherhood had succeeded not through militant labor policies and strikes, but because of the cheap insurance policies it secured for members. Debs was clearly no wild-eyed agitator, and in 1883 he wrote an editorial in the *Locomotive Firemen's Magazine* declaring that "we do not believe in violence and strikes as means by which wages are to be regulated, but that all differences must be settled by mutual understanding arrived at by calm reasoning." In a burst of enthusiasm that he would later rue, he even boasted that he had secured Pullman cars for the use of delegates travelling to the brotherhood's national convention.

---

* At this time there were four brotherhoods of railroad workers—engineers, firemen, conductors, and trainmen; eventually there would be six more; the last, that of sleeping car porters, organized in 1924. They had started out as benevolent associations to provide insurance and other benefits, and gradually began to act as unions. They eschewed association with the more conservative American Federation of Labor (although, like the AFL, they were organized by skills) as well as the more radical Knights of Labor. Despite the decline in importance of railroads in American economic life, they are still in existence and function primarily as labor unions.

The American Railway Union

In the late 1880s Debs began to move to the left on the labor/ political spectrum. The defeat of Chicago packinghouse workers in an 1885, strike as well as the loss of several strikes by railroad brotherhoods, seems to have led him to rethink his views. In particular, a disastrous strike against the Chicago, Burlington & Quincy Railroad, in which the firemen were involved, led Debs to change his mind. In February 1888 the engineers and firemen went out on strike, and management scurried to hire men to replace the striking workers. Realizing that the line might be run without them, the strikers tried to tie up the system with a boycott of all Burlington trains. Management then secured an injunction against such a tactic, and Debs watched as unemployed men eagerly lined up to take the place of the strikers, while the other brotherhoods ignored the picket lines. Within a few weeks the strike was completely broken.

Because of the failure of other unions to participate, Debs began to think that the railroad workers needed some form of federation, so that all the brotherhoods would back a strike. He rather naively believed that if all of the railroad workers united, there would be no strikes, because the owners would understand the strength of the union and agree to arbitration of disputes. But most of the brotherhoods did not believe in federation; they had a hierarchy of their own, and looked down upon people they considered unskilled, such as firemen.

So Debs left the brotherhoods to become president of the newly formed American Railway Union (ARU), an organization founded in Chicago in June 1893. Any Caucasian who worked for a railroad in any capacity, from janitor up to engineer, could join. Any ten workers could unite to form a local chapter, which could then affiliate with the national union. Although Debs still preached that there ought to be cooperation between labor and management, the ARU was from the beginning more confrontational than its predecessors, its members frustrated by the failures of the brotherhoods. In the spring of 1894 the ARU struck the Great Northern Railroad, which had ordered three pay cuts in the span of eight months. The owner of the Great Northern, James J. Hill, agreed to arbitration, and this victory brought even more members flooding into the ARU. Debs no doubt felt some vindication. The brotherhoods had spurned his idea of federation, and so he had turned to the ARU. Less than a year after its founding the ARU had 465 locals and 150,000 workers—far more than any of the brotherhoods—and Debs had overnight become one of the nation's most prominent labor leaders. Many workers, especially among the unskilled, believed that the type of industrial unionism that Debs preached—that is, a union covering all jobs, skilled as well as unskilled, in any industry—would bring them the pay and respect they deserved.

The Pullman Workers Strike

Following the pay cuts, when a delegation of Pullman employees complained of the low wages and sixteen-hour days, George Pullman declined even to talk with them, and had them all fired. His vision of a contented labor force living in a clean, healthful environment had no room for organized labor. When President Grover Cleveland later appointed a commission to look into the causes of the strike, workers said that when the town of Pullman had first been opened, the company fired any man who joined a union.

Pullman saw the labor contract as a deal between employer and employee. He wanted to buy labor on certain terms, and some workers were willing to sell their labor on those terms. Each party exercised free will, and the labor agreement represented freedom of choice on both sides. But the contract had no guaranteed duration. If Pullman disapproved of how a man worked, or if economic conditions dictated a reduction in the work-force or a lowering of wages, then Pullman could renegotiate the contract or just let the man go. Workers, in turn, also had options; if they did not like the new terms, they could leave and offer their labor to another employer.

Even in his own time Pullman was something of a dinosaur in terms of his thinking. Other employers emphasized not the labor contract but market conditions. The price of labor would be determined by the laws of supply and demand. If workers had skills that were in demand, employers would offer higher wages; if there was an oversupply of particular skills, the price (the wage) would drop. But even those employers who argued for a market standard did not call for unions. They understood that even by market standards they held the upper hand, and did not want unions to equalize the relationship. On this the market standard owners and the free labor barons like George Pullman agreed.

Following the ARU victory over the Great Northern, 35 percent of Pullman's workforce joined the union. They were eligible because some twenty miles of track ran into or through the company's plant, and the ARU charter said that anyone working in any capacity on railroad lines could join. After Pullman refused to negotiate with a committee, its members voted to strike. On the morning of May 11, 1894, Pullman's workers reported to the plant, but upon a signal by their leader they walked out. Management and labor disagreed about how many men worked at the plant at the time (the union said 4,300, management said 2,850) and how many wanted to keep working (the union said only 300, managers said twice that number), but as soon as the plant had emptied, company representatives posted signs at all the gates: "The works are closed until further notice."

Technically, the ARU had not yet been involved, but union officials had been in Pullman and at the meeting in which the strike vote had been taken, and Pullman workers undoubtedly believed that the ARU would back them. When the ARU gathered in Chicago in June for its first annual convention, the Pullman strike was *the* issue on the delegates' minds.

Debs, on the other hand, perhaps because of his experience with earlier railroad strikes, tried to get the delegates to understand that given the economic downturn and the fact that tens of thousands of workers were unemployed, Pullman would have little trouble getting men to replace those who had gone out. He warned the delegates to proceed cautiously, but few listened.

Instead, they paid more attention to representatives from the company, such as seamstress Jenny Curtis, who headed the "girls' union local"— those women who made carpets, drapes, linen, and seat coverings for the palace cars. Her father had worked for Pullman for thirteen years, she told the convention, and when he died the company demanded that she assume responsibility for the $60 he owed in back rent. When she refused, the company merely began taking deductions from her biweekly paycheck. She only earned between nine and ten dollars, and she paid seven of that for room and board in Pullman. "We ask you to come along with us," she declared, "because we are not just fighting for ourselves, but for decent conditions for workers everywhere." The delegates shouted back that they would. First they would try to talk to Pullman one last time, but the company owner refused to meet with them. Instead his lieutenant, Thomas Wickes, declared that the company would never negotiate with the ARU, and he informed the six members of the company on the delegates' committee that they were fired.

The Boycott

A great deal of sympathy existed in Chicago and elsewhere for the Pullman workers, common men and women tyrannized by an abusive employer and landlord. But how could the ARU support the workers, who, after all, did not exactly work on the railroads? One plan was to refuse to handle Pullman cars, unhitching them from the rest of the train; in fact, some ARU locals in St. Paul and elsewhere had sporadically cut Pullman cars out of trains. Another idea involved a total boycott of railroads using Pullman cars to force them to sever their ties with the Pullman Company.

Even people who supported the idea of a union and the right of workers to strike for better pay and conditions considered a boycott inappropriate. A boycott would affect all the roads, since they all utilized Pullman cars in their passenger trains. A strike was direct action by employees against their employer; a boycott was an indirect weapon that could hurt many more thousands of workers, passengers, and shippers, and in turn aggravate the already severe economic downturn. Debs said he did "not really like the term 'boycott.' . . . There is a deep-seated hostility in the country to the term 'boycott.'" After Pullman declined to talk to them, however, the ARU delegates on June 22 passed a motion to refuse to handle Pullman cars or any trains with Pullman cars unless the company responded to grievances by June 26, and then made the vote unanimous. They then jumped up and began to cheer loudly, although as one commentator noted, it was not certain whether in bravado or anxiety. The union president, Eugene Debs, certainly felt a great deal of anxiety.

Crucial to the success of any boycott would be the switchmen, but as it turned out, switchmen had joined the ARU in large numbers. Debs predicted that the switchmen would refuse to add Pullman cars or to remove them. The railroads would then fire the switchmen and try to replace them, and this in turn would lead other union members to walk out in solidarity, thus bringing more and more trains to a halt.

The scenario played out as Debs had predicted. On June 27, the day after the deadline for the Pullman Company to respond, 5,000 men left their jobs, and fifteen railroads were tied up. By the next day, 40,000 had walked off, and rail traffic was snarled on all lines west of Chicago. On the third day, the number of strikers had climbed to 100,000, and at least twenty lines were either tied up or completely stopped. By June 30, 125,000 workers on twenty-nine railroads had quit work rather than handle Pullman cars. The ARU had few locals in the East or the Old South, but the boycott seemed remarkably effective everywhere else.

Debs may have been pleased by the effectiveness of the boycott, but he was also alarmed by the anger expressed by the workers, anger he feared would break out into violence. He sent telegram after telegram to the locals, urging them to avoid violence and not to stop entire trains. He reminded them that the union was merely refusing to handle Pullman cars; it was not a strike against all railroads. In the course of the strike Debs sent out some 4,000 telegrams, hundreds every day, urging ARU members to eschew violence.

On June 29, Debs spoke at a large and peaceful gathering in Blue Island, Illinois, to get support from fellow railroad workers. After he left, however, groups within the crowd became enraged, set fire to nearby buildings, and derailed a locomotive. Unfortunately for the strikers, it was a mail train. This greatly upset President Grover Cleveland, in that the strike had now prevented the federal government from exercising one of its most important responsibilities, and he vowed that even a postcard deposited in the U.S. mail must be delivered. Even worse, from that point on, the ARU lost control of the situation.

Violence

The first hint of how bad things would get came when groups of strikers began stopping entire trains. Given that most of the 150,000 members of the ARU were either on strike or actively helping the strikers, that other unions had joined the cause, and that wildcat strikes were breaking out against individual lines, violence may have been inevitable. Certainly Debs continued to try to keep things under control, with nonstop telegrams urging locals to show restraint and to eschew violence. But it was no use.

When the sheriffs in Vermilion and Marion Counties informed Governor Altgeld that they feared that local situations would spiral out of control, Altgeld sent six companies of militia to Danville at the beginning of July and another three to Decatur, with orders to quell any rioting and clear the way for the trains.

In Chicago, mobs, which the U.S. Strike Commission (appointed by Cleveland after the strike had been quelled) described as "composed generally of hoodlums, women, a low class of foreigners, and recruits of the criminal classes," took possession of railroad yards, overturning and burning railroad cars and stealing whatever they could lay their hands on. When Mayor John P. Hopkins requested help, Governor Altgeld sent additional troops to Chicago on July 6, explaining that he had not sent them earlier because local authorities had not requested them.

Judge Grosscup Issues an Injunction

By then, however, the federal government had acted. In Washington a majority of the members of the president's cabinet supported Attorney General Richard Olney's demand that federal troops be sent into Chicago to end a "reign of terror." No evidence existed that the American Railway Union had any part in fomenting the violence. Nonetheless, a great deal of property had been destroyed, twelve people had been killed, and there had been a disruption of the mails.

Acting on orders from Attorney General Olney, federal attorney William A. Woods went into federal court to seek an injunction against the boycott. Woods chose a judge he knew had anti-union sentiments, Peter S. Grosscup, who on July 2 gladly issued an order preventing ARU leaders from "compelling or inducing by threats, intimidation, persuasion, force or violence, railway employees to refuse or fail to perform duties." The injunction, which Grosscup based on both the Sherman Antitrust Act and the Interstate Commerce Act, also prevented the ARU leadership from communicating with their subordinates. Debs, who had been trying to prevent violence, could no longer even send telegrams advising against violence.

For Grover Cleveland, with the derailing of a train carrying the mail and the issuance of an injunction by a federal court, the strike had now become a federal issue, and he ordered troops into Chicago on July 3. Altgeld was outraged when he learned that Cleveland had ordered in federal troops, and immediately wired the president, saying, "surely the facts have not been correctly presented to you in this case, or you would not have taken the step, for it seems to me unjustifiable. Waiving all questions of courtesy I will say that the State of Illinois is not only able to take care of itself, but it stands ready to furnish the federal Government any assistance it may need elsewhere." Despite Altgeld's repeated protests, Cleveland continued to send in troops, even though state militia seemed quite capable of handling the situation.

Nervous that, given the terms of the injunction, he could no longer exercise any control over the strikers, Debs at first welcomed the troops, thinking they might maintain order and allow the strike and boycott to proceed peacefully. Before long Debs realized that the federal troops were to make sure the trains moved and this would inevitably undermine the boycott. The troops were not a neutral peacekeeper, but an enforcer for the railroads.

The strikers reacted with outrage to the appearance of the troops, and what had been basically a peaceful strike (there had been little or no violence in the railroad yards) turned into mayhem. On July 4, strikers and their sympathizers set off fireworks and tipped over railcars. They then built blockades to prevent troops from reaching the rail yards. ARU leaders could do nothing, prevented by the injunction from any communication with the workers. On July 6, some 6,000 rioters destroyed 700 railroad cars and caused $340,000 of damage in the South Chicago Panhandle yards.

By this time there were 6,000 federal and state troops, 3,100 police, and 5,000 deputy marshals, but they could not contain the violence. On July 7, national guardsmen, after being assaulted, fired into a mob, killing at least four people (some estimates put it nearer to thirty) and wounding many others. With trains at a standstill, railroads lost $4.7 million in revenue ($120 million in current dollars), while the striking workers lost $1.4 million in wages. Violence led to further deaths, and then the strike ran out of steam. The ARU tried to enlist the help of the American Federation of Labor, but the craft unions had little use for the non-skilled ARU workers. Debs then tried to call off the strike, urging that all workers except those convicted of crimes be rehired without prejudice. The General Managers' Association, the federation of railroads that had overseen the response to the strike, refused and instead began hiring nonunion men. The strike dwindled, trains began to move with increasing frequency until normal schedules had been restored, and on August 2 the Pullman works reopened.

By then the original public sympathy for Pullman's workers had all but evaporated. At the peak of the walkout, as many as a quarter-million workers in twenty-seven states had gone on strike, disrupted rail traffic, or rioted. *Harper's Weekly* thought the nation was "fighting for its own existence just as truly as in suppressing the great rebellion." The disruption of the rail system had farmers worried about getting their crops to market, individuals concerned about the mails, and consumers apprehensive over what the strike would do to the price and availability of goods. Ministers preached against the boycott; Congress supported Cleveland's use of troops; and the press, in Chicago and elsewhere, turned against Debs, the union, and labor in general. During the violence the *Chicago Tribune* headed its story with "LAW IS TRAMPLED ON—RIOTOUS EMISSARIES OF DICTATOR DEBS." Jane Addams of Hull House, who supported the strike, had nonetheless been unable to reach her dying sister because of the rail disruption. She later wrote that the series of events "had dispelled the good nature which in happier times envelopes the ugliness of the industrial situation."

The Trial of Eugene V. Debs

On July 7, at the height of the violence, federal officers arrested Debs and four other ARU leaders for violating the terms of the injunction, and all five were soon released on a $10,000 bond. Debs and the others would face two trials, one in civil court for failing to obey the injunction and the other in criminal court for criminal conspiracy. Eventually the government abandoned the criminal charges, but Debs and his codefendants, all officers of the ARU, stood trial for violating the injunction.

At the heart of the government argument was a stack of telegrams Debs had sent, dozens every day, to ARU locals. Even though nearly all of them counseled restraint and abjured violence, they did urge union leaders to get the men to strike and boycott. "Tie up the roads that insist on handling boycotted cars," Debs wired A. P. Merriman in Memphis. "Every true man must quit now and remain out until the fight is won," he declared in identical messages to ARU locals in different parts of the country.

Debs and his counsel tried to argue that the union leadership itself had never been involved in seizing any railroad property or engaged in violence, and therefore they were not in contempt of court and had not violated the injunction. But the close ties among the government attorneys, the railroads, and federal judges made the union argument futile. On December 14, 1894, U.S. circuit court judge William A. Woods ruled that Debs and the others were in contempt of court for violating the original injunction issued on July 2. Woods, who clearly hoped that the trial would lead to a Supreme Court appointment, wrote an overly long opinion that said far more about his own anti-union credentials than it did about the case. He ordered the defendants to serve three to six months in the McHenry County Jail in Woodstock, Illinois. They could remain out on bail while their attorneys, who by now included Clarence Darrow, took an appeal to the U.S. Supreme Court.

The High Court Rules

On March 25 and 26, 1895, former senator Lyman Trumbull, Clarence Darrow, and the distinguished Chicago attorney Stephen Gregory argued for Debs and his fellow defendants. Attorney General Richard Olney, Assistant Attorney General Edward Whitney, and U.S. attorney Edwin Walker represented the government. The galleries of the Old Senate Chamber were packed, and according to the *Chicago Tribune,* "Laboring people thronged every available nook and corner of the courtroom."

Unlike in current practice, where each side presents its entire argument and then is followed by the other, in 1895 the government and defense attorneys took turns, so that the points raised by one could be rebutted by the following speaker. Although the attorneys, especially Darrow, spoke passionately, their arguments to the nine justices essentially followed what they had presented in their extensive briefs.

For the union men, three main points had been emphasized. First, the notion of a judge charging a man with an offense, even a civil offense, and then another judge finding guilt and imposing a jail sentence, deprived the defendants of one of their basic constitutional rights: trial by jury. Second, as Gregory put it, "this injunction was aimed at a strike; these men were imprisoned because they were leaders of a strike." The injunction had not been narrow, but was so broad that it struck at what everyone acknowledged to be part of the freedom of labor, the right to go on strike against intolerable conditions. Judge Grosscup had not been trying to prevent damage, but to cripple the ability of Debs and others to protest against the Pullman Company. Finally, Darrow attacked the very idea that the Sherman Act, aimed at the predatory practices of industrial corporations, had ever been meant to apply to labor unions.

The government argued that the case should never have been accepted by the Supreme Court, since it lacked jurisdiction. The contempt citation was "interlocutory"—that is, provisional or temporary, and not final—and only final decrees could be appealed to the Supreme Court. Everyone understood that this technical point was there only to give the justices a hook if they wanted to dismiss the case as improvidently accepted and thus avoid a ruling. The real heart of the government argument was that the Court indeed had the power to issue such a sweeping injunction, since the union leaders were challenging the authority of the federal government. The government had not only the power but the responsibility to protect interstate commerce and the delivery of the U.S. mail. The Supreme Court should affirm what the lower court had done, since "similar conditions are likely to arise in the future." The government also emphasized that this was not a criminal case; it was not trying to label a strike a "criminal conspiracy," and in fact the government abandoned its efforts to try Debs and the others under that charge.

On May 27, 1895, two months after oral argument, Justice David J. Brewer delivered the unanimous opinion of the Court, and as everyone had expected, upheld the government. He saw two important questions in the case. First, did the federal government have power to prevent obstructions of interstate commerce and the transportation of the mail? Second, did a federal court acting through its equity jurisdiction* have the authority to issue an injunction in support of those efforts to protect interstate commerce and mail delivery? It was clear by this point that the Court had completely rejected all of the arguments made by the defense team. This was how Richard Olney had wanted the case decided—not on whether workers had a right to strike, but on whether the federal government could respond.

Brewer left no doubt that the Constitution unambiguously gave the federal government powers relating to interstate commerce and the mail. "The entire strength of the nation may be used to enforce in any part of the land the full and free exercise of all national powers and the security of all rights entrusted by the Constitution to its care," he said. "The strong arm of the national government may be put forth to brush away all obstructions to the freedom of interstate commerce or the transportation of the mails." This "strong arm" included the army and state militia, which had in fact been called out against the strikers.

Two years earlier, in *Pettibone v. United States,* the Court had reversed a federal conviction for conspiracy to obstruct justice in a labor dispute, ruling that federal courts did not have jurisdiction, directly or indirectly, over a state's criminal process. Because Debs had been imprisoned by a federal court for an offense committed solely within Illinois, the *Pettibone* decision should have led to his release. But Brewer, who had dissented in *Pettibone,* as had all of the justices who had been in the majority in that case, ignored it.

Instead, Brewer developed the idea that the injunction was a special form of relief that could be used to prevent irreparable damage to property that could not be adequately compensated in later actions at law. This use of the injunction had long been available through equity to private parties, but Brewer expanded its use to protect public rights and punish public wrongs. In doing so, he significantly enlarged the federal courts' equity jurisdiction and gave the federal and state governments powerful tools to use against labor.

Brewer made no bones about his dislike of the strike. While one might admire the self-sacrifice of the workers,

---

* In England there were separate civil courts for law and equity. Law cases involved monetary damages, while judges in equity could impose nonmonetary remedies, such as an injunction, to resolve a conflict. The Constitution gave federal courts jurisdiction in both law and equity.

It is a lesson which cannot be learned too soon or too thoroughly under this government of and by the people that the means of redress of all wrongs are through the courts and at the ballot-box, and that no wrong, real or fancied, carries with it legal warrant to invite as a means of redress the cooperation of a mob, with its accompanying acts of violence.

The workers, the strikers, and the union leaders had all been wrong in the Pullman dispute; more generally, in an increasingly industrialized America, workers should rely on the courts and the legislatures to protect their interests. Brewer ignored the fact that most laborers in the country saw the courts and the legislatures as their enemies and not their protectors.

Aftermath

In re Debs was one of a trio of cases decided by the Supreme Court in 1895 that left a widespread impression that the Court was simply a tool of the wealthy and big business interests in the country. In *United States v. E. C. Knight Co.*, it had for all purposes emasculated the Sherman Antitrust Act by announcing such a narrow definition of interstate commerce as to make the act unenforceable. Then, in *Pollock v. Farmers' Loan & Trust Co.*, it had struck down as unconstitutional the income tax provision of the Wilson-Gorman Act of 1894.

The general outcry against the *Pollock* case led to the 1913 adoption of the Sixteenth Amendment, allowing Congress to levy income taxes, while changes of administration as well as personnel on the Court led to a more receptive judicial attitude on the meaning of antitrust law. The effects of the *Debs* case lingered longest, and for the next forty years business interests hostile to labor unions found the courts willing partners in suppressing strikes through injunction. Finally, Congress passed the Norris-LaGuardia Act in 1931, stripping federal courts of the power to issue injunctions in labor disputes.

George Pullman and his enterprises thrived in the years immediately following the strike. He headed a company that built the Metropolitan elevated railway system in New York, and his factory continued to build palace cars for the nation's rail system. The Pullman Company merged in 1930 with the Standard Steel Car Company to become Pullman-Standard, and it built its last car for Amtrak in 1982. After that the company faded away, its plants shut down, and the remaining assets were sold off in 1987.

Labor continued to revile Pullman, and when he died of a heart attack in 1897, he was buried at night in a lead-lined coffin within an elaborately reinforced steel-and-concrete vault. Workers then poured several tons of cement over the vault to prevent his body from being exhumed and desecrated by labor activists.

Debs and his codefendants surrendered themselves at the Woodstock jail in June 1895, and while confined, Debs began his journey from labor activism toward socialism. In January 1897 he formally announced his adoption of his new creed. "The issue," he declared, "is Socialism vs. Capitalism. I am for Socialism because I am for humanity. . . . The time has come to regenerate society—we are on the verge of a universal change."

Debs would lead American socialism for the next three decades, and be the Socialist Party's candidate for president five times. He would oppose American involvement in the First World War, and for his efforts would be convicted of sedition. This would send his case back to the Supreme Court, which once again ruled against him (*Debs v. United States* [1919]).

Cases Cited

Debs v. United States, 249 U.S. 211 (1919)
In re Debs, 158 U.S. 564 (1895)
Pettibone v. United States, 148 U.S. 197 (1893)
Pollock v. Farmers' Loan & Trust Co., 158 U.S. 601 (1895)
United States v. E. C. Knight Co., 156 U.S. 1 (1895)

For Further Reading

The best single book on the subject is David Ray Papke, *The Pullman Case: The Clash of Labor and Capital in Industrial America* (1999). For Pullman, see Liston Edgington Leyendecker, *Palace Car Prince: A Biography of George Mortimer Pullman* (1992), and for the town he built, Stanley Buder, *Pullman: An Experiment in Industrial Order and Community Planning, 1880–1930* (1967). For Debs, see the older but still valuable Ray Ginger, *The Bending Cross* (1949), and Nick Salvatore, *Eugene V. Debs: Citizen and Socialist* (1982). The labor troubles of this period are examined in many works; especially good is Gerald G. Eggert, *Railroad Labor Disputes: The Beginnings of Federal Strike Policy* (1967). There is an enormous amount of primary material in United States Strike Commission, *Report on the Chicago Strike of June–July, 1894* (1895).

The Case of the Almost-White Traveler

Plessy v. Ferguson (1896)

ON JUNE 7, 1892, Homer Plessy walked into the Press Street Depot in New Orleans, bought a first-class ticket to Covington, and boarded the East Louisiana Railroad's Number 8 train. Most passengers who buy tickets and get on a train or a bus or a plane assume that they have embarked on a journey to their destination. Homer Plessy had no such illusions. He expected that he would either be forced off the train or arrested or both, and he was not disappointed. As the train pulled away from the station the conductor asked the light-complected Plessy if he was a "colored man." Plessy said he was and the conductor told him to move to the colored car. Homer Plessy refused. "I am an American citizen," he told the trainman. "I have paid for a first-class ticket, and intend to ride to Covington in the first-class car." The conductor stopped the train, and Detective Christopher Cain boarded the car, arrested Plessy, and forcibly dragged him off the train with the help of a few other passengers. After a night in jail, Plessy appeared in criminal court before Judge John Howard Ferguson to answer charges of violating Section 2 of an 1890 Louisiana law mandating separate railroad cars for white and colored passengers. The case that bears their names gave birth to legalized apartheid in the United States, the era of Jim Crow.

The Freedmen after the Civil War

The Civil War and the Thirteenth Amendment brought an end to slavery, but did not give the former bondsmen either legal or political equality. In fact, the Southern state almost immediately passed a series of laws known as "Black Codes," which, if not enslaving the freedmen, severely restricted their freedoms and put them at the mercy of whites. Opposition to black freedom often took extra-legal forms as well, as the white-sheeted Ku Klux Klan rode the countryside harassing, brutalizing, and sometimes murdering former slaves.

The Reconstruction congresses tried to protect the freedmen through a series of civil rights and enforcement statutes, and also through two more amendments to the U.S. Constitution. The Fourteenth Amendment defined as a citizen of the United States any person born in the country or who had immigrated and been naturalized. It also prohibited the states from denying to any citizen the due process of law or the equal protection of the laws, or from abridging the privileges and immunities attached to citizenship. The Fifteenth Amendment declared that the right to vote could not be denied because of race. During the time when Union troops occupied the former Confederate states, the army protected the freedmen and enforced these rights, while white Southerners seethed with resentment.

A Confederate soldier who returned to New Orleans after the war wrote how he hoped "the day will come when we have the upper hand of those black scondrels [*sic*] and we will have no mercy for them. We will kill them like dogs." His sentiment reflected that of many other whites in the defeated South, but while Northerners evidenced less overt racial prejudice, for the most part white Americans, both North and South, disdained blacks as morally and intellectually inferior, people who would never be able to take their place as equals in the American polis.

By the 1870s the North had tired of the crusade. Slavery had been abolished, laws had been passed protecting the rights of those formerly enslaved, and the Constitution had been amended to safeguard the rights of citizenship. Now the former slaves and their former owners ought to be left alone to work out their new relationship. By the end of the century they had done so, but in a way that guaranteed future strife. The racism that afflicted society in general also affected the Supreme Court, which delivered a devastating blow to efforts to protect the rights of the freedmen in the *Civil Rights Cases* (1883).

In the last of the great Reconstruction statutes, the 1875 Civil Rights Act, the Republican majority in Congress tried to secure by law some semblance of racial equality that could be protected by the government and by courts. While no one expected that such legislation would change the prevailing racial attitudes held by both Northern and Southern whites, the law aimed to protect the freedmen from deprivation of the minimal rights of citizenship.

A critical provision of the Civil Rights Act prohibited racial discrimination in public places, what would later be called "public accommodations," which rested on Section 5—the enforcement clause—of the Fourteenth Amendment. Five cases testing the application of this section rose in both the North and South, and the Supreme Court combined them for a single hearing in March 1883. The government argued that the Thirteenth Amendment not only abolished slavery, but had conferred all the rights of free citizens on the former slaves, while the Fourteenth Amendment had given Congress the power to protect those rights through appropriate legislation.

In his opinion for an 8–1 Court, Justice Joseph Bradley denied both of the government's contentions, and by doing so, robbed the amendments of much of their meaning. Bradley stood on fairly firm ground when he noted that not every example of discrimination against Negroes could be interpreted as a renewal of slavery; therefore the Thirteenth Amendment could not be invoked as a ban on racial prejudice.

Although the Fourteenth Amendment had in fact been drafted specifically to ensure the freedmen's rights, Bradley denied that Congress had any affirmative powers under the amendment. Congress could only legislate in a remedial manner to correct an unconstitutional law. If a state enacted a law that restricted black rights, Congress could then act to right the injustice. In the absence of positive state action, Congress had no power to initiate action in this area. Bradley also held that if a state failed to take action, but by inaction tolerated discrimination—such as exclusion from hotels, restaurants, and clubs—Congress could still not legislate. By this decision the Court in one stroke nullified all congressional power under the Fourteenth Amendment to protect the freedmen and left their fate to the states. It also invited the Southern states not only to tolerate but to encourage private discrimination. The ruling would remain in force until the Court disavowed it in upholding the 1964 Civil Rights Act, nearly a hundred years after the Civil War ended.

Justice John Marshall Harlan entered the lone dissent in the *Civil Rights Cases,* pointing out correctly that the Court had eviscerated the Fourteenth Amendment of its meaning. He also noted the bias in the Court's judgment, since before the war the Court had accorded Congress comparable powers in upholding the various fugitive slave laws. Although he wrote in dissent, Harlan sketched out a theory of "state action" that would become the basis of civil rights jurisprudence several decades later. He utilized the idea of "affected with a public interest," which the Court had expressed in *Munn v. Illinois* (1876), and argued that facilities such as railroads, hotels, restaurants, and theaters filled a public function, a notion that had long been recognized in common law and which served as the basis for regulating these services. If such businesses discriminated, then they did so with the consent of the state; this constituted state action and could be reached under the Fourteenth Amendment, even using Bradley's crabbed view of Section 5 power. Harlan's ideas would be the basis on which the Court built up a civil rights jurisprudence after World War II.

Not only did the *Civil Rights Cases* bar Congress from taking affirmative steps against racial discrimination, but states could allow private discrimination simply by looking the other way. But what if states took positive steps to impose racial segregation? What if they not only tolerated private hotels and restaurants from excluding blacks but required them to do so? Theoretically Congress still had the power to reach this type of state action. But if Congress chose not to act—and by 1883 it was clear that Congress no longer had the will or the desire to interfere in the Southern states—would the courts find the state action in violation of the Fourteenth Amendment?

The Beginnings of Jim Crow

Prior to the Civil War the inferior status of slaves had made it unnecessary to pass laws segregating them from white people. Both races could work side by side so long as the slave recognized his or her subordinate place. In the cities, where most free Negroes lived, rudimentary forms of segregation existed prior to 1860, but no uniform pattern emerged. In the North free blacks also labored under harsh restrictions and often found an even more rigid segregation than in the South.

One might have expected the Southern states to have created some system to segregate the races immediately after the war, but this did not happen. Instead, the confusion of Reconstruction led to a number of trends, any one of which might have become dominant. In some states the legislatures imposed rigid separation, but only in certain areas; Texas, for example, required that every train have one car in which all people of color had to sit. The South had had no real system of public education prior to the Civil War, and as the postwar governments dominated by former slaves and carpetbaggers created public schools, these were as often as not segregated by race. Nonetheless, New Orleans had fully integrated schools until 1877, and in North Carolina former slaves routinely sat on juries alongside whites.

Inconsistent segregation practices dominated North and South well into the 1880s. The picture was far from rosy, however, as racial violence grew in the South and the lynching of blacks reached an all-time high in the 1880s and early 1890s. While upper-class whites may have wanted to find some peaceful accommodation with the freedmen, demagogues like Tom Watson of Georgia fomented racial hatred among poor whites.

But although the practices of segregation may have been inconsistent, the white South stood united in the belief that blacks belonged in a secondary status in society, in which they could not exercise political power and would not threaten the social hegemony of whites. Some historians have seen the beginnings of segregation on public transportation, such as steamboats and railroads, as at least in part gender-based. White women had always enjoyed separate first-class train accommodations, so they could be insulated against the crudeness of the men's smoking car, lower-class whites, and of course slaves and other African Americans, except those who traveled with their mistresses as maids or nannies. The men's equivalent had been the first-class smoking car, with its bar and spittoons. When freed blacks attempted to buy tickets for these cars, the railroads, sensitive to the patronage and power of their white clients, refused.

In 1878, the Supreme Court in *Hall v. DeCuir* ruled that states could not *prohibit* segregation on common carriers such as railroads, streetcars, or riverboats. A dozen years later it approved a Mississippi statute *requiring* segregation on intrastate carriers in *Louisville, New Orleans & Texas Railway v. Mississippi* (1890). In doing so the Court essentially acquiesced in the South's solution to the problems of race relations. Only Justices Harlan and Bradley dissented, on the grounds that such laws, even if confined to intrastate lines, had an inhibitive effect on interstate commerce.

From 1887 to 1892 nine states, including Louisiana, passed laws requiring separation on public conveyances, such as streetcars and railroads. Though they differed in detail, most of these statutes required equal accommodations for black passengers, and imposed fines and even jail terms on railroad employees who did not enforce these regulations. Five of the states also provided criminal fines or imprisonment for passengers who tried to sit in cars from which their race excluded them. The Louisiana Separate Car Act passed in July 1890. In order to "promote the comfort of passengers," railroads had to provide "equal but separate accommodations for the white and colored races" on lines running in the state.

Challenging the Separate Car Act

The measure marked a dramatic and humiliating reversal of fortune for the black and mulatto citizens of Louisiana. Although a slave state, Louisiana in general and New Orleans in particular had always had, because of their French origins, a more tolerant attitude toward people of color than did other Deep South states. In addition to the usual demarcation between black and white, since the 1700s, New Orleans had acknowledged a third class, *gens de couleur libre*, sometimes called Creoles, the freed descendants of European fathers and African mothers, who had enjoyed a great deal of autonomy. Although Louisiana, like most Southern states, had laws against marriage between slaves, it did allow free people of color, whites, and the *gens de couleur* to marry, testify in court against whites, and in some cases inherit property from their fathers. Some became slaveowners themselves, and apparently many of them accumulated significant property. Their social standing, especially in New Orleans, had insulated them from some of the white reaction following the war; for example, public schools in the city had been integrated until 1877. But when whites regained power after the end of Reconstruction in 1877, they saw only two races, and the privileged position of the *gens de couleur* evaporated; from then on they were black as far as the law was concerned.

Gens de couleur helped form the American Citizens Equal Rights Association when the Separate Car bill was introduced, and they pledged to fight it. Among the members of the committee was Louis A. Martinet, a Creole attorney and doctor who had also founded the *New Orleans Crusader,* and he and his newspaper became the leading opponents of the law. After its passage his paper called for both a legal challenge and a boycott of those railroads that had segregated cars. "We'll make a case, a test case," he editorialized in the *Crusader,* and "bring it before the Federal Court on the grounds of invasion of the right of a person to travel through the States unmolested."

Martinet received important help when Albion W. Tourgée, a white lawyer, offered his assistance. Tourgée had fought for the North (and been twice wounded and taken as a prisoner), and after the war had been a lawyer and judge in North Carolina. There he had seen the depredations wrought upon blacks by the Klan and other white terrorist groups, and as a carpetbagger had himself been the victim of some harrowing experiences. He moved back to New York, where he wrote a number of best-selling books, including *A Fool's Errand, by One of the Fools* (1879), a novel based on his experiences during Reconstruction. He used his newfound fame and fortune to advocate for black equality, and founded the National Citizens' Rights Association.

A citizens' committee drawn primarily from the Creole community raised $3,000 to fund a lawsuit, and Tourgée agreed to be lead counsel in the case. But they also needed a local lawyer, since the challenge to the law would have to go through state courts before it could be appealed to the federal system. A white lawyer, James Walker, finally agreed to take the case in December 1891 for a fee of $1,000. (Tourgée did not accept any fee for his involvement, which stretched over a five-year period.)

Martinet did not consider any of the black lawyers in New Orleans competent to raise a constitutional question, since, as he explained, they practiced almost entirely in the police courts.

Tourgée and Martinet considered several possibilities. They could have a black passenger buy a ticket outside of Louisiana and then travel into the state, thus raising a challenge to the law under the commerce clause. They might have a fair-skinned mulatto attempt to enter the ladies' car, but there they ran into the problem, as Martinet noted, that she might not be refused admission. In New Orleans, he wrote to Tourgée, "people of tolerably fair complexion, even if unmistakably colored, enjoy here a large degree of immunity from the accursed prejudice."

But Tourgée wanted someone who was an octoroon, a person who was "of not more than one eighth colored blood," because he believed the winning strategy would be to expose the ambiguities in the definition of race. How did the law, or a train conductor, determine the race of a passenger? "It is a question," Tourgée told his colleague, that the Supreme Court "may as well take up, if for nothing else, to let the court sharpen its wits on." Martinet agreed, and in New Orleans began talking to sympathetic railroad officials who wanted the law overturned for their own financial reasons. It would not do if their test passenger was merely excluded from boarding or even thrown off the train; he would have to be arrested so that a real case existed and he could claim injury in federal court. One railway informed him that it did not enforce the law, while another said that though it opposed the statute as too costly, it did not want to go against it publicly. Then the Louisville & Nashville line agreed to a test case. As it happened, for reasons neither Martinet nor Tourgée expected, their test case fizzled.

On February 24, 1892, the twenty-one-year-old Daniel Desdunes purchased a first-class ticket on the Louisville & Nashville from New Orleans to Mobile, Alabama, and took a seat in the whites-only car. He was arrested according to the plan, and charged with a criminal violation of the Separate Car Act. Tourgée, Martinet, and the local attorney, James Walker, filed a "plea of jurisdiction," arguing that since Desdunes was a passenger in interstate commerce, he had the right and privilege to travel free from any governmental regulation save that of the Congress. Tourgée also introduced his claim that the determination of race was a complex question of both science and law, and so could not be delegated to a train official. The lawyers assumed that their plea would be denied, Desdunes would be convicted, and then they would appeal. Then, on April 19, 1892, the presiding judge, Robert Marr, suddenly disappeared, and no one knew what had happened to him.

While Desdunes's attorney tried to figure out what to do next, on May 25 the Louisiana Supreme Court handed down its decision in

Louisiana ex rel. Abbott v. Hicks. A train conductor on the Texas and Pacific Railway had been prosecuted for seating a black passenger in a white car, and the railway argued that since the passenger was traveling between two states, either the Louisiana law did not apply to interstate travel or, if it did, then it was unconstitutional under the commerce clause. Much to everyone's surprise, the Louisiana high court agreed that regulations of the Separate Car Act could not apply to interstate passengers. Given this development, the new judge in Desdunes's case, John Ferguson, dismissed the case, and Martinet could not have been happier. "Reactionists may foam at the mouth," he trumpeted in the *Crusader,* "but Jim Crow is as dead as a door nail."

Enter Homer Adolphe Plessy

Martinet, of course, knew that the *Abbott* case did not apply to intrastate commerce, that is, travel entirely within the borders of Louisiana, and he and Tourgée began looking for another light-skinned black man to test the law. They found Homer Adolphe Plessy, a shoemaker, a friend of Desdunes's father, and a member of the citizens' committee. Thirty years old at the time, Plessy had already become well-known in the Creole community for his work in several local community betterment groups. Born to *gens de couleur,* Plessy's grandfather, a white Frenchman from Bordeaux, had come to New Orleans after the slave revolt in Haiti in the 1790s. Germaine Plessy married a free mulatto named Catherine Mathieu, and they had eight children, including Homer's father, Adolphe.

The Plessys were an artisan family, and all of the children spoke both English and French. Adolphe was a carpenter, and had he not died when Homer was five, the young Plessy might well have followed him in that trade. Three years after Adolphe's death, his widow Rosa married Victor M. Dupart, a post office clerk from a family of shoemakers. Young Homer chose to follow his stepfather's family and learn the shoemaking trade.

The Dupart family was also involved in a number of benevolent, religious, and social societies in the New Orleans Creole community. Victor had been an active member of the Unification Movement, a civil rights group formed in the 1870s. The group worked across racial lines seeking political equality for all and an end to discrimination, and this commitment influenced Homer. It also led to his acceptance in such socially prominent Creole groups as the Société des Francs-Amis (Society of French Friends), a Creole organization that had existed in New Orleans since the early nineteenth century and that provided medical and funeral expenses for its members.

His first venture into social activism had been in 1887, when he became involved in education reform as vice president of the Justice,

Protective, Educational, and Social Club. The group had unsuccessfully challenged the segregation of Orleans Parish public schools, despite a provision in the Louisiana state constitution that prohibited the establishment of separate schools on the basis of race. Because so many of the city's wealthier white families sent their children to one of nearly 200 private schools, the public schools were beset with financial difficulties and many black children just dropped out and wandered the streets. The Social Club committed its resources to establishing a library and trying to ensure good teachers for the black schools.

Like many of the *gens du couleur*, Plessy could easily have passed for white, and he described himself as "seven-eighths Caucasian and one-eighth African blood," which nonetheless made him colored under the terms of the Separate Car Act. But he and other light-complected Creoles chose not to turn their backs on their African ancestry, and tried to protect the rights they believed the Fourteenth Amendment had given them.

The Separate Car Act in the Courts

After the Committee to Test the Constitutionality of the Separate Car Act had posted a $500 bond so Plessy could be released, the legal maneuvers began. Plessy was not arraigned until October 1892, four months after his arrest, and interestingly the information (a form of indictment) did not include any reference to his race. Once again the trio of attorneys—Martinet, Walker, and Tourgée—entered a plea claiming the act was unconstitutional and therefore the court did not have jurisdiction to hear or determine the facts. And again they claimed that the matter of race, both as to fact and to law, was too complicated to permit the legislature to assign this determination to a railway conductor. They then got to the heart of the matter, the question they would argue on up to the U.S. Supreme Court:

> [The Act] establishes an insidious destinction [*sic*] and discriminates between citizens of the United States based on race which is obnoxious to the fundamental principles of national citizenship, perpetuates involuntary servitude as regards citizens of the colored race . . . and abridges the privileges and immunities of citizens of the United States and rights secured in the XIIIth and XIVth amendments.

After some jockeying among the lawyers, Judge Ferguson agreed with the district attorney that the defense had not established any basis to deny the legitimacy of the act. Plessy's lawyers immediately appealed this ruling to the state supreme court, effectively stopping the trial until that court ruled. In *Ex parte Plessy* (1893) the Louisiana Supreme Court held that the Separate Car Act did not violate either the Thirteenth or the Fourteenth Amendment. Citing the *Civil Rights Cases,* Justice Charles Fenner concluded that the law did not implicate rights guaranteed by the Thirteenth Amendment, since segregation in public facilities did not, in the court's view, constitute a badge (symbol) or an incident of slavery. The sole question at hand, according to Fenner, was whether the law violated some part of the Fourteenth Amendment, and it did not. Restricting passengers to accommodations on the basis of race rested on a well-established principle "that, in such matters, equality, and not identity or community, of accommodations is the extreme test of conformity to the requirements of the Amendment." Neither racially segregated schools nor racially separated facilities violated the equal protection clause even if motivated by some animus, because law did not involve itself in how people felt about persons of a different color or in how race affected social structure. The Separate Car Act was a reasonable exercise of the legislature's policy-making discretion.

The next step would have been an appeal to the federal courts, but Tourgée worried that the makeup of the Supreme Court did not bode well for them. "Of the whole number of Justices," he wrote Martinet, "there is but one who is known to favor the view we must stand on. . . . [Another four would] probably stay where they are until Gabriel blows his horn." That left four who might be persuaded, and Tourgée hoped that with the passage of time one or more of the diehards would be replaced by a justice favorable to their cause. But time did not prove helpful. Between the filing of the initial writ of appeal in 1893 and oral argument in Washington in April 1896, both the general climate and the attitude of the Court hardened. Throughout the country, but especially in the South, conditions for blacks deteriorated.

The Supreme Court Decides

On April 13, 1896, the Supreme Court heard arguments in *Plessy v. Ferguson.* Tourgée, in his brief, began with the claim that because the reputation of being white had considerable economic as well as social and political value, allowing a train employee to arbitrarily determine that a passenger was or was not white violated the constitutional guarantee against the taking of property without due process of law. He went on to describe why being white in the United States was so important and so valuable in terms of occupations open to whites, and the amount of property held by white people, and declared that being white "is the most valuable sort of property, being the master-key that unlocks the golden door of opportunity."

Because the statute also involved the loss of freedom as well as property, it had to rest on the certainty of racial classification, but as he had repeatedly claimed in the lower courts, that determination involved complex questions of law and science. One could not, he claimed, be at all certain in determining race, since over many generations there had been "race-intermixture" so that for great numbers of citizens "the preponderance of the blood of one race or another" was impossible to ascertain.

In the end, he argued, the law had failed to come up with a just standard. In many states even one drop of black blood caused that person to be counted as colored. "Why not count everyone as white in whom is visible any trace of white blood? There is but one reason to wit, the domination of the white race." Altogether, Tourgée listed some nineteen reasons why the Court should hold the Louisiana law unconstitutional, but all of them boiled down to the same basic claim: treating black people separately, forcing them to sit apart, violated both the spirit and the letter of the Fourteenth Amendment by depriving them of equal protection, due process, and the rights and immunities that citizens should enjoy. These clauses gave Homer Plessy affirmative rights, that is, they not only protected him against arbitrary state action but gave him the right to travel and to be treated with the same respect accorded to all citizens. "Justice is pictured as blind," he told the justices, "and her daughter the Law ought at least to be color-blind."

The brief filed by Louisiana attorney general Milton Cunningham essentially followed the arguments submitted to the state supreme court by Lionel Adams, the prosecutor who had handled the Plessy arraignment in Judge Ferguson's court. But Cunningham added a copy of the decision in that case, claiming that because of the short notice he had received he had not had time to prepare a new brief, but that the Louisiana court had answered all of the arguments raised by Plessy's lawyers. He also cited the *Civil Rights Cases* to deny any claim that somehow segregation by race violated the Thirteenth Amendment.

On May 18, 1896, five weeks after oral argument, the Court handed down its ruling, voting 7–1 to uphold the Louisiana law. (Justice David Brewer had been absent for the oral argument and so did not take part in the decision.) Only John Marshall Harlan dissented.

Justice Henry Billings Brown wrote the majority opinion, and it has distorted his historical portrait much as *Dred Scott* distorted that of Roger Taney. From our viewpoint, of course, the opinion reeks of racism and in essence told the South it could treat blacks pretty much as it pleased, as long as it provided equal facilities, even though separate. The decision does have these characteristics, but there is much more. Brown believed strongly in states' rights, and thought that in those provinces where the states had primary responsibility they should be free to act. A few years earlier he had written the majority decision in *Lawton v. Steele* (1894) upholding New York state's exercise of its police powers to control fishing on Lake Ontario, and progressives applauded him when he wrote the decision in *Holden v. Hardy* (1898), confirming Utah's power to regulate the hours of men working in mines. We can accuse Brown of insensitivity, but in terms of his judicial philosophy he was consistent; matters belonging to the states should be left to the policy judgments of the states themselves.

Brown made short work of Tourgée's claim that determining race was far beyond the technical ability of a train conductor. While the statute obviously gave the conductor the authority to make assignments by race, in this case no deprivation of due process occurred because the question of Plessy's race did not "properly arise on the record." The effort by his attorneys in the Supreme Court to make racial determination appear so complex had backfired because they had deliberately not mentioned Plessy's race at the trial court level. One could claim a lack of due process in reviewing an incorrect classification, since that claim had not been raised at the trial.

The reasoning is, of course, a bit disingenuous because everyone knew the whole case revolved around classifying Homer Plessy as white or black. The information against him had indicated that he had been assigned "to the coach used for the race to which he belonged," and the affidavit from Detective Cain described Plessy as "a passenger of the colored race." Plessy's race may not have been so identified in the formal record, but it permeated the case from the initial arrest. (On the other hand, a fact Tourgée carefully avoided, the conductor had not had to make a guess; he had asked Plessy his race, and Plessy had told him he was colored.) Brown did concede that racial reputation constituted a property interest, and had Plessy in fact been white and been forced to sit in the colored coach, the law allowed him to sue the train company for damages.

The crux of the opinion, and the only part that either party cared about, was the constitutionality of legally required separation on the basis of race. By the time of *Brown v. Board of Education* (1954), both the law and the preponderance of public opinion saw segregation as not only unlawful but also designed to categorize blacks as an inferior race. In 1896, however, that was far from the case. Although the Fourteenth Amendment had been intended to establish an absolute equality of all citizens of any color before the law, Brown asserted, "in the nature of things it could not have been intended to abolish distinctions based on color, or to enforce social, as distinguished from political, equality, or a commingling of the two races unsatisfactory to either." The Court considered racial separation by itself to be far different from racial subordination:

> We consider the underlying fallacy of the plaintiff's argument to consist in the assumption that the enforced separation of the two races stamps the colored race with the badge of inferiority. If this be so, it is not by reason of anything found in the act, but solely because the colored race chooses to put that construction upon it. The argument necessarily assumes that if, as has been more than once the case, the colored race should become the dominant power in the state legislature, and should act in precisely similar terms, it would thereby relegate the white race to an inferior position. We imagine that the white race, at least, would not acquiesce in this assumption. The argument also assumes that social prejudices may be overcome by legislation.... But legislation is powerless to eradicate racial instincts, or to abolish distinctions based on physical differences.

Although Brown's opinion has often been cited as the basis for the phrase "separate but equal," those words do not appear in the opinion. The Louisiana Separate Car Act, like most state segregation statutes, required equal facilities in order to claim the constitutional fig leaf that the law did not violate the equal protection clause.

Justice Harlan's Dissent

The lone dissent, by John Marshall Harlan, who had also dissented in the *Civil Rights Cases,* soon achieved mythic status, and he minced no words in rebutting Brown's assertions that the law did not harm those it relegated to separate facilities. "The Constitution does not permit any public authority to know the race of those entitled to be protected." Where Brown had said that all the law did was impose a minor distinction based on race, Harlan declared, "Every one knows that the statute in question had its origin in the purpose, not so much to exclude white persons from railroad cars occupied by blacks, as to exclude colored persons from coaches occupied by or assigned to white persons." The alleged provision of equal accommodations aimed at keeping blacks separate, and this ran directly counter to the constitutional promise that all citizens be treated alike.

The state could not argue the reasonableness of this required separation, since if this could be allowed, then the state could compel blacks and whites to walk on opposite sides of the street, require them to sit in different parts of a courtroom, and even segregate "native and naturalized citizens . . . or Protestants and Roman Catholics." Ironically, at least one of these hypotheticals became public policy in nearly all Southern states, with blacks not only required to sit either in the back of a courtroom or in the balcony but also to use a separate Bible when sworn in as witnesses.

Harlan understood the larger issue involved:

> The white race deems itself to be the dominant race in this country. And so it is, in prestige, in achievements, in education, in wealth, and in power. So, I doubt not, it will continue to be for all time, if it remains true to its great heritage, and holds fast to the principles of constitutional liberty. But in the view of the Constitution, in the eye of the law, there is in this country no superior, dominant, ruling class of citizens. There is no caste here. Our Constitution is color-blind, and neither knows nor tolerates classes among citizens. In respect of civil rights, all citizens are equal before the law.

It was not a question of social equality, as Brown had asserted, but of civil rights. In a phrase that would be taken up and validated six decades in the future, he condemned legal segregation of the races as a "badge of servitude wholly inconsistent with the civil freedom and the equality before the law established by the Constitution."

Finally, to illustrate what he considered the absurdity of the law, he noted that there existed a race of men "so different from our own" that Congress did not permit them to become citizens. But under the Louisiana statute a "Chinaman can ride in the same passenger coach with white citizens of the United States, while citizens of the black race who have all the legal rights that belong to white citizens are yet declared to be criminals if they ride in a public coach occupied by citizens of the white race."

The majority opinion not only was mistaken, Harlan declared, but "will in time prove to be quite as pernicious as the decision made by this tribunal in the *Dred Scott* case." The common government of all, he warned, should "not permit the seeds of race hate to be planted under the sanction of law."

Plessy's Bitter Fruits

Harlan's plea that the "Constitution is color-blind" (a phrase taken from Tourgée's brief for Plessy) fell on deaf ears, not only within the Court but in the country as well. Southern newspapers, of course, approved of the decision, while the black press denounced it. But the surest sign of the changing temper of the country was that where there had been a vociferous protest in the North over the *Civil Rights Cases* thirteen years earlier, the *Plessy* decision caused hardly a ripple. Not only was the response to the decision muted, but the case practically disappeared from the law books for the next half-century. It did not appear in any of the major constitutional law textbooks, or if it did, as only a footnote. Not until the National Association for the Advancement of Colored People began its attack on segregation in the 1940s did the *Plessy* doctrine come under close scrutiny.

In part this is due to the fact that the case really did not change anything at the time. The case affirmed a growing practice and gave it legitimacy. As one historian noted, "what followed *Plessy* then looked considerably like what preceded it." Segregation on public transportation had begun in 1887, and given the racial attitudes of the country at the time, few people expected the Court to try to stop it. The case did, however, give the green light to Southern states to expand the doctrine of segregation, and between 1896 and 1920, Jim Crow—the legal and systematic segregation of the races—triumphed throughout the former slave states. Signs marked "Whites Only" and "Colored" showed up everywhere—in theaters, restaurants, railroad cars, boardinghouses, and even over water fountains. South Carolina prohibited blacks and whites from working together in the same room in textile plants, and from using the same entryways, exits, or lavatories. Mississippi established segregation in hospitals, a practice soon adopted elsewhere, and even forbade white nurses from attending black patients.

Hundreds of Jim Crow laws existed on the books, but the laws themselves do not provide an adequate gauge of the extent of segregation, the harshness with which it was enforced, or the overall racial discrimination in the South. The laws established minimal requirements; in practice, segregation normally went well beyond what the statutes required. Institutionalized and legally enforced segregation bred hatred and distrust among both whites and blacks—just as Harlan had warned—attitudes that would not easily break down even after the Supreme Court reversed itself and declared segregation unconstitutional in 1954.

Coda

Shortly after the high court decided the case, Homer Plessy reported to Judge Ferguson's court to answer the charge of violating the Separate Car Act. He changed his plea to guilty, and paid the $25 fine. For the rest of his life, until he died in 1925, Plessy lived quietly in New Orleans, working as a laborer, warehouseman, and clerk. In 1910 he became a collector for a black-owned insurance company, and continued to be active in the African American community's benevolent and social organizations, such as the Société des Francs-Amis and the Cosmopolitan Mutual Aid Association. Upon his death he was buried in his mother's family tomb in the city's St. Louis Cemetery Number 1, and his obituary merely identified him as the "beloved husband of Louise Bordenave."

Justice Harlan died in October 1911, and in an article commemorating his friend and colleague, Justice Brown spoke about Harlan's dissenting opinion in *Plessy*. Brown conceded that perhaps Harlan had been right, and that the purpose of the law had been not just segregation of the races but subordination of black people.

Cases Cited

Brown v. Board of Education, 347 U.S. 483 (1954)
Civil Rights Cases, 109 U.S. 3 (1883)
Ex parte Plessy, 45 La. Ann. 80 (1893)
Hall v. DeCuir, 95 U.S. 485 (1878)
Holden v. Hardy, 169 U.S. 366 (1898)
Lawton v. Steele, 152 U.S. 133 (1894)
Louisiana ex rel. Abbott v. Hicks, 44 La. Ann. 770 (1892)
Louisville, New Orleans & Texas Railway v. Mississippi, 133 U.S. 587 (1890)
Munn v. Illinois, 94 U.S. 113 (1877)
Plessy v. Ferguson, 163 U.S. 537 (1896)

For Further Reading

The best single book on the case remains Charles A. Lofgren, *The Plessy Case: A Legal and Historical Interpretation* (1988), but one should also see Thomas Brook, ed., Plessy v. Ferguson: *A Brief History with Documents* (1996). For Tourgée see Mark Elliott, *Color-Blind Justice: Albion Tourgée and the Quest for Racial Equality from the Civil War to* Plessy v. Ferguson (2006). Treatment of the former slaves after the Civil War is explored in William Gillette, *Retreat from Reconstruction, 1869–1879* (1979). The starting point for a discussion of segregation is C. Vann Woodward's classic, *The Strange Career of Jim Crow*, which first appeared in 1955. The legal expansion of segregation can be traced in Pauli Murray, *State Laws on Race and Color* (1952). The story can be picked up in the works cited in connection with *Brown v. Board of Education* (ch. 18).

The Case of the Stubborn Baker

Lochner v. New York (1905)

IF *DRED SCOTT* gave its name to the most reviled case in the nineteenth century, then *Lochner v. New York* holds that dubious title for the first half of the twentieth century. For years *Lochner* stood as a code word for conservative activism by a judiciary out of touch with the realities of modern industrial life. Although there have been recent efforts to rehabilitate the jurisprudence of the majority opinion, for more than seven decades the case stood as the symbol of a reactionary court opposing progressive reform.

Industrialization and Protective Legislation

The industrialization of the United States in the decades after the Civil War brought great prosperity to the nation, but it also opened up a Pandora's box of social ills and economic disparities unknown in an earlier and mostly agrarian country. Railroads now crisscrossed the country and, with innovations such as the refrigerated car, opened up eastern markets to midwestern and southern farmers, making it possible to enjoy fresh fruit, vegetables, and meat on a regular basis in the nation's cities. Steel, a key element in building factories, railroads, ships, and machinery, dropped in price from $100 a ton in the mid-1870s to $12 a ton by 1890. The discovery of great quantities of coal made steam power inexpensive, and by 1900, 80 percent of the nation's factories relied on coal and steam rather than the older water power. Inventors like Thomas Edison not only developed new industries, such as the generation and distribution of electrical power, but also created products to be used in the home both to save labor and for recreation, such as sewing machines.

To operate these huge factories and mills entrepreneurs needed workers, and these came from both internal and external migration. Hundreds of thousands of men and women left American farms to work in factories, while millions of immigrants from Europe came to the United States seeking better lives and opportunities. Small cities grew large, while new cities such as Pittsburgh seemed to appear almost overnight. A nation of farms was becoming a nation of cities, a "smokestack America."

The growth and prosperity did not come without a human price. Working in mines, mills, and factories was often dangerous. Owners hired women and children, some as young as six, not only because of their nimbler fingers but also because they worked for lower wages than men. In many industries workers toiled ten or more hours a day, six or seven days a week; in the steel industry, for example, a twelve-hour day remained the norm until after World War I. The sick or injured simply lost their jobs, and if they had no resources of their own relied on family, friends, neighbors, or local charities to survive. A network of laws protected owners not only from efforts by workers to unionize, but even from paying damages to laborers hurt on the job. While life certainly improved for those in the middle and upper classes, it did so on the backs of laboring men, women, and children who seemingly had no voice in either society or politics.

The era of reform we call Progressivism arose in response to the evils that industrialization spawned. In one area in particular, "protective legislation," reformers tried to secure laws, mostly at the state level, to do away with child labor, limit the number of hours a person could work each day, establish safety standards in the workplace, set minimum wages, and create a safety net of employer liability and workmen's compensation to help those injured on the job. Although successful in a number of areas, the final accomplishment of many of these goals would not come until the New Deal in the 1930s. In the early part of the century reformers not only had to work to get their programs enacted by state legislatures, but they had to fight to secure judicial approval as well. In the courts the story of *Lochner*, and of all protective legislation, is a battle between conservative advocates of substantive due process and freedom of contract and reform proponents of the police power.

Substantive Due Process versus the Police Power

The due process clause of the Fourteenth Amendment, according to leading legal thinkers such as Judge Thomas Cooley of Michigan, dealt not only with procedural methods, but also had a substantive aspect that served to protect vested rights in property and prevent the government from any sort of regulation of the market, the workplace, or the labor contract between employer and employee. Another law writer, Christopher Tiedeman of Missouri, noted that the "power of constitutional limitations protects private rights against the radical experimentation of social reformers."

Many courts took this advice seriously. One judge noted disapprovingly the "sentiment favorable to paternalism in matters of legislation," while Judge Robert Earl, speaking for a unanimous New York Court of Appeals in *In re Jacobs* (1885), attacked a state law prohibiting the manufacture of cigars in tenements as trammeling "the application of [the worker's] industry and the disposition of his labor, and thus . . . it deprives him of his property and some portion of his personal liberty." A Georgia judge declared that he knew "of no right more precious, and one which laboring men ought to guard with more vigilance, than the right to fix by contract the terms upon which their labor shall be engaged."

Progressives and conservatives alike recognized that as part of its sovereign powers, a state could control both individual and property rights to preserve the health, safety, and welfare of the people. But while conservatives conceded the existence of this authority, they claimed it had very limited applicability. Progressives, on the other hand, saw the power as far more extensive, allowing the state to intervene actively on behalf of the oppressed and exploited. The police power, declared Oliver Wendell Holmes in *Noble State Bank v. Haskell* (1911), "may be put forth in aid of what is sanctioned by usage, or held by the prevailing morality, or strong and preponderant opinion to be greatly and immediately necessary to the public welfare." Under this expansive reading, the police power could reach almost anything the legislature wished to regulate.

In the police power lay the key to constitutional approval or denial of protective legislation. If courts took a narrow view of the police power, reform measures would face tough sledding; when judges adopted a more liberal interpretation, protective legislation would receive a sympathetic hearing. Merely declaring that certain policies promoted the public good did not by itself bring a statute within the sanction of the police power. The law had to relate specifically and directly to a clearly recognized health or safety objective. Some courts also demanded that the law be "reasonable" as well. Not only did there have to be a threat to the public welfare, but the response by the legislature had to appear appropriate in the eyes of the court. This, of course, meant that conservative judges who did not like any interference in the market could always find a reason to condemn legislation as unreasonable.

In recent years scholars have been revising the picture that progressives painted of a reactionary bench blocking progress. Although one can certainly find cases in which judges struck down protective legislation and invoked the sacred doctrines of freedom of contract and due process, a closer look discloses a different pattern. Common law—that is, judge-made law as opposed to statutes—typically operates after the fact, responding to rather than anticipating new situations and institutions. As society underwent significant changes in the latter nineteenth century, all agencies of government had to deal with these new facts. Even if judges had been prescient, it is unlikely that they would have rushed to approve a wide spectrum of innovative laws, especially since many proposals ran counter to long-established common law principles.

By 1905 a pattern had emerged. Initially, state courts typically reacted negatively to much protective legislation, but then grew accustomed to the idea and began approving it. They had no trouble with child labor laws for the simple reason that for centuries the law had seen minors as special wards of the state, which in its role as *parens patriae*—that is, of sovereign and guardian of children and other disadvantaged persons—could act to protect them. As the public view of child labor as a preventable evil gained public acceptance in the latter nineteenth century, state legislatures responded with a variety of laws mandating school attendance to a certain age or barring children from working in factories, and courts invariably approved them. Similarly, early efforts to establish maximum hours for people working in dangerous environments, such as mining, or for women, also met with judicial approval. But these groups—children, women, and men in dangerous occupations—all fit into classical legal categories of persons under a disability—that is, legally unequal in some respects—and therefore likely to need the protection of the state.

But what about men who were not in dangerous trades? Could the state limit the hours they worked? That is the question the courts asked in *Lochner.*

Bakeshops at the Turn of the Century

Baking was a growth industry in the second half of the nineteenth century. Prior to the Civil War most baking was done in the home, but industrialization drew many women to work in factories, and as fewer found the time to bake at home they turned to local bakeries for their bread. Urbanization contributed to this trend, since tenements usually had no ovens. Even in those apartments with ovens, the cramped conditions with two or more families often sharing quarters made home baking impossible. The number of wage earners in the baking industry went from fewer than 7,000 in 1850 to more than 60,000 in 1900, a rate of increase almost twice that of manufacturing in general. Because a majority of Americans still lived on farms or in small villages, home baking probably still accounted for three-fourths of the bread eaten in the United States; in cities like New York and Chicago, however, most bread came from bakeries.

At the beginning of the twentieth century commercial baking had two major divisions. One was known as the cracker industry, and supplied hardbread, crackers, and hardtack—nonperishable breadstuffs for ocean voyages and overland trips. Like many other industries, smaller firms began to merge with one another, and after a series of price wars culminated in the creation of the National Biscuit Company (Nabisco) in 1898, which controlled 70 percent of the cracker business.

Joseph Lochner was not part of the cracker trade. He owned Lochner's Home Bakery in Utica, New York, a business similar to hundreds of other small bakeries around the country that baked fresh bread and pastries to service a very localized clientele, the neighborhoods in which they were located. Most were very small, and three-fourths of them employed four or fewer people. Most of the owners of these shops were called master bakers, or "boss bakers," in that they had served terms as apprentices or journeymen to other bakers before striking out on their own. It took little capital to start up a bakery, and in many ways baking resembled the garment trades, with boss bakers serving as jobbers and hiring itinerant laborers.

Although there had been some inventions such as a mechanical mixer in 1880 and a molding machine in 1905, bread baking, unlike cracker-making, remained highly labor intensive. One study found that in 1899 only one bakery in ten used power machinery. A boss baker essentially needed only an oven and a place to put it. Since profit margins were low and, lacking any form of mass production, few opportunities existed to improve efficiency, about the only costs over which the boss baker had any sort of control were the wages he paid, how many hours he could work his men, and the rent he paid for his workspace. In cities, the cheapest places available were usually the cellars of the tenements. Since they could not normally be rented out for residence, cellars were often unused, and building owners eagerly accepted the additional income from the bakers. The majority of New York bakers—about 87 percent as late as 1912—worked out of tenement house cellars.

From the bakers' view, the rent was cheap and the floors, whether of wood, dirt, or occasionally concrete, were sturdy enough to support the weight of an oven. These spaces, however, had never been intended for commercial use—in fact, they had not been designed for any use other than storage. Whatever sanitary facilities the tenements had—sinks, baths, and toilets—all drained down to a sewer pipe in the cellar. In the 1880s, when many of the tenements had been constructed, the drain pipes had been made of clay and brick, and even the more modern iron pipes leaked and smelled foul, especially in the heat generated by the baking ovens. In the cellar bakeries the sewer pipes were often encased in wood and used for benches, storage, or even cooling racks for the loaves.

One could hardly imagine a worse place in which to prepare food, or even in which to work. The cellar floors were often damp, either from leaky sewers or rain seepage; dirt walls were the norm, and ceilings usually low. A factory inspector in 1895 reported that ceilings in cellar bakeries ran from a high of eight feet to as low as five and a half feet, a height in which most men would have to stoop to work. There were few windows, so even in daytime little light came in, and ventilation might often be no more than horizontal grates on the outside sidewalk. In the summer workers suffered intense heat, and in winter even the heat of the oven could not keep the place warm. The lack of ventilation also meant that flour dust and fumes, natural in any baking, could not escape. The cellar bakery in 1900 bore no resemblance to the modern bakeshop, with its light, airy workspace and clean, stainless-steel implements, or even to Grandma's kitchen. Everyone who visited these workplaces agreed that they were filthy and that the bread they produced posed a health hazard to consumers.

Working long hours in this environment could not have been beneficial to the health of the workers, either, and work long hours they did, much of it at night. A factory inspector reported that in one bakeshop he had visited the men worked 15 hours a day six days each week, and 24 hours on Thursdays, for a weekly total of 114 hours. (Bakeries in primarily Jewish neighborhoods would have been closed from sundown on Friday to sundown on Saturday.) New York bakers had gone on strike in 1881, and one of their demands was for a 12-hour day, meaning they would not have to work more than 72 or 84 hours a week. In 1895 the typical bakery worker labored 74 hours a week, but many worked longer. Moreover, in baking as elsewhere, nearly everyone worked by the day, not by the hour, and neither custom nor law required additional pay for added hours.

Clearly something had to be done, but what? Unlike industries with large factories, or even the sweatshops of the garment trades, health and safety regulations would be hard to devise and even harder to implement. Bread baking was a marginally profitable business but an essential one in an urban environment. So reformers set out to do what they could, and in 1895 the state assembly passed the New York Bakeshop Act.

Trying to Clean Up the Bakeshops

As with most protective legislation in the Progressive era, several reform groups backed the measure, which was modeled closely on the English Bakehouse Regulation Act of 1863. But while they all agreed that the cellar bakeries had to be cleaned up, the groups had differing agendas.

Public health advocates, for example, believed that both the work and the environment of the cellars led to what was then called *consumption*. That term included any wasting disease and lung disorder, including what we now label *tuberculosis*. Consumption was the most dreaded disease of the nineteenth century, and euphemisms included "captain of death" and "the white plague." Although prevalent, little was actually known about it, and curative potions such as Duffy's Pure Malt Whiskey were sold to prevent "the frightful ravages of these scourges which have so long baffled medical science." Even after the German scientist Robert Koch discovered the tubercle bacillus in 1892, proving that consumption was bacterial and spread by infection, controversy continued over its cause and cure. Not until 1907 did the New York City Health Department implement a program that recognized the bacterial source of tuberculosis and require the reporting of cases.

In 1894 common wisdom accepted the idea that unhealthy environments—like the cellar bakeries—caused consumption, and in fact bakery workers did seem to suffer from a variety of respiratory ailments that probably included tuberculosis but also included problems that we now know were caused by breathing flour dust and working with leaking sewage nearby. That year Edward Marshall, a muckraking reporter for the *New York Press,* wrote a series of stories detailing the unsanitary conditions in the bakeries. Marshall's stories led state factory inspectors to investigate, and they concluded that not only were the workers at risk, but so was the general public that bought and ate their bread:

> Cockroaches and other insects, some of them the peculiar development of foul bakeries and never seen elsewhere, abounded, and as chance willed became part of the salable products. Rats, which seemed not to fear the human denizens of these catacombs, ran back and forth between the piled up bread and their holes.

The inspectors noted that many of the bakers lived in the bakeries, and "hardly ever get out of their baking clothes, that they, as well as their bedding, are in a nauseating filthy condition, totally unfitted to serve as chief factors in the production of the staff of life." The Marshall exposé, confirmed by the state report, gave public health advocates powerful ammunition to push for reform.

Housing reformers wanted to provide safer and healthier housing, and doing away with unsanitary bakeshops in the cellars was a necessary step. In 1890 Jacob Riis published *How the Other Half Lives,* with vivid language and dramatic photographs documenting the crowded and unsanitary conditions in New York's tenement districts. In the two decades that followed reformers used a variety of approaches to try to improve the housing in which the cities' poor lived. Settlement houses organized home visitors to instruct the immigrants on cleanliness; others pushed for parks and playgrounds to alleviate the harsh slums; and, in an effort to ease overcrowding, cities and states passed laws limiting the number of people who could live in an apartment, although with a lack of sufficient inspectors, poor families who needed the rent of one or more boarders kept fitting in as many people as possible.

Reformers also tried to draw a line between work and home. This proved nigh impossible in the garment trades, where many men and women did their work at home. That, however, was "clean" work; cutting and sewing by poor light may have been bad for the eyes, but it did not attract vermin, and they could not sell dirty goods to their jobbers. Cellar baking, on the other hand, violated all of these precepts, and housing reformers also joined the fight to pass the Bakeshop Act.

Purely and simply, labor advocates wanted to reduce the long hours that men toiled in the cellar shops. In fact, when the bill was introduced in February 1895, bakers on New York's East Side were on strike to demand shorter hours and better working conditions. Unions led the fight for the new Bakeshop Act, and the law reflected labor's priorities.

While few bakeries ever grew to the size of the cracker factories, some bake shops, especially in the more middle-class sections of the city, operated at a level well above the cellar bakeries in terms of size and cleanliness, and the workers tended to be of German descent. Most of them belonged to the Bakery and Confectionary Workers International Union, and by the mid-1890s had negotiated contracts that established a ten-hour day and a six-day week. These bakeries— both the owners and their employees—worried about competition from the cellar operations, which could sell their breads at a lower rate because they paid less for labor and rent and worked their men far more than ten hours a day. An article in the *Bakers' Journal* condemned "the cheap labor of the green hand [recent immigrant] from foreign shores," which drove down wages for all and forced honest journeymen "into other walks of life, into the streets, the hospitals, alms houses, insane asylums, penitentiaries and finally death through poverty and desperation."

A key figure in the union was the charismatic Henry Weismann, a German immigrant who had started his American life in California, where he had been active in the union-sponsored Anti-Coolie League, which violently opposed Chinese workers in the United States. Police arrested Weismann for possession of explosives, and after a short jail term he moved to New York and became editor of the *Bakers' Journal*; by 1894 he had become the unofficial leader and spokesman for the union and played a key role in organizing union support for the Bakeshop Act.

The sanitary regulations followed the British law, and included prohibitions against keeping domestic animals in bakeries and workers sleeping in the bakeroom, and sought to establish minimum sanitary standards. The key provision of the New York law from labor's standpoint was a clause limiting biscuit, cake, and bread workers to ten hours of labor per day and sixty per week. The state's health commissioner, Cyrus Edson, endorsed the hours limit as a health measure: "The provision limiting the hours of worktime of the men is especially good from a sanitary standpoint. There is unmistakable evidence that these men are overworked, and that, in consequence of this, they are sickly and unfit to handle an article of food."

Gov. Levi P. Morton put his signature on the law on May 2, 1895, just a few days after it passed with wide margins in both houses of the assembly. Weismann's editorial in the *Bakers' Journal* proclaimed that this day "will stand forth as one of the most memorable days in the history of the great struggle of American bakers for better and more humane conditions." That optimism, however, soon turned sour in the face of reality. Factory inspectors found that most cellar bakeries ignored both the sanitary regulations as well as the limits on hours. For many men the bakery was not only where they worked but also where they lived, so they did not want to report violations, fearing their employer would fire them and evict them from the only home they knew. Reformers called for a new law abolishing cellar bakeries altogether, but that effort failed, as did a demand from boss bakers, tenement house owners, and flour merchants to weaken the law.

Joseph Lochner Challenges the Law

The scene now shifts from the lower East Side of New York, the site of so many of the cellar bakeries, to upstate Utica and Lochner's Home Bakery, which produced cookies, bread, and cakes primarily for early-morning customers on their way to work. A 1908 photograph of the bakery shows a relatively airy and mechanized shop on the first floor of a commercial building, one quite unlike the cellar bakeries sensationalized in Edward Marshall's articles. Because changes in the bread-baking trade occurred fairly rapidly at this time, there is no way to tell if the shop of 1908 is the same as it was in April 1901, when Lochner was charged with violating the Bakeshop Act.

Like most bakery owners, Lochner opposed the act, and in the years after its passage simply ignored it. His employees often had to work late into the night, sometimes sleeping in the bakery before getting up early to prepare for the morning rush. An inspector, probably through the Bakers Union, learned that one of Lochner's employees, Aman Schmitter, worked more than sixty hours one week and swore out a complaint against the bakery owner. Apparently this was not Lochner's first violation, but this time he decided to fight. No one was going to tell him how to run his business—not the workers, nor their union, nor the state of New York.

Although this was a civil rather than a criminal misdemeanor, in New York at that time there was little difference procedurally between the two, and so in October 1901 a grand jury of Oneida County indicted Lochner for violation of the Bakeshop Act. Lochner and his attorney, William S. Mackie, recognized that they had little hope of prevailing at the local or perhaps even the state level, and hoped they would be able to appeal to the Supreme Court. In a pretrial motion Mackie asked for dismissal on the grounds that the grand jury had not properly stated the charges, and that even if true, what his client had done did not constitute a crime. Judge W. T. Dunmore dismissed both objections, and at the beginning of the trial on February 12, 1902, asked Lochner whether he pleaded innocent or guilty. Lochner refused to do either and offered absolutely no defense to the charges, giving Dunmore no choice but to find him guilty and sentence him to pay $50 or spend fifty days in jail.

While the tactics may have been designed to move quickly into the appeals process, the plan did not display great lawyering skills on Mackie's part. He apparently did not take into account the fact that appeals courts do not hear evidence, but decide only questions of law. The facts that help them decide whether the law has been properly applied are supposed to have been determined during the trial, and constitute what is known as the record. Lochner's trial left no record of his defense, and all the state appeals courts had to go on was the unchallenged testimony from the state that one of Lochner's employees worked more than the sixty hours a week permitted by law.

Nevertheless, Lochner and Mackie believed that they would have better luck at the appellate level because New York courts had not been overly friendly to protective legislation. In the famous cigar makers case (*In re Jacobs* [1885]), the state's highest court had invalidated a law banning cigar manufacturing in tenements as a violation of due process.

More recently, the state court had struck down a requirement that state contractors pay their workers the "prevailing wages" (*People ex rel. Rodgers v. Coler* [1901]). But New York courts had also endorsed a wide range of labor regulations as within the police power.

The Appellate Division, the first step in the appeals process, split 3–2 in upholding the law. The judges dismissed the technical claim that the grand jury had not filed a proper indictment, and Judge John M. Davy distinguished the Bakeshop Law from the cigar makers case because the new law did not prohibit baking but merely imposed regulations on how the business was conducted, a legitimate expression of the police power. Two of the judges, however, dissented without filing an opinion, and one assumes that they agreed with Mackie's claim that the law violated due process by infringing too greatly on Lochner's business, especially the right to contract freely with his workers.

Lochner and Mackie then appealed to the Court of Appeals, New York's highest court, and lost in a 4–3 decision. Chief Judge Alton B. Parker declared it "beyond question" that the public had a right to have clean bakeries, and therefore the state could, under its police power, regulate the conduct of the business. Parker played down the fact that labor unions had been the prime movers in securing the hours limitation, and opined that the Bakeshop Act as a whole had clearly been intended to promote public health; the hours limitation was merely part of the overall plan to promote sanitary conditions. In fact, even if the law had not been intended to protect the public health, it still operated to guard the health of the bakers and therefore fell within the ambit of the police powers (*People v. Lochner* [1904]).

Three judges dissented, and two of them wrote opinions. Denis O'Brien believed the hours provision unduly paternalistic and an infringement of the liberty and property of citizens. Moreover, the hours provision, even if attached to a purported health measure, amounted to "class legislation"—that is, laws designed to benefit only one particular group and not all citizens equally. He found no connection between the hours regulations and the sanitary provisions, and could see no way that the hours limitation could be construed as a health measure. Edward Bartlett agreed with O'Brien and condemned the hours limitation as paternalistic and therefore null and void.

The Court of Appeals is the first forum in this case in which the larger battle of due process and freedom of contract came up against the police power. The trial court and the Appellate Division had not bothered to debate this point, the former because Lochner, aside from a pretrial objection, had not really articulated this claim, and the latter because it had not been part of any record. The Court of Appeals could easily have followed this approach, but at least three members of the state high court strongly believed in the concept of the negative state, one that had very few powers, and were willing to pose that against almost every effort by the state to regulate either the market or the workplace.

Union supporters were elated with the decision, but not with how close the vote had been, and realized that there would be an appeal to the Supreme Court. But, they believed, the Court would merely confirm the New York decision; there was nothing to worry about. The New York Association of Master Bakers, which had been paying for at least part of Lochner's legal costs, met shortly after the Court of Appeals decision, and decided to levy a one dollar assessment on each member to pay for the appeal to the Supreme Court. The association also decided to replace Mackie with Frank Harvey Field, a prominent Brooklyn attorney, and Henry Weismann.

Henry Weismann? The same Henry Weismann who had been elected international secretary of the bakers union and had been one of the masterminds in piloting the Bakeshop Act through the New York Assembly? Indeed, this was the same man, now arguing on the opposite side of the question. He had resigned only two years after gaining control of the union, complaining of unbearable antagonism and whispered vilifications. His opponents, however, claimed that he had been forced out because they had caught him with his hand in the till, and offered proof showing that Weismann and several others received kickbacks from the company that printed the *Bakers' Journal,* and that they had also skimmed off some of the money paid by advertisers.

Around this time (it is not clear if it was while he still headed the union or after he had been forced out in 1897), Weismann opened a bakery of his own and joined forces with his old enemies in the Retail Bakers' Association, the organization of bakery owners. He became a shrill critic of the Bakeshop Act, denouncing it through his new role as editor of the *Bakers' Review,* the journal of the bakery owners. He also studied law and passed the New York bar exam. He later wrote that as a master baker, he underwent "an intellectual revolution, saw where the law which I had succeeded in having passed was unjust to the employers." He would now have a chance to prove that in the nation's highest court, which had agreed to hear the case.

The Supreme Court Hands Down a Surprise Decision

Although the Supreme Court had struck down some protective legislation, Lochner's chances nonetheless appeared slim. In *Holden v. Hardy* (1898) the justices had upheld an hours law that applied to miners and men who worked in dangerous occupations. The majority had also upheld three statutes, based on the police power, which had been challenged as class legislation, with the dissenters never getting more than three votes. Even though the Court had within the last several years recognized a substantive due process that protected vested property rights and that freedom of contract also enjoyed constitutional protection, it had not used either of those stratagems to invalidate legislation passed under the police powers.

Field and Weismann decided, first, that their best chance lay in attacking the Bakeshop Act as prohibited class legislation. They condemned the hours provision as class legislation because it applied to some bakers and not to others, and claimed that between one-third and one-half of all bakers did not come within the law's compass. This group included bakery owners; bakers in hotels, restaurants, clubs, and boarding houses; or bakers who were seasonal workers.

Second, they maintained that the hours law did not fall within the legitimate purview of the police power because, unlike in *Holden v. Hardy,* where the law dealt with dangerous trades, baking was not the type of business that needed special regulation. Unlike mining, baking was a generally healthful occupation, and if the Court allowed the law to stand, that "would mean that all trades will eventually be held within the police power."

Third, Field and Weismann denied that the Bakeshop Act was a health measure. Its backers asserted that it had been modeled on the English Bakehouse Regulation Act of 1863, but that law had in fact been a sanitary measure and did not regulate adult working hours. The New York law, Field and Weismann declared, was really an hours regulation on which there had been tacked a few sanitary measures. While the state had the power to enforce true health provisions, it could not enact class legislation under the flimsy excuse of a few sanitary clauses.

Interestingly, the two lawyers also provided an appendix that in many ways anticipated the fact-laden brief that Louis Brandeis would submit a few years later in *Muller v. Oregon* (1908). In the New York Court of Appeals, Judge Irving G. Vann had concurred in upholding the law, but had emphasized that he considered it primarily a sanitary measure because baking was unhealthful. Field and Weismann presented mortality figures from England showing that bakers had a lower mortality rate than the general population. Another English study asserted that bakers had a mortality rate about equal to those of cabinet makers, masons, and clerks, and in the twenty-two occupations studied, bakers had the lowest rate of pulmonary disease. They also included excerpts from medical articles recommending better sanitation and ventilation in bakeries, but not shorter hours. All told, the brief for Lochner was thorough, well argued, and backed by factual data disputing the claim that the Bakeshop Act was a health measure.

In turn, Julius M. Mayer, the New York attorney general, filed only a short brief, probably because he considered it an easy case governed by *Holden v. Hardy*. Mayer made three points: first, Lochner had the burden of proving the statute unconstitutional, as opposed to New York having to prove it was valid; second, the purpose behind the Bakeshop Act had been and remained the protection of the public health and the health of bakery employees; third, since the law was so clearly a health measure, it fell within the legitimate purview of the police power.

The Court heard oral argument on February 23, 1905, and handed down its decision on April 17. Given the Court's recent history in upholding police power regulations, it came as a surprise when Lochner won, albeit by a close 5–4 vote. (There is evidence that in the initial vote the Court had sided 5–4 with New York, and Justice John Harlan had been assigned the opinion. Then one of the justices changed his mind, throwing the case to Lochner, and Harlan's opinion became a dissent.) Chief Justice Melville Fuller, David Brewer, and Rufus Peckham, as anticipated, voted to void the law; none of these three men had ever met a labor law he considered constitutional. More surprisingly, they were joined by Henry Brown and Joseph McKenna, neither of whom had previously voted to invalidate protective legislation. Why they did so in this case has been attributed by some to the creativity of the Field and Weismann brief, especially the appendix, arguing that baking was not an unhealthful profession.

Peckham delivered the majority opinion (there is some internal evidence that it had begun life as a dissent). Surprisingly, in light of Lochner's emphasis that the Bakeshop Act was class legislation, Peckham ignored that issue and employed a fundamental rights/due process analysis. The hours provision clearly interfered with the right of contract, he declared, which the Court had recognized in *Allgeyer v. Louisiana* (1897) as part of the liberty protected by the due process clause of the Fourteenth Amendment. Under *Holden* this liberty could be infringed to protect the public health or the health of workers at risk, but the law always favored liberty of contract. The only way the Bakeshop Act could be sustained was if in fact it protected workers' health, and Peckham clearly did not believe that it did. "Clean and wholesome bread," he asserted, "does not depend on whether the baker works but ten hours a day or only sixty hours per week."

Unlike children, women, or miners, bakers could not be considered a "necessitous" group needing special protection. So unless the state could prove that the hours provisions had been intended to address particular unhealthful aspects of bakery work, the law unconstitutionally violated the fundamental right of liberty of contract. Peckham then asked whether any proof existed to show baking as a dangerous or unhealthful trade, and concluded there was not; in fact, the scientific evidence seemed to say just the opposite. (Peckham here clearly relied on the factual appendix submitted by Field and Weismann, but did not cite it directly.)

Since the law clearly failed to qualify as a health measure, it could not be maintained as a valid exercise of the police power. The act is not, he declared, "within any fair meaning of the term, a health law, but is an illegal interference with the rights of individuals, both employers and employees, to make contracts regarding labor upon such terms as they may think best, or which they may agree upon with the other parties to such contracts." While the sanitary provisions of the law might be valid, the hours regulations definitely were not. He ended by warning state legislatures that the courts would determine whether purported health laws were in fact related to legitimate concerns of the state, and that merely describing a measure as a health law did not make it so. In other words, it did not matter whether state legislatures thought they were enacting health measures or not; that judgment would be made by the courts.

Justice John Marshall Harlan delivered the main dissent, joined by Edward White and William Day, and where Peckham had taken a crabbed view of the police power, Harlan took a far more expansive position. The police power, Harlan wrote, extends at least "to the protection of the lives, the health, and the safety of the public against the injurious exercise by any citizen of his own rights," and the Fourteenth Amendment had never been intended to interfere with this power. Liberty of contract certainly did exist, but it had to be subordinate to the police power. The Court should not be second-guessing the legislature as to the health benefits of a statute, and should only invalidate a purported health measure if it had "no real or substantial relation to those objects, or is, beyond all question, a plain, palpable invasion of rights secured by fundamental law."

Harlan in essence accepted Peckham's belief in freedom of contract as a basic, constitutionally protected right, but believed that when in conflict with a legitimate exercise of the police power, the latter took precedence. They also agreed that when a claimed health measure did not, in fact, deal with health issues, then it should be voided. They differed in that Peckham saw the Bakeshop Act as a labor regulation masquerading as a health measure, since he did not consider baking unhealthful, while Harlan accepted the rationale of the New York legislature that long hours did adversely affect both the health of the bakers and the safety of the public's bread.

Although Harlan's was a well-crafted dissent, for the most part we pay little attention to it today because it has been overshadowed by the brief but memorable dissent filed by Oliver Wendell Holmes Jr. Holmes's dissent instantly became the classic call for judicial restraint and an attack on judges who would substitute their policy preferences for those of the people's duly elected representatives. The majority opinion, he charged, was based on "an economic theory which a large part of the country does not entertain." The state's right to interfere with liberty of contract was well established in history, and he pointed to such examples as laws against usury or Sunday work. A constitution is not supposed to embody a particular economic theory, be it paternalism or laissez-faire. "The Fourteenth Amendment does not enact Mr. Herbert Spencer's *Social Statics*," a famous argument for laissez-faire. The whole idea of liberty, Holmes went on, is perverted whenever it is "held to prevent the natural outcome of a dominant opinion," except when everyone could agree that a particular statute infringed upon fundamental principles. That was not the case here, and he believed a reasonable person would find the hours provisions legitimately related to health, and therefore the law should be upheld.

Lochner's Aftermath

As one might expect, reaction varied according to where one stood in relation to protective legislation. Bakery owners and other businessmen applauded, while organized labor denounced Peckham's opinion as reactionary, confirming their view of the judiciary as a handmaiden to capitalist entrepreneurs and an enemy of working people. Legal scholars then and later condemned the majority opinion as mechanical jurisprudence, as abstract reasoning that did not take into account the facts of real life. Here they overlooked the presence of the factual appendix about bakers' mortality rates in Field and Weismann's brief, one that Peckham clearly relied on, and the fact that the state of New York made no effort to prove its assertion that the hours provision was in fact a health measure. *Lochner* was destined to become a symbol of judicial interference with the democratic process, where judges substituted their own judgment of policy choices for those of the people's elected assemblies. Holmes's dissent became a rallying cry for Progressives, and even though subsequent scholars have tried to show that a legitimate jurisprudential theory undergirded Peckham's opinion, "Lochner" and "Lochnerism" never lived down this odor.

Three years later, however, many reformers believed that the justices had recognized their "error" when a unanimous Court upheld a ten-hour-a-day, sixty-hour-week law for women in *Muller v. Oregon*. The noted Boston attorney and future Supreme Court justice Louis D. Brandeis submitted a brief designed to answer Peckham's arguments. Where Field and Weismann had put factual material into an appendix,

Brandeis made it the heart of his brief—nearly one hundred pages of abstracts from state and medical reports and only two pages of legal citation. The state of Oregon believed that limiting the number of hours women worked was a legitimate health measure, and Brandeis gave the Court proof that it was—proof that New York had failed to advance in support of the Bakeshop Act.

Muller seemed a turning point, and in the following decade the Court rarely overturned state statutes regulating labor. By the time the United States entered World War I most people thought of *Lochner* as a dead letter. In 1917 the Court upheld a maximum hours law applying to all workers, men as well as women (*Bunting v. Oregon*), and *Lochner* seemed to have been overruled *sub silentio*. In the 1920s, though, it came roaring back when the Taft Court, packed with conservatives opposed to protective regulation, struck down one reform law after another, narrowing the scope of the police power as well as how that power affected the public interest. In 1923 the Court struck down a federal minimum wage law that applied to the District of Columbia in *Adkins v. Children's Hospital,* and Justice Sutherland ignored nearly two decades of precedent to revive *Lochner* and the primacy of freedom of contract. That set the stage for the ongoing fight between reformers and conservatives that would reach its peak in the constitutional crisis of the mid-1930s. The road away from *Lochner* began in 1937, when the Court upheld a minimum wage law for women in *West Coast Hotel Co. v. Parrish* (see Chapter 16).

Debate continues today over *Lochner* and its jurisprudence, with the notion of substantive due process—once thought dead and buried—reincarnated to protect rights other than property. Much of the revolution in civil liberties, including the Court's enunciation of a right to privacy, finds its origin as liberty interests in the Fourteenth Amendment, and this presents a paradox for scholars who support those rights but denounce the *Lochner* Court as activist.

Unfortunately, we know little of the man who gave his name to the case. One assumes he rejoiced in his victory in the Supreme Court, and afterward continued to run Lochner's Home Bakery as he saw fit.

Cases Cited

Adkins v. Children's Hospital, 261 U.S. 525 (1923)
Allgeyer v. Louisiana, 165 U.S. 578 (1897)
Bunting v. Oregon, 243 U.S. 426 (1917)
Holden v. Hardy, 169 U.S. 366 (1898)
In re Jacobs, 98 N.Y. 98 (1885)
Lochner v. New York, 198 U.S. 45 (1905)

Muller v. Oregon, 208 U.S. 161 (1908)
Noble State Bank v. Haskell, 219 U.S. 104 (1911)
People ex rel. Rodgers v. Coler, 59 N.E. 716 (N.Y. 1901)
People v. Lochner, 69 N.E. 373 (N.Y. 1904)
West Coast Hotel Co. v. Parrish, 300 U.S. 379 (1937)

For Further Reading

The best single book on the case is Paul Kens, *Judicial Power and Reform Politics: The Anatomy of Lochner v. New York* (1990, rev. ed. 1998). There are few studies of the baking industry, but a useful account is William G. Panschar, *Baking in America* (2 vols., 1956). The fight of labor for shorter hours and the response of the law are examined in Christopher L. Tomlins, *The State and the Unions: Labor Relations, Law, and the Organized Labor Movement in America, 1880–1960* (1985). Sidney G. Tarrow first suggested that *Lochner* should be viewed more as a labor union case than as health or housing reform in "Lochner Versus New York: A Political Analysis," 5 *Labor History* 277 (1964). The most nuanced reexamination of the case and its aftermath is Howard Gillman, *The Constitution Besieged: The Rise and Demise of Lochner Era Police Powers Jurisprudence* (1993). An assertive defense of the majority opinion is David Bernstein, *Rehabilitating Lochner* (2011). To put the case in the larger context of jurisprudential development and change, see William M. Wiecek, *The Lost World of Classical Legal Thought: Law and Ideology in America, 1886–1937* (1998).

The Case of the Gentle Anarchist

Abrams v. United States (1919)

JACOB ABRAMOVSKY was only nineteen years old when he took part in the abortive revolution of 1905 against the czar of Russia. Three years later his sister Manya had saved enough money to bring him to the United States to join her. After his arrival at Ellis Island he changed his name to Abrams and went to work as a bookbinder in New York City, and soon became president of the local union. He remained a radical, and he met his future wife, Mary Damsky, a clothing goods worker, at a May Day rally in 1911. When World War I broke out Abrams became a follower of Peter Kropotkin's theory that capitalism had to be overthrown so it could be replaced by a society founded on principles of cooperation. It was not his anarchism, however, or even his pacifism that got him arrested, but his opposition to American military intervention to suppress the 1917 communist revolution in Russia. Convicted of violating the 1918 Sedition Act, Abrams and his colleagues took their fight all the way to the Supreme Court. Although they lost their appeal, that case began the revolution in free speech jurisprudence that eventually buried the crime of seditious libel and that is at the base of modern First Amendment doctrine.

World War I and Speech

Although World War I was hailed as the war "to make the world safe for democracy," it set off the worst invasion of civil liberties in the nation's history to that time. The government clearly had to protect itself from subversion by enemy agents, but there were few if any examples of

German agents at work in the United States. The laws passed by Congress at the behest of the Wilson administration seemed aimed more at suppressing radical criticism of the government's policies than at ferreting out spies.

In the Selective Service Act, for example, Congress authorized the jailing of anyone who obstructed the military draft. The Espionage Act of 1917, purportedly aimed primarily at treason, also punished anyone making false statements for the benefit of the enemy, seeking to cause disobedience in the armed services, or obstructing recruitment or enlistment in the nation's military branches.

The Trading with the Enemy Act of 1917 granted the postmaster general authority to ban foreign language and other publications from the mails, and Albert Sydney Burleson intended to make full use of those powers. The most conservative member of Woodrow Wilson's wartime cabinet, Burleson used his authority to block mailings of any publication he deemed subversive. When asked about his standards for allowable comment, he replied that it was impermissible to say "that this Government got in the war wrong, that it is in for the wrong purposes, or anything that will impugn the motives of the Government for going into the war," or that "the Government is controlled by Wall Street or munitions manufacturers," or even to criticize the Allies "improperly." When a newspaper, the *Milwaukee Leader*, did in fact raise such questions, Burleson revoked its second-class mailing privileges.

In addition, the 1918 Sedition Act, passed at the urging of western senators and modeled after Montana's statute to curb the radical Industrial Workers of the World, struck out at a variety of "undesirable" activities, and forbade "uttering, printing, writing, or publishing any disloyal, profane, scurrilous, or abusive language" about the American form of government, the U.S. Constitution, the armed forces, or the flag, or to use language designed to bring any of them into "contempt, scorn, contumely, or disrespect." More to the point, as Jacob Abrams would learn, the law did not allow anyone to "willfully urge, incite, or advocate any curtailment of production in this country of any thing or things . . . necessary or essential to the prosecution of the war . . . with intent by such curtailment to cripple or hinder the United States in the prosecution of the war."

Finally, the Immigration Act of 1917 permitted the deportation of alien anarchists or those who believed in the use of force to overthrow the government. In fact, the deportation of alien anarchists had been possible since 1903, and that power had been expanded in the Immigration Act of 1917.

As noted, it is certainly understandable that a government at war would wish to protect itself against subversion. But the evidence indicates that President Wilson, preoccupied first with mobilization and then with peacemaking, gave little thought to the problem and deferred to his conservative advisers, such as Burleson. And they took full advantage of the subjectivity of the laws to decide whom to prosecute, and what comments fell within the very broad definitions of the law.

Jacob Abrams Opposes the War

These laws and similar state statutes caught radicals, pacifists, and other dissenters in an extensive web that they could not escape. The total number of indictments ran into the thousands; the attorney general reported 877 convictions out of 1,956 cases commenced in 1919 and 1920. Four of those convicted were Jacob Abrams and his three codefendants, fellow Russian émigrés Samuel Lipman, Hyman Lachowsky, and Mollie Steimer.

After the war broke out in August 1914, Abrams became more determined to act on his anarchist and pacifist beliefs. He helped write and publish Yiddish-language newspapers that took stands on issues of the day. The first publication with which he was associated was *Der Shturm* (The Storm), succeeded in 1918 by *Frayhayt* (Freedom), which opposed war in general. "The only just war," the editors proclaimed, "is the social revolution."

Had Abrams been just a pacifist, he would not have run afoul of the law. The administration did not prosecute people such as Jane Addams, who opposed all wars. But Abrams also spoke out against American entry into the war, as well as Allied efforts to suppress the 1917 communist revolution in Russia. The *Frayhayt* group, like other anarchists, denounced the United States for sending troops to fight against the communist Red Army. In the summer of 1918 Abrams, Lipman, Lachowsky, and Steimer purchased a small printing press and rented a basement shop in New York's East Harlem. They printed two leaflets, "The Hypocrisy of the United States and Her Allies" and "Workers—Wake Up!" The former denounced President Wilson's decision to intervene in Russia in general terms, but the latter called for concrete action:

Workers, Russian emigrants, you who had the least belief in the honesty of our Government must now throw away all confidence, must spit in the face of false, hypocritical military propaganda which had fooled you so relentlessly, calling forth your sympathy, your help, to the prosecution of the war.

With the money which you have loaned, or are going to loan them [a reference to the war bond drives], they will make bullets not only for the Germans, but also for the Workers Soviets of Russia. Workers in the ammunition factories, you are producing bullets, bayonets, cannon, to murder not only the Germans, but also your dearest, best, who are in Russia and are fighting for freedom. . . .

Workers, our reply to the barbaric intervention has to be a general strike! An open challenge only will let the Government know that not only the Russian Worker fights for freedom, but also here in America lives the spirit of revolution.

Workers, we must not and shall not betray the brave fighters of Russia.

Workers—Wake UP!!

One did not have to be a reactionary to see these sentiments as violating the Sedition Act, and on August 23, 1918, federal agents arrested the four friends and charged them with breaking the law. Also arrested and tried with them was a printer, Hyman Rosnansky, accused of distributing the leaflets, and Gabriel Prober, a bookbinder charged with conspiracy but ultimately acquitted. A grand jury indicted them in September, and they stood trial the following month. Although their actions could hardly be considered a threat to the war effort, their trial garnered considerable attention in the press because of the highly prejudicial remarks of the presiding judge, Henry DeLamar Clayton Jr., a former congressman from Alabama. For his work in helping to pass the 1914 Antitrust Act that bears his name, Wilson rewarded Clayton with a federal judgeship. Because Alabama had few radicals, Clayton was in New York City in the summer and fall of 1918 to help relieve a crowded docket; many of the alleged radicals arrested and tried by the Justice Department lived and wrote in New York.

Abrams tried to explain that the United States itself had been the product of an uprising. "When our forefathers of the American Revolution—" Abrams began, only to be interrupted by Clayton: "Your what? . . . Do you mean to refer to the fathers of this nation as your forefathers?" At another point the judge told the defense lawyer, Harry Weinberger, "I have tried to out-talk an Irishman, and I never can do it, and the Lord knows I cannot out-talk a Jew." Twice Clayton asked the defendants, "Why don't you go back to Russia?" When he charged the jury, the judge declared, "If we have got to meet anarchy, let us meet it right now." It took the jurors little time to find the four guilty, and Clayton sentenced the three men—Abrams, Lipman, and Lachowsky— to twenty years in prison, and Mollie Steimer to fifteen. The four went free on bail pending their appeal.

Attorneys for Abrams and his codefendants based their appeal on the claim that the Sedition Act violated the First Amendment, which says that "Congress shall make no law . . . abridging the freedom of speech." Realistically, they could not have held out much hope for success, given the history of First Amendment jurisprudence in 1919.

Theories of Speech and the Bad Tendency

Various writers and groups had put forward theories that would in essence have taken the First Amendment free speech clause literally— there could be no censorship of any kind—and thus would have been extremely speech protective. They had had little success, in part because of who they were. The Industrial Workers of the World (IWW), the feared and radical "Wobblies," had developed an extensive rationale that would have made speech almost entirely free from governmental regulation. Today we would find that argument not very different from the rationale put forward by contemporary jurists and philosophers, but before World War I, only fellow radicals took the IWW's stance on free speech seriously.

The scholar David Rabban has identified what he terms a "lost tradition of libertarian radicalism," which defended as a primary value individual autonomy against the power of church and state. This tradition reaches back to before the Civil War and can be found in various movements including abolitionism, labor reform, and women's rights. After the passage of the Comstock Acts of 1873 and 1876, which censored materials moving through the mails, libertarian radicals organized in such groups as the National Defense Association (1878) and the Free Speech League (1902), the latter actively involved in defending those whose speech had somehow been restricted, such as Emma Goldman, the radical, and Margaret Sanger, the pioneer of birth control. The leader of the Free Speech League, Theodore Schroeder, worked out a philosophy of free speech premised on the belief that everyone had a right to say whatever they wished and that government had no business acting as a censor. Schroeder rejected theories of speech and of the press that would allow interference by the state should the speech have a "bad tendency," or which would allow publication but then punish the speaker.

Despite the best efforts of the Free Speech League, as well as of writers like Schroeder and law professor Ernst Freund, the overwhelming weight of judicial opinion at the time, in both federal and state jurisdictions, did not recognize the notion that the First Amendment meant exactly what it said—that is, that speech should not be abridged. The expression of unpopular or strange views received little sympathy either from the public at large or the men who sat on the bench.

Most judges relied on Sir William Blackstone, who more than one hundred years earlier in his *Commentaries on the Laws of England* (1765–1769) had argued that the right of free speech precluded prior restraint—that is, the government could not stop a person from speaking or publishing ideas, but the law could punish speakers and writers if their expressions tended to harm the public welfare—a subjective test that gave the British Crown and conservative jurists great leeway.

In the leading Supreme Court decision of this time, *Patterson v. Colorado* (1907), Justice Oliver Wendell Holmes Jr. followed Blackstone's analysis. Thomas Patterson could hardly be described as a radical. A U.S. senator from Colorado and a newspaper publisher, he had actively supported a referendum that provided home rule for Denver. He was outraged when the Republican legislature enlarged the state supreme court and packed it with judges who overturned the results of the popular referendum, and his newspapers published editorials, cartoons, and letters ridiculing the court. The state attorney general brought criminal contempt proceedings against Patterson on behalf of the state court, which in turn fined him and his publishing company $1,000, without allowing him any opportunity to prove the truth of his allegations.

Patterson appealed to the U.S. Supreme Court, but Holmes rejected all of his arguments about freedom of speech and the press. Earlier, as a state judge, Holmes had written, "For the legislature absolutely or conditionally to forbid public speaking in a highway or public park is no more an infringement of the rights of a member of the public than for the owner of a private house to forbid it in his house" (*Commonwealth v. Davis* [1895]). The First Amendment, Holmes wrote in *Patterson*, "prevents all previous restraints upon publications," but allows "the subsequent punishment of such as may be deemed contrary to the public welfare." Interestingly, Holmes dismissed the notion of truth as a defense: "The preliminary freedom extends to the false as to the true; the subsequent punishment may extend as well to the true as to the false." The Supreme Court heard only a few other First Amendment cases before the wartime convictions reached it on appeal in 1919, and all of them essentially followed Blackstone as explained by Holmes in *Patterson*.

Schenck and "Clear and Present Danger"

The first wartime case, *Schenck v. United States* (1919), involved the secretary of the Philadelphia Socialist Party, who had been indicted for urging resistance to the draft. He had mailed out circulars condemning conscription as despotic and unconstitutional, and calling on draftees to assert their rights by refusing induction. Under the terms of the Espionage Act, Schenck had urged unlawful behavior. But did the First Amendment's free speech clause protect him? The justices unanimously said no.

Holmes, probably assigned the case on the basis of his earlier speech opinions, tried to develop a standard based on the common law rule of "proximate causation"—that is, could the action reasonably be seen as the cause of an event? He also took a fairly traditional view of speech as a limited right. One could not, he pointed out, falsely shout "Fire!" in a crowded theater. In a famous passage Holmes attempted to define the limits of speech:

> The question in every case is whether the words are used in such circumstances and are of such a nature to create a clear and present danger that they will bring about the substantive evils that Congress has a right to prevent. It is a question of proximity and degree. When a nation is at war, many things that might be said in time of peace are such a hindrance to its effort that their utterance will not be endured so long as men fight and no Court could regard them as protected by any constitutional right.

The "clear and present danger" test became the starting point for all subsequent free speech cases, and within a week the Court sustained two other convictions under this rule. In *Frohwerk v. United States*, a German-language newspaper had run articles attacking the draft and challenging the constitutionality of the war. In *Debs v. United States*, Holmes accepted a jury finding that in a militant antiwar speech, the socialist leader Eugene V. Debs had intended to interfere with the nation's mobilization.

Holmes Learns from His Critics

The three decisions, as well as the clear and present danger test, upset defenders of free speech, especially because they had come from Holmes, a man they believed to be an ardent libertarian. Legal scholars such as Zechariah Chafee Jr., Ernst Freund, and others criticized Holmes for his insensitivity to the larger implications of free speech. "Tolerance of adverse opinion is not a matter of generosity," Freund declared, "but of political prudence." In an influential article, later expanded into a book, Chafee insisted that the Framers of the First Amendment had more in mind than simply banning censorship. Instead, they had intended to do away with the common law of sedition altogether and make it impossible to prosecute criticism of the government in the absence of any incitement to lawbreaking. In none of these cases, the Harvard professor maintained, could one argue that the defendants had been attempting to incite active violations of the law.

The attacks stung Holmes, not only for their unexpectedness and intensity, but because he thought of himself as the darling of younger progressives, and he greatly enjoyed the hero worship of men like Professor Felix Frankfurter of Harvard and the English political scientist Harold Laski. In correspondence with good friends, Holmes complained that the real problem lay not in his opinions, which adhered to established law, but in the fact that the government had brought these cases in the first place. Even Holmes's most ardent admirers have to admit that at this time his view of freedom of speech was, as one scholar described it, "primitive."

But even as he tried to defend the three opinions, Holmes's own attitude was undergoing a sea change. On a train trip to New York he had encountered Judge Learned Hand of the federal district court in New York, and the two men had a conversation about the First Amendment. Hand had written an opinion, greatly admired by libertarians, in a case entitled *Masses Publishing Co. v. Patten* (1917). The postmaster general had sought to exclude *The Masses* magazine from the mails under the Espionage Act, claiming that it had been willfully critical of the government. Hand had issued an injunction against the postmaster, and had also expounded a test for evaluating the constitutionality of First Amendment challenges to legislation that punished alleged "direct incitement to violent resistance." Instead of using the then-current standard of whether "the indirect result of the language might be to arouse a seditious disposition," a test of great subjectivity and guesswork on the part of judges and juries, Hand wanted them to ask whether "the language directly advocated resistance to the draft." Instead of guessing whether the language might or might not be interpreted one way or another, Hand wanted the trier of fact to ask whether the alleged incitement had any actual chance of success. Wild-eyed rantings by anarchists meant little and posed no dangers because they were not taken seriously, and therefore should be ignored. Hand argued that if the government wanted to prosecute, it had to prove that the words had a real chance of success. Under the Hand test, Jacob Abrams and his fellow anarchists would have gone free. Although the Second Circuit Court of Appeals overrode Hand's decision, Hand's continued correspondence with Holmes tried to move Holmes away from the *Schenck* test.

After the Court recessed Holmes headed for his summer cottage in Beverly, Massachusetts, and prepared, as he usually did, to settle in for three months of reading, not just his older favorites, such as Plato, but new works friends had sent him. According to his journal, in the summer of 1919 Holmes read at least eight works dealing with freedom of speech. His young friend Harold Laski sent him several works, including his own book, *Authority in the Modern State* (1919), in which he asserted that "no mind is in truth free, once a penalty is attached to thought." Although Holmes disagreed with much in E. S. P. Haynes, *The Decline of Liberty in England* (1916), he sympathized with the argument that "the whole collective tendency seems to be toward underrating or forgetting the safeguards in bills of rights that had to be fought for in their day and are still worth fighting for. . . . All of which is but a paraphrase of eternal vigilance is the price of freedom."

Then in late July 1919, Laski, who was then in America, invited the jurist to tea in Cambridge for the express purpose of meeting Zechariah Chafee, at that time an assistant professor at the Harvard Law School. Prior to the meeting Laski gave Holmes a copy of Chafee's June 1919 article in *The New Republic* criticizing the three speech opinions of the previous spring. Laski, whom Holmes respected, endorsed Chafee's argument, and at tea, the young academic—the scion of an aristocratic New England family—showed Holmes how he could take what he had written and convert it into a speech protective policy.

In his article, which he would expand into one of the most important books on speech in the United States, Chafee had said that, with the exception of *Debs*, the others were "clear cases of incitement to resist the draft" and thus covered by the Espionage Act, so no real issues of free speech were concerned. This was far from accurate, but matched Holmes's view. Chafee then went on to call the "clear and present danger" test the Supreme Court test for free speech, which in fact it would become—although after just two decisions, both on the same day, Chafee's characterization was a bit premature.

Chafee then engaged in an amazing bit of *legerdemain*. Earlier views of the First Amendment were incompatible with the "bad tendency" test, but fit in better with Learned Hand's direct incitement criterion. He then argued that Holmes's formula "substantially agreed" with the Hand test, as well as with the history and purpose of the First Amendment speech clause. Clear and present danger, according to Chafee, tracked the common law rule on incitement, "and clearly made the punishment of words for their bad tendency impossible." In fact, the Holmes opinion in *Schenck* does punish speech for a potential bad tendency, and the only way that Chafee could describe the *Schenck* decision as speech protective was to distort the facts of the case to make it appear that Schenck's words had been dangerous.

Debs, however, should have been decided the other way, and Holmes himself had been uncomfortable with it but felt he had to defer to the jury finding. If the clear and present danger test had been properly applied in that case, Chafee suggested, Eugene Debs would have been freed, since while Debs had spoken out against the war he had not urged his audience to break the law. For the test to be more than "a passing observation," it had to be used "to upset convictions for words when the trial judge did not insist that they must create a 'clear and present danger' of overt acts"—that is, in order for their convictions to be upheld, the defendants' words would clearly have to meet the Hand test of direct incitement, even in wartime.

Finally, Chafee talked about a value that had been completely absent from the Holmes opinions, "the social interest behind free speech." If Holmes wanted to utilize the clear and present danger test, then it would have to be applied rigorously, and there would have to be sufficient proof of inherent danger, not just the condemnation of unfamiliar ideas as a bad tendency. Speech had to be protected because "one of the most important purposes of society and government is the discovery and spread of truth." Chafee showed Holmes how to redirect the clear and present danger test, to make it more speech protective. The results of that tea in Cambridge could be seen in the dissent Holmes wrote a few months later in the *Abrams* case.

Abrams: Fighting Faiths

Where Schenck and Frohwerk had been charged under the 1917 Espionage Act, and the justices could limit their focus to draft resistance, the Abrams group had been convicted under the 1918 Sedition Act. Essentially, they had been found guilty of the crime of seditious libel, and thus the real crime was not one of action—trying to cripple the draft—but one of words. The government clearly sought to restrict speech itself. The majority, speaking through Justice John Clarke, however, found the trilogy of cases decided earlier that year to be controlling.

Clarke's opinion is interesting in that in addition to laying out the contents of the two pamphlets the defendants had published, he also attacked the defendants' lack of commitment to the United States. All of the defendants "were born in Russia. They were intelligent, had considerable schooling, and at the time they were arrested they had lived in the United States terms varying from five to ten years, but none of them had applied for naturalization." At the trial four of them had testified in their own behalf, and of these "three frankly avowed that they were 'rebels,' 'revolutionists,' 'anarchists,' that they did not believe in government in any form, and they declared that they had no interest in the government of the United States."

Clarke quoted extensively from the pamphlets, such as the one charging that President Wilson's "shameful, cowardly silence about the intervention in Russia reveals the hypocrisy of the Plutocratic gang in Washington and vicinity." The purpose of the two pamphlets, and of the one entitled "Workers—Wake Up!" especially, "obviously was to persuade the persons to whom it was addressed to turn a deaf ear to patriotic appeals of the government of the United States, and to cease to render it assistance in the prosecution of the war." Nor could the defendants claim, as they did at the trial, that all they wanted to do was prevent injury to the Russian cause, because the only way they could achieve that goal was "defeat of the war program of the United States."

Clarke spoke for seven of the nine justices. Only Oliver Wendell Holmes, joined by Louis Brandeis, dissented. Yet it is that dissent that we remember, not the majority opinion, because it is the beginning of a true speech-protective jurisprudence of the First Amendment.

Holmes briefly reviewed the two pamphlets, and essentially dismissed them as hyperbole, which even under the closest reading could not be thought to have had any chance of interrupting the American war effort. Moreover, if one took the pamphlets at face value, the defendants had been objecting primarily to interference in Russian affairs, and that end could have been achieved without any diminution of American prosecution of the war.

Holmes emphasized that he believed that on the facts the spring trilogy of cases—*Schenck, Frohwerk,* and *Debs*—had been rightly decided, and that the United States "constitutionally may punish speech that produces or is intended to produce a clear and imminent danger that it will bring about forthwith certain substantive evils that the United States constitutionally may seek to prevent. That power undoubtedly is greater in time of war than in time of peace." But after an extensive discussion on the common law of intent, Holmes concluded that the government had failed to prove the required intent. Had Holmes stopped here the case would have been forgotten, and the dissent seen as a muddled product of an aging jurist's mind.

But then Holmes began to talk about the First Amendment and the right of free speech in a way that had been completely absent in the earlier decisions. Even in war the right of free speech is there, as powerful as in peacetime, and government could abridge it only in the face of clear and imminent danger. To do that, however, the government had to prove that the speech would trigger an evil that was clearly dangerous as well as about to happen. That had not happened here. "Nobody can suppose that the surreptitious publishing of a silly leaflet by an unknown man, without more, would present any immediate danger that its opinions would hinder the success of the government arms or have any appreciable tendency to do so."

Holmes could not find the legal basis of intent, nor could he find the factual basis of a clear and present danger. Without proving that these existed, then government had no right to punish publication. "In this case sentences of twenty years' imprisonment have been imposed for the publishing of two leaflets that I believe the defendants had as much right to publish as the government has to publish the Constitution of the United States now vainly invoked by them," he said. Holmes thought the two leaflets not only silly but harmless, but "even if I am technically wrong, and enough can be squeezed from these poor and puny anonymities to turn the color of legal litmus paper," that at the most they deserved only a nominal punishment. As to the wisdom of their beliefs, that should not even have been raised at their trial.

Holmes understood, however, why the defendants and their ideas had been attacked. People who believed wholeheartedly in the logic of their premises opposed those who questioned them. The majority did not silence speech it considered impotent, such as a claim that someone has squared the circle. But they do fear speech that attacks their basic beliefs, even if ineffective, because history shows that new ideas can supplant older ones, and the whole idea of seditious libel—which Holmes argued the First Amendment eradicated—was to stop criticism of the established order.

Holmes's peroration, which some commentators have compared to another great work in defense of free speech, John Milton's *Areopagetica*, made the case for the necessity of a free flow of new ideas:

> When men have realized that time has upset many fighting faiths, they may come to believe even more than they believe the very foundations of their own conduct that the ultimate goal desired is better reached by free trade in ideas—that the best test of truth is the power of the thought to get itself accepted in the competition of the market; and that truth is the only ground upon which their wishes safely can be carried out. That, at any rate, is the theory of our Constitution. It is an experiment, as all life is an experiment. For every year, if not every day, we have to wager our salvation upon some prophecy based upon imperfect knowledge. While that experiment is part of our system I think that we should be eternally vigilant against attempts to check the expression of opinions that we

loathe and believe to be fraught with death, unless they so imminently threaten immediate interference with the lawful and pressing purposes of the law that an immediate check is required to save the country. I wholly disagree with the argument of the government that the First Amendment left the common law as to seditious libel in force. History seems to me against the notion. . . .

I regret that I cannot put into more impressive words my belief that in their conviction upon this indictment the defendants were deprived of their rights under the Constitution of the United States.

Reaction to Holmes's Dissent: Pro and Con

The same men who had criticized Holmes's opinions in the spring trilogy, and who had led him to rethink the issue of the summer, now rushed to praise him. None of his prior opinions, declared Laski, seemed "superior either in nobility or outlook, in dignity or phrasing, and in that quality the French call *justesse*." Felix Frankfurter spoke of "the pride I have in your dissent," while Zechariah Chafee devoted an article in the *Harvard Law Review* to the case, referring to "Justice Holmes's magnificent exposition of the philosophic basis" of the First Amendment. Justice Clarke and the majority had clearly used the clear and present danger test erroneously. Holmes had shown what it truly meant, and as reformulated by him, could not be taken as "marking the true limit of governmental interference with speech and writing under our constitution."

Not everyone proved so enthusiastic. Learned Hand, while happy that Holmes had moved toward a more speech-protective stance, found the effort to distinguish the facts in *Abrams* from those in *Schenck* disingenuous. Other writers, clearly influenced by their animus toward radical thought, attacked the dissent in harsher terms. One law review article called it "most unfortunate and indeed deplorable," and its point of view "a positive menace to society and to this Government." The sharpest attack came from Dean John H. Wigmore of Northwestern Law School, one of the most widely respected legal scholars in America. In an article entitled "*Abrams v. United States*: Freedom of Speech and Freedom of Thuggery in War-Time and Peace-Time" (*Illinois Law Review* [1920]), he warned against the efforts of alien agents to foment revolution in the United States. He never mentioned either Holmes or Brandeis by name, but he condemned the "minority of two" for their "obtuse indifference to the vital issues at stake in August, 1918, and it is ominous in its portent of like indifference to pending and coming issues." For Wigmore, freedom of speech could only be kept from becoming thuggery by limiting its use to those who held the right ideas about society—in other words, only for speech with which the majority of the good people agreed.

Holmes's opinion is still cited, for it is indeed elegant and eloquent. It also sets out a rationale for free speech that is very appealing, the idea of a "marketplace of ideas." In this market there are no "true" opinions, but rather they compete with one another until those with greater force of logic win out. It is the idea that in any competition of ideas, justice, freedom, and other values we prize in a democracy will win out.

But the notion of a marketplace, while appealing to the philosopher, really has little to say about the place of free speech in a democracy. In *Abrams* Louis D. Brandeis joined Holmes's dissent. Within a few years Brandeis had taken over writing dissents in free speech cases, and in his masterpiece, *Whitney v. California* (1927), Holmes joined in the Brandeis opinion. Where the Holmes market analogy is an abstraction, Brandeis in *Whitney* argued that in a democracy citizens had both rights and responsibilities. They had the important duty of taking part in debates over public policy, and they could only do this if they had access to all points of view—those acceptable to the majority as well as those that offended the majority. Only by hearing all these different perspectives could citizens then make up their minds on which policies to support, which candidates to vote for, and which causes to back. To Brandeis the First Amendment guarantee not only protected the speaker but, more importantly, protected the right of the citizen to hear a variety of views.

That notion eventually became the basis of modern First Amendment jurisprudence, building on what Holmes had written in *Abrams* and culminating in *Brandenburg v. Ohio* (1969), which finally put an end to the crime of seditious libel.

The Sad End of Jacob Abrams

What happened to Jacob Abrams? On learning that the Supreme Court had upheld their convictions, Abrams and Samuel Lipman fled to New Orleans, where they hoped to take a boat first to Mexico and then to the Soviet Union. Authorities quickly apprehended them and on December 26, 1919, Abrams, Lipman, and Hyman Lachowsky began serving their sentences at the federal penitentiary in Atlanta. During his time there Abrams worked first in the laundry, then as a typesetter on a prison paper, and also learned to play the banjo. His belief in anarchism never wavered, and he wrote to his wife that he was sustained by his faith in "the new world, the world that you and I dream about."

He served a little less than two years of his twenty-year sentence. His attorney managed to secure a presidential commutation on condition that he leave the country for the Soviet Union at his own expense, and that he never set foot in the United States again. On November 23, 1921, Abrams, his wife Mary, Lipman, Lachowsky, and Steimer sailed for Latvia and then traveled to Moscow. There they found that the revolution they had praised had not yielded the workers' paradise of which they had dreamed. After Lenin had taken power the fragile coalition between communists and anarchists had fallen apart, and the government now deported or even murdered outspoken anarchists. Abrams worked for a while in a steam laundry, but his disenchantment grew. In November 1925 he and Mary left for Paris, and eventually settled in Mexico City. Abrams, already fluent in Russian, Yiddish, and English, soon mastered Spanish as well.

In Mexico City Abrams edited a Yiddish-language newspaper, *The Voice*, but he and Mary were never happy. The terms of his commutation prevented him from even visiting the United States to see old friends, and in the 1930s the virus of anti-Semitism that infected Europe also infected Latin America. A chain smoker, Abrams was diagnosed in 1945 with throat cancer, and he sought a temporary visa that would allow him to go to Philadelphia for treatment at Temple University Hospital. He did not receive it until June 1952, and FBI agents kept him under surveillance during the entire time he was in the country. The treatment, as well as a subsequent operation in Mexico, proved of no avail; Jacob Abrams died on June 10, 1953, at age sixty-seven. Few people remembered him, although his name lives on in a case that helped make the promise of the First Amendment's speech clause a reality.

Cases Cited

Abrams v. United States, 250 U.S. 616 (1919)
Brandenburg v. Ohio, 395 U.S. 444 (1969)
Commonwealth v. Davis, 162 Mass. 510 (1895)
Debs v. United States, 249 U.S. 211 (1919)
Frohwerk v. United States, 249 U.S. 207 (1919)
Patterson v. Colorado, 205 U.S. 454 (1907)
Schenck v. United States, 249 U.S. 47 (1919)
Whitney v. California, 274 U.S. 357 (1927)

For Further Reading

A masterful retelling of the case and of Abrams's life and work is Richard Polenberg, *Fighting Faiths: The Abrams Case, The Supreme Court, and Free Speech* (1987). The Wilson administration's wartime policies and their effect on individual rights are examined in Paul L. Murphy, *World War I and the Origin of Civil Liberties in the United States* (1979). The best single book on free speech is Harry Kalven Jr., *A Worthy Tradition: Freedom of Speech in America* (1988), but the classic work, and the one most pertinent to this episode, is Zechariah Chafee Jr., *Free Speech in the United States* (1920, rev. ed. 1941). For Holmes, see G. Edward White, *Justice Oliver Wendell Holmes: Law and the Inner Life* (1993), especially chap. 12.

The Case of the High-Tech Bootlegger

Olmstead v. United States (1928)

L AW BY ITS VERY NATURE always lags behind societal changes, and this is particularly true when it comes to technological development. A new technology challenges the courts to find already existing rules that can then be applied to new circumstances. In the nineteenth century, for example, it took many years before courts could establish rules regarding railroads and the liability they had for damages from steam engines spewing out sparks as they crossed farmlands. Sometimes years, even decades, pass before judges can articulate a workable rule that marries modern technology to constitutional safeguards.

In 1928 Justice Louis Brandeis tackled the question of a new technology—the telephone—and in doing so laid the basis for one of the most important constitutional developments of the twentieth century— the emergence of a right to privacy. Government agents had put a wiretap on the phones of a suspected bootlegger, gaining the information used to convict him of violating the Prohibition Act. On appeal he raised issues of what the Fourth Amendment required in terms of a search, and although he lost, Brandeis's dissent would bear fruit over the next four decades until the Supreme Court adopted his reasoning and held that the Constitution did protect an individual's right to privacy.

The Road to the Noble Experiment

Olmstead v. United States grew out of the great failed experiment of Prohibition, one of the legacies of the Progressive reform ferment that marked American society in the two decades leading up to the nation's entry into World War I in 1917.

Americans always drank, and at least from colonial times there were those who viewed liquor as sinful. During the nineteenth and early twentieth centuries the prohibitionists won some notable victories, and by 1917 twenty-six states—more than half the Union—were legally dry—that is, they prohibited the manufacture, transportation, or sale of alcoholic beverages within their state borders. In addition, some of the so-called wet states permitted a local option allowing their rural areas to ban liquor. For those opposed to drink—and this included everything from beer to champagne to whiskey—all the problems of society resulted from drunkenness. The Anti-Saloon League claimed that each year, inebriated parents smothered some 3,000 infants in their cribs. Accidents on the job, broken families, husbands who deserted their wives, girls led to a life of debauchery—all arose from the same cause. Prohibitionists looked at a complex world through a single moral lens, and found liquor guilty of all they deemed wrong in America.

There were, of course, many problems confronting the United States in the early twentieth century. The great industrialization that had gathered steam after the Civil War reached its fruition around 1900, and the country was pockmarked by great factories spewing forth noxious gasses and employing thousands of workers. Many of those who toiled in the mills, mines, and plants had only recently arrived in the United States, part of the great wave of immigration from eastern and southern Europe between 1880 and 1920. What had been a nation of farms and small towns was rapidly transforming into a nation of cities, and by the 1920s the census would report that one-half of all Americans lived in urban areas. The cities, of course, with their more liberal attitudes on everything from politics to sex—and with a saloon allegedly on every corner—struck the rural Baptists and Methodists who made up the heart of the Prohibition movement as symbolic of all they believed wrong. Drink had sent God's country staggering into the arms of Satan!

The rural dries, however, would not have been able to secure passage of Prohibition without the help of urban progressives and the war itself. Many reformers believed that if drink did not actually cause the evils they fought, it certainly contributed to it. Not all factory workers picked up their pay on Friday and then drank it away in the saloon, but a few did. Not all accidents in the mills and sweatshops could be attributed to workers drunk on the job, but some could. Not all husbands who deserted their families did so because of habitual drunkenness, but there were enough stories to give the charge credence.

Moreover, middle-class reformers detested the big-city political machines like Tammany Hall in New York that had their precinct offices in saloons and that rewarded faithful voters with free drinks. The forces that made these machines powerful from the 1880s to the 1930s had much to do with the great changes sweeping the nation and very little to do with alcohol, but the prohibitionists had a single moral lens that ignored everything but Demon Rum. They hated the cities and all the cities stood for, and in their eyes liquor epitomized the city.

During the war the necessity to conserve grain for food, both on the home front and for the troops, led Congress to adopt a wartime prohibition on the production of alcohol. In December 1917 Congress passed a constitutional amendment to ban the "manufacture, sale, or transportation of intoxicating liquors within, the importation thereof into, or the exportation thereof from the United States," and gave both Congress and the states concurrent power to enforce the prohibition. By January 1919 thirty-six states had ratified the Eighteenth Amendment banning alcohol, and in October 1919 Congress, over President Woodrow Wilson's veto, enacted the Volstead Act to extend wartime prohibition and to define *alcoholic* as one-half of 1 percent alcohol by volume, a definition that could include partially fermented apple juice. On January 17, 1920, Prohibition—the so-called "Noble Experiment"—began.

Prohibition in Practice

In the decade that followed, it appears that drinking in general amongst the population declined, especially in the rural areas that had most fervently supported the ban. As a whole there were probably fewer arrests in the country resulting from drunkenness and few deaths from alcoholism. According to a 1920 study undertaken by *Survey* magazine of Grand Rapids, Michigan, drunkenness had disappeared, families spent more time together, the saloon was no longer the visitor's entry to the city, and the number of arrests for crime had dropped so much that the police force had been reduced—all as a result of Prohibition.

The study seems to have been overly optimistic, and may have reflected the support many people initially gave to Prohibition. It soon became apparent, however, that despite the ratification of the Eighteenth Amendment, many people in the country had little use for Prohibition. Even in rural areas, moonshine and hard cider abounded, while the cities were overwhelmingly opposed to the ban on drink. Before long, the Noble Experiment in social reform turned into a national nightmare of failed law enforcement and a widespread disdain for those agencies trying to enforce the ban.

Prior to 1919, Prohibition had been a state matter. The National Commission on Law Observance and Enforcement found state enforcement effective, while another study termed local law "fairly well obeyed and respected." In contrast, federal enforcement of Prohibition quickly turned into a "nation-wide scandal" that, in President Harding's words, was "the most demoralizing factor in our public life."

At the heart of the problem lay the impossible task mandated by the Eighteenth Amendment, the moral reform of a nation that had been drinking since colonial times. Prohibition stands as the premier example of law's inability to change the personal behavior of people who do not want to change. The amendment's division of responsibility left it unclear who had the primary responsibility for enforcement—the states or the national government. Section 2 reads, "The Congress and the several States shall have concurrent power to enforce this article by appropriate legislation." Did that mean that Congress could set up police functions inside the states? What if a state, such as Maryland, did not pass the necessary enforcement law or, as New York did in 1923, repeal its enforcement statute? Could states set up barricades to keep alcohol coming in from other states or from Canada? Who had the responsibility to patrol the shores to prevent smuggling? Did the federal government have the authority to conscript state law enforcement officers? The federalism that had been so essential a part of the American constitutional scheme for more than 130 years reeled from the onslaught of issues never imagined by the Framers of the Constitution.

The hastily thrown-together federal Prohibition agency (later the Bureau of Alcohol, Tobacco, and Firearms) lacked skilled personnel, and many of the "agents" were little more than political hacks, some of whom had criminal records, given their jobs by local bosses. They quickly aroused public resentment when they indiscriminately sprayed waterfront streets with bullets or invaded private houses without a search warrant. To many citizens, the agents seemed to be as lawless as the bootleggers they pursued.

Soon millions of Americans seemed to side with purveyors of illegal booze. On one occasion, thousands of weekend fun seekers at Coney Island in New York watched Coast Guard cutters chase rumrunners, and cheered as the latter opened a lead in escaping from the government boats. In Ocean City, Maryland, a mob of wets stormed the city jail to free two men arrested for drunkenness. In many big cities the agents seemed helpless. In New York, Chicago, or San Francisco, a stranger looking for a drink could stop a local policeman on the street who then politely pointed out the nearest speakeasy and also provided the magic words to get in—"Joe sent me." In 1929 a former assistant attorney general in charge of Prohibition prosecutions conceded that liquor could be bought "at almost any hour of the day or night, either in rural districts, the smaller towns, or the cities."

The American people, who prided themselves in their ingeniousness, came up with one device after another to get what the law said they could not have. Sophisticated chemical laboratories, hidden in warehouses, redistilled industrial alcohol (although the process, in less skilled hands, could yield products that poisoned, paralyzed, or killed thousands of people). Compliant druggists wrote prescriptions for alcohol that could then be blended with other ingredients. Many people brewed at home, and hardware stores openly displayed and sold the equipment needed. Boats smuggled in premium liquors from Europe and the Caribbean along New Jersey's Rum Row, while ice sleds easily crossed over from Canada in midwinter.

The worst aspects of Prohibition were the big city gangs that not only overwhelmed law enforcement agencies, but usually corrupted local governments as well. In 1920 "Scarface" Al Capone, a petty hoodlum from the Five Points area of New York, moved to Chicago and quickly built an empire based on alcohol, gambling, and prostitution. By 1927 his businesses grossed more than $60 million a year, and his army of nearly a thousand thugs "took care" of rival bootleggers who tried to cut in on Capone's territory. In 1926 and 1927 Chicago saw more than 130 gang murders, and police did not solve a single one of them.

In New York, Chicago, Philadelphia, and elsewhere, the real power in the city rested not with the elected municipal governments but with the gangs. As one commentator sarcastically noted, the gangs "eliminated waste, promoted efficiency, and replaced the disorder of obsolete individualism with rigorous discipline." It was an ideal that advocates of the "New Capitalism" such as Herbert Hoover promoted during that decade.

The Olmstead Ring in Seattle

Criminals quickly adapted the new technologies of telephones and automobiles to help them circumvent Prohibition. In Seattle, a police lieutenant named Roy Olmstead learned all about the bootlegging business while making arrests, and realized that the main problem of running an illegal business was lack of organization. There were too many unconnected pieces, too many mistakes arising from lack of information and communication, and lack of leadership. Olmstead left the police department and proceeded to put together a highly efficient organization to import and distribute liquor in violation of the Volstead Act. The "Olmstead Ring" could have served as a case study at the Harvard Business School. Olmstead himself put in $10,000 for working capital and acted as general manager, while eleven others put in $1,000 each; 50 percent of the profits went to Olmstead, and the other partners divided the balance. At its peak, the organization employed between fifty and seventy people; it leased two seagoing vessels to bring the liquor from British Columbia to Seattle, and several smaller boats to distribute alcohol up and down the Washington State coast.

Olmstead purchased a ranch outside of Seattle with large underground facilities to store the imported cases, as well as several apartments in the city from which his men would make deliveries to local consumers. The ring ran out of a central office manned by telephone operators, salesmen, deliverymen, dispatchers, bookkeepers, collectors, and even an attorney. As a former police officer, Olmstead had contacts—including his two brothers—in the Seattle police department who kept him apprised of possible raids, and also helped him to arrange the release of any of his men who might be arrested.

From early morning to late at night, operators manned the telephone bank at the main office, and either Olmstead or one of his managers would then take the orders and give them to a deliveryman, who would go to one of the local caches, pick up the requested items, and take them to the customers. On some days the operation delivered as many as two hundred cases of liquor. As the court records showed, even in a bad month sales amounted to $176,000, and annual income easily topped $2 million (equivalent to more than $25 million in current dollars).

Little of this was secret. The local press dubbed Olmstead the "King of the Puget Sound Bootleggers," and Olmstead made no effort to maintain a low public profile. In 1924 he divorced his first wife and married Elise Campbell, a vivacious young Englishwoman he met in Vancouver, Canada, while on a buying trip. He built her a beautiful mansion, which they dubbed the "snow white palace" in the exclusive Mount Baker neighborhood, overlooking Mount Rainier. The Olmsteads founded the American Radio Telephone Company, and brought in a young inventor, Alfred M. Hubbard, as a business partner. Together they built a large radio transmitter and one of Seattle's first commercial broadcasting studios, KFQX. Federal law enforcement agents were suspicious of Olmstead's real motives, and speculated that he used the station's broadcast of children's bedtime stories to send coded messages to his rum-running boats.

Federal agents utilized their own technology. They ran taps on the phones into the ring's main office as well as the lines at Olmstead's home and the residences of some of his partners. At the main office they set up a listening post table in the basement of the building, and attached earphones to the telephone wires using alligator clips. At the private residences they attached the wires either in the basements of apartment buildings, or on telephone poles outside houses. At no time did they enter the premises, nor did they have a warrant to eavesdrop—since neither police nor prosecution believed a warrant was necessary. One needed a warrant to enter a premise, but federal agents never actually did so; they listened from outside the office and the homes.

Over several months the federal agents came to know the bootleggers and their operations, and the difficulties they occasionally faced and overcame in their business. They learned the identities of the major customers, who the ring was paying off in the police department, and how Olmstead and his team responded when a ship was seized or storms delayed delivery. Over the course of the investigation the agents compiled 775 pages of transcriptions of telephone calls, and on that basis secured arrest warrants for Roy Olmstead and seventy other people. Some escaped, and at trial a few were acquitted. But juries in the federal court for the western district of Washington found Olmstead and seventeen of his partners and managers guilty, and the Court of Appeals for the Ninth Circuit affirmed the convictions and jail sentences.

The Meaning of the Fourth Amendment

From the beginning, Olmstead's lawyers had argued that the use of wiretap evidence obtained without a search warrant violated the Fourth Amendment to the Constitution, and they now brought that argument to the U.S. Supreme Court. His lead attorney, John F. Dore, claimed that the rights guaranteed under the Constitution are "indispensable to the full enjoyment of personal security, personal liberty, and private property," and therefore may not be trampled upon by the government. If the government used fraud or subterfuge to secure evidence, then it could not be admitted as evidence in a case. Dore also tried to convince the Court that even if there had not been an actual invasion of the physical premises, if the results were to force a person to furnish evidence against himself, then it violated the Fifth Amendment's prohibition against self-incrimination.

American Telephone & Telegraph, the nation's largest provider of phone service, as well as a number of smaller telephone firms, filed briefs as *amici curiae*, or friends of the court, protesting against the use of private conversations, secured through wiretaps, as violations of the Fourth and Fifth Amendments.

Olmstead had some good arguments on his side, but no case up to that time had actually dealt with the use of wiretap evidence. The Fourth Amendment, adopted as part of the Bill of Rights in 1791, held that "The right of the people to be secure in their persons, houses, papers, and effects, against unreasonable searches and seizures, shall not be violated, and no Warrants shall issue, but upon probable cause, supported by Oath or affirmation, and particularly describing the place to be searched and the persons or things to be seized." If nothing else, the amendment prohibited the general warrants common in the last years of colonial America, where the British Crown's agents could search anyone's home without showing cause or even telling a magistrate what they were seeking. Under the Fourth Amendment there could be no "fishing expeditions" of this type.

The Fifth Amendment included a number of safeguards for persons accused of crimes, including indictment by a grand jury and a ban on double jeopardy, but a key part read that no person "shall be compelled in any criminal case to be a witness against himself." When Olmstead's case reached the Supreme Court in February 1928, the jurisprudence of these protections could best be described as slim. The Court had heard a few cases, but not very many, and since lawyers both for the government as well as for Olmstead cited all of them, they clearly did not create a clear line of precedents. The Fourth Amendment thus became central to the arguments for both sides, and both relied on three earlier cases.

The Court first heard a Fourth Amendment challenge in 1886, and even then the argument was made that papers secured without a warrant not only violated the search and seizure clause of the Fourth Amendment, but also the self-incrimination clause of the Fifth Amendment. E. A. Boyd & Sons allegedly entered into an arrangement with Union Plate Glass Company to import plate glass with the intention of avoiding the tariffs imposed by the 1874 Customs Act. The U.S. attorney directed the Boyds to produce their invoices for the glass, and they challenged the validity of the order under the Fourth and Fifth Amendments. Eventually the Boyds handed over the documents, which the government used to secure a conviction for evasion of tariffs, and they appealed.

A unanimous Court reversed that conviction in *Boyd v. United States* (1886). Justice Joseph P. Bradley stated that the Fourth and Fifth Amendments protected the privacy of individuals from government intrusion, and applied not only in criminal cases but—and this was the most important part in regard to *Olmstead*—even where there had been no physical invasion of property. The Court struck down the provision of the Customs Act authorizing compulsory production of evidence as unconstitutional, and therefore the invoices could not be used against the Boyds.

Boyd led directly to the next major Fourth Amendment case, *Weeks v. United States* (1914), in which the Court expanded the protections of the Fourth Amendment. Federal marshals, aided by state officers, searched and arrested Freemont Weeks at the Union Station in Kansas City, Missouri. They had no warrant, but the papers they seized led to Weeks's conviction of using the mails to transport lottery tickets. Prior to his trial he demanded the return of his effects and objected to their use at the trial, thus laying a basis for appeal to the high court.

Speaking for a unanimous court, Justice William R. Day took a major step in providing for an enforcement mechanism against Fourth Amendment violations—the exclusionary rule. The warrantless search as well as the trial court's refusal to return Weeks's property had been a violation of his constitutional rights of personal security, personal liberty, and private property. Day relied exclusively on Fourth Amendment grounds to order the judgment reversed, and completely ignored the Fifth Amendment claims Weeks had raised.

A few years later the Court, disgusted by the methods of the government in the postwar Red Scare, signaled its displeasure at federal abuse of constitutionally protected rights in another Fourth Amendment case, *Silverthorne Lumber Company v. United States* (1920).

In *Silverthorne* two men had been arrested after indictment by a grand jury. Agents of the Justice Department, without a warrant, then ransacked their office, removing books, papers, and other documents. Justice Oliver Wendell Holmes Jr., writing for the Court, branded the government's action an "outrage" and blocked any use of the illegally seized material by the government in legal proceedings. Holmes's insistence that the documents "shall not be used at all" helped expand the exclusionary rule hinted at in *Boyd* and more fully enunciated in *Weeks*. The decision stressed two themes: the exclusionary rule provided the only effective means of protecting Fourth Amendment rights, and judicial integrity required that the courts not sanction illegal searches by admitting the fruits of this illegality into evidence.

Given this clear line of precedents, one would have thought that the Court in Olmstead's case would have precluded use of the warrantless wiretap evidence. A bare majority of the Court, however, refused to accept the Fourth Amendment argument, and instead agreed with the government's lawyer, Michael J. Doherty, that wiretapping did not constitute an unreasonable search and seizure within the meaning of the Fourth Amendment, and that evidence secured through a wiretap could be used at a trial.

Chief Justice Taft's Opinion

Chief Justice William Howard Taft wrote the majority opinion, joined by Justices Willis Van Devanter, James C. McReynolds, George Sutherland, and Edward T. Sanford. Taft tried to limit the decision to what he termed was the sole question that the Court had agreed to hear in accepting the case for review—whether "the use of evidence of private telephone conversations between the defendants and conversations between the defendants and others, intercepted by means of wire tapping, amounted to a violation of the 4th and 5th Amendments."

In what can only be described as a wooden opinion, Taft went over all of the Supreme Court's prior Fourth Amendment opinions and found them irrelevant to the *Olmstead* case. The precedents had all involved physical intrusion into the defendants' homes or offices, and in this instance the federal agents had done no more than listen in on conversations from positions outside the premises. "There was no evidence of compulsion to induce the defendants to talk over their many telephones," he said. "They were continually and voluntarily transacting business without knowledge of the interception." As for the alleged violations of the Fourth Amendment, Taft declared, "The Amendment does not forbid what was done here. There was no searching. There was no seizure. The evidence was secured by the use of the sense of hearing and that only. There was no entry of the houses or offices of the defendants."

Taft could find no means by which this activity violated the Fourth Amendment. "The language of the Amendment can not be extended and expanded to include telephone wires reaching to the whole world from the defendant's house or office," he said. "The intervening wires are not part of his house or office, any more than are the highways along which they are stretched." Then Taft, who in other cases had no problem in reaching out to make new law, adopted the posture of strict judicial restraint. Congress could, he noted, make evidence secured by wiretap inadmissible in federal trials, but "courts may not adopt such a policy by attributing an enlarged and unusual meaning to the Fourth Amendment."

Why did Taft, who certainly knew that the prior cases from *Boyd* to *Weeks* to *Silverthorne Lumber* had all strengthened the protections of the Fourth Amendment, write an opinion in *Olmstead* that weakened them? One answer is that a majority of the justices supported the Noble Experiment. Three members of the Court—Pierce Butler, George Sutherland, and James McReynolds—detested Prohibition because they opposed the expansion of the national administrative state; they also believed that positive law, i.e., statutory enactments, should not be used to overthrow established social values. Taft wrote to his brother that "Holmes, Van Devanter, Brandeis, Sanford and I are steady in the boat." Taft was not sure about the newest member of the Court, Harlan Fiske Stone: he "wobbles a good deal on the subject, and I don't quite see where he stands, and I am not quite sure that he does."

Holmes and Brandeis had bowed to the will of the people in accepting Prohibition, although in practice Holmes continued to enjoy his drink and to receive bottles from his friends. Brandeis had liked his beer and an occasional whiskey, and for many years at dinner he had served guests the good Kentucky bourbon that his brother Alfred regularly sent from Louisville. His views on democratic governance led him to support Prohibition after ratification, and in time he even came to be a fervent supporter of the ban on alcohol, believing it could improve the lives of working people. On the most extreme end, Taft and Van Devanter saw opposition to dryness as resistance to the legal order itself.

During the 1920s a majority of the Court consistently found in favor of the government in cases involving Prohibition. The Court had upheld the War-Time Prohibition Act, and then approved the Volstead Act that implemented the Eighteenth Amendment. Even the Tenth Amendment, which reserved powers to the states and which was a darling of conservative federalists, fell before the needs to banish Demon Rum. As Justice Sanford wrote in a 1924 case, *Everard's Breweries v. Day*, since Prohibition "is within the authority delegated to Congress by the Eighteenth Amendment, its validity is not impaired by reason of any power reserved to the States." Fear of overweening national authority, a bedrock of conservative as well as federalist thought since the founding of the Republic, vanished in the Taft Court's enthusiasm for the Noble Experiment.

In a variety of cases the Court majority allowed the government to close distilleries without compensation to the owners, ruled that the ban on double jeopardy did not apply when a person had been convicted of one crime for possessing alcohol and then convicted in another trial for selling the same liquor, permitted the government to confiscate an automobile that carried illegal alcohol, upheld a congressional ban on the common prescription of wine and liquor for medicinal purposes, and allowed searches of cars for contraband without a warrant.

Justices Butler and Holmes Dissent

The Taft opinion elicited dissents from Butler, Holmes, and Brandeis. In a well-reasoned historical analysis, the generally conservative Butler repudiated Taft's sterile interpretation of what the Fourth Amendment meant, although he agreed with Taft that the only question properly before the Court was whether the evidence itself could be used. Stone, who concurred in all of the dissents, did not agree with this part of Butler's writing. Although the grant of *certiorari* accepting the appeal identified a single issue, he believed that the Court was always free to consider any matter part of the record, and in this regard found himself in agreement with Holmes and Brandeis.

Holmes took a different tack from Butler and, in a comment that soon caught the liberal imagination, condemned wiretapping as a "dirty business." He identified two "objects of desire," noting that one could not have both. "It is desirable that criminals should be detected, and to that end all available evidence should be used. It also is desirable that the government should not itself foster and pay for other crimes, when they are the means by which the evidence is to be obtained." We have to choose, he declared, "and for my part I think it a less evil that some criminals should escape than that the government should play an ignoble part." Holmes had originally not intended to write an opinion at all, since "My brother Brandeis has given this case so exhaustive an examination," but he did so for two reasons. First, Brandeis had privately asked him to do so, and second, he did not completely agree with all that Brandeis said, especially that the Fourth and Fifth Amendments created rights of privacy that covered the defendant.

The Brandeis Dissent and the Right of Privacy

It was Justice Brandeis, however, whose dissenting opinion had the most profound and lasting impact on Fourth Amendment jurisprudence. Brandeis used his dissent to drive home several points. He clearly abhorred the methods used by the Prohibition agents, and the reason for his antipathy is one that should be read every day by government officials up to and including presidents:

> Decency, security and liberty alike demand that government officials shall be subjected to the same rules of conduct that are commands to the citizen. In a government of laws, existence of the government will be imperilled if it fails to observe the law scrupulously. Our Government is the potent, the omnipresent teacher. For good or for ill, it teaches the whole people by its example. Crime is contagious. If the Government becomes a lawbreaker, it breeds contempt for law; it invites every man to become a law unto himself; it invites anarchy. To declare that in the administration of the criminal law the end justifies the means—to declare that the Government may commit crimes in order to secure the conviction of a private criminal—would bring terrible retribution. Against that pernicious doctrine this Court should resolutely set its face.

But Brandeis had another argument to make, one that he had been advocating for nearly four decades—the right to privacy. In an 1890 article he had written with his law partner, Sam Warren, Brandeis had relied on common law private action and tort law, since the alleged violators of privacy had been the press and commercial actors. Now, because the government had been involved, he identified personal privacy as a matter of constitutional law, and married his earlier notion of the right to be let alone with the Fourth Amendment's ban on unreasonable search and seizure and the Fifth Amendment's protection against self-incrimination.

To justify reading privacy into these amendments, he assigned his law clerk that term, Henry J. Friendly, to researching the circumstances surrounding the drafting of the Fourth Amendment. Brandeis expected his clerks to argue with him, and when they did make a convincing argument, he would listen. At first the justice wanted to base his dissent on the violation of the Washington State statute against wiretapping, but Friendly convinced him that it must rest on a constitutional basis. The result is one of the landmark dissents in constitutional history.

Taft had emphasized that the Framers had nothing more in mind than the general warrants used by the British in the 1760s and 1770s, and the Fourth Amendment applied to little else. Brandeis cited Chief Justice Marshall's reminder that "We must never forget that it is a constitution we are expounding." Times had changed since 1791, and Brandeis cited case after case as well as historical treatises to show that the Court had constantly read constitutional provisions to take into account conditions never envisioned by the Framers. The technical nature of the federal agents' entry onto the defendant's property did not matter as much as the intent of the amendment to protect people in their homes and businesses. "Time works changes, brings into existence new conditions and purposes. Subtle and more far-reaching means of invading privacy have become available to the Government. Discovery and invention have made it possible for the Government, by means far more effective than stretching upon the rack, to obtain disclosure in court of what is whispered in the closet." (At this point Brandeis wanted to refer to a new device recently developed by the General Electric Company called "television," but removed the note in deference to Friendly's skepticism.)

He then went on to write one of the most eloquent—and most quoted—passages in American law:

> The makers of our Constitution undertook to secure conditions favorable to the pursuit of happiness. They recognized the significance of man's spiritual nature, of his feelings and of his intellect. They knew that only a part of the pain, pleasure and satisfactions of life are to be found in material things. They sought to protect Americans in their beliefs, their thoughts, their emotions and their sensations. They conferred, as against the Government, the right to be let alone—the most comprehensive of rights and the right most valued by civilized men. To protect that right, every unjustifiable intrusion by the Government upon the privacy of the individual, whatever the means employed, must be deemed a violation of the Fourth Amendment.

Brandeis dismissed Taft's mechanistic view that no intrusion had occurred, since it did not matter where the actual physical connection with the telephone wires took place:

> And it is also immaterial that the intrusion was in aid of law enforcement. Experience should teach us to be most on our guard to protect liberty when the Government's purposes are beneficent. Men born to freedom are naturally alert to repel invasion of their liberty by evil-minded rulers. The greatest dangers to liberty lurk in insidious encroachment by men of .zeal, well-meaning but without understanding.

In the *Olmstead* dissent Brandeis reinvented Fourth Amendment jurisprudence. Taft's majority opinion, as well as prior search and seizure cases, had been grounded in conceptions of property, whether or not police had actually entered the home or business. Brandeis shifted the emphasis from where the alleged wrong took place to how it affected the individual's rights. While Brandeis disliked the "dirty business" of wiretapping as much as Holmes, for him the more important issues were the conduct of the police and the individual's right to be let alone. If the police had probable cause to suspect a person of wrongdoing, the Constitution required that a warrant be secured. Warrantless searches, except in very special circumstances, could not be allowed.

Chief Justice Taft reacted furiously to the dissents. "If they think we are going to be frightened in our effort to stand by the law and give the public a chance to punish criminals," he told his brother, "they are mistaken, even though we are condemned for lack of high ideals." He believed that Brandeis had gone off on what he considered irrelevant ethical issues, and termed Brandeis "the lawless member of the Court" for having done so. Holmes had written "the nastiest opinion," and Taft claimed that Holmes had voted the other way "till Brandeis got after him and induced him to change." But, he told Justice Sutherland, "I hope that ultimately it will be seen that we in the majority were right."

Taft also was incensed that the dissents went beyond what he termed the only question that the Court had agreed to review. "Some of our number, departing from that order, have concluded that there is merit in the twofold objection overruled in both courts below that evidence obtained through intercepting of telephone messages by government agents was inadmissible because the mode of obtaining it was unethical and a misdemeanor under the law of Washington." Taft then went into a lengthy exposition of the law of evidence, citing various legal treatises all purporting that even evidence illegally obtained may be submitted without triggering any sort of constitutional violation. The fact that

Washington State law prohibited wiretapping did not control the behavior of federal agents, nor the validity of the evidence they gathered while listening in on conversations.

Taft's prediction proved wrong, although it took many years before Brandeis's dissent became established as a constitutional right in *Griswold v. Connecticut* (1965). Brandeis did, however, live to see Congress prohibit wiretapping evidence in federal courts in the Federal Communications Act of 1934, and the Court to partially reverse *Olmstead* in 1937. In 1967 the Supreme Court fully adopted Brandeis's position and overturned *Olmstead* completely, bringing wiretapping within the ambit of Fourth Amendment protection. That same year, Justice Potter Stewart explained the Court's new philosophy in words that grew directly out of Brandeis's dissent—"The Fourth Amendment protects people, not places." In a more recent case, *Kyllo v. United States* (2001), Justice Antonin Scalia used the logic of Brandeis's dissent to hold that federal agents could not use a new technology, thermal imaging, to look through the walls of Danny Lee Kyllo's house to determine if the occupant was growing marijuana. Even though the agents used the machine outside the premises, they had secured information about the inside, and could not use that evidence without a warrant.

Roy Olmstead Reforms

Following the Supreme Court's affirmation of the conviction, federal agents brought Roy Olmstead to the prison on McNeil Island to serve out his four-year term. On May 12, 1931, he was released with time off for good behavior. The Seattle he returned to was, of course, suffering from the Great Depression, but little had changed in the bootlegging business other than that a new group of rumrunners supplied liquor to the citizenry. Then in November 1932 Washington repealed all of its Prohibition enforcement laws, and a year later Franklin Roosevelt announced the ratification of the Twenty-first Amendment, repealing Prohibition altogether. On Christmas Day, 1935, President Roosevelt granted Olmstead a full presidential pardon, restoring his constitutional rights, and also remitted him $10,300 in costs.

During his time on McNeil Island Olmstead studied carpentry, and he also became a Christian Scientist. After his release he made his living for a while selling furniture, but he began devoting more and more time to his vocation as a Christian Science minister, visiting Seattle jails to talk and give solace to the inmates, and helping to rehabilitate some of them. He ran his ministry out of a small, unobtrusive office, but he remained a newsworthy personality throughout his life. He gave an interview to the *Seattle Post-Intelligencer* just a year before his death in 1966, at age eighty.

Cases Cited

Boyd v. United States, 116 U.S. 616 (1886)
Griswold v. Connecticut, 381 U.S. 419 (1965)
James Everard's Breweries v. Day, 265 U.S. 545 (1924)
Kyllo v. United States, 533 U.S. 27 (2001)
Olmstead v. United States, 277 U.S. 438 (1928)
Silverthorne Lumber Company v. United States, 251 U.S. 385 (1920)
Weeks v. United States, 232 U.S. 383 (1914)

For Further Reading

For Prohibition see Thomas R. Pegram, *Battling Demon Rum: The Struggle for a Dry America, 1800–1933* (1988), and Richard F. Hamm, *Shaping the Eighteenth Amendment: Temperance Reform, Legal Culture, and the Polity, 1880–1920* (1995). The history of the Fourth Amendment is explored in Thomas N. McInnis, *The Evolution of the Fourth Amendment* (2009), and its relation to privacy is developed in David L. Hudson, *The Right to Privacy* (2009), and Frederick S. Lane, *American Privacy* (2009). The effect of Prohibition on the Taft Court is examined in Robert Post, "Federalism, Positive Law, and the Emergence of the American Administrative State: Prohibition in the Taft Court Era," 48 *William and Mary Law Review* 1 (2006). For Brandeis and his concern about privacy, see Melvin I. Urofsky, *Louis D. Brandeis: A Life* (2009); the writing of the opinion is examined in Paul A. Freund, "The Evolution of a Brandeis Dissent," *Manuscripts* 10 (Spring 1958): 18–25, 34.

The Four Horsemen's Last Ride

The New Deal Cases (1930s)

IN 1929 THE UNITED STATES entered into the most severe economic depression in the nation's history. When Franklin Roosevelt took the oath of office as the nation's thirty-second president in March 1933, he promised action to bring relief to a nation in which one-third of the people were ill-housed, ill-clothed, and ill-fed. Moreover, in words that struck terror into the hearts of conservatives, he promised that if one program did not work, he would try something else, and he believed the Constitution gave the national government adequate power to confront what he called an emergency as grave as war itself.

While Roosevelt had large Democratic majorities in both houses of Congress and enormous popular support for the New Deal, four of the nine justices on the Supreme Court stood unalterably opposed to such an extensive involvement of the federal government in the economy and in the labor market. The Four Horsemen, as they were called, after the four horsemen of the Apocalypse—James McReynolds, Willis Van Devanter, George Sutherland, and Pierce Butler—could usually pick up a fifth vote from one of the two moderate conservatives, Chief Justice Charles Evans Hughes and Owen Roberts. Three members of the Court did not necessarily support the New Deal programs, but Louis D. Brandeis, Harlan Fiske Stone, and Benjamin Cardozo believed in judicial restraint, and found nothing in the Constitution to bar the administration from enacting its program.

The majority struck down one New Deal measure after another until finally, in frustration, Roosevelt embarked on an ill-advised scheme to "pack" the Court with justices friendly to his program. In the midst of the battle over the plan, the Supreme Court suddenly seemed to reverse course in a suit brought by a chambermaid, Elsie Parrish, seeking back wages and overtime pay under a Washington State minimum wage statute. At the time, many people thought the *Parrish* decision helped sink the Court-packing bill, but the story of the greatest constitutional crisis since the Civil War is far more complex.

The Great Depression

Facts can only tell us so much about the extent of the financial catastrophe that we know as the Great Depression. Between 1929 and 1932 factory production in the United States dropped more than 50 percent, while industrial construction fell from $949 million to a scant $74 million. Steel plants, the backbone of the economy, operated at 12 percent of capacity, and the stock market, which had stood at 452 on September 3, 1929, bottomed out at 52 in July 1932. Vast human suffering marked the real tragedy: thirteen million people unemployed; two million homeless, many of them riding the country in boxcars; people living in tarpaper shacks in clusters dubbed "Hoovervilles"; and families fighting outside the back doors of restaurants for garbage scraps. President Herbert Hoover tried to help, but could not transcend the limits of the laissez-faire ideology he held so dear, and he would not ask the government to interfere in the marketplace or provide relief—what he termed a "dole"—to those people out of work and starving. "The country needs," declared Roosevelt, the Democratic candidate for president in 1932, "and, unless I mistake its temper, the country demands bold, persistent experimentation."

Experimentation would be the hallmark of the New Deal. No other president had ever entered the White House committed to the idea of just trying something—anything—and if that did not work, trying something else. Some of the New Deal had been anticipated in Roosevelt's campaign speeches and in earlier strains of Progressivism: a reforestation program to employ youth, public power development, regulation of utilities and the stock market, economic planning and cooperation with business, and repeal of Prohibition. Yet some of the most striking activities of the Roosevelt administration seemingly came out of the blue: deficit spending, federal works, agricultural relief, massive expenditures for housing and slum clearance, the Tennessee Valley Authority, heavily progressive tax schemes, a labor relations board, and Social Security. All of these resulted both from Roosevelt's fertile mind and his willingness not only to listen to new ideas, but to act on them.

At the state level, people demanded action as well. Roosevelt, in fact, had come to national attention in part for his innovative use of state resources in New York to alleviate suffering. Governors such as C. Ben Ross in Idaho and Floyd Olsen in Minnesota personally intervened to prevent auctions of property when banks had foreclosed on mortgages. In a nation where farmers destroyed their unsalable crops while people went hungry, the sanctity of the marketplace—which conservatives had trumpeted as the keystone of American prosperity—no longer made sense, and state after state adopted measures regulating the market and the workplace that they hoped would do some good. The judicial response to state legislation proved far from consistent and anticipated the confused reaction of the courts to national New Deal legislation.

The Court and State Measures to Combat the Depression

The first Supreme Court case set the pattern for many to follow. The Depression had caused chaos in the ice-making business, with cut-throat competition causing many firms to fail. In an effort to bring some stability to the industry, Oklahoma had enacted a law declaring the manufacture of ice to be a public utility, and therefore requiring a state certificate of convenience and necessity before entering the business. The conservative majority, speaking through Justice Sutherland, denied that ice manufacture could be in any way considered as affected with the public interest, and therefore could not legitimately be regulated by the state. In addition, he charged, the law fostered monopoly (*New State Ice Co. v. Liebmann* [1932]).

With his well-known antipathy toward monopoly, Louis Brandeis might have been expected to vote against the regulation, but instead he entered a powerful dissent that would be cited time and again in the battles that followed. He criticized the majority for failing to take note of the conditions that had led Oklahoma to adopt this policy. It did not matter whether the members of the Court agreed with it, because that was not their prerogative: "The true principle is that the State's power extends to every regulation of any business reasonably required and appropriate for the public protection." A state might consider it necessary to limit certain types of business, and to regulate others in order to mitigate the effects of a depression. Whether such an approach would work he did not know, nor did it matter. The Court had the power to prevent experiments, ill-advised or otherwise, but it should use that power infrequently. "We must ever be on our guard," he warned, "lest we erect our prejudices into legal principles."

The Court seemed to respond to Brandeis's plea when it upheld a Minnesota mortgage moratorium law in *Home Building & Loan*

Assn. v. Blaisdell (1934). Clearly an emergency measure, it did not reduce creditors' rights, but it did provide debtors with more leeway and time to pay their notes. Continuing the trend in *Nebbia v. New York* (1934), Justice Roberts—who often sided with the Four Horsemen—seemingly accepted the argument that the public need, especially in emergencies, overrode traditional property rights. In trying to aid dairy farmers, New York had established a system of minimum prices, and Leo Nebbia had been arrested for selling milk below that price in his Rochester market. Was there any constitutional principle that prevented the state from attempting to alleviate problems caused by an aberrant economy? In words that chilled the conservatives, Roberts declared, "We think there is no such principle." The relation of a business to the public interest clearly depended on existing economic conditions, he claimed, and therefore any business might legitimately be deemed as affected with a public interest and regulated for its benefit—something the Four Horsemen strenuously opposed.

In his dissent, Justice McReynolds made it quite clear that he did not believe in judicial restraint. The Court had to look not only at whether constitutional provisions allowed or barred certain actions, but "this Court must have regard to the wisdom of the enactment" as well. The fact that the conservatives disagreed with much of the legislation coming out of the states and the New Deal meant that if the Four Horsemen could get just one more vote, they could strike down legislation they considered "unwise." Franklin Roosevelt's New Deal gave them a great deal of legislation they did not like.

The New Deal Begins

Because today we are so used to big-scale governmental programs, we may have difficulty understanding how limited the federal government was in 1933. The Interstate Commerce Commission, the Federal Trade Commission, and the Food and Drug Commission existed, but they were small and relatively powerless, and the other commissions that would form the regulatory state had yet to be created. The strongest government agency was probably the Federal Reserve System, yet it had only a fraction of the power it exercises today, and the type of intervention it took in 2008 and 2009 to counter that economic downturn would have been inconceivable in 1929. Social Security, unemployment insurance, Medicaid, food stamps, and other types of federal or state "safety net" programs did not exist. Although both the Senate and the House of Representatives had standing committees, they had few staff, and there was no overall budgeting procedure in place. After the enormous increase in the military during the Great War, the army and the navy had shrunk to their prewar levels, and had yet to come to terms with the airplane as a military instrument. As for helping people in need, that was the business of private charity. Herbert Hoover strongly believed in Grover Cleveland's aphorism that while the people should cheerfully support the government, the government should in no circumstances support the people.

Roosevelt's first hundred days in office still stand as the epitome of energetic executive leadership and accomplishment. First, he had to deal with the banking crisis, since in the month leading up to his inaugural banks had closed everywhere, even in New York, and the New York Stock Exchange also announced it would not open. Roosevelt knew that most of the banks in the country were sound, but had lost the confidence of the people, who had lined up to draw out their savings. So he announced a "bank holiday" under the rather dubious authority of the old 1917 Trading with the Enemy Act. All banks would close until federal bank examiners could go over their books, and only sound banks would open, banks in which the people's money would be safe.

The federal government lacked the people to carry out such a nationwide audit; at best it could make a rough assessment of banks in good health and those about to fail. But Roosevelt gave people the psychological assurances they so craved, and as banks began to reopen they found people queuing up to put money *into* their accounts. The gamble had worked, and people looked to Washington to see what the president would do next.

Unlike Abraham Lincoln, who kept Congress on the sidelines in the first months of the Civil War, Roosevelt had large Democratic majorities in both houses just waiting for the president to give them their marching orders. In addition to executive orders that took the U.S. dollar off the gold standard, Roosevelt sent fifteen major pieces of legislation to Congress, which enacted all of them in three months. Some of them would become cornerstones of a new administrative state and reconfigure certain aspects of the economy, such as agriculture. Others, like the Tennessee Valley Authority, still stand as monuments to how creative government can serve the people. These programs created jobs by building up an infrastructure of roads, dams, and other public works. For the first time the federal government exercised real regulatory control over the nation's banking and securities markets. Some of these laws were temporary measures, such as the Civilian Conservation Corps, which put young men to work planting trees and building trails in national parks. One conspicuous failure, the National Industrial Recovery Act (NIRA), generated a lot of sound and fury but in the end did little to revive the economy. It made no difference, since Roosevelt had said he would try something, and if it worked, well and good; if it did not, then another experiment would take its place.

Roosevelt had been trained as a lawyer, and he knew that even as Congress rushed to enact the New Deal, at some point the legislation would wind up before the Supreme Court. He had, however, a politician's pragmatic view of the Constitution, one akin to Lincoln's belief that the document gave the government adequate powers to confront any crisis that arose. In his inaugural address, Roosevelt explained that "our Constitution is so simple and practical that it is possible always to meet extraordinary needs by changes in emphasis and arrangements without loss of essential forms." He knew that the document forbade certain things no matter what the circumstances, but he had also seen how flexible it had proven in the Great War. He believed the Depression posed just as great a threat to the country as war, and that the old economic beliefs no longer worked. The Constitution, he believed, allowed the government to try new remedies for the ailing economy.

From another point of view, much of the legislation of the first hundred days rested on constitutional assumptions as questionable as the economic theories that animated those laws. The administration also faced hurdles in the fact that most of the statutes had been drafted by enthusiastic but inexperienced young lawyers under difficult time constraints. For example, Roosevelt had given the committee drafting the National Industrial Recovery Act just one week to overhaul the nation's business structure, and the defects in the bill it drafted later proved its undoing. The drafters claimed that the broad mandate of the commerce clause provided constitutional justification, but nothing in the history of commerce clause jurisprudence going back to John Marshall had ever been applied to such a massive program. When they did not know exactly how they wanted to structure a particular feature, the bill's drafters indicated a general goal and delegated authority to the president to work it out, thus ignoring traditional separation of powers not only between the executive and legislative branches, but between the states and the federal government as well.

'Even had there been no Four Horsemen on the bench, the difficulties of sloppy legislative drafting were compounded by the poor quality of lawyers in the Justice Department. Attorney General Homer Cummings, an old-line Democrat, saw the jobs under his control as patronage plums for deserving party hacks rather than career jobs for well-qualified candidates. To take one example, the solicitor general, J. Crawford Biggs, lost ten of the first seventeen cases he handled. Only those departments and agencies with political clout of their own could stand up to Cummings and use their own attorneys to defend New Deal programs.

Going Off the Gold Standard

It would be impossible to review every New Deal program and the judicial response to it in the space we have, but to understand the antagonism of the judicial conservatives on the high court we can look at three laws and the constitutional challenges they faced—the executive order and subsequent legislation to abandon the gold standard, the National Industrial Recovery Act, and the Agricultural Adjustment Act (AAA)—as well as state efforts to impose minimum wages.

The Depression caused a great deflation—that is, sharp drops in wages earned as well as prices paid for goods—and most economists believed that recovery depended at least in part on triggering a moderate inflation. Drive up wages so that people would have more money to spend, went the theory, and when they bought goods, manufacturers would hire more people to produce more goods. Most economists also believed that adherence to the gold standard as the basis for currency prevented inflation, and recommended that the country go off the gold standard, as many European nations had already done.

Shortly after taking office Roosevelt announced that the country would go off the gold standard, and Congress, by joint resolution, canceled clauses in both private and governmental bonds that called for repayment in gold. Even the House of Morgan agreed with this policy, and its head, Russell Leffingwell, praised Roosevelt for saving the country from "complete collapse." Many people who held bonds, however, believed that their investments would lose value if payment came in a devalued paper money rather than in gold, and they went to court, claiming that the government could not abrogate a contract, especially its own pledged word.

The first case, *Norman v. Baltimore & Ohio Railroad Company*, addressed the question of private bonds. By a 5–4 vote the Court sustained the government's power to define the value of the nation's money. Chief Justice Hughes explained that the contracts did nothing but define gold as a method of payment, and Congress had the authority to abrogate private contracts if they ran counter to a legitimate exercise of the national power.

In *Perry v. United States,* the government secured a technical victory, but at the cost of a tongue-lashing not seen in the Court since John Marshall had chastised Thomas Jefferson and James Madison in *Marbury v. Madison* (1803). Hughes distinguished between private bonds, which always had to bend to the public good, and government obligations, which represented the pledged word of the government of the United States. An observer in the courtroom that day reported that the Jovian Hughes thundered as if he were still secretary of state lecturing a banana republic on the necessity of keeping its word. Congress, declared the chief justice, could not break its promises, even in carrying out legitimate powers, and the Court ruled Congress's joint resolution unconstitutional insofar as it abrogated the gold clauses in government bonds. Recognizing that enforcement of that decision might well wreak havoc with the nation's finances, and that the administration would probably ignore it, Hughes then did as Marshall had done 130 years earlier—he found a way out of the quandary. The government had done a terrible thing, but since the plaintiff had suffered no real damages, he had no standing to sue. Justice McReynolds spoke for the Four Horsemen in such vitriolic terms that some of his comments did not appear in the formal record. At one point he bitterly commented, "This is Nero at his worst. The Constitution as we know it is gone."

The National Industrial Recovery Act

The heart of the First New Deal, as the 1933 measures came to be known, was the National Industrial Recovery Act, its most ambitious and also most ill-conceived act. The preamble read like a lawyer's brief, justifying the law as a legitimate method of removing the burdens on interstate commerce caused by the Depression. Everybody got something. Industries could draft business-wide codes regulating fair competition that would be exempt from antitrust prohibitions, although a later section declared that nothing in the bill should be construed as suspending the antitrust laws. Labor got section 7(a) guaranteeing the right to organize into unions and to bargain collectively, and ensuring this provision would appear in every one of the industrial codes, which also had to have provisions for maximum hours and minimum wages. Congress appropriated the then-unheard-of sum of $3.3 billion for public works with the clear aim of hiring the unemployed. A National Recovery Administration (NRA) would oversee the industrial codes and compliance. The bill was clearly modeled on the experience of the Great War, when labor, management, and government had worked in close and fruitful cooperation. If, however, businesses balked at signing the industrial codes, the NRA had the power, in the name of the president, to draft and impose codes on the recalcitrants. All codes, once approved by the president, had the force of law. As even those who supported the general ideas embodied in the bill admitted, it had been poorly drafted, the procedures were sloppy at best, and there were numerous internal contradictions.

The first case involving federal legislation to come before the Court—*Panama Refining Co. v. Ryan*—focused on one portion of the NRA that actually made good sense but which had all the defects of the larger measure. Several oil-producing states, in an effort to raise oil prices, had imposed maximum production limits on wells within their borders, but they had no power to control excess illegal production—so-called hot oil—from being sold in interstate commerce. Much to the satisfaction of these states, the NRA gave the president authority to bar interstate shipment of oil produced in excess of state laws. This idea seemed to have a sound constitutional basis, since the policy resembled that of the 1913 Webb-Kenyon Act, in which federal power had been used to keep liquor from being transported into states that had adopted Prohibition.

Whatever merits the idea may have had, the administration of the measure could not be justified. An amazed Court heard counsel for the oil producers relate how they had been unable to obtain copies of the regulations, and then how the rules, which had the force of law, had been promulgated in a careless and casual way. At one point Justice Brandeis asked the government attorney defending the law, "Is there any way by which to find out what is in these executive orders when they are issued?" The embarrassed lawyer admitted it would be difficult.

An 8–1 Court, with only Cardozo dissenting, invalidated the hot oil clause. Chief Justice Hughes did not deny that Congress had the power to regulate hot oil, but the Court just could not overlook the slipshod way it had gone about the job. Moreover, while agreeing that Congress could delegate power to the president, it had the responsibility of providing policy and standards to guide him. The ruling returned the oil industry to a condition of unregulated, cutthroat competition, which need not have happened had the bill been more carefully crafted. One positive result of *Panama Refining Co.* is that the government soon afterward began publishing the *Federal Register*, which has made government regulations available in an orderly and easily ascertainable form.

The *Schechter* Case

Although the decision did not touch upon the rest of the Recovery Act, the administration realized that the delegation of powers to the president in other programs could not measure up any better than had the hot oil arrangement, and it waited for the other shoe to drop. On so-called Black Monday, May 27, 1935, it did. The Supreme Court unanimously invalidated the National Recovery Act as well as the Frazier-Lemke Act that provided mortgage relief, and ruled that the president could not remove members of independent regulatory commissions.

Normally when multiple cases challenge the constitutionality of a federal statute, the Court allows the solicitor general to recommend which case should come up to the high court, and the government, naturally, will select that case in which it can make the strongest argument. In arguing the NRA, the government had originally planned on using the Lumber Code as its test case. A few large manufacturers dominated the industry, and so a code drawn by and then agreed to by the leaders would control the practices of the smaller companies as well—exactly how the NRA wanted the codes to function. The lumber code, however, had a number of anomalies relevant to the business that in the end would have prevented a resolution of the major constitutional questions, and the high court dismissed that suit in *United States v. Belcher* (1935). In looking for another test case, the solicitor general chose poorly in deciding to defend the poultry code.

Unlike lumber, the poultry business in the United States was heavily fragmented. Chickens were raised on thousands of farms, and then sold either to middlemen or directly to local butchers, depending on geography and the local market. There were no industry leaders, no large wholesale processors (such as the Perdue Company today), and thousands of local butcher shops. As a result, the government could look to no single company or even a group of them to act as industry leaders, and in 1934 the NRA itself drafted and then promulgated the Live Poultry Code. The code fixed the maximum number of hours employees could work, imposed a minimum wage, and banned certain methods of "unfair" competition.

If a market needed stability, the poultry business certainly qualified. The New York City area comprised one of the largest poultry markets in the nation, with sales of 190 million pounds in 1933. Farmers considered chickens as good as cash, since unlike seasonal crops such as corn—which could only be sold after a harvest—chickens could be sold any day of the year. Moreover, farmers could sell one or two chickens, or a dozen or more, whenever they needed cash. But the price per pound that farmers received had fallen by more than half from 1929 to 1933, from 30 cents to 14 cents. The Live Poultry Code for the New York area aimed at imposing controls on the market and raising the price that both farmers and butchers received for their product.

The Schechter brothers ran a kosher butcher shop in Brooklyn, New York. They purchased live poultry from wholesalers in New York and Philadelphia, slaughtered the chickens, and then sold the processed chickens to retail stores and to other butchers. The Schechters were charged with sixty counts of violating the code by selling "unfit" chickens, illegally selling chickens on an individual basis, avoiding inspections by local poultry regulators, falsifying records of sales, and selling chickens to nonlicensed purchasers. A federal district court jury found them guilty of nineteen counts, and the Court of Appeals for the Second Circuit affirmed the conviction.

Chicken markets, even fairly good-sized ones such as the Schechters operated, were primarily local stores, and catered not only to retail food outlets but also to neighbors who came in wanting a chicken. Although the code forbade it, the Schechters allowed their longtime customers to pick out which chicken they wanted, and then slaughtered it for them. They understood that there was no way a housewife in the straightened circumstances of the Depression was going to just take whatever chicken the butcher offered; it ran against the centuries-old customs of local markets in Europe as well as the United States. (Even now, consider going to the grocery store or a fruit market to buy apples or grapefruit. People examine the produce, handling individual pieces of fruit before deciding what they want to buy, and would not patronize a store or a fruit stand that would not let them make their own choices.)

The high court accepted the appeal, heard oral argument on May 2 and 3, and handed the decision down a little over three weeks later. Normally the Court tries to decide cases on as narrow a basis as possible. If there are two reasons to either approve or strike down a law, the Court will use the narrower one and not even discuss the other. But in *Schechter v. United States,* Chief Justice Hughes posed *three* broad questions, and then proceeded to answer them all. Did the economic crisis create extraordinary governmental powers? Had Congress lawfully delegated its powers to the president? Did the act exceed the government's authority under the commerce clause? This radical departure from the Court's customary procedures made it quite clear to many observers that not only Hughes, but the entire bench, wanted to make sure that after the Court invalidated the National Industrial Recovery Act it would stay dead.

In his earlier opinion in *Blaisdell* upholding the Minnesota mortgage moratorium, Hughes had clearly said that emergencies could call forth latent powers; he now reversed himself and declared that "extraordinary conditions do not create or enlarge constitutional power." The elaborate rationale in the Recovery Act's preamble tying the remedy to the Depression made no impression on the Court. As for the delegation of power, the chief justice reiterated the Court's objections in *Panama Refining Co.* Congress clearly could delegate power to the president, but it had to establish clear guidelines and standards. Here it had given the president a blank check to create and enforce codes or, worse yet, to enforce as the law of the land codes that were drafted by private parties. Justice Cardozo added a concurring opinion that captured the sense of the Court when he described the problem as "delegation running riot."

Had the delegation problem been the only difficulty with the Recovery Act, it could easily have been remedied. The ruling that emergencies did not create new or enlarge existing powers might have cramped the administration but would have been acceptable if the

Court had conceded the government's power to regulate these industries. But Hughes—joined by all of his colleagues—answered the third question, dealing with the reach of governmental authority under the commerce clause, in as narrow a manner as possible. He revived the old distinction that most scholars considered obsolete and discarded, between the direct and indirect effects of local activity on interstate commerce. Only those activities that directly affected interstate commerce could be regulated by the federal government. The Schechters' business had no direct effect—and in fact very little indirect effect—on interstate commerce and therefore could not be regulated by Congress. Even Justice Cardozo, who in his concurrence differed with Hughes over how one could determine the distinction between direct and indirect effect, could not find any connection between selling sick chickens in Brooklyn and interstate commerce.

Roosevelt received the news of Black Monday in astonishment, and could hardly believe that even the liberal members of the Court had gone against him: "Where was Ben Cardozo? And what about old Isaiah [Brandeis]?" To reporters he complained that the decision relegated the country to "the horse-and-buggy definition of interstate commerce." The president did not understand that even many of his liberal supporters thought the Recovery Act unconstitutional and in fact detested the emphasis of the early New Deal on large-scale planning.

The New Deal Farm Program and the Court

However, even those of Roosevelt's supporters who opposed the NRA believed that the New Deal's agricultural program not only justified, but in fact was working effectively to cure the ills plaguing the nation's farmers. They were to be sorely disappointed by the Court's next New Deal ruling. The agricultural sector had been depressed since 1921, and poverty on the nation's farms contrasted sharply with the general prosperity of the nation in the 1920s. Farming may have been the last "true" market in America—one in which the laws of supply and demand operated, and with no single buyer or seller, or even groups of buyers or sellers, able to influence prices. But as prices fell, farmers tried to make up the loss in their income by growing more, and this additional supply, without a corresponding rise in demand, only further depressed prices for farm goods. What needed to be done was to somehow limit farm production, and the New Deal embarked on this course in the Agricultural Adjustment Act (AAA) of 1933.

The AAA rested on the notion of "parity." The market would be regulated so as to ensure farmers the same purchasing power for their crops as they had in the base period of 1909–1914. Farmers accepting voluntary restrictions on production and the amount of acreage planted could participate in a government plan of price supports, and the entire scheme would be financed by a tax on food processors, such as the miller who converted wheat to flour. During Roosevelt's first term, farmers' gross income rose more than 50 percent, while rural debt fell sharply, although the droughts of 1934 and 1935 may deserve as much credit as the AAA for limiting production.

The constitutionality of the AAA was argued on December 9, 1935, and the Court handed down its decision in *United States v. Butler* on January 6, 1936. This time, however, the justices were far from unified.

Drafters of the bill had felt confident that in the food processing tax they could rely on a recognized federal power. Officials of the Hoosac Mills Corporation attacked the levy, which they characterized not as a true tax but as an integral part of an unconstitutional plan to regulate agricultural production. The government challenged their right to sue since the Court had, in several cases, held that taxpayers had no standing to question in court how the federal government spent its tax revenues. The conservatives on the Court brushed this argument aside, and according to Justice Roberts, the plaintiffs had challenged not just the tax and its uses, but the whole regulatory plan of which the tax "is a mere incident."

Roberts's majority opinion is tortured and confusing. He had to dismiss a long line of precedents to make out that the processing tax was not a "true" tax, merely because none of the proceeds went into the general coffers; instead, it purchased compliance with a program that exceeded congressional power. He ignored the nature of a modern economy by characterizing agriculture as purely a local enterprise, and therefore not subject to the commerce clause. Even if the sum of many local conditions had created a national problem, Congress could not "ignore constitutional limitations" imposed by the Tenth Amendment, which gave the states any powers not specifically granted to the national government.

The ruling brought forth strong protests from within and outside the Court. Harlan Fiske Stone, considered the most knowledgeable person on the bench regarding taxation, dissented sharply from what he considered Roberts's myopic view of the taxing power. Joined by Brandeis and Cardozo, Stone pointed out that the processing tax did nothing more than raise revenue; the regulatory part came through the appropriations process. He condemned Roberts's "tortured construction of the Constitution," and the majority's resort to the argument that if it allowed this program to stand then the government could regulate any area of the nation's economic life. Finally, he dismissed Roberts's claim that there was no personal judgment in his opinion, and attacked the majority for their hypocrisy in substituting their own judgment for that of Congress.

The Attack on the New Deal Continues

The attack by the Court's conservatives on the New Deal and on efforts by the states to address the Depression seemed relentless. After the *Schechter* decision Congress had tried to salvage part of the Recovery Act in the Guffy-Snyder Coal Conservation Act of 1935. The NRA coal code had brought a desperately needed stability to the mining industry, and the new law tried to reestablish that stability. Declaring coal production part of interstate commerce and "affected with a national public interest," Congress asserted that regulation was not only necessary but constitutionally justified. The conservative majority on the Court would have none of it, however.

In *Carter v. Carter Coal Company* (1936), Justice Sutherland declared the entire bill unconstitutional in a 5–4 ruling. He relied on *Schechter* for an extremely restrictive view of interstate commerce; while the transportation of coal might be interstate commerce, mining was local and therefore not subject to congressional control. Despite the clear intention of Congress to have the different parts of the bill treated separately through the use of a severability clause, Sutherland invalidated them all, including the labor provisions that had not even been at issue. All the provisions, he declared, were intertwined, all were terrible, and all were unconstitutional.

Even Chief Justice Hughes could not stomach this. In a separate opinion he agreed that even though the labor provisions were invalid, the Court should not ignore the congressional severability clause. Cardozo, speaking also for Brandeis and Stone, charged that the majority had turned its back on the realities outside the courtroom. If an industry as disrupted as coal, and so central to the nation's economic well-being, could not be federally regulated, then little hope remained for solving the country's economic woes.

The *Carter* decision that fanned the growing public protest against the Court was on the New Deal, and in the next few weeks the Four Horsemen—determined to kill what they considered radical governmental interference in business matters—added fuel to the flames. First, by a 5–4 majority, the Court struck down the Municipal Bankruptcy Act of 1934 as an infringement on states' rights. The act allowed local governments and agencies, with the permission of the states, to file for voluntary bankruptcy (bankruptcy being governed by national law). Justice McReynolds condemned the act as infringing on state sovereignty; Cardozo's dissent, joined by Hughes, Brandeis, and Stone, pointed out that since the states had to approve before a municipality could act, they lost nothing. Then in June, again by a 5–4 vote, the Court invalidated a New York State minimum wage statute as a violation of freedom of contract in *Morehead v. New York ex rel. Tipaldo.* Justice Butler's opinion emphasized that the doctrine of *Adkins v. Children's Hospital* (1923) still governed.

The New Deal's only victory in 1935 and 1936 came in Chief Justice Hughes's narrow ruling upholding the Tennessee Valley Authority. In *Ashwander v. Tennessee Valley Authority* (1936), the Court approved the sale of electrical power generated by a federal dam to a private power company on the grounds that the federal government had undisputed power to sell off not only the lands it owned, but also any byproducts of those lands such as minerals or power. At least for the time being the Court did not look into the extensive planning aspects of the TVA.

By the fall of 1936 the Four Horsemen, joined by Roberts, stood at the head of opposition to the New Deal and its programs. While liberals naturally protested the Court's failure to restrain itself and to stop meddling into the policymaking prerogatives of the legislature, even many conservatives felt the Court had gone too far. After the *Morehead* decision, former president Herbert Hoover complained that the Court had taken away powers from the states that they legitimately had. The Republican candidate for president in 1936, Alf Landon of Kansas, did as much as he could to distance himself from the Court. Members of both parties supported a constitutional amendment to affirm the states' authority to regulate working conditions.

In the election Franklin Roosevelt did not mention the Court; he did not have to, since everyone recognized that popular programs to put people back to work stood endangered by five men. Roosevelt promised to expand the New Deal and to heal America. In 1935 and 1936 Congress had enacted a whole series of measures, the so-called Second New Deal that included, among other bills, the Social Security program. All of these would come before the Court after the election, a fact everyone understood. That fall, the American people signaled their approval of the New Deal by giving Roosevelt the most sweeping margin of victory since James Monroe had run unopposed more than a century earlier. All but two states, Maine and Vermont, voted for Roosevelt, and he enjoyed strong Democratic majorities in both houses of Congress. With such a mandate, Roosevelt could not allow five old men, even justices of the Supreme Court, to stop the New Deal. Everyone knew he would have to do something, but the president gave no clue as to what he was considering.

The Court-Packing Plan

Two weeks after his second inaugural, Roosevelt, who had been mulling over several plans, decided to pack the Court with justices who would be friendly to New Deal measures. The number of justices is not spelled out in the Constitution, and over the years it had varied; but it had been nine since the 1870s. Roosevelt claimed that the Court had fallen behind its work because the aging justices no longer could keep up with the demands of their jobs. Six members of the Court were over seventy, and Brandeis—arguably the justice most accepting of the New Deal—was over eighty. Roosevelt proposed that for each member of the judiciary over seventy the president could appoint an additional member of the Court, with a maximum of six to the high court and forty-four to the district and appellate benches. The whole plan, he claimed, was designed to make the judiciary more efficient. Only later did he admit the true reason: "We cannot yield our constitutional destiny to the personal judgment of a few men who, fearful of the future, would deny us the necessary means of dealing with the present."

For once Roosevelt's famed political sagacity deserted him, and he totally misjudged both the sentiments of the country and of Congress. Had he come out and said from the beginning that a handful of old men should not be allowed to thwart the nation's will, there would have been opposition but he might have won; in fact, he almost did. But Roosevelt appeared too crafty, not trustworthy on this issue, and the longer the debate went on the less support he enjoyed. The famed editor of the *Emporia* (Kan.) *Gazette*, William Allen White, asked what would stop a future reactionary president "as charming, as eloquent and as irresistible as Roosevelt" from packing the Court to abridge the Bill of Rights.

Elsie Parrish Wants Her Money

The death blow to the Roosevelt plan came in a series of decisions beginning in late March 1937, starting with *West Coast Hotel v. Parrish*. Between 1933 and 1935 Elsie Parrish, a grandmother, had worked periodically as a chambermaid at the Cascadian Hotel in Wenatchee, Washington, a facility owned by the West Coast Hotel Company. The hotel paid her $12 per week, less than the minimum wage of $14.50 per week for a forty-eight-hour week as established by the state's Industrial Welfare Committee. When the hotel let her go she asked for both the back wages due on her regular hours as well as the time-and-a-half the law required for overtime, a total of $216. The hotel offered her $17, and she went to court.

Parrish lost in the trial court, which on the basis of *Adkins v. Children's Hospital* (1923) ruled the state minimum wage law unconstitutional. The Washington Supreme Court, however, distinguished the state law from the federal minimum wage law that had been struck down in *Adkins*, since it applied only to the District of Columbia. In citing that case, Judge Millard skipped over the majority holding and cited at length the dissents by William Howard Taft and Oliver Wendell Holmes arguing for the constitutionality of a minimum wage. Millard also noted that *Adkins* had not disturbed the decision in *Stettler v. O'Hara* (1917), which upheld an Oregon minimum wage law. The court found for Elsie Parrish, and the case went on appeal to the U.S. Supreme Court.

To nearly everyone's surprise, on March 29, 1937, the high court by a 5–4 vote upheld the Washington statute. Owen Roberts, who had written the decision invalidating a similar New York law a year earlier in *Morehead*, joined with Hughes and the liberals in an opinion that *Adkins* had been wrong and should be overruled. Hughes dismissed the *Morehead* case by asserting that at the time the Court had not been asked to reexamine *Adkins*, and therefore had used it as a determining precedent.

Roberts's change of heart led to a great deal of speculation, as well as the claim that the Court had reversed course to save itself from the Roosevelt reorganization and a loss of power. "A switch in time," contemporary wits chuckled, "saves nine." But in fact it appears fairly certain that Roosevelt's plan did not affect the Court's decision. Roberts had been unhappy with his *Morehead* opinion, but since New York had not challenged *Adkins*, Roberts, the least creative member of the bench, felt he could not raise it. When *Parrish* had been argued in December 1936, counsel for Washington had asked for a reversal of *Adkins*, and Roberts voted to sustain the law. Because of illness, Justice Stone had not voted and, wanting to avoid a 4–4 decision that would have left the Washington court decision in place but would not have struck down *Adkins*, Chief Justice Hughes postponed the vote. Had Stone not been ill, the opinion would have come down in January, before Roosevelt announced his plan, and in fact might have forestalled it.

After *Parrish* the Court moved back to the path it had been following prior to 1935, sustaining state regulations to bolster the economy under the broad rubric of the police power, and upholding New Deal measures through a liberal reading of the commerce clause and the taxing power. All of the important measures of the Second New Deal—Social Security, the Wagner Labor Relations Act, debtor relief, progressive taxation, unemployment insurance—received the Court's blessing, although usually with a strong dissent by the Four Horsemen. Then they began to retire, and by 1943 Roosevelt had appointed eight of the nine members of the Court. The Court-packing plan had failed, but Roosevelt claimed that while he might have lost that battle, he had won the war.

Cases Cited

Adkins v. Children's Hospital, 261 U.S. 525 (1923)
Ashwander v. Tennessee Valley Authority, 297 U.S. 288 (1936)
Carter v. Carter Coal Company, 298 U.S. 238 (1936)
Home Building & Loan Assn. v. Blaisdell, 290 U.S. 398 (1934)
Marbury v. Madison, 1 Cr. 137 (1803)
Morehead v. New York ex rel. Tipaldo, 298 U.S. 587 (1936)
Nebbia v. New York, 291 U.S. 502 (1934)
New State Ice Co. v. Liebmann, 285 U.S. 262 (1932)
Norman v. Baltimore & Ohio Railroad Co., 294 U.S. 240 (1935)
Panama Refining Co. v. Ryan, 292 U.S. 388 (1935)
Parrish v. West Coast Hotel Co., 185 Wash. 581 (1936)
Perry v. United States, 294 U.S. 330 (1935)
Schechter v. United States, 295 U.S. 495 (1935)
United States v. Belcher, 294 U.S. 736 (1935)
United States v. Butler, 297 U.S. 1 (1936)
West Coast Hotel Co. v. Parrish, 300 U.S. 379 (1937)

For Further Reading

Good general overviews of the New Deal court cases and the constitutional crisis they provoked are Marian McKenna, *Franklin Roosevelt and the Great Constitutional War: The Court-Packing Crisis of 1937* (2002), and Burt Solomon, *FDR v. the Constitution: The Court-Packing Fight and the Triumph of Democracy* (2009). The best political interpretations can be found in the essays in William E. Leuchtenburg, *The Supreme Court Reborn: The Constitutional Revolution in the Age of Roosevelt* (1995). Alternative interpretations are Barry Cushman, *Rethinking the New Deal Court: The Structure of a Constitutional Revolution* (1998), and Edward G. White, *The Constitution and the New Deal* (2000). Justice Roberts and his nonjurisprudence remain a puzzle to historians, and are examined in Charles A. Leonard, *A Search for a Judicial Philosophy: Mr. Justice Roberts and the Constitutional Revolution of 1937* (1971).

The Case of the Conscientious Schoolchildren

The Flag-Salute Cases (1940 and 1943)

FEW SYMBOLS OF OUR COUNTRY carry so much emotional and patriotic freight as does the American flag, and many people seem ready to deal out a harsh justice to those whom they consider disrespectful of Old Glory. Honoring that symbol can take many forms, but requiring a person to do so, and in a particular way, may also infringe upon that individual's religious beliefs. That is the story behind the flag-salute cases of 1940 and 1943, cases that are part of the beginning of rights consciousness in modern America. These and related cases all grew out of the tenacity of members of a small religious sect, the Jehovah's Witnesses, to cling to their beliefs despite public opprobrium and even physical danger. Justice Harlan Fiske Stone wrote to Chief Justice Charles Evans Hughes that "I think the Jehovah's Witnesses ought to have an endowment in view of the aid which they give in solving the legal problems of civil liberties."

Lillian Gobitas Acts on Her Faith

In October 1935 twelve-year-old Lillian Gobitas and her family, as they did every week, sat around their kitchen table and heard Joseph Rutherford, the head of the Jehovah's Witnesses, deliver his talk about their beliefs and what they meant for the Witnesses in their daily lives. On this day Rutherford implored the faithful not to salute the American flag, because in essence the salute was nothing more than idol worship prohibited by the Bible. Rutherford also spoke about the bravery of Witnesses in Germany who refused to salute Adolf Hitler, and the persecution they suffered for doing so. American Witnesses, he exhorted, should show the same courage as did their German coreligionists.

Lillian determined to practice what Rutherford had preached, and the next day she and her ten-year-old brother, William, along with another Witness child, Edmund Wasliewski, refused to participate in the morning flag-salute ceremony at their grade school in Minersville, Pennsylvania. As she later recalled, "[E]verybody in the class turned and looked. . . . Then they kind of ignored me after that." Once out of the classroom, however, the other students began to taunt the Witness children, and to pick on Lillian and her brother: "When I got to school each morning, a few boys would shout 'Here comes Jehovah!' and shower me with pebbles."

School officials also proved unsympathetic, although there was no regulation mandating that students participate in the flag salute. (It should be noted that at the time the form of salute was an outstretched arm, similar to the one used in Nazi Germany.) The head of the local school board, Charles Roudabush, dismissed pleas for religious tolerance from Lillian's father, Walter; the board then passed a rule requiring participation and expelled the children for their refusal to salute the flag. Walter Gobitas decided to fight the decision in court. He filed a suit on behalf of his children and on his own behalf, asking to be relieved of the financial burden of additional education costs. The state required that all children attend school, yet his children, because of their religious beliefs, could not attend the Minersville schools because of the local school board's regulations. He appealed to the Witness Watchtower Society for aid, and Joseph Rutherford, an able attorney, secured victories in 1938 in federal district court and afterward in the Court of Appeals for the Third Circuit.

The Witnesses in Federal Courts

Federal district judge Albert B. Maris, in what the Supreme Court called a "thoughtful opinion," granted the relief that Walter Gobitas sought. The school board then appealed, but the appellate court upheld Judge Maris's decision. The Third Circuit panel found that the flag salute impinged on the family's First Amendment right to free exercise of religion, as applied to the states through the Fourteenth Amendment's due process clause. During this process the courts, anticipating there would be appeals, did not order the school board to readmit the Witness children, and so they continued to go to a private school. After losing in the court of appeals, the school board decided to appeal to the Supreme Court. In that tribunal, the American Civil Liberties Union (ACLU) and the American Bar Association's Committee on the Bill of Rights both filed briefs supporting the family.

The fact that much of the jurisprudence that has developed about the First Amendment's free exercise clause came from litigation initiated by the Jehovah's Witnesses is somewhat paradoxical. Freedom of expression and conscience is not part of Witness beliefs, which—as a number of sources have testified—can be extremely repressive. The Witnesses practice a rigid faith that leaves practically no room for flexibility or dissent. Witnesses who openly question either the practices or the tenets of the faith can find themselves "disfellowshipped," or excommunicated and shunned by the others.

The group developed out of the late-nineteenth-century Bible study movement founded by Charles Taze Russell, with the formation of Zion's Watchtower Tract Society. Following various schisms and organizational changes, the group that won out imposed an authority structure, brought its evangelical practices under centralized control, and adopted the name Jehovah's Witnesses in 1931.

A central aspect of the movement is extensive study of the Bible, and the belief that in its passages can be found the guide to living today. Witnesses troubled by the flag salute found answers in the relevant passages of the Bible, especially Exodus 20:4–6, Matthew 22:21, and John 5:21. The passage from Exodus in particular seemed to speak directly to the matter by forbidding the worship of anything other than God:

> Thou shalt not make unto thee any graven image, or any likeness of any thing that is in heaven above, or that is in the earth beneath, or that is in the water under the earth. Thou shalt not bow down thyself to them, nor serve them: for I the Lord thy God am a jealous God, visiting the iniquity of the fathers upon the children unto the third and fourth generation of them that hate me.

Lillian recalled that her parents studied this passage with her and her brother and helped them to understand it, but they never pressured the children to do anything. That was to be their own decision, a decision that listening to Joseph Rutherford's radio address helped them to make. After much thought, Lillian and her brother determined that saluting the flag conflicted with their religious beliefs.

Another key tenet of Witness theology involved prosletyzing, a literal "witnessing" of their faith to others and trying to convince them of its truth. This included handing out tracts on street corners, ringing doorbells, talking with potential converts, and otherwise trying to win over adherents. The Witnesses practiced what they believed with such fervency that many townships considered them a nuisance and tried, by various means, to curtail their activities. (This conduct, however, did not seem to be what upset the Minersville School Board; it objected to the refusal of Witness children to salute the flag.)

The Witnesses in the High Court: Round I

The modern school flag-salute ceremony dated from 1892, and the first statute making the salute mandatory passed the New York legislature in 1898 on the day after the United States declared war on Spain. By 1940 thirty states had included the ritual as part of its daily school routine, and nearly all made participation mandatory. Attacks in the courts on the compulsory flag salute had been totally unsuccessful. At the time of the Minersville School Board's petition for review, the Supreme Court had already considered the question of a compulsory flag salute three times, and three times it had disposed of the issue in brief, unsigned *per curiam* (collectively written) memoranda that held the matter to be of local or at most a state matter, with no federal question involved. As recently as April 1939 the Court had unanimously denied an appeal from the Supreme Court of California, which had upheld a mandatory flag salute in public schools.

When the high court heard the *Minersville* case, Joseph Henderson, a pillar of the Philadelphia bar, represented the school board, and he made three points:

1. The expulsion of the Gobitas children did not violate their rights under the U.S. Constitution.
2. The expulsion did not violate their rights under the constitution of the Commonwealth of Pennsylvania.
3. The children's refusal to participate in the flag-salute exercise because they believed doing so would violate a law of God, as contained in the Bible, was not founded on a religious belief.

This last point by itself shows how greatly the majority of people at that time misunderstood the nature not only of what Jehovah's Witnesses believed, but of the great variety of religious beliefs that differed from mainstream Protestant thought. Baptists, Methodists, Episcopalians, and other Protestant groups had no problem with the flag salute; the many Americans who belonged to the mainline religions could not fathom how one could oppose the salute on religious grounds.

Professor George K. Gardner of the Harvard Law School and Joseph Rutherford himself led the team representing the Gobitas children. Their case rested on two assertions. First, man must be free to exercise his conscientious belief in God and according to what he believes to be the commands of God, and the state may not compel him to obey a rule that he conscientiously believes conflicts with God's law. Second, the regulation made and enforced by the Minersville School District violated the Fourteenth Amendment of the Constitution.

Lillian Gobitas and her family had traveled to Washington in April 1940 to hear oral argument in the case (the clerk of the Court misspelled the family name as "Gobitis," which it has remained in Court records and history books until this day), and she remembered the event in great detail:

> The nine judges heard another case before us. Some kind of corporate case and, oh, there were interruptions, dropping pencils and paper and this and that and interrupting the lawyers.... Then along came Joseph Rutherford and he argued from the Bible standpoint. And instead of all that shuffling and interruptions, there was not a sound. It was so awesome.... He compared the Witness Children to the three Hebrews that refused to bow down before Nebuchadnezzar's image and were ready to be thrown into the fiery furnace. Biblical examples like that.... Everyone just paid rapt attention and that surely included me.... And so we thought that because we had won in both [lower] courts, well it's a shoo-in.

It was not. Although Lillian may have been impressed by the performance of Gardner, Rutherford, and the society's legal counsel, Hayden Covington, legal scholars have considered both the briefs filed by the Watchtower Society as well as the oral argument as woefully inadequate. The historian David Manwaring described the Witnesses' effort as "a discouragingly bad brief. It ignored all the most crucial constitutional issues, and seemed calculated to produce a negative emotional effect with its repeated recourse to argument *ad hominem*." Full of hyperbole, it cast the proponents of the compulsory flag salute as champions of "arbitrary totalitarian rule of the state."

Although they did little good, the *amicus* briefs filed by the ACLU and the American Bar Association addressed what we now consider the key constitutional issues of the application and reach of the First Amendment's religion clauses. In 1940 the process of incorporation, by which the Fourteenth Amendment's due process clause applied the protections of the Bill of Rights to the states, had not progressed that far. The Court had applied the speech clause as well as the press clause, and in the infamous *Scottsboro* trial had also declared that states had to provide a fair jury trial, but no decision had yet applied the free exercise clause. The majority of the justices favored a cautious approach, since the idea that the due process clause applied the Bill of Rights to the states was, at least in the high court, a new concept.

This caution can be seen in *Palko v. Connecticut* (1937), where Justice Benjamin Cardozo laid down the guidelines for which constitutional rights should be incorporated and applied to the states. Cardozo included all of the protections of the First Amendment, for freedom of thought and speech "is the matrix, the indispensable condition, for nearly every other form of [freedom]." As for the Second through Eighth Amendments, the Court should apply only those that are "of the very essence of a scheme of ordered liberty," and "so rooted in the traditions and conscience of our people as to be ranked as fundamental." He did not, however, spell out which rights met these criteria.

At first blush it would seem that the free exercise clause of the First Amendment should be included and applicable to the states, since the notion of religious freedom certainly went far back in American history. Many of the early colonists had fled the Old World seeking to avoid religious persecution, and throughout the nineteenth and twentieth centuries other groups had come for the same reason. The immediate precursor of the religion clauses lay in the Virginia Statute for Religious Freedom of 1786, written by Thomas Jefferson and James Madison. The problem was that although the Court and the nation were familiar with the major Protestant religions, as well as with Catholicism and Judaism, they knew little about sects whose beliefs varied from the mainstream.

The Court had heard very few religion cases, and in 1940 the controlling precedent for the free exercise clause dated back to the 1879 decision of *Reynolds v. United States*. In 1862 Congress had passed a law prohibiting polygamy in the U.S. territories, an act clearly directed at the Mormons in Utah. George Reynolds challenged the law on the grounds that Congress had impaired his constitutional right to the free exercise of his beliefs, which included polygamy. A unanimous court disagreed. Chief Justice Morrison Waite drew the distinction between belief and practice. People could believe anything they wanted, and Congress could not punish them for those ideas, no matter how outlandish they might seem. Society, however, had the authority to define what it considered immoral or dangerous behavior, and the power to punish it. Reynolds certainly had the right to believe in multiple marriages, and the government equally had the power to put him in jail if he practiced it.

In the *Minersville* case, the ACLU and the American Bar Association wanted the Court to abandon or at least modify this dichotomy, and to recognize that if a person truly believed in some tenets, then he had to act on them, and had the right to do so if such acts did no harm to others.

The ACLU emphasized that the right "to entertain the belief, to adhere to the principle, and to teach the doctrine, that the act of saluting the flag contravenes the law of Almighty God, is a part of the liberty referred to in the Fourteenth Amendment." Beyond that the ACLU brief, like the opinion in the Third Circuit, questioned whether mandating the flag salute really fostered true patriotism. Would expelling the Witness children "instruct the youth of Pennsylvania in loyalty to the flag and Constitution of the United States"? In other words, did the flag-salute requirement accomplish its stated purpose?

The Bar Association committee in its brief claimed that no public need existed for the compulsory flag salute "as to justify the overriding of the religious scruples of the children." The conclusion challenged the Court to look at the world around it, and to adhere to the high ideals of the Constitution:

> The philosophy of free institutions is now being subjected to the most severe test it has ever undergone. Advocates of totalitarian government point to the speed and efficiency with which such systems are administered, and assert that democracy can offer nothing to outweigh these advantages. The answer is to be found in the value of certain basic individual rights and the assurance afforded by free institutions that these shall not be required to yield to majority pressure no matter how overwhelming.
>
> The worth of our system must ultimately be judged in terms of the importance of these values and the care with which they are safeguarded. We consider them immeasurably important. We believe that the letter as well as the spirit of our Constitution demand vindication of the individual liberties which are abridged by the challenged regulation.

The argument carried no weight with the justices. During oral argument Justice Felix Frankfurter passed a note to his colleague Frank Murphy questioning whether the Framers of the Bill of Rights "would have thought that a requirement to salute the flag violates the protection of 'the free exercise of religion'?" Frankfurter, a naturalized American citizen, took ideals of citizenship and patriotism very seriously, and he had little sympathy with those who, as he saw it, refused to meet their civic obligations. This may have been why Chief Justice Hughes assigned the opinion to Frankfurter.

In his opinion for the 8–1 majority, Frankfurter started by noting that when the Court "must reconcile the conflicting claims of liberty and authority, [and] when the liberty invoked is liberty of conscience, and the authority is authority to safeguard the nation's fellowship, judicial conscience is put to its severest test." But although he acknowledged the importance of free religious belief, Frankfurter claimed it had never been absolute, and had always been limited by laws of a general nature. He then framed the "precise" issue in terms of judicial restraint—that is, of the Court not second-guessing policies enacted by the elected branches—and called upon the Court to defer to the wisdom and prerogatives of local school authorities:

> To stigmatize legislative judgment in providing for this universal gesture of respect for the symbol of our national life in the setting of the common school as a lawless inroad on that freedom of conscience which the Constitution protects would amount to no less than the pronouncement of pedagogical and psychological dogma in a field where courts possess no marked and certainly no controlling competence. . . . To the legislature no less than to courts is committed the guardianship of deeply cherished liberties.

There is a formulaic quality to the opinion, and it reflects Frankfurter's long-held ideas on judicial restraint, a view he and other liberals had long argued when conservatives imposed their own economic biases to negate progressive reforms. Is the legislative end legitimate? Are the means chosen reasonable? If so, then it is not up to the courts to say there is a better way. The fact that this law affected religious beliefs did not matter to Frankfurter, who made no distinction between laws regulating the economy and laws regulating personal expression or speech. Even some of Frankfurter's admirers called this his "fall of France" opinion (the decision was announced during the Dunkirk evacuation of Allied soldiers from France after their defeat at the hands of the Germans), since he believed that the United States would soon be drawn into the European conflict and that fostering patriotism was a paramount objective of public schools.

Some of Frankfurter's defenders believe that in his heart he knew that the practice of mandating flag salutes was wrong, but that given what then existed as settled free exercise doctrine—and there was precious little of it—his core belief in judicial restraint compelled him to write as he did. Frankfurter may have been one of the smartest men ever to sit on the high court, but not one of its most creative. Where Holmes and Brandeis—whom he acknowledged as his heroes—could reach out and create new doctrines where the old ones had failed, Frankfurter could not.

Only Harlan Fiske Stone dissented, and followed the line of reasoning in his 1938 *Carolene Products* opinion, where he had declared that the Court had a special obligation to protect minorities. "The Constitution expresses more than the conviction of the people that democratic processes must be preserved at all costs," he wrote. "It is also an expression of faith and a command that freedom of mind and spirit must be preserved, which government must obey, if it is to adhere to that justice and moderation without which no free government can exist."

Where Frankfurter willingly left the protection of minority rights to the legislative branch, Stone recognized that the enforcement of liberties could not be left to the polls. The whole idea of the Bill of Rights was to shield minorities from the majority will, and that legislative "protection" of groups like the Witnesses would not be sufficient when a majority of voters felt their beliefs were incorrect, inappropriate, or even offensive.

The Violent Response to the Decision

The three most liberal members of the Court—Hugo Black, William Douglas, and Frank Murphy—voted with the majority but were troubled from the start. Black did not like the law but saw nothing in the Constitution to invalidate the measure. Douglas later claimed that if Stone had not been so late in circulating his dissent he might have joined it. When the Court convened after the summer recess, Douglas told Frankfurter that Black had second thoughts about his *Gobitis* vote. "Has Black been reading the Constitution?" Frankfurter asked sarcastically. "No," Douglas replied, "he has been reading the newspapers."

There Black—and everyone else—would have noted the Justice Department reports that in the weeks following the decision there had been hundreds of attacks on Witnesses, especially in small towns and rural areas, a pattern that continued for at least two more years. In Kennebunkport, Maine, the townspeople burned a Witness meeting hall, and in Rockville, Maryland, just outside the nation's capital, a mob attacked a Witness Bible meeting. A lawyer who represented the Witnesses in Connersville, Indiana, was beaten and driven out of town. The city council in Jackson, Mississippi, banned Witnesses from living there. Veterans were at the head of mobs in Arkansas, California, Texas, Wyoming, and other places that attacked Witnesses. In Litchfield, Illinois, a mob attacked a caravan of Witness automobiles, overturning and burning them. Several states moved against the group by seizing children who refused to salute the flag, and after local courts declared them delinquents, committing them to reformatories. The St. Louis

Post-Dispatch editorialized that while it would be a mistake to attribute all of the violence to the Supreme Court decision, "there can be little doubt that that most unfortunate decision will be an encouragement for self-appointed guardians of patriotism and the national moralists to take the law into their own hands."

Gobitis is one of the early cases in which the Court wrestled with how far the protection of the Bill of Rights—originally written to restrain the federal government—should apply to the states. In a famous footnote in the *Carolene Products* case, Justice Stone had written that courts had to look more intensely at issues involving individual rights than at economic regulations. Frankfurter's majority opinion denied that any difference existed, but at least four members of the Court—Stone, Black, Douglas, and Murphy—disagreed, and over the next few years, as the Witnesses brought one challenge after another to local regulations that they claimed impinged on their freedom of conscience, these four could sometimes pick up one or more votes to expand the meaning of the First Amendment guarantees, although some decisions still went against the Witnesses.

Expanding the Boundaries of the First Amendment

In *Cox v. New Hampshire* (1941), for example, a unanimous Court upheld a state regulation requiring permits for parades, even religious parades, and the following year sustained the conviction of a Witness who had gotten into a fight after calling a city marshal "a God-damned racketeer" and "a damned Fascist." Frank Murphy, normally the Court's champion of free speech, found these "fighting words" outside First Amendment protection (*Chaplinsky v. New Hampshire* [1942]).

The following term the Witnesses were back in Court after they refused to pay a municipal licensing fee for peddlers prior to selling their religious tracts. The issue in *Jones v. Opelika* (1942) was essentially the same as in *Gobitis*—the extent to which the government's acknowledged power to maintain public order impinged on the free exercise of religion. A majority voted to sustain the ordinance, but this time four judges dissented—Stone, Black, Douglas, and Murphy. Moreover, in an unprecedented step, the latter three appended a statement acknowledging *Opelika* as a logical extension of *Gobitis*, and said this was "an appropriate occasion" to confess that they had been wrong in the earlier case. The majority opinions in both decisions, they charged, suppresses or tends to suppress the free exercise of religion practiced by a minority group. This is but another step in the direction which *Minersville School District v. Gobitis* took against the same religious minority and is a logical extension of the principles upon which that decision rested. Since we joined in the opinion in the *Gobitis Case,* we think this is an appropriate occasion to state that we now believe that it was also wrongly decided. Certainly our democratic form of government functioning under the historic Bill of Rights has a high responsibility to accommodate itself to the religious views of minorities however unpopular and unorthodox those views may be. The First Amendment does not put the right freely to exercise religion in a subordinate position. We fear, however, that the opinions in these and the *Gobitis Case* do exactly that.

This recantation infuriated Frankfurter, who pointed out that *Gobitis* had not been challenged in the *Opelika* litigation or even mentioned in conference.

By this time many Americans had begun to rethink the implications of the earlier flag-salute case, especially after the country entered the war against fascism. The flag salute could hardly compare to the repression practiced in Nazi Germany (and it had been changed from an outstretched arm to one's hand over the heart in the meantime), but it did strike many people as a needless intrusion on personal liberty in the name of the state. Although Black and Frankfurter disagreed on many things, they did agree, as the latter told Justice Stanley Reed, that the Witness cases "are probably but the curtain raisers of future problems of [great] range and magnitude."

When Wiley Rutledge joined the Court in January 1943, the dissenters in *Opelika* finally had a majority. In May 1943 the Court by 5–4 majorities handed the Witnesses two victories on the same day. In *Murdock v. Pennsylvania,* it struck down a tax on peddlers of religious tracts, and in *Martin v. Struthers* invalidated an ordinance prohibiting door-to-door distribution of religious materials. In the first case Justice Douglas likened the levy to taxing a minister for the privilege of delivering a sermon, while in the latter Justice Black conceded the need for some police regulation but held that the preferred position of speech and religion took precedence.

Frankfurter, angry at seeing his *Gobitis* majority vanish, penned a furious dissent that attacked the majority for its "large, uncritical, congenial abstractions" that would confuse and mislead the American people. He also responded to critics who had suggested that he and his allies did not care about the protection of individual liberties. Frankfurter and those who voted with him cared for the Bill of Rights as much as the majority did, but felt themselves bound by the overarching principle of judicial restraint.

The High Court: Round II

These cases set the stage for the Court to revisit its decision in *Gobitis*. Challenges to the flag salute arose in several states, and the Court accepted an appeal from West Virginia. There the state Board of Education, pursuant to an act of the state legislature, required all schools—public, private, and parochial—to require courses "for the purpose of teaching, fostering and perpetuating the ideals, principles and spirit of Americanism, and increasing the knowledge of the organization and machinery of the government."

In a resolution dated January 9, 1942, and drawing heavily on Frankfurter's opinion in *Gobitis*, the school board ordered school authorities in each community to make the flag salute a regular part of the daily program. All teachers and pupils "shall be required to participate in the salute honoring the Nation represented by the flag," and refusal to salute would be "regarded as an act of insubordination, and shall be dealt with accordingly." Children were to be expelled, and not readmitted until they agreed to participate in the ritual. An expelled child not in school would be deemed a delinquent, and parents and guardians would be liable to fines and a jail term.

The draconian measure soon elicited a spate of lawsuits. Three Jehovah's Witnesses—Walter Barnette, Paul Stull, and Lucy McClure—brought suit on behalf of their children in federal district court in Charleston seeking an injunction against enforcement of the new rules (*West Virginia Board of Education v. Barnette* [1943]). The arguments mirrored those in the earlier case, with the parents claiming an unconstitutional abridgement of religious freedom and free speech for their children, while the school board asserted its authority over children in its care, and citing *Gobitis*, asked for the suit to be dismissed as without merit. Recognizing the importance of the case, the federal district court set up a special panel to hear it, two judges from the district and a third from the Court of Appeals for the Fourth Circuit, John J. Parker of North Carolina.

Although lower courts are required to adhere to Supreme Court decisions, in this case the judges chose not to follow *Gobitis*, even though it had been decided less than three years earlier. They noted that at least four members of the Supreme Court now believed the *Gobitis* ruling to be wrong, and that in *Jones v. Opelika* the majority had to a large measure ignored *Gobitis*. Judge Parker, speaking for the entire panel, wrote:

Under such circumstances and believing as we do that the flag salute here required is violative of religious liberty when required of persons holding the religious views of plaintiffs, we feel that we should be recreant to our duty as judges if through a blind following of a decision which the Supreme Court itself has thus impaired as authority, we should deny protection to rights which we regard as among the most sacred of those protected by constitutional guaranties.

The school board appealed to the Supreme Court, which heard oral argument on March 11, 1943. Many of the same names could be found on the briefs of the two parties, as well as those of the ABA Committee on the Bill of Rights and the American Civil Liberties Union. What had changed was the makeup of the high court. *Gobitis* had been decided by an 8–1 majority, with only Harlan Fiske Stone dissenting. In the subsequent Witness cases Hugo Black, William Douglas, and Frank Murphy had moved to Stone's side. When President Franklin Roosevelt elevated Harlan Stone to replace Hughes as chief justice and James Byrnes left the Court for an executive position in the war administration, the president named Robert H. Jackson and Wiley Rutledge to their seats. Rutledge had immediately sided with the Stone group, and helped achieve the victories in *Murdock* and *Struthers*. Jackson normally allied himself with Felix Frankfurter to uphold governmental regulation, but in this case he voted to support the Witnesses. Stone assigned the decision to Jackson, much to the chagrin of Black and Douglas, who wanted to proclaim the justice of their recantation.

After reviewing the facts, Jackson began by noting that the rights asserted by the Witness children did not bring them into any conflict with the rights of other individuals, the type of conflict that often involved courts weighing the issues, as in the polygamy case. Here "the sole conflict is between authority and rights of the individual."

Interestingly, Jackson only ventured partway onto the terrain of conscience protected by the free exercise clause. The ACLU in its brief, fearful that the justices might not want to get involved in freedom of conscience issues, had added a section that relied on the speech clause, suggesting that unless the religiously motivated behavior constituted a "clear and present danger" to the public, it could not be regulated, no matter how worthy or reasonable the legislative purpose. Jackson appears to have picked up on this argument, and the bulk of his decision reads as if it were a freedom of speech rather than a free exercise of religion issue. The use of the flag as a symbol, he explained, is a form of utterance, and likewise the decision not to salute the flag is also a type of expression. While the Witnesses objected to the flag salute because of religious beliefs, others could and did object to any form of government-coerced speech for a variety of reasons, all of which would be protected by the First Amendment's speech clause.

Where Frankfurter had said the rights involved were assigned to the protection of the legislature, and that courts should defer to legislative judgment, Jackson disagreed. "The very purpose of a Bill of Rights was to withdraw certain subjects from the vicissitudes of political controversy, to place them beyond the reach of majorities and officials and to establish them as legal principles to be applied by the courts," he maintained. "One's right to life, liberty, and property, to free speech, a free press, freedom of worship and assembly, and other fundamental rights may not be submitted to vote; they depend on the outcome of no elections."

Frankfurter had used "national unity" as the compelling government rationale to require the flag salute of all students. That national unity is an end that officials may foster by persuasion and example was not the question, Jackson stated. "The problem is whether under our Constitution compulsion as here employed is a permissible means for its achievement," and the majority thought not. Moreover, efforts to secure such unity by coercion were doomed to failure, and those "who begin coercive elimination of dissent soon find themselves exterminating dissenters. Compulsory unification of opinion achieves only the unanimity of the graveyard."

The issues, Jackson declared, were not difficult; the Court had been elucidating principles of free speech for more than two decades. Only the fact that the symbol involved was the American flag made the case a hard one. He concluded with what remains one of the most ennobling statements of American freedom ever penned by a Supreme Court justice: "If there is any fixed star in our constitutional constellation, it is that no official, high or petty, can prescribe what shall be orthodox in politics, nationalism, religion, or other matters of opinion or force citizens to confess by word or act their faith therein. If there are any circumstances which permit an exception, they do not now occur to us."

Justice Black, joined by Douglas, concurred, explaining that since they had voted with the majority in *Gobitis,* they felt compelled to add a few words of their own. Despite the many protections of the First Amendment, it did not go so far as to grant individuals "an absolute right to make final decisions, unassailable by the State, in everything they will or will not do." Nevertheless, while the state can certainly work to inculcate loyalty, it cannot do so by compulsion. "Love of country must spring from willing hearts and free minds," a sentiment expanded upon by Justice Murphy in an equally short concurrence.

Three members of the Court dissented. Justices Roberts and Reed merely noted that they believed *Gobitis* had been rightly decided and that the West Virginia case should have followed that precedent. Felix Frankfurter, however, entered an anguished dissent that began: "One who belongs to the most vilified and persecuted minority in history is not likely to be insensible to the freedoms guaranteed by our Constitution. Were my purely personal attitude relevant I should wholeheartedly associate myself with the general libertarian views in the Court's opinion, representing as they do the thought and action of a lifetime. But as judges we are neither Jew nor Gentile, neither Catholic nor agnostic."

He then went into a lengthy defense of judicial restraint, repeating the general ideas of his earlier opinion in *Gobitis* that courts should defer to the wisdom of the legislative branches. The truly astonishing aspect of Frankfurter's original opinion in *Gobitis* and his later dissent is that he completely ignored any difference between impingements upon individual liberties, even those protected by the Bill of Rights, and economic regulations. In both instances the judgment of the legislatures must be respected. The idea that courts had any special role to play in protecting individuals and groups from majoritarian prejudice, an idea that Holmes, Brandeis, and Stone had embraced, remained then and later foreign to Frankfurter.

Aftermath

When Lillian Gobitas heard the news, she experienced a deep sense of joy that the Witnesses had finally been victorious. "We were thrilled, absolutely thrilled. And you know, things began to wind down. Believe it or not, everything cooled down. The mobbings stopped. . . . It just wound down and everything got calm again. [Witness] kids went back to school." The Minersville School Board sent a letter reinstating the Gobitas children, but for Lillian it was a bit too late. By then she was twenty years old, and although she lacked that last year of high school, she had been accepted by and attended a local business college. As she put it, she and her brother had gone on with their lives.

Although the flag-salute cases remain an important part of our constitutional history, and of the history of religious freedom in the United States, they play less of a role in courses in constitutional law. The reason is fairly simple—the two cases were decided not on free exercise of religion grounds but on a free speech rationale, the clear and present danger test. In subsequent years the Court moved past this test in speech cases and developed a separate jurisprudence for evaluating the actions of individuals based on their religious beliefs against the needs of the state to maintain order. In *Sherbert v. Verner* (1963), the Court held that a Seventh-day Adventist who had been discharged from her job because she would not work on Saturdays could not be denied unemployment benefits by the state. In the case the Court established a balancing test that protected religious action as well as speech unless the government could show a compelling state interest to infringe on those actions. While *Sherbert* swung the pendulum to favor individual beliefs, in later years the Court seemed to back away from that, once again setting up the dichotomy between religious belief and action based on that belief, and allowing states to regulate the latter while protecting the former.

Unfortunately, we do not know much about what happened to the Barnettes, but Lillian Gobitas went on to have a very full life. She wanted very much to work at the headquarters of the Watchtower Society in New York City at a time when they "didn't take girls much at all," but because of her role in the case they made an exception for her. The time she spent there led her to do missionary work in Europe, where she met her husband, Erwin Klose, one of the brave German Witnesses who had inspired the young Lillian. At the same time that Lillian was standing up for her religious principles in Pennsylvania, Klose refused to serve in the German army or salute Hitler, because he believed doing so would be an act of worship of a false God. For this he wound up in a concentration camp. Looking back many years later she told an interviewer that "those things would not have happened otherwise. [The case] changed the course of our lives. I call it the storybook life."

Cases Cited

Chaplinsky v. New Hampshire, 315 U.S. 568 (1942)
Jones v. Opelika, 316 U.S. 584 (1942)
Martin v. Struthers, 319 U.S. 141 (1943)
Minersville School District v. Gobitis, 310 U.S. 586 (1940)
Murdock v. Pennsylvania, 319 U.S. 105 (1943)
Sherbert v. Verner, 374 U.S. 398 (1963)
United States v. Carolene Products Co., 304 U.S. 144 (1938)
West Virginia Board of Education v. Barnette, 319 U.S. 624 (1943)

For Further Reading

The best single volume on these cases and the related religious freedom decisions at the time is Shawn Francis Peters, *Judging Jehovah's Witnesses: Religious Persecution and the Dawn of the Rights Revolution* (2000). Older but still useful is David Manwaring, *Render unto Caesar: The Flag Salute Controversy* (1962). To understand the faith, see M. James Penton, *Apocalypse Delayed: The Story of Jehovah's Witnesses* (2nd ed., 1997). A good portrait of Lillian Gobitas Klose is in Peter Irons, *The Courage of Their Convictions* (1990), 25–35. For the Stone Court and its handling of these cases, and especially Felix Frankfurter's role, see Melvin I. Urofsky, *Division and Discord: The Supreme Court under Stone and Vinson, 1941–1953* (1997), chap. 3. A more negative view of the cases is Richard Morgan, "The Flag Salute Cases Reconsidered," 34 *Journal of Supreme Court History* 275 (2009).

The Case of Too-Long-Delayed Equality

Brown v. Board of Education (1954 and 1955)

No CASE IN AMERICAN HISTORY has had as much impact upon the social, political, and economic fabric of the nation as *Brown v. Board of Education of Topeka, Kansas,* in 1954. It did not wipe away three centuries of racism, nor did it immediately abolish racial segregation, which the Court had approved six decades earlier in *Plessy v. Ferguson* (1896). But it began the process, and a decade later Congress, in the 1964 Civil Rights Act, made all forms of racial separation in public places illegal. That law, and the Voting Rights Act of the following year, made it possible for African Americans to attend schools of their choice, vote for and elect public officials, and run for office themselves. *Brown* helped to transform the American landscape, so that in 2008 the United States could elect a black president. The opinion may not have the intellectual rigor and jurisprudential analysis of some of the Court's other great cases, but as Court of Appeals judge J. Harvey Wilkinson reminds us, *Brown* "was humane, among the most humane moments in all our history. It was . . . a great political achievement, both in its uniting of the Court and in the steady way it addressed the nation."

Linda Brown and the Other Plaintiffs

Linda Brown (born 1943) and her two sisters were happy and beloved children growing up in Topeka, Kansas. Their father, Oliver, was a boxcar welder at the Santa Fe Railroad, and also an ordained minister of the African Methodist Episcopal Church. They lived in a modest, multiracial neighborhood, and although housing was not highly segregated, the schools were. Linda later recalled that "I lived in a neighborhood that was integrated and I had playmates of all nationalities. . . . Then when school started we would go these opposite directions and, of course, your playmates who you played with everyday wanted to know, 'Well, why don't you go to school with us?'"

The Browns lived only seven blocks from the all-white Sumner Elementary School, but Linda had to attend the black Monroe Elementary School. To get there she had to leave her house an hour and twenty minutes before her school started, and walk through an active railway switching yard for five blocks to get to her bus station. The bus took a circuitous route to the school, and would occasionally arrive before school opened, leaving her and the other children to stand around in whatever weather the season brought—rain, snow, or heat.

In 1950 Oliver Brown tried to enroll Linda at Sumner so she would not have to make that long and dangerous trip, but he was turned away. Oliver Brown was no activist but he was mad, and he went to the local branch of the National Association for the Advancement of Colored People (NAACP) seeking help. The association's Legal Defense Fund (LDF) had reached the point where it felt ready to challenge the separate-but-equal doctrine the Supreme Court had approved in *Plessy v. Ferguson* (1896), and it was looking for test cases. Once the LDF accepted their case, the Brown family had little involvement with the case at trial or on appeal. In addition to the Linda Brown case in Kansas, the LDF began suits in Virginia, Delaware, South Carolina, and the District of Columbia.

In Farmville, Virginia, a sixteen-year-old student named Barbara Rose Johns secretly organized a student strike to protest the terrible conditions at the all-black Moton High School, which had no gymnasium, cafeteria, or teachers' rest rooms. Neither teachers nor students had desks or blackboards, and due to overcrowding some students had to take classes in an old and decrepit school bus parked on the grounds. Requests for supplies and additional funding had been turned down by the local, all-white school board. The NAACP of Virginia agreed to take on the case, and while Barbara Johns by rights should have been the lead plaintiff, the first name alphabetically belonged to another student plaintiff, Dorothy E. Davis (*Davis v. County School Board of Prince Edward County, Virginia*).

In Delaware the parents of Ethel Louise Belton sued the Claymont School District in New Castle County because their daughter had been refused admission to the Claymont High School solely because of her race, and were told to enroll her in the Carver Vocational School in Wilmington, nine miles away. The Beltons won in the state court, and the school district appealed (*Gebhart v. Belton*).

As a young child in Clarendon County, South Carolina, Harry Briggs Jr. experienced the horrible conditions of segregated black schools—poor heating, overcrowding, and lack of basic resources such as up-to-date textbooks. His parents, Harry and Eliza Briggs, filed suit against the school board, and many white South Carolinians did not take well to the suit. Harry Sr. lost his job, eventually having to move to Florida to seek work. Harry Jr. also had difficulty finding work later on when his relationship to the case became known (*Briggs v. Elliot*).

Gardner Bishop was the father of a student at the segregated Browne Junior High School in Washington, D.C. In 1947 school authorities responded to complaints about crowded conditions at Browne by reopening two run-down former elementary schools for satellite classes. The black parents objected, and demanded that the better white schools be opened to all students without reference to race. On September 11, 1950, Bishop took his son and ten other black students and attempted to enroll in the Sousa Junior High School. They were turned away, and the parents filed suit; Spottswood Bolling Jr. became the lead plaintiff simply because his name headed the alphabetical list (*Bolling v. Sharpe*).

The five cases wended their way through state and lower federal courts, and their appeals arrived at the U.S. Supreme Court in the fall of 1952. The Court consolidated the cases with the Kansas appeal of Brown's suit as the lead case so that, according to Justice Tom Clark, "the whole question would not smack of being a purely Southern one." By then, the LDF had been fighting racial segregation in the courts for more than twenty years, and had slowly been making inroads. But these five cases marked a major step for the organization; for the first time it would attack the doctrine of separate-but-equal head-on.

From *Plessy* to *Brown*

Following *Plessy*, segregation had infused every aspect of race relations in the South and in some border states as well. So-called Jim Crow laws enforced the complete segregation of blacks and whites. In addition to separate cars on railroads, trolleys, and buses, there were white and colored drinking fountains and toilets, and of course, schools. Where a locality could not afford completely separate facilities, such as hospitals or theaters, African Americans had to be treated in certain rooms or sit in particular areas. As for equality in accommodations, that did not exist either. White-owned restaurants refused to serve colored customers, and blacks had to sit in the balconies of theaters and at the back of buses. White-dominated legislatures and local school boards never provided equal funding or resources to black schools, which received "hand-me-down" textbooks when white schools got new ones.

In the late 1920s the NAACP launched a plan to attack Jim Crow in the courts on several fronts. One prong of the plan called for suits against segregation on interstate facilities, and in *Morgan v. Virginia* (1946), a 7–1 Court claimed that railroads operating in interstate travel had to have a uniform policy, and therefore could not separate passengers on the basis of race. A few years later, in *Henderson v. United States* (1950), the Court unanimously held that dining cars on interstate trains could not require black passengers to sit in a segregated area behind a screen.

A second part of the NAACP plan involved forcing states to provide more equal funding for black schools and teachers, and in dozens of suits the LDF almost always won when it offered as evidence the large disparities between per-pupil funding, salary differentials between similarly qualified black and white teachers, wide variations in the conditions of school buildings, and other aspects. In fact, by the time the Supreme Court heard *Brown,* salary differentials for teachers in most southern states had been equalized.

The real target, and the biggest problem, was how to attack segregation itself. The LDF decided that it would start in higher education, because while all states had black and white schools for elementary and secondary students, not all states had separate university facilities. In many states if a black student wanted to go to a law or medical or engineering school, the state went to extreme lengths to avoid integrating their facilities, preferring instead to provide a stipend so that the student could attend an out-of-state university.

The first breakthrough came in *Missouri ex rel. Gaines v. Canada* (1938), when Chief Justice Charles Evans Hughes startled the South by insisting that if it wanted to keep segregated schools, then it had to provide some form of similar or equal opportunity for black students. The Court did not have a chance to show how seriously it meant this until after World War II, when it heard the case of Ada Sipuel. After compiling an excellent record at the State College for Negroes in Langston, Oklahoma, she applied to the University of Oklahoma Law School, the only one in the state. The school refused to admit her. Thurgood Marshall, the head of the LDF, represented her at oral argument in early January 1948, and four days later a unanimous court issued an order directing Oklahoma to provide Sipuel with a legal education in conformity with the Fourteenth Amendment's equal protection clause. Unfortunately for Sipuel, the state set up a "black" law school in the basement of the state capital, and the justices, still leery of confronting segregation straightforwardly, refused to consider whether the state had in fact met its mandate.

At the second trial (over the quality of the rump law school) the NAACP called Professor Walter Gellhorn of Columbia University as an expert witness, and during a break Gellhorn got into a revealing conversation with Mac Williamson, the attorney general of Oklahoma, who was representing the university. Gellhorn said that even if the state could convince the court that this basement school was "equal," what was the state going to do when a Negro applied for a medical education—build him a whole medical school? Williamson suddenly smacked his head as the revelation hit him: "Oh, my God, suppose one of them wanted to be a petroleum engineer! Why, we've got the biggest petroleum-cracking laboratory in the country here."

A few years later the University of Oklahoma again tried to get around the rules. It had grudgingly admitted sixty-eight-year-old George McLaurin into its graduate school, where he hoped to earn a doctorate in education. But McLaurin had to sit in the corridor outside the regular classroom, use a separate desk on the mezzanine of the library, and eat alone in a dingy alcove in the cafeteria. When the NAACP challenged these rules, the university allowed McLaurin to sit inside the classroom but surrounded his seat with a railing that said "Reserved for Colored." A unanimous Court struck these rules down in *McLaurin v. Oklahoma State Regents* (1950) as imposing inequality on the petitioner.

Although the justices shied away from questioning *Plessy* in the Oklahoma case, they came near it in a case decided the same day. After Heman Marion Sweatt applied to the University of Texas Law School in 1946, a federal district court gave the state six months to establish a law school for blacks. The state created the School of Law at the Texas State University for Negroes, a makeshift classroom in an Austin basement. Although the physical plant and the library had grown by the time Thurgood Marshall carried the case to the Supreme Court in 1950, Marshall felt confident that he could show that the absence of a good library, well-known faculty, and all the other intangibles that made the University of Texas Law School a top-flight institution denied Sweatt an equal education.

If nothing else, the justices of the Supreme Court—especially Tom Clark, a graduate of the Texas Law School—knew what made a good law school, and in *Sweatt v. Painter* they unanimously rejected the Texas claim that it had provided equal facilities. Chief Justice Fred M. Vinson ordered Sweatt admitted to the University of Texas Law School, the first time the Supreme Court had ever ordered a black student admitted to a previously all-white school on the grounds that the state had failed to provide equal separate facilities.

For Thurgood Marshall and the LDF, the *Texas* opinion was "replete with road markings telling us where to go next" as they turned their attention to challenging segregation in the public schools. Seventeen southern and border states, as well as Washington, D.C., legally required segregation in public schools; another four states permitted it. The attack on segregation *per se*—and not just on the lack of equal facilities—had been the LDF goal for years, but Marshall and his colleagues faced formidable opposition. Many members of the NAACP opposed attacking segregation. Teachers had won the cases on equal pay and were better off than they had been; they feared they would lose not only these gains but their jobs as well. Others worried about the backlash if the LDF succeeded; it had not been all that long since black men were routinely lynched in the South.

There were also pressures to go ahead. Black servicemen who had fought for others' freedom overseas in World War II came back to find no freedom for themselves, and they chafed at the racial prejudice they found everywhere in the South as well as in many northern states. Harry Truman had ordered the armed forces to integrate, and in Korea for the first time black soldiers fought alongside their white comrades. The Cold War also aided the drive for civil rights, as the United States and the Soviet Union fought to win the support of unaligned nations in Africa and Asia. Black diplomats discovered that they could not find hotel rooms if they traveled in the South, and even in Washington many restaurants would not accept them as customers. Soviet propaganda harped incessantly on how badly the United States treated people of color, a point that Third World countries took seriously.

The Arguments

The Court heard oral argument on the five public school cases in the fall of 1952, but although a majority of the justices agreed that segregation was bad, they could not reach agreement on what constitutional authority they could use to strike it down. Although the equal protection clause seemed the logical choice, it had a cloudy history in the Court, and Oliver Wendell Holmes Jr. once dismissed it as the last resort in a losing case. So the justices looked for other grounds to support an opinion. In the spring of 1953 the Court requested that counsel reargue the case in December. Specifically, the justices wanted both sides to address whether Congress in proposing—and the states in adopting—the Fourteenth Amendment had intended to ban racial segregation in the schools. Furthermore, if the Court ruled against continued segregation, how should the decision be implemented?

On September 8, 1953, Chief Justice Vinson died unexpectedly of a heart attack, and speculation now focused on how the new chief, former California governor Earl Warren, would approach the problem of racial segregation. Warren had said little about the matter, but the NAACP knew that during World War II Warren had been vociferous in his demand that Japanese Americans be taken out of California and moved to inland relocation camps.

Instead of the usual one to two hours allotted for oral argument, the justices sat through ten hours spread over three days. John W. Davis, a former solicitor general of the United States, represented South Carolina. He defended racial segregation in an emotional coda to a long and distinguished career. Only Daniel Webster had argued more cases in the Supreme Court, and at the original argument the year before Thurgood Marshall believed that Davis had outlawyered him.

But Marshall was better prepared at reargument, and his very presence in the chamber symbolized what he demanded of the Court—equality for all people regardless of the color of their skin. (Although different lawyers represented the plaintiffs in the five cases, all were associated with the NAACP and looked to Marshall, who technically represented only Harry Briggs, as the lead attorney.)

The Decision

On May 16, 1954, Marshall received a telephone call from the clerk of the Court telling him that the decision would be handed down the next day. He took a train from New York to Washington, but no cab would pick him up at Union Station, so he ran the several blocks to the Court, arriving as the justices took their seats.

Considering its epochal significance, the decision in *Brown v. Board of Education* is deceptively simple, running a mere eleven pages. Chief Justice Warren wanted it to be short enough so that newspapers could reprint it in its entirety, and he read the whole opinion from the bench. He began by stating that the history of the Fourteenth Amendment and its relation to education, which the Court had asked both sides to argue, was "inconclusive"—in part because public education in the South in 1868 was almost nonexistent. Most white children at the time were privately educated, and black children not educated at all. He then briefly examined the *Plessy* doctrine, as well as the extent of segregation in northern and southern states. Times had changed, Warren declared, and "in approaching this problem we cannot turn the clock back to 1868 when the Amendment was adopted, or even to 1896 when *Plessy* was written. We must consider public education in the light of its full development and its present place in American life throughout the Nation." Education played a crucial role in training people to become productive members of society, and more importantly, to be citizens and to participate in civic life. When a state undertakes to provide education to its people, it must do so on equal terms to all.

Warren read through two-thirds of the opinion before he reached the crucial question: "Does segregation of children in public schools solely on the basis of race . . . deprive the children of the minority group of equal educational opportunities?" Pausing for a moment, he continued, "We unanimously believe it does." Reaffirming the eloquent dissent of the first Justice Harlan in *Plessy,* that separate could never be equal, Warren declared that to segregate black children

> from others of similar age and qualifications solely because of their race generates a feeling of inferiority as to their status in the community that may affect their hearts and minds in a way unlikely ever to be undone. . . . Segregation with the sanction of law, therefore, has a tendency to retard the educational and mental development of Negro children.

As a result, the Court concluded "that in the field of public education the doctrine of 'separate-but-equal' has no place. Separate educational facilities are inherently unequal." When Warren announced that the decision was unanimous, he later recalled, "a wave of emotion swept the room."

(Four of the cases dealt with state laws, but the fifth, *Bolling v. Sharpe,* arose in the District of Columbia, which was not under the mandate of the Fourteenth Amendment. Chief Justice Warren, while noting this fact, held that "to impose a lesser duty," i.e., to allow segregation to continue in the District, would be "unthinkable." The Court found its justification for ending segregation in the due process clause of the Fifth Amendment, which did apply to the federal government.)

Brown was, and remains, a testimonial to Earl Warren's innate humaneness and to his political skill. A majority of the justices had agreed early on that segregation was unconstitutional, and Warren had labored throughout the winter and spring to get them all to agree to decide the case on equal protection grounds, and also to have the vote unanimous. A decision of such import could be crippled if there were a dissent or a less than complete agreement. Noting the wide applicability of the decisions and the complexity of devising a solution, Warren invited the parties to assist the Court in fashioning an appropriate remedy. The "wide applicability" phrase broadcast the intention of the Court to order desegregation in all school districts—North and South, rural and urban. The reference to complexity signaled to the South that the justices recognized the social and psychological turmoil the decision would cause and that they intended to allow the states some time to accustom themselves to the idea. By inviting the parties to help compose a solution, the Court hoped that Jim Crow states would cooperate and thus avoid the necessity of having the judiciary impose a remedy. Finally, Warren carefully framed the opinion to apply to only one area, the legal segregation of children by race in primary and secondary public schools, a group most likely to win sympathy as victims of racism.

The Response

Within an hour of the opinion, the Voice of America beamed news of the decision around the world in more than thirty languages, emphasizing that the issue had been settled through a democratic process and not by dictatorial imposition or mob behavior. The immediate reaction from the international community was overwhelmingly positive. To take but one example, the Municipal Council of São Paulo, Brazil, sent a letter to the American embassy applauding the decision and joining in what it termed the universal rejoicing that had greeted news of *Brown.* By August 1954 the U.S. Information Agency reported to the National Security Council that "the decision is regarded as the greatest event since the Emancipation Proclamation, and it removes from Communist hands the most effective anti-American weapon they had in Black Africa."

Northern newspapers hailed the decision as "momentous." What the justices had done, declared the *Cincinnati Enquirer,* "is simply to act as the conscience of the American nation." The *New York Herald Tribune* proclaimed that "in the lives of nations there are moments when the ideal blazes forth with shattering intensity. Men see the truth they have known all along and yet have somewhat managed to deny. Such a moment comes with the clear, final decision of the Court." The *Des Moines Register* spoke of the Court's effort to begin "the erasure of one of American democracy's blackest marks."

Within the black community reaction was mixed, as leaders waited to see how the lofty words would translate into action. The *Chicago Defender,* a leading black newspaper, called the decision a "second emancipation proclamation . . . more important to our democracy than the atomic bomb or the hydrogen bomb." Local black columnist Nat Williams, writing in Memphis, said "there was no general 'hallelujah, 'tis done' hullabaloo. Beale Streeters are sorta skeptical about giving out with cheers yet." The Associated Negro Press (ANP), a national news service, while heralding the long-awaited ruling nonetheless wanted to see how the South would react, and whether some southern states "will take drastic action to circumvent" the ruling. The ANP reminded its readers that the governors of Georgia and South Carolina had promised to abolish public schools rather than abolish segregation (as indeed some localities later did).

Initially the South heard voices of moderation, more so than one might have expected. Gov. Thomas Stanley of Virginia called for "cool heads, calm study, and sound judgment." "Big Jim" Folsom, Alabama's governor, declared that "when the Supreme Court speaks, that's the law." The governor of Arkansas promised that "Arkansas will obey the law. It always has." The respected *Louisville Courier-Journal* assured its readers that "the end of the world has not come for the South or for the nation. The Supreme Court's ruling is not itself a revolution. It is rather acceptance of a process that has been going on for a long time." The editors urged southerners to follow the Court's example of moderation, advice akin to that of the *Atlanta Constitution,* which called on Georgians "to think clearly."

Warren's strategy assumed that the states would accept the inevitability of desegregation by the time the Court reconvened to devise an implementation plan, and initial signs seemed encouraging. Some southern communities did not wait for the Court to act. Baltimore adopted a freedom of choice plan, which enabled 3,000 blacks to attend previously all-white schools starting in September 1954. Louisville changed over its school system within a semester, while St. Louis initiated a two-year plan. Counties in West Virginia, junior colleges in Texas, and public schools in Washington, D.C., and Wilmington, Delaware, all enrolled blacks in previously segregated schools.

Initial optimism soon faded as ominous signs appeared. Governor Stanley abandoned his early moderation, and in June announced he would do everything possible to continue segregation in Virginia. In Mississippi, White Citizens Councils began to form in July, pledged to total war in defense of segregation. But no one knew exactly what the Court would demand in terms of implementation, and in the twelve months following the initial decree much of the South cautiously marked time.

Remedies and *Brown II*

The Court heard arguments on proposed remedies that winter and again in April. The problem was difficult and controversial on its own, but the justices also had to decide whether to abandon, at least in this instance, the Court's traditional policy of ruling only on the case before it. Normally, if a party raises a valid claim that his or her constitutional rights have been violated, the decree is directed only to that petitioner's case; other persons "similarly situated" do not immediately gain the benefit of the decision. Lower federal courts then take notice of the decision and apply it prospectively to future petitioners raising such a claim. In the school cases, however, that would mean that every black child wanting to enroll in a previously all-white school would have to go to court to secure the same rights that had been awarded to Linda Brown in Topeka. Determined states and localities, armed with sufficient resources, could tie up the desegregation process for years, even decades, by litigating each claim.

The Court also usually takes little notice of practical matters. Once a right has been defined, it has to be available to all citizens, despite institutional obstacles. Circumstances in public education, however, varied enormously from state to state, and even from locality to locality within a state. In some instances desegregation would mean just a few blacks sitting in predominantly white classrooms, and in other schools just the opposite—and this made a difference. Even recognizing the enormous emotional and logistical problems, how long could the Court give the South? Every day that black children attended inferior, segregated schools they suffered a loss of their constitutional rights. On the other hand, too precipitate an order could lead to widespread obstruction, even violence.

The NAACP wanted full integration in the shortest possible time. Blacks had been waiting three and a half centuries to be treated as equals and should not have their constitutional rights denied one more day.

Southern states were equally intransigent. Virginia urged the Court to face the "reality" of major differences between the two races, and offered statistics to prove the inferiority of blacks. Florida informed the justices that it had conducted a poll and only one out of seven police officers would enforce attendance at racially mixed schools.

The federal government, appearing as a "friend of the Court," suggested a middle position between "integration now" and "segregation forever." States should submit timetables within ninety days, and then implementation should be supervised by local federal district courts. The courts would have discretion to make adjustments in the schedules to reflect local conditions. An immediate start, however, would have to be made, and the decision would have to be enforced by all federal officials, all of whom had taken an oath to uphold the Constitution.

On May 31, 1955, Chief Justice Warren, again for a unanimous Court, handed down a seven-paragraph decision, commonly known as *Brown II*. School segregation had to be ended everywhere, but the Court recognized that differing local conditions required varying solutions. Local school districts must "make a prompt and reasonable start toward full compliance," and oversight would be lodged in federal district courts. Local judges should exercise "practical flexibility," but delay and noncompliance should not be allowed. Desegregation of public schools should proceed "with all deliberate speed."

The Court did not fix a date for the end of segregation, nor even require that initial plans be filed within ninety days, as the Justice Department had recommended. Why the Court did not demand more has been debated ever since, but some evidence indicates that Felix Frankfurter, worried about violent resistance, convinced Earl Warren that it would be better to go slowly at first, and suggested the "all deliberate speed" criterion.

The South exulted, since many had been braced for a specific schedule for the dismantling of segregation; now it looked as if real implementation could be delayed indefinitely. Assignment of primary responsibility to local federal courts led some southerners to assume that the decree could be totally ignored. Ernest Vandiver, lieutenant governor of Georgia, rejoiced when he heard the news. District judges, he announced, "are steeped in the same traditions that I am. . . . A 'reasonable time' can be construed as one year or two hundred. . . . Thank God we've got good Federal judges."

Moving—but Slowly

Most federal judges, however, soon made it clear that they took seriously their oath to support the Constitution. John Minor Wisdom, Elbert Tuttle, John R. Brown, and Richard Rives of the Court of Appeals for the Fifth Circuit (which covered a broad swath of southern states), as well as district court judges Frank Johnson of Alabama and J. Skelley Wright of Louisiana defied friends and death threats to become forceful advocates of desegregation. By January 1956 federal judges had rendered opinions in nineteen cases and in every one reaffirmed the Supreme Court's ruling in *Brown*.

The South dug in its heels. Refusing to enact statewide desegregation statutes, the states bitterly fought the NAACP in court, forcing one delay after another, so that as late as 1961 few school districts in the Deep South had faced a school desegregation suit. (In many places black plaintiffs were afraid to file suit, while the LDF, stretched beyond its resources, could only handle so many cases at once.) The southern press ground out articles and books purporting to show not only the inferiority of black people, but the unconstitutionality of the Court's decision. The White Citizen Council movement spread and soon claimed 500,000 members in eleven states. Whites and blacks who signed desegregation petitions lost their jobs and found they could not get credit from stores or banks. In 1956, 101 southern members of Congress, including all but three senators from the former Confederate states, signed a belligerent "Southern Manifesto" opposing the Court's decision.

In Virginia, usually seen as moderate in its race relations, Sen. Harry F. Byrd called for "massive resistance" to desegregation, and there and elsewhere in the South politicians resurrected the long-discredited theories of John C. Calhoun. Alabama claimed that it had the right to "interposition" in order to protect its citizens from unconstitutional federal action, and the state legislature resolved *Brown* to be "null, void and of no effect." Georgia, Mississippi, South Carolina, Louisiana, and North Carolina all adopted resolutions proclaiming that *Brown* had no legal force and they would ignore it.

Aside from the overblown rhetoric, southern states adopted numerous measures to thwart the courts and evade compliance. Georgia made it a felony for any school official to use tax money for mixed-race schools, while Mississippi declared it unlawful for the races to attend school together from kindergarten through high school. Mississippi and South Carolina amended their constitutions to abolish public schools, and all southern states designed one program after another to keep the races separate. John Temple Graves, an Alabama newspaperman, declared "there is not one way, but many" to nullify *Brown*.

The opening of school in September 1956 found that 723 districts in the seventeen southern and border states had accomplished some measure of desegregation, 186 more than the previous year. Three thousand school districts remained totally segregated. About 300,000 black students went to school in so-called integrated situations, which could mean many different things, but 2.4 million remained totally segregated. Total separation remained the rule in Alabama, Florida, Georgia, Louisiana, Mississippi, North and South Carolina, and Virginia. The Ku Klux Klan came alive again, and bombings, murder, and cross burnings spread across the southern states. All over the South, as the noted southern-born scholar C. Vann Woodward lamented, "the lights of reason and tolerance began to go out under the insistent demand for conformity and a malaise of fear spread over the region."

Ike and Little Rock

The Supreme Court, as Alexander Hamilton noted in *Federalist* No. 78, has neither the power of the purse nor the sword, and it must rely on the other branches of government as well as its own moral authority to enforce its decisions. Congress, dominated by southerners, refused to act, and so did President Dwight Eisenhower, who privately complained that he believed *Brown* had set back the cause of progress in the South by at least fifteen years. Yet Eisenhower had signed off on the government's *amicus* brief in *Brown,* and he knew from the State Department that continued segregation was hurting American foreign policy in Africa and Asia. The day after the Court handed down its decision he ordered the commissioners for the District of Columbia to set an example of peaceful integration in the city's schools. But Eisenhower, who enjoyed near-universal respect and admiration for his role as supreme commander of the Allied forces in World War II, did not provide any moral leadership to the nation or to the southern states in dealing with the shame of American apartheid. When officials at the University of Alabama defied a court order to admit a black student, all Eisenhower said was, "I certainly hope that we could avoid any interference."

Finally, events forced the reluctant Eisenhower to act. In the fall of 1957 the Little Rock, Arkansas, school board agreed to a court order to admit nine black students to Central High School. Gov. Orville Faubus, previously considered a moderate, called out the national guard to prevent blacks from entering the building. He withdrew the guard on a court order, but when the black students tried to enter Central High, a mob attacked the school. Eisenhower, who only two months earlier had said he could not envision any situation in which he would use federal troops, could no longer sit by passively and watch federal authority flouted. He ordered 1,000 paratroopers into Little Rock, and nationalized the 10,000 Arkansas national guardsmen to protect the black students and maintain order. The president who had tried for the past three years to ignore the growing racial tensions in the South had been forced to act, and he became the first president since Reconstruction to use federal troops to enforce black rights.

The Supreme Court, which had been silent on school matters since *Brown II,* now spoke in *Cooper v. Aaron* (1958) in an unusual, unanimous *per curiam* decision signed by all nine justices. *Cooper* not only reaffirmed *Brown,* but also reasserted the Court's authority as the ultimate interpreter of the Constitution. Arkansas had claimed not to be bound by *Brown* since it had not been a party to that case, and the justices could have limited themselves to a sharp reminder that states have no power to nullify federal court orders. Instead, they reminded Arkansas and the nation that ever since 1803 it had been, in Chief Justice John Marshall's words, "the province and duty of the judicial department to say what the law is." That principle remained in effect, and therefore the Court's interpretation of the Fourteenth Amendment in *Brown,* or for that matter of any constitutional provision in any case, became the supreme law of the land and bound not only federal officials but state governments as well.

The Beginnings of Desegregation

Not until the passage of the 1964 Civil Rights Acts and the 1965 Voting Rights Act did southern schools begin to desegregate. The growing infusion of federal money into primary and secondary education had became substantial in Lyndon Johnson's Great Society programs, and the Civil Rights Act denied federal funds to any school district that continued to enforce racial segregation. More important was the voting bill, which made African Americans a major political force in every southern state. As the federal government enforced the rights of blacks to register and to vote, they began electing black sheriffs, council members, and school boards, which did away with segregation. Even white southern officeholders recognized that blacks held the balance of electoral power in many districts and states, and they could not win if they antagonized those constituents.

Some southern schools never became truly integrated. In some areas the overwhelming population made even integrated schools predominantly black. In many places middle-class whites took their children out of public schools and enrolled them in all-white private academies, or moved to the suburbs where blacks could not afford housing. But even if *de facto* segregation remained in many parts of the nation, *de jure* separation—segregation mandated by and enforced by the law—ceased to exist.

Linda Brown remembered the day the case bearing her name was decided, with the whole family excited. Her father rushed in from work, embraced his wife, and said, "Thanks be to God for this." Linda went on to become a civil rights activist in her own right. At age thirty-six, in protest at the failure of the Topeka School District to completely desegregate the system, she asked the local court to reopen *Brown v. Board of Education* on behalf of her own children. Her son, Charles, said, "I had a funny feeling when I heard the judge agreed to reopen the case. I began to wonder whether my kids will be in this lawsuit too someday." She won the suit, and in 1994 Topeka agreed to a new plan that aimed at a truly integrated school system. Since then she has been involved in the Brown Family Foundation, which works to provide educational resources regarding the significance of the original decision.

Cases Cited

Bolling v. Sharpe, 347 U.S. 497 (1954)
Brown v. Board of Education I, 347 U.S. 483 (1954)
Brown v. Board of Education II, 349 U.S. 294 (1955)
Cooper v. Aaron, 358 U.S. 1 (1958)
Henderson v. United States, 339 U.S. 816 (1950)
McLaurin v. Oklahoma State Regents for Higher Education, 339 U.S. 637 (1950)
Missouri ex rel. Gaines v. Canada, 305 U.S. 337 (1938)
Morgan v. Virginia, 328 U.S. 373 (1946)
Plessy v. Ferguson, 163 U.S. 537 (1896)
Sipuel v. Oklahoma State Board of Regents, 332 U.S. 631 (1948)
Sweatt v. Painter, 339 U.S. 626 (1950)

For Further Reading

The literature on *Brown* and its progeny continues to grow, but two books serve as good starting points. Richard Kluger, *Simple Justice: The History of Brown v. Board of Education and Black America's Struggle for Equality* (1976) is a classic, but should be supplemented by Robert J. Cottrol, Raymond T. Diamond, and Leland B. Ware, *Brown v. Board of Education: Caste, Culture, and the Constitution* (2003), which brings in more recent scholarship and also has a broader understanding of the social, economic, and cultural concerns of the African American community at the time. The NAACP's role is detailed in Mark V. Tushnet, *The NAACP's Strategy against Segregated Education, 1925–1950* (1987), and *Making Civil Rights Law: Thurgood Marshall and the Supreme Court, 1936–1961* (1994). The best biography is Juan Williams, *Thurgood Marshall: American Revolutionary* (1998). A rather unique perspective can be found in Paul E. Wilson, *A Time to Lose: Representing Kansas in Brown v. Board of Education* (1995). The role of the Eisenhower administration is explored in David A. Nichols, *A Matter of Justice: Eisenhower and the Beginnings of the Civil Rights Revolution* (2007). For Little Rock, see Tony A. Freyer, *Little Rock on Trial: Cooper v. Aaron and School Desegregation* (2007). The importance of foreign policy in the case is detailed in Mary L. Dudziak, *Cold War Civil Rights: Race and the Image of American Democracy* (2000). The response to *Brown II* is explored in a series of essays in Brian J. Daugherty and Charles C. Bolton, *With All Deliberate Speed: Implementing Brown v. Board of Education* (2008).

The Case of the Robust Press

New York Times v. Sullivan (1964)

Full-PAGE ADVERTISEMENTS in newspapers are common, and involve far more than selling merchandise. Some are political in nature, endorsing candidates for public office or urging support for particular positions, and may often include a request for funds to further the cause. Such an ad appeared in the *New York Times* at the end of March 1960, and asked readers to send in money to help civil rights activists in their struggle to end racial segregation in the South. The ad detailed some of the dangers facing Martin Luther King Jr. and others, and also alleged several acts of violence against King and student activists.

The advertisement led the Montgomery, Alabama, commissioner of public safety, L. B. Sullivan, to file a libel suit against the *Times,* and the decision is a landmark in the development of freedom of the press as guaranteed in the First Amendment. But one has to look at the *Sullivan* case not just in terms of the press clause, but in the larger context of the civil rights revolution then taking place in America.

Merton Nachman Reads the Newspaper

Not too many people read the *New York Times* in Montgomery, Alabama, but in early April 1960, a few who did became greatly upset. One of them was Merton Roland Nachman, the preeminent libel lawyer in Montgomery, and certainly one of the best in the state. Although he considered himself a political moderate, Nachman, like many others in the

South, felt increasingly frustrated by the attention northern newspapers like the *Times* gave to the actions of what he considered a radical minority causing all the trouble. He immediately spotted some factual errors in the ad that might be enough to make it libelous *per se* under Alabama law. He cut out the page and took it over to the three city commissioners, and told the police commissioner, L. B. Sullivan, that there was no doubt that even though he had not been directly named in the ad, he could bring an action against the *Times*. The ad cast aspersions on Sullivan because it attributed to the police force the lead complicity in bombing the home of Martin Luther King Jr., and more generally in fomenting a police-state terrorism that left blacks fearful for their lives not only from roving mobs but also from police who either directly aided the rioters or who stood by passively and did nothing to protect African American citizens.

Sullivan and the other city commissioners needed no convincing. On the one hand they were frustrated by their inability to put an end to the civil rights uprising, and on the other they objected to how the northern media, supposedly without real knowledge of life in the South, portrayed them as bullies and terrorists. Nachman began proceedings on behalf of the commissioners in state court, but before he was finished he would be arguing before the U.S. Supreme Court, and its decision would mark a new day in the interpretation of the First Amendment's press clause.

The Struggle for Civil Rights in Alabama

Although known primarily for its ruling on the meaning of freedom of the press, *New York Times v. Sullivan* (1964) is as much a civil rights case as a First Amendment opinion. The Court's landmark decision in *Brown v. Board of Education* (1954) did not cause the civil rights movement, but it fanned the spark that had been there into a roaring flame. Moderate voices on both sides were soon drowned out, and diehard southern whites clashed frequently with African Americans no longer willing to live in a segregated society. Although relatively peaceful compared to the battles that had to be fought to end apartheid in South Africa, the civil rights movement in the United States saw its share of violence and bloodshed.

Immediately following the decision in *Brown,* three states—South Carolina, Georgia, and Mississippi—adopted constitutional amendments authorizing the legislature to end public education rather than desegregate the schools. The governors and attorneys general of Alabama, Mississippi, and other Deep South states refused the Court's invitation to file briefs in the implementation hearings, a clear signal they did not intend to be bound by those decisions. In Virginia, Sen. Harry F. Byrd called for "massive resistance," while Gov. James Byrnes of South Carolina, a former member of the high court, declared bluntly that "South Carolina will not now nor for some years come to mix white and colored children in our schools." In Georgia, Herman Talmadge pledged that as long as he occupied the governor's mansion there would be no "Negroes and whites associating with each other socially or in our school systems." In addition to the rhetoric, one southern state after another enacted measures to frustrate the courts and prevent desegregation of the schools.

Most ominously, the level of violence escalated. Eight black men were lynched in 1955, and several others killed for daring to assert their rights. In Belzoni, Mississippi, whites shot the Rev. George Lee at point-blank range for insisting on his right to vote. When Authorine Lucy tried to enroll at the University of Alabama in February 1956, white students rioted and almost lynched her; she had to flee and then was formally expelled. In Birmingham a mob attacked the great black singer Nat "King" Cole when he sang at a whites-only concert in the city auditorium. The Ku Klux Klan, the white-sheeted nightriders who had been quiescent in the South since the 1920s, sprang back to life and burned crosses throughout the South. In Alabama a group of whites savagely beat and castrated a black man and then told him, "This is what will happen if Negroes try to integrate the schools." When eight black students tried to enter Central High School in Little Rock, Arkansas, under a court order, Gov. Orville Faubus used the national guard to prevent them from doing so, leading President Dwight Eisenhower to send in the 101st Airborne Division to restore order and to protect minority students—the first time federal troops had been deployed on southern soil since Reconstruction. All over the South, as the noted southern-born historian C. Vann Woodward lamented, "the lights of reason and tolerance began to go out under the insistent demand for conformity and a malaise of fear spread over the region."

Montgomery, Alabama, became a major battleground in the struggle, epitomized by the famous bus boycott that began on December 1, 1955, when a black seamstress, Rosa Parks, boarded the Cleveland Avenue bus at City Square and took a seat in the white section. A few stops later the bus driver ordered her to surrender her place in favor of a white rider, and she refused. Within a few days the city's African American population organized itself to boycott the city's bus lines and either to walk or find alternative ways to get to work and then home again. The Montgomery Improvement Association (MIA), a group of black civic leaders working to improve the lot of the black community, named a newcomer to town, the twenty-six-year-old Rev. Martin Luther King Jr., as its head. At first the MIA hoped the economic pressure would lead the city's white power structure to seek a compromise, but that failed to happen, and then in late January 1956, King's home was bombed by unknown persons. Recognizing that the boycott by itself would not be enough, and worried that the bombing was just the first omen of an escalating violence, the MIA then filed suit in federal court seeking an end to bus segregation.

In turn the white leaders of the community filed suit in state court under the Alabama Anti-Boycott Act of 1921, and on February 21, 1956, a grand jury returned indictments against eighty-nine African Americans, twenty-four of whom were ministers, for the misdemeanor of conspiring to boycott a lawful business. So far the fight had stayed relatively peaceful, with the exception of the bombing of King's home, with each side trying to win its case in the courts. Northern media, however, flocked to cover the boycott, and instead of reporting on what southern whites saw as the prevailing civility between the two groups, focused on Klan violence and the hostility of lower-class segregationists. When the Supreme Court mandated the end of segregation on the bus lines in *Gayle v. Browder* in December 1956, die-hard segregationists turned to other methods to counter civil rights activity.

By early 1958 the largest organization in Montgomery was the White Citizens' Council, which demanded absolute subservience by whites to the segregationist line. When, for example, a group of white women organized a series of weekly interracial prayer meetings at a black Roman Catholic hospital, the council singled them out for public ridicule. After they all received threats that their husbands' businesses would be destroyed, most of the white women publicly recanted their racially moderate beliefs, though one of them, librarian Juliette Morgan, committed suicide rather than do so.

In local and state elections die-hard segregationists played the race card for all it was worth, and easily defeated moderates who wanted to find an accommodation with the court orders. In 1958 former attorney general John Patterson won election as Alabama governor by conducting a campaign of unalloyed racism that handed George C. Wallace, the favorite, a surprising loss. In the wake of Patterson's victory, Wallace declared that he would "never be out-niggered again." Patterson got a local state judge, Walter Burwyn Jones, to issue a court order outlawing in Alabama the National Association for the Advancement of Colored People (NAACP), the nation's oldest civil rights group, which sponsored nearly all of the lawsuits attacking segregation. Finally, in January 1959 Montgomery city officials made clear that they were not going to retreat from their hard line, and ordered that all thirteen city parks and the city zoo be sold as a way of evading a federal court order mandating their integration.

L. B. Sullivan and Law Enforcement in Montgomery

In March 1959, segregationist power surfaced again in the Montgomery municipal elections, and white racists took special satisfaction from the election of Lester Bruce (L. B.) Sullivan over incumbent police commissioner Clyde Sellers.

L. B. Sullivan was born in Records, Kentucky, on March 5, 1921, the son of a farmer and a schoolteacher. In 1941 he entered the Army Air Force and, following his father's example, joined the military police, where he rose to the rank of sergeant while stationed at Maxwell Field in Montgomery. Following World War II, Sullivan remained in Montgomery, where he raised a family of three children and held several different jobs. Sullivan gradually made helpful political connections, attaching himself to the rising political fortunes of Gordon Persons, who would later be elected governor of Alabama. In 1947 Sullivan was chosen by the Alabama Public Service Commission to be first inspector and then chief inspector of field activities. In 1951 Governor Persons appointed Sullivan director of public safety for Alabama, a position he held until 1955.

By 1954 Sullivan enjoyed considerable public notice for his role in cleaning up Phenix City, Alabama, a small town immediately across the Chattahoochee River from Columbus, Georgia, and the Fort Benning military reservation. Phenix City had earned the title of "the most corrupt city in America." Its problems were mostly economic; it was the poor relation of prosperous Columbus, which benefited directly from the army's massive presence. Phenix City, positioned as it was on the wrong side of the river, derived only the indirect consequences of the U. S. Army's presence: gambling, prostitution, illegal liquor sales, and loan sharking. Sullivan, as head of the state police, helped conduct a highly successful cleanup campaign that led Phenix City to win an All-American City award in 1955, and gave Sullivan a reputation as an effective and honest law officer.

Sullivan left his post as director of public safety, returning temporarily to private life. From 1955 to 1957 he worked as a consultant for the International Association of Chiefs of Police, attended the Federal Bureau of Investigation Police Academy, and graduated from the Northwestern University Traffic Institute.

Through his personal life, Sullivan spun a web of politically useful contacts among the middle and lower-middle classes of the city's eastside. He was an active club worker, holding memberships in the Alcazar Shrine, the American Legion, the Elks, the Eagles, and the Andrew Jackson Lodge of the Masonic Order. His religious fundamentalism complemented and reinforced his racism; he was at once a Baptist and a member of the Ku Klux Klan. In his 1959 campaign for Montgomery police commissioner, Sullivan promised voters "the continuation of Southern traditions and customs" at the same time that he also declared his intention to promote "industrial growth and development for our city, county, and state." White moderates distrusted Sullivan and his political ambitions. He was, according to one local businessman, "smooth, polished, relatively sophisticated for Montgomery. He had read a few books." He was also pragmatic and opportunistic, qualities that he demonstrated in his campaign.

Sullivan succeeded in painting his opponent, the ardent segregationist Clyde Sellers, as weak on the race issue and public order because of an incident involving Martin Luther King Jr. During the summer of 1958, King's closest associate and friend, the Rev. Ralph D. Abernathy, had an affair with one of his female parishioners. On August 29 the woman's husband, Edward Davis, attacked Abernathy in the basement of the minister's office, first with a hatchet and then a gun. The minister fled from his church onto the street, where fortuitously two Montgomery police officers took Davis into custody. When King arrived at the courthouse to aid Abernathy, Montgomery police, already ruffled by the bizarre behavior of both Davis and Abernathy, arrested King for loitering. He was convicted and fined ten dollars. Police Commissioner Sellers, however, decided to pay King's fine rather than have him jailed as a martyr. In the 1959 commission race, Sullivan effectively exploited this incident, charging Sellers with using "kid gloves to handle social agitators."

Once in office Sullivan implemented the reform of the police department designed to fulfill his campaign pledge to undertake "fair and impartial enforcement of laws." The new commissioner reorganized internal police operations, created neighborhood patrols, developed outreach programs through the police department for the city's youth, and established a police reserve "composed of people from all walks of life." These reforms coincided with a growing level of civil rights disturbances in the Alabama capital that placed great pressure on the police force and on Sullivan's leadership.

The Sit-in Movement Comes to Alabama

Sullivan's first major crisis occurred in February 1960, when the sit-in movement reached Montgomery. The first black sit-in, protesting segregated restaurant facilities, began at the F. W. Woolworth lunch counter in Greensboro, North Carolina, on the first of the month. Within days the protest spread through the rest of the upper South, moving to Charlotte, Raleigh, then Rockhill, North Carolina, and on to Orangeburg, South Carolina, and Nashville, Tennessee. The movement was unique, and in its novelty lay a source of profound concern for the white South. Until the sit-in movement began, whites had largely inspired and led most of the major civil rights battles. There were, of course, the exceptions, of which the bus boycott in Montgomery was the most notable. But in the sit-ins young blacks began taking an aggressive role that captured the attention of the national media, including the *New York Times*, whose editors dispatched, as they had done during the bus boycott, additional correspondents to cover breaking civil rights developments.

On February 25, thirty-five students from all-black Alabama State College sought service at the snack bar in the basement of the Montgomery County Courthouse. The students were rebuffed and arrested. The following day Gov. John Patterson, who was also the ex officio chairman of the State Board of Education, demanded expulsion of the students from the public college. On February 27, most of the eight hundred students at Alabama State marched to the state capitol to protest Patterson's actions. Governor Patterson and Commissioner Sullivan decided to apply officially sanctioned force and intimidation against the students. While state and Montgomery police stood idly by, bat-wielding Klansmen waded into the group of black students. The attack went unpunished, even though the *Montgomery Advertiser* ran pictures of the incident, with several members of the mob clearly identified. The *Advertiser*'s editor, Grove Hall Jr., condemned the attack and rebuked Sullivan for failing to halt it and to seek arrests of those who had perpetrated it. At the same time, the extremist press praised the incident. The *Montgomery Home News*, for example, observed that "the crisp crack of a hickory bat on a Negro head snapped the people out of their apathy into the realization that the steady, cold siege against their way of life was now breaking out in . . . obviously Communist-inspired racial strife." It served, the editor said, as "a signal for the white Christian race to stand up and be counted."

"Heed Their Rising Voices"

The civic culture of Montgomery, therefore, was already under considerable stress when the *New York Times* published a full-page ad, titled "Heed Their Rising Voices," on March 29, 1960.

Prominent northern civil rights leaders had no qualms about raising money to defend Martin Luther King Jr. and the other activists arrested in the South. A group including such civil rights veterans as Bayard Rustin, A. Phillip Randolph, and the Rev. Harry Emerson Fosdick determined to take out a full-page ad in the *Times* that would not only condemn the violence in Montgomery but also raise funds for the cause. There had to be at least enough money generated to cover the $4,552 the *Times* charged for a full-page ad. Rustin wanted the ad to be hard-hitting, and he prodded the author, John Murray, to liven it up, telling him to add the names of a number of prominent people as endorsers to make it more appealing. When Murray protested that they had not been contacted, Rustin assured him that there would be no problem, since they had all been involved in the movement and had lent their names previously. Although the *Times* had a department to check on the accuracy of ads submitted to it, the man staffing that office when the copy came in signed off without questioning the material, because it "was endorsed by a number of people who are well known and whose reputation I had no reason to question."

The first four of the ten paragraphs in the ad dealt specifically with the sit-in movement. Appealing to the Constitution and the Bill of Rights, it told how "thousands of Southern Negro students . . . engaged in widespread non-violent demonstrations . . . had boldly stepped forth as the protagonists of democracy." The third paragraph dealt specifically with events in Montgomery. It claimed that eight hundred students from Alabama State College had marched to the state capitol and on its steps had sung "My Country 'Tis of Thee," after which the student leaders had been expelled from the college. It also claimed that "truckloads of police armed with shotguns and tear-gas" then "ringed the Alabama State College campus." When students protested these actions by refusing to reregister for classes, "their dining hall was padlocked in an attempt to starve them into submission."

The fifth and sixth paragraphs focused on the plight of Martin Luther King Jr. So-called "Southern violators of the Constitution" were determined to destroy King and to answer his "peaceful protests with intimidation and violence." The sixth paragraph in particular claimed that they had "bombed [King's] home almost killing his wife and child," that they had "assaulted his person," and had him arrested "seven times—for 'speeding,' 'loitering,' and similar 'offenses.'"

The remaining four paragraphs pleaded not just for moral support "but material help so urgently needed by those who are taking the risks, facing jail, and even death in a glorious re-affirmation of our Constitution and its Bill of Rights." Below these paragraphs were two blocks of endorsements. The first contained sixty-four names, including such prominent figures as Eleanor Roosevelt, Marlon Brando, Harry Belafonte, Shelley Winters, Nat King Cole, and Frank Sinatra. The second block listed ministers associated with the Southern Christian

Leadership Conference, including four from Alabama. To the right was a coupon to be clipped and returned with a contribution.

There is no question why the committee chose to purchase a page in the *Times* or to whom they were directing their appeal. Founded in 1851, the *New York Times* was the most prestigious newspaper in the country. It had an average daily circulation of 650,000, a number that doubled on Sunday. Most of these were sold in the New York City area and the northeast corridor stretching from Boston to Washington, D.C. Elsewhere far fewer copies circulated, with most of them sold to libraries, colleges, and to a few individuals. On an average weekday in Alabama, the *Times* sold about 390 papers and about 2,500 on Sunday; of this, only about 35 were sold in Montgomery County.

Rustin and his colleagues directed their ad not at the South, but at the sympathetic white, progressive, and intellectual leadership of the North. The invocation of "Southern violators" echoed prevailing northern stereotypes of Dixie as a racist, violent, and backward area. The ad named no individuals and made no reference to any officeholder, but painted a damaging picture of police forces in the South, who were in fact earning a reputation for their brutality in dealing with civil rights demonstrators. The group had no idea that the ad would have any effect in the South.

It would not, at least in the terms that its signers anticipated—a check sent in with the coupon. But thanks to Merton Nachman, the *Times* and several of the signers soon found themselves facing libel charges in Alabama court.

A Brief History of Libel Law

The law of defamation traces back at least to the thirteenth century, and has its roots deep in feudal society. If one lord of the realm impugned the reputation of another, the result would be a fight to the death as the insulted baron defended his honor by the sword. To remove questions of reputation from the tilting field to the courts prompted the enactment of *De Scandalis Magnatum* in 1275. Reenacted and enlarged several times, the law made it a crime to slander the peers of the realm. In 1606 Sir Edmund Coke prosecuted a printer who had published a poem making fun of two archbishops of Canterbury. The case, *De Libellis Famosis*, set out the standard that a person may libel another by harming their reputation, even by saying things that are true, whether the object of the libel is a public official or a private person, or whether he be dead or alive (one of the archbishops was in fact dead at the time the poem had been published). The punishment for libel could be fine, imprisonment, or cutting off the ears of the offender.

From these beginnings grew the laws of libel. Two forms of libel—blasphemy, or libel against religion, and obscenity, libel against the moral norms of society—need not detain us here. Seditious libel, the criticism of the government or its officials for either policy or actions, had been used against protesters during the First World War (see Chapter 14). Subsequent court decisions had made it harder to use seditious libel against critics of the government, and in any event it was a charge that could only be brought by a government against an individual. The Alabama case involved the fourth form, private libel, or the defamation of an individual, and that person's recourse under law. Private libel is an area of tort law that is still very much alive today, although somewhat circumscribed following the decision in the *Sullivan* case. Much of the law of defamation is state law, both statutory and common, and is a descendant of centuries of haphazard and often baffling evolution.

Reputation has always been an important consideration in society, and in the Middle Ages punishment for slander could be terrible indeed. The Laws of Alfred the Great, compiled in the late ninth century in England, held that "if anyone is guilty of public slander, and it is proved against him, it is to be compensated with no lighter penalty than the cutting off of his tongue." By the thirteenth century recourse had been moved to ecclesiastical courts, which treated slander as a spiritual offense, but after the English Reformation jurisdiction moved to the common law courts, where it has remained since.

The law of defamation crossed the Atlantic with the English colonists, and according to some scholars took up a good part of the business of colonial courts. Truth initially mattered not, only whether the defendant had said or printed something maligning the reputation of the plaintiff. Traditionally such suits had two parts. In one, dealing with the "law of the case," the judge ruled whether the statement was libelous; in the second, known as "the facts of the case," a jury ruled whether the defendant was indeed the culprit who had uttered the malicious remarks. There had to be evidence that a third party had heard or read the comments. If Tom charged Dick with cheating at cards, that did not constitute a libel. If, however, Tom publicly told Harry that Dick cheated, that was a libel—even if Dick actually *had* cheated.

A major change to libel law occurred in the American trial of John Peter Zenger in 1735, when Zenger's lawyer, Andrew Hamilton, got a jury to agree that it, and not the judge, would determine if a statement were libelous, and that in its considerations, truth would be a complete defense. That is, if the defendant could show that what had been said was true, there was no libel. To use the example above, if Dick sued Tom, Tom would be held innocent if he could in fact prove that Dick had cheated. In the two centuries between *Zenger* and *Sullivan*, truth as a defense became embedded in American libel law, but with significant provisions to protect the reputations of individuals.

Among those provisions were what some scholars have called "galloping presumptions." To begin with, defamatory statements were presumed false, so the burden was not on the plaintiff to prove that what had been said was false, but on the defendant to prove that it was true. Truth, however, is not always easy to discern. Facts can be determined, i.e., the attack on the World Trade Center took place on September 11, 2001, is a fact and is not under dispute. But how does one prove that the mayor of a town awarded municipal contracts based on cronyism? Just because John is a friend of the mayor does not mean that his company is not better qualified to do the work than others.

A second rule involved intent. In criminal law intent is an essential element of a crime; if someone knows or should know that a particular act violates the law, and does it anyway, that constitutes criminal intent. In libel law, historically, whether the statement resulted from malice, ignorance, negligence, or just plain misfortune did not matter. One published at one's peril, and the law presumed malice—evil intent— from the simple fact of speech or publication.

Third, the aggrieved party did not have to show any actual injury to reputation, since this too was inferred from publication. Nor did the plaintiff have to prove any specific monetary damage, but could claim almost any amount. It would then be up to the jury to determine how much money, if any, would be awarded for damages.

All these rules, of course, gave the advantage to the plaintiffs. Most states recognized a difference between fact and opinion and protected the right to express an opinion, but only so far as the factual basis of the opinion was accurate. Here again the burden of proof of accuracy lay with the speaker or publisher, who would lose this privilege if any of his statements proved factually incorrect. A few states allowed the privilege if there were only minor errors in fact made either through inadvertence or in the good-faith belief that they were correct. Alabama, however, took a stricter view, and this is why Merton Nachman was so certain that under Alabama law his clients had a sure-fire libel suit against the *New York Times*.

The *Sullivan* Case

Nachman's confidence grew out of his knowledge that the ad did indeed contain factual errors. The students sang "The Star-Spangled Banner" and not "My Country 'Tis of Thee" on the state capitol steps. Students had been expelled from Alabama State College not in connection with the protest at the capitol, but after seeking service at the Montgomery County Court House. Police were deployed in large numbers, but they did not "ring" the campus, and there had been absolutely no effort to padlock the dining hall. King had been arrested four times, not seven, and four of the ministers listed as sponsors testified that they had never seen the ad, and that their names had been used without their permission. Under Alabama law the expression of opinion was protected only so far as it rested on a completely accurate factual basis. Even one error could open the speaker to libel charges, and Nachman had more than one error to rely upon.

Although the *Times* quickly sent an apology to Sullivan and others, it did no good. The paper faced multiple suits from the three Montgomery city commissioners, the city commissioners of Birmingham and Bessemer, and Governor Patterson. Each plaintiff sought $500,000 in damages, except for the governor, who sought $1 million. Although the suits also named four of the ministers who signed the ad, the main target was clearly the northern press. If the *Times* could be forced to pay out several million dollars in damages, all of the northern media—and not just the *Times*—would become very wary of how they covered the civil rights disturbances in the South. L. B. Sullivan and others may have felt aggrieved at their depiction as "Southern violators," but they also knew they would have a far easier time putting down civil rights activism without the press reporting their every move.

Nachman's confidence proved well-founded. The *Sullivan* trial took less than three days, and the jury brought in a verdict for the plaintiff in just two hours and twenty minutes for the full amount that Sullivan had demanded—$500,000. The next day, to drive home the point, the (Montgomery) *Alabama Journal* noted that the verdict "could have the effect of causing reckless publishers of the North . . . to make a re-survey of their habit of permitting anything detrimental to the South and its people to appear in their columns." On appeal, the Alabama Supreme Court upheld the judgment on August 30, 1962.

The *Times*, of course, had to appeal the verdict on up to the U.S. Supreme Court, and to do so had to find grounds that would somehow nullify Alabama's harsh libel law. While the suit no doubt had the added objective of silencing the press, L. B. Sullivan had in fact been libeled as state law defined it at that time, and in a community where one's good name meant a great deal. Although the civil rights movement had triggered many legal stratagems by southern states to block desegregation, in this case Alabama had not concocted a new law, but had simply applied a customary rule as to fair comment—a rule, by the way, similar to libel law in most other states, northern as well as southern, at the time.

The Supreme Court and the Press Clause

The *Times* brought in a noted constitutional scholar, Herbert Wechsler of the Columbia Law School—a man, as one reporter described him, "of formidable intellect and formidable presence." Wechsler's job would be to convince the U.S. Supreme Court that the First Amendment's press clause protected newspapers against the type of libel suit brought by L. B. Sullivan. It would be a challenging task, as he had very little precedent to rely upon.

The First Amendment applied literally to the federal government—Congress shall make no law—but the Court had incorporated it and applied the press clause to the states as well in *Near v. Minnesota* (1931). But while the states could no longer deny the press rights granted to it under the Constitution, the Supreme Court had pretty much left libel laws intact and under the jurisdiction of the states. The only prior high court case dealing with libel had been *Beauharnais v. Illinois* in 1952, when a 5–4 Court had upheld the conviction of white supremacist Joseph Beauharnais under an Illinois statute prohibiting group libel, i.e., defamation of a group or class of people. Speaking for the majority, Justice Felix Frankfurter declared "libelous utterances are not within the area of constitutionally protected speech." In a dissent that seems prescient in the context of the *Sullivan* case, Justice William O. Douglas noted that "today a white man stands convicted for protesting in unseemly language against our decisions invalidating restrictive covenants. Tomorrow a Negro will be hauled before a court for denouncing lynch law in heated terms." And, in fact, the next libel case the Court would hear involved African Americans protesting the violence they faced in Alabama, and the *New York Times* carrying an advertisement about that violence.

Had it been a simple libel case, the Court might not have even taken it. But the case involved the nation's preeminent newspaper and centered on the civil rights movement that had been triggered in large part by the Court's own rulings. The Court had little choice, and observers believed that in taking the case the justices would overrule the lower court verdict. The trick would be in how to do that, given the lack of precedent in this area.

"Debate on Public Issues Should Be Uninhibited, Robust, and Wide-Open"

On March 9, 1964, Justice William Brennan delivered the opinion of the Court. In his first sentence he noted how rarely the high court decides to take a fresh look at a whole body of law. "We are required in this case to determine for the first time the extent to which the constitutional protections for speech and press limit a State's power to award damages in a libel action brought by a public official against critics of his official conduct." After reviewing the facts of the case, the errors in the advertisement, and the lower court judgments, Brennan announced: "We reverse the judgment. We hold that the rule of law applied by the Alabama courts is constitutionally deficient for failure to provide the safeguards for freedom of speech and of the press that are required by the First and Fourteenth Amendments in a libel action brought by a public official against critics of his official conduct."

Brennan quickly disposed of Sullivan's reliance on earlier decisions of the Court that had left libel law to state jurisdiction, saying that in none of them had criticism of public officials and their policies been at issue. In addition, the Court had often looked past labels such as *contempt* or *breach of the peace* to see how the conduct fit into the larger scheme of constitutional safeguards, and today it did so with the label of *libel.* He then went into a history of the expansion of First Amendment protections in the previous four decades, and quoted at length from Justice Brandeis's opinion in *Whitney v. California* (1927). In that case the majority had upheld Anita Whitney's conviction for allegedly calling for the violent overthrow of the government. Brennan termed Brandeis's dissent the "classic formulation" defining the meaning of free speech. Several subsequent cases had then expanded the parameters of First Amendment protection, and from them he drew this conclusion:

> We consider this case against the background of a profound national commitment to the principle that debate on public issues should be uninhibited, robust, and wide-open, and that it may well include vehement, caustic, and sometimes unpleasantly sharp attacks on government and public officials. . . . The present advertisement, as an expression of grievance and protest on one of the major public issues of our time, would seem clearly to qualify for the constitutional protection.

The notion that public debate should be "uninhibited, robust, and wide-open" proved to be the most-quoted phrase of the decision, because it summed up what Holmes and Brandeis and other champions of free speech had intended—that in a democracy all opinions, even unpleasant ones or ones delivered unpleasantly, had to be allowed so that full debate could take place on important issues. In 1964 no issue affected American society more than civil rights, and outdated technicalities of state tort law could not be used to silence that debate.

Brennan also used the case to review prior efforts to limit speech, such as the Sedition Act of 1798, which although "never tested in this Court, the attack upon its validity has carried the day in the court of history." Although it would be another five years before the Court once and for all buried the crime of seditious libel in *Brandenburg v. Ohio*, for all practical purposes that ancient offense could no longer be prosecuted in the United States after *Sullivan*.

Recognizing that Sullivan and others might try again in a new libel suit, Brennan then added another layer of protection to critics of governmental actions by noting that appellate courts had the power, because of the constitutional issues involved, to review the facts in libel cases to ensure that local juries had not decided improperly. Normally appellate courts only review questions of law, but here the Court was essentially warning states that it would not allow attacks on the press because of technicalities such as the matter of minor errors. Such errors, if made in good faith and were indeed minor, could not be used as a launching pad for libel suits. Only deliberate distortions of the facts, made with evil intent, could be the basis for a suit. The majority did not give the press total immunity from libel, but absent actual malice in deliberately falsifying information, honest criticism and reporting, even with some factual errors, would be protected.

Brennan reversed the judgment of the Supreme Court of Alabama, and remanded the case to that court for further proceedings "not inconsistent with this opinion." Given the tenor of the ruling, there was little the Alabama court could do except overturn the judgment and dismiss the case.

Although all nine justices supported Brennan's conclusions, only five others signed onto it. Three members of the Court—Hugo Black, William O. Douglas, and Arthur Goldberg—believed the First Amendment went even further to create an absolute privilege for critics of official conduct, even if that criticism was maliciously false.

Black, joined by Douglas, charged that the facts of the case showed that "state libel laws threaten the very existence of an American press virile enough to publish unpopular views on public affairs and bold enough to criticize the conduct of public officials." He believed that the suits against the newspaper had but one purpose—to harass those who criticized Montgomery officials' actions against civil rights activists. While this case involved race, it could be used in any situation in which newspapers or television shone a spotlight on questionable governmental policies. The Constitution dealt with this threat, he claimed, by granting an absolute immunity to the press for any criticism of government officeholders.

Justice Goldberg also entered a concurrence, in which Douglas joined, in which he argued that even if the press did not have the total immunity suggested by Black, it had a greater level of constitutional protection than the Court majority allowed. "In a democratic society," he wrote, "one who assumes to act for the citizens in an executive, legislative, or judicial capacity must expect that his official acts will be commented upon and criticized. Such criticism cannot, in my opinion, be muzzled or deterred by the courts at the instance of public officials under the label of libel."

Aftermath

The decision is important in two areas. First, the underlying rationale of unfettered speech as an essential part of political dialogue greatly expanded the meaning of the First Amendment, both in terms of speech and press. By bringing criticism of government policy and officials within the ambit of protection, it enormously broadened the parameters of free speech and press. Second, Brennan's opinion took what had previously been regarded as purely private law, a matter left to each state's common law, and constitutionalized the tort law of defamation. In subsequent cases the Court would refine just how far protection of the press went and what still remained in state law to protect the reputation of truly private citizens.

As the excesses of white racists mounted, many southern moderates decided that the time had come to abandon the old ways, and they turned against the symbols of hard-line resistance like L. B. Sullivan. He lost his bid for reelection to a third term in 1967, but when George Wallace won election as Alabama's governor in 1971 on a platform of "segregation now, segregation forever," he named Sullivan as commissioner of state prisons. These were not happy years for Sullivan, as he was buffeted on one side by demands from reformers for massive changes in the antiquated prison system and on the other by legislators unwilling to provide funds for the much-needed overhauls. He resigned on July 24, 1975, just five days before federal court hearings began that culminated in orders directing the state to end overcrowding and physical violence in the prisons.

Sullivan served for a while as deputy commissioner of prisons and then became executive assistant to Alabama attorney general Bill Baxley. Sullivan died of a heart attack at home on June 12, 1977, but in death as in life he proved controversial. When he was inducted into the Alabama Peace Officers Hall of Fame in 1989, some black city officials in Montgomery protested, labeling Sullivan as "a famous racist and hater of black people and anything they stood for." In 1998 the Alabama Senate passed a resolution to name a new prison after Sullivan, but this gesture also evoked a strong response from the black community. The Rev. Joseph Lowery, one of the ministers Sullivan had sued over the *Times* advertisement, declared that Sullivan had represented "the Old South, with all the venom and vitriol and oppression" that it contained.

Cases Cited

Beauharnais v. Illinois, 343 U.S. 250 (1952)
Brandenburg v. Ohio, 359 U.S. 444 (1969)
Brown v. Board of Education, 347 U.S. 483 (1954)
De Libellis Famosis, 3 James 1 (Star Chamber, 1606)
Gayle v. Browder, 352 U.S. 903 (1956)
Near v. Minnesota, 283 U.S. 697 (1931)
New York Times v. Sullivan, 376 U.S. 254 (1964)

For Further Reading

For a broad overview of the First Amendment and its development, see Harry Kalven Jr., *A Worthy Tradition: Freedom of Speech in America* (1988). Libel is explored in Norman L. Rosenberg, *Protecting the Best Men: An Interpretive History of the Law of Libel* (1986). Anthony Lewis, *Make No Law: The Sullivan Case and the First Amendment* (1991), provides a fine case study, but one should also see Kermit L. Hall, "Cultural History and the First Amendment: *New York Times v. Sullivan* and Its Times," in Sandra F. VanBurkleo et al., eds., *Constitutionalism and American Culture: Writing the New Constitutional History* (2002), 267–306, for a better understanding of the southern notion of "honor" and how it influenced the case in Alabama.

The Case of the Uninformed Rapist

Miranda v. Arizona (1966)

WINSTON CHURCHILL once commented that a great deal could be learned about a society by examining how it treated persons accused of a crime. In the United States one might have assumed, merely from reading the Fourth, Fifth, Sixth, and Eighth Amendments to the Constitution, that the country treated accused criminals fairly, that its adversarial justice system—in which the state has to prove the guilt of the defendant—respected individual rights greatly.

But prior to the 1960s, the treatment accorded to a suspected criminal varied enormously from state to state. The Bill of Rights was originally applicable only to the national government, and persons accused of violating a federal criminal law did receive all of their constitutional protections. Many states had similar protections in their state constitutions, but actual practice bore little resemblance to constitutional guarantees. Starting in 1963, however, the U.S. Supreme Court "incorporated" the criminal provisions of the Bill of Rights so that they applied to the states as well as to the federal government. The Court set minimal standards that all states had to follow, and thus nationalized the rights of the accused. This so-called revolution in due process was not without its critics, who charged that the Court exceeded its authority and that its decisions hindered police work and coddled criminals. No case in this area was attacked more severely than *Miranda v. Arizona* (1966).

The Victim

Around midnight on March 3, 1963, an eighteen-year-old woman finished working her shift at the concession stand at the Paramount Theatre in downtown Phoenix. She took a bus, and had just gotten off to walk the few blocks to her house when a car pulled out of a parking lot and almost hit her. The car stopped, the driver got out, walked up to her, and grabbed her. Telling her not to scream, he forced her into the back seat of his car. He tied her hands and ankles, and holding some sharp object against her throat, said, "Feel this." She later testified that it all happened so suddenly that she did not have time to do anything.

The man then drove some twenty minutes and stopped in the desert just outside of town, untied her hands and feet, and told her to take off her clothes. When she refused he forcibly took off her clothes, undressed himself, and then raped her. She told the police, "I was pushing against him with my hands. I kept screaming, I was trying to get away but he was a lot stronger than I was, and I couldn't do anything." After the man had finished, he got dressed and drove his victim back to within a few blocks of her home, during which time she managed to get her clothes on. When he let her out of the car, he asked her to pray for him.

The victim, who lived with her mother and a married sister, arrived home shortly after 2:00 a.m., disheveled and hysterical. Her sister calmed her down long enough to discover what had happened and immediately called the police. Although the young woman, who was slightly retarded (she had the intelligence of a twelve- or thirteen-year-old), did not know her assailant and gave somewhat conflicting accounts of the event to the police, she did provide a description that the police matched up to twenty-three-year-old Ernesto Miranda.

On March 13 the police arrested Miranda and placed him in a lineup, where the victim identified him as the man who had abducted and raped her. In addition, another woman identified him as the man who had robbed her at knifepoint of eight dollars several months earlier.

Ernesto Miranda and His Confession

Miranda's father had emigrated from Mexico and worked as a house painter, and Ernesto grew up in poor but not desperate circumstances. His mother died when he was six, and his father remarried. He never adjusted to the stepmother who reared him, and did not have close ties to his father or brothers. He frequently skipped school, and dropped out completely halfway through the ninth grade. Once on the streets he soon ran afoul of the law.

Police arrested him in 1954 at age fourteen for stealing a car, and he spent six months in a reform school. He had barely gotten out when he was arrested and convicted for attempted rape and assault, but spent only a short time in jail. When Miranda was seventeen Los Angeles police charged him for being a Peeping Tom, but because of his youth he was placed on probation. Unable to get or hold a regular job, he proved no more successful as a criminal, and was arrested twice more, for armed robbery. He apparently escaped prosecution by enlisting in the army in 1958, but any hopes for a new start soon faded. He went AWOL from the army, and after getting caught peeping again spent several months in a stockade before the army gave him a dishonorable discharge. Back in civilian life he drifted until he was arrested while driving a stolen car, and this time he spent two years in a federal penitentiary.

After his release in early 1961, he met Twila Hoffman and moved in with her. She was several years older than he and had two children. Although separated from her husband, she could not afford a divorce. They moved to Phoenix to try to start fresh, had a daughter, and Miranda got a job driving a truck for a produce company. Things seemed to be going well, and his employer described Miranda as one of his best workers. Less than two years later he was charged with kidnapping and rape.

After the victim had identified him in the lineup, the officers investigating the case took Miranda to an interrogation room and told him that he had been identified, not only by the rape victim but also by the woman he had earlier robbed. At this point Miranda confessed to both the abduction and rape as well as the robbery, and his account of the events matched those provided by the two women. He signed a written statement that the confession had been made "voluntarily" and with "full knowledge" of his legal rights. He had no opportunity to see a lawyer, nor did he ask for one. The question of whether someone in his situation could waive his legal right against self-incrimination without the advice of an attorney would become the central issue of this case three years later when it reached the high court.

Initially pursuing an insanity defense, Miranda's court-appointed attorney, Alvin Moore, requested a sanity hearing. The two psychiatrists who examined Miranda while he was awaiting trial agreed that he had normal intelligence, knew right from wrong, and understood the nature of the crimes at the time they had been committed. They also agreed that he had emotional disorders, but disagreed on their extent. Both reports proved consistent with the alleged rape, which psychologist Nicholas Groth classified as "power" rape. This is the most common form of sexual attack, and is motivated by feelings of inadequacy and the need to demonstrate one's manhood. Neither of the two doctors, however, provided any groundwork for an insanity defense.

Moore needed a different strategy. At the trial, he called no witnesses, nor did he put Miranda on the stand; instead he focused entirely on trying to have the judge throw out the confession. In cross-examining the police officers who had interrogated Miranda, he asked, "Did you ever advise the defendant he was entitled to the services of an attorney?" They responded that they had not. The trial judge, Yale McFate, overruled Moore's objection to the confession and allowed it into evidence. Moore also tried to discredit other prosecution witnesses, and, using cross-examination techniques no longer allowed today, accused the rape victim of not really trying to fight back. He ended his summation with an allegation that criminologists now dismiss as a myth, that a woman cannot be raped unless she permits it.

The jury deliberated for five hours and found Miranda guilty. On June 27, 1963, Judge McFate sentenced him to two concurrent sentences of twenty to thirty years, one for kidnapping and the other for rape. In a separate trial Miranda had also been convicted of robbery, for which he received an additional sentence of twenty to twenty-five years to be served after the rape sentence; all together Ernesto Miranda faced up to fifty-five years in prison. The Arizona Supreme Court affirmed the conviction, and rejected Moore's claim that the confession should have been excluded. The judges unanimously ruled that it had been made voluntarily, and that Miranda understood his rights even without a lawyer present. Because Miranda understood his rights, the court did not have to examine the question of whether the police should have offered him the opportunity to consult a lawyer.

The Supreme Court accepted the case, along with similar cases from New York, Ohio, California, and a federal case from the Ninth Circuit, and heard oral argument on February 28 and March 1, 1966. The *Miranda* case gave the justices the opportunity to tie loose ends together from earlier cases that all explored the Fifth Amendment's protection against self-incrimination and the Sixth Amendment's right to counsel.

The Due Process Revolution Begins:
Gideon v. Wainwright

The case that began the Warren Court's so-called "due process revolution" in criminal procedure was the landmark decision in *Gideon v. Wainwright* (1963). The right to counsel had been one of the first to be nationalized and applied to the states in *Powell v. Alabama* (1932), a case resulting from the infamous Scottsboro affair, in which nine black teenagers had been convicted of raping two white girls, and in which for all practical purposes the defendants were not represented by counsel. Ten years later, however, in *Betts v. Brady* (1942), the Court backed off and declared that the Fourteenth Amendment had not incorporated the specific guarantees of the Sixth Amendment. A majority held that counsel for indigent defendants did not constitute a fundamental right essential to a fair trial. Rather, the justices would make a case-by-case inquiry into the totality of the circumstances to see if the lack of counsel had deprived the defendants of a fair trial. Over the next twenty years the Court heard many cases alleging special circumstances, and in nearly all of them ruled that a lawyer should have been provided to ensure fairness. In *Chewning v. Cunningham* (1962), for example, the Court reversed a conviction under a recidivist statute (one adding extra penalties to repeat offenders), holding that due process had been denied because the legal questions in the case presented too great a potential for prejudice without a lawyer's assistance.

By then a majority of the Court was ready to overrule *Betts,* and they chose to do so in *Gideon.* Justice Black, who had dissented in *Betts,* spoke for a unanimous Court in *Gideon,* which did away with case-by-case determination and held that the presence of counsel was a fundamental right essential to a fair trial. In his biography of Chief Justice Warren, Ed Cray wrote: "No tale so affirmed the American democracy. No story broadcast around the world so clearly proclaimed that not just the rich received justice in American courts." The Court also took the unusual step of applying *Gideon* retroactively, so that states that had not originally provided counsel in felony cases either had to retry the defendants properly, or—as often proved the case, with witnesses dispersed and evidence cold—let them go. (Clarence Earl Gideon, with the benefit of a lawyer in his retrial, was found not guilty.)

The Fifth Amendment's "Great Right"

The Fifth Amendment includes what has sometimes been called the "Great Right," that no person "shall be compelled in any criminal case to be a witness against himself." The origins of this right go back to objections against the inquisitorial proceedings of the medieval ecclesiastic tribunals as well as the Courts of Star Chamber. By the late seventeenth century the maxim of *nemo tenetur prodere seipsum*—no man is bound to accuse himself—had been adopted by common law courts and expanded to mean that a person did not have to answer any questions about his or her activities. The state could prosecute a person but could not require that he or she assist in the practice. The British colonies in North America carried this doctrine over as part of the received common law, and after the Revolution many states wrote it into their early bills of rights. James Madison included it as a matter of course when he drafted the federal Bill of Rights.

The privilege came under severe criticism from conservative groups during the 1950s Red Scare, when one witness after another, accused of having communist sympathies (and thus being "red"), refused to answer Sen. Joseph McCarthy's questions about their activities on the grounds of possible self-incrimination. Many people associated the phrase "taking the Fifth" (i.e., relying on the Fifth Amendment's protection against governmental abuse of power) with communists, believing that if a person were truly innocent, whether of being a communist or of a crime, he or she should have no problem telling the truth. Legal journals and the popular press carried articles on whether this constitutional right to avoid self-incrimination, which allegedly sheltered only guilty persons, should be amended or even abolished.

The Supreme Court had taken an expansive view of this right ever since the late nineteenth century, and had expanded the privilege against self-incrimination to apply to both criminal and civil cases in which testimony might later be used in criminal proceedings. The privilege is not absolute. For example, persons may not refuse to be fingerprinted; to have blood samples, voice recordings, or other physical evidence taken; or to submit to sobriety tests—even though all of these may prove incriminating. At trial, however, an accused has the right to remain silent, and any adverse comment on a defendant's silence, either by judge or prosecutor, violates the constitutional protection.

Although people may not be forced to testify against themselves, they may voluntarily confess, and that confession may be used in evidence, as it was in Ernesto Miranda's case. Over the years, the Court has steadily expanded the meaning of *voluntary*, and has thrown out confessions secured by physical torture such as whipping or psychological brutality, such as the case where police tell a suspect that thirty to forty people are waiting to "get him" if he does not confess.

Connecting the Fifth and Sixth Amendments:
Massiah

Starting in 1964, the Warren Court connected the Fifth Amendment privilege against self-incrimination to the Sixth Amendment right to counsel on the grounds that only if the accused had been properly informed of his or her rights, including the right to remain silent, could a resulting confession be valid and admissible. In a key case, *Massiah v. United States* (1964), the defendant had been indicted for smuggling drugs in violation of federal law. Winston Massiah had retained a lawyer, pled not guilty, and been released on bail. Unbeknownst to him, one of his codefendants, Jesse Colson, had decided to cooperate with federal agents and agreed to have his car wiretapped. A government agent in a nearby car overheard the conversation between the two in which Massiah admitted his guilt. The conversation was later admitted as evidence and Massiah was convicted. No doubt the "confession" had been voluntary, in that it had not been coerced out of him, and yet the Court held it inadmissible by a 6–3 vote.

In that opinion, Justice Potter Stewart held that the confession could not be admitted because if Massiah's lawyer had been present he would have advised him not to talk to his codefendant or to anyone else about the crime. The key to the ruling seems to have been that Massiah had already retained a lawyer, and was therefore entitled to his advice from that time forward. By surreptitiously taping what Massiah thought had been a private conversation, he "was denied the basic protection of counsel when there was used against him at trial evidence of his own incriminating words, which federal agents had deliberately elicited from him after he had been indicted and in the absence of his counsel."

Although the three dissenters had an easy time showing that the confession had not been coerced and that it, by previous standards, ought to be considered voluntary, the majority seemed intent on pressing home the point about confessions in the absence of counsel. Had the federal agents taped a similar conversation before Massiah had been indicted, or before he had asked for an attorney, that recording would have been admissible not as a post-arrest confession but as part of the evidence collected during an investigation. (This balance between thorough police investigation and eliciting confessions became a critical question after the *Miranda* decision.)

The Court's majority seemed to be suggesting that the government should not rely so much on confessions to prove guilt—a concept alien to most law enforcement officials, for whom confessions were a time-honored mainstay of police work. *Massiah* expanded *Gideon* by requiring a lawyer's advice not just at trial, but back to the time of indictment or even when an accused person first retained counsel. For the first time it also tied together the rights in the Fifth and Sixth Amendments, linking the right to avoid self-incrimination to legal counsel. This became clear in the explosive case of *Escobedo v. Illinois* (1964), which involved murder, not just drug smuggling, as *Massiah* had. Justice Arthur Goldberg's opinion for a 5–4 Court showed the majority's apparent disdain for use of confessions as evidence in criminal trials, and to a lesser extent, for many contemporary police procedures as well.

Strengthening the Connection: *Escobedo*

Danny Escobedo had been brought in for questioning regarding the murder of his brother-in-law, and had asked to see his lawyer. The lawyer was already at the police station and demanding to see his client when Escobedo confessed. It appeared that Escobedo had not been coerced into confessing, but without one lie and an equally important bit of silence on the part of the police, Escobedo might not have confessed. In the interrogation detectives told Escobedo that he could go home if he implicated another man (the lie) but did not tell him that if he did implicate the other, he was in fact implicating himself as well, since under Illinois law the admission of complicity in a murder was legally as damaging as a confession of firing the fatal shots (the silence). Escobedo's admission that his accomplice had committed the murder was, in effect, a confession of his own involvement.

Escobedo's lawyer, picking up on the *Massiah* ruling, argued that police refusal to allow his client to see him during the course of an interrogation constituted a denial of the assistance of counsel assured by the Sixth Amendment and made mandatory upon the states by the Fourteenth, and thus any incriminating statements Escobedo made without a lawyer present could not be used in his trial. Illinois argued, as any state or local police department would have, that voluntary confessions are an essential police tool, and placing a lawyer in the process would reduce significantly the number of criminals who confess.

The Court agreed with the Illinois argument, but then noted that it cut both ways; it overturned Escobedo's conviction because it underscored how critical the interrogation stage is to the whole criminal process. The right to counsel, if it is to mean anything, must attach at the critical stage of interrogation—otherwise a lawyer's aid is useless. If this meant that, with lawyers present, there would be fewer confessions, then police would have to investigate cases more thoroughly. "We have learned the lesson of history, ancient and modern," Goldberg declared. "A system of criminal law enforcement which comes to depend on the 'confession' will, in the long run, be less reliable and more subject to abuses than a system which depends on extrinsic evidence independently secured through skillful investigation." Beyond that, "no system of criminal justice can, or should, survive if it comes to depend for its continued effectiveness on the citizens' abdication through unawareness of their constitutional rights." Once police moved from the investigating stage to the accusatory, the adversarial system at the heart of American justice comes into play and the accused person has the right to counsel.

Justices Harlan, Stewart, and White dissented, with White hitting the most important point—that in fear of forced confessions, the Court's majority wanted practically to do away with them altogether. He found nothing in the Constitution to justify such an argument, and believed the remedy lay in what had been the Court's practice for many years—case-by-case review utilizing a totality of the circumstances standard.

Following this decision the Los Angeles police chief claimed, "If the police are required . . . to . . . establish that the defendant was apprised of his constitutional guarantees of silence and legal counsel prior to the uttering of any admission or confession, and that he intelligently waived these guarantees . . . a whole Pandora's box is opened as to under what circumstances . . . can a defendant intelligently waive these rights. . . . Allegations that modern criminal investigation can compensate for the lack of a confession or admission in every criminal case is totally absurd!" The Los Angeles district attorney, on the other hand, stated, "It begins to appear that many of these seemingly restrictive decisions are going to contribute directly to a more effective, efficient and professional level of law enforcement." The former police commissioner of New York, Michael J. Murphy, charged that "what the Court is doing is akin to requiring one boxer to fight by Marquis [*sic*] of Queensbury rules while permitting the other to butt, gouge and bite." On the other hand, former U.S. attorney for the District of Columbia David C. Acheson, who by then was directly in charge of the Secret Service and the Bureau of Narcotics, observed, "Prosecution procedure has, at most, only the most remote causal connection with crime."

Previous rulings of the Warren Court had prompted criticism in the political arena, but *Escobedo*, as one historian noted, "raised the storm against the Court to gale force." Republican presidential candidate Barry Goldwater claimed that it was "no wonder our law enforcement officers have been demoralized and rendered ineffective in their jobs." Cars sported bumper stickers that read "Impeach Earl Warren" and "Support Your Local Police." As riots erupted in New York and Los Angeles, and student protest over the Vietnam War escalated, often into violent clashes with authorities, many people wondered if indeed there was a correlation between the Court's alleged permissiveness and escalating crime and violence.

The reaction to *Escobedo*, however, paled in comparison to public response to *Miranda v. Arizona*, which, if not the most controversial decision of the Warren Court (that distinction belongs either to *Brown v. Board of Education* [1954], ending racial segregation in schools, or *Engel v. Vitale* [1962], prohibiting mandatory prayer in schools), was certainly the most controversial criminal procedure decision the Court had ever handed down. *Gideon* had required only five states to change their practices; *Miranda* would make all fifty states institute a new procedure.

"You Have the Right to Remain Silent"

The *Massiah* and *Escobedo* decisions clearly required some sort of remedial prescription, a step usually taken by legislatures. Congress, however, had its hands full with Lyndon Johnson's Great Society proposals, especially his "war on poverty," while state legislatures, which normally enacted codes governing police procedures, showed little interest in responding to the Court. From what could be discerned, state legislators and their constituents seemed more than satisfied with what the police were doing. The prestigious American Law Institute undertook to propose a model code of pre-arraignment procedures, but even though it allowed police up to four hours to question a suspect without a lawyer present, it aroused little interest among the states. Both *Massiah* and *Escobedo* stayed in effect without any significant challenges from the legislatures, nor any effective implementing action either.

In the summer of 1965 Chief Justice Warren told his incoming clerks that given the failure of either Congress or the states to respond to the Court's confession cases, "I think we are going to end up taking an *Escobedo* case this year." In fact the Court took five, of which *Miranda* was the lead case. Part of the uproar over the 5–4 decision is the legislative nature of Warren's opinion for the Court, which is, as many commentators have shown, rather weak on judicial precedent and strong on the type of specifics typical of statutes. The extensive reference to police manuals demonstrating how interrogators were to secure confessions might have made more sense if there had been proof that any of the police departments involved, or any of the detectives assigned to these specific cases, had in fact relied on those manuals. Of all the decisions of the Warren Court, *Miranda* most justifies charges of judicial activism and legislating.

Nevertheless, the majority did have good reason to push through a solution. From a jurisprudential standpoint, while the decisions in *Massiah, Escobedo,* and other confession cases had begun the process of tying together the Fifth Amendment protection against self-incrimination and the Sixth Amendment right to counsel, many questions remained over just how the two actually worked together. When did the right to counsel begin? Were confessions absolutely forbidden? At what point could police begin questioning suspects?

The *Miranda* decision answered these questions. Early in the opinion Chief Justice Warren declared that constitutional rights attach when police begin custodial interrogation immediately after a person has been taken into custody or otherwise deprived of his or her freedom. Police are free to question anyone about a crime, but once they detain a suspect, they have to follow certain procedural safeguards:

Prior to any questioning, the person must be warned that he has a right to remain silent, that any statement he does make may be used as evidence against him, and that he has a right to the presence of an attorney, either retained or appointed. The defendant may waive effectuation of these rights, provided the waiver is made voluntarily, knowingly and intelligently. If, however, he indicates in any manner and at any stage of the process that he wishes to consult with an attorney before speaking there can be no questioning. Likewise, if the individual is alone and indicates in any manner that he does not wish to be interrogated, the police may not question him. The mere fact that he may have answered some questions or volunteered some statements on his own does not deprive him of the right to refrain from answering any further inquiries until he has consulted with an attorney and thereafter consents to be questioned.

The four dissenters—Harlan, White, Stewart, and Clark—protested against replacing the flexible totality of circumstances approach with what they considered to be rigid and inappropriate rules.

The decision certainly had an anticonfession cast, but far more muted than Goldberg's *Escobedo* opinion, perhaps because Warren himself, a former district attorney, was less anticonfession than he was pro-professionalism. He once commented that "I think [the police] are a bunch of lazy people who aren't getting their work done because they are too lazy to get it right." He had, in fact, during his time in California upgraded the quality of police work in his jurisdiction, and rightly or wrongly, he believed that during his tenure the police and the prosecutors had been both professional and civil liberties conscious. Further-more, he had the example of the Federal Bureau of Investigation. The FBI warned suspects of their rights and still got convictions. If the national government could do it right, then so could the states. As far as Warren was concerned, the *Miranda* warnings were cost effective; whereas lazy cops got convictions via confessions, professionals got theirs through serious detective work. Both got their man, but, he believed, the pro always got the right one.

In fact, Warren offered police a prophylactic method of making sure that evidence they gathered through interrogation, whether corroborating (i.e, supportive of a conclusion but not conclusive by itself) or confessional, would stand up in court, and here one can see the old district attorney at work. No prosecutor wants a case to fail at trial because the evidence the police have presented is flawed—due to lack of a search warrant or a less than voluntary confession. In essence, Warren told the police, take the fifteen seconds or so that it takes to read the warning, and then if the suspect still wants to talk without a lawyer, that confession is voluntary and admissible. Although both he and Goldberg seemed against all confessions, they did understand that in many cases the perpetrator, if not a habitual criminal, may want to confess, especially in many domestic violence cases. If Mary comes home and finds her husband in bed with her best friend, gets the hunting rifle out of the hall closet, and kills both of them, when the police arrive their problem is trying to keep Mary quiet long enough to read her the warning before she confesses, not trying to trick her into confessing. A professional killer is well aware that he should not talk; people like Mary, on the other hand, usually want to confess what they have done. The *Miranda* warnings would make those confessions admissible as evidence in court.

The Success of *Miranda*

Predictably, police and political conservatives disagreed with the decision even more forcefully than they had with *Escobedo*. Mayor Sam Yorty of Los Angeles condemned *Miranda* as "another set of handcuffs on the police department," while Edmund McNamara, Boston's police commissioner, complained that "criminal trials no longer will be about a search for truth, but search for technical error." North Carolina senator Sam Ervin, a former state-court judge, charged that "enough has been done for those who murder and rape and rob! It is time to do something for those who do not wish to be murdered or raped or robbed." The executive director of the International Association of Chiefs of Police complained that "I guess now we'll have to supply all squad cars with lawyers."

Yet within a very short time, despite all the screaming about the Court being soft on crime and handcuffing the police, *Miranda* embedded itself in the popular consciousness. The 1970s saw the comeback of detective programs on television, such as *Hawaii Five-O*, that made the *Miranda* warnings familiar to everyone. The main character, Steve McGarrett, viewed *Miranda* exactly as Earl Warren had wanted, as doing the police a service by making them more professional. It seemed to take no time for everyone from preteens on up to be aware of and to memorize the warnings.

The more progressive police departments in the country quickly realized the positive aspects of the decision, and some lost little time in announcing that they had been following similar practices for years. For police officers in these jurisdictions, adjustment meant little more than memorizing or carrying a card to make sure they used the right phrases.

Felons who wanted to confess did so anyway; in other instances the lack of confession merely required more effective police work to find the guilty party. As to charges that the decision caused crime rates to increase, Attorney General Ramsey Clark explained that "court rules do not cause crime." Many U.S. attorneys agreed, and one commented that "changes in court decisions and procedural practice have about the same effect on the crime rate as an aspirin would have on a tumor of the brain."

In fact, in the years since *Miranda,* police departments have indeed learned to use enhanced investigative techniques to secure convictions, and crime rates have gone down in many cities. New technology has aided police immensely in carrying out the prophylactic purpose of the *Miranda* warnings. Nearly all police cruisers now carry video cameras to record what happens at the scene of a crime when the police arrive. These cameras can also be used to film officers reading a suspect his or her rights, thus allowing the ensuing comments, confessional or otherwise, to be admitted. A person taken into a police station is usually questioned with either a tape recorder or a video camera present, again confirming that the suspect has voluntarily agreed to talk, or has asked for a lawyer. In all instances, the affirmation of the *Miranda* procedure validates the evidence.

Refining *Miranda*

Over the years the Court has reaffirmed *Miranda* on a number of occasions, although it has carved out some commonsense exceptions, such as *New York v. Quarles* (1984). In that case, a woman ran up to a police car saying that she had been raped, and that her assailant had fled into a nearby supermarket. She also told the police that the man was armed. Police apprehended the suspect, but before reading him his rights asked him the whereabouts of the gun, to which Quarles replied, "It is over there." The police retrieved a loaded .38-calibre revolver from an empty carton, formally arrested Quarles, and then read him his rights. He then said that he would answer questions without an attorney and acknowledged that the gun was his. He later appealed on the grounds that the police had interrogated him (asking him about the gun) before they had given the required warning.

The Court ruled against Quarles and found that the police had acted properly. Although the high court agreed that once police had apprehended Quarles he was in a custodial situation, the circumstances could not be ignored. There had been a concealed weapon, there might have been an accomplice, and reading the *Miranda* warnings immediately might have led the suspect to remain silent and thus endanger both the police and the public. Police officials had an obligation to control the situation, and retrieving a loaded weapon constituted their highest priority. It is a small carve-out to the rule, but one that does not endanger its basic holding.

In 2000 the Court reaffirmed *Miranda* in a rather unusual case. Shortly after the Warren Court had handed down its decision, Congress passed the Omnibus Crime Control Act of 1968, part of which explicitly aimed at overturning the ruling. Known as Section 3501, it essentially provided a very broad and loose definition of what constituted a voluntary confession in federal cases. No administration ever tried to use Section 3501, or even defend it in court, believing that it would not stand up to constitutional scrutiny. In the late 1990s, however, a conservative public advocacy group filed a friend of the court brief in the Court of Appeals for the Fourth Circuit, and a three-judge panel accepted the argument that Section 3501 overrode *Miranda*. In *Dickerson v. United States* (2000), Chief Justice William Rehnquist, who had often been a critic of *Miranda,* nonetheless wrote for a 7–2 majority holding that *Miranda* was a "constitutional rule" and therefore not subject to a congressional override.

In the most recent case decided, a 5–4 majority held that even if the police read the *Miranda* warnings, the suspect must affirmatively invoke the rights involved, i.e., he or she cannot remain silent but actually say, "I do not want to talk." The suspect must invoke his or her *Miranda* rights unambiguously. The Court's then-newest justice, Sonia Sotomayor, strongly dissented, joined by Justices Stevens, Ginsburg, and Breyer. The decision, she charged, "turns *Miranda* upside down" (*Berghuis v. Thompkins* [2010]). Although critics have charged that this is another example of the Roberts Court chipping away at the constitutional rights of individuals, it is unclear yet just how this decision will play out in practice. Police departments have become used to dealing with *Miranda* as the Warren Court had intended, and since the results have been positive—more convictions based on more effective investigation—it is unlikely they will change those procedures.

Miranda's End

After the high court decision of his case, Ernesto Miranda still remained in custody, because he had appealed only the abduction and rape conviction and not that of robbery. The prosecutor immediately announced he would be retried on the first two charges, and the hearings began in February 1967. The new trial replicated the first go-round, but without the introduction of the confession as evidence.

The victim and her sister testified again, but the prosecutor had additional damning evidence. While Miranda had been in jail, his common-law wife, Twila Hoffman, had borne a child with another man. An incensed Miranda, who thought that after the Supreme Court decision he would be a free man, had written to social service authorities charging that Hoffman was not a fit mother. Scared of what Miranda might do if he were released, Hoffman agreed to testify that Miranda had told her while he was in jail awaiting the first trial that he had in fact abducted and raped the young woman. Again the jury found him guilty, and again he received concurrent sentences of twenty to thirty years.

He only served five years, and after his release from prison in 1972 on parole soon found himself again in trouble with the law. He served more time for violating his parole. He complained that he had been cheated because he had not made any money off the case, and tried to peddle autographed cards that had the *Miranda* warnings on them. In 1976 he was killed in a skid row bar in Phoenix in a fight over a three-dollar poker bet. The police read the *Miranda* warnings to his alleged killer, who then exercised his right to remain silent.

Cases Cited

Berghuis v. Thompkins, 2010 U.S. Lexis 4379 (2010)
Betts v. Brady, 316 U.S. 455 (1942)
Brown v. Board of Education, 337 U.S. 483 (1954)
Dickerson v. United States, 530 U.S. 428 (2000)
Engel v. Vitale, 370 U.S. 421 (1962)
Escobedo v. Illinois, 378 U.S. 478 (1964)
Gideon v. Wainwright, 372 U.S. 335 (1963)
Massiah v. United States, 377 U.S. 201 (1964)
Miranda v. Arizona, 384 U.S. 436 (1966)
New York v. Quarles, 467 U.S. 649 (1984)

For Further Reading

For the case itself, see Liva Baker, *Miranda: Crime, Law, and Politics* (1983), and Richard C. Cortner and Clifford M. Lytle, *Constitutional Law and Politics: Three Arizona Cases* (1971). The broader context of the Warren Court is well examined in L. A. Scot Powe, *The Warren Court and American Politics* (2000), while Fred Graham, *The Due Process Revolution* (1970), casts a somewhat critical eye on the various Warren Court criminal decisions. A good article for the earlier cases is Arnold N. Enken and Sheldon H. Elsen, "Counsel for the Suspect: *Massiah v. United States* and *Escobedo v. Illinois,*" 49 *Minnesota Law Review* 47 (1964).

The Case That Aroused Great Passions

Roe v. Wade (1973)

THERE HAVE BEEN FEW CASES in the Supreme Court's history that have aroused such passionate and sustained criticism as the 1973 decision holding that, as part of her right to privacy, a woman had a constitutionally protected right to secure an abortion. Nearly four decades after Justice Harry Blackmun wrote the 7–2 opinion, it is still at the center of controversies over the extent of the Court's powers, constitutional interpretation, and judicial activism. Every nominee to the Supreme Court in the last thirty years has been questioned on his or her opinion on the case, and all of them have evaded giving a straightforward answer. Despite efforts by state legislatures to get around the holding and by conservative presidents to appoint justices willing to overrule *Roe v. Wade,* it remains on the books, shorthand for other issues involved in the culture wars, particularly feminism's demand for equal rights for women.

Abortion Legislation: A Brief History

In the late 1960s Texas, like many states, had laws prohibiting abortion that dated back to the latter part of the nineteenth century. Abortion—the inducement of a miscarriage in order to terminate a pregnancy—had been a fairly common option in most parts of the world since antiquity. The women of ancient Greece, Rome, and Egypt ate substances derived from plants such as silphium, Queen Anne's lace, and acacia gum to end unwanted pregnancies, and those societies viewed abortion not as a crime but as a form of birth control. Women had abortions in Tudor and Stuart England, and took the practice with them to the New World. The reasons women chose to have abortions then are pretty much the same reasons as now; they wanted to end pregnancies caused by rape or incest, or that posed a danger to their physical or mental health. Poor families chose abortions because they could not feed another mouth, and at a time when society frowned on having a child out of wedlock, single women who got pregnant had abortions rather than face the type of social stigma Nathaniel Hawthorne depicted in *The Scarlet Letter.*

In colonial and early republican times society viewed abortion as a private matter, but we do know from the available historical documents that it was not that rare. Women used methods they got from friends and relatives, or went to folk healers or midwives for help. Common abortifacients often involved toxic plants like juniper, which Native Americans had traditionally used for the same purpose. After the Revolution the United States continued to follow English common law, which allowed women to have abortions up until the time they could feel the fetus move, the so-called "quickening," which often occurred in the fourth month of gestation. In an era before pregnancy tests and regular visits to a doctor, the quickening might be the first sign for some women that they were even pregnant; symptoms such as fatigue, weight gain, nausea, or even the cessation of menses might well have been attributed to other health issues.

Quickening played an important role in the law and in public attitudes regarding abortion. Some religious traditions believed that at the time of quickening the fetus received its soul from God. American law considered quickening the point at which a fetus could be considered a human being for certain purposes. For example, if an assault caused a woman to miscarry, her husband could sue the attacker for loss of his property interest in the unborn child. Most states, however, did not consider a fetus a full person until birth, so while the attacker might be liable for damages, he would not be subject to criminal penalties for murder or manslaughter. If a woman took steps to end a pregnancy before quickening, neither church nor society considered it a sin or a crime.

In 1821 Connecticut became the first state to make it illegal for a woman to have an abortion, but only after quickening. Since it was nearly impossible to prove that quickening had occurred without the woman's cooperation, the law proved extremely difficult to enforce. From the records it appears that abortion providers faced criminal action only when the pregnant woman died or had serious health consequences afterward.

In the years that followed other states passed laws that went beyond the Connecticut statute. In 1828 Illinois, Missouri, and New York made all abortions illegal, even in the early stages of pregnancy, in order to protect women from incompetent abortion providers. These laws viewed pregnant women as victims of the crime, and the women themselves could not be prosecuted either for seeking an abortion or for performing one on themselves. Other states passed similar laws in the 1830s and early 1840s. In 1845 New York amended its statute so that a woman could be charged with a crime if she tried to obtain an abortion or performed one on herself at any stage of the pregnancy. The new laws were impossible to enforce without the testimony of the women involved. According to some studies, even as more states passed laws against abortion, women continued to have them. In 1845 Chief Justice Lemuel Shaw of Massachusetts, where abortion was still legal prior to quickening, dismissed a case against abortionist Luceba Parker. There was no evidence that the fetus had quickened, and therefore no way to prove that an abortion had been intended.

In the 1840s a Massachusetts physician, Charles Knowlton, became the country's best-known advocate of abortion rights, arguing in newspaper interviews, magazine articles, and books that abortion constituted a necessary part of family planning. (One needs to recall that at this time neither condoms nor any other form of birth control, aside from abstinence, were available.) American society would benefit, Knowlton argued, if all parents were happy and healthy and all children wanted and well cared for. If an additional child would be a burden, then parents should be allowed to end the pregnancy.

In the light of Knowlton's campaign, women's health clinics opened in many cities that provided abortion, although they disguised this fact to avoid running afoul of the law. They treated, they said, diseases specific to women, and in an age when custom dictated that middle- and upper-class women not go out of the house once their pregnancy showed, few men—even those in government—were going to ask many questions about these "diseases." At the same time, newspapers and magazines carried advertisements for mail-order drugs to cleanse a woman's reproductive tract and restore normal menstruation.

How many abortions took place cannot be known, but one estimate is that by the Civil War there was one abortion for every four live births. An even more significant and verifiable statistic is that the fertility rate for American women declined by 50 percent between 1800 and 1900, from an average of 7 to 3.5 children. For many, perhaps most American women, abortion provided the only means of birth control available to them.

Not everyone approved, and in the years following the Civil War the American Medical Association (AMA), founded in 1847, took the lead in opposing abortion. Doctors claimed that abortion posed unnecessary risks to women's lives and health, and it is true that many women who had abortions suffered from infections and other dangerous complications afterward. But a good part of the opposition grew out of the fact that most surgical abortions were performed by midwives, and doctors wanted to gain greater control over the practice of medicine. The AMA lobbied both the federal and state governments to bar anyone but a licensed physician from performing an abortion.

Some Americans opposed abortion on moral grounds, and argued that a woman's fundamental duty and purpose was to bear children, and women who had abortions, therefore, selfishly refused to accept their "natural" roles as wives and mothers. The criminalization of abortion, like many other laws in this period, asserted that women had to be protected against their own weaknesses, as well as the immorality of conceiving unwanted children and then trying to get rid of them. Some religious groups also began to condemn the practice, and the Catholic Church in 1869 abandoned the concept of quickening and declared human life sacred from conception. Catholic leaders began denouncing abortion as a moral evil.

Some white Protestant leaders opposed abortion because they feared the country was being overrun by immigrants from southern and eastern Europe, who typically had higher birth rates. It was the duty of educated middle-class, old-stock women, they argued, to have as many children as possible in order to keep America safe from these new groups. Joining them was Anthony Comstock, who saw abortion as a result of promiscuous sex—even among married people—and wanted to prohibit not only abortions but even information about the crude contraceptives then becoming available.

Beginning in the 1860s the campaign made rapid headway throughout the United States. Connecticut passed an anti-abortion law eliminating the quickening standard, and made abortion a crime for both those who performed it as well as for women who obtained one. The Connecticut statute became a model, and by 1890 every state in the Union, as well as the remaining territories, had given in to the antivice crusaders and the doctors, and abortion was now a crime. While most states outlawed the procedure at any stage of the pregnancy, they also allowed so-called "therapeutic" abortions if the woman's life was at risk from the pregnancy. Hospitals established abortion review committees, and if a doctor wanted to perform a therapeutic procedure he needed permission from the committee. Four states—Louisiana, Massachusetts, New Jersey, and Pennsylvania—did not have any exceptions in their laws, not even if an abortion was necessary to save the woman's life.

These were the laws on the books until the 1960s.

Growing Support for Abortion Rights

During this period enforcement varied considerably. Initially, police and prosecution cracked down on abortion providers, particularly midwives, and especially when a death or injury occurred. Then in the 1920s sexual attitudes began to liberalize, and police enforcement slackened considerably. The Great Depression also changed attitudes, as massive unemployment and poverty made it difficult for many families to provide for the children they already had much less for new mouths to feed. Abortion became more acceptable, even for married women, and in many parts of the country police just looked the other way. At the same time, many doctors performed abortions in their offices without asking a hospital committee's permission. While again it is difficult to provide accurate numbers, studies indicate that during the Depression some 600,000 to 800,000 abortions—nearly all of them technically illegal—took place. Many of these occurred in "back alley" clinics and often led to infection or worse; estimates are that between 8,000 and 17,000 women a year died at the hands of these incompetent and uncaring abortion providers, most of whom were little more than charlatans.

As doctors realized that they could perform safe abortions, and that their patients desperately needed help, they began to call for repeal of the harsh laws on the books. But then came World War II, and after the peace couples who had delayed families suddenly rushed to make up for lost time. As part of the postwar "baby boom," women were exhorted to leave jobs and return to their "natural" role as wives and mothers. Police again raided the same clinics where only a few years earlier they had steered women in need of help. The crackdown on abortion also fit in with the social conservatism of the 1950s. When the Soviet Union legalized abortion in the mid-1950s, anti-red crusaders in the United States linked abortion to support for communism! The prosecution and conviction of some doctors, such as the highly regarded Baltimore physician George Timanus, also served to scare doctors who had previously been willing to perform abortions. At the same time, there seemed to be a rising demand from women for abortion services, and in the absence of trained physicians, women sought other sources.

If a woman had means, then she had opportunities, and a quick trip to Europe could combine both a short vacation as well as a medically safe abortion. Ironically, two heavily Catholic outposts in the

Western Hemisphere also provided legal abortions, Puerto Rico and Mexico. Every Friday afternoon a charter plane took off from Dallas for Mexico, with the passengers—all women, some of the younger ones with their mothers—going to "shop." The plane returned on Sunday afternoon, and while all the passengers carried something they had bought, they also were no longer pregnant. Even within the United States some women could obtain safe abortions. As one doctor noted, "as long as you were the banker's daughter, the doctor's daughter, the golf buddy's daughter, an unwanted pregnancy was always taken care of."

But those without means, or those who could not travel because of fear of parents or husbands, had to turn to the back alley providers, where unskilled and often disreputable people preyed on them. As one scholar described it, those entering the practice included "motorcycle mechanics, bartenders, and real-estate agents, who knew little more than that women needed abortions and that inducing them was profitable." From this era we have stories of women meeting intermediaries who blindfolded them and then drove them to secret places where unknown people performed abortions. There may have been as many as one million abortions a year during the 1950s and early 1960s, and a shockingly high number of deaths. One estimate put such abortions as the cause for more than 40 percent of maternal deaths.

Then change occurred, precipitated on the one hand by doctors appalled at the carnage untrained abortionists wreaked on helpless women, and on the other from the growing women's rights movement, which began to see access to birth control and abortion as key to women's control over their own bodies.

Two events in the early 1960s also prodded both the public and doctors to rethink the accepted notions regarding abortion. Sherri Finkbine, the Phoenix host of *Romper Room*, a national children's show, was happily married and pregnant. Then she learned that a drug she had been taking to alleviate sleeplessness and morning nausea was thalidomide, which had been linked to severe birth defects. The Finkbines' doctor recommended a therapeutic abortion, and the local hospital committee approved. Wanting to alert other women to the dangers of the drug, Sherri alerted the local press. The wire services picked up the story, and the Finkbines soon found themselves in a media circus, inundated with letters both supporting and attacking them. *Romper Room* fired her, the local hospital committee withdrew its approval, and the Finkbines, because they had the resources, traveled to Sweden. There she had a safe and legal abortion of a fetus that was too deformed to have lived. On their return home the Finkbines publicly defended their decision as best for themselves and their other children. A Gallup poll conducted a month after her return indicated that 52 percent of the respondents thought she had done the right thing, and only 32 percent said she had been wrong. Even one-third of the Catholics agreed with her decision.

Around the same time the country witnessed an epidemic of rubella, or German measles, and it was established medical knowledge by then that pregnant women contracting the disease faced a high risk of birth defects. Between 1962 and 1965 approximately 15,000 babies were born with birth defects linked to rubella. Most doctors and hospital review committees supported abortions for pregnant women with rubella, but in 1966 an anti-abortion member of the California Board of Medical Examiners forced the San Francisco district attorney's office to prosecute nine well-known obstetricians because they had performed hospital abortions on women with the disease. The story once again got national media attention, and doctors around the country protested, including the deans of one hundred medical schools. All this attention forced the district attorney to drop the charges, but it made doctors aware that even when the law allowed therapeutic abortions for good medical reasons, the vagaries of local regimes might leave them open to prosecution.

By then, however, the first steps had been taken toward reforming abortion laws that a good part of the public and most of the medical profession considered archaic. The Planned Parenthood Association, the country's leading advocate for birth control information and the reform of abortion laws, had sponsored a national conference in 1955, and the papers from that meeting, all urging repeal of the laws and making safe and legal abortion more available, received favorable notice in both the scientific and legal communities. Four years later the prestigious American Law Institute (ALI), whose members—judges, lawyers, and law professors—suggested "model" codes, largely adopted the findings of the Planned Parenthood meeting, and recommended that the criminal provisions regarding abortion be dropped from all state penal codes. The ALI did not endorse making abortion more available, and physicians remained concerned that local prejudices and prosecutors trying to make a reputation could still override their professional judgment.

Since most states pay close attention to ALI recommendations, many began reviewing their abortion statutes. California began the process in 1962, and although the Catholic lobby managed to kill a reform bill then and the following year, the idea of safe and legalized abortions gathered momentum and the assembly passed a reform measure in 1967. Thirty other states debated reform, and over the next few years nine other states passed ALI-style reform statutes. Even after states passed such measures, however, abortion providers often ran into opposition. The Catholic Church opposed abortions and brought pressure on local hospital committees not to approve the procedure; other hospitals, not wanting to be labeled as "abortion mills," put quotas on the number of procedures they would allow.

At the same time, the women's rights movement was gaining strength throughout the country, and one of its key demands was a woman's control over her own body. This included decisions as to whether or not to use contraceptives (the oral contraceptive had just been introduced in 1960) and whether to continue or terminate an unwanted pregnancy. Although initially many media outlets treated the women's rights movement as a joke and focused on some of the more radical groups, eventually the mainstream press and television began treating women's demands seriously. Discussion of reproductive control moved from a taboo area to the front pages, and numerous articles in women's magazines began exploring the matter for the first time. Interestingly, while doctors opposed a ban on abortion because it interfered with their professional judgment, many women argued that selecting whether to abort or not should be their decision, not the doctor's. By 1969 a Harris poll found that 64 percent of Americans, including 60 percent of Catholics, believed that abortion should not be a legal question but a private decision between a woman and her doctor.

In the early 1970s other states followed California in repealing their old abortion statutes. The battle that caught the most headlines occurred in New York, a heavily Catholic state where the Church lobbied relentlessly and brought a great deal of pressure on Catholic members of the assembly. At first it appeared that the measure had fallen one vote shy, but then George Michaels asked to change his "no" vote to "yes." He acknowledged that, given the Church's influence in his district, this would probably mean the end of his political career, but he could not in good conscience vote to kill a bill so important to women's health. The bill passed the assembly and the next day the Senate followed suit, with Gov. Nelson A. Rockefeller signing it into law in April 1970.

The New York law was a true repeal law, and essentially removed abortion from the criminal code. In addition, it was not restricted to New York residents, nor did it require that abortions take place in hospitals. In 1973 the number of legal abortions in New York outnumbered live births, and thanks to groups like Planned Parenthood that set up safe and clean clinics, back alley providers practically disappeared. But then the reform movement faltered. Opposition to repeal in other states prevented any other significant changes, and advocates decided to look to the courts.

Establishing the Right to Privacy

During the 1950s and 1960s, the Supreme Court under Chief Justice Earl Warren had struck down state-sponsored racial segregation, declared state legislative malapportionment unconstitutional, breathed life into those portions of the Bill of Rights protecting persons accused of crimes, and made the First Amendment into a shield as well as a sword of democratic government. Moreover, it had determined that a constitutional right to privacy existed in the landmark case of *Griswold v. Connecticut* (1965).

Justice Louis D. Brandeis had argued in *Olmstead v. United States* (1928) that the Constitution included a right to privacy, a right to be let alone from government interference, but the full Court did not accept this notion for four decades. *Griswold* involved an 1879 statute prohibiting the use of any drug or device to prevent conception, and penalizing any person who advised on or provided contraceptive materials. Civil libertarians had tried twice before without success to get the high court to review this law, and in its most recent attempt the Court had turned away the challenge because no one had been prosecuted under it for years. In his dissent in *Poe v. Ullman* (1961), however, Justice John Marshall Harlan II had suggested that a liberty interest in personal privacy—that is, an individual right that came within the protection of the Fourteenth Amendment—existed that deserved judicial protection.

Shortly afterward New Haven officials prosecuted Estelle Griswold, the executive director of the Connecticut Planned Parenthood League, for violating the 1879 law. In *Griswold* Justice William Douglas, speaking for a 7–2 majority, wrote one of the most creative opinions in the Court's history, reversing the conviction and voiding the law. Although Harlan in *Poe* had suggested that a right to privacy existed in the Fourteenth Amendment's due process clause, utilizing that clause would have meant resurrecting the idea of substantive due process, the doctrine that had killed so much reform legislation and which still had a bad odor even after the Court had disavowed it in the late 1930s (see Chapters 13 and 16). Rather than rely on substantive due process, though, which actually made sense and which the Court had from time to time used to protect rights, Douglas instead cobbled together justifications from various parts of the Bill of Rights. The amendments, he declared, "have penumbras, formed by emanations from those guarantees that help give them life and substance." Taken together (in what one wit termed Amendment 3 and a half), they form a constitutionally protected right of privacy, and no privacy could be more sacred or deserving of protection from intrusion than the marital chamber.

Although Douglas did not mention abortion in his opinion, and even though he tried to shy away from substantive due process, it soon became clear that the due process/liberty interest argument, which Justice Harlan spelled out in his concurrence in *Griswold,* might be the key to getting the abortion question before the courts. Harlan argued that the Fourteenth Amendment due process clause did in fact include substantive rights, and that one of these was a liberty interest in one's own body, and the right of the individual, not the government, to make decisions regarding one's own health and physical welfare.

In New York a law school student named Roy Lucas, spurred on by the fact that he had had to take his girlfriend to Puerto Rico to get a safe and legal abortion, wrote a term paper that he then published and which was studied carefully by abortion rights activists. Lucas located a right to an abortion in the same set of constitutional protections that Douglas had expounded in *Griswold.* He listed a number of cases in which the Court had identified individual liberty rights and argued that for a woman, the decision to terminate a pregnancy was a liberty and privacy matter as important as any of those previously identified by the Court, such as how to raise and educate one's child. Lucas went on to reject the argument that a fetus is a legal human being, since that position had no basis in Anglo-American law. The state had a legitimate interest in protecting the health and safety of women, and this would warrant some regulation, such as requiring that the procedure be carried out by licensed physicians. As for those states that allowed therapeutic abortions, Lucas believed they could be challenged as too vague to satisfy due process requirements. There should, he declared, be "a frontal attack on the very assumptions of abortion legislation . . . through judicial enforcement of the guarantees of human rights found in the amendments to the United States Constitution." Lucas also prepared a model legal brief that he believed could be used in attacks on abortion legislation.

One of the people who read the Lucas article was Sarah Ragle Weddington.

Sarah Weddington Meets Norma McCorvey

While Sarah Ragle had been a third-year student at the University of Texas Law School in Austin, she discovered that she was pregnant by

Ron Weddington, a fellow student who later became her husband. The couple recognized that she would not be able to get an abortion in Texas, where the law prohibited the procedure except to save the life of the mother, so they went to the Mexican border town of Piedras Negras, where they found a competent doctor. She finished her law degree but then found it hard to get a job because most firms would not hire women, so she accepted a nonpracticing position with the American Bar Association. Her experience with gender bias led Weddington to become active with women's rights groups, birth control counseling, and referring women to safe abortion clinics in Mexico.

She later claimed that *Roe v. Wade* "started at a garage sale, amid paltry castoffs," to raise money for a women's liberation consciousness-raising group. Two of the women, Judy Smith and Bea Durden, were actively involved in the underground abortion referral service, and worried whether their activities might lead to their prosecution as accomplices under the Texas criminal abortion statute. Although the topic had never been mentioned in her law school classes, her own personal history led Weddington to agree to do some legal research for her friends.

Weddington, it should be noted, was not the only lawyer in the country then doing research on the possibility of challenging a state abortion statute, nor the only one who read the Lucas article, but she was the one who, despite being only a few years out of law school, successfully brought a case to the U.S. Supreme Court.

Her research convinced her that it would be possible to mount a constitutional challenge to the Texas statute, and she asked her friend and fellow law school classmate, Linda Coffee (who had also run into gender discrimination in looking for a job), to help her. Coffee agreed, and they began looking for a pregnant woman who could serve as a plaintiff. In January 1970 they met twenty-two-year-old Norma McCorvey.

McCorvey had had a difficult life. Her parents constantly fought, and when at age ten she was kicked out of a Catholic boarding school for "rebellious behavior," she wound up in a reform school in Gainesville, Texas. She spent four years at the all-girls institution, years she would later call the happiest ones of her childhood. She was returned to her home at age fourteen, and her mother arranged for her to stay at the home of a relative. He raped her every night for three weeks until her mother found out and brought her home. Norma worked as a waitress in a Dallas restaurant, and in 1964 the sixteen-year-old married Woody McCorvey. They moved to California, and when McCorvey found out his wife was pregnant he beat her and she left and went home to her mother. She gave birth to a girl and ceded her parental rights to her mother, who raised Melissa and for the most part tried to keep Melissa away from Norma.

Although she divorced Woody she kept her married name, and floated from one job to another, one man to another, and occasionally one woman to another. She got pregnant again, and gave her second child up for adoption. "Every time I go to bed with a man," she explained, "I get pregnant," and she was pregnant again in 1969, this time by an aging gambler working as a carnival ticket-taker. She went to a doctor and said she wanted him to "take my baby away," but aware of the law, he quickly showed her out of his office. Trying to induce a miscarriage, she ate quantities of peanuts and castor oil, but only wound up getting sick. She tried other doctors and lawyers, and when she finally got the name of a clandestine abortion clinic she found it locked. Finally, a sympathetic doctor referred her to Henry McCluskey, a lawyer specializing in adoptions, and he sent her to see Linda Coffee.

When McCorvey, Coffee, and Weddington met at a pizza parlor in northeast Dallas, the two lawyers liked what they saw—a petite, visibly pregnant woman with an air of naiveté—one who would be an appealing plaintiff in the courtroom. At the time, McCorvey still wanted to get an abortion, but Weddington and Coffee wanted a test case, and they convinced her to become "Jane Roe." A few months later McCorvey delivered a healthy son, and gave it to McCluskey for adoption. McCorvey then, as she later recalled, "stayed invisible, burying myself in drugs and alcohol, as Linda and Sarah made history in my name."

Jane Roe Wins Round One

In March 1970 the two lawyers filed their initial suit in federal court against Henry Wade, the district attorney for Dallas County, with Coffee paying the filing fees out of her own pocket. She also asked that the case be heard by a three-judge panel consisting of both district and circuit court judges, a procedure then allowed when challenging the validity of a statute on federal constitutional grounds. In addition to getting a more varied panel, one could appeal the results directly to the U.S. Supreme Court. To their surprise, the request was granted, and the panel that would hear the case could not, from their point of view, have been better.

They got one of the few women on the federal bench at that time, Sarah Hughes, who after the assassination of John F. Kennedy in November 1963 had sworn in Lyndon Johnson as president aboard Air Force One. In addition, district court judge William Taylor had a reputation as fair and open-minded, while Court of Appeals judge Irving Goldberg had issued several pioneering decisions on civil rights.

The two lawyers had been meeting with the Dallas Committee for the Study of Abortion, which wanted to enlarge the suit to include married as well as single women. *Roe v. Wade* would thus be a class action suit as well as an individual case, speaking for all women denied access to legal abortion in situations where the state had no compelling reason to deny it. To bolster these claims, two other parties joined the suit. Dr. James H. Hallford contended that the Texas law infringed on his right as a doctor to provide his patients with the treatment that in his judgment they needed. "John and Mary Doe," pseudonyms for David and Marsha King, joined the case to argue for a married couple's right to terminate a pregnancy.

The panel heard the case on May 22, 1970. Weddington's legal experience up until this time had consisted of a few uncontested divorces, so Coffee handled most of the oral argument. But Weddington handled the crux of the constitutional case. The Texas law, she claimed, infringed on Jane Roe's "right to safe and adequate medical advice pertaining to the decision of whether to carry a given pregnancy to term" and upon "the fundamental right of all women to choose whether to bear children." When the hearing ended, Weddington and her allies had no idea which way the court would decide. "Most lawyers leave the courtroom knowing they will simply have to wait for the decision. That is just the way it is. We began to wait."

Less than a month later they had their decision in the first stage of *Roe v. Wade*. The panel issued a unanimous *per curiam* decision (a memorandum from the entire court that does not bear a single author's name) holding the statute too vague to be enforced. But the court also went on to address the broader issue, and ruled that "the Texas abortion laws infringe upon plaintiffs' fundamental right to choose whether to have children." The panel relied on *Griswold,* but not on the Douglas opinion. Instead they turned to Justice Arthur Goldberg's concurrence, which used the Ninth Amendment's provision of rights retained by the people as a basis for the right of privacy. The panel also refused to issue an injunction preventing further prosecutions, on the assumption that no district attorney would prosecute a law deemed unconstitutional.

The decision made the front pages of all the Texas papers, and even received some attention in other parts of the country. The Kings, speaking as the Does, naturally applauded the decision; no word came from Jane Roe. Even the president of the Catholic Women of the Dallas Diocese agreed that the court could not have reached any other decision, because as it stood the law was too vague, and she hoped the legislature would craft a better statute with more carefully defined health exemptions. District Attorney Henry Wade announced that he would not only appeal the decision, but until the Supreme Court spoke he would continue prosecutions under the law.

Abortion in the Supreme Court before *Roe*

We focus on *Roe* because it was the case decided by the Supreme Court, but in the summer of 1970 there were more than twenty lower court cases challenging abortion statutes in the states and in the District of Columbia. Some people have argued that the Court should not have taken up the matter until the reform movement in the states had run its course. Reform, however, not only seemed stalled, but few states went as far as New York had done. Some of the "reform" statutes did not give women a full right to terminate a pregnancy, but placed limits on how and when an abortion could be secured. In addition, prosecutorial discretion threw a wild card into the mix; a woman seeking an abortion in one jurisdiction might well be ignored by a prosecutor, while in the next district over she and her doctor could be arrested and tried. Moreover, some of the state courts had begun declaring that, based on *Griswold*, a constitutional right to privacy existed that included a woman's option to have an abortion. Given this situation, the only question was how soon the Court would grapple with the issue.

The first abortion case the justices heard involved a District of Columbia statute. U.S. District judge Gerhard Gesell, an eminent and highly respected jurist, struck down the law banning abortions on the grounds that the "health" and "life" exceptions to the ban were too vague. He went on to note that "as a secular matter a woman's liberty and right of privacy extends to family, marriage and sex matters and may well include the right to remove an unwanted child at least in the early stages of pregnancy."

The Supreme Court reversed Gesell in *United States v. Vuitch* in 1971 (Milan Vuitch was a doctor who performed abortions in the Washington, D.C., area), but in a highly fractured opinion that tried to duck the privacy question. Hugo Black delivered the majority opinion that the health provisions of the statute were not overly vague, and he was joined in part by Burger, Douglas, Stewart, and White, and then joined in another part by Burger, Harlan, White, and Blackmun. White and Douglas both agreed that the statute was not vague, but Douglas dissented on the grounds that the statute did not meet due process requirements because it opened a physician's judgment to the vagaries of a jury trial. Harlan, joined by Brennan, Marshall, and Blackmun, dissented on jurisdictional grounds, claiming that the appeal should not have been allowed. Then

Harlan, speaking only for himself, said that despite the jurisdictional issue, on the merits he would agree with the majority; Blackmun said something similar. Only Potter Stewart believed that a physician should not be subject to prosecution for performing an abortion that in the doctor's opinion was necessary either for health reasons or to save a patient's life. None of the nine justices ventured into the privacy terrain.

Roe v. Wade and *Doe v. Bolton*

The Court could have chosen appeals from any of a half-dozen states, but it took the one from Texas because that state's law represented the older type of statute, one that banned nearly all abortions, and it also took *Doe v. Bolton,* an appeal from a Georgia reform statute passed in 1968. Unlike the Texas law, Georgia did not make all abortions criminal except those necessary to save the life of the woman. Instead, abortion was legal when two sets of criteria were met. First, an abortion was permissible if a licensed physician, "in his best clinical judgment," deemed an abortion necessary because the woman's health or life was in danger, the baby was likely to have a serious birth defect, or the pregnancy was the result of rape. Second, the decision had to be approved by two other licensed doctors and a hospital abortion committee, and be performed in a hospital. While far more lenient than the Texas law, it still left the decision to abort in the hands of doctors and committees, not with women.

The plaintiff in the Georgia case, Sandra Bensing, had a story similar to that of Norma McCorvey—a ninth-grade dropout who married a drifter and rapidly had two children. He beat her and the children, who were eventually taken away and placed in foster care for their protection. She got pregnant again during a stormy period in their marriage, and decided to leave her husband and put the child up for adoption if she could not get an abortion. Her attorney, Margie Hames, conferred frequently with Weddington and Coffee, and they assisted each other with the appeals briefs.

On May 21, 1971, the Court announced that it would hear the two cases with briefs due over the summer. Weddington at this time was working for the city attorney of Fort Worth, and he refused to give her time to work on the case, so she and her husband decided she should quit and devote herself full-time to preparing for the high court, which heard oral argument on December 13, 1971. There were, however, only seven justices on the bench, since President Nixon was having trouble replacing Hugo Black and John Marshall Harlan II, who had both retired in ill health in September. At conference five justices voted to overturn the Texas statute, but there was no clear majority in the Georgia case. Chief Justice Burger assigned the case to Harry Blackmun, who was known as a notoriously slow writer, and in the summer of 1972 Blackmun buried himself in the medical library at the Mayo Clinic and worked on a draft. Because the justices recognized the important issues involved, they decided to reschedule oral argument in both cases when there would be a full bench. With the addition of William Rehnquist and Lewis Powell, nine justices heard reargument on October 11, 1972, and handed down their decision on January 22, 1973.

By a 7–2 vote in both cases, the Court struck down the two state laws. In his opinion Justice Blackmun first reviewed the history of anti-abortion legislation, as well as numerous ethical, philosophical, and religious writings on the subject. He concluded that the laws of most states, including Texas, were out of touch with medical advances and history. More importantly, he found that they violated the constitutional right to privacy.

Conceding that the document "does not explicitly mention any right of privacy," Blackmun cited a dozen or so cases going back more than eighty years to assert that the Constitution protected such a right in a variety of ways. The Court "has recognized that a right of personal privacy, or a guarantee of certain areas or zones of privacy" exist under the Constitution. This right of privacy "is broad enough to encompass a woman's decision whether or not to terminate her pregnancy." The state imposed a great burden upon a woman when it denied her this decision, subjecting her to potential medical harms, as well as financial and emotional harms.

The state, however, also had an interest in protecting life, and he set out a three-stage standard to determine when a woman's privacy right trumped the state's interest, and when the state could restrict the woman's right. During the first trimester, the decision of whether to continue the pregnancy rested entirely with the woman and her physician. During the second trimester, a state had a right to regulate abortions to protect the health and safety of a pregnant woman, but the decision of whether to have an abortion still remained with the woman. Only in the third trimester did the state gain a paramount interest in preventing an abortion. The reason was that "the fetus then presumably has the capability of meaningful life outside the mother's womb," and state protection thus has a logical and biological justification. During this third trimester a state could prohibit abortion "except when it is necessary to preserve the life or health of the mother." (The trimester scheme had not been suggested in any of the briefs; Blackmun developed it out of his own research.)

Two justices dissented. William Rehnquist believed that the Court should not have heard the case at all, because Roe's pregnancy was over, and while a party "may vindicate his own constitutional rights, he may not seek vindication for the rights of others." Blackmun answered this argument when he noted that pregnancy litigation will seldom survive the trial stage, and appellate review would be effectively denied. Pregnancy provided a classic example of "capable of repetition, yet evading review," and the law should not be that rigid.

Byron White also dissented, claiming that nothing in the language or history of the Constitution supported the Court's judgment, and that the majority had simply fashioned a new right for pregnant mothers with scarcely any reason or authority to justify it. Moreover, it had now taken away from the states—where it belonged—the power to fashion policy in this area.

In the companion case of *Doe v. Bolton* challenging the Georgia law, the Court set aside the requirements that interfered with a woman's decision to terminate a pregnancy, namely that abortions had to take place in accredited hospitals rather than clinics, and that a committee had to approve the procedure before a doctor could act. For all practical purposes, abortion laws in some forty states were effectively nullified.

The Response to the Decisions

The decisions were not particularly controversial when announced. The death of former president Lyndon Johnson that day pushed news of *Roe* to the inside pages, and some states, notably New York and California, had already adopted laws that met Blackmun's criteria. Moreover, to many people the decision seemed the logical conclusion of a set of cases that had been expanding not only the right of privacy, but the rights of women that recognized changing societal views of the family and of child-bearing. *Roe* seemed a very modern decision, much like *Brown v. Board of Education* (1954), that liberated a large class of people—in this case women—from antiquated laws. Women's groups, needless to say, were elated.

There was no immediate large-scale public outcry against it, and much of the mainstream press applauded. The *New York Times* called it a "major contribution to the preservation of individual liberties." Although the conservative *Wall Street Journal* worried that Blackmun's trimester scheme might tread on the toes of state lawmakers, on the whole it praised the decision, and said the Court had "struck a reasonable balance on an exceedingly difficult question." Social and legal conservatives, on the other hand, thought the Court had gone too far.

Professor (and later appellate judge) John Noonan believed that not only had the justices misread history, but they had created a right where none existed.

It is in this last area that *Roe* received the heaviest criticism, even from liberals who favored abortion rights. Professor John Hart Ely, who had been one of Earl Warren's law clerks, wrote what many consider the most devastating analysis and concluded that one could not find in the Fourteenth Amendment's due process clause any justification or logic to extend an umbrella of protection giving women the right to terminate a pregnancy. When Ruth Bader Ginsburg was named to the high court, she repeated at her confirmation hearings her earlier criticism that the Court should have issued a narrower ruling, overturning the Texas statute but leaving other laws restricting abortions in place. This stratagem, Ginsburg believed, would not have aroused such a strong backlash, and the question would have been left in the hands of state legislatures.

Within a few years the climate changed, when religious groups— notably Roman Catholics and fundamentalist Protestants—began a campaign against the decision. The National Conference of Catholic Bishops had denounced the opinion immediately, but it had done so from a religious perspective, and its opposition was aimed primarily at Catholic women, whom it urged not to commit such a sin as they considered abortion to be. But as conservative Protestant groups such as the Christian Coalition entered the political arena, opposition to abortion— even by those who did not share the Christian Coalition's beliefs— became their chief rallying cry. Some state legislatures, responding to this pressure, tried to evade *Roe,* but while the Court approved some restrictions on abortions, it kept the basic holding of *Roe* in place. Conservatives hoped that with the appointment of the Reagan and Bush justices the decision would be overturned, and they thought that time had come when the Court heard *Planned Parenthood of Southeastern Pennsylvania v. Casey* in 1992. But three of the Reagan-Bush justices— Sandra Day O'Connor, Anthony Kennedy, and David Souter—wrote a joint opinion reaffirming the "essential holding" of *Roe,* namely, that women had a constitutionally protected right to an abortion in the early stages of a pregnancy.

If *Lochner* was the *bête noire* of liberal reformers in the 1920s and 1930s, *Roe v. Wade* has been the target of conservative ire for more than three decades. The debate, as one legal scholar has called it, is a clash of absolutes, with neither side willing to admit any justice on the part of the other. For social conservatives and Christian anti-abortion groups, it is not only an example of judicial usurpation of the legislature's primacy in policymaking, but it is also immoral, since it dismisses the unborn as nonpeople without souls. For legal conservatives it ignores the plain meaning of the Constitution, and hijacks the due process clause to tack on not only a right to privacy, but a right to abortion, into a document that never had nor was meant to have such ideas. Political conservatives see it as judicial activism run rampant, and at every judicial nomination hearing Republican senators use their speaking time both to attack and to try to get the nominees to disavow it.

Aftermath

Between the first and second arguments of *Roe*, Sarah Weddington decided to run for the Texas House of Representatives, and thanks to the name recognition she had earned as the lawyer in the case, won a seat in November 1972. She served three terms, and later recalled as one of her proudest achievements a bill that stemmed from another personal incident of gender bias. A credit card company refused to issue her a card in her own name without her husband's signature. So she sponsored the Texas Equal Credit bill, and after it passed, went back to the company, which now had no choice but to issue her a card in her name.

After service in the Texas legislature she worked for the Carter administration as general counsel to the Department of Agriculture, and in 1978 became the president's special assistant on women's issues. In the 1980s she taught first at Texas Women's University, and then joined her alma mater, the University of Texas Law School. Using that base she has remained active in the campaign for women's rights.

Norma McCorvey felt herself rather ill-used by Weddington, who treated the Kings as her main client, and McCorvey never attended any of the sessions of the proceedings; she did not even know when the case was being argued before the Supreme Court. In fact, when the decision came down McCorvey learned of it reading a newspaper; Weddington had been unable to find her. For much of the 1970s and 1980s she led a quiet existence. She began a long-term and stable lesbian relationship with Connie Gonzales, and the two women ran a successful apartment cleaning and rehabilitation business. In 1984 she revealed that she had been "Jane Roe," but did not become widely known as such until 1989, when she took part in a pro-choice rally in Washington, D.C.

After Weddington published her story of the case in 1992, McCorvey decided to tell her side. A publisher bought the proposal, and then assigned a writer to help her; the result was *I Am Roe: My Life, Roe v. Wade, and Freedom of Choice,* which came out in 1994. In it she claimed that "the lawsuit was not really for me. It was about me, and maybe all the women who'd come before me, but it was really for all the women who are coming after me."

The following year, however, she publicly announced that she had become a born-again Christian and no longer believed in abortion. The dramatic change came about, she said, after the pro-life Operation Rescue opened offices next door to a Dallas family services clinic where she did volunteer work. She spent the next two years as an activist for Operation Rescue, but left the organization in 1997 because she had grown increasingly uncomfortable with the group's confrontational tactics. She has remained strongly pro-life and claims that she ended her sexual relations with Gonzales, although the two women continue to live together. In 1998 she joined the Catholic Church. She serves as executive director of the Crossing Over Ministry, formerly the Roe No More Ministry, dedicated to reversing the 1973 decision.

(Sandra Bensing, who had been the "Jane Doe" in the Georgia case, also became a born-again Christian, and affiliated with the militant Operation Rescue in the late 1980s. She claimed her role in the case had been a huge mistake resulting from mental instability.)

In 2005 McCorvey asked the Supreme Court to overturn *Roe v. Wade* on the grounds that new evidence exists that the procedure harms women, but the Court denied the petition in *McCorvey v. Hill.*

Cases Cited

Brown v. Board of Education, 347 U.S. 483 (1954)
Doe v. Bolton, 410 U.S. 179 (1973)
Griswold v. Connecticut, 381 U.S. 419 (1965)
Lochner v. New York, 198 U.S. 45 (1905)
McCorvey v. Hill, 543 U.S. 1154 (2005)
Olmstead v. United States, 277 U.S. 438 (1928)
Planned Parenthood of Southeastern Pennsylvania v. Casey, 505 U.S. 833 (1992)
Poe v. Ullman, 367 U.S. 497 (1961)
Roe v. Wade, 314 F.Supp. 1217 (N.D. Texas 1970)
Roe v. Wade, 410 U.S. 113 (1973)
United States v. Vuitch, 402 U.S. 62 (1971)

For Further Reading

The literature on the case is immense, but a good overall summary is N. E. H. Hull and Peter Charles Hoffer, *Roe v. Wade: The Abortion Rights Controversy in American*

History (2001). Together with Williamjames Hoffer, they have edited *The Abortion Rights Controversy in America: A Legal Reader* (2004). The status of abortion laws in the states is examined in Leslie J. Reagan, *When Abortion Was a Crime: Women, Medicine, and Law in the United States, 1867–1973* (1997). David J. Garrow, *Liberty and Sexuality: The Right to Privacy and the Making of Roe v. Wade* (1994), emphasizes the case as a privacy matter. An interesting take is Jack M. Balkin, ed., *What Roe v. Wade Should Have Said* (2005), in which many of the nation's top legal experts "rewrote" the case. For personal reminiscences of the two women most responsible, see Sarah Weddington, *A Question of Choice* (1992), and Norma McCorvey, with Andy Meisler, *I Am Roe: My Life, Roe v. Wade, and Freedom of Choice* (1994). For McCorvey's later change of views, see her *Won by Love* (1998), written with Gary Thomas.

Coming Out of the Closet and into the Courts

The Gay Rights Cases (1986–2003)

ONE CANNOT HIDE one's gender or the color of one's skin, but for many years gays and lesbians in America had to hide their sexual orientation because of widespread prejudice against homosexuality. The civil rights revolution and then the women's movement emboldened gay groups to follow the same path—stand up openly, demand full rights, and go to court when those rights were denied. Public opinion had been ready to respond to calls for equality for women and people of color, but perhaps because many Americans were unfamiliar with homosexuality, and because religious groups condemned it as a sin, the fight for gay rights took a different turn. In examining how the Supreme Court responded starting with its first encounter with gay and lesbian demands we can also see how far the general public changed as well.

Michael Hardwick Is Arrested

One morning in August 1982 a police officer knocked on the front door of Michael Hardwick's home in the Virginia Highland section of Atlanta, Georgia, carrying a warrant for Hardwick's arrest for failure to appear in court on a charge of drinking in public. The officer, K. R. Torick, later alleged in his official report that when he arrived, one of Hardwick's housemates answered the door and admitted him. The man told Torick he did not know if Michael was home, but the officer could look for him. Torick started walking down the hallway, and through an

347

open bedroom door saw Hardwick and a male companion engaged in sex, and he promptly arrested both of them for violating Georgia's sodomy statute.

Thus began a series of cases that brought the issue of gay rights before the Supreme Court five times in the next two decades, and saw the high court extend a measure of constitutional protection to homosexual Americans for the first time. In doing so the justices added still more fuel to the culture wars roiling America, the struggle between those who clung to what they considered traditional virtues and notions of right and wrong, and those who embraced a new world without what they saw as outdated prejudices and morals.

Michael Hardwick had been born and raised in Miami, and studied at Florida State University with the goal of becoming a landscape architect. At college he was something of a spiritual recluse, and even considered becoming a Buddhist monk, much to his Catholic family's chagrin. "They were actually relieved when I told them I was coming out instead," he recalled. "Their attitude was, 'Thank God!'" He opened a small landscaping business and did well, but then decided he needed more time for himself and moved to Gatlinburg, Tennessee, in the Smoky Mountains and ran a health food store. At the urging of some friends he later moved to Atlanta, where he found work at a gay bar that was getting ready to open as a discotheque. Atlanta was less than welcoming to gays, and one evening when he came home three men were waiting for him and beat him up. Because of renovations at the bar, Hardwick often worked late, and one time was there until seven in the morning. He went outside with a bottle of beer to relax, but threw it into a trash can just as Officer Torick pulled up. Once Hardwick told him where he worked Torick knew that he was gay, and hassled him, eventually giving him a ticket for drinking in public. Hardwick decided not to challenge the ticket. In fact, the warrant that Torick had with him on August 3 was not even valid, because Hardwick had already paid the $50 fine.

Hardwick was in for more bad treatment after Torick hauled him and his friend down to the police station. Even though they had offered no resistance Torick put them both into handcuffs, and after they had been booked and fingerprinted, officers threw them into the holding tank, informing both guards and the other prisoners that the two guys were gay and what they had been doing when they were arrested. They spent most of the day there until friends found out what happened and posted bail for their release.

Paradoxically, the district attorney's office in Atlanta had been trying to develop better relations with the city's gay community, and unless there were other factors, such as drunkenness or disorderly conduct, had told police to leave gays and lesbians alone. In fact, until Hardwick's arrest the local prosecutor had never used the sodomy statute against people simply having sex. Not all of the police favored this policy, and many of the more homophobic managed to hassle gays whenever they could. According to Hardwick's testimony, Torick went out of his way to arrest him for drinking in public when he had already tossed the beer bottle away.

Three days after the arrest Clint Sumrall of the American Civil Liberties Union (ACLU) contacted Hardwick. The ACLU had been seeking a test case to challenge Georgia's sodomy law on the basis that it violated a constitutionally protected right to privacy. Hardwick agreed to meet with other ACLU staff and lawyers. Although they made it clear that if he went forward with the case and lost he could be sentenced up to the maximum twenty-years in prison that the law allowed, Hardwick agreed to proceed with the case, and the ACLU assigned Kathy Wilde as his lawyer. She filed suit on Hardwick's behalf against both the police commissioner of Atlanta and the state attorney, Michael Bowers. Since most of the practices banned in the sodomy statutes of Georgia and other states, such as anal sex, fellatio, and cunnilingus, were enjoyed by straight as well as gay men and women, Wilde also brought in John and Mary Doe, a pseudonymous heterosexual couple, to claim that Torick's arrest of Hardwick had had a chilling effect on their own personal relationship.

Hardwick Goes to Court— Charting Unfamiliar Territory

The ACLU took the suit to federal district court, where Judge Robert H. Hall threw it out, ruling that Hardwick had no legitimate cause to plead. Wilde then took the case to the Court of Appeals for the Eleventh Circuit, which had very little guidance in terms of Supreme Court precedent.

In 1985 the high court had heard only one case in which the litigants claimed that state laws against sodomy violated the right to privacy. In 1975 a three-judge district court in Virginia, by a vote of 2–1, had upheld that state's sodomy law on the grounds that *Griswold v. Connecticut* (1965) only extended the right of privacy in intimate matters to married couples. The sole dissenter, Judge Robert Merhige Jr., believed that privacy applied to everyone: "To say, as the majority does, that the right of privacy, which every citizen has, is limited to matters of marital, home, or family life is unwarranted under the law."

On appeal the Supreme Court in *Doe v. Commonwealth's Attorney* (1976), by a 6–3 vote, affirmed the lower court decision without opinion, and only three justices—William Brennan, Thurgood Marshall, and

John Paul Stevens—indicated that they would have accepted the case to hear its merits. With the firestorm generated by the Court's decision in *Roe v. Wade* only three years earlier still building, however, it is likely that the justices wanted to avoid another controversial case.

In considering Hardwick's case, the Eleventh Circuit noted that because the Supreme Court had not given any reasons for its decision in affirming *Doe*, established judicial procedure meant that lower courts were not bound by the results of the Virginia panel. Moreover, according to Judge Frank M. Johnson, recent decisions by the high court in abortion cases seemed to indicate that a wider interpretation of the right to privacy might be in order. He then concluded that "the Georgia sodomy statute infringes upon the fundamental constitutional rights of Michael Hardwick." Johnson ordered the case to go back to the district court, where in order for the law to be upheld, Georgia would have to "demonstrate a compelling interest in restricting the right and must show that the sodomy statute is a properly restrained method of safeguarding [the state's] interests" (*Hardwick v. Bowers* [1985]).

Georgia, however, had no interest in retrying the case in district court, and took an appeal to the U.S. Supreme Court, which accepted the case on November 4, 1985, and heard oral argument on March 31, 1986. On the last day of the term, June 30, 1986, a 5–4 Court ruled that the due process clause of the Fourteenth Amendment did not confer any fundamental right on homosexuals to engage in acts of consensual sodomy. Perhaps the only surprise was the closeness of the ruling and the fact that there were five separate opinions.

In the decades following World War II the Supreme Court had undertaken a judicial revolution in the meaning of civil rights and civil liberties. It had struck down state-sanctioned racial segregation, done away with malapportioned state legislatures that effectively robbed minorities of their representation, expanded the meaning of due process and equal protection, and reinterpreted the Bill of Rights and its guaranties, especially in the areas of free expression and criminal procedure. Although the Equal Rights Amendment had failed to be ratified by the necessary three-fourths of the states, the Court in a series of decisions had essentially implemented its purpose, giving women full and equal rights before the law.

The Gay Rights Movement

At least one group, however, had not benefited from this revolution— homosexuals. The law had traditionally viewed homosexuality as both a moral sin and a criminal act. The detestation could be seen in how the great English law writer, Sir William Blackstone, treated it at the time of the founding of the American republic. Blackstone hesitated to even discuss something "the very mention of which is a disgrace to human nature . . . a crime not fit to be named." Laws criminalizing homosexual acts had been brought over by the colonists from the Mother Country, and after the American Revolution, all of the states had written such strictures into their legal codes. This historic view of homosexuality as a crime against nature, a moral evil condemned by the common law, played a major role in the majority opinion in *Bowers v. Hardwick.*

According to some commentators, part of the reason is that gay and lesbian protests for civil rights came later than the movements to secure civil rights to people of color or equality to women. Homosexuality remains misunderstood by many people even in the early twenty-first century; ignorance, fear, and loathing were even more widespread prior to the Stonewall riots of June 28, 1969, which prompted many gay and lesbian groups to agitate for equal protection of their rights under law. In fact, the Supreme Court—with its previous rulings on civil rights and freedom of speech—made that protest possible.

Gay and lesbian groups also noted that compared to Europe, the United States remained the most homophobic of all Western democracies. France and the Netherlands had decriminalized gay and lesbian sex as early as 1810, Belgium in 1867, Italy in 1889, Spain in 1932, the Scandinavian countries between 1930 and 1970, Great Britain in 1967, and Germany in 1969. In 1981 the European Court of Human Rights had ruled in *Dudgeon v. United Kingdom* that statutes outlawing homosexual sex acts were invalid under the European Convention on Human Rights, a ruling binding on all twenty-one nations then belonging to the Council of Europe.

In addition, thanks to gay and lesbian legal activists, some state courts had begun to consider whether the right to privacy—as articulated either in the federal Constitution, state constitutions, or the common law—extended to private sexual behavior by consenting adults. In 1980 the highest court in New York had agreed that the right to privacy protected by the New York constitution rendered invalid that state's sodomy law (*People v. Onofre*). The Model Penal Code proposed by the National Conference of Commissioners on Uniform State Laws in 1970 did away with sodomy among consenting adults as a crime, and between 1971 and 1983, nearly two-thirds of the states considering adoption of the Model Penal Code repealed their sodomy statutes. Just as gay and lesbian rights groups thought they might be turning the legal corner, however, the AIDS epidemic hit, and suddenly homosexuals had to deal with one more stigma as thousands of gay men began to sicken and die from the disease. Fear of contagion, and belief that the epidemic was God's retribution for gay lifestyles, added to the onus of homosexuality. AIDS stalled reform dead in its tracks; between 1984 and 1991, not a single one of the states considering the Model Penal Code repealed its sodomy laws, and in some states there was agitation to reinstate such laws.

Conservatives in the 1980s had also stepped up their attack on much of the postwar constitutional expansion of rights, especially the right of privacy in general and of a woman's right to an abortion in particular. In addition, some moderates who agreed with the substance of the Court's ruling in *Roe v. Wade* nevertheless questioned the wisdom of the Court's decision to hear that case at a time when many state legislatures were already successfully modernizing their nineteenth-century laws and making safe and legal abortions available to women. Other scholars raised additional questions not just about the legitimacy of a right to privacy, but if it did exist, what its limits were. There is no question that the justices had this concern in mind when they agreed to hear *Bowers v. Hardwick*.

Hardwick in the Supreme Court

Gay and lesbian activists saw the growing antipathy toward the expansion of rights as a reason to press their attack on sodomy laws. The facts of the case—two men arrested in the privacy of their home for behavior that hurt no one, the apparent targeting of a discrete group by police, and the fact that the acts defined in the Georgia law, although they applied to all persons, were only enforced against homosexuals—all seemed to fit with the type of rights the Court had articulated over the previous two decades. The Court had grown more conservative with the addition of justices appointed by Richard Nixon and Ronald Reagan; one or two more such appointments and there might be no chance of winning rights for homosexuals in the foreseeable future.

By refusing to hear the Virginia case, *Doe v. Commonwealth's Attorney,* the Court had avoided the issue because the lower court had upheld the Virginia statute; it was impossible to do so in *Bowers v. Hardwick,* since refusing to hear the case would have meant upholding the decision that sodomy laws violated an individual's fundamental rights. At least two justices, White and Rehnquist, wanted to take the *Hardwick* case in an effort to limit *Roe* and quash efforts to extend the right of privacy. More liberal justices, including Brennan and Marshall, who had dissented in *Doe,* thought there might be five justices favorable to Hardwick. Nearly everyone believed that the critical vote would be that of Justice Lewis F. Powell Jr. In oral argument he closely questioned Professor Lawrence Tribe of Harvard, who argued Hardwick's case, about the limits of his claim. Did Tribe want to strike down every law against consensual sexual behavior? Did he want to do away with prohibitions against incest or bigamy or prostitution? Tribe had attempted to show that all Hardwick wanted was the same right to privacy regarding his sex life that straight people enjoyed for theirs. At the time, no one knew that one of Powell's law clerks, Michael Mosman, a conservative Mormon, had given the justice a twelve-page memorandum arguing against the extension of a constitutional right to privacy to homosexuals. One phrase in Mosman's memo caught Powell's eye. If Hardwick won, Mosman said, it would open the doors to unchecked sexual freedom because "no limiting principle comes to mind." The idea of "no limiting principle" drove Powell's questioning of Tribe.

Nonetheless, at their conference the following Wednesday, Powell voted to affirm the lower court decision invalidating the antisodomy law. As a matter of course Powell preferred not to overrule lower courts unless there was a clear and convincing reason to do so. He may also have been swayed by the comments of Brennan, Marshall, and Harry Blackmun, who believed that the case was controlled by two strong precedents—*Loving v. Virginia* (1967), which struck down antimiscegenation laws and upheld the right of people to marry whom they loved, even across racial lines, and *Stanley v. Georgia* (1969), which had voided an obscenity statute on the grounds that people could read or view whatever they wanted in the privacy of their homes. It appeared as if "the privacy of their homes" was the type of limiting principle Powell needed. But he remained torn. While he favored the right to privacy he knew little about homosexuality and believed he knew no gay men, although as it happened one of his clerks was gay. He played with the idea of the Eighth Amendment ban against cruel and unusual punishment, since the Georgia statute criminalized behavior that contemporary psychiatric thought believed beyond the control of the individual.

With Justice John Paul Stevens joining them, five votes existed to overturn Georgia's sodomy statute, along with those of other states that still criminalized such behavior. Chief Justice Burger and Justices White, Rehnquist, and O'Connor voted to overturn the appellate court and sustain the law. As the senior justice in the majority, Brennan assigned the opinion to Blackmun.

Powell, however, had not fully made up his mind, and in the days following the conference he came under increasing pressure to change sides. Chief Justice Warren Burger wrote a long letter to Powell attacking the American Psychiatric Association's depiction of homosexuality as an uncontrollable addiction. At the top of the page, Powell wrote, "There is both sense and non-sense in this letter—mostly the latter." But if Burger did not sway him, Mosman did. He wrote a second memo urging Powell to change his vote, and argued that the only real issue before the Court was whether homosexual sodomy was a fundamental right. The justice, he knew, did not believe it was, and the question of whether such acts should be criminalized, Mosman argued, should be left for another day. Powell agreed, and changed his vote, giving the supporters of the Georgia law a one-vote majority. Burger reassigned the case to Byron White, who quickly wrote an opinion that would have cheered the most homophobic heart.

White began by denying that the Constitution conferred any fundamental right upon homosexuals to engage in sodomy: "Moreover, any claim . . . that any kind of private sexual conduct between consenting adults is constitutionally insulated from state proscription is unsupportable." While admitting that the courts had expanded the protection of the Bill of Rights through the due process clause of the Fourteenth Amendment, only rights "deeply rooted in the Nation's history and tradition" or "implicit in the concept of ordered liberty" could be included. White noted that until 1961 all fifty states outlawed sodomy and that twenty-four states as well as the District of Columbia continued to do so in 1985. Against this history, he dismissed the assertion that sexual freedom was a fundamental right as "at best, facetious."

As for the argument that because such conduct had taken place in one's home it was somehow entitled to greater protection, White would have none of it. *Stanley,* he claimed, had protected certain activities within the home, but it had been firmly grounded in the First Amendment. If the Court were to approve of homosexual sexual activity on the grounds of a right to privacy in one's home, then it would also have to insulate against prosecution for adultery, incest, and other sexual crimes that took place in the home, and this the Court was unwilling to do. As one commentator noted, not a single sentence of White's opinion "expressed any understanding of the fact that the case involves human beings who have needs for intimacy, love and sexual expression like the rest of us. Not a single sentence acknowledges the human anguish that anti-homosexual statutes can create." Many people noted that White seemed to be gunning not so much for homosexuals as for the very idea of a constitutional right to privacy in the first place.

The harshness of White's opinion drove Powell to write separately, but he did not withdraw his vote, thus making White's opinion authoritative for the next two decades. Powell issued a two-paragraph concurrence that while upholding the law he believed that homosexual conduct ought not to be punished by incarceration, since that would violate the Eighth Amendment's ban against cruel or unusual punishment. The concurrence, as his biographer noted, was "justly ignored." The chief justice also entered a short concurrence, emphasizing his belief that absolutely nothing in the Constitution could be construed to prohibit a state from outlawing such behavior.

Both of the dissenting opinions, one by Blackmun and the other by Stevens, emphasized the right of privacy as the key issue in the case, rather than the fact that the behavior in question was that of homosexual sex. Blackmun did depict gays as victims of prejudice and as individuals worthy of constitutional respect. Both justices spent most of their dissents discussing the nature and extent of what they considered a basic constitutional right, rather than explaining why Georgia's law did not meet the standards necessary for state action to impinge on fundamental rights. Quoting Louis Brandeis in *Olmstead v. United States* (1928), Blackmun said "this case is about 'the most comprehensive of rights and the right most valued by civilized men,' namely, 'the right to be let alone.'"

The contrast between the majority and dissenting opinions could not be sharper. Where White had been harsh in dismissing the claims of gays to be secure in their personal choices, and practically dismissive of a constitutional right to privacy, the dissents emphasized the personal anguish of those affected by the law and the powerful protections embodied in constitutional rights to protect minorities against the bigotry or conventional moral standards of the majority. Unless one could show that harm would result to others, the right of personal autonomy should be fully protected.

Years later, in 1990, after he had retired from the bench, Powell told students at New York University Law School that his vote in the case had probably been a "mistake," although he also asserted that because no one had actually been prosecuted under the law Hardwick's was a frivolous case. That confession hardly consoled gay and lesbian activists. Thomas Stoddard, the executive director of the Lambda Legal Defense and Education Fund, declared that "for the gay rights movement, this is our *Dred Scott* case." The nation's highest court, he said, "has expressed a certain distaste for gay men and women and suggested that they may be treated differently from other Americans."

Michael Hardwick did not serve any jail time, and in the years following the decision became an activist for gay rights. On October 13, 1987, in a carefully staged, six-hour display of civil disobedience, Hardwick and 571 other demonstrators were arrested in front of the Supreme Court for protesting against the decision that bore his name. He moved back to Florida, where he died in 1991 at the age of thirty-seven, purportedly from AIDS.

The Court Tries to Find Its Way

Over the next several years lower courts relied on *Hardwick* to dismiss claims of unconstitutional discrimination against gays and lesbians; a group constitutionally subject to criminal penalties for its behavior could reasonably be distinguished from other groups. The one bright spot for gays and lesbians was that not a single state that had earlier done away with its sodomy statutes recriminalized the practice after the decision, and in fact, as the AIDS crisis eased, other states actually began repealing their laws or seeing state courts strike them down under state constitutional grounds, as had happened in *Onofre*. Gay and lesbian groups continued to push for equal rights, and saw their efforts rewarded with numerous state and local ordinances prohibiting discrimination on the basis of sexual preference. In a first step toward acceptance of gays and lesbians in the military, President Bill Clinton secured the "don't ask, don't tell" policy that recognized gays were of value in serving their country. Also, unlike Presidents Reagan and George H. W. Bush, Clinton saw and treated gays as an important political group. The campaign to secure gay rights would take another great leap forward in 2003, when the Supreme Court reversed *Bowers v. Hardwick* in *Lawrence v. Texas*. Before the justices got there, however, they decided three intervening cases that, at best, sent mixed signals to the gay community and also to its adversaries.

The first of these cases, *Hurley v. Irish-American Gay, Lesbian, and Bisexual Group of Boston* (1995), involved a Massachusetts law forbidding discrimination on the basis of sexual orientation in a place of public accommodation. A coalition of gay and lesbian groups had successfully argued in state court that the law applied to the annual St. Patrick's Day parade in Boston; they wanted to participate and to carry a banner declaring who they were. On appeal Justice David Souter (appointed to the Court in 1992 to replace William Brennan) spoke for a unanimous bench in holding that the state law could not be applied to the expressive decisions of a private parade; the free speech rights of the organizers of the parade permitted them to include or exclude whom they wanted. The coalition's attempt at public expression was overridden by the rights of the parade organizers.

Five years later, in *Boy Scouts of America v. Dale,* Chief Justice Rehnquist (who took over the center chair from Burger in 1986) had a bare 5–4 majority upholding a similar claim against the Scouts. James Dale had been a model Scout, reaching the highest rank of Eagle and then becoming an assistant troop leader. While a student at Rutgers University, Dale had come out of the closet and announced that he was gay. After the leaders of the local Boy Scout council learned this, and that Dale had become president of a gay rights group at Rutgers, they expelled him from his leadership position. Dale went to court and successfully argued that a New Jersey civil rights law prohibited any "public accommodation" from discriminating on the basis of sexual orientation. The Scouts pointed to their own policy statements depicting homosexual conduct as inconsistent with the requirement that a Scout be "morally straight" and "clean." In other states the Scouts, facing similar suits, had argued that it was a private club and not a public accommodation, and that as such, it enjoyed a First Amendment freedom of association to include or exclude whomever it pleased.

After losing in state court the Boy Scouts appealed to the Supreme Court and won a ruling that kept the antigay policy intact. Rehnquist acknowledged that the government can override a group's associational rights to promote a compelling interest, but courts should also defer to a private group's view of what might interfere with its constitutionally protected expression. "Dale's presence in the Boy Scouts would, at the very least, force the organization to send a message . . . that the Boy Scouts accept homosexual conduct as a legitimate form of behavior."

The two dissenting opinions by Stevens and Souter—both of whom had joined the majority in *Hurley*—did not disagree so much with Rehnquist's interpretation of the law but of the facts. Quoting from the Scouts' handbook, Stevens declared that "it is plain as the light of day that neither one of these principles, 'morally straight' and 'clean,' says the slightest thing about homosexuality." Since the Scouts had not proclaimed any antigay policy in its official handbook, then *Hurley* was not controlling. Dale did not flout his sexual orientation, and no evidence existed that he wanted to send any kind of message.

There is a certain blindness in the opinions in both *Hurley* and *Boy Scouts* as to the so-called "private" nature of both organizations. While the parade-organizing group may have been a private entity, the parade itself was far from it, requiring massive support from the city of Boston in the form of traffic control, fire and police protection, and cleanup of the massive amount of debris generated by the event. Since St. Patrick's Day long ago lost any semblance of an all-Irish or all-Catholic event, there had been non-Irish groups participating for years. In fact, following a state court ruling the same gay group had marched uneventfully in the 1992 parade, along with 10,000 other participants before a crowd estimated at 750,000 people.

Similarly, the Boy Scouts of America hold a charter of incorporation from Congress, and Boy Scout troops as well as the younger division of Cub Scouts meet around the country in a variety of public places, including schools and community centers. Their promotional materials make no mention of discriminating against gays, and in fact emphasize that they welcome all boys as members. The two cases are the direct descendants of *Bowers,* and continued the antigay bias of that Court.

A Ray of Hope—*Romer v. Evans*

In between these two decisions came *Romer v. Evans* (1996), giving gay activists their first real glimmer of hope that the Supreme Court might be moving away from its earlier stance.

The political activity of gay and lesbian advocacy groups in Colorado had met with success in the form of numerous municipal ordinances that banned discrimination in jobs and housing on the basis of race, gender, or sexual orientation. In addition, the state legislature had repealed its sodomy statute so that gay sexual activity was no longer subject to criminal penalties. In the late 1980s, however, Colorado Springs saw an influx of socially conservative evangelical Christian groups, who stood opposed to the legal and political gains made by homosexuals. Had they merely opposed the local laws and worked to repeal them they would have been within the accepted American political tradition. Instead, they did something so extraordinary that it shocked many people, including some of the justices on the Supreme Court.

By circulating and signing petitions, these groups got a constitutional amendment on the fall ballot, which specifically repealed any state or local law that protected people who were "Homosexual, Lesbian or [of] Bisexual Orientation," and prohibited the passage of any legislation in the future that would protect such people in their "conduct, practices or relationships." In November 1992, 53 percent of the voters of Colorado approved Amendment 2. Richard G. Evans, an administrator in Denver, one of the cities whose antidiscrimination laws had just been voided, declared "it was as if 800,000 people had said [to homosexuals] 'You're not equal to us.'" He sued Roy Romer, the governor of Colorado, to have Amendment 2 nullified as a violation of the Fourteenth Amendment's equal protection clause. The Colorado Supreme Court agreed with the trial court that Amendment 2 was unconstitutional in that it named a specific class, and the state appealed to the Supreme Court.

In oral argument both Timothy Tymkovich, the attorney general of Colorado, and Jean Dubovsky, the lawyer arguing for Evans, came in for heavy questioning, but Tymkovich, as one witness observed, had his head handed to him, especially by Anthony Kennedy. The justice appeared visibly appalled by Amendment 2, which in effect closed off all of the normal political venues by which any citizen or group of citizens could seek redress of grievances. In essence, it read gays, lesbians, and homosexuals out of the social and political order. This fact did not seem to bother the attorneys general of Alabama, California, Idaho, Nebraska, South Carolina, South Dakota, or Virginia, who filed *amici* briefs urging the justices to overturn the Colorado high court, and they were joined by such conservative stalwarts as the American Center for Law and Justice, the Christian Legal Society, and the Family Research Council.

A far greater number of friend of the court briefs urged the affirmation of the Colorado decision, and these included the attorneys general of Oregon, Iowa, Minnesota, Nevada, Washington, and Maryland. Briefs also came from the District of Columbia and from a number of cities like Atlanta, which also had antidiscrimination measures, as well as from some of the leading constitutional scholars in the country, including Lawrence Tribe of Harvard; John Hart Ely, the former dean of Stanford Law; Philip B. Kurland of the University of Chicago; and Kathleen M. Sullivan of Stanford. The wide range of *amici* briefs pointed up not only how successful gay and lesbian groups had been in advocating for equal rights, but also how that success had inflamed fears of social conservatives and many conservative Christian groups. According to one of his clerks, Kennedy was particularly impressed by the brief filed by Professor Tribe, who had been the losing counsel in *Hardwick*. A majority of the justices also seemed impressed by the argument that the Court could strike down Amendment 2 without revisiting *Hardwick*; the debate over Amendment 2 did not deal with sexual practice, but with political and social rights.

In a clear departure from the tone that had marked that earlier case, Kennedy spoke for six of the justices—himself and Justices Stevens, O'Connor, Souter, Ginsburg, and Breyer—in striking down Amendment 2 and affirming the decision of the Colorado court. The opening sentence showed exactly where the Court was going: "One century ago, the first Justice Harlan admonished this Court that the Constitution 'neither knows nor tolerates classes among citizens.' Unheeded then, those words now are understood to state a commitment to the law's neutrality where the rights of persons are at stake. The Equal Protection Clause enforces this principle and today requires us to hold invalid [Amendment 2]."

Kennedy seemed especially outraged by the notion that the law cut off any avenue by which homosexuals could seek political or judicial recourse against discrimination. Moreover, a fair reading of the wording in Amendment 2 could lead to the conclusion that "it deprives gays and lesbians even of the protection of general laws and policies that prohibit arbitrary discrimination in governmental and private settings." Quoting from an earlier opinion of Justice Brennan, the constitutional idea of equal protection unequivocally tells us this "cannot constitute a *legitimate* governmental interest." Not once in his opinion did Kennedy refer to *Hardwick*, although he referenced many of the leading cases in civil rights.

Justice Antonin Scalia, joined by Chief Justice Rehnquist and Justice Clarence Thomas, referred almost immediately to *Hardwick*, and he saw no harm in what he described as "a modest attempt by seemingly tolerant Coloradans to preserve traditional sexual mores against the efforts of a politically powerful minority to reverse those mores through use of the laws." That objective, as far as he was concerned, was "unimpeachable under any constitutional doctrine." He then attacked Kennedy's opinion on a point-by-point basis, but underlying the entire dissent was a belief that what was really at issue was not an unconscionable effort to deny some group equal rights, but the vile nature of that group's sexual practices, which offended many people. Scalia felt that *Hardwick* should have been the deciding precedent, and not the civil rights cases cited by Kennedy.

Romer v. Evans is seen by many as a major turning point in the battle for gay rights. Kennedy gave advocates what they had been seeking all along: recognition that prejudice on the basis of sexual orientation was no more acceptable under the Constitution than discrimination because of race or religion. Where Scalia indicated that the criminalizing of their sexual activity was sufficient constitutional justification for setting gays and lesbians apart as a class, Kennedy countered by citing several nineteenth-century cases that had approved harsh treatment of Mormons—then a vilified sect—and which had long been disavowed by the Court. No group, Kennedy argued, could be made inferior and discriminated against under the equal protection clause. Even though a closely divided Court in 2000 would uphold the right of the Boy Scouts to keep gays out of leadership positions, *Romer* showed that a majority of the Court no longer shared the homophobic sentiment that had seemingly animated *Hardwick*. Gay and lesbian advocacy groups believed they could secure a reversal of *Hardwick*, and they set out to find the right test case.

John Geddes Lawrence Is Arrested

On September 17, 1998, police officers responding to a reported weapons disturbance in an outskirt of Houston, Texas, entered an apartment occupied by John Geddes Lawrence, a fifty-five-year-old medical technician. The complaint came from a neighbor, Robert Royce Eubanks, who told the police that because of a domestic fight or a robbery there was a man with a gun "going crazy." Harris County deputy sheriff Joseph Quinn entered the unlocked apartment with his gun drawn. (The lack of a warrant did not figure in any of the subsequent litigation.) Once in the apartment they found Lawrence engaging in sex with his thirty-one-year-old companion, Tyrone Garner. Police arrested both men, held them in custody overnight, and then charged them under a Texas criminal statute that forbade "deviate sexual intercourse" between parties of the same sex. They were tried, found guilty, and fined $200 apiece. The neighbor, Eubanks, who had earlier been accused of harassing Lawrence and with whom Garner was also romantically involved, later admitted that he had been lying, pleaded no contest to charges of filing a false police report, and served fifteen days in jail.

The Lambda Legal Defense and Education Fund took on their case, and appealed it up through the Texas court system on grounds that it violated the due process of law protected by the Fourteenth

Amendment and the state constitution, as well as the right to privacy. As expected, they lost at each stage, with the courts relying on *Bowers v. Hardwick,* but they believed that after *Romer* they now had a chance to get the Supreme Court to reverse that decision. The justices accepted the case on December 2, 2002, and heard oral argument on March 26, 2003; three months later they handed down their decision in *Lawrence v. Texas.* Paul Smith, the lawyer who represented Lawrence, had once been a law clerk to Lewis Powell, and later in life had come out of the closet to acknowledge that he was gay.

The Court asked counsel to address three questions:

1. Whether the petitioners' criminal convictions under the Texas "Homosexual Conduct" law—which criminalizes sexual intimacy by same-sex couples, but not identical behavior by different-sex couples—violated the Fourteenth Amendment guarantee of equal protection of the laws;
2. Whether the petitioners' criminal convictions for adult consensual sexual intimacy in their home violate their vital interests in liberty and privacy protected by the due process clause of the Fourteenth Amendment; and
3. Whether *Bowers v. Hardwick* should be overruled.

Unlike the Georgia statute, which had penalized acts defined as sodomy no matter who committed them, the Texas law applied only to same-sex practices, and thus specifically targeted homosexuals. If the Court had meant what it said in *Romer,* this by itself should have been enough to overturn the Texas law as well as similar prohibitions in twelve other states. The justices recognized that, unlike in *Romer,* they could hardly strike down the Texas law and leave *Hardwick* in place. The question mark was Justice Sandra Day O'Connor, who had been in the majority in *Hardwick* and also in *Romer,* and was widely considered the swing vote on the Court, the fifth vote to make a majority. She would probably be willing to strike down the Texas statute because it was so obviously discriminatory, but would she be willing to overrule *Hardwick?*

The Supreme Court Decides

In the conference five justices—Stevens, Kennedy, Souter, Ginsburg, and Breyer—voted not only that the Texas law should be struck down, but that *Hardwick* should be overruled as well. O'Connor agreed with the first point but not the second, while Chief Justice Rehnquist, along with Justices Scalia and Thomas, would have upheld the law. With the chief justice in the minority, John Paul Stevens as the senior justice in the majority had the authority to assign the case. He might well have wanted to keep it for himself, since he had written such a forceful dissent in *Hardwick,* but he chose Anthony Kennedy for two reasons. First, Kennedy's opinion in *Romer* formed the jurisprudential basis of the decision in this case. Second, Kennedy was considered a moderate conservative; a decision that would upset social conservatives and evangelical Christians would be better received if it came from a conservative rather than a liberal (although Stevens never saw himself as a liberal; he always said he never changed but that the Court moved to the right). In the end, Stevens got exactly what he hoped for—an analytically powerful opinion that also rang with moral fervor.

Courts are as a rule reluctant to overturn precedents, especially in cases that had been decided recently. *Hardwick* was less than two decades old, and three of the justices in that case still sat on the Court. Kennedy understood that in order to justify such a step, he had to show that the earlier opinion failed on jurisprudential as well as societal grounds. He began with what is the boldest statement of a right to privacy articulated by a modern Court (some of whose members denied even the existence of such a right):

> Liberty protects the person from unwarranted government intrusions into a dwelling or other private places. In our tradition the State is not omnipresent in the home. And there are other spheres of our lives and existence, outside the home, where the State should not be a dominant presence. Freedom extends beyond spatial bounds. Liberty presumes an autonomy of self that includes freedom of thought, belief, expression, and certain intimate conduct. The instant case involves liberty of the person both in its spatial and more transcendent dimensions.

After reviewing the facts, Kennedy went to the nub of the case. The only way that the Court could agree that the sexual conduct of two consenting adults fell within the liberty provisions of the due process clause was to reexamine *Hardwick*. He questioned White's framing the issue as whether the Constitution "confers a fundamental right upon homosexuals to engage in sodomy," and charged that how White phrased the issue "discloses the Court's own failure to appreciate the extent of the liberty at stake." The very wording "demeans the claim of the individual put forward, just as it would demean a married couple were it to be said marriage is simply about the right to have sexual intercourse." Kennedy went on to compare White's objectification of gay and lesbian sexuality to the way anti-Semitism and racial prejudice reduced the sexuality of Jews and blacks to hateful terms.

A fair-minded understanding of the basic constitutional right of privacy, Kennedy declared, would take seriously, in gay as well as straight sexual relations, the accompanying integrity of the connection between sexual expression and companionate friendship and love. "When sexuality finds overt expression in intimate conduct with another person," Kennedy wrote, "the conduct can be but one element in a personal bond that is more enduring. The liberty protected by the Constitution allows homosexual persons the right to make this choice." The state, he concluded, "cannot demean [homosexual] existence or control their destiny by making their private sexual conduct a crime."

For those who argued that the Constitution mentioned neither privacy nor rights given to gays, Kennedy responded that the Framers had not drafted the document in specific terms, because they did not claim to know "the components of liberty in its manifold possibilities," but were themselves open—as the Court needed to be—to new arguments and experiences. "They knew times can blind us to certain truths and later generations can see that laws once thought necessary and proper in fact serve only to oppress. As the Constitution endures, persons in every generation can invoke its principles in their own search for greater freedom."

The majority held the Texas statute unconstitutional in that it penalized only acts committed by same-sex couples, that acts between consenting adults in the privacy of their home is a liberty and privacy interest protected by the due process clause, and that *Bowers v. Hardwick* was overruled.

Justice O'Connor concurred in that part of the opinion overturning the Texas statute because it discriminated against homosexuals, but she defended the right of a state to outlaw certain types of acts, provided it applied the ban on a nondiscriminatory basis. For her the case should have been decided not on a right to privacy embedded in the due process clause, but on the manner in which the law was enforced measured against the equal protection clause.

Justice Scalia, dissenting for himself, Rehnquist, and Thomas, attacked the majority for its inconsistency. It had refused to overturn *Roe v. Wade*, a bad decision, but had no qualms in reversing what he considered a perfectly good precedent in *Bowers v. Hardwick*. Essentially, Scalia, like White, did not believe in a constitutional right to privacy in general or its application to support either abortion or sodomy in particular. He dismissed Kennedy's careful historical analysis that showed how attitudes toward homosexuals had changed over the years, because he considered that constitutionally irrelevant; originalist intent was all that mattered, and a strict construction of the Constitution and the intent of its Framers would make clear that laws prohibiting abortion as well as sodomy were perfectly acceptable. Only a change in the Constitution itself could alter that fact.

Much of Scalia's hostility is aimed at the fact that Kennedy and O'Connor had coauthored the opinion in *Planned Parenthood of Southeastern*

Pennsylvania v. Casey (1992), which had kept the basic premise of *Roe v. Wade* intact, and much of his dissent is aimed at *Roe* and the idea of privacy as a constitutional right. But it also shares White's disdain of homosexuals and the idea that as a group they enjoy any particular rights. "The matters appropriate for this Court's resolution are only three," he concluded. "Texas's prohibition of sodomy neither infringes a 'fundamental right' (which the Court does not dispute), nor is unsupported by a rational relation to what the Constitution considers a legitimate state interest, nor denies the equal protection of the laws. I dissent."

Justice Clarence Thomas entered a short dissent of his own in which he termed the Texas law "uncommonly silly." Were he a member of the Texas legislature, he "would vote to repeal it. Punishing someone for expressing his sexual preference through noncommercial consensual conduct with another adult does not appear to be a worthy way to expend valuable law enforcement resources." But he could find no constitutional objection to Texas doing so.

The Aftermath of *Lawrence*

Supporters of gay rights as well as opponents reacted vociferously to the decision, because both sides in the "culture wars" over the place of gays and lesbians in American society considered the maintenance or defeat of sodomy laws as central, at least symbolically, to their causes. Elizabeth Birch, the executive director of the Human Rights Campaign, the nation's largest gay lobby, declared, "This is a historic day for fair-minded Americans everywhere. We are elated." The executive director of Lambda Legal rejoiced that the *Lawrence* decision "closed the door on an era of intolerance and ushered in a new era of respect and equal treatment for gay Americans."

Opposition groups looked at matters differently. Tom Minnery, a vice president at Focus on the Family, a conservative religious group, attacked the Court for continuing to "pillage its way through the moral norms of our country." The American Society for the Defense of Tradition, Family, and Property saw the consequences of *Lawrence* as even worse than those of *Roe v. Wade,* for in granting constitutional protection to sodomy, the Court "renounced the duty imposed by Natural Law on every government to uphold morality in striving for the common good."

What both sides agreed upon, but reacted to far differently, was the belief that *Lawrence* would be the opening wedge in a campaign to constitutionalize same-sex marriage. David Smith of the Human Rights Campaign called the case a giant step forward, and "contained in there are links to marriage, child-rearing . . . it's just not too far a leap." Jan LaRue, chief counsel for Concerned Women for America, a conservative

Christian political action group, had no doubt that "homosexual activists will try to bootstrap this decision into a mandate for same-sex marriage. Any attempt to equate sexual perversion with the institution that is the very foundation of society is as baseless as this ruling."

In fact, Justice Kennedy's opinion did not mention same sex-marriage, although Justice Scalia's dissent implied that if you struck down the sodomy laws then there were all sorts of other laws regarding sex and homosexuality that could also be challenged. The Court's ruling did trigger a backlash as several states adopted so-called defense of marriage laws or even state constitutional amendments banning same-sex marriage. On October 3, 2003, President George W. Bush proclaimed October 12–18 Marriage Protection Week, and declared that marriage is "a union between a man and a woman." His administration, he promised, would work to support that institution.

Then on November 18, 2003, the worst fears of the conservatives seemed to come to life as the Supreme Judicial Court of Massachusetts ruled that the Commonwealth had failed to "identify any constitutionally adequate reason" to deny gay or lesbian couples the right to marry. In the ensuing legal conflict, both sides would look to *Lawrence* for either confirmation of their claims for equality or as evidence of the moral disintegration of the nation.

In recent years, however, the momentum seems to be shifting in favor of gay marriage. Attorney General Eric Holder announced that the Obama administration would no longer support the federal Defense of Marriage Act in court. After California voters passed a state constitutional amendment banning marriage between gays, a federal district court ruled the amendment unconstitutional in that it violated the equal protection clause. Recent polls showed for the first time that more than 50 percent of the nation supported gay marriage, and among younger people that number was 70 percent. Then in June 2011 the New York legislature enacted a statute permitting marriage between gays. It is likely that the California case, because it involves the Fourteenth Amendment and is already in the federal courts, may eventually wind up in the Supreme Court. But the New York statute should stand, since there is apparently no constitutional bar to a state defining marriage, a power traditionally seen as part of the state's sovereign authority.

Cases Cited

Bowers v. Hardwick, 478 U.S. 186 (1986)
Boy Scouts of America v. Dale, 530 U.S. 640 (2000)
Doe v. Commonwealth's Attorney, 425 U.S. 901 (1976)
Dudgeon v. United Kingdom, 45 Eur. Ct. H.R. (1981) P52

Griswold v. Connecticut, 381 U.S. 479 (1965)
Hardwick v. Bowers, 760 F.2d 1202 (11th Cir. 1985)
Hurley v. Irish-American Gay, Lesbian, and Bisexual Group of Boston, 515 U.S. 557 (1995)
Lawrence v. Texas, 539 U.S. 558 (2003)
Loving v. Virginia, 388 U.S. 1 (1967)
Olmstead v. United States, 277 U.S. 438 (1928)
People v. Onofre, 51 N.Y.2d 476 (1980)
Planned Parenthood of Southeastern Pennsylvania v. Casey, 505 U.S. 833 (1992)
Roe v. Wade, 410 U.S. 113 (1973)
Romer v. Evans, 517 U.S. 620 (1996)
Stanley v. Georgia, 394 U.S. 557 (1969)

For Further Reading

The best single volume covering the issues from Hardwick to Lawrence is *The Sodomy Cases* (2009), by David A. J. Richards, although the older *Courting Justice: Gay Men and Lesbians v. The Supreme Court,* by Joyce Murdoch and Deb Price (2001), is quite useful. Michael Hardwick talks about his experience in Peter Irons, *The Courage of Their Convictions* (1988), chap. 16. Justice Powell's role is treated in John C. Jeffries Jr., *Justice Lewis F. Powell, Jr.: A Biography* (1994), while Justice Kennedy's views are examined in Helen J. Knowles, *The Tie Goes to Freedom: Justice Anthony M. Kennedy on Liberty* (2009), and Frank J. Colucci, *Justice Kennedy's Jurisprudence: The Full and Necessary Meaning of Liberty* (2009). For the role of lawyers in gay rights litigation, see Ellen Ann Anderson, *Out of the Closets and into the Courts* (2006).

The Constitution Besieged

The War on Terror Cases (2000s)

ON SEPTEMBER 11, 2001, nineteen Muslim extremists hijacked four passenger planes and flew two of them into the Twin Towers of the World Trade Center in New York and the third into the Pentagon outside Washington, D.C. Passengers on the fourth plane, once they realized what had happened, overpowered the terrorists but lost their lives as the plane crashed in rural Pennsylvania. The assaults took 2,974 lives, mostly civilians and mainly Americans, but among the dead were nationals from more than ninety countries. The attack—the first foreign assault on American soil since World War II and the first on the mainland since the War of 1812—demanded action by the administration of George W. Bush, who had been elected less than a year earlier. The response included a war against al-Qaeda in Afghanistan, the invasion of Iraq, and a variety of measures designed to locate terrorists and their sympathizers in the United States. The last program raised a number of constitutional issues, most of which the administration chose to ignore; in some areas the government took actions contrary to the restraints that the Constitution specifically imposed on national authority. During much of this period Congress acted as a rubber stamp—often with many Democrats voting with the Republican majority—for presidential proposals; only the Supreme Court opposed the administration's policies toward men the president labeled as "enemy combatants."

Rounding Up Suspected Aliens

Following the September 11 attacks, Attorney General John Ashcroft vowed that the federal government would use its full might and "every available statute" to hunt down and punish "the terrorists among us." In a roundup conducted over the next month with wartime urgency and secrecy, the administration detained more than 1,200 people suspected of a variety of crimes, from violating immigration laws to being material witnesses to aiding the enemy. As it turned out, with the exception of a small percentage who had violated immigration laws, most of the people seized had done nothing, but it took the government nearly a year before it released more than 1,000 of the detainees.

The arrests, however, spawned dozens of lawsuits in the lower federal courts, with Ashcroft and federal prosecutors on one side arguing that the war powers of the president trumped any civil liberties protections of the Bill of Rights, while a combination of public defenders, immigration lawyers, civil libertarians, and constitutional scholars argued just the opposite, that while civilian courts remain open—as they surely were in this country—then the Constitution remained in effect.

There were three major groupings of cases. First, people held primarily for violation of the immigration laws objected to new rules requiring their cases to be heard in secret, and broadened their arguments into an attack on what they claimed was unconstitutional preventive detention. Second, people jailed as material witnesses, because the government believed they had information about terrorist plots, argued that they should not have been held in order to give grand jury testimony, since that had not been the practice in any other type of criminal case. Third, Yaser Esam Hamdi and José Padilla, whom the administration labeled "enemy combatants," sought what they claimed to be the fundamental rights of Americans, such as representation by a lawyer and being able to challenge their detention before a civilian judge.

Ten days after the September 11 attacks, Judge Michael J. Creppy, the nation's chief immigration judge, issued sweeping instructions to hundreds of magistrates around the country regarding "special interest" immigration cases. "Each of these cases is to be heard separately from all other cases on the docket," Creppy ordered. "The courtroom must be closed for these cases—no visitors, no family, and no press." Then in an absolutely Orwellian line, he wrote, "This restriction includes confirming or denying whether such a case is on the docket." Although the administration refused to explain how it decided which cases would be tried in this manner, it turned out that all of them involved Arab and Muslim men detained in a fairly haphazard manner. They had not been arrested for terrorist activities but had been picked up for traffic violations or tips from neighbors *before* September 11.

On August 27, 2002, a federal appeals court ruled that the press and the public must be allowed to witness immigration hearings, and strongly rebuked the Bush administration for its secrecy policy. A three-judge panel of the Court of Appeals for the Sixth Circuit in Cincinnati held that the news media and ordinary citizens have a constitutional "right of access." The executive branch "seeks to uproot people's lives, outside the public eye, and behind a closed door," wrote Senior Judge Damon J. Keith. "Democracies die behind closed doors. The First Amendment, through a free press, protects the people's right to know that their government acts fairly, lawfully, and accurately in deportation proceedings."

Although the government said it would appeal the ruling, it did not, since it recognized that it most likely would have lost. Moreover, in unrelated immigration cases, the Supreme Court indicated that it would not look favorably on the administration policy. In *Demore v. Kim* (2003), for example, the justices by a 5–4 vote held that legal aliens who commit certain crimes can be imprisoned pending their deportation hearings; however, by a separate 6–3 vote, they ruled that federal courts have jurisdiction to review a congressional statute in the context of a *habeas corpus* petition filed by someone detained under it. The case dealt with one aspect of the 1996 Illegal Immigration Reform and Immigration Responsibility Act, and the persons detained were not being held for terrorist activities. But the decision did allow the government to hold suspected terrorists in jail pending deportation or other criminal hearings, albeit openly, and with the prisoner having the right to file a *habeas* petition.

The administration faced another rebuff in a non-terrorist-related case when the Court refused to take on appeal *Snyder v. Rosales-Garcia* (2003). The Court of Appeals for the Sixth Circuit sided with Mario Rosales-Garcia and Reynero Carballo, two Cuban nationals first detained in 1980 as they tried to enter the United States. They had at the time been deemed excludable—that is, ineligible to seek asylum— and jailed, but were at times released on parole, during which they accumulated criminal records in the United States, primarily for drug and burglary charges. The government revoked their paroles and sought to deport them, but because Cuba would not accept them, they had been detained indefinitely by the Immigration and Naturalization Service (INS).

Their *habeas* petition received a boost following the Supreme Court decision in *Zadvydas v. Davis* (2001), which held that permanent resident aliens could not be kept in prison longer than six months while efforts were made to find a country that would receive them. Although the government argued in *Snyder* that the class of immigrants in *Zadvydas* differed from excludable persons, the Sixth Circuit found that "excludable aliens—like all aliens—are clearly protected by the due process clauses of the Fifth and Fourteenth Amendments."

Since this case touched directly upon the Bush administration's policy of detaining people indefinitely without hearings, the Justice Department immediately asked the high court to review the Sixth Circuit decision, but apparently all nine justices agreed to leave the lower court ruling in place, and the *Snyder* ruling held.

Zacarias Moussaoui

The most notorious of all the terrorism cases involved Zacarias Moussaoui, a French citizen who had been arrested prior to September 11 but then charged with a terrorism-related crime: he allegedly would have been the replacement for the twentieth hijacker. (Since three of the four planes had five hijackers, it was assumed that one additional hijacker was missing from the fourth plane.) French authorities had monitored Moussaoui ever since 1996, when he had been observed meeting with Islamic extremists in London. He had traveled to Malaysia in 2000, and there had allegedly received terrorist training and become part of the 9/11 plot. He then entered the United States on a student visa, and between February and May 2001 attended flight-training courses in Norman, Oklahoma. Although he flunked out of the program and never flew solo, he met with two of the men who piloted the planes into the Twin Towers.

Moussaoui demanded, as a constitutional right, to be allowed to question a senior al-Qaeda leader held in U.S. custody, on the grounds that the man's testimony would clear him of terrorism charges. The government refused to allow Moussaoui to contact the man, Ramzi Binalshibh, through a video hookup to Guantánamo Base in Cuba, where Binalshibh was being held incommunicado. "The damage to the United States will be immediate and irreparable," argued then–assistant attorney general Michael Chertoff, but he was unable to convince U.S. District Judge Leonie Brinkema, who agreed with Moussaoui's attorneys that he could not receive a fair trial without full access to an accused fellow terrorist he said could help disprove the government's claim.

The government proved no more able to convince a federal appeals court than it had Judge Brinkema. The Court of Appeals for the Fourth Circuit dismissed the appeal on jurisdictional grounds, throwing the case back to the district court, where unless the government had agreed to allow access, the entire case against Moussaoui might well have been thrown out. The proceedings then took a bizarre turn, with Moussaoui insisting on representing himself, pleading first guilty, then recanting, then admitting that he was part of an al-Qaeda plot—not of the 9/11 events but of an attack that would come later. In May 2006 a jury found him guilty of multiple acts of terrorism, and the judge sentenced him to six consecutive life sentences.

The Moussaoui case was not the only one in which the administration had been pulled up short by the courts. A federal magistrate in northern Virginia ordered the government to release from custody four men accused of having links to a Kashmiri terrorist group until their trials. Judge T. Rawles Jones Jr. said the government had not convinced him that the men posed any danger to the community or a risk of fleeing before their trial, and he also raised doubts about the government's case against them. In New York, Judge Michael B. Mukasey dressed down then–deputy solicitor general Paul Clement for asking the court without good reason to reconsider an earlier ruling that enemy combatant José Padilla—an American citizen whose case would later play an important role—could consult with counsel to discuss his petition for a writ of *habeas corpus.* The administration had argued here, as it would in all of the terrorism cases, that captured enemy fighters—even American citizens—were not entitled to the protections afforded to defendants in criminal cases in regular civilian courts. The most difficult issues, however, arose with respect to so-called "enemy combatants" captured in Afghanistan and Iraq, and then detained at the U.S. naval base at Guantánamo, Cuba.

Enemy Combatants

In his book on civil liberties in wartime, *All the Laws but One,* Chief Justice William Rehnquist wrote that when bullets fly, "laws speak with a somewhat different voice." Traditionally, when the nation had been at war, the courts had been unusually—some would say excessively— deferential to the policymaking prerogatives of the executive and legislative branches. Normally, the high court would not hear a challenge to wartime actions until after the end of the fighting, unless requested to do so by the administration. To take a few examples, the Court did not rule on the constitutionality of price-fixing until after the end of World War I, but it expedited a review of the draft act, since the Wilson administration had to be certain of its constitutional authority in this area. In the Second World War it upheld the wartime exclusion of Japanese Americans from the West Coast and their forced relocation into detention camps. The war on terror, however, is a different kind of war, and as a result the courts do not have the luxury of postponing decisions until after the fighting has stopped. In the war on terror the fighting may never stop, so courts will have to rule on constitutional questions when they arise, and hope that their decisions will have no adverse repercussions on war-related policies.

When the Bush administration began hostilities against al-Qaeda and the Taliban in Afghanistan and then later attacked Iraq, the army captured prisoners, and the administration labeled a number of them as "enemy combatants." Traditionally, that term refers to members of the armed forces of a state with which another state is at war. When they are captured, they are considered prisoners of war and their treatment is defined under a series of Geneva Agreements to which the United States is a signatory. But since the war on terror is not directed against another state but an entity, al-Qaeda, and the prisoners were not part of an official military force, the Bush administration decided that they would not be treated as prisoners of war (POWs), but rather held incommunicado and without redress to American courts, even if they were American citizens. In 2001 international law defined how POWs were to be treated, but since the Bush administration refused to define captured fighters as POWs, they needed another label and a policy of how to treat them.

On November 26, 2002, the general counsel of the Defense Department defined "enemy combatant" as "an individual who, under the laws and customs of war, may be detained for the duration of an armed conflict." The term included "a member, agent, or associate of al-Qaeda or the Taliban"—a description so broad it could include even noncombatants. The Defense Department relied on a single Supreme Court decision to justify its policy, *Ex parte Quirin* (1942), the case involving Nazi saboteurs who landed on Long Island with the intent of attacking American munitions plants, and who were almost immediately arrested. After a military tribunal found them guilty and ordered them executed, their military lawyers took an appeal to the Supreme Court. It heard the case and confirmed the judgment. In the opinion, Chief Justice Harlan Fiske Stone defined enemy combatants as "citizens who associate themselves with the military arm of the enemy government, and with its aid, guidance, and direction enter this country bent on hostile acts." The definition included foreign nationals as well as U.S. citizens. The Bush administration insisted that American citizens could also be held incommunicado, and relied on the war powers granted to the president by Congress for justification.

Although the Nazi saboteurs had been tried by a military tribunal, the army had assigned them lawyers, and those lawyers had been able to take an appeal to the Supreme Court. The Bush administration, on the other hand, intended that there be no trial for the new enemy combatants, and no access to lawyers. Had the administration treated the foreign nationals as prisoners of war there would have been no expectation of a trial, but the war on terror is unlike conventional wars. In a regular war, even one that lasts several years, prisoners on both sides assume that when an armistice or a peace treaty is signed, they will be repatriated. Their time in a prison camp may be indefinite, but it is determined by the length of the war itself. The war on terror, however, as nearly everyone agrees, will not have a defined ending. There will be no peace treaty, and since it is not waged between armies, will involve civilian groups both as terrorists and as victims. To rule that prisoners accused of terrorism can be held incommunicado, and indefinitely, without any chance of proving themselves innocent of the charges against them, flies in the face of centuries of Anglo-American legal and constitutional tradition. Cases attacking this policy began almost immediately, with a majority of the lower courts ruling that the administration had exceeded its authority even under the war powers. The first of these cases reached the Supreme Court in 2004, despite strong efforts by the Justice Department to prevent any courts from hearing them.

It was inconceivable that the judiciary would allow itself to be cut out of a process that involved at heart the most cherished of American rights. Civil libertarians had denounced the Bush administration for gross violations of basic human rights, while its supporters claimed that the Bush position had been "far more modest and restrained than the actions of the Lincoln and [Franklin] Roosevelt administrations." John Yoo, a member of the Bush Justice Department from 2001 to 2003, argued that "the government is by no means pushing the envelope." Whether one agreed with the civil libertarians or with the administration's defenders, however, one could not doubt that at some point these issues would be decided in court.

Ironically, when civil libertarians first began warning about the rights of captured enemy combatants, one member of the Bush administration took action to investigate. Defense Secretary Donald Rumsfeld convened a panel of constitutional lawyers aware of the wartime mistakes of previous presidents, and they helped draft a policy that gave accused noncitizens the right to counsel before military tribunals, a public trial, appellate review, and other protections embodied in the Uniform Code of Military Justice. Then–attorney general John Ashcroft, who of all recent holders of that position had been least interested in protecting civil liberties, dug in his heels, refused to accept the policy, and went further to condemn civil libertarians for aiding the terrorists. The confrontation in the courts might easily have been avoided if Ashcroft had paid attention to the proposed policy instead of ignoring it.

The Prisoners of Guantánamo

Two of the cases, *Rasul v. Bush* and *Al Odah v. United States*, arose from the detainees kept at the Guantánamo Naval Base in Cuba. During the Spanish-American War of 1898, the U.S. Navy attacking Santiago, Cuba, needed shelter during the summer hurricane season, and chose Guantánamo Harbor on the southeastern part of the island, a large natural harbor surrounded by steep hills. Following the war the United States declared that it had no territorial ambitions to control Cuba, but the 1903 Cuban-American Treaty granted the United States a perpetual lease of the area. The Cuban government today insists that the treaty was procured by force and that continued American occupation is illegal. The naval base there has a brig, or prison, and this suited the needs of the Bush administration lawyers perfectly since, they believed, Guantánamo was not U.S. territory, and therefore beyond the reach of constitutional requirements.

This was not a new argument, and had been played out in the Supreme Court over a century earlier in the so-called Insular Cases, which held that the Constitution did not necessarily "follow the flag"— that is, extend to areas outside the United States but under American control. The government claimed that the Court had no business even ruling on the legality of detaining aliens captured abroad at a base that is outside U.S. sovereign territory. Solicitor General Theodore Olsen's brief even complained about "judicial interference with military affairs" and the "truly dangerous precedent of judicial second-guessing of quintessentially military decisions." Although the Court had in previous cases paid great attention to the impact of international accords and treaties such as the Geneva Convention, Olsen brushed them aside and denied that the administration had any obligation under international law to give the Guantánamo detainees access to the courts. "Our government reserves that judgment to the political branches which, unlike the courts, may be held politically accountable for that judgment," he said.

In essence, the administration did not ask that the Court uphold its position, but said that the Court had no authority even to hear the case. Given how strenuously the Rehnquist Court had argued that the high court—and not the political branches—is the ultimate interpreter of the Constitution, some commentators saw this as practically waving a red flag at the justices to provoke them.

The government had a subtler and even more problematic position to defend in the cases of Yaser Esam Hamdi and José Padilla, both U.S. citizens designated as enemy combatants. Hamdi was born in 1980 to Saudi Arabian parents in Baton Rouge, Louisiana, and as a child he left the United States with his parents to live in Saudi Arabia. As a teenager he ran away and joined the Taliban in Afghanistan, and in November 2001 he was captured by Afghanistan's Northern Alliance forces and turned over to American authorities. José Padilla was born in Brooklyn and later moved to Chicago, where as a gang member he got into trouble with the law and served a prison sentence for manslaughter. He later converted to Islam, took the name Muhajir Abdullah, and became associated with an Islamic terrorist cell. Both men were eventually sent to Guantánamo, and ordered held without trial.

Since both men were American citizens, the administration did not attempt to claim that U.S. courts should stay out of these two cases, and in fact conceded that review by the judiciary was appropriate. That review, however, should be minimal. Moreover, the administration claimed that neither man had a right to see counsel, although it later reversed itself and agreed to let them consult lawyers after considerable public criticism of its position, especially by conservative groups such as the American Bar Association and former federal judges who filed a brief on their behalf and that of other Guantánamo detainees.

Legal scholars seemed to agree that the administration could designate people, even U.S. citizens, as enemy combatants, and in the 1942 German saboteurs case, one of those seized was an American citizen. The German saboteurs were tried before a military court and had the benefit of court-appointed lawyers; the Bush administration, however, claimed that it could seize and hold citizens designated as enemy combatants indefinitely, and without granting them access either to lawyers or to the courts.

In *All the Laws but One*, Chief Justice Rehnquist predicted that "there is no reason to think that future wartime presidents will act differently from Lincoln, Wilson or Roosevelt, or that future justices of the Supreme Court will decide questions differently from their predecessors." But, he noted, in the more recent wartime cases the Court has proven less tolerant of the "least justified" restrictions on civil liberties. "It is both desirable and likely," he went on, "that more careful attention will be paid by the courts to the basis for the government's claims of necessity as a basis for curtailing liberty." Rehnquist's assumptions proved fairly accurate.

The Guantánamo cases initially involved a technical question— namely, whether federal courts had jurisdiction to hear appeals from the detainees being held outside the country. The administration, and a lower court, relied on a 1950 case, *Johnson v. Eisentrager,* which involved German prisoners seized by the United States in China and tried by an American military tribunal in Germany after the Second World War. At the time the high court ruled that because the Germans were aliens and were not on U.S. soil, they had no right to seek *habeas* review in American courts. The Bush administration claimed that the Guantánamo detainees were the same as the Germans in *Eisentrager,* enemy aliens on foreign soil. But lawyers representing the detainees asserted that Guantánamo was hardly foreign soil, since it was under the *de facto* control of the United States. Moreover, unlike the Germans, the aliens held there had not been charged with any offense or even found to fit the definition of an "enemy alien" or a "combatant." Thomas Wilner, representing the Kuwaiti nationals held at the base, charged that American treatment of the aliens was "radically at odds with any constitutional regime of due process or the rule of law."

The Supreme Court Issues a Warning

In *Rasul v. Bush* (2004), decided along with *Al Odah v. United States,* a 6–3 majority made it clear that the Bush administration had gone too far in seeking unchecked power to detain and interrogate individuals in its war on terror. The detainees were entitled to *habeas* review by neutral adjudicators, and in a direct rebuff to the administration and especially the solicitor general (who sat glumly in the courtroom as the decisions were read on the next-to-last day of the term), reminded them that the Supreme Court, and no one else, is the final arbiter of the boundaries between the branches of government, in wartime as well as in peace.

The Court was even more explicit in *Hamdi v. Rumsfeld* (2004), regarding the American citizen captured with the Taliban in Afghanistan. "We have long since made clear that a state of war is not a blank check when it comes to the rights of the nation's citizens," wrote Justice Sandra Day O'Connor. "The threats to military operations posed by a basic system of independent review is not so weighty as to trump a citizen's core rights to challenge meaningfully the government's case and to be heard by an independent adjudicator." Hamdi "unquestionably" had the right of access to a lawyer.

Although Justice Scalia, joined in a rare pairing with Justice Stevens, dissented from the reasoning in O'Connor's opinion in *Hamdi,* the two went even further in rejecting the administration's position. Reading from his partial dissent, Scalia said the Constitution offered only one way to achieve the administration's goal—suspension of *habeas corpus* by a vote of Congress, a step that had not been taken in the contiguous states since the end of Reconstruction. "If civil rights are to be curtailed during wartime," Scalia wrote, "it must be done openly and democratically as the Constitution requires."

In the case of José Padilla, the Court sidestepped the issues in his case by declaring that he had sought *habeas* relief in the wrong court. By a 5–4 vote, the Court ruled that a federal court in New York where Padilla had brought suit lacked jurisdiction over him, and he should have brought the case in South Carolina, where he had been held in a military jail. The four dissenters said they would have decided the merits of the case, and Justice Stevens accused the majority of shirking its duty: "At stake in this case is nothing less than the essence of a free society."

About the only victory the administration gleaned from these decisions is that O'Connor agreed that the government had a *limited* right to detain people it suspected of involvement in terrorism, but although she did not indicate any hard rule on the length of this detention, she implied that it could not be indefinite or overlong.

The administration tried to make the best of the decisions, but one could not ignore that the Court had issued a sharp rebuff to Bush's policy. Following the decisions the army began making immediate preparation for setting up military tribunals at Guantánamo, and allowed the detainees there access to lawyers for the first time. Then the administration began dragging its feet. Civil rights groups attacked these hearings as shams and as completely lacking in due process either under a civilian or a military justice standard. Clearly the administration was trying to get around the rulings, and just as clearly the issue would come back to the high court.

Hamdan v. Rumsfeld

Although the federal courts, especially at the lower level, did not wish to be seen as obstructionist in the early years of the war on terror, the message that went out constantly to the Bush administration was that prisoners taken in the war, whether called enemy combatants or something else, were entitled to at least some minimal considerations of due process. They could not be jailed indefinitely without recourse to some legal system, military or civilian; they had to be informed of the charges against them; and they had to be given an opportunity to refute those charges. To all of this the administration paid either no heed or lip service, and instead got Congress to pass legislation denying federal courts jurisdiction over the detainees. The case of *Hamdan v. Rumsfeld* (2006) thus raised core constitutional questions regarding both separation of powers as well as fundamental individual rights, including:

- Did Congress and the executive branch have the power to strip federal courts and the Supreme Court of jurisdiction?

- Did the executive have the authority, under the president's war powers, to lock up individuals indefinitely, without benefit of traditional protections such as a jury trial, the right to cross-examine accusers, and the right to appeal?

- Did international treaties—specifically the Geneva Conventions on the treatment of prisoners of war—apply to those the government called "enemy combatants"?

The case involved Salim Ahmed Hamdan, a Yemeni with acknowledged links to al-Qaeda, and imprisoned at Guantánamo. Hamdan admitted that he had been a driver and bodyguard to al-Qaeda leader Osama bin Laden, but denied that he had any role in planning or executing the attacks on September 11, 2001. The only charge the government could come up with was "conspiracy," a crime not recognized either in the Geneva Conventions or in American military law.

In *Hamdan v. Rumsfeld* (2006), the Court by a 5–3 vote (Chief Justice John Roberts had voted in this case in the Circuit Court and so recused himself) declared that the military tribunals convened by the Defense Department did not measure up to any standards provided for either under civilian courts or military courts convened under the Military Justice Act (the basic law setting forth the Code of Military Justice that governs the American armed forces), and in fact lacked any constitutional base whatsoever. Speaking for the majority, Justice John Paul Stevens used a separation of powers argument to note that Congress and the executive could not strip federal courts, and especially the Supreme Court, of jurisdiction to hear cases involving basic rights. In addition, the justices cited both earlier Supreme Court cases as well as the various Geneva Conventions to drive home the point that the administration had failed to live up to any standards of recognized law in treating the prisoners held at Guantánamo. For the administration to proceed, Congress would now have to authorize some form of tribunal.

The decision was widely seen as a rebuke to the Bush administration, not only on this issue but also on the president's claim that under the Constitution's Article II war powers clause he had authority to do whatever he considered necessary regardless of existing law, international treaties, or even the Constitution. Given the decisions in the two 2004 cases (*Rasul* and *Hamdi*), as well as the Court's refusal to dismiss Hamdan's *habeas* appeal when it first came up in January, the ruling may have shocked the Bush people but came as no surprise to those outside the government.

Moreover, the entire theory of an all-powerful presidency in which the war powers trumped any and all constitutional limitations on the chief executive came under increasing attack. Immediately after September 11, few people in or out of the government wanted to criticize the president's handling of the war on terror. But the war was not going well, and Bush's approval ratings stood well below the 50 percent mark during most of his second term. Not only had his overall handling of foreign and domestic policy been questioned, but critics, including many Republicans, had increasingly condemned the president's claims of expansive powers.

When it became known in 2005 that the National Security Agency had conducted widespread wiretapping of American telephone communications, in defiance of the law and without consulting with the appropriate congressional committees, not only did civil rights activists protest, but so too did many conservative Republicans. U.S. District Judge James Robertson, one of eleven members of the secret Foreign

Intelligence Surveillance Court that should have heard applications for such wiretaps, resigned in protest. Republican senators Chuck Hagel of Nebraska, Olympia Snowe of Maine, and Arlen Specter of Pennsylvania promised hearings on the matter, and Specter thought that there should and would be a court case on the subject.

Members of Congress also grew upset over "signing statements" Bush made when approving legislation, in effect reserving his right to ignore the laws. This practice came to light after Bush signed a law banning the torture of detainees. The law, sponsored by a former Vietnam War POW, Republican senator John McCain of Arizona, had such large backing in Congress that its supporters could easily have overridden a presidential veto. So Bush signed it, and at the same time quietly initialed a "signing statement" reserving his right to ignore the law. McCain and many other lawmakers were furious. Had Bush tried to ignore a duly passed statute, there surely would have been a court case, and since past Court decisions on presidential responsibility to enforce duly enacted legislation indicated Bush had little support for his constitutional views, the administration likely would have lost.

Bush was not a lawyer, but he relied on a cadre of attorneys in both the Justice Department and White House who advised him that he had practically unlimited authority as commander in chief. While other presidents had acted under a liberal interpretation of this authority, none of them, including Abraham Lincoln and Franklin Roosevelt, claimed as Bush did that he could ignore duly enacted legislation. (The administration's lawyers also wrote memoranda that justified the use of torture by the army and CIA agents despite both American law and international conventions forbidding the practice.)

Bush, under the mantle of his war powers, waged the war on terror as he saw fit. If the intelligence agencies wanted to eavesdrop without warrants, he told them to go ahead. If the military wanted to hold detainees without trial or subject them to torture, Bush had no problems. The Court's decision in *Hamdan* at the very least should have served as a warning to the president that the nation is governed under a Constitution; Bush seemed unwilling to recognize that signal, and so the Supreme Court had to act still one more time.

Another Rebuke from the Court

In *Boumediene v. Bush* (2008), the Court again rebuked the Bush administration for its handling of the rights of prisoners confined at Guantánamo, declaring that those in custody there had a constitutional right to challenge their detention. The case had been brought by Lakhdar Boumediene, a citizen of Bosnia and Herzegovina born in

Algeria, who was arrested with five other men for allegedly planning to blow up the American embassy in Bosnia in October 2001. In January 2002 the Supreme Court of Bosnia ruled there was no evidence to hold the men and ordered them released. American troops, part of a peace-keeping mission in Bosnia, were waiting for them as they emerged from prison; they then captured and transported them to the prison in Guantánamo. There Boumediene was tried under the newly created military tribunals, and his lawyer took an appeal to federal courts challenging the validity of the military panels.

By a 5–4 vote the Court struck down sections of the 2006 Military Commission Act (the act that authorized the military tribunals), which stripped American courts of jurisdiction over *habeas corpus* petitions filed by foreign nationals held at Guantánamo, and ordered quick *habeas* hearings for them. As many as two hundred detainees had *habeas* petitions pending. This was the third consecutive rebuke for the administration in its policy of treating the detainees as nonpersons devoid of any rights protected by the Constitution.

Writing for the majority, Justice Anthony Kennedy said the review provided by the 2005 Detainee Treatment Act "falls short of being a constitutionally adequate substitute" because it failed to offer "the fundamental procedural protections of *habeas corpus*." The laws and the Constitution, he declared, "are designed to survive, and remain in force, in extraordinary times." To ensure that constitutional guarantees could be enforced, civilian courts would hear *habeas* petitions. While the decision left open many questions, it was categorical in its rejection of the administration's basic arguments. It repudiated the legal basis for the strategy adopted after 9/11 of housing prisoners captured in Afghanistan and elsewhere at Guantánamo where, according to advice given by Justice Department lawyers to the White House, domestic American law would not reach.

Normally the Court, having decided that the right to *habeas* existed, would have sent the case back to the appeals court for further review of the procedures involved. But the "gravity of the separation-of-powers issues raised by these cases and the fact that these detainees have been denied meaningful access to a judicial forum for a period of years render these cases exceptional," and required that the high court itself make these determinations. The majority concluded that the procedures devised by the administration and Congress had major flaws. For example, a detainee could not present evidence that might clear him of blame because that evidence was withheld from the record or presented after the hearing.

Justice Kennedy took the unusual step of orally delivering much of his opinion, which included a lengthy history of *habeas corpus*. He was followed by Justice Scalia, who also read aloud from his bitter dissent and charged that the majority opinion "will almost certainly cause more Americans to be killed. . . . The decision is devastating." Justice Roberts also dissented, and criticized the majority for dismissing out of hand the efforts of the other two branches to respond to the Court's prior rulings. He claimed that "this decision is not really about the detainees at all, but about control of federal policy regarding enemy combatants." (Solicitor General Paul Clement, who had argued the case, told the justices that "the political branch has spoken," an argument that at least five of the justices rejected.)

Paradoxically, given the deep split in *Boumediene,* the justices stood unanimously in a second *habeas* ruling the same day. Two men, Mohammad Munaf and Shawqi Ahmad Omar, both American citizens, faced criminal charges in Iraq and were being held prisoners in an American camp. The administration claimed that because the men were technically held by the twenty-six-nation multinational force in Iraq, federal courts did not have jurisdiction to hear their *habeas corpus* petitions.

All nine justices rejected the Bush administration's position in *Munaf v. Geren.* The men were being held in an American military prison, and what mattered was that they were held by American soldiers subject to a U.S. chain of command. They thus had the right to file a *habeas* petition. But, after rejecting the administration position, the chief justice ruled against the two men on the merits of their case, stating that their release through *habeas* "would interfere with the sovereign authority of Iraq to punish offenses against its laws committed within its borders."

Aftermath

The Bush administration left office in January 2009, with its policies toward detainees, torture, and claims of overriding executive privilege condemned by all but the most militant neoconservatives, some of whom had planned and then pushed the administration into wars in Afghanistan and Iraq. The new president, Barack Obama, promised that he would follow the law banning torture, and that the prison at Guantánamo would be closed. While the torture has ceased, the prison was still open at the time this chapter was written, since Congress has refused to appropriate the necessary money. Issues have also arisen as to where the prisoners would be transferred for trial, and what to do about a small number of men who cannot be tried but who are too dangerous to release. In some areas the Obama administration has continued Bush-era policies, albeit without the claim of unlimited presidential authority.

The Court cases reaffirmed that even in an unusual type of war, one not involving a nation-state as the enemy and without any conceivable time limits, constitutional protections cannot be ignored. In most instances the prisoners at Guantánamo could have been tried either in civilian or military tribunals, and either convicted or released and deported back to their home countries. In those few instances where the claim that allowing defendants to see evidence against them would breach national security concerns, judicial procedures have long been in place to view such materials *in camera* by the judge. It is possible that a few real terrorists might have slipped through this net, but the damage they might have done seems small compared to that perpetrated against the Constitution itself in the name of national security. As Louis Brandeis wrote long ago, "Experience should teach us to be most on our guard to protect liberty when the Government's purposes are beneficent. . . . The greatest dangers to liberty lurk in insidious encroachment by men of zeal, well-meaning but without understanding" (*Olmstead v. United States* [1928]).

Cases Cited

Al Odah v. United States, 553 U.S. 723 (2008)
Boumediene v. Bush, 553 U.S. 723 (2008)
Demore v. Kim, 538 U.S. 510 (2003)
Ex parte Quirin, 317 U.S. 1 (1942)
Hamdan v. Rumsfeld, 548 U.S. 557 (2006)
Hamdi v. Rumsfeld, 542 U.S. 507 (2004)
Johnson v. Eisentrager, 339 U.S. 763 (1950)
Munaf v. Geren, 553 U.S. 674 (2008)
Olmstead v. United States, 277 U.S. 438 (1928)
Rasul v. Bush, 542 U.S. 466 (2004)
Snyder v. Rosales-Garcia, 322 F.3d 386 (6th Cir., 2003), cert. denied, 539 U.S. 941 (2003)
Zadvydas v. Davis, 533 U.S. 678 (2001)

For Further Reading

The literature on the war on terror is expanding at a rapid pace, but a good place to start is Louis Fisher, *The Constitution and 9/11: Recurring Threats to America's Freedoms* (2008), which provides a broad but critical look at how the government responded to 9/11, and historical antecedents for certain policies. See also Richard M. Pious, *The War on Terror and the Rule of Law* (2006), and for a differing view, Richard A. Posner, *Not a Suicide Pact: The Constitution in Times of National Emergency* (2006). Specific studies include Jonathan Mahler, *The Challenge: Hamdan v. Rumsfeld and the Fight over Presidential Power* (2008); Joseph Margolies, *Guantánamo and the Abuse of Presidential Power* (2006); Howard Ball, *Bush, the Detainees, and the Constitution: The Battle over Presidential Power in the War on Terror* (2007); and David Cole, *Enemy Aliens: Double Standards and Constitutional Freedoms in the War on Terror* (2003). John Yoo, who wrote a number of the memos regarding presidential power and interrogation techniques, defended his position in *The Powers of War and Peace: The Constitution and Foreign Affairs after 9/11* (2005); see his article as well as other viewpoints in the Hoover Institution's symposium, *Terrorism, the Laws of War, and the Constitution: Debating the Enemy Combatant Cases* (2005).

Constitution of the United States

WE THE PEOPLE of the United States, in Order to form a more perfect Union, establish Justice, insure domestic Tranquility, provide for the common defence, promote the general Welfare, and secure the Blessings of Liberty to ourselves and our Posterity, do ordain and establish this Constitution for the United States of America.

ARTICLE I

Section 1. All legislative Powers herein granted shall be vested in a Congress of the United States, which shall consist of a Senate and House of Representatives.

Section 2. The House of Representatives shall be composed of Members chosen every second Year by the People of the several States, and the Electors in each State shall have the Qualifications requisite for Electors of the most numerous Branch of the State Legislature.

No Person shall be a Representative who shall not have attained to the age of twenty five Years, and been seven Years a Citizen of the United States, and who shall not, when elected, be an Inhabitant of that State in which he shall be chosen.

[Representatives and direct Taxes shall be apportioned among the several States which may be included within this Union, according to their respective Numbers, which shall be determined by adding to the whole Number of free Persons, including those bound to Service for a Term of Years, and excluding Indians not taxed, three fifths of all other Persons.][1] The actual Enumeration shall be made within three Years after the first Meeting of the Congress of the United States, and within every subsequent Term of ten Years, in such Manner as they shall by Law direct. The Number of Representatives shall not exceed one for every thirty Thousand, but each State shall have at Least one Representative; and until such enumeration shall be made, the State of New Hampshire shall be entitled to chuse three, Massachusetts eight, Rhode-Island and Providence Plantations one, Connecticut five, New-York six, New Jersey four, Pennsylvania eight, Delaware one, Maryland six, Virginia ten, North Carolina five, South Carolina five, and Georgia three.

When vacancies happen in the Representation from any State, the Executive Authority thereof shall issue Writs of Election to fill such Vacancies.

The House of Representatives shall chuse their Speaker and other Officers; and shall have the sole Power of Impeachment.

Section 3. The Senate of the United States shall be composed of two Senators from each State, [chosen by the Legislature thereof,]² for six Years; and each Senator shall have one Vote.

Immediately after they shall be assembled in Consequence of the first Election, they shall be divided as equally as may be into three Classes. The Seats of the Senators of the first Class shall be vacated at the Expiration of the second Year, of the second Class at the Expiration of the fourth Year, and of the third Class at the Expiration of the sixth Year, so that one third may be chosen every second Year; [and if Vacancies happen by Resignation, or otherwise, during the Recess of the Legislature of any State, the Executive thereof may make temporary Appointments until the next Meeting of the Legislature, which shall then fill such Vacancies].³

No Person shall be a Senator who shall not have attained to the Age of thirty Years, and been nine Years a Citizen of the United States, and who shall not, when elected, be an Inhabitant of that State for which he shall be chosen.

The Vice President of the United States shall be President of the Senate, but shall have no Vote, unless they be equally divided.

The Senate shall chuse their other Officers, and also a President pro tempore, in the Absence of the Vice President, or when he shall exercise the Office of President of the United States.

The Senate shall have the sole Power to try all Impeachments. When sitting for that Purpose, they shall be on Oath or Affirmation. When the President of the United States is tried, the Chief Justice shall preside: And no Person shall be convicted without the Concurrence of two thirds of the Members present.

Judgment in Cases of Impeachment shall not extend further than to removal from Office, and disqualification to hold and enjoy any Office of honor, Trust or Profit under the United States: but the Party convicted shall nevertheless be liable and subject to Indictment, Trial, Judgment and Punishment, according to Law.

Section 4. The Times, Places and Manner of holding Elections for Senators and Representatives, shall be prescribed in each State by the Legislature thereof; but the Congress may at any time by Law make or alter such Regulations, except as to the Places of chusing Senators.

The Congress shall assemble at least once in every Year, and such Meeting shall [be on the first Monday in December],[4] unless they shall by Law appoint a different Day.

Section 5. Each House shall be the Judge of the Elections, Returns and Qualifications of its own Members, and a Majority of each shall constitute a Quorum to do Business; but a smaller Number may adjourn from day to day, and may be authorized to compel the Attendance of absent Members, in such Manner, and under such Penalties as each House may provide.

Each House may determine the Rules of its Proceedings, punish its Members for disorderly Behaviour, and, with the Concurrence of two thirds, expel a Member.

Each House shall keep a Journal of its Proceedings, and from time to time publish the same, excepting such Parts as may in their Judgment require Secrecy; and the Yeas and Nays of the Members of either House on any question shall, at the Desire of one fifth of those Present, be entered on the Journal.

Neither House, during the Session of Congress, shall, without the Consent of the other, adjourn for more than three days, nor to any other Place than that in which the two Houses shall be sitting.

Section 6. The Senators and Representatives shall receive a Compensation for their Services, to be ascertained by Law, and paid out of the Treasury of the United States. They shall in all Cases, except Treason, Felony and Breach of the Peace, be privileged from Arrest during their Attendance at the Session of their respective Houses, and in going to and returning from the same; and for any Speech or Debate in either House, they shall not be questioned in any other Place.

No Senator or Representative shall, during the Time for which he was elected, be appointed to any civil Office under the Authority of the United States, which shall have been created, or the Emoluments whereof shall have been encreased during such time; and no Person holding any Office under the United States, shall be a Member of either House during his Continuance in Office.

Section 7. All Bills for raising Revenue shall originate in the House of Representatives; but the Senate may propose or concur with Amendments as on other Bills.

Every Bill which shall have passed the House of Representatives and the Senate, shall, before it become a Law, be presented to the President of the United States; If he approve he shall sign it, but if not he shall return it, with his Objections to that House in which it shall have originated, who shall enter the Objections at large on their Journal, and proceed to reconsider it. If after such Reconsideration two thirds of that House shall agree to pass the Bill, it shall be sent, together with the Objections, to the other House, by which it shall likewise be reconsidered, and if approved by two thirds of that House, it shall become a Law. But in all such Cases the Votes of both Houses shall be determined by yeas and Nays, and the Names of the Persons voting for and against the Bill shall be entered on the Journal of each House respectively. If any Bill shall not be returned by the President within ten Days (Sundays excepted) after it shall have been presented to him, the Same shall be a Law, in like Manner as if he had signed it, unless the Congress by their Adjournment prevent its Return, in which Case it shall not be a Law.

Every Order, Resolution, or Vote to which the Concurrence of the Senate and House of Representatives may be necessary (except on a question of Adjournment) shall be presented to the President of the United States; and before the Same shall take Effect, shall be approved by him, or being disapproved by him, shall be repassed by two thirds of the Senate and House of Representatives, according to the Rules and Limitations prescribed in the Case of a Bill.

Section 8. The Congress shall have Power To lay and collect Taxes, Duties, Imposts and Excises, to pay the Debts and provide for the common Defence and general Welfare of the United States; but all Duties, Imposts and Excises shall be uniform throughout the United States;

To borrow Money on the credit of the United States;

To regulate Commerce with foreign Nations, and among the several States, and with the Indian Tribes;

To establish an uniform Rule of Naturalization, and uniform Laws on the subject of Bankruptcies throughout the United States;

To coin Money, regulate the Value thereof, and of foreign Coin, and fix the Standard of Weights and Measures;

To provide for the Punishment of counterfeiting the Securities and current Coin of the United States;

To establish Post Offices and post Roads;

To promote the Progress of Science and useful Arts, by securing for limited Times to Authors and Inventors the exclusive Right to their respective Writings and Discoveries;

To constitute Tribunals inferior to the supreme Court;

To define and punish Piracies and Felonies committed on the high Seas, and Offences against the Law of Nations;

To declare War, grant Letters of Marque and Reprisal, and make Rules concerning Captures on Land and Water;

To raise and support Armies, but no Appropriation of Money to that Use shall be for a longer Term than two Years;

To provide and maintain a Navy;

To make Rules for the Government and Regulation of the land and naval Forces;

To provide for calling forth the Militia to execute the Laws of the Union, suppress Insurrections and repel Invasions;

To provide for organizing, arming, and disciplining, the Militia, and for governing such Part of them as may be employed in the Service of the United States, reserving to the States respectively, the Appointment of the Officers, and the Authority of training the Militia according to the discipline prescribed by Congress;

To exercise exclusive Legislation in all Cases whatsoever, over such District (not exceeding ten Miles square) as may, by Cession of particular States, and the Acceptance of Congress, become the Seat of the Government of the United States, and to exercise like Authority over all Places purchased by the Consent of the Legislature of the State in which the Same shall be, for the Erection of Forts, Magazines, Arsenals, dock-Yards, and other needful Buildings;—And

To make all Laws which shall be necessary and proper for carrying into Execution the foregoing Powers, and all other Powers vested by this Constitution in the Government of the United States, or in any Department or Officer thereof.

Section 9. The Migration or Importation of such Persons as any of the States now existing shall think proper to admit, shall not be prohibited by the Congress prior to the Year one thousand eight hundred and eight, but a Tax or duty may be imposed on such Importation, not exceeding ten dollars for each Person.

The Privilege of the Writ of Habeas Corpus shall not be suspended, unless when in Cases of Rebellion or Invasion the public Safety may require it.

No Bill of Attainder or ex post facto Law shall be passed.

No Capitation, or other direct, Tax shall be laid, unless in Proportion to the Census or Enumeration herein before directed to be taken.[5]

No Tax or Duty shall be laid on Articles exported from any State.

No Preference shall be given by any Regulation of Commerce or Revenue to the Ports of one State over those of another; nor shall Vessels bound to, or from, one State, be obliged to enter, clear, or pay Duties in another.

No Money shall be drawn from the Treasury, but in Consequence of Appropriations made by Law; and a regular Statement and Account of the Receipts and Expenditures of all public Money shall be published from time to time.

No Title of Nobility shall be granted by the United States: And no Person holding any Office of Profit or Trust under them, shall, without the Consent of the Congress, accept of any present, Emolument, Office, or Title, of any kind whatever, from any King, Prince, or foreign State.

Section 10. No State shall enter into any Treaty, Alliance, or Confederation; grant Letters of Marque and Reprisal; coin Money; emit Bills of Credit; make any Thing but gold and silver Coin a Tender in Payment of Debts; pass any Bill of Attainder, ex post facto Law, or Law impairing the Obligation of Contracts, or grant any Title of Nobility.

No State shall, without the Consent of the Congress, lay any Imposts or Duties on Imports or Exports, except what may be absolutely necessary for executing its inspection Laws: and the net Produce of all Duties and Imposts, laid by any State on Imports or Exports, shall be for the Use of the Treasury of the United States; and all such Laws shall be subject to the Revision and Controul of the Congress.

No State shall, without the Consent of Congress, lay any Duty of Tonnage, keep Troops, or Ships of War in time of Peace, enter into any Agreement or Compact with another State, or with a foreign Power, or engage in War, unless actually invaded, or in such imminent Danger as will not admit of delay.

ARTICLE II

Section 1. The executive Power shall be vested in a President of the United States of America. He shall hold his Office during the Term of four Years, and, together with the Vice President, chosen for the same Term, be elected, as follows:

Each State shall appoint, in such Manner as the Legislature thereof may direct, a Number of Electors, equal to the whole Number of Senators and Representatives to which the State may be entitled in the Congress: but no Senator or Representative, or Person holding an Office of Trust or Profit under the United States, shall be appointed an Elector.

[The Electors shall meet in their respective States, and vote by Ballot for two Persons, of whom one at least shall not be an Inhabitant of the same State with themselves. And they shall make a List of all the Persons voted for, and of the Number of Votes for each; which List they shall sign and certify, and transmit sealed to the Seat of the Government of the United States, directed to the President of the Senate. The President of the Senate shall, in the Presence of the Senate and House of Representatives, open all the Certificates, and the Votes shall then be counted. The Person having the greatest Number of Votes shall be the President, if such Number be a Majority of the whole Number of Electors appointed; and if there be more than one who have such Majority, and have an equal Number of Votes, then the House of Representatives shall immediately chuse by Ballot one of them for President; and if no Person have a Majority, then from the five highest on the list the said House shall in like Manner chuse the President. But in chusing the President, the Votes shall be taken by States, the Representation from each State having one Vote; A quorum for this Purpose shall consist of a Member or Members from two thirds of the States, and a Majority of all the States shall be necessary to a Choice. In every Case, after the Choice of the President, the Person having the greatest Number of Votes of the Electors shall be the Vice President. But if there should remain two or more who have equal Votes, the Senate shall chuse from them by Ballot the Vice President.][6]

The Congress may determine the Time of chusing the Electors, and the Day on which they shall give their Votes; which Day shall be the same throughout the United States.

No Person except a natural born Citizen, or a Citizen of the United States, at the time of the Adoption of this Constitution, shall be eligible to the Office of President; neither shall any Person be eligible to that Office who shall not have attained to the Age of thirty five Years, and been fourteen Years a Resident within the United States.

In Case of the Removal of the President from Office, or of his Death, Resignation, or Inability to discharge the Powers and Duties of the said Office,[7] the Same shall devolve on the Vice President, and the Congress may by Law provide for the Case of Removal, Death, Resignation or Inability, both of the President and Vice President, declaring what Officer shall then act as President, and such Officer shall act accordingly, until the Disability be removed, or a President shall be elected.

The President shall, at stated Times, receive for his Services, a Compensation, which shall neither be encreased nor diminished during the Period for which he shall have been elected, and he shall not receive within that Period any other Emolument from the United States, or any of them.

Before he enter on the Execution of his Office, he shall take the following Oath or Affirmation:—"I do solemnly swear (or affirm) that I will faithfully execute the Office of President of the United States, and will to the best of my Ability, preserve, protect and defend the Constitution of the United States."

Section 2. The President shall be Commander in Chief of the Army and Navy of the United States, and of the Militia of the several States, when called into the actual Service of the United States; he may require the Opinion, in writing, of the principal Officer in each of the executive Departments, upon any Subject relating to the Duties of their respective

Offices, and he shall have Power to grant Reprieves and Pardons for Offences against the United States, except in Cases of Impeachment.

He shall have Power, by and with the Advice and Consent of the Senate, to make Treaties, provided two thirds of the Senators present concur; and he shall nominate, and by and with the Advice and Consent of the Senate, shall appoint Ambassadors, other public Ministers and Consuls, Judges of the supreme Court, and all other Officers of the United States, whose Appointments are not herein otherwise provided for, and which shall be established by Law: but the Congress may by Law vest the Appointment of such inferior Officers, as they think proper, in the President alone, in the Courts of Law, or in the Heads of Departments.

The President shall have Power to fill up all Vacancies that may happen during the Recess of the Senate, by granting Commissions which shall expire at the End of their next Session.

Section 3. He shall from time to time give to the Congress Information of the State of the Union, and recommend to their Consideration such Measures as he shall judge necessary and expedient; he may, on extraordinary Occasions, convene both Houses, or either of them, and in Case of Disagreement between them, with Respect to the Time of Adjournment, he may adjourn them to such Time as he shall think proper; he shall receive Ambassadors and other public Ministers; he shall take Care that the Laws be faithfully executed, and shall Commission all the Officers of the United States.

Section 4. The President, Vice President and all civil Officers of the United States, shall be removed from Office on Impeachment for, and Conviction of, Treason, Bribery, or other high Crimes and Misdemeanors.

ARTICLE III

Section 1. The judicial Power of the United States, shall be vested in one supreme Court, and in such inferior Courts as the Congress may from time to time ordain and establish. The Judges, both of the supreme and inferior Courts, shall hold their Offices during good Behaviour, and shall, at stated Times, receive for their Services, a Compensation, which shall not be diminished during their Continuance in Office.

Section 2. The judicial Power shall extend to all Cases, in Law and Equity, arising under this Constitution, the Laws of the United States, and Treaties made, or which shall be made, under their Authority;—to all Cases affecting Ambassadors, other public Ministers and Consuls;— to all Cases of admiralty and maritime Jurisdiction;—to Controversies to which the United States shall be a Party;—to Controversies between two or more States;—between a State and Citizens of another State;—

between Citizens of different States;—between Citizens of the same State claiming Lands under Grants of different States, and between a State, or the Citizens thereof, and foreign States, Citizens or Subjects.[8]

In all Cases affecting Ambassadors, other public Ministers and Consuls, and those in which a State shall be Party, the supreme Court shall have original Jurisdiction. In all the other Cases before mentioned, the supreme Court shall have appellate Jurisdiction, both as to Law and Fact, with such Exceptions, and under such Regulations as the Congress shall make.

The Trial of all Crimes, except in Cases of Impeachment, shall be by Jury; and such Trial shall be held in the State where the said Crimes shall have been committed; but when not committed within any State, the Trial shall be at such Place or Places as the Congress may by Law have directed.

Section 3. Treason against the United States, shall consist only in levying War against them, or in adhering to their Enemies, giving them Aid and Comfort. No Person shall be convicted of Treason unless on the Testimony of two Witnesses to the same overt Act, or on Confession in open Court.

The Congress shall have Power to declare the Punishment of Treason, but no Attainder of Treason shall work Corruption of Blood, or Forfeiture except during the Life of the Person attainted.

ARTICLE IV

Section 1. Full Faith and Credit shall be given in each State to the public Acts, Records, and judicial Proceedings of every other State. And the Congress may by general Laws prescribe the Manner in which such Acts, Records and Proceedings shall be proved, and the Effect thereof.

Section 2. The Citizens of each State shall be entitled to all Privileges and Immunities of Citizens in the several States.

A Person charged in any State with Treason, Felony, or other Crime, who shall flee from Justice, and be found in another State, shall on Demand of the executive Authority of the State from which he fled, be delivered up, to be removed to the State having Jurisdiction of the Crime.

[No Person held to Service or Labour in one State, under the Laws thereof, escaping into another, shall, in Consequence of any Law or Regulation therein, be discharged from such Service or Labour, but shall be delivered up on Claim of the Party to whom such Service or Labour may be due.][9]

Section 3. New States may be admitted by the Congress into this Union; but no new State shall be formed or erected within the Jurisdiction of any other State; nor any State be formed by the Junction of two or more States, or Parts of States, without the Consent of the Legislatures of the States concerned as well as of the Congress.

The Congress shall have Power to dispose of and make all needful Rules and Regulations respecting the Territory or other Property belonging to the United States; and nothing in this Constitution shall be so construed as to Prejudice any Claims of the United States, or of any particular State.

Section 4. The United States shall guarantee to every State in this Union a Republican Form of Government, and shall protect each of them against Invasion; and on Application of the Legislature, or of the Executive (when the Legislature cannot be convened) against domestic Violence.

ARTICLE V

The Congress, whenever two thirds of both Houses shall deem it necessary, shall propose Amendments to this Constitution, or, on the Application of the Legislatures of two thirds of the several States, shall call a Convention for proposing Amendments, which, in either Case, shall be valid to all Intents and Purposes, as Part of this Constitution, when ratified by the Legislatures of three fourths of the several States, or by Conventions in three fourths thereof, as the one or the other Mode of Ratification may be proposed by the Congress; Provided [that no Amendment which may be made prior to the Year One thousand eight hundred and eight shall in any Manner affect the first and fourth Clauses in the Ninth Section of the first Article; and][10] that no State, without its Consent, shall be deprived of its equal Suffrage in the Senate.

ARTICLE VI

All Debts contracted and Engagements entered into, before the Adoption of this Constitution, shall be as valid against the United States under this Constitution, as under the Confederation.

This Constitution, and the Laws of the United States which shall be made in Pursuance thereof; and all Treaties made, or which shall be made, under the Authority of the United States, shall be the supreme Law of the Land; and the Judges in every State shall be bound thereby, any Thing in the Constitution or Laws of any State to the Contrary notwithstanding.

The Senators and Representatives before mentioned, and the Members of the several State Legislatures, and all executive and judicial Officers, both of the United States and of the several States, shall be bound by Oath or Affirmation, to support this Constitution; but no religious Test shall ever be required as a Qualification to any Office or public Trust under the United States.

ARTICLE VII

The Ratification of the Conventions of nine States, shall be sufficient for the Establishment of this Constitution between the States so ratifying the Same.

Done in Convention by the Unanimous Consent of the States present the Seventeenth Day of September in the Year of our Lord one thousand seven hundred and Eighty seven and of the Independence of the United States of America the Twelfth. IN WITNESS whereof We have hereunto subscribed our Names,

George Washington, President and deputy from Virginia, and thirty-eight other delegates.

[The language of the original Constitution, not including the Amendments, was adopted by a convention of the states on September 17, 1787, and was subsequently ratified by the states on the following dates: Delaware, December 7, 1787; Pennsylvania, December 12, 1787; New Jersey, December 18, 1787; Georgia, January 2, 1788; Connecticut, January 9, 1788; Massachusetts, February 6, 1788; Maryland, April 28, 1788; South Carolina, May 23, 1788; New Hampshire, June 21, 1788.

Ratification was completed on June 21, 1788.

The Constitution subsequently was ratified by Virginia, June 25, 1788; New York, July 26, 1788; North Carolina, November 21, 1789; Rhode Island, May 29, 1790; and Vermont, January 10, 1791.]

AMENDMENTS

AMENDMENT I

(First ten amendments ratified December 15, 1791.)

Congress shall make no law respecting an establishment of religion, or prohibiting the free exercise thereof; or abridging the freedom of speech, or of the press; or the right of the people peaceably to assemble, and to petition the Government for a redress of grievances.

AMENDMENT II

A well regulated Militia, being necessary to the security of a free State, the right of the people to keep and bear Arms, shall not be infringed.

AMENDMENT III

No Soldier shall, in time of peace be quartered in any house, without the consent of the Owner, nor in time of war, but in a manner to be prescribed by law.

AMENDMENT IV

The right of the people to be secure in their persons, houses, papers, and effects, against unreasonable searches and seizures, shall not be violated, and no Warrants shall issue, but upon probable cause, supported by Oath or affirmation, and particularly describing the place to be searched, and the persons or things to be seized.

AMENDMENT V

No person shall be held to answer for a capital, or otherwise infamous crime, unless on a presentment or indictment of a Grand Jury, except in cases arising in the land or naval forces, or in the Militia, when in actual service in time of War or public danger; nor shall any person be subject for the same offence to be twice put in jeopardy of life or limb; nor shall be compelled in any criminal case to be a witness against himself, nor be deprived of life, liberty, or property, without due process of law; nor shall private property be taken for public use, without just compensation.

AMENDMENT VI

In all criminal prosecutions, the accused shall enjoy the right to a speedy and public trial, by an impartial jury of the State and district wherein the crime shall have been committed, which district shall have been previously ascertained by law, and to be informed of the nature and cause of the accusation; to be confronted with the witnesses against him; to have compulsory process for obtaining witnesses in his favor, and to have the Assistance of Counsel for his defence.

AMENDMENT VII

In Suits at common law, where the value in controversy shall exceed twenty dollars, the right of trial by jury shall be preserved, and no fact tried by a jury, shall be otherwise re-examined in any Court of the United States, than according to the rules of the common law.

AMENDMENT VIII

Excessive bail shall not be required, nor excessive fines imposed, nor cruel and unusual punishments inflicted.

AMENDMENT IX

The enumeration in the Constitution, of certain rights, shall not be construed to deny or disparage others retained by the people.

AMENDMENT X

The powers not delegated to the United States by the Constitution, nor prohibited by it to the States, are reserved to the States respectively, or to the people.

AMENDMENT XI (Ratified February 7, 1795)

The Judicial power of the United States shall not be construed to extend to any suit in law or equity, commenced or prosecuted against one of the United States by Citizens of another State, or by Citizens or Subjects of any Foreign State.

AMENDMENT XII (Ratified June 15, 1804)

The Electors shall meet in their respective states and vote by ballot for President and Vice-President, one of whom, at least, shall not be an inhabitant of the same state with themselves; they shall name in their ballots the person voted for as President, and in distinct ballots the person voted for as Vice-President, and they shall make distinct lists of all persons voted for as President, and of all persons voted for as Vice-President, and of the number of votes for each, which lists they shall sign and certify, and transmit sealed to the seat of the government of the United States, directed to the President of the Senate;—The President of the Senate shall, in the presence of the Senate and House of Representatives, open all the certificates and the votes shall then be counted;—The person having the greatest number of votes for President, shall be the President, if such number be a majority of the whole number of Electors appointed; and if no person have such majority, then from the persons having the highest numbers not exceeding three on the list of those voted for as President, the House of Representatives shall choose immediately, by ballot, the President. But in choosing the President, the votes shall be taken by states, the representation from each state having one vote; a quorum for this purpose shall consist of a member or members from two-thirds of the states, and a majority of all the states shall be necessary to a choice. [And if the House of Representatives shall not choose a President whenever the right of choice shall devolve upon them, before the fourth day of March next following, then the Vice-President shall act as President, as in the case of the death or other constitutional disability of the President. —][11] The person having the greatest number of votes as Vice-President, shall be the Vice-President, if such number be a majority of the whole number of Electors appointed, and if no person have a majority, then from the two highest numbers on the list, the Senate shall choose the Vice-President; a quorum for the purpose shall consist of two-thirds of the whole number of Senators, and a majority of the whole number shall be necessary to a choice. But no person constitutionally ineligible to the office of President shall be eligible to that of Vice-President of the United States.

AMENDMENT XIII (Ratified December 6, 1865)

Section 1.
Neither slavery nor involuntary servitude, except as a punishment for crime whereof the party shall have been duly convicted, shall exist within the United States, or any place subject to their jurisdiction.

Section 2.
Congress shall have power to enforce this article by appropriate legislation.

AMENDMENT XIV (Ratified July 9, 1868)

Section 1. All persons born or naturalized in the United States, and subject to the jurisdiction thereof, are citizens of the United States and of the State wherein they reside. No State shall make or enforce any law which shall abridge the privileges or immunities of citizens of the United States; nor shall any State deprive any person of life, liberty, or property, without due process of law; nor deny to any person within its jurisdiction the equal protection of the laws.

Section 2. Representatives shall be apportioned among the several States according to their respective numbers, counting the whole number of persons in each State, excluding Indians not taxed. But when the right to vote at any election for the choice of electors for President and Vice President of the United States, Representatives in Congress, the Executive and Judicial officers of a State, or the members of the Legislature thereof, is denied to any of the male inhabitants of such State, being twenty-one years of age,[12] and citizens of the United States, or in any way abridged, except for participation in rebellion, or other crime, the basis of representation therein shall be reduced in the proportion which the number of such male citizens shall bear to the whole number of male citizens twenty-one years of age in such State.

Section 3. No person shall be a Senator or Representative in Congress, or elector of President and Vice President, or hold any Office, civil or military, under the United States, or under any State, who, having previously taken an oath, as a member of Congress, or as an officer of the United States, or as a member of any State legislature, or as an executive or judicial officer of any State, to support the Constitution of the United States, shall have engaged in insurrection or rebellion against the same, or given aid or comfort to the enemies thereof. But Congress may by a vote of two-thirds of each House, remove such disability.

Section 4. The validity of the public debt of the United States, authorized by law, including debts incurred for payment of pensions and bounties for services in suppressing insurrection or rebellion, shall not be questioned. But neither the United States nor any State shall assume or pay any debt or obligation incurred in aid of insurrection or rebellion against the United States, or any claim for the loss or emancipation of any slave; but all such debts, obligations and claims shall be held illegal and void.

Section 5. The Congress shall have power to enforce, by appropriate legislation, the provisions of this article.

AMENDMENT XV (Ratified February 3, 1870)

Section 1. The right of citizens of the United States to vote shall not be denied or abridged by the United States or by any State on account of race, color, or previous condition of servitude.

Section 2. The Congress shall have power to enforce this article by appropriate legislation.

AMENDMENT XVI (Ratified February 3, 1913)

The Congress shall have power to lay and collect taxes on incomes, from whatever source derived, without apportionment among the several States, and without regard to any census or enumeration.

AMENDMENT XVII (Ratified April 8, 1913)

The Senate of the United States shall be composed of two Senators from each State, elected by the people thereof, for six years; and each

Senator shall have one vote. The electors in each State shall have the qualifications requisite for electors of the most numerous branch of the State legislatures.

When vacancies happen in the representation of any State in the Senate, the executive authority of such State shall issue writs of election to fill such vacancies: Provided, That the legislature of any State may empower the executive thereof to make temporary appointments until the people fill the vacancies by election as the legislature may direct.

This amendment shall not be so construed as to affect the election or term of any Senator chosen before it becomes valid as part of the Constitution.

AMENDMENT XVIII (Ratified January 16, 1919)

Section 1. After one year from the ratification of this article the manufacture, sale, or transportation of intoxicating liquors within, the importation thereof into, or the exportation thereof from the United States and all territory subject to the jurisdiction thereof for beverage purposes is hereby prohibited.

Section 2. The Congress and the several States shall have concurrent power to enforce this article by appropriate legislation.

Section 3. This article shall be inoperative unless it shall have been ratified as an amendment to the Constitution by the legislatures of the several States, as provided in the Constitution, within seven years from the date of the submission hereof to the States by the Congress.[13]

AMENDMENT XIX (Ratified August 18, 1920)

The right of citizens of the United States to vote shall not be denied or abridged by the United States or by any State on account of sex.

Congress shall have power to enforce this article by appropriate legislation.

AMENDMENT XX (Ratified January 23, 1933)

Section 1. The terms of the President and Vice President shall end at noon on the 20th day of January, and the terms of Senators and Representatives at noon on the 3d day of January, of the years in which such terms would have ended if this article had not been ratified; and the terms of their successors shall then begin.

Section 2. The Congress shall assemble at least once in every year, and such meeting shall begin at noon on the 3d day of January, unless they shall by law appoint a different day.

Section 3.[14] If, at the time fixed for the beginning of the term of the President, the President elect shall have died, the Vice President elect shall become President. If a President shall not have been chosen before the time fixed for the beginning of his term, or if the President elect shall have failed to qualify, then the Vice President elect shall act as President until a President shall have qualified; and the Congress may by law provide for the case wherein neither a President elect nor a Vice President elect shall have qualified, declaring who shall then act as President, or the manner in which one who is to act shall be selected, and such person shall act accordingly until a President or Vice President shall have qualified.

Section 4. The Congress may by law provide for the case of the death of any of the persons from whom the House of Representatives may choose a President whenever the right of choice shall have devolved upon them, and for the case of the death of any of the persons from whom the Senate may choose a Vice President whenever the right of choice shall have devolved upon them.

Section 5. Sections 1 and 2 shall take effect on the 15th day of October following the ratification of this article.

Section 6. This article shall be inoperative unless it shall have been ratified as an amendment to the Constitution by the legislatures of three-fourths of the several States within seven years from the date of its submission.

AMENDMENT XXI (Ratified December 5, 1933)

Section 1. The eighteenth article of amendment to the Constitution of the United States is hereby repealed.

Section 2. The transportation or importation into any State, Territory, or possession of the United States for delivery or use therein of intoxicating liquors, in violation of the laws thereof, is hereby prohibited.

Section 3. This article shall be inoperative unless it shall have been ratified as an amendment to the Constitution by conventions in the several States, as provided in the Constitution, within seven years from the date of the submission hereof to the States by the Congress.

AMENDMENT XXII (Ratified February 27, 1951)

Section 1. No person shall be elected to the office of the President more than twice, and no person who has held the office of President, or acted as President, for more than two years of a term to which some other person was elected President shall be elected to the office of the President more than once. But this Article shall not apply to any person holding the office of President when this Article was proposed by the Congress, and shall not prevent any person who may be holding the office of President, or acting as President, during the term within which this Article becomes operative from holding the office of President or acting as President during the remainder of such term.

Section 2. This article shall be inoperative unless it shall have been ratified as an amendment to the Constitution by the legislatures of three-fourths of the several States within seven years from the date of its submission to the States by the Congress.

AMENDMENT XXIII (Ratified March 29, 1961)

Section 1. The District constituting the seat of Government of the United States shall appoint in such manner as the Congress may direct:

A number of electors of President and Vice President equal to the whole number of Senators and Representatives in Congress to which the District would be entitled if it were a State, but in no event more than the least populous State; they shall be in addition to those appointed by the States, but they shall be considered, for the purposes of the election of President and Vice President, to be electors appointed by a State; and they shall meet in the District and perform such duties as provided by the twelfth article of amendment.

Section 2. The Congress shall have power to enforce this article by appropriate legislation.

AMENDMENT XXIV (Ratified January 23, 1964)

Section 1. The right of citizens of the United States to vote in any primary or other election for President or Vice President, for electors for President or Vice President, or for Senator or Representative in Congress, shall not be denied or abridged by the United States or any State by reason of failure to pay any poll tax or other tax.

Section 2. The Congress shall have power to enforce this article by appropriate legislation.

AMENDMENT XXV (Ratified February 10, 1967)

Section 1. In case of the removal of the President from office or of his death or resignation, the Vice President shall become President.

Section 2. Whenever there is a vacancy in the office of the Vice President, the President shall nominate a Vice President who shall take office upon confirmation by a majority vote of both Houses of Congress.

Section 3. Whenever the President transmits to the President pro tempore of the Senate and the Speaker of the House of Representatives his written declaration that he is unable to discharge the powers and duties of his office, and until he transmits to them a written declaration to the contrary, such powers and duties shall be discharged by the Vice President as Acting President.

Section 4. Whenever the Vice President and a majority of either the principal officers of the executive departments or of such other body as Congress may by law provide, transmit to the President pro tempore of the Senate and the Speaker of the House of Representatives their written declaration that the President is unable to discharge the powers and duties of his office, the Vice President shall immediately assume the powers and duties of the office as Acting President.

Thereafter, when the President transmits to the President pro tempore of the Senate and the Speaker of the House of Representatives his written declaration that no inability exists, he shall resume the powers and duties of his office unless the Vice President and a majority of either the principal officers of the executive departments or of such other body as Congress may by law provide, transmit within four days to the President pro tempore of the Senate and the Speaker of the House of Representatives their written declaration that the President is unable to discharge the powers and duties of his office. Thereupon Congress shall decide the issue, assembling within forty-eight hours for that purpose if not in session. If the Congress, within twenty-one days after receipt of the latter written declaration, or, if Congress is not in session, within twenty-one days after Congress is required to assemble, determines by two-thirds vote of both Houses that the President is unable to discharge the powers and duties of his office, the Vice President shall continue to discharge the same as Acting President; otherwise, the President shall resume the powers and duties of his office.

AMENDMENT XXVI (Ratified July 1, 1971)

Section 1. The right of citizens of the United States, who are eighteen years of age or older, to vote shall not be denied or abridged by the United States or by any State on account of age.

Section 2. The Congress shall have power to enforce this article by appropriate legislation.

AMENDMENT XXVII (Ratified May 7, 1992)

No law varying the compensation for the services of the Senators and Representatives shall take effect, until an election of Representatives shall have intervened.

Source: U.S. Congress, House, Committee on the Judiciary, *The Constitution of the United States of America, as Amended,* 100th Cong., 1st sess., 1987, H Doc 100-94.

Notes

1. The part in brackets was changed by section 2 of the Fourteenth Amendment.
2. The part in brackets was changed by the first paragraph of the Seventeenth Amendment.
3. The part in brackets was changed by the second paragraph of the Seventeenth Amendment.
4. The part in brackets was changed by section 2 of the Twentieth Amendment.
5. The Sixteenth Amendment gave Congress the power to tax incomes.
6. The material in brackets was superseded by the Twelfth Amendment.
7. This provision was affected by the Twenty-fifth Amendment.
8. These clauses were affected by the Eleventh Amendment.
9. This paragraph was superseded by the Thirteenth Amendment.
10. Obsolete.
11. The part in brackets was superseded by section 3 of the Twentieth Amendment.
12. See the Nineteenth and Twenty-sixth Amendments.
13. This amendment was repealed by section 1 of the Twenty-first Amendment.
14. See the Twenty-fifth Amendment.

Glossary

Affidavit. A declaration in writing made upon oath for use as evidence in legal proceedings.

Affirmative power. Power granted explicitly in either the Constitution or through legislation.

Amici curiae. Friends of the court, used to denote groups filing supportive briefs in the Supreme Court who are not parties to the litigation.

Appeal. A request to a higher (appellate) court to review the decision of a trial court of a lower appellate court.

Appellate court. A court with the power to rule on an appeal of a trial court or other lower tribunal, normally only reviewing questions of law.

Articles of Confederation. The 1781 compact among the thirteen original states that formed the basis of the first national government of the United States until it was supplanted by the Constitution.

Bad tendency test. A test in seditious libel cases from English Common law that asks whether the words spoken have a "tendency to bring about evil consequences."

Belief-action dichotomy. Distinction regarding the First Amendment's Free Exercise Clause, suggesting that the clause protects against the government's efforts to restrict beliefs but does not prevent the state from forbidding specific actions that might threaten public safety, even if undertaken because of religious beliefs.

Black codes. Laws enacted by southern legislatures after the Civil War that severely restricted the freedoms of former slaves and put them at the mercy of whites.

***Certiorari*, writ of.** An order that is given by a superior court to a lower court directing it to send up the record of a case for review; the primary means by which the Supreme Court determines what cases it will hear.

Circuit court of appeals. In the federal system, the court that hears appeals and reviews judgments of the district courts, and whose decisions may be appealed to the Supreme Court. The thirteen courts of appeals form the intermediate branch of the federal judicial system.

Class legislation. Laws allegedly designed to benefit only one particular group and not all citizens equally.

Clear and present danger test. A test devised by Justice Holmes in 1919 and used for the next fifty years to determine whether the state could punish people for speech that might bring about "an immediate substantive evil."

Comity. Legal reciprocity, or the principle that one state will extend certain courtesies to and recognize the jurisdiction, laws, and judicial decisions of other states.

Commerce clause. The provision in Article I, Section 8 of the Constitution that gives Congress the authority to regulate commerce with other nations, among the states, and with native tribes.

Common law. Judge-made law as opposed to statutes.

Concurring opinion. A written opinion by a judge who agrees with the majority decision of the court but disagrees with the rationale for reaching that decision.

Confession. An admission to the police by a suspect that he or she has committed a criminal act.

Construction (regarding the Constitution). The method by which the various clauses of the Constitution are construed.

Contempt of court. A commission or omission that hinders the orderly administration of justice or impairs the dignity of a court or otherwise shows contempt for its authority.

Coverture. The legal term for the status of a married woman.

Cruel and unusual punishment. Criminal penalties that a society does not consider appropriate, involve torture, or could result in death when the death penalty had not been ordered.

Cy pres. Ancient common law doctrine under which if a charitable trust could not be fulfilled according to its terms, the state would apply it to purposes most close to that of the original intent.

De facto **segregation.** Segregation that results from practice rather than law.

Defamation. Speech or print that publicly traduces the reputation of another.

De jure **segregation.** Separation on the basis of race enacted into law and imposed by the government.

Dissenting opinion. The written opinion of one or more judges who disagree with the ruling of the majority.

Double jeopardy. The subjecting of a person to a second trial or punishment for the same offense for which the person has already been tried or punished.

Due process. Judicial procedural rights, as given by the Constitution, statutes, regulation, and common law.

Eleventh Amendment. An amendment prohibiting suits by citizens against a state in federal court.

Enemy combatant. An individual who is not a uniformed member of the military of a recognized nation state but who engages in acts of terrorism or combat against the United States, and who, under the laws and customs of war, may be detained for the duration of an armed conflict.

Enforcement clauses. Provisions in the Thirteenth, Fourteenth, and Fifteenth Amendments allowing the extension of the powers of Congress such that they could enforce these articles by providing appropriate legislation.

Enumerated powers. A list of items found in Article I, Section 8 of the Constitution that set forth the authoritative capacity of the Congress.

Equal protection clause. A Fourteenth Amendment clause assuring that all citizens will be treated equally by the government in its laws.

Equity. That branch of law which deals in nonmonetary remedies, with the goal of establishing just and fair solutions to civil wrongs.

Establishment of religion clause. A clause given in the First Amendment prohibiting the national government from recognizing one church or religion as the official religion of the nation.

Exclusionary rule. A judicial rule prohibiting the police from using at trial evidence obtained through illegal search and seizure.

Ex parte. Literally "from one party," a hearing in which the court hears only one side of a controversy, as in the case of a temporary restraining order.

Federal court. A court of the U.S. national government.

Federalism. A political system in which powers and responsibilities are allocated between states and a national government.

Femme sole. Prior to the emancipation of women, a term applied to a woman who was legally entitled to carry out business contracts without the express consent of her husband.

Fifteenth Amendment. This amendment declared that the right to vote could not be denied because of race.

Fifth Amendment. This amendment protects against abuse of government authority in a legal procedure.

Four Horsemen. A name given to New Deal–era conservative Justices James McReynolds, Willis Van Devanter, George Sutherland, and Pierce Butler, alluding to the four horsemen of the Apocalypse.

Fourteenth Amendment. This amendment defined as a citizen of the United States any person born in the country or who had immigrated and been naturalized, and it prohibited states from denying any citizen the due process of law and equal protection under the law.

Fourth Amendment. This amendment guards against unreasonable searches and seizures and requires any warrant to be judicially sanctioned and supported by probable cause.

Freedom of contract. Parties capable of entering into a contract and giving their consent to its terms ought not to be curbed by the state, save to protect the health, welfare, and morals of the community or to prevent criminal activities.

Free exercise clause. The second clause of the First Amendment, which forbids the national government from interfering with the religious beliefs of a person.

Fugitive slave law. An 1850 law compelling northerners to honor southerners' property claims to slaves and to aid in capturing and returning runaway slaves.

Full faith and credit clause. From Article IV, Section 1 of the Constitution, this clause requires states to honor the legal actions taken in other states.

Great Right. A clause in the Fifth Amendment safeguarding persons from being compelled to be a witness against him or herself in a criminal proceeding. See Fifth Amendment.

Habeas corpus. A writ or legal action that releases a prisoner from unlawful detention based on insufficient cause or evidence.

Hand test. Developed by Judge Learned Hand to evaluate the constitutionality of First Amendment challenges, this asked whether "the language directly advocated resistance to the draft."

Impeachment. A proceeding brought against the president or federal judges to remove them from office.

Imperium in imperio. A state within a state.

Implied powers. Those powers authorized by the Constitution that, though not explicitly stated, are necessary to implement powers expressly stated.

Incorporation of the Bill of Rights. The process by which the courts have applied portions of the Bill of Rights to the states.

Injunctions. Judicial orders to cease certain actions.

Interlocutory. Provisional or temporary, and not final; only final decrees can be appealed to the Supreme Court.

Jim Crow laws. Southern state laws mandating segregation of blacks and whites.

Judicial restraint. Theory of interpretation that encourages a judge to limit the exercise of judicial power.

Judicial review. The doctrine under which legislative and executive actions are subject to review and possible invalidation by the judiciary.

Jurisdiction. The authority of a court to decide particular cases or questions of law.

Jurisprudence. The philosophy or science of law.

Libel. A published falsehood or statement resulting in the defamation of someone's character.

Mandamus, **writ of.** A court-issued writ commanding a public official to carry out a specific act or duty.

Manumission. The act of freeing a person from slavery or involuntary servitude.

Married women's property acts. Mid-nineteenth-century laws allowing married women to own property in their own names.

Martial law. The rule of law established and maintained by the military in the absence of civil law.

Merits (of a case). The strengths of a judicial case that make the matter worth pursuing legally.

Military tribunal. A military court designed to try member of enemy forces during wartime, operating outside the scope of conventional criminal proceedings.

Minority rights. Collective rights afforded to minority groups.

Miranda **rights.** Requirement that the police inform suspects that they have a right to remain silent and to have counsel while being interrogated.

Missouri Compromise. An 1820 law that prohibited slaves above the southern border of Missouri in the Louisiana Territory.

Natural law. Any system of law that is purportedly determined by nature and thus is universal.

Necessary and proper clause. The last clause of Article I, Section 8 of the Constitution, which grants Congress the authority to make all laws that are required to exercise its designated powers.

Nemo tenetur prodere seipsum. No man is bound to accuse himself.

Nineteenth Amendment. This amendment granted women the right to vote.

Ninth Amendment. This amendment described rights retained by the people as a basis for the right of privacy.

Obiter dicta. The comments provided in an opinion, as opposed to a finding of law.

Originalism. A theory of constitutional interpretation that tries to determine and reflect the intent of the Constitution's Framers.

Parens patriae. The role of the state as "parent" to guard the interest of children and other persons under legal disabilities.

Peculiar institution. A euphemism for slavery and its effects on the social and economic realms.

Peonage laws. Passed in nearly all southern states, laws dictating that if a black man ran afoul of the law, even for loitering, he could be sentenced to jail and his labor sold to a white man.

Per curiam. Collectively written; a memorandum from the entire court that does not bear a single author's name.

Personal liberty laws. Laws in northern states that gave runaway slaves the right to appointed counsel, jury trials, habeas corpus, and even the writ of personal replevin in order to fight being returned to their owners.

Personal replevin, **writ of.** An old procedural device to free a person from prison or from the custody of another.

Pluralism. A theory describing a political system in which all significant social interests freely compete with one another for influence over the government's policy decisions.

Police power. The power of the state to protect the lives, health, and safety of the public.

Popular sovereignty. Citizens' delegation of authority to their agents in government, with the ability to rescind that authority.

Positive law. Statutory enactments; man-made laws as opposed to common, or judge-made, law.

Precedent. A principle or rule established in a legal case that other courts or judicial bodies may apply when deciding subsequent cases with similar issues or facts.

Preemption (e.g., preemption doctrine, federal preemption). A rule forbidding states from acting in any way contrary to federal policy.

Privileges and immunities clause. The clause in Section 1 of the Fourteenth Amendment that guarantees all U.S. citizens certain basic rights.

Procedural rights. Rules governing how actions of the government, such as a jury trial, may be carried out.

Protective legislation. Legislations in which reformers tried to secure laws, mostly at the state level, to eradicate child labor, limit the number of hours a person could work each day, establish safety standards in the workplace, set minimum wages, and create a safety net of employer liability and workmen's compensation to help those injured on the job.

Recidivist statute. Law adding extra penalties to repeat offenders.

Reconstruction Amendments. The Thirteenth, Fourteenth, and Fifteenth Amendments. Also known as the Civil War Amendments.

Remedial legislation. Legislation that provides remedies to counter certain wrongs or abuses, and also to correct defects in previous legislation.

Search and seizure. In law enforcement, an exploratory investigation of a premises or a person and the taking into custody of property of an individual in the interest of gaining evidence of unlawful activity or guilt.

Section 3501. A law, since held unconstitutional, that allowed statements to be used against suspects in a federal prosecution, even if the police had given no *Miranda* warnings, as long as the suspect supposedly gave the confession voluntarily to the police.

Segregation. The political and social practice of separating whites and blacks into dual and highly unequal schools, hospitals, prisons, public parks, housing, and public transportation. (See also Jim Crow laws.)

Separate but equal doctrine. The Supreme Court–initiated doctrine stating that separate facilities for blacks and whites are constitutional provided they are equal.

Separation of powers. The distribution of government powers among several institutions—in the United States: legislative, executive, and judicial.

Seriatim. Judicial decisions in which each justice writes a separate opinion.

Severability clause. A clause in a contract or a statute that allows for the terms of the contract or statute to be independent of one another so that if a court deems one term unenforceable or unconstitutional, the contract or law as a whole will remain in force.

Signing statement. A written pronouncement issued by the U.S. president that is intended to modify implementation or ignore altogether provisions of a new law.

Sixth Amendment. This amendment provides the right for counsel on the grounds that a resulting confession can be valid and admissible only if the accused had been properly informed of his or her rights.

Sixteenth Amendment. This amendment allows the Congress to levy an income tax without apportioning it among the states or basing it on Census results.

Slander. False and malicious oral statements that damage another person's reputation.

Sovereignty. The power that inheres in government.

Stare decisis. The authority of prior decisions in ruling in a new case.

State paper. A document kept by a government to record discussions, options, and decisions by government officials, departments, and civil servants.

States' rights. Powers reserved to the states and denied to the federal government.

Stationary despotism. Term used by reformers and liberal politicians to describe slavery.

Sub silentio. Under silence; without notice being taken or without making a particular point of the matter in question. If a case is decided against precedent, the newer case is said to have overruled the previous decision *sub silentio.*

Substantive due process. The theory of law through which courts enforce limits on legislative and executive powers and authority.

Substantive law. The statutory law that defines rights, duties, and responsibilities.

Substantive rights. Basic human rights, including those granted by both natural and positive law.

Supremacy clause. From Article VI of the Constitution, establishing a hierarchy of law, with the Constitution taking precedence over legislation, thereby giving courts the power to nullify legislative acts.

Taking the Fifth. Relying on the Fifth Amendment's protection to avoid testifying about one's prior activities.

Tenth Amendment. This amendment establishes that powers not granted to the federal government nor prohibited to the states by the Constitution are reserved, respectively, to the states or the people.

Thirteenth Amendment. This amendment officially abolished and continues to prohibit slavery.

Tort. In common law, a wrong that involves a breach of a civil duty, other than a contractual duty, owed to someone else.

Unlawful cohabitation. An offense, created by the Edmunds Act, that required no proof of marriage but merely proof that a man lived in the same household with two or more women; designed to get around the legal distinction between bigamy and polygamy.

Vested rights. Rights that have accrued or are secured to their possessor and are not contingent on any change in the law.

War powers. The president's claims under the Constitution's Article II, which empowers him to have authority as commander-in-chief to do whatever he considers necessary regardless of existing law, international treaties, or even the Constitution.

Index

ABA. *See* American Bar Association

Abernathy, Rev. Ralph D., 296

Abortion
and due process, 333–334
and right to privacy, 333–334, 337, 338, 339, 340, 350, 352, 363–364
and substantive due process, 333–334

Abortion cases, 338–339. See also *Roe v. Wade*

Abortion legislation, 325–329

Abortion rights, 329–333

Abrams, Jacob, 209, 222–223
and war, opposition to, 211–213

Abrams v. United States, 218–221, 221–222
and clear and present danger, 221
and freedom of speech, 209–211
and seditious libel, 209, 218, 220–221, 222

Access, right of, and immigration cases, 368–369

Acheson, David C., 317

ACLU. *See* American Civil Liberties Union

"An Act to Protect the Health of the City of New Orleans, and to Locate the Stock Landings and Slaughterhouses." *See* Slaughterhouse Act of 1869

Adams, John, 1, 2, 3, 4, 132

Adams, John Quincy, 21, 49, 50, 69

Adams, Lionel, 185

Addison, Alexander, 10

Adkins v. Children's Hospital, 207, 255, 256–257

Afghanistan War, 104–105

Agricultural Adjustment Act, 252–254

Agricultural production, authority to regulate, 252–254

Al Odah v. United States, 104, 373

Alabama, civil rights struggle in, 292–297

Allgeyer v. Louisiana, 204

Altgeld, John Peter, 159, 168–169

American Bar Association (ABA), 261, 263–264, 264–265, 271, 375

American Civil Liberties Union (ACLU), 261, 263–264, 264–265, 271, 349

American Railway Union, 164. See also *Debs, In re;* Pullman workers strike

Anderson, John, 77

Anthony, Susan B., 130, 136

Anti-Boycott Act of 1921, 294

Arthur, Chester A., 151

Ashcroft, John, 367–368, 373

Ashmore, John, 65

Ashwander v. Tennessee Valley Authority, 255

Authority to abrogate private contracts, 247–248

Authority to permit monopolies, 243

Authority to regulate agricultural production, 252–254

Authority to regulate banking, 245

Authority to regulate business, 243–244

Authority to regulate coal industry, 254

Authority to regulate oil industry, 248–249

Authority to regulate work standards
 and *Lochner v. New York*, 194, 198–199, 205, 206–207
 and *New Deal Cases*, 242, 250, 255, 256–257
 See also Protective legislation

Authority to sell off lands and byproducts, 255

Bad tendency test, 213–214, 217, 218. *See also* Freedom of speech

Bakeshop Act of 1895, 196, 198–199, 202
 Lochner's violation of, 199–201
 violation of, and due process, 201
 See also *Lochner v. New York*

Bakeshops, and sanitation, 194–196, 197–199, 205–206. See also *Lochner v. New York*

Bank Bill of 1791, 17–20

Bank charter, 17, 18–20. See also *M'Culloch v. Maryland;* Second Bank of the United States

Bank of the United States, 18, 19–20. *See also* Second Bank of the United States

Banking, authority to regulate, 245

Bankruptcy, 254–255

Banks. See *M'Culloch v. Maryland;* Second Bank of the United States

Barnette, Walter, 270, 274

Bartlett, Edward, 201

Baxley, Bill, 306

Beauharnais v. Illinois, 303

Beemis, Nathan, 65–66

Belden, Simon, 118

Bensing, Sandra, 339, 344

Betts v. Brady, 313

Biddle, Nicholas, 30

Biggs, J. Crawford, 246

Binalshibh, Ramzi, 370

Birch, Elizabeth, 364

Bishop, Gardner, 277

Black, Hugo, 305–306, 313, 338
 and *Flag-Salute Cases*, 267, 268, 269, 271, 272

Black, Jeremiah S., 100, 101

Black Codes, 176. *See also* Racial discrimination

Blackmun, Harry, 325, 340, 353, 355
 and abortion cases, 338–339, 341

Blackstone, Sir William, 214, 351

Blair, Montgomery, 83–84

Blow family, 82, 87, 89

Bolling, Spottswood, Jr., 277

Bolling v. Sharpe, 277, 282

Bootlegging, 228, 229–231, 239. See also *Olmstead v. United States*

Boumediene v. Bush, 379–381
 and habeas corpus, 380–381

Bowers, Michael, 349

Bowers v. Hardwick, 350, 351, 352–355, 363

Bowles, William, 95

Boy Scouts of America v. Dale, 356–357

Boyd v. United States, 232, 233

Bradley, Joseph, 115, 120, 124, 177, 232
 and Bradwell case, 139–140, 141

Bradwell, James, 128–130, 133

Bradwell, Myra, 127–128, 128–130, 134, 142
 and right to practice law, 133–136
 (see also *Bradwell v. Illinois*)
 and women's suffrage, 130–131, 136

Bradwell v. Illinois, 127
 and contracts, right to make, 136–138
 and coverture, 128, 131–132, 134, 137–138
 decision in, 138–141
 and equal rights for women, 139–140
 and privileges and immunities, 136–138, 138–139, 141
 in Supreme Court, 136–138
 See also Legal discrimination; Right of women to practice law; Right of women to practice a profession

Brandeis, Louis, 206–207, 225, 241, 304, 382
 and *Abrams* case, 222
 and New Deal, 254–255, 256
 and *New Deal Cases*, 243, 249
 and *Olmstead* case, 236–238, 239, 333
 and *Panama* case, 249
 and Prohibition, 234–235

Brandenburg v. Ohio, 222, 305

Breckinridge, John, 4–5

Brennan, William, 303–305, 306, 338, 349–350, 353
Brewer, David, 155, 172–173, 204
Breyer, Stephen, 322, 359, 361
Briggs, Harry, Jr., 277
Briggs v. Elliot, 277
Brinkema, Leonie, 370
Brockenbrough, William, 28–29
Brown, Henry Billings, 185–187, 190, 204
Brown, John R., 286
Brown family, 275–276, 289
Brown v. Board of Education I, 186, 275, 280–281, 317
   consolidated cases in, 276–277
   decision in, 281–282
   decision in, reaction to, 292–293
   decision in, response to, 283–284
   and equal protection clause, 280, 281–282
   in Little Rock, Arkansas, 287–288
   resistance to, 286–289
   and separate-but-equal doctrine, 282
   See also Racial segregation
Brown v. Board of Education II, 284–286
Brown v. Maryland, 43–44
Bruce, Lester, 295
Buchanan, James, 85
Buchannan, James A., 21, 30–31
Bunting v. Oregon, 207
Burger, Warren, 16, 338, 353–354
Burleson, Albert Sydney, 210, 211
Burr, Aaron, 1, 12, 13–15
Bush, George H. W., 356
Bush, George W., 365, 378, 379, 380.
      See also *Boumediene v. Bush; Rasul v. Bush*
Bush (George W.) administration, 104–105, 370
   and enemy combatants, 371–373
   and Guantánamo cases, 374, 375
   and *War on Terror Cases,* 368–369, 369–370, 377, 378, 379, 381
Business, authority to regulate, 243–244
Butler, Benjamin, 100, 109
Butler, Elizur, 54, 59–60
Butler, Pierce, 234, 235–236, 241, 255
Byrd, Harry F., 286–287, 293
Byrnes, James, 271, 293

Cadwalader, George, 97
Cain, Christopher, 175
Calder v. Bull, 114
Calhoun, John C., 49, 58, 87, 115, 286–287
Callender, James, 11
Campbell, John, 85, 115, 118, 119–120, 121–122, 123
Cannon, Angus, 153
Cannon, George Q., 147, 151
Cardozo, Benjamin, 241, 249, 251, 252, 254–255, 264
Carolene Products case, 267, 268
Carpenter, Matthew Hale, 136–138, 141
Carrington, Henry, 95
Carter v. Carter Coal Company, 254
Case of Monopolies, 122
Catron, John, 85
Chafee, Zechariah, Jr., 215–216, 217, 218, 221
Chaffee, Calvin, 78, 89
Chaplinsky v. New Hampshire, 268
Charter. *See* Bank charter
Chase, Salmon, 65, 103, 124, 141
Chase, Samuel, 1, 5, 11–13, 114
Cherokee, 58–60. See also *Cherokee Nation v. Georgia;* Indian removal; Indian sovereignty
Cherokee Nation v. Georgia, 51–52, 56
Chertoff, Michael, 370
Chester, Elisha W., 55
Chewning v. Cunningham, 313
Child labor laws, 194
Chisholm v. Georgia, 55
Civil court, v. military tribunal, 95–96, 100, 101, 102–103, 103–105. See also *Merryman, Ex parte; Milligan, Ex parte; Vallandigham, Ex parte*
Civil rights
   in Alabama, 292–297
   and *Milligan* case, 103
   and *Slaughterhouse Cases,* 119–120, 123–124, 125
Civil Rights Act of 1866, 119–120
Civil Rights Act of 1875, 176–177
Civil Rights Act of 1964, 177, 275, 288–289
Civil Rights Act of 1965, 275, 288–289

Civil Rights Cases, 176, 177–178, 184–185, 186, 188, 190, 362

Civil War, 89, 91, 92
 and military tribunal v. civil court, 95–96, 100, 101, 102–103, 103–105 (see also *Merryman, Ex parte; Milligan, Ex parte; Vallandigham, Ex parte*)
 opposition to, 93–95 (see also *Milligan, Ex parte*)
 racial discrimination after, 175–178
 and Reconstruction policy, 100, 103

Civil War Amendments, 107

Civilian Conservation Corps, 245

Clark, Ramsey, 321

Clark, Tom, 277, 279, 319

Clarke, John, 218–219, 221

Clawson v. United States, 153

Clay, Henry, 71, 80

Clayton, Henry DeLamar, Jr., 212

Clear and present danger
 and *Abrams* case, 221
 and *Flag-Salute Cases,* 271, 272, 273
 and freedom of speech, 214–215, 215–216, 217–218, 219–220, 221
 and *Schenck* case, 214–215, 219

Clement, Paul, 371

Cleveland, Grover, 159, 167, 168–169, 245

Clifford, Nathan, 120

Clinton, Bill, 356

Coal industry, authority to regulate, 254

Coasting Act of 1793, 40, 41, 43

Codes, authority to create and enforce, 248, 250–252

Coffee, Linda, 335, 336, 339

Cohabitation law, 151, 152–153

Cole, Nat "King," 293

Colson, Jesse, 315

Commerce clause
 and *Debs, In re,* 159, 171–173
 and *Gibbons v. Ogden* (1824), 36, 37, 45
 and *New Deal Cases,* 248–249, 252, 254 (*see also* National Industrial Recovery Act)
 and Separate Car Act, 182

Commonwealth v. Alger, 111

Commonwealth v. Aves, 63

Commonwealth v. Davis, 214

Compromise of 1850, 72, 80–81

Comstock, Anthony, 328

Comstock Act of 1873, 213

Comstock Act of 1876, 213

Constitution, U.S., interpretation of, 18–19

Contract freedom
 and *Lochner* case, 192, 193, 194, 201, 203–206, 207
 and *People v. Lochner,* 201–202

Contracts
 authority to abrogate private, 247–248
 women's right to make, 136–138

Cooley, William H., 112

Cooper, Thomas, 11

Cooper v. Aaron, 288

Corn Tassels, George, 51

Counsel, right to. *See* Right to counsel

Court-packing plan, 255–256, 257

Coverture, 129, 131–132, 134, 137–138. *See also* Legal discrimination against women

Covington, Hayden, 263

Cox v. New Hampshire, 268

Creppy, Michael J., 368

Cuban-American Treaty, 373–374

Cummings, Homer, 246

Cummings, v. Missouri, 137

Cunningham, Milton, 185

Curtis, Benjamin R., 85, 87

Curtis, Jenny, 166

Customs Act of 1874, 232

Dallas, Alexander J., 10

Daniel, Peter V., 85

Darcy v. Allein, 122

Darrow, Clarence, 170, 171

Dartmouth College case, 154

Davis, David, 102

Davis, Dorothy E., 276

Davis, Edward, 296

Davis, John W., 281

Davis v. Beason, 154

Davis v. County School Board of Prince Edward County, Virginia, 276

Davy, John M., 201

Day, William R., 233

Dayton, Jonathan, 39

Debs, Eugene, 162–163, 164, 166–167, 215, 218
  and injunction, violating terms of, 170
  and Pullman workers strike, 166, 168, 169, 170
  See also *Debs, In re*
Debs, In re
  aftermath of, 173–174
  and commerce clause, 159, 171–173
  decision in, 172–173
  and injunction, suppression of strikes through, 159, 171–173
Debs v. United States, 174, 215, 217, 218, 219
Defense of Marriage Act, 365
Demore v. Kim, 369
Desdunes, Daniel, 181
Dickerson v. United States, 322
District of Columbia Organic Act of 1801, 2
Dodd, Harrison H., 93–94
Doe v. Bolton, 339–341
Doe v. Commonwealth's Attorney, 349–350, 352
Doherty, Michael J., 233
Dore, John F., 231
Douglas, Stephen, 84, 86, 88–89
Douglas, William, 303, 305–306, 333–334, 338
  and *Flag-Salute Cases,* 267, 268, 269, 271, 272
Douglass, Frederick, 72
Dred Scott v. Sandford, 61, 73, 75
  aftermath of, 87–90
  decision in, 85–87, 114, 149
  in federal court, 82–83
  in state courts, 77–79
  in state supreme court, 81, 82
  in Supreme Court, 83–85
  See also Scott, Dred; Slavery
Dubovsky, Jean, 358
Dudgeon v. United Kingdom, 351
Due process
  and abortion, 333–334
  and Bakeshop Act, violation of, 201
  and *Gideon* case, 312–313
  and Guantánamo cases, 375, 377
  and immigration cases, 369
  and *Milligan* case, 95

and *People v. Lochner,* 201–202
and *Plessy v. Ferguson,* 184, 185, 186
and polygamy, 153–154
and *Slaughterhouse Cases,* 114–115, 124, 125
Dunmore, W. T., 200
Durant, Thomas, 122–123
Durden, Bea, 335

Eakin v. Raub, 9
Earl, Robert, 193
Edmunds Act of 1882, 151–152, 154
Edmunds-Tucker Act, 152, 153
Edson, Cyrus, 199
Eisenhower, Dwight, 287–288, 293
Election of 1800, 1, 3
Elkinson v. Deliesseline, 43
Ely, John Hart, 342, 359
Ely, Richard, 161
Emancipation Proclamation, 93–94
Emerson, Irene (née Sanford), 76, 77, 78, 82, 89
Emerson, John, 75–77
Emerson, Ralph Waldo, 72
Emmet, Thomas A., 41
Employees, and work hours. *See* Authority to regulate work standards
Employment Division v. Smith, 156
Enemy combatants, 367, 368, 377
  and Guantánamo cases, 374–375
  and *War on Terror Cases,* 371–373
  See also Indefinite detainment
Engel v. Vitale, 317
English Bakehouse Regulation Act of 1863, 197
Equal protection clause
  and *Brown I,* 280, 281–282
  and *Plessy* case, 184, 185, 187
  and school segregation, 278–279
Equal rights for women, 139–140. *See also* Women's rights
Ervin, Sam, 320
Escobedo, Danny, 316
Escobedo v. Illinois, 315, 316–317, 318, 319
Espionage Act of 1917, 210, 215, 216, 217, 218. See also *Frohwerk v. United States; Schenck v. United States*
Eubanks, Robert Royce, 360

Evans, Richard G., 358
Everand's Breweries v. Day, 235

Faubus, Orville, 288, 293
Federal Reserve Act of 1913, 20
Federal Reserve System, 31
Fenner, Charles, 184
Ferguson, John Howard, 175, 183–184, 185
Field, David Dudley, 100, 101
Field, Frank Harvey, 202, 203, 205, 206–207
Field, Roswell, 82
Field, Stephen, 124–125, 155
Fillmore, Millard, 80, 81
Finkbine, Sherri, 330–331
Fitch, John, 34, 35, 37
Flag-Salute Cases, 259
    aftermath of, 273–274
    and clear and present danger, 271, 272, 273
    and freedom of religion, 260–261, 262–266, 270–273
    and freedom of speech, 263–264, 266, 270, 271–272, 273
    See also *Minersville School District v. Gobitas; West Virginia Board of Education v. Barnette*
Fletcher v. Peck, 121
Folsom, "Big Jim," 283
Fosdick, Rev. Harry Emerson, 298
Four Horsemen. *See* Butler, Pierce; McReynolds, James; Sutherland, George; Van Devanter, Willis
Frankfurter, Felix, 140, 221, 285, 303
    and *Flag-Salute Cases*, 265–266, 267, 269–270, 272–273
Franklin, Benjamin, 34
Frazier-Lemke Act, 249
Freedmen, statutes to protect, 176–177
Freedom of religion, 268–270
    and *Flag-Salute Cases*, 260–261, 262–266, 270–273
    and *Reynolds* case, 143, 148–150
Freedom of speech
    and *Abrams* case, 209–211
    and bad tendency test, 213–214, 217, 218

and clear and present danger, 214–215, 215–216, 217–218, 219–220, 221
    and *Flag-Salute Cases*, 263–264, 266, 270, 271–272, 273
    and *Schenck* case, 214–215, 219
    and World War I, 209–213
    See also Libel; Seditious libel
Freedom of the press, and libel, 291. See also *New York Times v. Sullivan*
Freeport Doctrine, 89
Freund, Ernst, 213, 215
Friendly, Henry J., 237
Frohwerk v. United States, 215, 218, 219
Fugitive Slave Act of 1793, 62, 67–68, 70
    constitutionality of, 64–65, 66
    See also *Prigg v. Pennsylvania*; Slavery
Fugitive Slave Act of 1850, 71–73
Fugitive slaves, 62, 63–65, 67–69. *See also* Slavery
Full faith and credit clause, 64
Fuller, Melville, 155, 204
Fulton, Robert
    and patent rights, 35
    and steamboat design, 33–34, 34–35
    See also Fulton-Livingston group; *Gibbons v. Ogden; Livingston v. Van Ingen*; Steamboat navigation monopoly rights
Fulton-Livingston group, 38–40
    and steamboat navigation monopoly rights, 35–38

Gardner, George K., 263
Garfield, James A., 100
Garland, Hugh, 83
Garner, Tyrone, 360
Garrison, William Lloyd, 69, 70
Gay Rights Cases, 347
    in lower courts, 355–357
    See also *Bowers v. Hardwick; Hardwick v. Bowers; Lawrence v. Texas; Romer v. Evans*; Sodomy, and right to privacy
Gay rights movement, 350–352
Gayle v. Browder, 294
Gebhart v. Belton, 276–277
Gellhorn, Walter, 278–279

Gender bias, and right of women to practice law, 135, 138. *See also Bradwell v. Illinois*
Gessell, Gerhard, 338
Geyer, Henry S., 83–84
Gibbons, Thomas, 39–40, 44, 45
Gibbons v. Ogden (1820), 40–41
Gibbons v. Ogden (1824), 33, 41–42
  and commerce clause, 36, 37, 45
  decision in, 42–43
  legacy of, 43–45
  See also Steamboat navigation monopoly rights
Gibson, John Bannister, 9
Gideon v. Wainwright, 312–313, 315
Giles, William, 4, 12, 15
Giles, William F., 97
Gilmore, George R., 54
Ginsburg, Ruth Bader, 322, 342, 359, 361
Gobitas case. See *Minersville School District v. Gobitas*
Gobitas family, 259–260, 261, 273, 274
Goesart v. Cleary, 140
Gold standard, 245, 247–248
Goldberg, Arthur, 305–306, 315, 319, 320, 337
Goldberg, Irving, 337
Goldman, Emma, 213
Goldwater, Barry, 317
Gompers, Samuel, 163
Graham, Thomas, 48
Graves, John Temple, 287
Gray, James B., 70
Great Depression, 242–243. *See also* New Deal
Greeley, Horace, 87
Gregory, Stephen, 171
Grier, Robert, 85
Griswold, Estelle, 333
Griswold v. Connecticut, 239, 333–334, 349
Grosscup, Peter S., 168, 171
Groth, Nicholas, 311–312
Groves v. Slaughter, 67
Guantánamo cases, 373–375, 379–381
  aftermath of, 381–382
  and due process, 375, 377
  and enemy combatants, 374–375
  and habeas corpus, 375, 376–377
  See also *Al Odah v. United States; Boumediene v. Bush; Hamdan v. Rumsfeld; Rasul v. Bush; War on Terror Cases*
Guffy-Snyder Coal Conservation Act of 1935, 254

Habeas corpus, 104
  and *Boumediene v. Bush,* 380–381
  and Guantánamo cases, 375, 376–377
  and *Hamdan* case, 378
  and immigration cases, 369–370
  and *Merryman* case, 96–98
  and *Milligan* case, 102
  and *War on Terror Cases,* 371
Habeas Corpus Act of 1863, 103
Hagel, Chuck, 379
Hall, Grovel, Jr., 297
Hall v. DeCuir, 179
Hallford, James H., 337
Hamdan, Salim Ahmed, 377–378
Hamdan v. Rumsfeld, 104–105, 377–379
  and habeas corpus, 378
Hamdi, Yasser Esam, 368, 374–375
Hamdi v. Rumsfeld, 104, 376, 378
Hames, Margie, 339
Hamilton, Alexander, 9, 11, 13, 17–20
Hamilton, Andrew, 300–301
Hand, Learned, 9, 216, 217, 221
Harding, Warren, 228
Hardwick, Michael, 347–349
Hardwick v. Bowers, 349–350
Harlan, John Marshall, 177, 190, 204, 205, 316, 319
  and *Plessy* case, 185, 187–188, 282
Harlan, John Marshall, II, 333–334, 338–339
Hay, George, 15
Haynes, E. S. P.
Henderson, Joseph, 262
Henderson v. United States, 278
Hepp, William, 108–109
Hirabayashi v. United States, 103–104
Hoffman, Twila, 311, 323
Holden v. Hardy, 186, 202–203, 204
Holder, Eric, 365

Holmes, Oliver Wendell, 193, 233, 234, 280, 304
  and *Abrams* case, 219–221, 221–222
  and freedom of speech, 214, 215–218
  and *Lochner* case, 205–206
  and *New Deal Cases*, 257
  and *Olmstead* case, 235–236, 238
  and *Schenck* case, 215
Holston Treaty, 51
Home Building and Loan v. Blaisdell, 243–244, 251
Hoover, Herbert, 229, 242–243, 245, 255. See also *Ashwander v. Tennessee Valley Authority*
Hopewell Treaty, 51
Hopkins, John P., 168
Hopkinson, Joseph, 23–24
Hornblower, Joseph C., 65
Horsey, Stephen, 95
Hoyt v. Florida, 140–141
Hubbard, Alfred M., 230
Hughes, Charles Evans, 75, 241, 249, 254–255, 259, 278
  and *New Deal Cases*, 247–248, 249, 251, 252, 254, 257
Hughes, Sarah, 336
Hulett, Alta, 141
Humphreys, Andrew, 95
Hunt, Randell, 118–119
Hunt, Ward, 120
Hunt, William, 119–120
Hurley v. Irish-American Gay, Lesbian, and Bisexual Group of Boston, 356, 357

Illegal Immigration Reform and Immigration Responsibility Act of 1996, 369
Immigration Act of 1917, 210
Immigration Act of 1918, 210
Immigration and Naturalization Service, 369
Immigration cases
  and due process, 369
  and habeas corpus, 369–370
  and indefinite detainment, 369–370
  and right of access, 368–369
  See also *War on Terror Cases*

Indefinite detainment, 369–370, 372–373, 375, 376, 377. *See also* Enemy combatants; Habeas corpus
Indian removal, 47–48, 48–51, 53–54, 58, 59. See also *Cherokee Nation v. Georgia; Worcester v. Georgia*
Indian Removal Act of 1830, 49, 54
Indian sovereignty, 52, 53–54, 55. See also *Cherokee Nation v. Georgia; Worcester v. Georgia*
Indian Springs Treaty, 49, 50
Injunction, suppression of strikes through. See *Debs, In re*
Interstate Commerce Act, 168
Iraq War, 104–105

Jackson, Andrew, 31, 57–58
  and Indian removal, 48–49, 51, 53–54, 58, 59
Jackson, Robert H., 271–272
Jacobs, In re, 193, 200
James, John, 22
Jefferson, Thomas, 1, 9, 12, 13–15, 28, 34, 79, 132
  and Bank Bill of 1791, 18–20, 20n
  and Constitution, U.S., interpretation of, 18–19
  and freedom of religion, 149, 150
  and Indian removal, 48
  and judges, removal of, 10–11, 13
  and Judiciary Act of 1801, 2, 3, 4–5
  and *Marbury* case, 6–8, 15–16
Jehovah's Witnesses, 259. See also *Flag-Salute Cases*
Jim Crow laws, 178–179, 189, 277–278. *See also* Racial segregation
Johns, Barbara Rose, 276
Johnson, Andrew, 95, 100
Johnson, Frank, 286
Johnson, Frank M., 350
Johnson, Joshua, 48
Johnson, Lyndon, 288–289
Johnson, Reverdy, 83–84
Johnson, Thomas, 48
Johnson, v. Eisentrager, 375
Johnson, William, 27, 43
Johnson and Graham's Lessee v. M'Intosh, 47–48

Jones, T. Rawles, Jr., 371
Jones, Walter, 24
Jones, Walter Burwyn, 294
Jones, William, 22, 24
Jones v. Opelika, 268–269, 270
Judges, removal/impeachment of,
     10–11, 11–13
Judicial power, 8–9. See also *Marbury v.*
     Madison
Judicial review, 8–9. See also *Marbury v.*
     Madison
Judiciary, 1. *See also* Judges; *Marbury v.*
     Madison
Judiciary Act of 1789, 3, 7, 82
Judiciary Act of 1801, 2, 3–5, 12
Judiciary Act of 1802, 5
Julian, George W., 72

Kaiser, John, 109
Kansas-Nebraska Act, 73, 86
Keith, Damon, J., 369
Kennedy, Anthony, 342, 380
     and Gay Rights Cases, 358, 359–360,
     361, 362–363
Kent, James, 36, 37–38, 40–41, 114
Kepley, Ada, 141
Kimball, Heber, 144–145
King, David, 337
King, Marsha, 337
King, Martin Luther, Jr., 291, 293–294,
     296, 298, 302
Klose, Erwin, 274
Knowlton, Charles, 327
Koch, Robert, 197
Korematsu v. United States, 103–104
Kurland, Philip B., 359
Kyllo v. United States, 239

Labor, and protective legislation, 191–
     192. See also *Lochner v. New York*
Labor unions, 162–163, 248
     and injunction, suppression of strikes
     through, 159, 171–173 (see also
     Debs, In re)
Lachowsky, Hyman, 211–213, 222, 223
Lamar, Lucius Q. C., 155
Landon, Alf, 255
Lands, authority to sell off, 255

Lansing, John, Jr., 36
LaRue, Jan, 364–365
Laski, Harold, 217
The Late Corporation of the Church of Jesus
     Christ of Latter-Day Saints v. United
     States, 154–155
Latimer, George, 70
Latimer Law, 70
Lawrence, John Geddes, 360–361
Lawrence, Matilda, 65
Lawrence v. Texas, 356
     aftermath of, 364–365
     in lower courts, 360–361
     in Supreme Court, 361–364
Lawton v. Steele, 186
LDF. *See* Legal Defense Fund
LeBeaume, Charles Edmund, 82
Lee, Charles, 6
Lee, Rev. George, 293
Leffingwell, Russell, 247
Legal Defense Fund (LDF), 276, 277,
     278–279, 279–280
Legal discrimination against women,
     127, 129, 131–132, 140. *See also*
     Coverture; *Bradwell v. Illinois*
Lemmon v. The People, 63, 88
Lewis, E. S., 108
Libel, 299–301. *See also* Freedom of
     speech; *New York Times v. Sullivan;*
     Seditious libel
Lincoln, Abraham, 1, 88–89, 93–94, 95,
     245, 246
     and *Merryman* case, 96–98
     and *Milligan* case, 103
     and *Vallandigham* case, 98–99
Lincoln-Douglas debates, 88–89
Lipman, Samuel, 211–213, 222, 223
Livingston, Henry Brockholst, 36
Livingston, Robert, 33–34, 35, 40. *See also*
     Fulton-Livingston group; *Gibbons*
     v. Ogden; Livingston v. Van Ingen;
     Steamboat navigation monopoly
     rights
Livingston v. Van Ingen, 36–38, 44
     decision in, 37–38, 40
Lochner, Joseph, 195
     and Bakeshop Act, violation of,
     199–201

Lochner v. New York, 191, 202–206
  aftermath of, 206–207
  and contract freedom, 192, 193, 194,
    201, 203–206, 207
  decision in, 204–205
  and due process, 204
  See also Authority to regulate work
    standards; Bakeshop Act; *People v.
    Lochner;* Police power; Protective
    legislation; Public health
Louisiana ex rel. Abbott v. Hicks, 182
*Louisville, New Orleans and Texas Railway
    v. Mississippi,* 179
Loving v. Virginia, 353
Lowery, Rev. Joseph, 307
Lucas, Roy, 334
Lucy, Authorine, 293
Ludeling, John, 119
Lumpkin, Wilson, 58
Luther v. Borden, 97, 121

Mackie, William S., 200, 202
Madison, James, 3, 7, 18, 19–20
Marbury, William, 1, 2–3, 6–7, 15–16
Marbury v. Madison, 5, 6–8, 247
  aftermath of, 15–16
  decision in, 8–9
  and judicial review, 8–9
Maris, Albert B., 260
Married women's property acts, 132
Marshall, Edward, 197–198
Marshall, James, 2
Marshall, John, 1, 14–15, 28, 37–38, 66,
    237, 288
  and *Brown v. Maryland,* 44
  and *Cherokee Nation* case, 51–52, 56
  and *Fletcher* case, 121
  and *Gibbons* case (1824), 33, 42–43
  and *Johnson* case, 48
  and Judiciary Act of 1801, 2, 3, 4, 5
  and *Marbury* case, 6–8, 8–9, 16
  and *M'Culloch* case, 17, 25–27, 29–30,
    64
  and *Osborne* case, 27
  and *Worcester* case, 56–57
Marshall, Thurgood, 278, 279, 338,
    349–350
Marshall, Wilson, 44

Martial law, 96, 102, 103. See also
    *Merryman, Ex parte; Milligan, Ex
    parte; Vallandigham, Ex parte*
Martin, Luther, 24
Martin v. Struthers, 269, 271
Martinet, Louis A., 180–181, 183–184
Masses Publishing Co. v. Patten, 216
Massiah, Winston, 315
Massiah v. United States, 314–315, 318
Mayer, Julius M., 204
McCain, John, 379
McCarthy, Joseph, 314
McClur, Lucy, 270
McCluskey, Henry, 336
McCorvey, Norma, 335–336, 343–344
McCorvey v. Hill, 344
McCulloh, James (aka McCulloch;
    M'Culloch), 17, 20–22, 30–31. See
    also *M'Culloch v. Maryland*
McDonald, Joseph Ewing, 100, 101
McFate, Yale, 312
McHenry, Jerry, 72
McKenna, Joseph, 204
McLaurin, George, 279
McLaurin v. Oklahoma State Regents, 279
McLean, John, 67, 69, 85, 87
McNamara, Edmund, 320
McReynolds, James, 233, 234, 241, 244,
    248, 254
M'Culloch v. Maryland, 22–25, 64, 118
  decision in, 25–27
  decision in, defense of, 29–30
  impact of, 27
  and necessary and proper clause,
    18–19, 64
  and states' rights, 28–29
  See also Bank charter; McCulloh,
    James; Second Bank of the United
    States
Merhige, Robert, Jr., 349
Merryman, Ex parte, 96–98, 100
Merryman, John, 97–98, 102
Michaels, George, 332
Midnight Judges, 2. *See also* Judiciary Act
    of 1801
Military Justice Act, 104–105, 378
Military tribunal, v. civil court, 95–96,
    100, 101, 102–103, 103–105. See

also *Merryman, Ex parte; Milligan, Ex parte; Vallandigham, Ex parte*
Miller, Samuel, 115, 123–124, 138–140, 141
Miller, W. H. H., 142
Miller, Zell, 59–60
Milligan, Ex parte, 98, 100–101
aftermath of, 105
decision in, 102–103
legacy of, 103–105
Milligan, Lambdin, 91–93, 95–96, 98, 99, 105
as antiwar agitator, 93–95
Minersville School District v. Gobitas, 269–270, 270–273
aftermath of, 273–274
decision in, 267–268
in federal courts, 260–262
in Supreme Court, 262–267
Minimum wage law, 207. *See also* Authority to regulate work standards
Minnery, Tom, 364
Minor v. Happensett, 136
M'Intosh, William, 48
Miranda, Ernesto, 310–312, 314, 322–323
Miranda v. Arizona, 317, 318–320
aftermath of, 321–322
and right against self-incrimination, 311
success of, 320–321
Miranda warnings, 318–320, 321–322. *See also* Right to counsel; Right against self-incrimination
Missouri Compromise of 1820, 61, 63, 76, 80, 82, 83–84, 85, 86. *See also* Slavery
Missouri ex rel. Gaines v. Canada, 278
Monopolies, 34, 243
and slaughterhouses (see *Slaughterhouse Cases*)
and steamboat navigation (*see* Steamboat navigation monopoly rights)
Monroe, James, 5
Montgomery, Alabama, bus boycott, 293
Moore, Alvin, 311–312

Morehead v. New York ex rel. Tipaldo, 255, 257
Morgan, Juliette, 294
Morgan, Margaret, 65–66, 69
Morgan v. Virginia, 278
Mormonism, 143–145, 145–146. *See also* Polygamy
Morrill, Justin, 145
Morrill Anti-Polygamy Act of 1862, 145–146, 151, 154
Mortgage moratorium law, 243–244
Morton, Levi P., 199
Morton, Oliver P., 95, 105
Mosman, Michael, 353–354
Moussaoui, Zacarias, 370–371
Mukasey, Michael B., 371
Muller v. Oregon, 203, 206–207
Munaf, Mohammad, 381
Munaf v. Geren, 381
Municipal Bankruptcy Act of 1934, 254
Munn v. Illinois, 177–178
Murdock v. Pennsylvania, 269, 271
Murphy, Frank, 265, 267, 268, 271, 272
Murphy, Michael J., 317
Murphy v. Ramsey, 153–154
Murray, John, 298

NAACP. *See* National Association for the Advancement of Colored People
Nachman, Merton, 291–292, 299, 301–302
National Association for the Advancement of Colored People (NAACP), 276, 278–279, 280–281, 285, 294
National Industrial Recovery Act, 245–246, 248–249, 254
challenge to (see *Schechter v. United States*)
Native Americans. See *Cherokee Nation v. Georgia;* Cherokee; *Worcester v. Georgia*
Near v. Minnesota, 303
Nebbia, Leo, 244
Nebbia v. New York, 244
Necessary and proper clause, 18–19, 64
Nelson, Samuel, 85
New Deal, 192

New Deal (*continued*)
  continuing attack on, 254–255
  and court-packing plan, 255–256, 257
  and Great Depression, 242–243
  programs, 242–243, 244–246
New Deal Cases, 241, 243–244
  and authority to abrogate private contracts, 247–248
  and authority to create and enforce codes, 248, 250–252
  and authority to permit monopolies, 243
  and authority to regulate agricultural production, 252–254
  and authority to regulate banking, 245
  and authority to regulate business, 243–244
  and authority to regulate coal industry, 254
  and authority to regulate oil industry, 248–249
  and authority to regulate work standards, 242, 248, 250, 255, 256–257
  and authority to sell off lands and byproducts, 255
  and bankruptcy, 254–255
  and commerce clause, 248–249, 252, 254 (*see also* National Industrial Recovery Act)
  and gold standard, 245, 247–248
  and union rights, 248
  See also *Schechter v. United States; West Coast Hotel Co. v. Parrish*
New State Ice Co. v. Liebmann, 243
New York Times, libel suit against. See *New York Times v. Sullivan*
New York Times v. Sullivan, 292, 297–299
  aftermath of, 306–307
  decision in, 303–306
  and freedom of the press, 291, 292, 303, 304, 306
  in lower court, 301–302
  in Supreme Court, 303
New York v. Quarles, 321–322
Noble State Bank v. Haskell, 193
Noonan, John, 342

Norman v. Baltimore and Ohio Railroad Company, 247
Norris-LaGuardia Act of 1931, 173
Northwest Ordinance of 1787, 76

Oakley, Thomas J., 41
Obama, Barack, 381
Obama administration, 365
O'Brien, Denis, 201
O'Connor, Sandra Day, 104, 342, 353, 361, 363, 376
Ogden, Aaron, 38–40, 44. See also *Gibbons v. Ogden* (1824)
Oil industry, authority to regulate, 248–249
Olmstead, Roy, 229–231, 239
Olmstead v. United States, 33, 355, 382
  decision in, 233–235, 237, 238–239
  dissent in, 235–239
  and Olmstead bootlegging ring, 229–231
  and right against self-incrimination, 231, 232, 236–237
  and right to privacy, 225, 232, 236, 238
  and search and seizure, 225, 231–233, 234, 235, 236, 238
  and search warrants, 230–231, 231–233, 235, 237, 238, 239
  in Supreme Court, 232–233
  and wiretapping, 225, 230–231, 233–234, 235–236, 237, 238–239
Olney, Richard, 168, 171
Olsen, Theodore, 374
Omar, Shawqi Ahmad, 381
Omnibus Crime Control Act of 1968, 322
Organic Act of 1801, 2
Osborne v. Bank of the United States, 27

Padilla, José, 368, 371, 374–375, 376. See *also* Enemy combatants
Palko v. Connecticut, 264
Panama Refining Co. v. Ryan, 248–249, 251
Panic of 1818, 27
Parker, Alton B., 201
Parker, John J., 270–271
Parker, Luceba, 327

Parks, Rosa, 293
Parrish, Elsie, 242
Parrish v. West Coast Hotel Co., 242
Patent rights, 34, 37
Paterson, William, 5
Patterson, John, 294, 297
Patterson, Thomas, 214
Patterson v. Colorado, 214
Peace Democrats, 92–93
Peckham, Rufus, 204–205, 206
People ex rel. Rodgers v. Coler, 201
People v. Lochner
   and contract freedom, 201–202
   and due process, 201–202
   See also Bakeshop Act
People v. Onofre, 351, 356
Perry v. United States, 247–248
Personal liberty laws, 63–64, 67. *See also*
   Slavery
Persons, Gordon, 295
Peters, Richard, 12
Pettibone v. United States, 172
Pickering, John, 10–11
Pierce, Franklin, 115
Pinkney, William, 24–25
Planned Parenthood of Southeastern
   Pennsylvania v. Casey, 342, 363–364
Plessy, Ex parte, 183–184
Plessy, Homer, 175, 182–183, 189–190
Plessy v. Ferguson, 275, 277, 281–282
   aftermath of, 188–189
   and dissent in, 187–188
   and due process, 184, 185, 186
   and equal protection, 184, 185, 187
   and privileges and immunities, 185
   in Supreme court, 184–187
   See also Racial segregation
Pochelu, Raymond, 108
Poe v. Ullman, 33
Poland Act of 1874, 146, 147
Police power, 201, 203–205, 207
   v. substantive due process, 192–194
   See also *Lochner v. New York*
Pollock v. Farmers' Loan and Trust Co., 173
Polygamy (in Mormonism), 144–145,
   156
   after *Reynolds* case, 151–154
   and cohabitation law, 151, 152–153
   and due process, 153–154

   end of, 154–156
   legislation against, 145–146, 151–152
   test case against, 147–148
   See also *Reynolds v. United States*
Postal service, and commerce clause,
   159, 171–173. See also *Debs, In re*
Powderly, Terence V., 163
Powell, Lewis, 340, 352–354
Press. *See* Freedom of the press
Prigg, Edward, 65–66
Prigg v. Pennsylvania, 61, 73
   aftermath of, 70–71
   decision in, 66–69
   See also Slavery
Privacy. *See* Right to privacy
Privileges and immunities
   and *Bradwell case,* 136–138, 138–139,
   141
   and *Plessy v. Ferguson,* 185
   and *Slaughterhouse Cases,* 116, 120,
   123–124, 138, 139, 141
Probable cause, and search warrants,
   231–232, 238
Prober, Gabriel, 212
Prohibition, 225–229, 234–235, 239. See
   also *Olmstead v. United States*
Property rights. See *The Late Corporation*
   of the Church of Jesus Christ of Latter-
   Day Saints
Protective legislation, 191–192, 192–194,
   197, 200, 202–203, 204, 206
   and contract freedom, 192, 193, 194,
   201, 203–206, 207
   and substantive due process, 192–193,
   194
   See also *Lochner v. New York*
Public health
   and bakeshops, 193, 196, 197–198,
   199, 201, 203–206, 206–207 (see
   also *Lochner v. New York*)
   and slaughterhouses, 108–110, 111,
   117–119, 120–122, 124, 125 (see
   also *Slaughterhouse Cases*)
Public works programs, 245
Pullman, George, 159–162, 165–166,
   166–167, 173–174
Pullman Palace Car Company, 159–161
Pullman workers strike, 159, 162,
   165–166

Pullman workers strike (*continued*)
  injunction against, 168–169, 170
  and railroad boycott, 166–170
  and violence, 167–168, 169–170

Quinn, Joseph, 360
Quirin, Ex parte, 372

Rabban, David, 213
Rachel v. Walker, 78, 81
Racial discrimination, post-Civil War,
    175–178. *See also* Slavery
Racial segregation, 275, 276, 277–279.
    See also Brown v. Board of Education;
    Jim Crow laws; *Plessy v. Ferguson*
Randolph, A. Phillip, 298
Randolph, Edmund, 18
Randolph, John, 12, 13
Rasul v. Bush, 104, 373, 378
Reagan, Ronald, 356
Reconstruction, 100, 103, 121. *See also*
    Civil War
Reconstruction Act of 1867, 110
Reconstruction Amendments, 107, 121
Reed, Stanley, 271
Reed v. Reed, 141
Rehnquist, William, 322, 340, 341, 371,
    375
  and Gay Rights Cases, 353, 356–357,
    359–360, 361
Religion. *See* Freedom of religion
Religious belief v. action, 149–150
Reynolds, Amelia, 148
Reynolds, George, 143, 146–147,
    147–148, 264
  incarceration of, 150, 151, 156–157
Reynolds v. United States, 264
  aftermath of, 151–154
  decision in, 149–150
  decision in, reaction to, 150–151
  and freedom of religion, 143, 148–150
  and religious belief v. action, 149–150
  See also Polygamy
Right against self-incrimination, 311,
    312, 313–314, 314–315, 316–317,
    318–320
  and wiretapping (see *Olmstead v.
    United States*)
  See also *Miranda* warnings

Right of access, and immigration cases,
    368–369
Right of women to practice a profession,
    136–137, 141–142. See also *Bradwell
    v. Illinois*
Right of women to practice law, 133–136,
    138–140, 141–142
  and coverture, 128, 131–132, 134,
    137–138
  and state supreme court, 134–136
  See also *Bradwell v. Illinois*
Right to counsel, 312–313, 314–315, 316.
    See also *Miranda* warnings
Right to privacy
  and abortion, 333–334, 337, 338, 339,
    340, 350, 352, 363–364 (see also *Roe
    v. Wade*)
  and sodomy, 348–349, 349–350,
    351–352, 352–355, 361–364 (see
    also *Gay Rights Cases*)
  and wiretapping, 225, 230–231,
    233–234, 235–236, 237, 238–239
    (see also *Olmstead v. United States*)
Riis, Jacob, 198
Rives, Richard, 286
Roberts, John, 378, 381
Roberts, Owen, 241, 244, 253, 255, 257,
    272
Roberts v. Boston, 63
Robertson, James, 378–379
Robinson, Harriet. *See* Scott, Harriet
Rochereau, Albin, 108–109
Rockefeller, Nelson A., 332
Roe v. Wade, 325, 335, 339–340, 350, 352,
    363–364
  aftermath of, 343–344
  decision in, 341–343
  in lower court, 336–338
  See also Abortion
Romer, Roy, 358
Romer v. Evans, 357–360
Roosevelt, Franklin, 239
  and court-packing plan, 255–256, 257
  and New Deal, 241, 242–243, 245–246,
    255
  and Second New Deal, 255, 257
Roosevelt, Nicholas, 34
Rosnansky, Hyman, 212
Roundabush, Charles, 260

Rumsey, James, 34
Rumsfeld, Donald, 373. See also *Hamdan v. Rumsfeld; Hamdi v. Rumsfeld*
Runaway slaves. *See* Fugitive slaves
Russell, Charles Taze, 261
Rustin, Bayard, 298
Rutherford, Joseph, 259–260, 261, 263
Rutledge, Wiley, 269, 271

Same-sex marriage, 365
Sanford, Edward, 233, 234
Sanford, Eliza Irene. *See* Emerson, Irene
Sanford, John F. A., 78, 82–83
Sanger, Margaret, 213
Sanitation
    in bakeshops, 194–196, 197–199, 205–206 (see also *Lochner v. New York*)
    in slaughterhouses, 108, 113 (see also *Slaughterhouse Cases*)
Scalia, Antonin, 104, 156, 239, 376, 380–381
    and *Gay Rights Cases*, 359–360, 361, 363–364
Schechter v. United States, 249–252, 254
Schenck v. United States, 217
    and clear and present danger, 214–215, 219
    and freedom of speech, 214–215, 219
Schmitter, Aman, 200
Schofield, Amelia Jane, 146–147
School segregation, 63, 275–277
    and separate but equal doctrine, 277, 278–279, 279–280
    See also *Brown v. Board of Education*
School segregation cases, 278–280
Schroeder, Theodore, 213
Scott, Dred, 75–77, 87, 89–90. See also *Dred Scott v. Sandford*
Scott, Harriet (née Robinson), 76, 77, 89–90
Scott, William, 81
Scott v. Emerson, 81
Scottsboro case, 264
Search and seizure. See under *Olmstead v. United States*
Search warrants, 228
    and probable cause, 231–232, 238
    See also under *Olmstead v. United States*

Second Bank of the United States
    conspiracy to defraud, 20–22, 30–31
    constitutionality of, 22
    See also Bank of the United States; *M'Culloch v. Maryland*
Second New Deal, 255, 257
Sedition Act of 1917, 209
Sedition Act of 1918, 210, 212–213, 218. See also *Abrams v. United States*
Seditious libel, 209, 218, 220–221, 222, 300, 305. See also *Abrams v. United States;* Freedom of Speech; Libel
Selective Service Act, 210
Self-incrimination, right against. See Right against self-incrimination
Sellers, Clyde, 295, 296
Separate Car Act, 179–182, 183–184
Separate-but-equal doctrine, 187
    and *Brown I*, 282
    and racial segregation, 276
    and school segregation, 277, 278–279, 279–280
    See also *Brown v. Board of Education; Plessy v. Ferguson*
Sergeant, John, 54–55, 55–56
Seward, William H., 72
Shaw, Lemuel, 63, 70, 111, 327
Sherbert v. Verner, 156, 273–274
Sherman Antitrust Act, 168, 171, 173
Shrader, Ex parte, 111
Silverthorne Lumber Company v. United States, 233
Sipuel, Ada, 278
Sit-in movement, in Alabama, 296–297
Slaughterhouse Act of 1869, 121–123
    butchers' challenge to, 113–116
    butchers' protest against, 110–113
Slaughterhouse Cases, 108
    aftermath of, 125–126
    and civil rights, 123–124, 125
    decision in, 123–125
    and due process, 114–115, 124, 125
    in federal court, 119–120
    and privileges and immunities, 116, 120, 123–124, 138, 139, 141
    in the state courts, 116–119
    in state supreme court, 118–119
    in the Supreme Court, 120–123

Slaughterhouses
  and monopolies, 108, 117–119, 120,
    122, 123, 125
  and public health, 108–110, 111,
    117–119, 120, 122, 124, 125
  sanitation in, 108, 113
  See also *Slaughterhouse Cases*
Slavery, 61, 62, 75, 79–80, 89, 102
  and Civil War, 91, 92
  and Emancipation Proclamation,
    93–94
  in the Northern states, 63
  See also Compromise of 1850; Dred
    Scott v. Sandford; Fugitive Slave
    acts; Missouri Compromise;
    Personal liberty laws; *Prigg v.
    Pennsylvania; Scott v. Emerson;* Scott,
    Dred
Smith, David, 364
Smith, Joseph, Jr., 143–144
Smith, Judy, 335
Snow, In re, 153
Snow, Lorenzo, 153
Snowe, Olympia, 379
Snyder v. Rosales-Garcia, 369–370
Social Security program, 242, 255, 257
Sodomy, and right to privacy, 348–349,
    349–350, 351–352, 352–355,
    361–364. See also *Gay Rights Cases*
Somerset v. Stewart, 78
Sotomayor, Sonia, 322
Souter, David, 342, 359, 361
Specter, Arlen, 379
Speech. *See* Freedom of speech
Speed, James, 100
Stanbery, Henry, 100
Stanley, Thomas, 283–284
Stanley v. Georgia, 353, 354
Stanton, Edwin, 95, 103
Stanton, Elizabeth Cady, 130
States' rights, 28–29
Steamboat navigation monopoly rights,
    35–38
  lower court challenge to, 36–38
  See also *Gibbons v. Ogden (1824);
    Livingston v. Van Ingen*
Steimer, Mollie, 211–213, 223
Stettler v. O'Hara, 257
Stevens, John, 34

Stevens, John Paul, 105, 322, 350, 376,
    378
  and *Gay Rights Cases,* 359, 361–362
Stewart, Potter, 239, 316, 319, 338, 339
  and *Massiah* case, 315, 317
Stidger, Felix, 95
Stoddard, Thomas, 355
Stone, Harlan Fiske, 234, 235, 241,
    253–254, 254–255, 372
  and *Flag-Salute Cases,* 259, 267, 268,
    271
Story, Joseph, 22, 52, 56–57, 114
  and *Prigg* case, 67–69, 70, 71
Stuart v. Laird, 5
Stull, Paul, 270
Substantive due process, 207
  and abortion, 333–334
  v. police power, 192–194
Sullivan, Kathleen M., 359
Sullivan, L. B., 291, 292, 295–296, 302,
    306–307
  and sit-in movement, in Alabama,
    296–297
Sumner, Charles, 89
Sumrall, Clint, 349
Sutherland, George, 207, 233, 234, 241,
    254
Swayne, Noah H., 124
Sweatt, Heman Marion, 279
Sweatt v. Painter, 279

Taft, William Howard
  and *New Deal Cases,* 257
  and *Olmstead* case, 233–235, 237,
    238–239
Taliaferro, Lawrence, 76
Tallmadge, James, Jr., 79
Tallmadge amendment, 79
Talmadge, Herman, 293
Taney, Roger Brooks, 24, 73, 75, 83, 85,
    89, 121
  and *Dred Scott* case, 85–87, 114,
    149
  and *Merryman* case, 97
  and *Prigg* case, 69, 70
Taylor, William, 336–337
Taylor, Zachary, 80
Telephone, and right to privacy. *See*
    Wiretapping

Tennessee Valley Authority, 242, 255.
   See also *Ashwander v. Tennessee
   Valley Authority*
Thomas, Clarence, 359–360, 361, 364
Thompson, Smith, 37, 44, 52
Three-fifths compromise, 62, 79
Timanus, George, 329
Toombs, Robert, 88
Torick, K. R., 347–349
Torture, 379, 381. See also *War on Terror
   Cases*
Tourgée, Albion W., 180–181, 183–184
Trading with the Enemy Act of 1917,
   210, 245
Tribe, Lawrence, 352–354, 359
Troup, George M., 49, 51
Truman, Harry, 280
Trumbull, Lyman, 171
Tuddenham, Mary Ann, 146
Tuttle, Elbert, 286
Tymkovich, Timothy, 358

United States v. Belcher, 250
United States v. Butler, 253
United States v. Cannon, 153
United States v. E. C. Knight Co., 173
United States v. Lopez, 45
United States v. Morrison, 45
United States v. Vuitch, 338–339

Vallandigham, Clement, 98–99
Vallandigham, Ex Parte, 98–99, 100
Van Buren, Martin, 47, 58
Van Devanter, Willis, 233, 234, 241
Van Ingen, James, 36–38
Vanderbilt, Cornelius, 45
Vandiver, Ernest, 286
Vann, Irving G., 203
Vinson, Fred M., 279, 280
Volstead Act, 227, 229, 235
Voting Rights Act of 1965, 275, 288–289
Vuitch, Milan, 338

Wade, Henry, 336
Wagner Labor Relations Act, 257
Waite, Morrison, 149–150, 264
Walker, Edwin, 171
Walker, James, 180, 181, 183–184
Walker, John C., 93

Wallace, George, 294, 306
War on Terror Cases
   aftermath of, 381–382
   and enemy combatants, 367, 368,
      371–373
   and habeas corpus, 371
   and Moussaoui, Zacarias, 370–371
   and presidential authority, 378, 379,
      380
   and torture, 379, 381
   and wiretapping, 378–379
   See also Immigration cases;
      Guantánamo cases
Warmoth, Henry C., 111–112, 113
Warren, Earl, 313, 333
   and *Brown I,* 280, 281–282, 284
   and *Brown II,* 285
   and *Miranda* case, 318–319, 319–320
War-Time Prohibition Act, 235
Washington, George, 11, 18, 19, 101
Washington Treaty, 49
Wasliewski, Edmund, 260
Watson, Tom, 178
Wayne, James, 85
Wayne, James Moore, 99
Webster, Daniel, 22–23, 40, 41–42, 281
Wechsler, Herbert, 303
Weddington, Sarah, 334–336, 339
Weeks v. United States, 232–233
Weinberger, Harry, 212
Weismann, Henry, 199, 202, 203, 205,
   206–207
Weld, Theodore Dwight, 69
Wells, Robert W., 83
West Coast Hotel Co. v. Parrish, 207,
   256–257
West Virginia Board of Education v. Barnette
   in lower courts, 270–271
   in Supreme Court, 271–273
Whiskey Rebellion of 1794, 101
White, Byron, 319, 338, 341, 353
   and *Bowers* case, 354, 355
   and *Escobedo* case, 316–317
Whitney, Edward, 171
Whitney v. California, 222, 304
Wigmore, John H., 221–222
Wilde, Kathy, 349
Wilkinson, J. Harvey, 275
Wilkinson, James, 14

Williams, George, 21–22, 30–31
Williamson, Mac, 279
Willson v. Black Bird Creek Marsh Co., 44
Wilner, Thomas, 375
Wilson, Woodrow, 210–211, 227
Wilson-Gorman Act of 1894, 173
Winny v. Whitesides, 77, 78, 81
Wiretapping
    and *Olmstead v. United States*, 225,
        230–231, 233–234, 235–236, 237,
        238–239
    and *War on Terror Cases,* 378–379
Wirt, William, 24, 40, 41–42, 54–55, 56
Wisconsin Enabling Act, 76
Wisdom, John Minor, 286
Women's rights, 139–140
    and coverture, 128, 131–132, 134,
        137–138
    and legal discrimination, 127, 129,
        131–132, 140 (see also *Bradwell v.*
        Illinois)
    and married women's property acts,
        132
    and right to practice a profession,
        136–137, 141–142 (see also *Bradwell*
        v. Illinois)
    and right to practice law, 133–136,
        138–140, 141–142 (see also *Bradwell*
        v. Illinois)
Women's suffrage, 130–131, 132, 136,
    140
    and polygamy, 152

Woodruff, George, 150–151
Woodruff, Wilford, 155, 157
Woods, William A., 168, 170
Woodward, C. Vann, 287, 293
Worcester, Samuel, 52–54, 56–57, 58,
    59–60
Worcester v. Georgia, 54–56
    decision in, 56–57
    decision in, enforcement of, 57–58
    and Indian removal, 47–48, 48–51,
        53–54, 58, 59
    and Indian sovereignty, 52, 53–54,
        55
Work hours. *See* Authority to regulate
    work standards
Work standards. *See* Authority to regulate
    work standards
World War I, and freedom of speech,
    209–213
Wright, J. Skelley, 286
Writs of mandamus, 3
Wynehamer v. People, 114

Yates, Joseph, 37
Yoo, John, 373
Yorty, Sam, 320
Young, Ann Eliza, 146, 147
Young, Brigham, 144–145, 146

Zadvydas v. Davis, 369
Zenger, John Peter, 300–301
Zenger case, 300–301